Contents

KU-487-092

Introduction   15

1 **H. G. Wells**
from *Joan and Peter: The Story of an Education* (1918)   19

2 **C. C. Perry**
from 'Our Undisciplined Brains: The War Test' (1901)   20

3 **Sir H. E. Roscoe**
from 'The Outlook for British Trade' (1901)   23

4 **O. Eltzbacher**
from 'The Disadvantages of Education' (1903)   27

5 **F. H. Doolan**
from a letter to the *Sunday Times* (1970)   32

6 **Sir J. Crichton-Browne**
from *Parcimony in Nutrition* (1909)   32

7 **Committee on Physical Deterioration**
from 'Overcrowding' (1904)   33

8 **Committee on Physical Deterioration**
from 'Pollution of Atmosphere' (1904)   35

9 **Committee on Physical Deterioration**
from 'Conditions of Employment' (1904)   36

10 **Committee on Physical Deterioration**
from 'Infant Mortality' (1904)   37

11 **General Sir Frederick Maurice**
from Evidence to the Committee on Physical Deterioration
(1904)   38

6 Contents

12 Charles Booth
from Evidence to the Committee on Physical Deterioration
(1904) 44

13 Fabian Society
'The Education Muddle and the Way Out' (1901) 55

14 Robert L. Morant
from 'The Organization of Education in Switzerland' (1898) 72

15 A. J. Balfour
Opening Speech introducing the Education Bill (1902) 73

16 Education Act (1902) 90

17 Board of Education
from the *Code of Regulations for Public Elementary Schools*
(1904) 94

18 Board of Education
from Prefatory Memorandum, *Regulations for Secondary
Schools* (1904) 98

19 Board of Education
from 'Courses of Instruction', *Regulations for Secondary
Schools* (1904) 104

20 Sidney Webb
'The Making of a University' (1903) 105

21 Richard Burdon, Lord Haldane
from *An Autobiography* (1929) 114

22 Katherine Bathurst
from 'The Need for National Nurseries' (1905) 119

23 Board of Education
from the Report upon Questions affecting Higher Elementary
Schools (1906) 126

R. Vinta

Penguin Education

Education, the Child and Society
A Documentary History 1900–1973

Edited by Willem van der Eyken

Education, the Child and Society

A Documentary History 1900–1973

Edited by Willem van der Eyken

Penguin Education

Penguin Education,
A Division of Penguin Books Ltd,
Harmondsworth, Middlesex, England
Penguin Books Inc, 7110 Ambassador Road,
Baltimore, Md 21207, USA
Penguin Books Australia Ltd,
Ringwood, Victoria, Australia

First published 1973
This selection copyright © Willem van der Eyken, 1973
Introduction and notes copyright © Willem van der Eyken, 1973

Made and printed in Great Britain by
Cox & Wyman Ltd, London, Reading and Fakenham
Set in Monotype Plantin

24 **Board of Education**
from the Report upon Questions affecting Higher Elementary
Schools (1906)   137

25 **H. Ward**
from Divisional Inspector's Report upon Elementary
Education in Lancashire (1915)   139

26 **Sir Samuel Hoare**
Question Time, House of Commons (1911)   143

27 **Edmond Holmes**
from *What Is and What Might Be* (1911)   144

28 **H. G. Wells**
from *Joan and Peter: The Story of an Education* (1918)   147

29 **Board of Education**
from the Annual Report of the Chief Medical Officer of the
Board, 1908 (1910)   148

30 **J. H. Palin**
from 'The Feeding of School Children: Bradford's
Experience' (1908)   150

31 **Margaret McMillan**
from 'London's Children: How to Feed Them and How not to
Feed Them' (1909)   156

32 **Board of Education**
from the Report on Attendance at Continuation Schools (1909)   162

33 **Board of Education**
from the Report on Attendance at Continuation Schools (1909)   164

34 **H. Caldwell Cook**
from *The Play Way: An Essay in Educational Method* (1917)   173

35 **Homer Lane**
Paper read to the Little Commonwealth Committee after the
Rawlinson Inquiry (1918)   175

36 **Désirée Welby**
from 'The Child and the Nation' (1913)   189

37 **R. Blair**
Prefatory Memorandum (1917)   195

38 **An Officer Wounded on the Somme**
'A National College of All Souls: The True War Memorial'
(1917)   201

39 **Board of Education**
from the Final Report on Juvenile Education After the
War (1917)   206

40 **F. Potter, Ben Turner, W. McG. Eagar and the
Rev. R. R. Hyde**
from Evidence to the Departmental Committee on Juvenile
Education after the War (1917)   213

41 **H. A. L. Fisher**
Introduction of the 1917 Education Bill (1917)   219

42 **Lieutenant-Commander J. C. Wedgwood**
from the debate on the 1917 Education Bill (1917)   232

43 **Sir Henry Hibbert**
from House of Commons, *Parliamentary Debates* (1918)   238

44 **London County Council**
from a Memorandum on the Education Act 1918 (1920)   239

45 **London County Council**
from a Memorandum on the Education Act 1918 (1920)   245

46 **London County Council**
from a Memorandum on the Education Act 1918 (1920)   249

47 **Lord Percy of Newcastle**
from *Some Memories* (1958)   250

48 **R. H. Tawney**
'Keep the Workers' Children in their Place' (1918)   251

49 Labour Party
'Nursery Schools' (1919) 255

50 Board of Education
'The Question of Free Secondary Education' (1920) 258

51 R. H. Tawney
from *Secondary Education for All: A Policy for Labour* (1922) 264

52 H. A. L. Fisher
from *An Unfinished Autobiography* (1940) 268

53 Royal Commission on Oxford and Cambridge Universities (1922) 270

54 Committee on National Expenditure (Geddes)
from the First Interim Report (1922) 276

55 Lord Percy of Newcastle
from *Some Memories* (1958) 287

56 Board of Education
Circular 1371 (1925) 288

57 Advertisement, *New Statesman* (1924) 290

58 Susan Isaacs
from *Intellectual Growth in Young Children* (1930) 291

59 Nathan Isaacs
'Critical Notice' (1966) 295

60 Board of Education
from the Report on the Training of Teachers for Public Elementary Schools (1925) 302

61 Lord Percy of Newcastle
from *Some Memories* (1958) 305

62 Consultative Committee on the Education of the Adolescent (Hadow)
from the Report (1926) 306

63 **Board of Education**
from 'The New Prospect in Education' (1928) 308

64 **Lord Percy of Newcastle**
'The School Leaving Age' (1929) 314

65 **Consultative Committee on the Primary School (Hadow)**
from the Report (1931) 320

66 **A. S. Neill**
'Freedom' (1937) 321

67 **Committee on National Expenditure**
from the Report (1931) 327

68 **Committee on National Expenditure**
from the Report (1931) 332

69 **Board of Education**
Circular 1421 (1932) 339

70 **George Orwell**
'The Private School' (1935) 341

71 **Board of Education**
from the Report on Private Schools (1932) 348

72 **Cyril Burt and Susan Isaacs**
'The Emotional Development of Children up to the Age of
Seven Plus' (1933) 354

73 **G. C. M. M'Gonicle and J. Kirby**
from 'The Physical Condition of Elementary School
Children' (1936) 363

74 **Education Act (1936)** 366

75 **Committee on Secondary Education (Spens)**
from the Report (1938) 369

76 **Committee of Secondary Education (Spens)**
from the Report (1938) 371

77 **Committee on Curriculum and Examinations in Secondary Schools (Norwood)**
from the Report (1943)   372

78 **Committee on Curriculum and Examinations in Secondary Schools (Norwood)**
from the Report (1943)   376

79 **George Orwell**
from 'The Lion and the Unicorn' (1941)   379

80 **Sir William Beveridge**
from the Report on Social Insurance and Allied Services (1942)   381

81 **Board of Education**
from the White Paper on Educational Reconstruction (1943)   384

82 **Board of Education**
from the White Paper on Educational Reconstruction (1943)   390

83 **Board of Education**
from the White Paper on Educational Reconstruction (1943)   393

84 **Lord Percy of Newcastle**
from *Some Memories* (1958)   395

85 **Education Act (1944)**
'The Three Stages of the System'   396

86 **Education Act (1944)**
'Compulsory Attendance'   398

87 **Education Act (1944)**
'Further Education'   399

88 **National Association of Labour Teachers**
'The Comprehensive School: Its History and Character' (1948)   404

89 **Marion Richardson**
from *Art and the Child* (1948)   413

12 Contents

90 Ministry of Education
from *Primary Education* (1959)   417

91 Central Advisory Council for Education (Crowther)
'Why the School Leaving Age should be Raised: The Benefit
to the Individual' (1959)   422

92 Ministry of Education
from Circular 8/60 (1960)   431

93 Jean Floud, A. H. Halsey and F. M. Martin
from *Social Class and Educational Opportunity* (1957)   432

94 C. A. R. Crosland
from *The Future of Socialism*   440

95 J. W. B. Douglas
from *The Home and the School* (1964)   452

96 Committee on Higher Education (Robbins)
'The Pool of Ability' (1963)   453

97 Committee on Higher Education (Robbins)
'The Total Number of Places for Home Students' (1963)   460

98 Central Advisory Council for Education (Newsom)
from *Half Our Future* (1963)   461

99 Ministry of Education
from the Report on Schools' Curricula and Examinations
(1964)   463

100 C. A. R. Crosland
from the Woolwich Polytechnic Speech (1965)   468

101 Department of Education and Science
from Circular 10/65 (1965)   474

102 Central Advisory Council for Education (Plowden)
from *Children and Their Primary Schools* (1967)   480

103 Central Advisory Council for Education (Plowden)
from *Children and Their Primary Schools* (1967)   500

104 J. W. B. Douglas, J. M. Ross and H. R. Simpson
from *All Our Future* (1968)   502

105 Schools Council
from *Raising the School Leaving Age* (1965)   504

106 Schools Council
from *Inquiry 1* (1968)   511

107 Department of Education and Science
from *Education: A Framework for Expansion* (1972)   512

108 Department of Education and Science
Circular 2/73, 'Nursery Education' (1973)   515

Further Reading   523

Acknowledgements   527

Index   529

Introduction

The intention of this collection of documents and extracts is to place conveniently before the student, the teacher and the interested layman a selection of snapshots, kaleidoscopic in form and chronological in time, which provide a documentary history of educational development in England and Wales this century.

In doing so, it tries to pick out the main lines of political, economic, social and scientific thought which influenced – and sometimes significantly failed to influence – subsequent policy, so that the reader, from these extracts, should be able to gain an intuitive feel for the growth of State education.

I say 'intuitive' because this is by no means a collection of record. It makes no claim to be either comprehensive or other than biased. Nor does it in any way seek to compete with an invaluable collection of official reports like Stuart Maclure's *Educational Documents*. Rather, it provides a complement to such a volume.

This is, nevertheless, a catholic collection. I have not strayed too far from the main thread of educational development. Indeed, it could be said that in many respects I have not adequately represented the realm of adult education, say, or technical education. There is little here on art education, or the education of the professions. Instead, I have tried to indicate the rich tapestry of debate about the central issues; the shaping of first primary, and then secondary, schooling for all, the rise of the universities as the tertiary stage of education and, most important of all, the shifting national philosophy of the child, from the determinist views that held sway at the turn of the century to the modern concept of the child as a dynamic, evolving personality.

The knowledgeable critic will inevitably quarrel with my selection. We may be agreed about the central importance of the 1902 Act or the concept of Educational Priority Areas in the Plowden Report; about the influence of the Hadow Report on the schooling of the adolescent and the philosophy contained in the Robbins Report on Higher Education. We might even agree that Sidney Webb's pamphlet on 'The Education Muddle and the Way Out' was an important factor in the shaping of the 1902 Act, and that the evidence of Professor Cyril Burt was central to the thinking of the Hadow reports. But I have tried to go beyond these documents to capture some of the flavour of the educational climate and to bring in, wherever possible, the image of the child and the conditions under which he lived. Here the choices are inevitably more contentious, and I have given fuller reign to my own prejudices. For me, no document says more about elementary schooling than Katherine Bathurst's pitiful description of three year olds falling asleep on their hard benches and cracking their foreheads on the seats in front of them. No official report has the graphic power of J. H. Palin's recollections about child poverty in Bradford. No report reflects the venomous fury of Tawney's attack on the National Federation of British Industry. No committee can match George Orwell's lacerating picture of the private school in the 1930s. Only the individual prose of A. S. Neill can fully capture the vision that prompted so many of the educational experiments of that period. And it takes the wit of an H. G. Wells to do justice to the Mainwearings of this world.

Where possible, therefore, I have tried to include the individual viewpoint – including, I may say, those who considered education rather less than a priority. In doing so, I have had to steer a rather cautious approach between producing a Reader and a collection of historical documents. Though fiction does very occasionally break in, I hope that it is clear that its foundation lies firmly within the realm of fact. But I have inevitably left myself open to two major charges: that I have included the esoteric, and done so at the expense of more important landmarks. I had better admit right away that I am guilty on both counts. I feel perhaps most concerned about the abstentions. There is nothing here from Cecil Reddie of Abbotsholme, or from Dorothy and Leonard Elmhirst of Dartington, or from J. H. Badley of Bedales; nothing from Albert Mansbridge or of Henry Morris. Nothing from A. D. Lindsay and Keele. Only a glimpse of the McMillan sisters. And, on the official side, not a mention of perhaps the most undervalued document of recent times, the Gittins Report on primary education in Wales.

All, regrettably, true. That is to repeat that this is not a comprehensive collection, but a map in which, inevitably, important details are missing. The real test is whether the map contains enough fundamental information to allow the stranger to explore the terrain for himself. I appreciate of course that confession, though no doubt disarming, does not necessarily lead to redemption. In selecting the documents which signpost this particular map, which might be said to have influenced educational policy, how does one measure the 'influence'? It is not in dispute, to pick a simple example, that the impact of mental measurement in the twenties profoundly affected educational thinking – both the Hadow and Spens committees depended much on the evidence of the psychologists, and in particular on that of

Professor Cyril Burt. What is more difficult to decide is which document, in the vast literature of educational psychology, qualifies as the critical one. I have not sought to resolve such imponderables, but instead, have looked for the representative statement. The analogy with 'signposts' is a useful one. Undoubtedly, others would have chosen differently. That is part of the fascination of history. If there are points to criticize about the selection, there are others to be made about the choice of length of extract. Which document should be quoted in full, which reduced to a few paragraphs ? Here I have borne two criteria in mind : its rarity value, and its internal content. Where a document sets out a reasonably full and important argument, such as the pamphlet issued in 1948 by the Association of Labour Teachers on the need for comprehensive schools, I have kept the full text. The argument for Educational Priority Areas in Plowden, again, is a concentrated and important discussion that is edited with peril. Nathan Isaacs's lucid discussion of the differences between the Montessori and Susan Isaacs approach to young children demands the full text. The Fabian Society's pamphlet on the education muddle pre-1902 is difficult to obtain, and is therefore reproduced complete. The cogent argument for raising the school leaving age to sixteen in Crowther demands full treatment though the price in this case was to lose the second part, arguing the case from the national interest. The economic discussions contained in the Geddes and May reports on national economies are again not readily available to the general reader, and have an intrinsic value.

But the corollary to this approach has been that where a document is relatively easily accessible, I have not tried to do other than indicate some crucial passages (the 1944 Act is one, the Hadow Report of 1926 is another) in the hope that this collection, if it has any merit, will prompt the reader in the direction of his own library to make his personal assessment of the evidence. In that way, we can begin to produce rather better and more detailed maps.

Although this collection is very much a personal choice, it rests on the work of others, whose scholarship has drawn our attention to the complexity of educational policy-making. If a list of such studies would have seemed unpalatably pretentious here, it remains true that their work has influenced this collection considerably. More directly, I could not have begun to bring this volume together without the assistance of Miss D. M. Jepson and her staff in the library of the Department of Education and Science. Their courtesy and cooperation, even while the library was physically being moved from one part of London to another, was unfailing. I am particularly indebted to Mr Mark Staunton, to whose personal involvement and professional skill this book owes much. I owe a similar debt of gratitude to the staff of the State Papers Room in the British Museum. Equally, I am grateful to Professor Brian Simon, of Leicester University, and Professor David Pritchard, of the University College of Swansea, for reading some of the material and making both useful and encouraging suggestions about it. To my friends at Penguin Education, Jonathan Croall and Kate Woodhouse, I am indebted for their constant encouragement and professional editing skills.

Most official papers fall into the Command Paper series. From 1836 to 1869, documents were simply given a number, ranging from 1 to 4222. Between 1870 and 1899 the numbers were prefixed by a C, and ranged from C 1 to C 9550. Between 1900 and 1918 documents were prefixed by the letters Cd, and ranged from Cd 1 to Cd 9239 Between 1919 and 1956 documents were prefixed by the code Cmd, and ranged from Cmd 1 to Cmd 9889. From 1956 to the present day documents are coded with the prefix Cmnd.

[. . .] means that material has been omitted.

1 H. G. Wells

from *Joan and Peter: The Story of an Education*, 1918, pp. 268–9.

The Boer War was England's Vietnam. At the turn of the century, the most powerful nation in the world was militarily defied by a colony of farmers, who exposed the limitations of its technologically superior forces and the training of its much-vaunted army. The repercussions were traumatic. England was forced into atrocities which provoked the public criticism of its allies. The military reverses brought about a decline in national morale, shook a complacent nation out of its lethargy, and raised fundamental questions about the fabric of its society. Wells summarized the spirit of bewilderment, anger and frustration that followed in the wake of Colenso, Modder River and Stormberg.

The South African war laid bare an amazing and terrifying amount of national incompetence. The Empire was not only hustled into a war for which there was no occasion, but that was planned with a lack of intelligent foresight and conducted with a lack of soundness that dismayed every thoughtful Englishman. After a monstrous wasteful struggle the national resources brought it at last to a not very decisive victory. The outstanding fact became evident that the British army tradition was far gone in decay, that the army was feebly organized and equipped and that a large proportion of its officers were under-educated men, narrow and conventional, inferior in imagination and initiative to the farmers, layers, cattle-drovers, and such like leaders against whom their wits were pitted. Behind the rejoicings that hailed the belated peace was a real and unprecedented national humiliation. For the first time the educated British were inquiring whether all was well with the national system if so small a conquest seemed so great a task. Upon minds thus sensitized came the realization of an ever more vigorous and ever more successful industrial and trade competition from Germany and the United States: Great Britain was losing her metallurgical ascendancy, dropping far behind in the chemical industries and no longer supreme upon the seas. For the first time a threat was apparent in the methods of Germany. Germany was launching liner after liner to challenge the British merchantile ascendancy, and she was increasing her navy with a passionate vigour. What did it mean?

2 C. C. Perry

from 'Our Undisciplined Brains: The War Test', *Nineteenth Century and After*, December 1901, pp. 897–901.

The concern about England's declining military efficiency led naturally to an examination of her intellectual vigour, and to demands for a national education system to compete with the growing power of Germany, recognized as the real threat to late Victorian England.

The innate rottenness of the British Army, its deficiency in that intellectual light and leading which is at once the most refined and the most awe-inspiring feature of modern warfare, has long been an accepted belief amongst our neighbours. To a great extent, no doubt, the thoughtlessness and *insouciance* of the British officer is to be explained by social causes. By many young Englishmen the military life which they look forward to entering has never been regarded in the light of a serious profession, or indeed as a profession at all. If we compare the English with the German officer, we cannot fail to be struck with the great difference in the degree of moral intensity in their respective conceptions of the duties which they have undertaken. Allowing for notable exceptions which may be said to prove the rule, it is practically the distinction existing between the amateur and the professional, the sportsman and the soldier.

Nor is this great difference of view difficult to account for. In either case the conception of military life is the direct and necessary outcome of the political and social development of the people. To the man ignorant of the history of Germany and unconscious of the tremendous forces to which her military system owes its birth, the grim rigour of German military life remains an enigma, as great an enigma as to the average German appears our own *laissez-aller* system, which leaves the vital interests of the country to be the sport of political expediency and official incompetence. In each country the present condition of things is the natural result of definite causes. The German, who, with an affectation of profundity, gibes at English laxity, and the Englishman, who, secure in his fool's paradise, can find no excuse for German severity, show equal ignorance. Unfortunately for the peace of the world the two conceptions of military duties, though equally intelligible from an historical point of view, are, under the actual condition of things, not equally reasonable or defensible. The present political state of Europe, which has proved our own carelessness to be dangerous and suicidal, has confirmed the wisdom of German thoroughness. The exceptional prosperity and security which we have for so many centuries enjoyed have blinded us to the demands of the age.

The enormous advance of science has practically shifted the centre of civilized life and has changed its very conception. Literature, art, manners, the various refinements of social intercourse, are no longer the only or indeed the chief characteristics which distinguish the civilized from the uncivilized man; nor is it in these, even when combined with natural gallantry and valour in the field, that the actual power of a modern nation can be said chiefly to reside. A want of science and method in a nation is practically a state of savagery which must necessarily succumb in the long run to the new civilization of scientific and technical attainment. If we deliberately choose to take our stand on mere physical excellence, on innate intelligence, on the untrained gifts of the natural man, our position is precisely that of the untutored native of the American prairie or African jungle, who with bow and arrow sets himself to resist the advent of a new race. An indifference, or positive aversion to the modern scientific spirit is all the more dangerous when, as in England, such aversion is specially characteristic of the aristocratic and ruling classes of the country. A dislike of detail and accuracy, an impatience of precision in statement as savouring of priggishness and punctiliousness, a careless disbelief in the value of re-search, a readiness to sink the professional in the amateur, the soldier in the civilian, are all typical of this attitude of mind. To know more than other people, if those people be our daily companions and comrades, comes to be regarded as treason to that spirit of good-fellowship, which, it is felt, ought to prevail among men equally careless and equally ignorant, a treason to be punished by unpopularity and dislike. A silent contempt, or at least dis-regard, of knowledge and high scientific attainment may be considered as one of the keynotes of the military spirit. [. . .]

For an unmilitary nation like ourselves it requires, no doubt, an effort to realize that the scientific calculation and technical knowledge necessary for the perfecting of a modern army form part and parcel of the intellectual life of a nation, that military incapacity means mental incapacity, and that there can be no better test of the practical intelligence of a nation than the conduct of a campaign. The course of our political development has in-evitably tended to produce a real, though unconscious, antagonism between military ideas and associations on the one hand and the intellectual life of the student and the thinker on the other. We hardly recognize indeed that there can be anything in common between the learned professions and the military life. Proud as we are of military success and of the national power which it represents, there has always been a tendency to regard the army as something apart from the nation itself, if not as a positive evil and a standing menace to civil liberty. Of that development of the military idea which has in all great Continental States made the people and the army almost convertible terms, and which has placed the very highest intellectual power in the country at the service of the combatant forces, we practically know nothing. No inconsistency in the English national character strikes the foreigner more than our bestowal of lavish praises in times of emergency upon a force which in times of peace we regard as almost beyond the pale of intellectual and social sympathy. It is this spirit which lies at the root of our military incapacity and our military disasters. No modern army can hope to be efficient which is not based on the intelligence as well as on the pride of a people. Continental militarism, whatever its evils, at least forms part of the national life and vigour. Its force and intelligence is not that of a caste or section, but of the people at large. It has created a community of interest such as never existed before between the military and the intellectual life of the country. The soldier and the civilian, whatever the external distinctions that may divide them, are animated by one and the same spirit of order, method and science. Universal schooling on the one hand, and universal conscription on the other, are the two pillars on which the most powerful State of Europe is raised. The most military State in the world is at the same time the most intellectual one. 'It is the Prussian schoolmaster who has defeated us,' remarked a distinguished Austrian general in the war of 1866 to one of the victors. It was from an intellectual point of view, as a masterpiece of scientific calculation and precision, that the Franco-German campaign of 1870 is chiefly entitled to the admiration of the world, and this campaign was practically the work of one man who united within himself all the best attributes of the student and the soldier.

The first step in finding a cure for those defects which the present campaign in South Africa has brought into such sharp relief is to recognize the fact that the real root of the evil does not lie in the condition of what is called military education, but in a general deficiency in the mental training of the English youth at large. [. . .]

It is, however, not with our universities, or with popular conceptions of education, that we are now more immediately concerned, but with those great institutions known by the name of public schools, to whom the education of our ruling classes is committed. It is these which must be held responsible for the initial stages of our military as well as of our general education. How far can the average instruction given at these schools – and it is the average not the abnormal result, the rule not the exception, that we are dealing with – conduce to the awakening of practical intelligence, and herein more especially to the development of logical thought and logical expression? No English observer who has opportunities of studying the youth of foreign lands as well as that of his own country can fail to observe that one of the most striking characteristics of the English as compared with the foreign boy is his peculiar distaste for consecutive thought or speech, his positive aversion on the one hand to any mental process, and on the other to the articulate expression of any such process. We are admittedly a silent nation and averse to reveal the current of our thoughts, and, so far as this reserve arises from an inward conviction of the uselessness of words in themselves, it is, no doubt, an excellent quality, yet youth at least is not the time nor is school the place for fostering by sheer want of mental discipline a characteristic which is due quite as often to mere intellectual sluggishness as to constitutional reserve.

3 Sir H. E. Roscoe

from 'The Outlook for British Trade', *Monthly Review*, May 1901, pp. 76–87.

At the heart of the debate about the war and about education lay a basic concern about England's trade position. For trade, it was recognized, meant power, influence, and independence. England was losing ground in the very sphere in which she had once been supreme. The battleground between nations had shifted, from the barracks and the high seas to the centres of learning.

A national system of secondary education has, so far at least, proved to be past praying for. Chaos still reigns supreme. Divergent interests are hard to reconcile. Vested interests are strong, and any government which undertakes to unravel the tangle must not only have its heart in the work, but be powerful enough to carry it through. Under these untoward conditions what course, then, ought a boy to take who has either the brains or the position, or both, to fit himself to be a man of light and leading in the world of English industry ? The old plan was to turn the lad as soon as he could read and write and cipher decently into the shops of his father's or his friend's factory. He must work like any other boy; he must be there at six o'clock every morning till six at night, and hammer and file or spin and weave with his fellow 'hands'. Thus he learnt his trade. To send him to one of our great public schools and afterwards to the university, was in his father's eyes, and the father was a keen-sighted person, certain ruin to his prospects as far as industrial life was concerned. So such boys grew up to man's estate in a narrow groove, and it was only in the rare case of exceptional ability or under exceptionally favourable conditions that one was able to successfully carry out any new move; the rest could do no more than hold their own or perhaps extend their trade on the lines laid down by their predecessors. So long as they had command of the trade, so long as they had no competitors treading on their heels, so long were they successful, practical, sound English manufacturers, who made their fortunes without much trouble or thought, and who expected their sons to go and do likewise. But things did not continue to go on so smoothly; the foreigner made his appearance on the stage and proved to be an important character, and by no means a mere walking gentleman. Then our practical man opens his eyes and finds the line blocked.

Are we, however, to admit that the public school and the university education, with the absence of any real teaching of modern languages, is inimical to a successful industrial career? If this be so it reveals a serious state of things, for it is undeniable that for a leader of men, for the head of a great and growing manufacturing concern, public-school training ought for many great and cogent reasons to be the best preparation. It may be said that the manufacturers have only recently been disabused of the notion of the unfitness of the public school and university as training for their sons, and that the time has not yet come when those who have thus been trained can show their mettle. In the meanwhile, however, our trade is slipping away from us, and he would be a bold man who could with confidence assert that it would be safe to trust to men trained in the present system of those schools to win it back again. For whilst amongst those eminent in the church, in the army, in the higher civil service, in the legislatures, public school and university men predominate, the examples will be found to be few and far between of men with that training who have made their mark as leaders in industry or even in commerce. Hence, we are forced to the conclusion that, be the reasons what they may, that which for argument's sake we may call our only national system of secondary and higher education is unfitted to, or at any rate does not, supply a great and crying national want, namely, for men fitted to cope with the danger we run of losing our pre-eminence in industry and commerce.

Look at the question from another point of view. Consider for a moment the long list of names of men who have advanced our old industries, who have founded new ones, who have by their achievements revolutionized society, and then ask how many of these men (one might easily name a hundred) have had a public-school and university training. Scarcely any. Most of them have, of course, had no school training worth talking about; they have risen to the first rank by their innate powers of brain and will; their school has been the workshop, their university the world. Then, it may be replied, if your great saviours of society have been self-made men, why all this educational fervour? Simply, again, because the conditions of things are changed. Old things have passed away and given place to the new. The engineers, the chemists of the past, had much less complex problems to deal with than their brethren of today. The roads, the bridges, the railways, the steam engines which were built by our English engineers in the past were simple matters compared with the construction of the Forth Bridge or the elaboration of an electric-light station. The manufacture of soap or alkali on a large scale demanded only a moderate amount of knowledge of scientific chemistry, but for the economic production of artificial indigo an intimate acquaintance with, and a perfect command over, the highest and most complicated problems of organic chemistry is essential. To advance science, whether pure or applied in the early stages of scientific history, was comparatively easy; to make discoveries of equal importance in the more advanced stage demands not only a thorough knowledge of what has gone before, but especially a complete training in the methods by which these results have been obtained. To be a leader in new paths the outfit must now be full: an inadequate provision rapidly brings the traveller to grief.

Here it is then that the want of system and the absence of provision is most strikingly felt. It is a systematized training for the men who are to be the officers of the industrial army which is lacking. Moreover, their preliminary preparation has hitherto been so incomplete that they are unable to take full advantage of the higher instruction, or to study with profit the special sciences which they are bound thoroughly to master in such institutions as exist. Not only, however, must justice be done, but full credit awarded, to those far-sighted persons who, whether acting as representing corporate bodies or as private individuals, whether as members of the profession of teachers or as a portion of the general public, have taken steps to set up and to maintain in various parts of the kingdom new universities, as Victoria and Birmingham, with university colleges and high schools of science and research, as well as the older studies, where, under the hands of able teachers, the competent man may not only carry on his scientific education up to the highest limits of the known, but where he can learn what is even more important – namely, the methods by which excursions may be made into the unknown.

This latter is, indeed, the essence of a scientific training; it is to fit the mind of the learner so that he may understand how to approach the investigation of a new problem, how to overcome the difficulties with which it is beset, and how to carry such work to a successful issue. Nothing but training in scientific research can possibly provide this necessary outfit No distinction in scholarship, no amount of book learning, still less the much-coveted 'blue', can supply this, and the misfortune from which the country suffers is that, whilst public honour is generally paid and support given to pre-eminence in the above, any acknowledgement of the value of the study of scientific method, or recognition of the services of those who are masters of that method, is but very occasionally met with. This position of affairs carries with it grave consequences. The most important of these is that our statesmen who, so it is said, cannot act in advance of public opinion and without its support, are unwilling to take steps which the governments of other nations have long ago deemed necessary of giving State recognition by the establishment and importance of at least one complete and thoroughly organized High School of Science. We should have one equipped on a big scale, to do for English industries what the Federal Technicum at Zurich has done for those of Switzerland and what the Reichs-Anstalt at Charlottenburg is doing for those of Germany. The establishment of such a seat of scientific training and research, say in the Metropolis, would not merely enable the requisite education of the highest type to be given in all branches in one institution, though not necessarily in one building, which now exists only sporadically and inadequately (though, so far as it goes, efficiently), in independent centres, but it would at once give a stamp of Imperial importance to these essential studies which, though acknowledged as State possessions in other countries, are, as such, here almost unrecognized. This can, however, best be done by paying due regard to the claims of existing institutions and by taking care that proper use is made of the educational advantages which such institutions afford to the Metropolis, by coordination and additions where necessary, rather than by the establishment of entirely new schools.

Against such a proposal we have at once the cry raised by the so-called economists, and by the older school of statesmen: 'Why should the nation pay for the education of persons who can quite well afford to pay for it themselves? The less government meddles with the higher education the better for the country. All that a government can be legitimately called upon to do is to help those who cannot help themselves,' and so on. This argument will not hold water. Does not Parliament at the present moment vote very large grants to the Scottish universities? Are not similar though much smaller grants voted to the English and Welsh university colleges? Are not the Royal Colleges of Science in London and in Dublin supported by government? Then large grants are made to the British museums and many other institutions of a more or less educational character, which benefit many besides those 'who cannot help themselves'. Indeed, the question may well be asked, Why does the nation pay away its millions for free elementary education? Surely not out of commiseration for the struggles for existence of the poor, but entirely because it rightly believes that it is for the benefit of our people as a whole that all should be delivered from the consequences arising out of national ignorance. The national elementary schools are not for the poor alone; they are for everybody, and the pity is that we in England do not act, as do our brethren across the sea, upon the great principle of equality before the schoolmaster. If, then, it can be proved – and proved it can be – that the establishment and maintenance of a perfectly equipped High School for Science – a scientific university – is a step which must be taken as one means of warding off the danger which threatens our industrial well-being; if it can be further shown that the necessity for taking such a step is immediate, and that to wait until public opinion is so far awakened to the state of the case that private munificence steps in to the rescue is to court ruin; if these things are true, what defence can an intelligent government make against founding or assisting to found so necessary an institution?

The University of London is at this moment being reconstructed. Is the present, then, not a favourable opportunity for the Government to come forward, and to assist the University, which has no funds for this purpose, in establishing such a complete High School for Science, and to place England in this respect at least on a level with little Switzerland?

The nation is prodigal of its wealth and of its life when duty calls. We are spending a hundred millions to save our Empire in South Africa; and the lives of thousands of brave men on both sides have been sacrificed in the cause. Our educational war is also waged to save the Empire. It requires no sacrifice of life, and its cost is a trifle compared with that called for month by month by the Commander-in-Chief in South Africa. Moreover, if all this is true, if England by her supineness and blindness is running even a remote risk of losing her trade and her industrial position, surely we are not asking too great a boon from a Government which has proved itself so alive to its responsibilities as to pay dearly for the honour and welfare of the Empire, when we say help us to combat the enemy not by shooting him down, but by proving to him in peaceful contest that the Englishmen is the better man.

4 O. Eltzbacher

from 'The Disadvantages of Education', *Nineteenth Century and After*, February 1903, pp. 315–18.

The debate was not totally one-sided. There were plenty of voices raised against the idea of spending more money on education, and some even presented interesting arguments of logic against the claimed benefits of education at all.

Education, after having been more or less neglected for a long time in Great Britain, has now become an all-powerful panacea in the eyes of the British public and of the British politician. As the alchemists of the dark ages expected to be able to turn any base metal into gold with the help of the philosopher's stone, even so the politicians of the present day expect education to work wonders in Great Britain and to benefit the nation most marvellously in every direction. And, as in the Middle Ages unenlightened princes often subjected their entire States to the fantastic experiments of astrologers and alchemists, half crack-brained mystics not entirely innocent of fraud, half nebulous scientists full of extravagant superstitions, in the hope of benefiting their people thereby, even so the patient British nation is to be experimented upon by the schoolmaster at the bidding of the politician, and education is to work wonders in every way. The stagnation of British commerce is to be converted into commercial triumphs by commercial education. Our former industrial supremacy is to return at the hand of technical education, improved military education is to endow us with capable officers – in fact, the whole nation will have to put its nose in a book. But may not the nation become shortsighted, in the literal and in the metaphorical sense, from too much study, and may not the promised blessings of the schoolmaster's activity prove largely an illusion? At present it seems as if we were going to fall from the Scylla of under-education into the perhaps more dangerous Charybdis of over-education.

Whilst educational enthusiasts in and out of politics are strenuously advocating the 'training' of leaders of men in every field of human activity, it is useful to consider occasionally the limitations of education, and to remember how few of the leaders of men have been 'trained' to their leadership by third parties either in schools or otherwise.

It is an old experience that the most prominent men in nearly every province of human activity have been amateurs, and that is one of the reasons why amateurs, and not professionals, are selected to rule our great public departments. Our great administrators have nearly all been amateurs and autodidacts. To take a few of the best known examples: Cromwell was a farmer, Warren Hastings and Clive were clerks, Mr Chamberlain was brought up for trade, Lord Goschen for commerce and Lord Cromer for the army. Other countries have had the same experience with self-taught amateurs. Prince Bismarck was brought up for law, failed twice to pass his examination, became a country squire, and drifted without any training into the Prussian diplomatic service and the cabinet, and founded the German Empire. George Washington was a surveyor, Benjamin Franklin a printer, Abraham Lincoln a lumberman, M. de Witte a railway official.

In a less exalted sphere we meet with the same phenomenon. Sir William Herschell was a musician, Faraday a bookbinder, Scott a lawyer's clerk, Murat a student of theology, Ney a notary's clerk, Arkwright the inventor of the spinning machine and the first cotton manufacturer, a barber, Spinoza a glass-blower, Adam Smith a clergyman, Lord Armstrong an attorney, Herbert Spencer an engineer, Pasteur, the father of modern medicine and chirurgy, a chemist, Edison a newsvendor; George Stephenson and most of the great inventors and creators of industry of his time were ordinary working men.

When we look round we find not only that many leaders of men were devoid of a highly specialized training in that particular branch of human activity in which they excel, that they were self-taught amateurs, but that many of the ablest politicians and of the most successful business men have not even had the advantage of a fair general education. Abraham Lincoln had learned at school only the three R's, and those very incompletely, President Garfield worked with a boatman when only ten years old, President Jackson was a saddler and never spelled correctly, President Benjamin Harrison started life as a farmer, and President Andrew Johnson, a former tailor, visited no school, and learned reading only from his wife. George Peabody started work when only eleven years old, the late Sir Edward Harland was apprenticed at the age of fifteen years, Andrew Carnegie began his commercial career when twelve years old, as a factory hand, Charles Schwab, president of the United States Steel Corporation, drove a coach as a boy, and then became a stake-driver at an iron works. Josiah Wedgwood started work when only eleven years old; Arkwright, the father of our cotton industry, was never at school, Edison was engaged in selling papers when twelve years of age, and Sir Hiram Maxim was with a carriage builder when he was fourteen. 'Commodore' Cornelius Vanderbilt, the railway king, who left more than a hundred million dollars, started as a ferryman at a tender age; the founder of the wealth of the Astors was a butcher's boy, Baron Amsel Mayer von Rothschild a pedlar, Alfred Krupp a smith, Rockefeller, the head of the Standard Oil Trust, a clerk. All these most successful men were autodidacts. People well acquainted with the City can name a goodly number of millionaires who occasionally drop an 'h', the only evidence left of an arduous career from the bottom rung of the ladder.

Why have so few eminently successful men been school-trained? Because the acceptance of ready-made opinions kills the original thinking power and unbiased resourcefulness of the mind, and paramount success cannot be achieved by docile scholars and imitators, but only by pioneers. Besides, the independent spirits who are predestined for future greatness are usually impatient of the restraint of schools, and of their formal and largely unpractical tuition, and wish to be free to follow their own instincts towards success.

In view of these numerous well-known instances of greatness achieved by men unaided, but also unspoiled by education, who taught themselves what they found necessary to learn, which instances might be multiplied *ad infinitum*, it is only natural to find a strong opposition to education among the unlearned men whose native shrewd common sense has not been affected by the reading of books. But even the learned begin to waver and to ask themselves whether the much-vaunted benefits of learning have not been largely over-estimated, and whether the undoubted advantages of education are not more than counterbalanced by corresponding dis-advantages.

The doubts as to the advantages of education have been considerably strengthened by our experiences in the South African war. Many observers have been struck by the curious phenomenon that our most highly edu-cated officers had on the whole so little success against the Boer officers, who were not only quite unlearned in the science of war, but also mostly uneducated, and sometimes grossly ignorant in elementary knowledge, peasants who had perhaps not even heard the names of Frederick the Great, Napoleon and Moltke, whose every battle our erudite officers had at their fingers' ends.

The highest military school in Great Britain is the Staff College. The officers who have succeeded in passing through that institution are con-sidered to be the most intellectual, and are marked out for future employ-ment in the most responsible positions. They are our most scientific soldiers and represent the flower of learning in the army. Consequently it might be expected that our most distinguished generals should be Staff College men. However, if we look through the Army List, it appears that our most successful officers in the Boer war – Lord Roberts, Lord Kitchener, Sir John French, Sir George White, Sir Archibald Hunter, Sir Ian Hamilton, Lord Dundonald, Sir Hector Macdonald, and General Baden-Powell – have not passed the Staff College. On the other hand, we find that the late General Colley, who lost Majuba, was a prominent military scientist and Staff College professor, and that General Gatacre, who was defeated at Stormberg, and Generals Kelly-Kenny, Hildyard, Hart and Barton, who also took part in the South African war, though not with conspicuous success, have the much-coveted P.S.C. (passed Staff

College) printed before their names. In the South African war it came to pass, as some crusty old colonels had prophesied, that the officers who were brimful of scientific military knowledge, and who could talk so learnedly on strategy and tactics, achieved nothing on the field of battle. Those who achieved something had not been 'trained' to generalship in the Staff College, and had not had their natural thinking power, their common sense, crowded out of existence by the absorption of a huge store of book-learning.

After some of our initial defeats a distinguished general was sent out, and it was reported that wherever he went a large library of military works, strategical, tactical and historical, went with him. He and his library went to Africa to save the situation, but not many months after, that distinguished scientific general returned in disgrace to England, together with his library. His imposing book knowledge, with which he could talk down any mere fighting officer, had availed him nothing in the field.

Our 'highly trained' professional intelligence officers proved also of very little value until they had unlearned in Africa what they had been taught at home, whilst quite unlearned Transvaal peasants made splendid intelligence officers. On the other hand, 'Colonel' Wools-Sampson, by far our best intelligence officer, was a civilian.

Our politicians have unfortunately not yet learned the lessons of the South African war. Instead of investigating why the unlearned peasant officers defeated so often the flower of our military scientists, who were fortified with the most profound military education, and who had a most extensive knowledge of the battles, the strategy and tactics of all periods, from the time of Hannibal onwards, a committee of gentlemen innocent of war was deputed to inquire into the education of our officers. Naturally enough their verdict was condemnatory of the present system, and various suggestions were made by it how to improve the education of our officers. Lord Kitchener, General French, Christian de Wet and Louis Botha, fighting officers who are no doubt the most competent judges of the qualifications required in an officer for war, were, unfortunately, not asked for their opinion on such a vital matter. It would have been interesting to learn how much or how little weight practical authorities of unrivalled weight, such as these, attach to school education of officers as practised in Great Britain, and what, according to their opinion, the effect of that school education is upon their common sense.

5 F. H. Doolan

from a letter to the *Sunday Times*, 1 November 1970.

*For the generation about whom the debate raged, the dominant feature of
life was not the Boer War, or trade, or Germany's growing industrial might.
It was sheer, naked poverty.*

I was born in 1903 in the slum areas of Walsall. Where we lived, eighteen
families shared six outside lavatories and one water tap. We had no gaslight
only an oil lamp or candle. We slept five to a bed; two children at the bottom
and mother, father and baby on the top. The average wage was about
eighteen shillings a week. My mother told me: 'If ever you bring home a
golden sovereign, I'll have it framed.' To pick up a few coppers, I would sell
evening papers, barefoot. On Saturday evenings we took two pence in an
enamel bowl to the cooked meat shop for the leavings. This would be our
Sunday dinner. We would look with envy at clothes in a second-hand shop.
I never had a new suit until I put on Army uniform. When school photographs were taken all the poor kids were at the back because we were so
ragged. To keep our homes in fuel we boys would go to the canal near the
ironworks, where the water was warm, and dive in to collect coal that had
fallen off the boats.

6 Sir J. Crichton-Browne

from *Parcimony in Nutrition*, 1909, quoted in J. C. Drummond and
A. Wilbraham, *The Englishman's Food*, 1958, p. 410.

*It was not only the obviously destitute who suffered. Some children of the
so-called upper classes, who attended private boarding schools, fared little
better. The following is an extract of a letter of a friend of Sir James
Crichton-Browne.*

There were fifteen of us boarders. We paid £150 a year, and we never had
enough to eat. We rose at 7 a.m. and had breakfast at 8.30, consisting of
weak tea, a thick bit of bread with a thin smear of butter. Butterine was
substituted for butter until complaints were made, and then we had salt
butter. Once a month a boiled egg was given at breakfast. Dinner, which
came at one o'clock, consisted of two courses, soup and meat, or meat and
pudding, vegetables being always served with the meat. But the meat was

doled out in very small portions, and although second helpings were nominally allowed, they were regarded with disapprobation, and were scarcely worth asking for. . . . Tea at six o'clock consisted of weak tea and bread and butter as at breakfast, but occasionally jam of a livid complexion was substituted for butter. We were always hungry, and all our pocket money went on food. I was growing fast, and often felt faint and ill, but it would not do to complain, for a girl on the sick list was isolated and fed on gruel or arrowroot made with water.

7 Committee on Physical Deterioration

'Overcrowding', from the Report of the Inter-Departmental Committee vol. 1, Cd 2175, 1904, pp. 16–17.

Growing concern about the conditions of life among the urban poor, highlighted by the work of men like Charles Booth and Seebohm Rowntree, led to the first major report into the physical health of the nation. It ran to three volumes, and was only one of many reports which between 1902 and 1906 examined problems of child employment, physical condition, diet, housing and industrial conditions at the time. They all told the same story.

Overcrowding still stands out most prominent with its attendant evils of uncleanliness, foul air and bad sanitation.

The problem is by no means a new one, however its conditions may have become aggravated in recent times. So long ago as the year 1598 the Privy Council addressed a letter to the Justices of Middlesex, inveighing against the owners of tenement houses for the abuses they encouraged;

the remedie whereof cannot be sufficientlie provided in havinge an eye to these persons that take those howses, beinge so great a nomber, and they cannot be justlie corrected untill they be taken with some offence, but in severe punyshinge those landlords that lett out those small tenements (parcells of howses and chambers) unto unknowne and base people and from weeke to weeke, not regardinge what the persones are that take the same, but to rayse a vile and unconscionable lucre.

This is not quite the official language of the present day, but among the opinions collected by the most modern investigator occur the following: 'Overcrowding is the great cause of degeneracy'; 'Drink is fostered by bad houses'; 'Crowded homes send men to the public-houses'; 'Crowding the main cause of drink and vice'.

The permanent difficulties that attach to the problem reside, as the same witness has shown, in the character of the people themselves (their feebleness and indifference, their reluctance to move, and their incapability of moving), and in the obstacle this presents to the best directed efforts on the part of the local authority to employ their powers.

It has been suggested that interference 'by administrative action and penalties at each point at which life falls below a minimum accepted standard' is the way by which the problem must be approached, and the occupation of overcrowded tenements seems to afford the best opportunity for the application of the doctrine. The evil is, of course, greatest in one-roomed tenements, the overcrowding there being among persons usually of the lowest type, steeped in every kind of degradation and cynically indifferent to the vile surroundings engendered by their filthy habits, and to the pollution of the young brought up in such an atmosphere. The general death-rate in these tenements in Glasgow is nearly twice that of the whole city, and the death-rate from pulmonary tuberculosis is 2·4 per thousand in one-roomed tenements, 1·8 in two-roomed tenements, and 0·7 in all the other houses. In Finsbury, again, where the population of one-roomed tenements is 14,516, the death-rate per thousand in 1903 was 38·9, yet the rate among occupants of four or more rooms was only 5·6, and for the whole borough 19·6. Similarly, a comparison between the population of Hampstead and Southwark, in respect of their ability to withstand disease and death, shows an expectation of life very largely in favour of Hampstead, at birth the relative figures being 50·8 and 36·5 years, at five, 57·4 and 48·7, illustrating the waste of material during the first years of life. From another table, furnished by Mr Shirley Murphy, the Medical Officer of Health for the administrative County of London, it appears that in seven groups of districts with an increasing amount of population living in over-crowded tenements the infant death-rate has followed the increase; that is to say, in districts with under 10 per cent of the population living under these conditions the death-rate was 142 per thousand, and then, as the proportion of people living in overcrowded tenements increases, so does the infant death-rate, going from 180 to 196, and then to 193, and then going on to 210, 222 and 223.

8 Committee on Physical Deterioration

'Pollution of Atmosphere', from the Report of the Inter-Departmental Committee, vol. I, Cd 2175, 1904, p. 20.

The attention of the Committee was prominently called to the effect on public health of the pollution of the atmosphere.

In dealing with the Manchester district one witness said,

The pollution of the air is worse than ever. I should trace much of the anaemia to the deprivation of sunlight and to the lessening of the vivifying qualities of the air. You have execrable air for the people to breathe.

Another gave similar testimony,

The condition of the air by its direct effect on lungs and skin is the cause of much disease and physical deterioration. By cutting off much of the scant supply of sunlight which is all that Manchester at best would be allowed by its gloomy climate to receive, it injures health. The filthiness of the air makes those inhabitants of all parts of Manchester who value cleanliness most unwilling to ventilate their dwellings. By killing nearly all vegetation and by its other effects, the foulness of the air contributes much to that general gloominess of the town which led Mr Justice Day to say in explanation of the prevalence of drunkenness in the town, that to get drunk 'is the shortest way out of Manchester'.

To this influence is attributed the removal of all well-to-do persons from the town, which the same witness stated to be a most fruitful cause of the ignorance and bad habits of the poor, and of the failure on the part of the authorities to take sufficient cognizance of those districts in which the poor are congregated without admixture of other classes.

The chief causes of this pollution are alleged to be the non-enforcement of the law for the prevention of smoke from factories, the imposition of inadequate penalties, the neglect to limit works which produce noxious vapours to special areas where they can be closely supervised and so do the least possible amount of harm; and lastly, the absence of any provision in the law compelling the occupants of dwellings to produce the least possible quantity of smoke.

On the point of prosecutions, it was stated that there are people in Manchester who systematically pollute the air and pay the fine, finding it much cheaper to do so than to put up new plant. The trial of such cases before benches of magistrates composed of manufacturers or their friends creates an atmosphere of sympathy for the accused, and it was alleged that magistrates who had sought to give effect to the law encountered the indifference and sometimes the positive opposition of their colleagues. It was explained that although careless stoking is often responsible for the evil, the production of smoke is really the result of overdriven furnaces; with adequate room for boiler and furnace, and a well paid fireman under careful supervision, smoke can be prevented without any special appliances, but the greater part of the smoke is produced by furnaces that are too small for their work.

9 Committee on Physical Deterioration

'Conditions of Employment', from the Report of the Inter-Departmental Committee, vol. 1, Cd 2175, 1904, pp. 26–7.

With the changes in occupation attending the rapid urbanization of the people, it is obvious that the conditions of employment must enter largely into the causes that determine physique.

No one will deny that coincident with the large increase in the number of factory workers great amelioration has taken place in the circumstances of labour, but causes prejudicial to health cannot be altogether eliminated, and under the most favourable conditions degenerative agencies will continue at work. Moreover, it seems to be the case that the advance has been more in the direction of combating the effects of dangerous trades, which, after all, only affect a comparatively small section of the working population. Describing the life of a boy of fourteen in a textile district, who has probably been bred in an unwholesome environment and nourished on unnatural food, Mr Wilson, HM Inspector of Factories, said,

The hours will be long, fifty-five per week, and the atmosphere he breathes very confined, perchance also dusty. Employment of this character, especially if carried on in high temperatures, rarely fosters growth or development; the stunted child elongates slightly in time, but remains very thin, loses colour, the muscles remain small, especially those of the upper limbs, the legs are inclined to become bowed, more particularly if heavy weights have to be habitually carried, the arch of the foot flattens and the teeth decay rapidly.

He continues,

The girls exhibit the same shortness of stature, the same miserable development, and they possess the same sallow cheeks and carious teeth. I have also observed that at an age when girls brought up under wholesome conditions usually possess a luxuriant growth of hair, these factory girls have a scanty crop which, when tied back, is simply a wisp or 'rat's tail'.

10 Committee on Physical Deterioration

'Infant Mortality', from the Report of the Inter-Departmental Committee, vol. 1, Cd 2175, 1904, pp. 44-5.

Among the more highly organized nations, where the tendency to a decrease in the birth-rate becomes more or less noticeable, the means by which infant mortality can be averted present a social problem of the first importance. Unfortunately in the volume of vital statistics, from which so many consolatory reflections are drawn, infant mortality remains a dark page. The Registrar-General in his last report lays down that 'the mortality among infants and very young children has always been regarded as a valuable test of salubrity'. Since the date of that report, Dr Tatham has caused to be prepared, at the Committee's request, certain interesting statistics respecting infantile mortality in England and Wales, at two quinquennial periods a quarter of a century apart. The tables, six in number, show the mortality among male and female infants separately (a) in town as distinguished from country; (b) among legitimate as distinguished from illegitimate infants. He has also furnished the Committee with a careful analysis of the tabular returns, and as this analysis is very full, it is only necessary to refer to the appendix, where will be found the six tables referred to, and also Dr Tatham's remarks upon them.

Three facts stand out prominently as the result of this investigation: first, that infantile mortality in this country has not decreased materially during the last twenty-five years, notwithstanding that the general death-rate has fallen considerably; secondly, that the mortality among illegitimate children is enormously greater than among children born in wedlock: thirdly, that about one-half the mortality occurs in the first three months of life.

The evidence furnished by a variety of witnesses is confirmatory of the conclusions to which these figures point. According to Dr Chalmers, of Glasgow, where the infant death-rate varies in different districts from sixty-three to 217 per thousand births (that for the whole city being 141), 'Quite one-third of the infant deaths occur in the first four weeks of life'. In certain parts of London, where the proportion of persons living in one or two-roomed tenements exceeds 35 per cent, it has already been seen that this death-rate reaches 223. Preston, with nearly half its female population occupied (30 per cent being married), has an average rate for the ten years to 1900 of 236, Burnley of 210, and Blackburn, with a still higher percentage of married women employed, of 200. In Sheffield, where the general rate in 1901 was 201, it went up in one district to 234 and there is no doubt that, in parts of the country, during certain seasons of the year, such rates are vastly exceeded.

Coming to particulars illustrative of these conditions, Mr Wilson speaking of Dundee, said: 'It was quite a common thing to find a woman had had as many as thirteen children, and had lost eleven or twelve out of that number, in some cases the whole of them.' Mrs Greenwood, in a paper submitted relating to Sheffield, says: 'One woman I know has buried seventeen out of eighteen children, another has had sixteen sons, of whom only six are living', though neither of them had worked out of their homes since marriage. Nor, in her opinion, is such waste necessarily connected with poverty; deaths from diseases of the respiratory organs constantly occur owing to the practice of even well-to-do mothers exposing imperfectly clad children to cold while gossiping with neighbours. Among a certain number of mothers questioned in Hanley and Longton, it appeared that 38 per cent of the children born to them had died in infancy, and the state of the case in many Lancashire towns is certainly no better; thus in Burnley one woman is said to have had twenty children and buried sixteen, all having died between one and eleven months of age; in this case the father was a collier in good wages and the mother stayed at home. At Accrington things have become so bad as to lead to vigorous action on the part of a conference convened by the Mayor, as the result of which exhaustive inquiry into the conditions under which children are brought up has been demanded.

11 General Sir Frederick Maurice

from Evidence to the Inter-Departmental Committee on Physical Deterioration, vol. 2, 1904, pp. 11–13.

Part of the concern with physical deterioration was the poor physical standards of recruits to the army. One man who drew particular attention to this, and who investigated the matter further, was General Sir Frederick Maurice, who gave evidence to the Committee on Physical Deterioration.

CHAIRMAN: 'You were for some years a General Officer Commanding at Woolwich?'

'Yes, for seven years.' [. . .]

'It was during those years that your attention was drawn in a somewhat special manner to the question of the physical health of the classes from which we draw recruits?'

'Yes.'

'And, in consequence of what came under your observation at that time, you had some interviews with the Inspector-General Borrett of recruiting thereon?'

'Yes.'

'Could you favour us with what passed on those occasions?'

'I had been very much struck by the fact that we were taking some very bad bargains into the Service, who had evidently cost a great deal of money, and who would never make soldiers at all, and, therefore, I went to see, the Inspector-General of Recruiting thereon, General Borrett. I called his attention to certain men who had been passed into the Service, and he immediately drew my attention to the fact that his great difficulty was, that if he stopped the recruiting doctors from taking these men by making their examination more strict, they rejected much too freely. I learnt that in the course of conversation.'

'Was that before the war?'

'Yes, and also after the war had begun; and, in fact, a good deal was subsequently to the war. I used generally to have my attention called to a bad case, and I would go and have a talk to him; I would at a single inspection at the Herbert Hospital find half-a-dozen men perfectly unfit for military or civil life. I very soon found that the practical point was that the doctors had had such bad recruiting subjects before them that their eyes had got wearied with the classes they were inspecting, and they passed those men in because, relatively to some of the others they had been seeing, they were not so bad.'

'In a spirit of sheer exhaustion?'

'Yes, and also that the standard of their eyes was lowered by the men they had been seeing. That, of course, rather alarmed me as to the class from whom we were getting our recruits. Then the question arose, whether it was simply that we were getting only refuse for the Army, or whether the failure in physique did not affect other classes, whether my experience was not applicable to these also.'

'The question was whether the condition indicated applied only to the loafing classes, or to the poorer classes generally?'

'Yes. After that I began to get a good deal of evidence from other people in Woolwich, and I found two most startling cases in my own family; that is to say, a daughter-in-law of my own engaged for a short time a temporary cook who is a married woman, and the house was kept awake at night by the screams of a baby in arms, night after night. We very soon found that the reason of this was that the mother was giving her six-month-old baby habitually for supper cold cabbage, though the woman was quite able to give it proper food.' [. . .]

'Did the child survive?'

'It was not dead at the time I speak of. But I was perfectly convinced that that would have an effect upon young men at eighteen years of age if that was the way they were treated when babies in arms. Then the question arose whether the case was exceptional or representative. I naturally went about among the ladies who visited the homes of the people, such as district visitors, clergymen's wives and others who had experience, and I found that it was their experience that the children were fed in that way, that the ordinary answers of the mothers when they were speaking of the feeding of their children was, "They eats just what we does".'

'You say that the universal testimony was that parents feed them off their own plates, and include raw herrings, pickles, fried fish and the like?'

'Yes. I found also that the societies which sent out children into the country districts, on the system of giving town children a few weeks of country air and country food, habitually received reports that the children could not eat the food natural for their time of life, because in their town life they had been accustomed to what they called relishes, the kind of unwholesome food of which I have spoken.'

'The things that were stimulating to the palate?'

'Yes. The other case arose from my own experience in my own family. My second son was very suddenly taken with scarlet fever, and before the infectious stage it became necessary to have him taken out of the house, and I had to send him to a hospital. At that time one could not put anyone into a paying ward, and he had to go into the ordinary ward at Blackheath; and, as he was always fond of looking after children, as soon as he was well, he helped the nurses to look after the children in the hospital. There was one little puny three-year-old child, who had had a penny given to him to play with, and the poor little wretch held out his hand to every visitor with this penny in it asking them to get him with it "just a ha'porth of gin". It was his one idea of the way to use the penny. Gin was his ideal of happiness. That led me to make inquiries, among nurses and doctors, as to their experience in this matter, and the answer I got was that livers diseased by gin, "gin-livers", for children under three years of age, were a common experience of hospital practice.'

'That's what you call a representative case?'

'Yes. The question was whether those cases were exceptional or representative, and I came to the conclusion that they were representative. That led me to write, not that article which you have before you but an earlier one. [. . .] The point of view, from what I had at that time learnt which then impressed me was that it was no use our talking of compulsory service; or of universal service; or of any other mode of increasing the inducements for getting soldiers for the Army if there were men in numbers quite sufficient for us ready to enlist, if they were only in fit condition to make soldiers. Obviously the cases that were coming under my observation showed that many who were willing were not fit, not from any hereditary deterioration, or from any thing of that kind, but that the children who could have been healthy soldiers, or anything else in civil life were being destroyed in their earlier years owing to their being improperly nurtured from the time of their being babies in arms, and so on. I therefore drew attention to the question in an article under the title of "Where to get Men". [. . .] It so happened that the Civic Society of Glasgow, which is a society formed partly from the university and partly from the chief people in the town interested in general social questions, had some time earlier asked me to deliver the inaugural lecture of their season, in September or October of last year. I wanted to deal with quite a different subject, but some of them had known that "Where to get Men" was by me, and they insisted on my taking up the subject again. I put this to you to show how very little I myself have had anything to do with the agitation of the question more than flying a kite that everybody has shot at. They were so interested already from their experience in Glasgow, and from what they had been concerned with on the question of health or deterioration (whichever way it may be put) that they insisted upon my taking up this subject, and it was solely on their urgent desire that I gave the lecture, the substance of which I brought into the article now before you.'

'It may be taken for granted, I suppose, that the conditions of existence in Glasgow are perhaps worse for the great mass of the population than those in any other town in the British Isles?'

'In many ways that is true, but in many ways it is true as a consequence that there is a more serious effort made to combat these evils in Glasgow than in almost any other town. I rather think a point I shall come to presently is closely connected with the point you raise. I do not think that our most serious danger arises from places where the conditions are most difficult, and most attention is drawn to them, but in those places where the thing has gradually arisen and nobody has looked after it. But I did find this in Glasgow, and there was one particular part of the question which, as it seemed to me, had been practically solved in Glasgow; that is to say, we all know the London County Council and other bodies have endeavoured to meet the difficulty of children not being properly fed who have to go to school. But the people who really know the poor, and who are in close touch with them, are alarmed at the idea of your pauperizing, if you feed the children.'

'If you feed them gratuitously?'

'I shall come to the gratuitous part of it in a moment. There was quite an agitation in London because they said that the immediate effect of feeding the children was to reward the careless parent and to take away his responsibility. But in Glasgow what they have done is this. They have worked with the Charity Organization Society and the police. They have made it a rule that the children should be fed. They then brought home the responsibility, and the practical result was that what they had done had diminished the applications for gratuitous food and not increased them. [. . .] It so happens, after the article in the *Contemporary Review* appeared, I received a similar request to go to Manchester, and without entering into all the circumstances of what I said down at Manchester, I may say that I found that there was another side of the question that appeared to me to have been most admirably solved, and that is as to the looking after the mothers in the feeding of their children and the nurture of their children. There they had a system of ladies, who work under the direction of medical men and who get into touch with the homes as soon as they are notified of a birth. The evidence is very completely given in a little report that I certainly think ought to be before your Committee – that is, the report of the Jubilee Meeting of the Manchester Sanitary Association.'

DR TATHAM: 'That is the Ladies' Health Society, is it not?'

'Yes. The point I want to make is this: that Manchester, as far as I am able to see, has practically solved that question if they could do it on a sufficient scale. Manchester is working on very small means as compared with the wealth of Manchester, but still the principle is solved, and the evidence is not only as to the great benefit to the children, but as to the fact that the mothers welcome the coming of the ladies who act under the instructions of the doctors. Of course it is necessary that you should have ladies selected who will exercise a good deal of tact, and where that has been done, the mothers actually welcomed their coming and were proud to show the improvement in their babies.'

CHAIRMAN: 'Is that commensurate to the cost in Manchester?'

'The cost is ridiculously small. You will see the figures in the report of the Jubilee Conference. Of course there has been a great deal of voluntary work which costs the town nothing. [. . .] My point is, that so far as I was able to see whilst in Manchester, the question of the feeding of the children at their homes has been most admirably solved; the question of the feeding of the children in the schools has likewise been solved in Glasgow. Therefore, I think that the great thing that is wanted is something that will bring the experience of Manchester to bear upon Glasgow, and the experience of Glasgow to bear upon Manchester.'

'And the experience of the two brought to bear upon the whole country?'

'Yes. One of the most alarming features of that report of the Jubilee Conference in Manchester is the statement made by the Chairman of the Medical Health Board of the County Council of Chester (because for this Jubilee those most conversant with the facts came from all parts of the country), that the most terrible conditions prevail in the large villages, and small towns that have been growing up without any kind of organization to look after them. You will find his statement there, and it is most frightful. He says that the death-rate in many of those places is not, as in many places, 200 or 300 per thousand: but that of all children born of all classes (of course that practically shows a higher percentage yet for the poorer classes), but he takes the whole birth-rate of all children born during certain months of the year, and he finds the death-rate is 800 per thousand. You can see the statement and the authority. All I can do is to give you the best evidence the case admits of.'

'That is under one year old?'

'Yes; and then, what he says is, that so far from that slaughter being discriminating, that is leaving a survival of the fittest – on the contrary the very causes that have led to the slaughter lead to the result that those who have escaped the slaughter are being brought up under conditions in which it is quite impossible to be virile.'

'Permanently unfitted for life?'

'Yes. That was very much confirmed by the view of Dr Ashby, who I think is acknowledged by almost all the profession as having devoted more special care to the culture of children than almost anyone else. He was speaking at the opening ceremony of the "Infants' Hospital" at Blackheath, as to which I might hand to you this paper. He was speaking *à propos* to that article of mine about the 11,000 people who offered themselves for enlistment in Manchester in 1899, of whom 8000 were rejected straight off, and he said: "I am prepared to produce, so as to account for every one of those 8000 recruits who were rejected, 8000 children now in Manchester at quite a young age who are rickety and unfit to make soldiers, or anything else, because of their improper nurture and improper care." '

'Is that owing to malnutrition?'

'I am not prepared to say that altogether. One other frequent cause of failure in physique, for instance is "flat feet", representing another form of want of care, because the greater number of flat feet are due to want of proper care and there would be very few cases of flat feet if the mothers properly treated them. The same is true of bad teeth, resulting both from improper feeding and improper care during childhood.'

12 Charles Booth

from Evidence to the Inter-Departmental Committee on Physical
Deterioration, vol. 11, 1904, pp. 50–55.

'Of course you know our Inquiry was originally initiated owing to the
extremely unsatisfactory condition of the recruits?'

'Exactly.'

'Would you say that those recruits were probably mainly derived from
the failures, from the class that are below the steady workers?'

'I think, on the whole, the Army is recruited from a lower class than
the average, but not by any means only or exceptionally from the lowest
class.'

'The two ruling conditions which would affect the health of the lower
classes, mainly, would be bad sanitary conditions and bad food, would it
not?'

'Yes, including largely in bad sanitary conditions, insufficient fresh air,
insufficient opportunity of getting out of town into the country.'

'Now you think, on the whole, sanitary conditions are admittedly
improving?'

'Clearly.'

'In spite of the increase of urban population there is an increased
improvement in the sanitary conditions?'

'Yes.'

'Would you say the same of the modern conditions of food, especially in
child life?'

'I think that they are bad.'

'Worse than they used to be?'

'I have not made the inquiry. My inquiry has not compared the past with
the present, and therefore it is only an opinion. I think so: I think that the
conditions as to food are worse.'

'Owing to the greater facilities of getting bad unwholesome food, such as
tinned food?'

'There is less home cookery, I should think, just as there is less home
dressmaking. It is the same thing. Things are done more cheaply in a
wholesale way, and no one makes their own clothes, and the poor hardly
mend them, and fewer people cook their own food.'

'Any remedies for improving the food conditions of the lower classes
concern not merely the supply of food, but the proper preparation of it
when they have got it?'

'I think the cookery centres of the educational bodies are very useful in teaching to cook, but by far the most important cause would be if there was less woman labour.'

'Especially, I suppose, immediately before and immediately after child-bearing?'

'That has not to do with the preparation of the food, but it has to do with the health of the women and the vigour of their children.'

'In those two great agencies, the Salvation Army and the Church Army, do you know what does become of the families of the people who go to their Homes?'

'They have not got them. They are people who have left their families, or never had them. They pose as single men and probably in many cases are so.'

'Are you in favour of similar efforts being made by direct State interference beyond those two voluntary agencies?'

'I have certainly thought that some Poor Law action should be taken in that direction.'

'It would be very difficult, would it not?'

'It would be very difficult.'

'It would be direct interference with the liberty of the subject to a certain extent, and it would be so difficult to draw a line when the State had the right to interfere with a man's personal liberty and when it had not?'

'It is extremely difficult. There are very interesting attempts made, as you know, in Germany, the experience of which might be used, but I entirely agree it is exceedingly difficult to do.'

MR LEGGE: 'With regard to this question of female labour and its deleterious effect on domestic life, have you formed any judgement as to whether the disinclination to attend to one's home is growing among the poorer classes, the women of the poorer classes?'

'I think they do tend to neglect their homes more.'

'Do you think that is because nowadays girls are sent to school so early and kept at school so long, and see so little of their homes?'

'No; I should not think that.'

'Would you see any objection, from the social point of view, of the movement in favour of keeping girls of all classes full time at school until they reach the age of fourteen?'

'A year more than now?'

'Yes?'

'I should not desire it.'

'At full time?'

'I should not think it desirable to extend the time.'

'The present age?'

'No.'

'You would think it still more wrong to extend the age to sixteen for girls?'

'I should not suggest it.'

'Would you be in favour of girls being allowed greater relaxation than boys in the way of half-time provided their employment were domestic?'

'I have not studied the way in which the half-time is worked. You mean factory half-time, of course?'

'No. I meant allowing only half-time attendance at school, provided they went home for the rest of the day to work with their mothers at domestic work?'

'That would be, on the whole, very desirable, I think.'

'There has been a recent tendency in London, as indeed in most big towns in England, to build large tenements for the housing of the poorer classes, improved Peabody buildings. Do you think that the conditions of life in them are better than in the one-storey or two-storey little tenements, of which you get acres upon acres in the East End?'

'In some cases they are and in some cases they are not. In themselves the extra height and absence of space around are certainly evils; on the other hand there are excellently arranged blocks, infinitely better than the ill-arranged cottages.'

'The advantages compensate for the disadvantages?'

'I think in the more recent and improved buildings probably that is so. There were some of the earlier ones that are atrocious.'

'Now, with regard to State interference, especially connected with Mr Lindsell's last two questions. I rather gather from what you said that you prefer municipal action to State action?'

'Each has its own role to play.'

'Yes. It is one of your points that you want considerable powers vested in the hands of municipalities or county councils?'

'Yes. I do not think we know exactly what will be best to do, or are at all prepared for a centralized uniform system. The experimental influence of local bodies who are trying to feel their way is, I think, more important, as I do not think we really know what is the best course to pursue.'

'You think that having large powers of central government a department, such as the Home Office or the Local Government Board, regulating any particular detail of administration, should be very shy of checking local authorities in trying experiments?'

'It is very difficult to say exactly what limit there should be to their action. It could be in some cases an advantage and in some cases they stimulate, but

I should wish that freedom were given as much as possible to the local authority.'

'At the same time I rather gather from the reference to the Salvation Army and the Church Army, that you would like those municipal authorities in their turn to allow as free a hand as possible to such reasonable and well-conducted voluntary associations?'

'I do not think they do interfere at all.'

'Have you seen the correspondence with regard to the London County Council's action in reference to the shelters of the Salvation Army, forcing them, for instance, to substitute bedsteads for bunks?'

'I do not think that because work of that sort is done from charitable motives it ought to rest upon any other regulations than would be enforced if it were done for profit. I do not think that there is any reason for allowing a shelter to be carried on, because it is a charity, in a different way from what you would if it was being done as a commercial undertaking – you should enforce the law exactly the same.' [. . .]

'Then with regard to the question of the disposal of the children and females, all those who might conceivably under some future dispensation be placed in labour colonies, you are aware no doubt that under the existing Industrial Schools Acts, children can be sent to industrial schools with no criminal taint whatever, who were simply the children of parents who neglect them and who have been very unfortunate?'

'I thought there were special schools for those children and that they were only sent to those schools in special cases. I did not know that the people who are not criminal could be sent to those schools. I thought in some towns there were schools that had been adopted, and that they gave them another name, but I was not aware that it was the case that children who have committed no fault can be sent to the schools to which the young criminals go.'

'Yes, but "criminals" is a hard term to apply to a child under ten?'

'But are children under ten sent?'

'A certain number are.'

'But they have committed theft or something – they have been convicted.'

'No. No child is supposed to have been convicted who is sent to an industrial school. They have been charged and they have been ordered to go to an industrial school, but it does not rank technically as a conviction. However, I need not press that point. With regard to Part VI of the Factory Act, you said very truly that it contains stringent regulations prohibiting home work in places where there is infectious disease, but you will no doubt recall also section 108 of the Act. That provides that where an outworker is working in unwholesome premises, after due notice and after investigation by a court, the occupier of any factory or workshop may render himself liable to suffer penalties if he sends in more outwork to be done in those premises ?'

'Yes, but it is work in the homes.'

'As you point out, that does not extend to ordinary home work; it must be home work which is done in connection with the factory or workshop ?'

'It is done for a centre.'

'Exactly. So that it is limited in its extent, so far as it applies to homes at all. And, furthermore, it has no direct reference to, or effect upon, the occupier or the tenant or the landlord of the house in which the work is being done ?'

'It acts directly upon the employer. It would stimulate him to see the way in which sanitary conditions were not observed.'

'Yes, but you wish to secure somehow some extension of that sort of influence ?'

'It is not an extension, it is an entirely different point, the object being to make it possible to apply the law with regard to factory work sufficiently to cover the small workshop – which is otherwise apt to escape and be under very bad conditions. It was on that account that it suggested itself to me that the proper engine for pressure was the landlord. But it covers an entirely different point. Those who are outworkers, working entirely in their own premises, not employing others, probably female workers who are given their work from some industrial centre, either a workshop or factory, or a giver-out of work – they are the classes that are covered here, are they not ?' [. . .]

'The last point is that question of statistics. You yourself have been conducting a tremendous inquiry for the last seventeen years or so. Do you not think it would be a good thing if there were some central authority whose business it should be not to allow such a piece of work as yours to lapse, either collecting itself or directing through various agencies the collection of similar information to the mass you have got together ?'

'I think a great deal more might be done from the Government centres to put together valuable statistics. But their powers and their line of inquiry would be very different from such as an individual is able or thinks it desirable to carry out. I do not think that an inquiry like mine would be at all desirable to prolong or go on with.'

'But it has brought out certain facts which might be tested from time to time ?'

'And especially tested in other ways.'

'No doubt, when I speak of the Government collecting information, the

Government in many cases might work through bodies such as Educational Committees, certifying surgeons all over the country, and so on?

'Yes.'

'You would be in favour of some method of coordinating all this work as well as keeping it alive?'

'Oh, certainly; but I do not know what shape the Government would desire it to take. It is difficult to say what part should be best played by the central authority or by the local authority or by philanthropic authorities. I could not say how it would be best. I have a great belief in the value of statistics.'

COLONEL ONSLOW: 'Do you consider that the existing laws of sanitation, overcrowding, inspection of food, and all those matters, both natural food, say meat and milk and anything else like that, and also the made-up foods, are sufficiently strong, if the local authorities or other authorities put them into force, to counteract evils which have been brought to light by your investigations and by Mr Rowntree's investigations?'

'I should say that they are stronger than can be at present enforced, and if they could be enforced they probably would be altered in various ways because the actual information would be got. We cannot enforce them, and therefore it is very hard to judge whether, they might be made stronger.

'Why could not you enforce them?'

'The circumstances are so difficult in dealing with home life.'

'Surely with sanitary inspection, for instance, the provision of proper sanitary arrangements in the houses, it should not be possible as it is in York for one midden privy to be at the disposal of some fourteen houses – surely that could be altered?'

'Yes, I think so.'

'Have the local authorities sufficient power to enforce landlords to build better?'

'They undoubtedly have. They can get those powers. I do not know what the powers are in York. But Parliament would give those powers and does give them. One difficulty lies in the fact that people are poor and need to get very cheap accommodation, the result being that they aggregate to the worst accommodation, and then if you try to deal with a centre you have a mass of wretchedly poor people whose habits are exceedingly bad. If you give them good appliances they destroy them, so that you have an evil that is very difficult to deal with, and I think can only be dealt with by many means and slowly.'

'Still as a matter of fact, the law is strong enough really to counteract all those things?'

'The law is as strong as it can be used at present.'

'As regards the inspection of those made-up foods, the patent foods for children. Do you think it is strong enough?'

'I do not know enough about that to say.'

'Then again, regarding the children, it is granted that many parents are bound to go out early – they have no time or the opportunity to prepare proper food, or to look after the children before going to school – would it be possible to give meals at all board schools, etc., for children, making the parents pay where they are able?'

'I should like to see it done.'

'Would you like to make it universal?'

'Yes, as far as I can see, I am in favour of every board school being also a restaurant or having a restaurant in connection with it where suitable food such as children like, but at the same time is also good for them, is sold at the minimum price – not with any intention of giving it away.'

'Not to pauperize them?'

'Quite so. The parents now of that class who have money give their children quantities of pennies to spend on sweets and so on; and if they could be induced instead of doing that to give their children tickets that would not be available anywhere except for their midday meal, they might be better fed and have better cookery, and it would have an excellent effect. If a system of that sort were established it would be the easiest way of providing for those children who do need the charity, and although I do recognize the objection of encouraging the parents to trust to such a thing, yet I believe the advantages would counterbalance any disadvantages.'

'It would be an advantage to those who are not able, either from poverty or stress of work, to look after their children?'

'Yes.'

CHAIRMAN: 'But the provision of the midday meal would not touch the case of a great number of school children who have to go out in the early morning with an empty stomach?'

'I suppose not. But that might be got over by giving them oatmeal, which none of them would be eager to take. I think a ration of oatmeal might be given as a breakfast with sugar or something. I think that they might have that given them. They much prefer to have their parents' food. The commonest plan in London is for the father to go away before breakfast, to take something with him, and come home to his one nice meal after his work at six o'clock, or some time like that, and the children enjoy the share they can get at that time. And the mother does not cook for herself, and the children get bread, or bread and dripping, or bread and butter, or bread and tea, in the middle of the day. A school restaurant would, I believe, not decrease the amount of cooking in the houses, and would give the children better food.

MR STRUTHERS: 'You think that would be the tendency? At present the mother very often prepares a meal in the morning or in the middle of the day for the sake of the children. They come home to have it, and she gets it with them. But if the children get it at a restaurant, she might herself become underfed?'

'Oh, certainly, that is so. I fully recognize that possible view – that it might do more to undermine the habits of the mother in cooking a midday meal. I would chance it.' [. . .]

'Perhaps you will not mind my asking you a question which has been asked already. But I want to be perfectly clear as to what is your opinion as to the physical state in a given area like Southwark – as to whether it is worse today than it was twenty or thirty years ago?'

'No, I do not think it would be correct to say that. But if you take the whole population of England, you will find a larger urban population, and, therefore, an extension of the evils which I trace to urban conditions.'

'But taking a given urban district which was fully populated twenty or thirty years ago, and that same district now, is the condition of the children worse than it was?'

'I should not expect it.'

'You are not aware of any statistics to prove that?'

'No.'

'And your view is that, though there is a larger proportion of urban population to the whole population of the country, there is a chance of greater improvement?'

'Yes.'

'Although there are a larger proportion living under urban conditions?'

'Yes.'

'You do not happen to have made inquiries as to the condition of life in the country at any time?'

'No. I live in the country a considerable part of my time. I see the people, but that is all.'

'Of course, as has been already said the sanitation has distinctly improved from what it was.'

'Yes.'

'So that it is only a question of food and fresh air that makes the difference between the country and the town at all in the matter of physique?'

'Food and fresh air and habits generally.'

'But chiefly those two things?'

'Yes, I suppose it is chiefly those two things.'

'It would be rather important to have some direct evidence as to what the physique of the inhabitants of the country village is, as compared with the town population.'

'Yes.'

'One assumes that the country population should be healthier and better physically than in the towns, but I do not think that there is much in the way of evidence as to that?'

'I think not.'

'Not beyond the general impression. But one finds, and I have known myself distinct cases where one's impression of the physique of the inhabitants of the country village was unfavourable, that on the whole it was not better than that of a pretty populous urban district?'

'Yes.'

'So you think it would be rather good to get a little evidence as to what is the physique and what are the conditions of life of a population in certain country districts?'

'It would. The evidence that I have in the matter is the far greater physical force of those who come into the city from the country. The country, whatever those who are left may be, does send the finest men to the towns, which cannot produce them.'

'I think in the town you say from 18s. to 21s. is what is necessary to support life decently in the case of a man with a wife and three children?'

'I rather arbitrarily fixed that as a line. I had to make a line on which you might call the people in poverty, and below which they were tending to extreme poverty, and above which you reach the ordinary comfortable condition of the working classes. But it is an arbitrary line, and cannot be definitely drawn.'

'But your impression was that 18s. to 21s. was necessary to support life decently?'

'Yes, for a man and his wife and a couple of children.'

'What proportion of that 18s. to 21s. would be paid in rent?'

'It would vary in the district they were living in and how they were housed.'

'Would it be a very wide range?'

'The range would be from 3s. to 6s. – I am speaking rather off-hand.

'But you think that 7s. would be quite a high figure for a family with an income of 21s. to pay in rent? It would be rather a high figure, would it not?'

'Yes, certainly.'

'So that that would leave them 14s. for food and other things?'

'Yes.'

'I do not know whether you have seen the returns that have been collected, I think it would be by the Board of Trade, of the wages of agricultural labourers in various parts of the country?'

'I have not.'

'But there I find that in many counties the total wage of the labourer in full employment, taking it all the year round, of course, is 13s.; 14s. is about the average; and there are very few counties which go much beyond that. So that they do not seem to have nearly so much to spend on food as your urban family, which seems to be well above the poverty line?'

'Country conditions are very different, both as to the way in which they try to live and as to the extra chances they have in garden produce, and so on. I am not able to give you a comparison.'

COLONEL FOX: 'Do you consider that the poverty amongst the lower classes is attributable very much to drink?'

'Yes.'

'Do you think that a man would drink less if he had good things – food at a low price – do you think that he would be less inclined to drink or "booze", or to spend the whole of the time in a "boozing" place?'

'Yes.'

'Would not that have a great effect upon the families also, and very likely the children would be better fed if most of the money was not used in drink?'

'Yes.'

'Well, then, we are told that the Jewish children, both boys and girls, of the age of twelve are much taller, considerably taller and considerably heavier, than the Christian children – you are aware of that?'

'I was not aware of that.'

'We have been told that, and we have had statistics about it. To what do you attribute that?'

'To the fact that the Jewish mothers do not work.'

'Why is it that the Jewish children should be heavier and taller than the Christian children?'

'Because the mothers do not work.'

'Is it attributable to the better food the Jewish children get, or what?'

'It is due to the more complete home life; they are undoubtedly better fed. [. . .]

CHAIRMAN: There are one or two points which have arisen I should like to ask you a few questions upon. With regard to this drink question, have you ever considered the evil effects of tea are perhaps worse than those of gin?'

'I do not think that they would be worse.'

'Is it not the case that a great many children are both anaemic and neurotic, solely from the abuse of the consumption of tea?'

'It is quite possible.'

'Should not you say from the chemical constituents of tea that it would be deleterious?'

'I have really no knowledge on the subject, but I think the way that they keep it constantly going cannot be good for them. What I doubt is whether children take very much of it.'

'I am told they do. Don't you think if we contemplated a new Tariff that a large relief to the taxation on tea might therefore have a very deleterious effect on the health of the nation?'

'I see – like a decreased tax on gin.'

'Don't you think that to remove the imposts on tea – I am putting this question seriously – might have a very deleterious effect?'

'I never have thought that the freeing of the tax on tea was any particular benefit, or what is called a free breakfast table.' [. . .]

'I was a little surprised in the course of your evidence to hear you speak so tolerantly of local inaction in dealing with the evils which we are considering. Of course I admit in regard to overcrowding the difficulty of disposing of the evil is a very great one?'

'It rather is a question from what impulse or authority the action is to spring, and it ought to spring indigenously in the district, and not be rammed down its throat by any outside authority.'

'Take the Public Health Act of 1875, which has been nearly thirty years in operation. Amongst the duties cast upon the local authorities is the obligation to inspect nuisances, and a nuisance is defined as "Any house or part of a house so overcrowded as to be dangerous or injurious to the health of the inmates, whether or not members of the same family." And then again another provision of the Act is the power to apply in certain cases, that is to say, after two convictions, to a Court of Summary Jurisdiction, for the closing of the house for such period as the court may deem necessary. Should you say that anything like a proper proportion of cases have arisen under which these provisions have been applied by local authorities, having regard to the extent of the evil?'

'What I have seen in London, an increasing activity in that direction, is immediately traceable to the more democratic of the local bodies. There is a distinctly greater activity; I think in many cases there has been a fresh and strong effort to deal with these evils.'

'Of course that Public Health Act was anterior to the Local Government Acts, and it is since that time that these powers have been to a much greater extent made use of, in your opinion?'

'In London it is so, I think.'

'Do you think in local areas generally in the country that has been so?'

'Yes, I should think so.'

'Touching that point, with regard to the condition in the country, here is a letter also in *The Times* of today, also from a lady, who signs herself "A Woman", in which she describes the condition of two or three cottages in the country, and she says here "Man, wife and large family of young children. No water fit to drink anywhere. Woman boils and skims pond water. While drinking it children constantly require medicine, have no appetite, skin becomes yellow and suffer in other ways. Whenever possible the water is kept in wooden tubs, and when children drink this they (with the exception of the eldest boy who is never well) recover their normal health. House built many years after the passing of the Public Health (Water) Act 1878." [...] I presume that there are ample powers to deal with conditions such as are described there?'

'I do not know what the powers of the rural authority are. They are very shy of using their authority here.'

13 Fabian Society

'The Education Muddle and the Way Out', Fabian Tract No. 106, January 1901, pp. 3–18.

Sidney Webb's pamphlet setting out the problems facing educational administrators at the turn of the century was perhaps the most influential on the final shape of the 1902 Act; copies were passed around the Cabinet, and it had a sale of more than 20,000.

Our educational machinery in England has got into a notable mess. Some places have two or three public authorities spending rates and taxes on different sorts of schools, whilst others have none at all. In one town the clever boy or girl finds in the infant school the lowest rung of an unbroken ladder to the university; whilst in the very next county there is no rescue for talented poverty from the shop or plough. Some school districts are too small to maintain a decent primary school; others are large enough to run a university. The central organization is as chaotic as the local. The various educational institutions in the United Kingdom – taking only those supported out of the rates and taxes – are officially under the charge of no fewer than ten separate Cabinet Ministers; and their several departments usually scorn to consult together.

The result is that, although we spend on education in the United Kingdom every year nearly twenty million pounds of public money of one sort or another, from rates, taxes or public endowments, we get a very inadequate return for it. In English education today, waste and want go hand in hand.[1]

The local authorities
The present muddle

There are, in England today, two distinct sets of local educational authorities, acting on the same areas, and sharing the provision of schools between them. These are (i) the school boards, (ii) the county, borough and urban district councils.

The school boards, of which there are now 2527, have unlimited powers of rating, but are, in other respects, narrowly restricted in their scope. They can maintain only 'elementary' schools, as defined by the Acts and by the Day and Evening 'Codes' annually issued by the Education Department. But they do not maintain or control even all the elementary schools. More than half the children in elementary day schools, and more than one-third of the young people in evening continuation schools, are in the so-called 'voluntary' or denominational schools. Where a school board exists, it is responsible for enforcing attendance at school upon all the children of the district, whether they go to board or voluntary schools. But in more than one-third of England (measured by population) no school board exists. Over this large area, the children must attend denominational schools, and these are under no local public control. In these parishes the duty of enforcing school attendance is entrusted to the local sanitary authority – that is, in rural parts, the persons who are the Guardians of the Poor. Even in the two-thirds of England in which school boards exist, they are not allowed to have schools of their own if there is already a sufficient supply of places in 'voluntary' schools, however unsuitable such schools may be for the special educational needs or religious opinions of the locality. The effect of this is that in over 10,000 parishes there is none but a denominational school. These 'voluntary schools' (though four-fifths of their cost is provided from taxes) are nominally governed by 'boards of managers', who are practically self-elected; whilst the real work of administration is usually performed by the minister of religion (Anglican or Roman Catholic) to whom the school 'belongs'. The Government puts the school boards, the

1. The proposals of this Tract relate exclusively to England. Scotland and Ireland have entirely distinct educational machinery, widely differing from that of England, but in an equal muddle. Wales, including for this purpose Monmouthshire, is included with England for elementary education, but has a system of its own for secondary schools and universities, and must be separately reorganized.

public educational authorities within their respective districts, exactly on the same footing as these little nominal committees of managers. Moreover, by a piece of official pedantry, every alteration in the Code intended to improve a village school under this irresponsible private management, is made to apply equally and identically to the largest and most efficient borough school board. The school boards were, in fact, established by Mr Forster in 1870 merely to 'fill up the gaps' in the then existing system of 'voluntary' schools, and they have been treated as stop-gaps ever since. They are closely scrutinized by jealous eyes in order to prevent them from providing 'secondary' or 'technical' education, however much their constituents may need or desire this. Nevertheless, so numerous are the children of school age that the English school boards in 1899–1900 spent about £9,500,000, an amount which had increased in each of the two preceding years by about 4 per cent. The English voluntary schools in the same year spent about £5,300,000, which had increased in each of the two preceding years by about 10 per cent. Of the totals the Government found about £3,600,000 and £4,150,000.

The county, borough and urban district councils, on the other hand, whilst narrowly limited in the amount they can spend on education, enjoy a large freedom as to its kind or scope. The Technical Instruction Acts, 1889 and 1891, prohibit their teaching any child who is in the standards of an elementary school, but impose no upward limit of any kind. Hence the London County Council, like the town councils of Manchester, Nottingham, Bristol, Newcastle, etc., can help to maintain a university. The instruction must be confined to 'technical education', but this has been so defined as legally to include every subject of study except 'theology, Greek and Shakespeare'.[2] The result is that town and county councils now maintain and aid hundreds of schools (above the elementary standards) of every kind – grammar schools, science and art schools, commercial schools, cookery schools, trade schools, and what not. In most towns, the town and county councils do not, in fact, confine themselves to anything that can properly be described as technical education. They have, without express statutory warrant, assumed the position of secondary education, and even university authorities; and in this they have been encouraged by the Education Department. But though they have thus stretched their powers, and enlarged their responsibilities, their funds are strictly limited.

The county councils (fifty-one in England) and county boroughs (sixty-two) can spend on 'technical education' what is known as the

2. Even these subjects may legally be taught in town or county council schools, if a proportional part of the expense is covered, as it always may be, by sources of income (such as fees or endowments) other than the town or county council grant.

'whiskey money' (the additional duties on beer and spirits imposed by the Local Taxation Act, 1890), and in 1899–1900 they did so spend £804,000 out of £867,000. They can spend also up to a penny in the pound from the county or county-borough rates. In 1899–1900, twenty-two county boroughs added in this way £44,960 to their whiskey money expenditure. No county council has yet levied a rate on the whole county for education, but in a few cases the council levies a rate on a part of the county at the request and for the benefit of the rural districts concerned. The non-county boroughs and urban district councils can, in addition, levy a penny rate of their own for technical education, and 262 of them now do so, to the extent of £36,894 a year.[3]

The total expenditure on education by these municipal bodies now amounts to about a million sterling, and it is increasing at the rate of about 5 per cent a year. In addition, they exercise, by their inspection and grants, more or less control over about a million sterling a year of educational endowments devoted to secondary and higher education.

Conflict and overlapping

These two distinct sets of local authorities come everywhere into more or less acute rivalry and conflict. The school boards were the earlier in the field, and they have frequently provided 'higher grade schools' and evening continuation schools of high type, scarcely to be distinguished from those started by the town and county councils. But this occasional overlapping is not, of itself, a serious evil, and, moreover, it is one which mutual consultation and consideration might easily set right. Nor is the waste of public money owing to this overlapping at all large in amount. What is serious is the educational chaos caused by the arbitrary separation of one part of education from another; the total absence of any considered scheme for fulfilling the whole educational needs of any one district; the lack of any coherent system for the promotion of scholars from school to school; the stupendous inequality between one district and another; and the deadening effect upon the primary schools of their confinement within rigid limits, and the exclusion of their teachers from the opportunity of being transferred to other branches of education. What is wanted, in the interests alike of the public, the children and the teachers, is administrative unity.

3. There may also be expended under the Public Libraries Acts 1892 and 1895, a penny rate (in Manchester and twenty-one other towns, enlarged by local Act to 2d., and in four towns unlimited) on 'public libraries, public museums, schools for science, art galleries and schools for art'. In addition, the Museums and Gymnasiums Act 1891, enables any town or urban district councils to spend up to a halfpenny rate on museums, and another halfpenny rate on gymnasiums.

Administrative unity

There ought to be, in each district of convenient size, one public educational authority, and one only; responsible for providing and controlling all the education maintained in the district out of public funds, whether it be literary, scientific, commercial, artistic or technological in type – whether it be, for any of these types, primary, secondary or university in grade.

The policy of drift

But there is, as yet, apparently not much chance of our getting this administrative unity. Having 'drifted' into the present muddle, the only easy course is to go on drifting; and this is what nearly everybody, statesman and schoolmaster alike, is vigorously doing. The last Liberal Government did nothing but 'drift', so far as education was concerned, the short time it was in power; and Mr Acland, unable to gain the ear of the Cabinet for so dull a subject, was reduced to making untiring administrative attempts to patch up a crazy structure.

In 1896 the Conservative Government half-heartedly attempted to unify local educational administration by forming 'education authorities' from the councils of counties and county boroughs. They did not believe it possible to abolish the school boards, and preferred, on the line of least resistance, to subordinate them to the new authorities. The Bill passed its second reading by an immense majority, but was lost owing to the revolt of the smaller or non-county boroughs, who objected to the surrender of their independence, and joined the opponents of the clauses intended to strengthen denominational education. Since then the chiefs of the Department have announced their intention of securing the objects of the defeated Bill, by a combination of administrative action and small Bills. This means that they have given up any serious attempt to think out the problem as a whole, and that the policy of least resistance has slipped back into a policy of drift. The school boards are weak; therefore bit by bit their power is being taken from them – but they are still retained in existence. The county councils are strong; therefore bit by bit their powers are being increased, but there is no suggestion that they should receive that unrestricted rating power and that control of all educational grades which alone would make them efficient educational authorities. The Church is powerful and the Church schools are in want of money. Therefore a new source of confusion is introduced by the creation of 'associations of voluntary schools', which secure the control of an important section of education to the official hierarchy of the various denominations.

Year after year we are promised a Secondary Education Bill, and it is safe to assume that it too will follow the line of least resistance and least thought. The school boards may unfortunately still further be restricted both in their day and in their evening schools, and the councils may be given increased power, but will still be subject to a narrow rating limitation, and still confined to special educational grades. But just as easy writing makes bad reading, so easy legislation makes bad administration. The school boards and the denominational school managers would still be in charge of the education of nearly three million children, and an expenditure of over twelve millions sterling annually, whilst every year the educational results of that expenditure would be endangered or even gravely impaired. Already it is difficult to create public interest in school board elections. Already it is common to find only one-fifth of the electorate taking the trouble to vote, and as the school boards are elbowed out by their stronger municipal rivals, this decay of public interest must increase. A body elected on a small poll is always in peril. The board schools have bitter enemies. In all sections of the community there are to be found many who think that to provide anything beyond the 'Three R's' for the manual labourers is illegitimate and absurd, whilst they dismiss with contempt the claim of elementary teachers to be or to become an educated class. As long as the county and town councils are kept without responsibility for or knowledge of the primary schools, they will tend to believe that the only real education is to be found in the technical schools which they maintain, or in endowed secondary schools which they inspect and aid, and which are open to all who can afford to pay the fees, and to a selected few of those who cannot. Their natural partisanship for their own schools inevitably tends (even if unconsciously) to reinforce that powerful social prejudice which resists any development of 'primary' education beyond the preparation for a life of hewing wood and drawing water. It has been suggested that this might be prevented by giving the school boards the statutory rights to a few representatives on the education committees of the councils. But such representatives would be in a permanent and helpless minority, and their presence would do little except increase friction; while the division of the responsibility of the councils might tend to produce that decreased interest which is the result of indirect election.

One method, however, of connecting the councils with primary education is so perfectly consistent with the policy of drift that it has been already foreshadowed, and may be adopted at any moment. The councils, while still separated from the Board schools, may be empowered or required to assist efficient 'voluntary', that is denominational, schools in their district. This would make the position of the board schools absolutely impossible. The councils would tend to become partisans not only of the social interests of the technical and secondary schools, but also of the religious interests of the denominational schools, and religious tolerance for teachers would, like the teaching of French or algebra to children without fee or scholarship, seem to be one of the 'fads' of an unreasonable and discredited faction.

Thus, whilst reform is difficult, delay is dangerous. The 'policy of drift' will not save the school boards, and will probably destroy all chance of an enlightened development of elementary education for the mass of the people.[4] Every year the town and county councils become stronger and more grasping; every year the importunities of the Anglicans and the Roman Catholics for increased grants of public money for their denominational schools become more pressing; every year the muddle increases.

The claim of the school boards to be the sole educational authorities

If the 'policy of drift' is thus so dangerous to elementary education, and if everything points to unification as the remedy, why should we not adopt the Liberal and Nonconformist cry of 'School boards everywhere and for everything?' This proposal – to place the whole of public education in each district under the control of the body already elected by the citizens to manage the greater part of it – seems at first sight irresistible. Closer consideration proves, however, that it is impracticable as a solution of the present difficulties, and that even if it were possible, it would not be desirable. We simply *cannot* make the school board the universal authority for secondary and technical education, because:

1. In one-third of England school boards do not exist. It was exactly for this reason that the school board was ignored in the Technical Instruction Act of 1889, and the new powers were given to the county, borough and urban district councils, which together cover all England.

2. School boards are so fiercely hated by large sections of the people, so little desired by the ordinary man, and so energetically opposed by positive majorities of the local electors, that their compulsory establishment in places where they are not petitioned for, and where they are not absolutely required to provide new schools, is politically impossible – even if it could be defended on principles of democracy and local self-government.

3. Even where school boards exist, their districts are, in the vast majority of

4. In December 1900, this peril was made both imminent and apparent. The Court of Queen's Bench decided (in *R.* v. *Cockerton*) that the London School Board could not, out of the school board rate, conduct classes for the examinations and grants of the old Science and Art Department, or go beyond the Code of the Education Department, or give instruction of any kind to adults, whether in day or evening schools. This decision may perhaps be appealed against, but it will certainly be accepted by the Government as definitely limiting the powers of the school boards.

cases, absolutely unsuitable for anything beyond elementary education. Out of 2527 existing school boards, 2085 govern populations of less than 5000. It will certainly be impossible for many years to come in England to maintain even one good secondary school for boys and girls in a population as small as 20,000. Only about 300 out of the 2527 existing school boards deal with such a population. Higher education, and more specialized education would, of course, be outside the possibilities of many even of these larger boards. To make the school board the sole authority for all education within its district would necessarily involve abolishing nine-tenths of the existing school boards, and creating new bodies for much larger districts than single parishes, or even than small boroughs. There would still remain the difficulty of providing for the purely rural areas divorced from their urban centres. But even if it were possible to adopt the existing school boards as the authorities for secondary and technical education, it would not be desirable, because school boards have inevitably become the scene of religious quarrels, and experience shows that their election is almost always made the occasion for a struggle between religious denominations. No one would wish to infect secondary and technical education – hitherto mainly free from sectarian squabbles – with this deplorable strife.

The case for a new educational authority

Many defenders of school boards now admit with regret that it is politically and geographically impossible to make the existing school boards the sole educational authorities for their respective districts. They urge that the best way to secure administrative unity in education is to create a brand-new body; to divest the county, borough and urban district councils of all their present educational powers; to abolish all school boards; to divide England up afresh into suitable districts; and to make each district elect an education council, to which should be entrusted all the education within its area. But this too, on examination, is found to be both impracticable and undesirable, because,

1. It would involve the maximum of disturbance of local property, finances and vested interests, and would combine in one irresistible opposition (i) the 2527 school boards and the 1200 county, borough and urban district councils, all objecting to having their freehold schools taken away from them, (ii) all their officials whose salaries would be disturbed and their very places jeopardized, (iii) all the members of Parliament, not understanding what it was about, but desperately wirepulled by the aforesaid local bodies and their officials, and (iv) all the ratepayers who would expect their rates to be raised by the change. No House of Commons would look twice at such a Bill; and no Cabinet would propose it.

2. It would almost certainly transfer to the elections of the new bodies, and so enlarge and perpetuate, the religious animosities and sectarian strife that now dominate school board elections and obstruct educational progress. All experience indicates that, at any rate in the England of this generation, public bodies directly elected to manage schools will be elected largely on theological grounds. The proposed new educational councils, though elected for wider educational functions, and often for larger areas, would tend to be merely the existing school boards under a new name.

We come thus into direct conflict with those who, so far as matters educational are concerned, still cherish a belief in the necessity of an *ad hoc* body. This demands separate consideration.

The story of the ad hoc *body*

It is now often urged, in support of the school boards, or of the proposal to create elected educational councils, that the business of providing and managing schools is of so special a nature that it is best entrusted to a separate public body elected *ad hoc* (that is to say, for this special business only). This is not the reason why school boards were invented. Whatever good arguments there may be for an *ad hoc* body for school management, the school board, as we know it, is merely one of the few survivors of what was once a large class. A hundred years ago most of the local government of the English towns was carried on by *ad hoc* bodies, chosen in all sorts of ways, for all sorts of different functions. During the eighteenth century, as the urban population increased, it became absolutely necessary to provide for more local government. No statesman thought out any general system. What happened was that one bit after another was stuck upon the structure of the old township government – in one place a special board of commissioners was appointed to drain the marshes; in another a separate body of governors and directors of the poor was elected to provide a workhouse; elsewhere a board of trustees was set to keep a road in repair; or a special 'lamp board' would be constituted to pave and light the streets. It was the age of *ad hoc* bodies, elected, coopted, appointed or constituted in every conceivable way, and literally thousands of them came into existence. In 1834, when the Poor Law was reformed, there was no public body either in the rural districts, or in the unorganized urban districts, to which the new work could possibly have been given. A new *ad hoc* body had therefore to be created. The result of this historical accident is that there are people today who have come honestly to believe that the management of a workhouse and the administration of relief is a matter of so special a nature that it must be entrusted to an *ad hoc* body. When, in 1870, Mr Forster carried the Education Act, efficient town councils existed in the boroughs, and it was at first proposed that the school board should be nominated by these town councils, of which they would virtually have been statutory committees, with independent powers. But in the rural districts no responsible local authority could be found, and the great population of London was in the hands of the Vestries. Indirect election was objected to by the Radicals, and the various denominational bodies insisted on 'a representation of all parties and all religions'. So Mr Forster gave way, and directly elected school boards were created. Now many people have come to feel that there is something inherently reasonable and natural in having a separate elected body to look after schools. This is not the opinion of Germany or Austria, France or Switzerland, where they know something about education. In all these countries the public body that manages other local affairs also manages the schools. The hesitation to carry the *ad hoc* theory to its logical conclusion shows an inherent doubt in its validity. Mr Chaplin's proposal to create a special authority for defective poor-law children met with universal condemnation, and during the debates on the London Government Bill 1899, the suggestion that Boards of Guardians should be abolished and their duties handed over to municipal authorities, met with general acceptance, especially from experts like Canon Barnett. We have, in fact, ceased to believe in the need for *ad hoc* authorities. During the last sixty years they have been as far as possible absorbed and abolished.[5]

The success of town and county councils, with their varied functions, is evidence that separate bodies for separate services are superfluous. There is at least as much difference between main drains and lunatic asylums, between street sweeping and technical education, between prevention of infectious disease and providing music in the parks as there is between 'purely municipal', poor law and educational functions – problems no less difficult, duties no less important, are involved in the actual work of a modern municipality as in any of the three separate services.

The way out

If, then, it is impracticable and undesirable, either to make the school boards the sole educational authorities, or to supersede them and all other existing educational bodies by brand-new educational councils, how are we to get administrative unity ? What we have to work towards is the concentration in a single elected body for each locality of all the public business entrusted to that locality. Leaving Poor Law aside, as outside the purpose of

5. The one case in which such authorities have been approved and multiplied – that of Port and Harbour Trusts – is not really an exception.

the present Tract, let us consider how, on this principle, we can get out of the education muddle.

First, as to the unit of area. It is at once clear that the large towns must be kept as distinct educational units. Birmingham and Manchester, Liverpool and Leeds, can neither be broken up nor merged. Outside the large towns, seeing that we want unity of all grades of education, the unit of area must, it is clear, be much larger than the parish; and as a large part of the educational machinery is already organized by the county, it does not seem either practicable or desirable to adopt any other area.

Leaving out of account for a moment London and the county boroughs, we propose that, in the fifty administrative counties which make up the rest of England, the county council should be made responsible for the provision and maintenance of every kind and grade of education within its area. All school boards existing within the county should be abolished, and their schools transferred to the county council. The annual cost of maintaining these and other public schools should become an equal charge throughout the county, levied in the ordinary county rate. The first duty of the county council should be to prepare and submit to the Board of Education for criticism (but not for control) a complete survey of the existing educational provision for the whole county, from the elementary school to the university, coupled with a plan for its completion and improvement. The council should have full and free powers to experiment in schools and subjects, and of initiation in new forms of instruction, subject only to the consent of the Board of Education. Finally, it should control any public educational endowments belonging to the locality, administer the 'whiskey money', and have unlimited powers to levy rates for the aiding and supplying of every description of education within its district.[6]

We have here the basis of a complete and systematic organization of education (outside London and the sixty-two county boroughs), based on the principle of administrative unity. But there are difficulties in the way, and objections to be overcome, with which we must deal one by one.

(a) *The non-county borough.* The first difficulty that confronts us is the claim of the non-county borough and the large urban district to escape from the county, and to be made, like the county borough, a completely independent

6. The six English universities would remain, as at present, independent of the local authorities, except in so far as these might aid them by grants, in which event conditions would naturally be mutually agreed. But the universities, no less than other educational bodies, should be subject to inspection, criticism and public report by the Board of Education itself. Such endowed, 'non-local' schools as Eton and Harrow, and the various unattached colleges and specialized educational institutions, would occupy a similar position.

educational unit. On the one hand it is undesirable even to appear to limit the activity of an energetic and growing town. On the other, we have the practical impossibility of disturbing the 'whiskey money' distribution, which now goes to the counties and county boroughs; and cutting off from the counties nearly all their schools and institutes, which have naturally been placed in the urban centres. The solution must be found in a proper organization of functions and powers. The educational system of the county must be organized as a whole, the little market towns taking in it their proper place as educational centres for the adjacent districts. But, in this system, the local administration, including the whole management of the institutions in the towns, should be delegated by the county council to a responsible local committee for each non-county borough or urban district. This local committee might consist, in the main, of persons nominated by the borough or urban district council, together with the county councillors for the district, at least two women, and possibly other persons interested in education. These committees could be allowed, subject to the ultimate control of the county council, to spend a definite sum annually allotted to them by the council, plus any special rate in their own area that the borough or urban district council could be induced to levy.

(b) *The absence of women, and often of persons with educational experience, from county and borough councils.* It is said that county and borough councils, though they usually contain some experienced administrators, are unfit to manage schools, because (i) they often include no men of educational experience or interested in the subject, and (ii) women are not eligible to sit upon them.[7] To get over this real difficulty, and also to facilitate efficient administration, the county and borough councils should be required by statute to appoint special educational committees. Under the Technical Instruction Acts the town and county councils have spontaneously developed this organization for educational purposes, entrusting the execution of their powers to committees on which are coopted persons whose presence and advice may be, for one reason or another, desired. This system has worked so well that it ought to be continued. The local authorities for education would then be the town and county councils acting each through a statutory committee consisting of a majority of councillors and of certain coopted individuals. In order to preserve unity of control, no other authority or body of persons should have a statutory claim to representation thereon; but, if only (pending an alteration of the law) to ensure the presence of women, the town or county council should be required to sub-

7. The law should, of course, be changed, so as to make women eligible for election to both town and county councils. See Fabian Tract no. 93.

mit for the approval of the Board of Education the proposed composition of its committees. These committees, like other committees, should not have the power to levy a rate, otherwise all the simplification of finance would be lost. At the beginning of the financial year the committee would present a budget, and after getting it passed would administer the allotted funds without further interference by the Council.

(*c*) *The need for local supervision*. But the county is a large area, and it is rightly urged that no county council can properly undertake the actual management of the schools in all its parishes. It is not suggested that it should do so. The work of the education committee of the county council would be to frame a scheme for providing and maintaining such schools, of such grades and types, and in such localities as the circumstances of the county require. It should provide both the capital cost and the annual maintenance of these schools; frame regulations for their government; inspect them by its officials; and appoint all the headmasters. But the detailed administration of the several institutions, the selection of assistant-masters, and as much else as possible should be delegated to a local committee, appointed by the county council for each parish or for each institution. For this local committee, two alternatives present themselves. Either the county council might be required to appoint the local parish council, or the county council might be left to appoint whom it chose among the local residents, with the addition of two or more members nominated by the parish council.

(*d*) *How to deal with the voluntary schools*. Every county council would find the greater part of the elementary education in its district in the hands of voluntary schools, owning no allegiance to it or to any other local authority; but often starving for lack of funds, and grossly below any reasonable standard of educational efficiency. It is politically impossible to abolish these voluntary schools; and whatever we may think of the theological reasons for their establishment, their separate and practically individual management does incidentally afford what ought to be, in any public system of education, most jealously safeguarded, namely, variety, and the opportunity of experiment. What we have to do with the voluntary schools is to put them under the control of the local educational authority; to improve and strengthen their committees of management; to raise their efficiency; and especially to provide better salaries for their teachers; to make impossible the tyrannical vagaries of foolish clergymen in the village schools; and to bring these into coordination with the rest of the educational system.

We propose that the county council should be allowed to offer a grant in aid up to, say, five or even ten shillings per head per annum to all the voluntary schools in the county, to be spent in increasing the salaries of the teaching staff, or otherwise raising the efficiency of the schools; and in all cases subject to the following conditions, viz.

1. The county council to be allowed to inspect the schools, frame regulations for their administration, and audit their accounts.

2. All future appointments and dismissals of teachers to be subject to its confirmation.

3. The appointment, subject to its approval, of a committee of managers, which should invariably include two members to be annually nominated by the parish (or urban district or borough) council; meet at least once in every term, appoint its own chairman and clerk, and have brought before it all school business (including the appointment, suspension or dismissal of teachers, the school log and the school accounts); be responsible for the whole management of the school; and transmit copies of its minutes annually to the county council.

The education committee of the county council should be empowered to provide additional school places when in its opinion the existing denominational school accommodation, though sufficient, was unsuitable to the demands of the district. In this way the Church schools would remain strong where the Church was strong, but a sufficient remedy would be provided for substantial Nonconformist grievances. A right of appeal to the Board of Education should also be reserved to the managers of any 'voluntary' school in any case of complaint against the local authority. With this freer system of grants the 'special aid grant' should be merged in the other government grants in aid and the voluntary associations for its administration should be abolished as unnecessary and inconsistent with county districts.

London and the county boroughs

We have reserved the case of London and the sixty-two county boroughs, where the need for educational improvement is less crying than in the rural districts, and the problem of unification more difficult. The administrative unity of all grades of education is, however, no less desirable in London and the large towns than in the country, and the malign influence of sectarian quarrels at school board elections is apt to be even more severely felt. On the other hand the school boards in these large towns are usually at least as efficient as the municipal authorities; the work to be done is large – in London colossal; and there would be some danger that unification would lead not, as in the counties, to an increased expenditure on education, but to some slackening in the present rate of increase, if not to a positive limit. The school boards in London and the county boroughs should therefore for the most part be left untouched. The county council in London and the town councils in the county boroughs would become the authorities for all education outside the powers of the school boards, with spending powers in this department of their work as unlimited as in drainage or water supply. They should, of course, retain all their existing powers, and they should, moreover, have the same enlarged powers of providing new schools as are given to the rural county councils.

These considerations do not apply to such county boroughs as Bury, Chester, Lincoln, Preston, St Helens and Stockport, which have no school board. Nor need they apply to county boroughs like Wigan, where the school board has no school; or like Blackburn, Oxford or Worcester, where only 5 to 10 per cent of the children are in board schools; or like Bath or Exeter, where the board schools contain fewer than 2000 children. In all these cases the school board should be abolished, and the town council at once made responsible for all grades of education. This would leave about forty-seven county boroughs in which, as in London, the school board system may be deemed to have so firmly established itself, as to be entitled to be untouched. But even in these cases it should be open to the school board, if it should come to think it desirable, to terminate its own existence, and transfer its schools and powers to the municipality.[8] Meanwhile the school board should be strongly represented on the education committee of the municipal body; and the management of the proposed grant in aid of voluntary schools should be dealt with by a statutory sub-committee, of which the school board members should form one half.

The central authority
The present drift

The Board of Education Act of 1899 has substituted the Board of Education for the Education Department, the Department of Science and Art, the Charity Commissioners and the Board of Agriculture, but no provision has so far been made for the rearrangement of their overlapping powers or for the internal organization of the new Department. The powers of the Treasury over university colleges, of the Local Government Board over poor law schools, of the Home Office over industrial schools and reforma-

8. In 1900–1901 Nottingham Town Council put a clause in a bill which it was promoting, for the complete merging of the School Board in the Town Council. The School Board passed a resolution (January 1901) that the Bill was 'premature', and desired its withdrawal 'for the present'. But the board is understood to be not unfavourable to the principle.

tories, and through the Prisons Commissioners, over prison schools, of the India Office over the Engineering College at Cooper's Hill, of the Board of Agriculture over the agricultural colleges, and of the War Office and Admiralty over their own primary schools in garrison towns, and over military and naval schools, are still continued to these departments. A consultative committee has been created, but without specific powers beyond the framing of a register of teachers. So far as can be seen, the present intention is to organize the Board of Education solely into primary and secondary divisions, the latter being illogically sub-divided into 'technical education' and 'secondary schools'. Such a plan may easily reduce the whole 'reform' to a merely mechanical concentration of existing departments under a single roof. This is of no use if no real unity and no organic relation between the various kinds and grades of education is created. Failure to secure this would be particularly bad for elementary education, which it is the fashion to regard as mechanical and suitable for assignment to lower-grade minds. The education of the great mass of the people must not be isolated from the general intellectual movement either locally or at the centre.

Our plan

The Board of Education should have, subject to the authority of Parliament, powers of inspection, criticism and audit of all education of every kind and grade, which is maintained or aided out of monies provided by Parliament, or from endowments or trust funds derived from persons deceased; and the Board should therefore take cognizance, not only of such primary and secondary education as it controls, but also of universities and university colleges, non-local schools, and other endowed educational institutions, army and navy schools, training colleges, poor law schools, and industrial and reformatory schools and schoolships.

The official staff should be unified and divided primarily into departments on a geographical basis, so that the section of the office dealing with each area should take within its purview all the grades of education, whether elementary, secondary or university, and all subjects of study, whether literary, scientific, technological or commercial, carried on in the day or in the evening, under public authorities or bodies of managers or trustees. Only in this way can we ensure a complete view of all the needs of the district, the organic unity of education within that district, and a differentiation of the requirements of different districts. This fundamental organization of the central department should be into ten or twelve 'provinces', each including all public education within a well-defined geographical area, such as London, Lancashire and Cheshire, Devon and Cornwall, the south-eastern counties and so on.

Each of these ten or twelve geographical sections should be under an official of high standing and varied experience, who might be called Provincial Superintendent. Through his hands should pass all the reports and other papers relating to any part of the education of his district, which should have its own staff of inspectors for different kinds of schools and different subjects of study. Each province would have its own special needs, and special difficulties, which should be treated without any striving after rigid uniformity.

But in order to secure the highest specialist efficiency, no less than national unity, all important proposals should pass from the heads of the geographical departments to one of three or four staff officers, of the rank of Assistant Under-Secretary of State, who should devote themselves each to one kind of education, and should deal with that kind of education all over the country. From him the papers would go, through the permanent Under-Secretary of State to the Board, that is the Minister for Education, for final decision.

The Board of Education should require (i) the provision of at least a prescribed minimum supply of all grades of education by each local authority separately or in conjunction with other local authorities; and (ii) the provision of an adequate educational and administrative staff.

The Board of Education should make the following grants: (i) a fixed grant based upon a calculation of two-thirds of the necessary minimum expenditure on each grade; and (ii) a variable grant based upon one-half of the additional expenditure on any grade up to a fixed maximum. In this way efficiency and enterprise would be promoted, and at the same time extravagance checked. If any educational authority expended less than the minimum in order to save the rates, that is, raised by rate less than one-third of the minimum expenditure, the Board should have power, in the first instance, to fine the locality by reducing or withholding all or part of its grant, *and of supplying the deficiency thus caused by ordering a special local rate to be levied*. If this failed to ensure the provision of the 'National Minimum' of education in the particular locality, the Board should have power, in the last resort, to remove the defaulting local authority from office, and appoint, for a short term of years, Government Commissioners in its stead, with power to rate. But such a drastic course would never be necessary. Meanwhile the Board's inspector should have the right to attend at all full meetings of the authority.

Conclusion

The democratic ideal in education is not merely that a ladder should be provided, whereby a few students may climb unimpeded from the elemen-

tary school to the university; though even this ideal has little chance of
realization so long as some rungs of the ladder are under no one's care, and
competing guardians squabble for the right to look after others. What the
national well-being demands, and what we must insist upon, is that every
child, dull or clever, rich or poor, should receive all the education requisite
for the full development of its faculties. For every child, in every part of the
country, at least a 'national minimum' of education must be compulsorily
provided. Above and beyond that minimum we must see that ample provision is made for varying faculties and divergent tastes. Our plan is to
extend popular control and popular assistance to every branch of education;
to combine all the scattered and over-lapping authorities; and to link
together the municipal life of our local authorities with the intellectual life
of the schools by the concentration of all local services under one local body.
This plan, it is true, requires the surrender of some cherished illusions, and
involves some delicate adjustments to suit transitory forms of organization,
but if these difficulties are faced and met on the lines sketched out in this
Tract, we shall bring the schools into intimate connection with the everyday life of the country and secure so far as official machinery is concerned a
sound and efficient educational system.

   The still more important and more difficult problems of what to teach and
how to educate, remain for separate consideration.

14 Robert L. Morant

from 'The Organization of Education in Switzerland', Educational
Department, Special Reports on Educational Subjects, vol. 3, no. 1, 1898,
p. 47.

The Cockerton Judgement is one of the causes célèbres *in British educational
history. Robert Morant, as Assistant Director of Special Inquiries in
the Education Department, introduced into his study of Swiss education a
number of paragraphs which were to lead to the London School Board
being fined for illegally using rates money to support secondary education,
when the law only allowed provision to be made for elementary education.
The man who heard the evidence, and gave the verdict against the London
School Board was the Government Auditor, Mr T. B. Cockerton; hence
the Cockerton Judgement.*

As far as the *minimum* expenditure of a locality is concerned, the Central
Authority has the right of seeing that certain general conditions (e.g. as to

teaching staff, buildings and curriculum) are adequate and satisfactory. But the Central Authority has not, as with us, any voice in limiting any additional efforts that the Commune may desire to make, out of its own funds, towards extending the educational advantages of its members, or towards making any higher developments of its educational supply. This at once suggests a vital difference between Swiss and English conceptions. For instance, in England many school boards have desired to improve their higher elementary education and to extend its scope by providing day schools of a higher grade; but they have frequently been told by the central authority that they cannot take any such steps as would involve the school board in any expense for this purpose, that it would be illegal to spend their rates in such a manner, inasmuch as they were only empowered by the Act of 1870 to use the rates to provide elementary education.

Similarly when, twenty years later, it was decided that in England and Wales the provision of evening schools giving purely continuative or higher education (instead of mainly elementary as before) might advisedly be made a function of the primary education authorities, it was necessary, in order that this might be done, that a special act should be passed (1890) to give this specific authorization, by removing from school boards the disability previously entailed on them under section 14 (1) of the Act of 1870 taken in connection with section 3, which required that in every school maintained by a school board 'the principal part of the Education given must be elementary'. Moreover, even when this considerable extension of school board powers into higher education was given, it was specifically stated to be for the provision of *evening* schools: no mention was made of its extension to the provision of day schools for a similar purpose.

15 A. J. Balfour

Opening Speech introducing the Education Bill, 24 March 1902.
Parliamentary Debates, House of Commons, 4th series, vol. 105, 1902, cols. 846–68.

The 1902 Education Bill is probably the most notable example of the work of an administrator turned innovator. Mr (later Sir) Robert Morant, who rose in seven years from being an obscure civil servant to be permanent secretary at the Board of Education, sat in the public gallery when Balfour, First Lord of the Treasury and Leader of the House, and very soon to be Prime Minister, introduced the Bill. Towards the end of that introduction, Balfour made a prophetic remark. 'We are agreed about secular education.

*We are not agreed about religious education.' The religious issue was, indeed,
to hang over educational policy until the 1944 Act.*

I rise on behalf of the Government to fulfil a pledge given in the King's
Speech that a Bill should be introduced dealing not merely with secondary
education or with primary education in their isolation, but dealing with
both in one measure and with the view of their better coordination. Nobody
can be more impressed than I am with the difficulty of the task which the
Government have undertaken; and certainly no Ministry, and I think no
House of Commons, would lightly engage in the controversies which any
attempt like that on which we are engaged must necessarily involve. It is
only because we feel that the necessity with which this Bill is intended to
deal is a pressing necessity, it is only because we are of the opinion that it
cannot with national credit be much longer delayed, that we have resolved to
lay before the House our solution of the great problem which, for so many
years past, education has embarrassed the Legislature and the reformer.
Perhaps the House will allow me, in order to make clear the position in
which we now find ourselves, to make a very short retrospect of the course
of events which have, in the first place, brought us to our present position
in regard to primary education, and, in the second place, brought us to our
present position in regard to what I may best describe as higher education –
including in that term secondary and technical instruction, but, for the
most part, excluding the work of the universities.

So far as primary education is concerned, it will be remembered that the
system under which we now work is practically the system adopted by this
House and by Parliament more than a generation ago. Before 1870, there
was indeed a system of education, but it was entirely voluntary in its
character. There was some Government inspection and some Government
support, but there was nothing in existence which could in any sense be
properly described as a national system of primary education. The Legislature in 1870 undertook a gigantic task, but it was a task which, however
great in magnitude, was yet simple in its character. The task they undertook was the task of 'provision' – of providing schools. They aimed at
supplying a gap, an omission from which the existing system suffered. They
desired to provide for every child in this country a school where he might
hope to obtain an adequate elementary education. But they did not desire
to substitute a new plan for an old plan, nor to sweep away what existed and
put something new in its place. Their policy was the very different one of
filling up the vacuum which voluntary effort had left empty, and doing by
local and State effort that which private effort had failed completely to
effect. It was for that object, and that object alone, that school boards were

called into existence. I have indeed seen a statement to the effect that it was intended by the then Government and the then Legislature to make the school board system as it were, the basis of our educational system, the ideal towards which all educational change should move; but I venture to say that is historically inaccurate, and that, in the opinion of Mr Gladstone and Mr Forster, school boards were designed to supplement, not to supplant, the voluntary schools already in existence.

The Act of 1870 successfully carried out this great, if in some respects limited, object. Schools were provided in every district in England, and every child in England henceforth had within its reach the means of elementary education. But two unforeseen consequences arose out of the arrangement, and three considerable omissions made themselves felt as time went on. The first of the two unforeseen consequences was the embarrassment into which the voluntary schools were thrown by the rivalry of the rate-aided board schools. It is perfectly well known that Mr Forster and the Government of that day greatly underrated the probable cost of elementary education. Mr Forster contemplated that a three penny rate would do all that had to be done; and this was no mere casual estimate embodied in an incidental observation. It was repeated more than once by Mr Forster in the 1870 debates. The estimate, as we all know, was entirely erroneous. But one result of that error was that there was a wholly unexpected expenditure by school boards on board schools, and that the voluntary schools were subjected to a competition which, however good for education, was certainly neither anticipated nor desired by the framers of the Act of 1870. The second result was that a strain, or at all events a burden, was put upon local finances in school-board areas, through the action of a body responsible indeed to the community so far as regards education, but having no responsibility for the general expenditure, which was, of course, in the hands of the local authority.

There were the two unexpected consequences. Let me just enumerate hurriedly the three important omissions to which I have referred. In the first place, the Act of 1870 provided no organization for voluntary schools. Board schools in boarding-school districts were organized under the school boards. But voluntary schools, whether in board-school districts or in other parts of the country, were isolated and unconnected. Something has been done by the Act of 1896 to remedy that. The Association of Voluntary Schools, which grew out of that Act, has been of much service in this connection; but even now organization necessarily remains imperfect. The second omission was one with which I shall have to deal more fully a little later on – that there was no sufficient provision for the education of the great staff of teachers required for our national schools. And the third omission was that our primary system was put in no kind of rational or organic connection with our system of secondary education, and through the system of secondary education, with the university education which crowns the whole educational edifice.

Now, may I ask the House to accompany me with equal or even greater rapidity over the history of higher education – education other than elementary ? We have really only to consider, as far as the activity of Parliament is concerned, two measures in connection with education above the elementary standards. One was the reform of the endowed schools. It was a great work. It substituted good schemes for bad schemes, efficient schools for inefficient schools, over a great part of the country; but it did nothing either to supplement the deficiency in secondary education, which everybody admits, or to see that such provision for it as existed was distributed to the best advantage. The other intervention by Parliament was secondary education, and on the whole, I am inclined to think, even more important and more fruitful. The Act of 1889, which gave to county councils and town councils certain duties in connection with higher technical education, was the first great step taken in the direction of municipalizing education.

The work they have done is valuable, and I shall have to say something about it directly; but, again, I have to point out there were and there are omissions and defects in the scheme I have described which it is the bounden duty of Parliament to remedy. One of these is, as I have said, the insufficiency of the supply of secondary education. Another is that by the very fact that you have given to county councils and borough councils the right and the duty to intervene in respect of technical instruction, but of technical instruction alone, the normal and healthy growth of a true scheme of secondary education has been inevitably warped. Higher technical instruction can only do its work – that is the belief and experience of every nation in Europe – it can only do its work well when that work is based on a sound general secondary education. The very fact that you have given your authority ample power to assist technical education, but only imperfect powers to assist a true secondary education, has had, and could not but have, the effect to a certain extent of preventing and warping the natural growth of a sound secondary system.

Well, the net result is as follows: we find dealing with education, secondary and primary, two elective authorities – the county councils and the borough councils on the one side, and in certain cases the school boards on the other. They are, and must be, to a certain extent, in rivalry. Not in hostility necessarily, not in hostility usually; but still, with a long, undefined frontier between the two, which must inevitably produce much confusion and some collision. Around these two rival authorities, but in no connection with them, are scattered independent endowed schools and independent voluntary schools, neither of them organized, neither brought into connection with the central primary authority or the central secondary authority, any more than they are brought into connection with each other.

Well, that is, I believe, a summary of the present state of things; but there are certain aspects of it so important that I hope the House will allow me to describe them a little more fully. To begin with one of the evils I have briefly alluded to. We now have, as I have said, two elective authorities having dealings with the rates, one of which has the power of drawing unlimitedly on the rates for educational purposes without rendering any account to the other, which is, nevertheless, responsible for the general working of the local finances. I cannot believe that is a sound system of local government. It is not a system we should tolerate in any other administrative branch of our business. It will be said that education is so important a subject, of such vital necessity for the well-being of the nation, that the authority entrusted with the duty ought not to be limited in the means placed at its disposal. Yes, but is there not even a more important, even a greater national need than education, and that is national defence? What on earth should we think of a system which gave to the experts of the Navy and Army, for purposes of national defence, unlimited power of drawing cheques on the national exchequer? We groan under the magnitude of the cost of the great spending departments; but what those groans would be if they possessed the financial powers of a school board the imagination fails to picture. I do not believe that this system of *ad hoc* authority with unlimited rating is one which really has any important experimental endorsement behind it at all. There is an hon. friend of mine on the other side of the House who takes great interest in this question. I refer to the hon. Member for Rossendale, who has quoted America as an instance of how such a system may find acceptance in a great community. I have looked as well as I can into the facts as they relate to America; and taking twenty-five of the chief cities of the United States, I find that a majority, a bare majority, I admit – thirteen of the twenty-five – have not an *ad hoc* authority at all, and of the remaining twelve which have such an authority only four are permitted unlimited rating power. In all the other cases where an *ad hoc* authority is established, that authority is strictly tied down in the demands it may make on the rates. We suffer under a different system, and this is one of the evils we ought to endeavour to cure in any measure dealing with the subject we submit to the House.

The second of the evils, already referred to, on which I wish to say a further word, relates to the imperfect coordination of educational effort above the limiting line of elementary education. Sir, I am not one of those who throw blame on school boards because they have, in many cases, trespassed on the territories of secondary education. It has turned out, no doubt, that they were guilty of illegality; but there was a great vacuum to fill, a great omission to make up; and it was most natural that keen educationists, seeing a great unoccupied territory, should – however ill-equipped for the enterprise – do what they could to settle it. Therefore, I throw no blame on the efforts of school boards; but frankly, I must add that so far as I have been able to make myself acquainted with the facts, these authorities for primary education have exaggerated their capacity for dealing with the problem of secondary education. Many of them seem to suppose that by merely putting at the top of an elementary school a certain number of classes dealing with subjects higher than elementary, a system of secondary education was thereby immediately established. But this is a profound mistake. Such classes may have done, within narrow limits, work useful and even necessary; but if we are considering the whole system of secondary education, *to* which the youth of the country come from elementary schools, and *from* which, if their abilities and circumstances warrant it, they go to technical institutes or the University – if that is the scheme we have to reform, no mere addition of higher classes at the top of elementary schools will carry out the objects we have in view. They can only be carried out by secondary schools, properly so called, to which children go at the age of thirteen or fourteen, and where they may spend three or four years in preparation for the work of life or for higher grades of education. Therefore, when we hear that, in spite of all the money the London County Council has spent upon secondary education, nevertheless the number of scholars in the true secondary schools, instead of increasing, has diminished, and they have been really robbed by the higher grade schools of the London School Board –

DR MACNAMARA (Camberwell, N.): How have they been robbed?

MR A. J. BALFOUR: I am not attacking the School Board. I am only showing that in attempting a task it is not qualified to perform, it is not serving the cause of education, and that it is a pity to induce scholars to stay at the higher grade primary schools under the mistaken impression that they are going through a training properly to be described as secondary education.

Now, the third defect of the present system, on which I would like to say a word or two, has relation to the education of teachers. I am the last man to undervalue the admirable service the army of teachers in primary schools have done for the community. Nor do I wholly attack the system of pupil teachers; there is something to be said for bringing future teachers into very early contact with the responsibilities of school life and accustoming him or her to dealing with children. But I cannot bring myself to believe that we ought to be content with this as the sole or even the principal method of training those who are to train our children. At this moment any child who wishes to become a teacher gets made a pupil teacher, and when he has reached that *status* half his time goes to teaching and the other half is given to learning – and what sort of learning? Neither the State nor the local authority provides for them schooling between the ages of thirteen and eighteen. They work with the stimulus of examination before them, picking up a little learning with the help of the master in the school; when they are in country districts, perhaps with the help of the clergyman of the parish, possibly with the aid of what is known as 'education by correspondence' – a deplorable system; in towns they may go to a pupil centre; and in country districts county councils have, in certain cases, established centres where, on Saturday afternoons, they may also go to eke out their slender means of obtaining the necessary education.

What is the result of such a system? I find that 36 per cent of the existing teachers have never got through the examination for the certificate, and I find that 55 per cent of the existing teachers have never been to a training college of any sort, kind or description. In other words, nothing has been done for them during the years which should have been devoted to secondary education; and training colleges, which come in at a later age, only assist 45 per cent of those who are actually engaged in teaching. We spend £18,000,000 a year on elementary education. Can anybody believe that under the system I have described we get the best results or can expect to get the best results for so vast an expenditure? For my own part, reasoning either from theory or from the example of America, or Germany or France, or any other country which devotes itself to educational problems, I am forced to the conclusion that ours is the most antiquated, the most ineffectual and the most wasteful method yet invented for providing a national education.

There is yet a third point on which I wish to say a word or two. It relates to the deplorable starvation of voluntary schools. Some of the opponents of voluntary schools put down their difficulties to the want of liberality on the part of the subscribers. I do not think there is any justification for that charge. I think it is perfectly marvellous what has been done under circumstances which, as I have already told the House, were never foreseen when the Act of 1870 was brought into existence. It will be remembered that the Government passed in 1897 – not wholly I am afraid, with the approval of hon. Gentlemen opposite – the aid grant to voluntary schools. It was freely prophesied at that time that this would lead to the wholesale diminution of subscriptions. It has not done so. The subscriptions have been maintained – I believe, so far as the Church of England is concerned, subscriptions have even been increased. The whole of the 5s. has gone, not to the relief of the subscriber, but to the improvement of education in voluntary schools. But the fact, nevertheless, remains that, after all these great efforts on the part of the voluntary subscriber, and after all the aid given from the National Exchequer, the voluntary schools are in many cases not adequately equipped and are not as well fitted as they should be to carry out the great part which they are inevitably destined to play in our system of national education. I say inevitably destined to play, because the idea of the voluntary schools being swept away by an Act of Parliament, or by any other method, is absurd. The mere magnitude of the forces with which you have got to deal renders it impossible. The mere magnitude of the gap which would be created in the system of national education renders it impossible. Let me remind the House that at this moment the number of voluntary schools is over 14,000, as compared with about 5700 board schools, and that, while the board schools educate 2,600,000 odd, the voluntary schools educate over 3,000,000. In other words, the majority of our children are at this moment educated in the voluntary schools of the country. And, if I turn from the number of children to the cost that would necessarily fall on the community in some form or another if the buildings of the voluntary schools were no longer available for the purposes of education, I find that, if we take the cost of provision throughout the country, excluding London, at £12 10s. per child, and if we cut that figure down, as we certainly ought to cut it down, in order to find the cost that would fall upon us if we had to provide accommodation for the children at present in voluntary schools to £7, even then, at that very cautious estimate, the cost to the community would be no less than £26,000,000 sterling. I do not take the case of London, because the provision in London would raise this average of £12 10s. to a much higher figure, and, though it might appear to strengthen my case, I am not quite sure that it would be fair, and I, therefore base my calculation on the more moderate estimate of the average cost of provision as we find it outside the metropolitan area.

I cannot leave this topic of the necessity of the voluntary schools without saying that, in my opinion, they are necessary also for another and a very different reason. What is the theory which, on both sides of the House, as I think – I do not recognize any difference of principle in this matter between us – we ought to adopt with regard to denominational education in public schools ? We do not insist, as everybody knows, upon teaching the children of this country a particular religion. We do insist upon teaching them a recognized arithmetic, a recognized geography, history and so forth. In the one case we decline responsibility, leaving the responsibility to the parents ; and in the other we are agreed that the State may properly take the responsibility of saying to every parent, so far as secular education is concerned, 'Your child shall learn what we think fit to teach it.' Of course, the reason of this difference is known to all. We are agreed about secular education. We are not agreed about religious education. Whatever be the historic origin of the present state of things, we have, as a community, repudiated responsibility for teaching a particular form of religion. We maintain the responsibility, we gladly assume the responsibility, for teaching secular learning. As we have thus left to the parents the responsibility for choosing what religion their children are to learn, surely we ought, as far as we can consistently with the inevitable limitations which the practical necessities of the case put upon us, to make our system as elastic as we can in order to meet their wishes. I do not stand here to plead for any particular form of denominational religion. I do stand here to say that we ought, as far as we can, to see that every parent gets the kind of religious training for his child that he desires. Here, then, is another reason, and by no means the least, why it is needful to maintain – I do not say maintain in its present shape – the possibility of giving denominational training in our elementary schools. I do not believe that anybody, thinking over the rather abstract train of argument I have ventured to lay before the House, will easily find any defect in the reasoning; and I am quite sure they will not charge me, or those who think with me in this matter, with any narrowness of spirit or with any inclination to proselytize in favour of any particular creed. The interests we desire to safeguard are the interests of the parents, and it is the wishes of the parents which, as far as possible, ought to be consulted.

From this long preface, then, I draw the following conclusions. Our reform, if it is to be adequate, must, in the first place, establish one authority for education – technical, secondary, primary – possessed of powers which may enable it to provide for the adequate training of teachers, and for the welding of higher technical and higher secondary education on to the university system. In the second place, I conclude that this one authority for education, being, as it is, responsible for a heavy cost to the ratepayers, should be the rating authority of the district. In the third place, I lay down that the voluntary schools must be placed in a position in which they can worthily play their necessary and inevitable part in the scheme of national education. These are debatable propositions. I add to them two others which, as I conceive, are not debatable – namely, that, as far as we can, our system should be one which will not encourage for the future the perpetual introduction of denominational squabbles into our local and municipal life; and that the education authority should have at its disposal all the educational skill which the district over which it presides can supply.

I will now proceed very briefly to describe the headings of our Bill; and I hope that, while describing it, I may be spared those natural, but, I think, rather inconvenient questions which I know it is not easy to restrain, but which must rather interrupt the general view of our scheme, which is all I intend to give to the House today. I, or some of my friends, will, later in the evening, be glad to answer the questions which will doubtless be put to me in the debate, and hon. Gentlemen will have the Bill itself in their hands in a few days. But I deliberately abstain from dwelling on some of the smaller details of the Bill in order that I may give a clearer general view of our general proposals. As the House will have anticipated, our education authority is the county council in counties, and the borough council in county boroughs. They will work through a committee or committees. The committees are to be framed by a scheme to be approved of by the education authorities at Whitehall; they will contain at least a majority of members appointed by the council; and another portion, appointed on the nomination of other bodies, will consist of persons experienced in education and acquainted with the needs of the various kinds of schools in the area. I ought to mention an exception with regard to Wales. Wales at this moment has a secondary education authority of its own, which has done quite admirable work, and the mere existence of which ought to allay any fears lest the authority should prove incapable of dealing with secondary education. If the Welsh people prefer, instead of committees of the county councils, to keep the existing authority, they are permitted by the Bill to do so. As regards secondary education, our provisions are practically identical with those with which the House is familiar, and which were embodied in the Bill of last year. The county councils and the borough councils will have a 2d. rate to work upon, but I am convinced that in many places that will be insufficient. There is power for any county council by provisional order to get that limit raised. I have said that the authority is the county council or the county borough council. This is the rule. But there is an exception. We think it impossible to deprive boroughs over 10,000 population, or urban districts over 20,000, of their existing jurisdiction over technical education; nor do we think they can be subordinated to the county in respect of primary education. We therefore leave them as they are with regard to the first; and make them autonomous with regard to the second.

SIR ALBERT ROLLIT (Islington, S.): I desire to know how the non-municipal element is to be appointed, whether by cooption from within the Committee, as in the former Bills, or by nomination from without, by external bodies, which is a new, and from the municipal point of view, a very different thing.

MR A. J. BALFOUR: I will show my hon. friend the exact words.

SIR CHARLES DILKE (Gloucestershire, Forest of Dean): Will the right hon. Gentleman repeat his last passage. We did not understand his last passage.

MR A. J. BALFOUR: I think I can put the matter in a very few words, beginning as it were from the other end. The councils of boroughs of over 10,000, and of urban districts of over 20,000, if they please, may become the absolute authority as regards primary education. They retain their existing powers as to technical education, and they also become the authority for secondary education concurrently with the county councils. The county council of course is the authority over all the district outside the areas I have mentioned.

So much for the authority. Now for its powers. We lay it down in the most absolute terms that the new education authority is, in the words of the Bill 'To control all secular instruction in public elementary schools in their district'. Whether those schools are voluntary, or whether they are rate-erected, in future, if this Bill becomes law, the local education authority which we create will be absolute master of the whole scheme of secular education in every elementary school in its district, voluntary or otherwise. The mode in which they will acquire that control in the case of rate-erected schools, of course, is simple enough. They acquire it as heirs of the school boards. As regards the voluntary schools, they obtain it partly by the explicit mandate contained in the Bill, which I have just quoted; partly by the right given them in the Bill of appointing one-third of the managers; partly by the right of inspection; and partly by the power of the purse. They also obtain it by the right of refusing on educational grounds to sanction the appointment of any teachers whom they think unfitted to carry on the work of secular education. It will be seen, therefore, that under our plan we create a single master of the whole of the primary educational machinery in each district, and that master is an absolute master. It is quite plain that this complete control carries with it the obligation of maintenance, and we propose that on the county or borough rate shall be thrown the whole cost of maintaining every school under the local authority. The managers of the voluntary schools will be required to devote their buildings to educational purposes, to keep them in good repair, and to make all reasonable alterations and improvements. Of course, when we lay down that the local authority is to bear all the charge of maintenance in the district, this can only be in respect of schools which are necessary, and by a necessary school we mean (following the precedent already set by the Code) a school which contains thirty children, or which, having accommodation for less than thirty, is full.

I have now explained that part of the scheme which deals with maintenance. But, as everybody knows, there are even thornier questions connected with what is known as provision – the supply of new schools as population increases, migrates or shifts. The existing system is both arbitrary and anomalous. I will endeavour to explain it, although it is so absurd that it may take some hon. Gentlemen somewhat by surprise. A school board is now, by the law and practice of the Department, not allowed to build a school in a district where there are already a sufficient number of places in existing schools for the children in the district. The schools may be wholly unsuited to the wishes of the district. There may be – to take an extreme case – nothing but Roman Catholic schools within reach of Protestant children. It makes no difference. As long as there are already provided a sufficient number of places for the children of the district, there no school board, even if one is called into existence, is allowed to find more suitable accommodation. There is a correlative absurdity on the other side. In the district where there is a school board, it is not, or until recently was not, in the power of any voluntary body to provide one, however much a denominational school might be required by the parents, unless the school board gave their consent. That is quite unjustifiable in theory, and occasionally productive of much hardship in practice. We propose to abrogate both these conditions. If the real needs of a district require a kind of education not given by the voluntary schools, we fail to see why it should be out of the power of the rate-payers to erect another school, just as we fail to see why a majority of the rate-payers should have it in their power to say to a minority of the parents in any area, 'You want a denominational school, and your children are sufficient in number to fill it; but we do not mean to let you have it.' We make a clean sweep of both these limitations, which make the existing system inequitable in practice and indefensible in theory; and we permit, under reasonable limitation, new schools to be erected in both cases. In case of dispute as to whether it is proper for the new school to be erected, the Education Department is made the arbiter between the parties, and what the Department has to take into account is the economy of rates, the interests of education, and the wishes of the parents. I do not know whether I shall help my case by taking extreme examples of the way in which this may conceivably work. Let us imagine a district in which a Roman Catholic school has been built for a Roman Catholic population, and from which, owing to some change in the industrial condition of the neighbourhood, the whole Roman Catholic population has migrated. Supposing that a Protestant population has come into the district, but that, notwithstanding, the Roman Catholic school has been kept up. Under the existing system the absurdity, or worse than absurdity, is irremediable. It could be remedied under the system we propose. Take the opposite case, which we often hear of, though I hope it is not often found in practice. I heard of one only the other day, in which there was a large Roman Catholic population within a school area ready and anxious to provide a school for their children, but absolutely prevented from doing so owing to the opposition of the school board. Both of those cases of hardship may arise, and sometimes do arise, under our existing system; both will be swept away under the system which we propose to substitute for it. I need only add on this branch of my subject that though, of course, you may in theory imagine that under this system there will be an undue multiplication of small schools, I believe common sense, the needs of economy, and the difficulty of finding the necessary funds will keep either undenominational or denominational zeal, as the case may be, within due bounds.

Sir, the scheme I have described is a scheme which we think suitable for the whole country with two very important, but I hope transitory, limitations, which I now proceed to describe to the House. The first of these limitations relates to London. London is not dealt with in this Bill. London could not, of course, in this case, as London cannot in almost any case, be dealt with as if it were in precisely the same condition as other parts of the country. I believe that my right hon. friend near me, the Home Secretary – in the Local Government Bill of 1888 – is almost the only person who has been able to deal with London in a Bill affecting the whole of England and Wales without making very special provisions for it. In fact, as we all know, London was treated differently from the rest of the country in the Act of 1870, though it was dealt with in the same Bill; it exists under a different set of sanitary laws; it exists under a different set of police laws; legislation affecting its constituent boroughs is different from the legislation affecting any other borough in the kingdom. I might go on multiplying examples, if it were necessary, in order to show that, if there be anything in precedent, London could not be left to the ordinary provisions of this Bill; that it would require a separate portion of the Bill to itself. I do not know what the House thinks – to me it seems evident that the Bill we have introduced is quite big enough for the remainder of the present session; and though the London problem must therefore be postponed, we shall approach it next session with all the advantage which the discussion upon the present measure gives us, and I am convinced that London will lose nothing, while the rest of the country will gain a great deal, by deferring the London portion of the Bill to next year.

The second limitation requires more explanation. I recognize, and I am sure the House recognizes, that whether they like the scheme we have proposed or whether they dislike it, it is, at all events, a far-reaching scheme. It touches an enormous number of controverted problems; it may rake up the ashes of many old controversies, and it may excite administrative disquiet, even alarm, in many portions of the country. I do not know that even now it has been brought home to the minds of everybody everywhere how vital is the need for some great reform, such as we propose; and we can hardly hope to succeed in our object unless we carry with us the local authorities on whom the burden and responsibility of working the Bill will fall. We think it will be most undesirable to drive or force them, with but brief consideration, and possibly against their will, into accepting our plan. We, therefore, propose to leave it to the councils of the various districts to adopt the portion of this Act dealing with elementary education if and when they please. My conviction is that but very few years will elapse before they all do so. I feel tolerably confident that, as it is steadily brought home to them that only by adopting this Act in its entirety can they really hope to deal with the education problem as a whole, they will all adopt it. How much better to attain that result through their free and untrammelled action than to force it upon them, it may be, prematurely. And, Sir, we have, I think, in the sphere of education itself, a good example of how valuable this cautious procedure may prove. It may be in the recollection of the older Members of the House that it was not until 1876 that the non-school-board areas were given the right to pass by-laws for making attendance at school compulsory. They were not obliged to exercise the right, but they were given it. Had they been obliged to make attendance at school compulsory, they would undoubtedly in many cases have bitterly resisted the obligation. Fortunately it was made a voluntary Act. Four years elapsed, and, without a word, without the smallest objection in any quarter of the House or from any part of the country, universal and obligatory school attendance was made by statute the universal rule. I augur well from this precedent; and I believe that, while the voluntary element which we introduce into our Bill will relieve a great many fears, smooth over many difficulties, and prevent many prejudices being harshly interfered with, it will not delay for any long or important period the universal adoption of this Act in every part of England and Wales.

Now, Sir, that is broadly, our scheme. I am aware that it will be looked at with very different eyes by different people according as one aspect or another of the complex education problem chiefly affects them. There are, for instance, some gentlemen who look at this question more from the ratepayers' point of view than from the educational point of view, or the denominational point of view, and I cannot deny that one effect of this measure will be to throw some burden on the rates at present borne elsewhere. But let me remind those who speak in the interests of the ratepayers, that, if this Bill carries out all we hope from it, or anything like all we hope from it, it will give them far better value for their money than they get now; that it will immensely increase the efficiency of our education system, and, by increasing its efficiency, increase its economy. Let them also remember that this Bill sweeps away, once and for all, that considerable and most useless expenditure of money which takes place in the election of school boards and the administration of small areas. Let me further remind them that, if they have been in the habit of complaining of the minute and petty interference of the Board of Education at Whitehall – interference which is alleged, rightly or wrongly I know not, to have thrown a quite unnecessary burden upon many schools – let them, I say, remember that interference from Whitehall will no longer be with individual schools; it will be with the county council. It is the county council which will receive the Imperial subvention; it is to the county councils that all complaints will have to be made; it is by the county council they will have to be remedied. If half the grumbling I have heard about the Education Department at Whitehall be justified, this will prove no small relief to a very large number of long-suffering managers. And, lastly, let it never be forgotten that, if the maintenance of voluntary schools throws a new burden on the rates, this is trifling compared with the burden the rates will have to bear if the voluntary schools be allowed to perish. From the ratepayers' point of view there cannot be a better investment.

So much for the ratepayers. Then, Sir, there is the enthusiast for local government. To him I would say that he need not be afraid that the county councils under this scheme will be overworked. They will carry out their great responsibilities largely through the new committees; and such experiences as we have of the admirable work they have done in regard to secondary education, I think, may relieve us of all anxieties as to their fitness for their new duties. If, moreover, the Bill adds to the work of county councils and borough councils, undoubtedly it will also add great dignity, it will increase the importance of their functions – I believe it will induce some persons to seek civic honours who have never thought of doing so before. Let me add that one great advantage which I foresee from the local government point of view is that education will now be largely decentralized, and that it will be for each district to determine what is the species of education most needed by the children in it to fit them for their work, which, after all, no central department could so well judge of as those whom their parents elect and who are acquainted with the circumstances in which they live.

Then there is another set of possible objectors I have to deal with, whom I hardly dare to hope I shall placate – the ardent believers in school boards. I am the first to recognize what admirable work the school boards in this country have done; but I think that even those who most admire them will admit that the present system of minority election and all the circumstances of canvassing which attend the election of the school board do not really conduce to the interests of education, but are, indeed, very prejudicial to it. I would point out to them also that under our plan all the best educational elements in the country will be turned on to the work of education. They will not have to go through this elaborate electoral process, or not necessarily; and we shall be able for our educational needs to reach strata of experts not now accessible – representatives of universities, of higher education in all its forms, who now cannot, from the nature of the case, submit themselves to the laborious tests of a school board election. Finally, I would say to them that, though they may prefer an *ad hoc* authority, they must surely know that no *ad hoc* authority now can cover the whole ground of education. The last hope of such a consummation was swept away when this House passed the Act of 1889 and when the new municipalities throughout the country took advantage of it. Higher technical education and some outlying portions of secondary education have since then been in the grip of the municipalities; and no practical man will tell me across the floor of this House that he expects that Parliament or the country will ever deprive the municipalities of powers they have so admirably used. I would therefore say to the advocate of the school boards that the school board can never become the universal education authority, and if he wants a universal authority – one which can really co-ordinate education – it can only be to the municipalities that he can turn his gaze.

Then I come to the militant denominationalists and the militant anti-denominationalists. The militant denominationalists, I admit, lose the complete control of their schools which they have hitherto enjoyed. The school managers will no longer be free from responsibility to anyone except His Majesty's Inspector of Schools and the Department at Whitehall. They will have to fall into line, so far as secular instruction is concerned, with other schools, and take such part as they may be ordered to take in the general scheme of education. But the strain of maintenance will be removed. No longer will the unfortunate supporter of voluntary schools [ironical opposition cheers] while freely paying his rates for the rival school over the way, have to beg subscriptions in order to keep his own school going – a position which I think even the hon. Gentleman who ironically cheered just now will admit was a hard one. And, lastly, the denominationalists will for the first time have a clear right to provide schools where the necessity for such schools can be shown to exist.

So much for the militant denominationalists. Now for the militant anti-denominationalists. I admit that they may dislike this Bill. Nevertheless, they will also gain something by it. There are two grievances in the present position of the English Nonconformists which have given rise to complaints which seem to me unanswerable. I hope in practice they do not weigh very heavily on any portion of the population, but still in theory they are unquestionably grievances which we ought to remedy as far as we can. The first is what I may call the grievance of the single school. In some districts there is but one school within reach, and that school is not conducted, so far as religious education is concerned, on lines pleasing to the Nonconformists. I do not say that this grievance is wholly removed, but it is greatly mitigated by a plan which in cases of real need will allow a school to be built although there be adequate accommodation already in the district – a school to be built which may be satisfactory to the Nonconformist parents of the children who go to it. There is yet a second grievance which I have heard stated, of the exact weight of which I am unable to judge, but which, upon paper at all events, seems genuine enough. It is said that there are whole regions of the country where, as all the schools, or nearly all of them, are practically Church schools, the child of a Nonconformist parent anxious to enter the teaching profession finds it almost impossible to obtain the necessary facilities. Again, by creating a local authority which will certainly have it in its power to deal with the whole question of the education and provision of teachers, this grievance also, if not removed, will be very largely mitigated. So I might even say to the militant Nonconformist that he also gets something out of the Bill – gets some of the grievances of which he has so long and so loudly complained diminished or removed. He also, I trust, therefore, may be induced to look with less malevolent eyes on the present educational reform which the Government is attempting.

To the educationist I think I need make no apologies and offer no excuses. From him I anticipate, and I believe I shall obtain, the heartiest support. He has long seen a vast expenditure of public money, which has yet left this country behind all its Continental and American rivals in the matter of education. He has seen a huge average cost per child in our elementary schools, and yet at the same time many of those schools half starved, inadequately equipped, imperfectly staffed. He has seen in the last ten or fifteen years a development of university life by private liberality which has no parallel except in America, which has covered, and is still covering, our great industrial centres with universities and university colleges where the very highest type of university instruction is given by men well qualified for their duty. He has seen technological institutions which I am afraid do not yet rival those which America and Germany have produced, but which yet in their measure and within their limits are admirable. He has seen them erected at a vast cost in every great industrial centre. Yet these university colleges and these great technological institutions do not, cannot, and never will effect all they might do so long as our secondary education, which is their necessary preparation, is in the imperfect condition in which we find it. Therefore I think I may make my appeal, to the educationist at least, with perfect confidence. I think I might go further. It is not upon the opinions or wishes of any particular section of opinion in this House or in the country that the fate of this Bill depends. It depends upon the common sense of the great body of the people, on their growing perception of the need of a really national system of education. If the country is determined on reform in this matter – and I believe its determination to be unalterable – then I say with some confidence that it is upon the lines of this Bill, and only upon the lines of this Bill, that that great reform can proceed. No other scheme – be it what you like – will give to the educational evils of this country the complete, radical and final cure which this Bill will give. I count upon the support of our countrymen to enable us to close for ever these barren controversies which for too long have occupied our time, and in the interests alike of parental liberty and of educational efficiency to terminate the present system of costly confusion.

Motion made, and Question proposed, 'That leave be given to bring in a Bill to make further provision with respect to education in England and Wales.'

16 Education Act (1902)

pp. 3–7.

The Act of 1902 opened a new chapter in the history of English education. It imposed upon the 'muddle' described by Webb a coherent framework leading from elementary school to university by way of the scholarship system. It created local education authority control and, by decentralizing the system, gave English education a characteristic which has remained distinctive in European development.

Elementary education

5 The local education authority shall throughout their area have the powers and duties of a school board and school attendance committee under the Elementary Education Acts 1870 to 1900, and any other Acts, including local Acts, and shall also be responsible for and have the control of all secular instruction in public elementary schools not provided by them, and school boards and school attendance committees shall be abolished.

6 1. All public elementary schools provided by the local education authority shall, where the local education authority are the council of a county, have a body of managers consisting of a number of managers not exceeding four appointed by that council, together with a number not exceeding two appointed by the minor local authority.

Where the local education authority are the council of a borough or urban district they may, if they think fit appoint for any school provided by them a body of managers consisting of such number of managers as they may determine.

2. All public elementary schools not provided by the local education authority shall, in place of the existing managers, have a body of managers consisting of a number of foundation managers not exceeding four appointed as provided by this Act, together with a number of managers not exceeding two appointed

(a) Where the local education authority are the council of a county, one by that council and one by the minor local authority; and

(b) Where the local education authority are the council of a borough or urban district, both by that authority.

3. Notwithstanding anything in this section –

(a) Schools may be grouped under one body of managers in manner provided by this Act; and

(b) Where the local education authority consider that the circumstances of any school require a larger body of managers than that provided under this section, that authority may increase the total number of managers, so, however, that the number of each class of managers is proportionately increased.

7 1. The local education authority shall maintain and keep efficient all public elementary schools within their area which are necessary, and have the control of all expenditure required for that purpose, other than expenditure for which, under this Act, provision is to be made by the managers; but, in the case of a school not provided by them, only so long as the following conditions and provisions are complied with

(a) The managers of the school shall carry out any directions of the local education authority as to the secular instruction to be given in the school, including any directions with respect to the number and educational qualifications of the teachers to be employed for such instruction, and for the dismissal of any teacher on educational grounds, and if the managers fail to carry out any such direction the local education authority shall in addition to their other powers, have the power themselves to carry out the direction in question as if they were the managers; but no direction given under this provision shall be such as to interfere with reasonable facilities for religious instruction during school hours.

(b) The local education authority shall have power to inspect the school.

(c) The consent of the local education authority shall be required to the appointment of teachers, but that consent shall not be withheld except on educational grounds; and the consent of the authority shall also be required to the dismissal of a teacher unless the dismissal be on grounds connected with the giving of religious instruction in the school.

(d) The managers of the school shall provide the school house free of any charge, except for the teacher's dwelling-house (if any), to the local education authority for use as a public elementary school, and shall, out of funds provided by them, keep the school house in good repair, and make such alterations and improvements in the buildings as may be reasonably required by the local education authority; provided that such damage as the local authority consider to be due to fair wear and tear in the use of any room in the school house for the purpose of a public elementary school shall be made good by the local education authority.

(e) The managers of the school shall, if the local education authority have no suitable accommodation in schools provided by them, allow that authority to use any room in the school house out of school hours free of charge for any educational purpose, but this obligation shall not extend to more than three days in the week.

2. The managers of a school maintained but not provided by the local education authority, in respect of the use by them of the school furniture out of school hours, and the local education authority in respect of the use by them of any room in the school house out of school hours, shall be liable to make good any damage caused to the furniture or the room, as the case may be, by reason of that use (other than damage arising from fair wear and tear), and the managers shall take care that, after the use of a room in the school house by them, the room is left in a proper condition for school purposes.

3. If any question arises under this section between the local education authority and the managers of a school not provided by the authority, that question shall be determined by the Board of Education.

4. One of the conditions required to be fulfilled by an elementary school in order to obtain a parliamentary grant shall be that it is maintained under and complies with the provisions of this section.

5. In public elementary schools maintained but not provided by the local

education authority, assistant teachers and pupil teachers may be appointed, if it is thought fit, without reference to religious creed and denomination, and, in any case in which there are more candidates for the post of pupil teacher than there are places to be filled, the appointment shall be made by the local education authority, and they shall determine the respective qualifications of the candidates by examination or otherwise.

6. Religious instruction given in a public elementary school not provided by the local education authority shall, as regards its character, be in accordance with the provisions (if any) of the trust deed relating thereto, and shall be under the control of the managers: provided that nothing in this subsection shall affect any provision in a trust deed for reference to the bishop or superior ecclesiastical or other denominational authority so far as such provision gives to the bishop or authority the power of deciding whether the character of the religious instruction is or is not in accordance with the provisions of the trust deed.

7. The managers of a school maintained but not provided by the local education authority shall have all powers of management required for the purpose of carrying out this Act, and shall (subject to the powers of the local education authority under this section) have the exclusive power of appointing and dismissing teachers.

8 1. Where the local education authority or any other persons propose to provide a new public elementary school, they shall give public notice of their intention to do so, and the managers of any existing school, or the local education authority (where they are not themselves the persons proposing to provide the school), or any ten ratepayers in the area for which it is proposed to provide the school, may, within three months after the notice is given, appeal to the Board of Education on the ground that the proposed school is not required, or that a school provided by the local education authority, or not so provided, as the case may be, is better suited to meet the wants of the district than the school proposed to be provided, and any school built in contravention of the decision of the Board of Education on such appeal shall be treated as unnecessary.

2. If, in the opinion of the Board of Education, any enlargement of a public elementary school is such as to amount to the provision of a new school, that enlargement shall be so treated for the purposes of this section.

3. Any transfer of a public elementary school to or from a local education authority shall for the purposes of this section be treated as the provision of a new school.

9 The Board of Education shall, without unnecessary delay, determine, in case of dispute, whether a school is necessary or not, and, in so determining, and also in deciding on any appeal as to the provision of a new school, shall have regard to the interest of secular instruction, to the wishes of parents as to the education of their children, and to the economy of the rates; but a school for the time being recognized as a public elementary school shall not be considered unnecessary in which the number of scholars in average attendance, as computed by the Board of Education, is not less than thirty.

10 1. In lieu of the grants under the Voluntary Schools Act 1897, and under section 97 of the Elementary Education Act 1870, as amended by the Elementary Education Act 1897, there shall be annually paid to every local education authority, out of moneys provided by Parliament
(a) A sum equal to four shillings per scholar; and
(b) An additional sum of three halfpence per scholar for every complete twopence per scholar by which the amount which would be produced by a penny rate on the area of the authority falls short of ten shillings a scholar; provided that, in estimating the produce of a penny rate in the area of a local education authority not being a county borough, the rate shall be calculated upon the county rate basis, which, in cases where part only of a parish is situated in the area of the local education authority, shall be apportioned in such manner as the Board of Education think just.

But if in any year the total amount of parliamentary grants payable to a local education authority would make the amount payable out of other sources by that authority on account of their expenses under this Part of this Act less than the amount which would be produced by a rate of threepence in the pound, the parliamentary grants shall be decreased, and the amount payable out of other sources shall be increased by a sum equal in each case to half the difference.

17 Board of Education

from the *Code of Regulations for Public Elementary Schools*, Cd 2074, 1904, pp. i–3.

Following the 1902 Act, Morant drafted a series of regulations which set the pattern for both the elementary and secondary schools. His Code for Public Elementary Schools *set the scene for an imaginative new concept of primary education, and embodies a philosophy of teaching which still influences schools today.*

Introduction

The purpose of the public elementary school is to form and strengthen the character and to develop the intelligence of the children entrusted to it, and to make the best use of the school years available, in assisting both girls and boys, according to their different needs, to fit themselves, practically as well as intellectually, for the work of life.

With this purpose in view it will be the aim of the school to train the children carefully in habits of observation and clear reasoning, so that they may gain an intelligent acquaintance with some of the facts and laws of nature; to arouse in them a living interest in the ideals and achievements of mankind, and to bring them to some familiarity with the literature and history of their own country; to give them some power over language as an instrument of thought and expression, and, while making them conscious of the limitations of their knowledge, to develop in them such a taste for good reading and thoughtful study as will enable them to increase that knowledge in after years by their own efforts.

The school must at the same time encourage to the utmost the children's natural activities of hand and eye by suitable forms of practical work and manual instruction; and afford them every opportunity for the healthy development of their bodies, not only by training them in appropriate physical exercises and encouraging them in organized games, but also by instructing them in the working of some of the simpler laws of health.

It will be an important though subsidiary object of the school to discover individual children who show promise of exceptional capacity, and to develop their special gifts (so far as this can be done without sacrificing the interests of the majority of the children), so that they may be qualified to pass at the proper age into secondary schools, and be able to derive the maximum of benefit from the education there offered them.

And, though their opportunities are but brief, the teachers can yet do much to lay the foundations of conduct. They can endeavour, by example and influence, aided by the sense of discipline which should pervade the school, to implant in the children habits of industry, self-control and courageous perseverance in the face of difficulties; they can teach them to reverence what is noble, to be ready for self-sacrifice, and to strive their utmost after purity and truth; they can foster a strong respect for duty, and that consideration and respect for others which must be the foundation of unselfishness and the true basis of all good manners; while the corporate life of the school, especially in the playground, should develop that instinct for fair-play and for loyalty to one another which is the germ of a wider sense of honour in later life.

In all these endeavours the school should enlist, as far as possible, the interest and cooperation of the parents and the home in a united effort to enable the children not merely to reach their full development as individuals, but also to become upright and useful members of the community in which they live, and worthy sons and daughters of the country to which they belong.

Course of instruction, syllabus and timetable

1. The education given in every public elementary school should be based on a graduated course of instruction, suitable to the age and capacity of the scholars, in the following subjects:

(a) *The English language*, including speaking with correct pronunciation, reading aloud with intelligence and clear enunciation, writing, oral and written composition, and grammar. At each stage recitation of pieces of literary merit should be practised.

(b) *Arithmetic*, including practice in oral and written descriptions of the processes used.

(c) *Knowledge of the common phenomena of the external world*, with special reference to the formation of a habit of intelligent and accurate observation, and to the application of that habit – in conjunction with simple forms of experiment – in the daily life and surroundings of the scholars.

(d) *Geography*, advancing from first notions to an outline knowledge of the chief physical features of the earth, and specially of the British Isles, and the British Dominions beyond the seas.

(e) *History*, comprising a general knowledge of the great persons and events in English history and of the growth of the British Empire.

(f) *Drawing*, including drawing from actual objects, memory drawing and brush drawing; together with other simple hand and eye training.

(g) *Singing*, which should, as a rule, be taught by note and should include practice in proper breathing.

(h) *Physical exercises*, according to an approved system.

(i) *Plain needlework*, for girls, including in the later years lessons in cutting out.

It is desirable that as far as possible subjects (a) to (f) should be taught in relation to each other and with reference to the surroundings of the children. The instruction should afford frequent opportunities for the practice of oral and written composition.

Part of the instruction of infants should be given by means of appropriate and varied occupations, and to a less extent the same methods should find a place in the teaching of the younger scholars (Article 3). Instruction in history and geography need not be given to infants.

One or more of the above subjects of instruction may be partly or wholly omitted in any class in which the Board are satisfied that there is good reason for the omission.[1]

2. The instruction under Article 1 must be in accordance with a syllabus which the Inspector may require to be submitted to him at any time. The Board may require the modification of any portion of the syllabus which is considered unsuitable.

The syllabus should show the amount of time allotted to each subject, and should ordinarily provide for a full year's instruction, but that year need not be identical with the school year (Article 27), or with the educational year adopted for any special subject (Schedule III, Rule I).

Specimen schemes of instruction suited to schools in various circumstances may be obtained on application to the Board.

3. The classification of scholars for instruction under Article 1 should not be based on a precise separation according to age; but scholars who, at the close of the course of instruction for the year, will not have completed their seventh year should generally be regarded as 'infants'. Other scholars should generally be regarded as 'younger scholars' until the close of the year of instruction in which they complete their eleventh year, and afterwards should generally be regarded as 'older scholars'.

4. Instruction in the following subjects (for which special grants are made on the conditions specified in Articles 34–6) may also be given to scholars in the upper classes under the regulations of Schedule III, where adequate equipment and efficient teachers are available: for boys – handicraft, gardening and (in schools in seaport towns, with the special consent of the Board) cookery. For girls – cookery, laundrywork, dairywork and household management.

5. One or two subjects other than those named in Articles 1 and 4 may often be taught with advantage to older scholars. The Inspector will satisfy himself (1) that any subject thus taken is suitable to the age, circumstances and capacities of those scholars who take it, (2) that it can be taken without interfering with the general course of instruction, (3) that it can be efficiently taught, and (4) that the instruction will be given in accordance with a suitably graduated scheme.

6. Instruction may be given in religious subjects but no grant is made in

1. Information and suggestions concerning the various subjects of the school course, and the methods of instruction suitable to each, will be found in the companion volume to the Code to be issued shortly.

T–ECS–D

respect of such instruction (section 97 (1), Elementary Education Act 1870).

7. The time during which instruction is given in each subject taken under this Code, whether at the school or elsewhere, must be entered in the timetable and is subject to the approval of the Inspector on behalf of the Board.

The timetable must be open at any reasonable time, except the ordinary school hours, to the inspection of the parent of any scholar attending the school who makes a written application to see it.

The timetable must be kept permanently and conspicuously affixed in every school-room (section 7 (2) Elementary Education Act 1870).

18 Board of Education
from Prefatory Memorandum, *Regulations for Secondary Schools*, Cd 2128, 1904, pp. 5–11.

Morant's Regulations for Secondary Schools *embodied his view that the education system was a dual one, in which the secondary element was to be based on the style and curriculum of the public schools, and that its objectives were strongly academic. In the event, the organization of secondary education was largely divisive, and its heavy emphasis on academic work at the expense of technical or practical activities influenced education throughout the century.*

The following regulations have been framed with the view of promoting the provision and organization of secondary schools, each of which shall have a clearly defined purpose, and a well considered scheme of instruction, suiting it to take its proper place in an organized system of national education.

1. Until recent years, the only direct aid given by the State towards the education of boys and girls other than those in elementary schools was in respect of instruction in science and in art, whether given as a portion of the curriculum of a secondary school or in special classes. The regulations for secondary schools have grown up round the old provisions of the Science and Art Directory. The sporadic science classes were gradually built up into schools of science; and the schools of science were subsequently widened into schools of what was known as the Division A type, providing a course of instruction in science in connection with, and as part of, a course of general education. Aid has also been recently given on a smaller scale to

schools in which science formed an important, but not a preponderating element in the instruction, known under the name of Division B schools. At the same time grants continued to be made directly towards the instruction in science and in art of classes in day schools as well as of evening classes and of classes held in technical institutions.

2. The duty laid on the Board by recent legislation, of superintending and promoting the supply of education other than elementary by local education authorities, makes it a matter of urgent necessity to place the administration of grants to secondary schools upon a wider and firmer basis. Some confusion exists in this country with regard to the precise function of the various schools and institutions purporting to provide secondary education. That term itself is not exempt from criticism. Of French origin, it had originally a meaning both logical and precise. It was that portion of the complete course of education necessary or desirable for the full intellectual development of the individual citizen which lay between the primary education, beyond which circumstances forbade the majority of the population to advance, and the tertiary education which succeeded and completed it from the age and standard of acquirement at which the scholar becomes the student, acquires rather than receives, and works with the fuller responsibility of adolescence and the more specialized scope required as a preparation for the occupations of mature life and the exercise of active citizenship.

3. The term primary as applied to education, though still occasionally used, has since the legislation of 1870 been almost wholly superseded alike in official and in popular language by the term elementary. The term tertiary has at no time come into acceptance in this country at all. The intermediate term of secondary, as applied to education, has consequently been left in the air; and to this fact in no small measure may be attributed the extreme vagueness with which the word is used and the actual misuse of it which may be often observed. Parliament in recent legislation has refrained from employing the term at all; and the Board do not consider that any precise definition of the term secondary education is immediately practicable. But a definition of the term 'secondary school' – which has come to have a recognized meaning in English education – has become indispensable in order to give to secondary schools a definite place in the wide and vague scheme of 'education other than elementary', with the provision and organization of which the local education authorities under the Act of 1902 have been charged, and in respect of which they obtain financial aid and administrative regulation from the Board of Education.

4. In order to arrive at a proper differentiation of functions, it is important

for purposes of central and of local administration, and in particular for considering and properly planning courses of instruction, to distinguish secondary schools, on the one hand, from technical institutes and classes which devote themselves mainly to giving specialized instruction and training in certain subjects to young persons and adults who should previously have completed a sound general education, and on the other, from evening schools and classes which, though they may offer instruction to some students in subjects of a general kind and to others in subjects of art or of pure and applied science, do not provide a consecutive and complete course of general education, to be followed by each student who attends the school.

5. For the purposes of these Regulations, therefore, the term 'secondary school' will be held to include any day or boarding school which offers to each of its scholars, up to and beyond the age of sixteen, a general education, physical, mental and moral, given through a complete graded course of instruction of wider scope and more advanced degree than that given in elementary schools. The Board desire to emphasize the three following points as being essential to this course of instruction:

(a) The instruction must be general; i.e. must be such as gives a reasonable degree of exercise and development to the whole of the faculties, and does not confine this development to a particular channel, whether that of pure and applied science, of literary and linguistic study, or of that kind of acquirement which is directed simply at fitting a boy or girl to enter business in a subordinate capacity with some previous knowledge of what he or she will be set to do. A secondary school should keep in view the development and exercise of all the faculties involved in these different kinds of training, and will fail to give a sound general education to its scholars in so far as it sends them out, whether to further study or to the business of life, with one or other of these faculties neglected, or with one developed at the expense of the rest. Specialization in any of these directions should only begin after the general education has been carried to a point at which the habit of exercising all these faculties has been formed and a certain solid basis for life has been laid in acquaintance with the structure and laws of the physical world, in the accurate use of thought and language, and in practical ability to begin dealing with affairs.

(b) The course of instruction must be complete; i.e. must be so planned as to lead up to a definite standard of acquirement in the various branches of instruction indicated above, and not stop short at a merely superficial introduction to any one of them. Secondary schools are of different types, suited to the different requirements of the scholars, to their place in the social organization, and to the means of the parents and the age at which the regular education of the scholars is obliged to stop short, as well as to the occupations and opportunities of development to which they may or should look forward in later life. But in no case can the course of a secondary school be considered complete which is not so planned as to carry on the scholars to such a point as they may reasonably be expected to reach at the age of sixteen. It may begin at the age of eight or nine, or even earlier. Scholars may pass into it from elementary schools at various ages beyond this, up to twelve or thirteen; and in schools of a high grade, which give an education leading directly on to the universities, it may be continued up to the age even of eighteen or nineteen. But as a rule the years from twelve or thirteen up to sixteen or seventeen will be those during which it is most important that it should be carried on in accordance with a systematic and complete scheme.

(c) The instruction must be graded in its various branches. A defect which is notorious in many schools is that in certain subjects (often from causes for which the school authorities are not responsible) instruction of the scholars is cut down to 'marking time' or the repetition of lessons already learned. Instruction which is not progressive, while it may be of some use as drill and discipline, is of little real educational value. It gives only a superficial and transitory acquirement, while at the same time it fails to interest or to stimulate the scholar.

6. In view at once of the capital importance of this central period of education, and of the limited sum which Parliament at present places at the disposal of the Board for grants in aid of education other than elementary, the grants payable under these Regulations are made in respect of a four years' course only. No school will be considered eligible for these grants which does not provide at least this amount of education. But the earlier education leading up to this course, and the further education (if any) given beyond it, are regarded by the Board as forming together with it a single organic and progressive system. The Regulations, therefore, require that the curriculum of the whole school must be submitted for approval; that the instruction in the preliminary stages must be such as will prepare scholars fully for proceeding to the main course; and that such further instruction as is provided beyond the limits of the main course shall be an adequate continuation of that general education which it is the function of the secondary school to provide, and shall not check the general development of the scholar's faculties by excessive or premature specialization.

7. All secondary schools receiving grants from the Board will in future have

to satisfy these conditions, as set forth more at large in the following Regulations. The rules there laid down have been framed with the view of ensuring that the education given shall be general in its nature, while leaving greater freedom than hitherto for schools to frame curricula of varying kinds, as may be required or rendered possible by local conditions. A certain minimum number of hours in each week must be given, in each year of the course, to the group of subjects commonly classed as 'English', and including the English language and literature, geography and history; to languages, ancient or modern, other than the native language of the scholars; and to mathematics and to science. Ample time is left for a well planned curriculum to add considerably to this minimum in one or more of these groups of subjects, as well as to include adequate provision for systematic physical exercises; for drawing, singing and manual training; for the instruction of girls in the elements of housewifery; and for such other subjects as may profitably be included in the curriculum of any particular school.

8. In respect of this complete course of graded instruction grants will be made on a simple and uniform scale which is set forth in paragraph 32 of the Regulations. This grant applies alike to all the types of school which come within the general definition of a secondary school as above given. These types fall, broadly speaking, into three main classes, whether regarded from the side of the standard or of the kind of general education which the school is meant to provide. In the former aspect they fall into one or other of the three grades of the Schools Inquiry Commission of 1864 and the Secondary Education Commission of 1894: the first-grade schools, leading up directly to the universities and the colleges of university rank; the second-grade schools, which stop short of that point as regards the bulk of their scholars; and the third-grade schools, which do not attempt to carry education much beyond the age of sixteen, and the object of which is to turn out scholars adequately equipped for commerce and business, for entering upon apprenticeship to the teaching profession, or for proceeding, with a sound preliminary general training, into technical and industrial pursuits. In the latter aspect, in respect of the kind of education offered, they may roughly be discriminated into what are known in ordinary usage as the literary, the scientific and the commercial types of school; the first of these paying special regard to the development of the higher powers of thought and expression, and that discriminating appreciation of what is best in the thought and art of the world, in other ages and countries as well as in our own, which forms the basis of all human culture; the second, to the training of the intellect towards understanding and applying the laws of the

physical universe; and the third, to the equipment of the scholars for practical life in the commercial and industrial community of which they are members.

9. The Board desire it to be clearly understood, that the fact of a uniform scale of grant being given to all these grades and types of school, implies no belief that they are of equal importance or have indiscriminate claims to State aid. Still less does it imply the assumption that the cost of maintaining one grade or type of school is the same as that of maintaining any other with a similar number of scholars, or that the return to the State per scholar in the form of trained material for citizenship is estimable in uniform terms of so many shillings a head. The uniform scale of aid given is designed to give impartial encouragement to all well-considered local effort towards developing a general system of secondary schools through many channels and in varying directions. Much of the work that has to be done in establishing such a system is experimental and will have to be reconsidered later in the light of its results. The secondary schools are in a sense the educational laboratory of the nation; and the case of elementary schools shows how difficult it is, even after a generation of practical working, to reach any certain conclusion as to the relative efficacy of different subjects and methods, and as to the exact point at which the control or influence of the state ceases to be an expanding and stimulating force and tends to fetter or to sterilize individual genius and local patriotism.

10. To this uniform scale of grants, however, one exception is at present retained as justified on historical and practical grounds and as necessary towards continuity of administration. The schools hitherto known as 'Division A schools' form an important element in the provision for higher education, and have grown into existence by the direct encouragement and special aid of the Board. A special imperial grant towards aiding the teaching of pure and applied science has for many years been one of the accepted liabilities of the State. This type of school is one which, in the words of previous Regulations, 'provides a thorough and progressive course in science forming a part of a general education' and including individual manual instruction and practical laboratory work. The instruction given in it is, upon this side of its work, somewhat more advanced and somewhat more specialized than that of ordinary secondary schools even of a high grade: and the cost of maintenance is correspondingly enhanced by the more expensive nature of its apparatus and general organization. For this type of school a special grant is made in addition to the ordinary grant which it receives as a secondary school complying with the general conditions prescribed for all such schools. The amount of this special grant will be

fixed by the Board with regard to the circumstances of each school, upon a scale which is the practical equivalent of the scale previously applicable to schools of this type, and may reach a maximum which doubles the total amount of the ordinary grant.

19 Board of Education

from 'Courses of Instruction', *Regulations for Secondary Schools*, Cd 2128, 1904, pp. 17–18.

1. The curriculum of the school must include an approved course of general instruction extending over at least four years.

2. In classes in the school below those taking the course the curriculum must be such as will prepare the scholars fully for entering on the course. It must include English, geography, history, arithmetic, writing, drawing and physical exercises. It should also make provision for work to develop accuracy of observation and skill of hand, and for singing.

3. The average age of the scholars in any class commencing the course must be not less than twelve years, and the Inspector must be satisfied that the class as a whole is qualified to commence the course.

4. The course should provide for instruction in the English language and literature, at least one language other than English, geography, history, mathematics, science and drawing, with due provision for manual work and physical exercises, and, in a girls' school, for housewifery. Not less than four and a half hours per week must be allotted to English, geography and history; not less than three and a half hours to the language where only one is taken or less than six hours where two are taken; and not less than seven and a half hours to science and mathematics, of which at least three must be for science. The instruction in science must be both theoretical and practical. Where two languages other than English are taken, and Latin is not one of them, the Board will require to be satisfied that the omission of Latin is for the advantage of the school.

5. In a girls' school in which the total number of hours of instruction is less than twenty-two per week, the time given to science and mathematics may be reduced to one-third of that total, provided that at least three hours are given to science.

6. By special permission of the Board, languages other than English may be omitted in a school which can satisfy the Board that its English course provides adequate linguistic and literary training, and that the staff is

specially qualified to give such instruction. In this case not less than
seven and a half hours per week must be allotted to English, geography and
history.

20 Sidney Webb

'The Making of a University', *Cornhill Magazine*, April 1903, pp. 530–40.

*Although the early twentieth century marked the foundation of a national
system of education, it also saw the creation – largely unheralded, as Sidney
Webb complained – of the civic universities, to break the monopoly of
Oxford and Cambridge in the field of higher education. Two men who
played a major role in that development later described the events that
produced a Golden Age in university-making.*

In the middle of February a few of the London newspapers reported,
briefly and obscurely enough, an official decision of no small moment to the
future of English education. The other newspapers did not notice it at all,
and public opinion is still unaware that a decisive step in national policy has
been taken. The decision was that of a special committee of the Privy
Council, consisting of the Duke of Devonshire, Lord Rosebery, Lord James
of Hereford, Lord Balfour of Burleigh and Sir Edward Fry, in favour of the
dissolution of the examining board known as the Victoria University, and
the establishment of separate teaching universities at Liverpool, at Manchester and for Yorkshire. Taken in conjunction with the complete reorganization of the University of London on a teaching basis (1898–1900),
with the statutory creation of a university at Birmingham (1900), and with
the recognition by the Government of new university colleges at Reading
and Southampton (1902), this simultaneous approval of the creation of three
new universities in the northern counties may fairly be said to mark an
epoch. We are actually engaged, on no small scale, in the business of making
universities. We are evidently going, during the next few years, to endow
each part of England with its own local university.

Now there are still many people, not otherwise ill-informed, to whom this
movement for the making of universities is little better than foolishness. To
them, a university means Oxford or Cambridge, and they are unable even
to imagine either the desirability or the possibility of creating a new university, or of establishing such a thing anywhere else than at Oxford or
Cambridge. There is, however, a very real and rapidly growing demand
for new universities. It is not a demand for additional Oxfords or new

Cambridges, but for something essentially different. It would plainly be hopeless, even if it were desirable, to attempt to create in London or at Birmingham the traditions, the atmosphere, the charm, or the grace of collegiate life on the Isis or the Cam. Nor do those who ask for additional universities seek to compete for the boys from Eton or Harrow, with two or three hundred a year to spend in pocket money. The new universities are demanded, and they will be paid for, not in order that a tiny section of the community, whether picked by means or by scholarship ability, may obtain the hallmark of a certain distinctive culture, but – to use terms which will certainly be misunderstood – in the twofold capacity of intellectual workshops and technical schools. What middle-class public opinion is now demanding is that there should be, on the one hand, adequate provision of complete intellectual training and professional instruction, cheap and easily accessible, for every boy or girl destined for a brain-working occupation; and, on the other, that there should be set going additional centres of the 'Advancement in Learning' in the Baconian sense, not necessarily the perfect acquaintance with what has been written in the past, but the discovery of new truth and the achievement of new conquests by man over his environment.

For both these purposes the making of new universities in England has become imperative. Other nations are rapidly increasing both the number and the proportion of their citizens equipped with the highest scientific and professional advantages. The proportion of university students is going up in Holland and the United States at the rate of 5 per cent per annum; in Germany and Belgium, by 6 per cent; in Switzerland, by more than 7 per cent; whilst in France, Italy, Austria and Russia the annual increase cannot fall behind these figures. On the other hand, in the United Kingdom the proportion of the population for whom we provide the highest training is at best stationary, and in some years actually declines. We may still believe that man for man an Englishman is superior to the citizen of any other country, but not even the most sanguine patriot can ignore the advantages of education. Even in the realm of public administration and business enterprise the world is passing out of the 'unskilled labour' stage, when our healthy English gentleman could by innate capacity for command easily distance every rival. We have come, at the opening of the twentieth century, to an era of professional expertness, in which the merely cultivated amateur is hopelessly beaten out of the field.

The world is requiring, year by year, not only more and more doctors and lawyers of scientific attainments and professional expertness of the highest standard of excellence, but also incomparably more engineers and chemists, architects and surveyors, teachers and civil servants, clerks and business managers, journalists and authors, who have quite certainly got to be edu-

cated up to a point far beyond that contemplated by the Oxford of a generation ago. In England, as things are, these tens of thousands of aspirants to
higher education cannot go to Oxford or Cambridge (it would be supremely
unwise of Oxford and Cambridge to seek to accommodate them), and for
lack of local universities their education is now usually prematurely broken
off, or lacks direction and stimulus – fails, above all, in subtle cultivation of
the imagination and generosity of aim – because there are not in England,
as there are in every other civilized country, local universities dispersed
throughout the land in such a way as to be genuinely accessible to at least
one per thousand of the population, instead, of, as at Oxford and Cambridge,
to less than one-fifth of that proportion.

It is important that the nature of the demand for new universities should
be understood, as misapprehension both arouses opposition on the part
of those who are concerned for the older universities and also perverts the
making of the new universities themselves. These new universities are not,
and should never be intended to become, the rivals of Oxford and Cambridge. They have different aims and different methods, and they will
appeal to different classes. The parent able to afford to send his son or
daughter to spend three or four years at Oxford or Cambridge will in nearly
every case continue to prefer to do so. The undergraduates of the new
universities will in the main be composed of persons who would not in any
event have found their way to these ancient haunts of learning. They will
include (a) those resident in or near the seat of the university, and thus able
to continue to live inexpensively at home; (b) the country students attracted
to the great urban centres by their exceptional opportunities for the study
of medicine, engineering or economics, or for professional training as
schoolmasters or lawyers. With the exception of a tiny proportion of local
residents and of these country students, the undergraduate class of the new
universities will, we may infer, be confined practically to those coming from
homes maintained on incomes of less than £1500 a year, whilst all of them,
without exception, will be intending to earn their bread in the practical
work of the world.

This is what is meant by saying that the new universities, besides being
centres for the advancement of learning, will be technical schools. We need
not dispute the advantage of spending three or four years in general culture
before even beginning professional training. It is most desirable that Oxford
and Cambridge should continue to provide this advantage for the select few
who can afford it, and should not tamper with their ideals with any vain
hope of attracting *les nouvelles couches sociales* of the educational world. It is,
however, plain that the tens of thousands of engineers and chemists, teachers
and lawyers, businessmen and journalists, for whom we have to provide

higher education cannot afford so leisurely a curriculum. By the age of twenty-two they must at any rate have got well forward with their specialized instruction and professional training; we must therefore necessarily organize our university courses in such a way as to turn out the graduate fully equipped, not only as a cultivated citizen, but also, so far as may be possible, as a trained professional. Hence it is exactly true, however much the term may be disliked, that the new universities will, apart from their higher purpose of being centres of scientific investigation and research, inevitably take on the character of technical schools for all the brainworking professions of the time – as, indeed, the most celebrated universities of the world, from Bologna and Salerno, through medieval Paris and Oxford, down to nineteenth-century Berlin and Heidelberg, have always been.

These conditions and limitations of the new universities imply, first, that they will rapidly become large and numerously frequented institutions; and, secondly, that the standard of their teaching will be extremely high. They will be large, because their *clientèle*, comprising, as it very shortly will do, all those intending to enter the less aristocratic brain-working occupations, will be enormous; and because a university course will soon be an indispensable qualification for every teacher, as well as for every chemist and every engineer. When we remember that Paris and Berlin have each over twelve thousand undergraduates, we may look to twenty thousand for London, and at least one or two thousand apiece for such centres as Manchester and Birmingham. Nor will the arts faculty lag far behind those of science, engineering and economics. The city of Liverpool alone, will need to engage for its own schools about two hundred new teachers every year, and must therefore, if it is to give them a three years' course, provide for three times that number of undergraduates in pedagogy alone. Moreover, the very fact that the undergraduates of the new universities will be young professionals, eager to master their subjects in order to apply them to gain their livelihood, will inevitably compel an intensive study of each department of learning unknown to the average passman. It is a very different thing for the economics professor, for instance, to lecture on banking and currency at Oxford, even to 'honours men'; and to deal with the same subject day after day before a class of bank clerks and branch managers in such a way as to retain their respect and convey instruction. The very practical character of the new universities will inevitably 'stretch' their professors – will force them, that is, to a much higher standard of knowledge and suggestiveness than is demanded of those who are giving courses intended only to produce a cultivated understanding of the whole realm of knowledge.

But the most important work of the professor in the new universities will be not so much his large undergraduate classes as the tiny group of graduate students who, in his laboratory or otherwise under his direction, are pursuing original research. The twentieth-century university will be most proud of and will gain most renown by its post-graduation work. This, too, will be aided by the very limitations and conditions of the new seats of learning. As they will necessarily have to deal with large numbers, the professorial staff will be numerous; and we therefore at once leave behind the 'early-Victorian' notion of a college in which there is a single professor for each subject, assumed to be able to teach the whole of it. In place of the venerable figure of this single-handed professor we get the faculty, or, as it is sometimes termed, the board of studies – the little group of able researchers, each keen on some particular branch of the subject, and knowing that branch with a minuteness impossible to anyone obliged to deal with so vast a field of learning as one science or one subject has now become. And in the faculty as a group of specialized experts collectively covering the whole field, together with the graduate students already engaged in the practical work of the world, or bringing with them from other universities the stimulating criticism of different traditions and new methods, we get the chance of a university society and a university atmosphere on the Thames or the Mersey which may not give us quite the literary grace or cultured charm of the old universities, but which is calculated to be, of all others, the most fertile in scientific discovery.

Let us apply these considerations to the new university which is plainly destined to be the greatest of them all, that of London, charged with the provision of tertiary education for seven millions of people. Here we have the pioneer work done, the legal formalities accomplished, the framework of a university constructed – even two million pounds' worth of buildings, plant and endowment in full going order – and yet scarcely more than the nucleus of a university. The twenty-five distinct and separate 'schools of the university', the five hundred university professors already at work in those schools, and the hundred or so more who are giving university courses in other institutions, together with the six thousand students in all these classes, amount as yet to little more than excellent material for a university, which needs a great deal of pulling together before it can take its place as the intellectual centre of the metropolis of the Empire. What London University needs, to put it briefly, is money, and the stimulating impulse of a great ideal. We shall the more easily understand this need if we pass in review the eight faculties of which the university is composed. These faculties, though they include among their six or seven hundred professors men of the highest distinction in almost every branch, have not yet taken their proper place as, for their several subjects, the inspiring and organizing committees of the supreme governing body. They have not in any one instance yet taken the lead in surveying the whole field of their subject, ascertaining what reorganization and what additional resources are needed to deal with it adequately throughout the whole 2730 square miles of the university sphere, for all its seven millions of people; and then placing these needs imperatively before public opinion and the authorities. Paid as they are by the separate governing bodies, they are still under the shadow of the older grouping of London education by colleges and institutions; they are as yet scarcely conscious of themselves as organs of a university which is organized by faculties, and not by colleges; and they seem, consequently, still unaware either of their proper place in the university, or of their great responsibilities. But they will serve us, for the moment, as categories in which we may classify the most urgent requirements of the university as a whole.

Let us begin with science, in which London is clearly destined to be exceptionally strong. Here we have some sixty or seventy professors, scattered irregularly over half-a-dozen 'schools' and half-a-dozen other institutions of the university, without either geographical or graded coordination, nearly all owning allegiance to particular governing bodies, and jealously concerned rather to maintain their own science teaching in that particular institution than to organize each branch of science for the whole seven millions of people who are their real clients. A beginning has been made by the appointment and payment by the Senate itself of professors of chemistry, located for the present at University College. But before this coordination can be completed even for chemistry; before it can be applied to the other sciences; before an adequately equipped and duly specialized centre for the advanced and post-graduation work of the faculty can be provided, to which a stream of able young researchers from other universities will be attracted; before the necessary provision of undergraduate teaching can be made for the outlying districts, with their thousands of potential students – there is a great deal of work to be done, and a great deal of money to be raised. It will take at least £50,000 a year to set the science faculty properly on its feet, put it in due relation to the university as a whole, provide at all efficiently for research, and at the same time supply the rapidly growing demand for undergraduate instruction over the whole thirty miles radius of the university area.

The new engineering faculty, with fewer than a score of professors, is in what we must call an infantile condition. Dispersed among three 'schools' and half-a-dozen other institutions, the faculty has to leave at present practically unprovided for such whole branches as marine engineering, naval architecture, hydraulics, and railway and tramway construction, in which London University ought to lead the world. Here, too, the need for a fully equipped and duly specialized post-graduation centre for the faculty is severely felt. The existing professors find themselves fully occupied with the grind of daily lectures to undergraduate classes; and the advanced mechanical student is, as a matter of fact, advised by the practical man to go to McGill University at Montreal, or to the Polytechnikum at Zurich, to find opportunities which London apparently cannot afford him. On the other hand, the rapid growth of the demand for undergraduate teaching makes urgent the multiplication of centres of 'first-degree' instruction, which the university cannot at present provide. In these new centres there are interesting experiments waiting to be tried – the six months' session alternating with six months spent in the workshop; the half-time course with a twelve months' session served by relays of teachers; or, on the other hand, an unprecedented development of the evening-class system. It is difficult to put a figure to the needs of the engineering faculty, dependent, as it is, on the provision of science instruction. But it is certain that a donation of a round million would not more than suffice for the work which is actually waiting to be done.

There is, however, one concrete need, connected with both the science and engineering faculties, which demands special notice. Neither London nor any other centre in the British Empire has anything comparable with the great Technical High School at Charlottenburg, near Berlin, where a capital expenditure of half a million, supported by an annual subsidy of £50,000 a year, provides for the German Empire the most advanced instruction, and the most highly specialized research in every branch of technology. We badly want a Charlottenburg in London, established on the four or five acres of vacant land at South Kensington, where it could work in close cooperation with the Royal College of Science and the Central Technical College, and where it could deal with such branches of the application of science to industry as are yet practically untouched by the university. To establish such a highly specialized and elaborately equipped institution, appealing scarcely at all for the attendance and fees of the undergraduate, involves a capital outlay of half a million, and an endowment of twice that amount.

The medical faculty, at present counting half the professors and a third of the students of the whole university, has one paramount and very simple need. At present the science teaching of the medical undergraduate is dispersed among twelve inadequately equipped medical schools, where twelve scanty staffs attempt the elementary instruction of twelve small classes in each subject. Imperfect as is this provision, it puts a strain on the hospitals and medical schools which seriously hinders the more important advanced medical teaching and clinical research. We shall not give our medical investigators a chance of discovering the causes of gout and cancer until we can relieve them of this strain. London is badly in want of a great university school of science for the medical faculty, so as to take off the hands of the hospitals the first two years of the medical undergraduate course. For this, too, there is vacant land at South Kensington, and the scheme awaits only a donation of a quarter of a million for building and twice that sum for endowment.

In the economic faculty, which includes 'industry', 'commerce' and 'political science', the university has its centre and its nucleus provided, by the munificence of Mr Passmore Edwards, at the London School of Economics at Clare Market. What is here wanted is professorships and scholarships in such subjects as insurance, banking, railway administration, foreign trade, commercial and international law and public administration. With these should come the expansion of the present nucleus of palaeography into an effective *école des chartes*, for the scientific study of history, for which London with its wealth of records offers the best opportunities in the world. Ten thousand pounds would endow, poorly enough, a single chair; and at least a score more chairs are needed.

The faculty of law is as yet an incorporeal entity, if not a 'chose in action'. The remnants of law teaching, with the Inns of Court holding aloof, were not deemed worthy to be collected into a faculty. But there are now funds available, from the proceeds of the sale of New Inn and the prospective yield of Clifford's Inn, out of which it is hoped that the Attorney-General will create a great school of law in organic connection with the university. The faculty of music has started with a donation of £5000 from Trinity College (London) for a professorship. The faculty of theology, with half-a-dozen 'schools' of various denominations, gets along as a veritable 'happy family', with no troubles or dissensions other than the chronic need of each of the seminaries for funds. But for these funds they do not look to the university; and the Church of England side at King's College has been fortunate enough to secure a new endowment from ecclesiastical funds.

There remains the arts faculty, the mother of all the rest, but fallen, in London, on rather evil days. The undergraduate classes in arts are few and scantily attended, while the specialist courses, of which London might have the best in the world, are spasmodic, uncoordinated and badly advertised. Apart from philosophy, which should set up as a separate faculty, and the large possibilities offered by archaeology, salvation is to be found for the arts faculty in two different directions, either of which ought to suffice to restore it to the premier position in the university. We want, in the metropolis of the Empire, a gigantic school of languages, based on comparative philology, not forgetting the ancient Oriental and classical literatures, but serving also the manifold needs of the trader, the official and the missionary. There are fifty different tongues to be taught, fifty different philologies to be scientifically investigated, and nearly as many literatures to be studied. Twenty thousand pounds would not endow more than one of the fifty, so that donors and benefactors of all tastes – those interested in the classical literatures of the Mediterranean, those touched by the subtle magic or practical needs of the East, those concerned for what may be called the missionary tongues of Africa and the Pacific, and those stirred rather by the modern Babel of commerce and twentieth-century authorship, must all cooperate to create the great school of languages which will one day be the pride of the Imperial university.

The other opportunity for the arts faculty in London is local, if not parochial in its aim. London engages for its primary and secondary schools more than fifteen hundred new teachers every year, and it will, at no distant date have to provide each of these, between eighteen and twenty-one, with a three years' course of 'training', nine-tenths of which is merely the general education of the undergraduate in arts, science or economics. For its own sake, as well as for theirs, the university must take in these four or five thousand students destined for the most extensive of all the brain-working professions of our time. The alternative of relegating them to closely segregated seminaries, apart from all university influence, cannot be contemplated with equanimity. It is therefore clear that, great as will be in London the faculties of medicine, science and engineering, that of arts will once again be numerically the greatest of them all.

London University stands therefore in urgent need of very large sums. To set it on its feet, and equip it with the necessary endowment to enable it to cope with its task, requires at least five millions sterling. Each of the nine other new local universities required by the different provinces of England needs perhaps a tenth of this sum. Within the next decade we have, in fact, to provide, for England alone, for what we may call tertiary education and the advancement of learning, the equivalent of ten millions sterling, which is about as much as we shall spend in the decade on three or four Admiralty works at Gibraltar, Simon's Bay, and other places which the taxpayer could not even find on a map of the world.

But unlike the £10,000,000 for Admiralty stone and concrete, the £10,000,000 required to set England up in universities need not come wholly out of the Budget of the Chancellor of the Exchequer. The Education Act of 1902 has made university education a public function no less than elementary education, and has given it a claim of equal strength to aid and support from the new local authorities. Already Nottingham, Birmingham, Liverpool and London contribute largely to the support of their local university institutions. A rate of no more than a penny in the pound – less than a tenth of what is gaily voted to the primary schools – would give the new local universities an annual income of something like half a million. If the Chancellor of the Exchequer would but pluck up courage to expand the present Government grant of £27,000 a year to English university colleges into one of £270,000 a year, on condition that at least an equal contribution was made from private donations or local funds – and no step that a Government could take would be more widely popular – this would very promptly give us the equivalent of ten or fifteen millions sterling, and enable England to be provided with ten strong universities for the several districts – in London and its thirty miles radius; at Manchester, Liverpool, Birmingham and Durham (with Newcastle-on-Tyne); for Yorkshire, for the East Midlands (with Nottingham), for East Anglia, for the South-Western Counties (with Bristol, Exeter and, it may be hoped, Plymouth), and for the South (with Reading and Southampton).

21 Richard Burdon, Lord Haldane

from *An Autobiography*, 1929, pp. 139–47.

But I must now return to the university question. My relations with Balfour over this question had become rather close ever since the London and Irish problems had engaged our efforts. But with these results I could not rest, and I went to him again about what was new. The old-fashioned view was that Oxford and Cambridge could not be reproduced and ought not to be even imitated. Nothing higher than university colleges, of the type which already to some extent existed, could be fashioned without detriment to the ideal of a university. Matthew Arnold himself had given some countenance to the restriction, and even Liberal thinkers like Bryce had to some extent followed him. The latter had, so far as my recollection serves me, originated the phrase 'Lilliputian universities'. Durham was pointed to as a restricted institution under clerical influences, and the Victoria University at Manchester was described as being little more than a federal body with functions which did not go beyond examining what were hardly more than external students from a group of colleges which included the University College at Liverpool and Leeds as well as that in Manchester itself. It was said that any attempt of a more ambitious kind was destined to fail. All these prognostications have now passed into oblivion, but they counted for much in the beginning of the present century.

I was of a different opinion. I had discussed the problem with men like

Sir William McCormick, afterwards to be the guiding spirit of the Treasury Committee on University Education. There was no such committee in these days, and there were no State grants for any such purpose. I had convinced myself that a civic university was a possible institution, and that if called into being it would have a great moulding influence and a high standard under the impulse of the local patriotism of the great cities where it was to be established. I found that Joseph Chamberlain was strongly with me in this view.

But the counter-battery of criticism was strong, and Parliament was quite indifferent from want of authoritative leading. Balfour asked me whether I could suggest a means of ascertaining the truth authoritatively and of overcoming the public apathy. I said that if he would select a very strong committee of the Privy Council to examine and report on the principle there might result a great instrument which he could use. And I pointed out that occasion had arisen for the appointment of such a committee. Liverpool, where my friend A. F. Warr, the local MP, and I had been at work, was ready to petition for a charter for the establishment of a separate University of its own for Liverpool. It would raise its own funds, the teachers were ready on the spot, and the only question was whether the Government would be prepared to overrule opposition and grant the Charter if recommended to do so by the Privy Council. Balfour agreed to take this course, and the Government assembled the Committee in December 1902. The petition of Liverpool was referred to it for report. Manchester somewhat half-heartedly supported the prayer of Liverpool, but Leeds strongly opposed it, and was backed by a number of persons who were eminent in the field of higher education in those days. The question was whether Liverpool, Manchester and Leeds were to have their own civic universities or whether the Victoria University at Manchester was to remain a federal body, with the three local university colleges under it.

It was settled that the President of the Council, the late Duke of Devonshire, should preside over the Committee of the Privy Council and have four colleagues. These included Lord Rosebery, the ex-Prime Minister, who was not unnaturally much interested on my account. The other members were the late Lord Balfour of Burleigh, the Secretary for Scotland, who knew the system in Scotland, where there were four universities for the population of four millions, while England had only four for about thirty-five millions; Lord James of Hereford, a Cabinet Minister; and Sir Edward Fry, the well known ex-Lord Justice of Appeal.

The hearing occupied 17, 18 and 19 December 1902. It was conducted like an appeal to the Judicial Committee. Eminent counsel appeared for the parties, and each side called witnesses. I had told Liverpool that if they desired it I would assume my wig and gown and lead as their advocate, but on one condition only, that as the work would be a labour of love, and from my point of view a very important one, I would accept no pecuniary reward.

But just before the case came on I found an unexpected letter from Lord Salisbury, the Prime Minister, proposing that I should be a Privy Councillor. King Edward, who had just succeeded, had specially asked that Sir Edward Grey and myself should be added to the Council. I had not been a Minister of the Crown, but I had come into a good deal of contact with the King in the course of the negotiations for the establishment of the Imperial College of Science and Technology, to which I have already referred. King Edward had accepted the view that it was the desire of his father, Prince Albert, that the valuable site of the Great Exhibition should be used in part for the establishment of some such institution for higher technical education, for a London 'Charlottenburg' in fact. He was very helpful and was instrumental in procuring for us the grant of the requisite land from the Exhibition Commissioners.

King Edward, while still Prince of Wales, had also been keenly interested in the Imperial Institute. This had got into difficulties, and was lapsing into insolvency notwithstanding the exertions of its acting head, the late Lord Herschell. The Prince, who had heard of the success of my efforts towards the reform of the University of London, sent for me in 1898 and asked me to get the newly constituted University to consent to have a part of the building of the Imperial Institute at South Kensington for its headquarters. 'You alone,' he said, 'can get over the opposition to a plan which will deliver the Imperial Institute and be good for the University.' I took the matter in hand, and brought the Prince to a meeting with the Senate, and terms were ultimately arranged with the assent of the Treasury.

Lord Knollys, who was then the Prince's Secretary, wrote to me on 8 July 1899:

My dear Mr Haldane,
The Prince of Wales has learned with great pleasure that the Senate of the University of London have accepted the Government proposals regarding the University and the Imperial Institute, and he trusts that all the details connected with the question will now be speedily settled.

His Royal Highness will naturally take a great interest in the future prosperity of the University, and if it is at any time thought he can be of use to it in any way, he hopes that the Governing Body will not hesitate to apply for his assistance.

Believe me, yours very truly,
Francis Knollys

When the Prince succeeded to the throne he acted up to his promise by promoting in every way he could the interests of the new Imperial College of Science. The result of all this was to bring me much into his society. I saw him very often in the end of the century and the beginning of the next.

With the plan for the new College of Science and Technology in the University there were others who gave help that was indispensable. I had called on Mr Wernher, of the great firm of Wernher, Beit & Co., whom and his partners I did not know excepting as public-spirited men of German origin and as impressed with the necessity for this country of German scientific training. I found him and Alfred Beit and the other members of his firm at their office. They were highly appreciative, and at once offered £100,000 for the scheme. To this they added later on other very large sums. I lunched at Beit's house in Park Lane to meet Cecil Rhodes, who had heard of the scheme for the reconstruction of London University into an intellectual centre for the students of the Empire. He and I went down to Tring Park to spend a weekend with Rothschild. I had much talk with Rhodes, who assisted in getting his South African friends to help further. He impressed me, not as an idealist of the kind to which I had been accustomed to look up to most, but as a splendidly energetic man of affairs, with a wide outlook and great capacity for getting things through. Sir Ernest Cassel, a man of the same type, in his turn gave a large contribution, and so did the Rothschilds.

Another who helped in a different way but most materially was the Permanent Head of the Treasury, Francis Mowatt. He was one of the largest-minded officials I ever came across. He negotiated the transfer to the new college of the Government College at South Kensington, and the increase of its already large annual endowment. He was a man who never failed to take the bigger side of things into account, and to look to the future, even when considering questions of economy for the State.

Anyhow I became a Privy Councillor just before the Liverpool case came on for hearing, and this precluded me from appearing as Counsel at the Bar. For although an advocate who is a Privy Councillor may conduct cases before the Judicial Committee, because it is a special Committee from which the general body of Privy Councillors are excluded, he cannot appear before a Committee of the full Council. However, this did not cause any real difficulty, for I said that I would go into the box as the first witness for Liverpool and state its case. I advised that the city should retain as one of its advocates Alfred Lyttelton, who knew little about higher education but was tactful and also well known to the members of the Committee. I also suggested Sidney Webb, who knew the subject thoroughly, and my old friend Kemp, who was one of my 'devils' at Lincoln's Inn in those days. The arrangement was carried out, and I stated the case for Liverpool as its witness with fulness. Lord Spencer was there in a very critical capacity on behalf of the Victoria University, of which he was Chancellor. Lord Ripon, who was the head of the Leeds College, was also present and opposed Liverpool vehemently. In order to get our views informally the Committee used to have us three to lunch with them at Downing Street while the sittings were taking place. Liverpool had this advantage, that we had worked out and knew our educational case more thoroughly than our opponents had been able to do.

At the close of the hearing the Committee of the Privy Council deliberated. On 10 February 1903 its Report, having been made, was embodied in an Order in Council of that date. It was pronounced that the case was made out for the grant of charters for full university status to Liverpool and Manchester. Leeds had not petitioned for such a charter, but it was made obvious that if she chose to do so later on she would receive one likewise. The principle laid down was a general one and a new one. It was added in the Report that the step of granting these charters involved issues of great moment, for dealing with which preparation should be made, especially in respect to the points upon which, having regard to the great importance of the matter, and the effect of the changes proposed on the future of higher education in the north of England, cooperation was expedient between universities of a common type and with cognate aims.

It has always seemed to me that this decision of the Government as advised by the Privy Council in 1903 was a step of the first importance in the history of higher education. Little notice was, however, taken of it by the public or by writers about English education. The thick printed volumes containing the documents and the evidence repose undisturbed in the library of the Judicial Office in Downing Street. None the less the decision gave rise to immediate results. Further new universities were set up with all possible speed. Besides Liverpool, Manchester and Leeds, Birmingham, Bristol and Sheffield received charters. Durham was expanded and transformed by the addition of colleges in Newcastle, so as to become a university of the new type. Later on Reading was to follow, and Wales was to have a wholly reconstituted university system. In Birmingham Chamberlain took the lead at once. He had told me that no other city would be able to found a university before his city, and he worked at the plan for Birmingham with characteristic energy and success. Besides all this, new university colleges were founded elsewhere in England.

Thus early in the century there were established teaching universities controlled within the great cities to which they belonged. The civic communities had reached a stage at which they had resolved to be content in higher education with nothing short of what was highest. Bristol, in which I had taken a keen interest, was a case in point. Along with other prominent citizens, the Wills family, who had derived great fortunes from the manufacture of tobacco, endowed the new university with magnificent buildings and gifts of money. In 1912 I was chosen to be Chancellor of that University, an office which I have held for many years, and which has given me the opportunity of watching the stimulating effect of the new and developed university life upon the educational institutions of the city and in places around it.

22 Katherine Bathurst

from 'The Need for National Nurseries', *Nineteenth Century and After*, May 1905, pp. 818–24.

The 1902 Act left local authorities free to take in children under five into elementary schools, or to debar them from entry. No provision, however, existed for providing separate facilities and a different style of teaching for these very young children. Of those who pressed for better conditions for the under-fives, Katherine Bathurst, an Inspector with the Board of Education, was the most outspoken. Apart from this article, she contributed to a special report presented to the Board of Education on the problem.

I wish to give in this article, in as vivid a manner as possible, some description of what is now going on inside elementary schools, and I shall start with the assumption that my readers are entirely ignorant of the subject. I will begin with large town schools, and reference will be made to some of those which I have actually visited in my official capacity. My object is a very simple one. I am anxious to interest women in these little children. Only women can deal satisfactorily with the present difficulties, and most of the evils I describe are produced by the absence of the quality known as 'motherliness'. Under existing regulations children of three years old cannot be refused admittance into elementary schools, and the attendance of all children over five is compulsory. The infants attending schools in this country numbered in 1903 no fewer than 2,044,902. Their number has, of course, now increased. I am unable to say exactly what proportion of these children would be under five years of age, but, judging from some statistics obtained in Manchester, I think the estimate of one-fourth would be a fairly accurate one. The usual age for promotion to schools for older children is between seven and eight, but as the Government has hitherto given a bigger grant per head on attendance for older scholars, there is a distinct desire on the part of the local authorities to promote at as early an age as possible. In Manchester the rule is that all children who will become seven before the expiration of the school year must be promoted at the beginning of the school year, unless special circumstances exist to prevent the arrangement. We therefore often get children of only six years and three months old who are being taught in schools for older scholars, and are thereby deprived of every opportunity for manual employment or kindergarten occupations.

To return to the infant schools. If my calculation is correct, there were last year some 500,000 children under five years of age who were attending school regularly. In the eyes of both central and local authorities a school is a place where children learn to sit still, to obey orders, and where they receive instruction in reading, writing and arithmetic; for the little girls the extra subject of needlework is added. Besides these, it is now customary to provide what are known as varied occupations, and on this topic many words of wisdom are spoken, and even books are published. The theories of great men, such as Pestalozzi and Froebel, are built upon them, and the teachers who can produce a certificate saying that they have passed an examination in kindergarten methods have a better chance than their fellows of preferment or of head-teacherships. The old-fashioned manager or inspector looks upon these things as 'fads'; the beginning and end of elementary education in his eyes is 'Teach 'em to read', and the amount of time devoted to other things in any particular place will depend practically upon his personal bias.

Let us now follow the baby of three years through part of one day of school life. He is placed on a hard wooden seat (sometimes it is only the step of a gallery), with a desk in front of him and a window behind him, which is too high up to be instrumental in providing such amusement as watching the passers-by. He often cannot reach the floor with his feet, and in many cases he has no back to lean against. He is told to fold his arms and sit quiet. He is surrounded by a large number of other babies all under similar alarming and incomprehensible conditions, and the effort to fold his arms is by no means conducive to comfort or well-being. They are too short in proportion to his body to be placed anywhere but in a tight crossbar over his chest. The difficulty of breathing in this constrained position is considerable, but he hunches his shoulders bravely to make his arms longer, and his back assumes the pleasing shape of a curved bow. He is very shortly attacked by the sensation of pins and needles in his legs, due to the lack of support for his feet, and the cap and coat which had reconciled him to this new venture in life are removed and hung on a peg out of sight. I heard of one motherly teacher who, realizing the value set by the child on these possessions, allowed him to have them hung well within view till he was accustomed to his new surroundings. Why a baby should attach this importance to his cap I cannot say. Whether it is a guarantee that his present state of life is temporary, and that he will one day, by placing it on his head, return to the mother who made it, I know not, but so it is. A newcomer will always settle down more patiently if allowed to hug, or at least see, his out-of-door garments. Without these he has no protection from the gaze of his fellows, and the bigger brother or sister who escorted him to school has disappeared into another room. He is alone with strangers, and must endure existence as best he may. He usually spends the first day or two in tears, rising at times to sobs of so disturbing a character that he has to be sent into the playground, in charge of an older scholar, to make a noise where it will not interrupt the work of the other children. If he cries quietly, he becomes aware of the following proceedings. A blackboard has been produced, and hieroglyphics are drawn upon it by the teacher. At a given signal every child in the class begins calling out mysterious sounds: 'Letter A, letter A,' in a sing-song voice, or 'Letter A says Ah, letter A says Ah,' as the case may be. To the uninitiated I may here explain that No. 1 is the beginning of spelling, and No. 2 is the groundwork of word-building. Hoary-headed men will spend hours discussing whether 'c-a-t' or 'ke-ar-te' are the best means of conveying the knowledge of how to read cat. I must own to indifference on the point myself, and I sympathize with teachers who are not allowed to settle it for themselves.

The word 'Stop!' from the teacher, accompanied by an alarming motion of the pointer in her hand towards the class, reduces it to silence, the pointer then indicates a second hieroglyphic on the blackboard, which is followed by a second outburst, and the repetition of 'Letter B, letter B,' etc., chanted by the whole class. This occupation lasts perhaps twenty minutes, but of time our baby has no knowledge; it is many, many years since he left the delicious liberty and enchanting variety of the gutter. The many-coloured world has changed into one monotonous hue, and people say one thing so many times that it makes him sleepy. 'Wake up, Johnnie; it's not time to go to sleep yet. Be a good boy and watch teacher.' More hieroglyphics are placed on the blackboard, and more sounds follow in the same sing-song voices, for the arithmetic lesson now begins. 'Figure 1, figure 1, figure 1, figure 2, figure 2, figure 2,' replace the words 'Letter A, letter B,' etc.; otherwise there seems to be no difference between one lesson and the next, and no ray of light illumines Johnnie's gloom. I have actually heard a baby class repeat one sound a hundred and twenty times continuously, and from fourteen to twenty times is a matter of common occurrence. With the exception of a little drill or marching between the subjects, it is an incontrovertible fact that lessons unbroken by a single manual occupation are actually in progress the whole morning in many of our baby classes in the big infant schools; and without attempting to follow further the effect on the poor child's brain, I would most earnestly discuss the uselessness – nay, worse, the harmfulness – of the whole system.

What possible good is there in forcing a little child to master the names of letters and numbers at this age? The strain on the teachers is terrific. Even when modern methods are in vogue and each child is provided with coloured counters, shells, beads or a ball frame, the intellectual effort of combining three plus one to make four, or two plus two for the same total, has no value at such an age. The nervous strain must reduce the child's physical capacity, and this, again, reacts unfavourably on the condition of the teeth, eyes and digestion. In the long summer afternoons things are at their worst. Baby after baby, overcome by sleep in the heated atmosphere, falls forward off his seat, banging his forehead against the desk in front, and awakes in tears to find such misfortunes are too common an occurrence for much comfort to be his portion. All that the hard-pressed and exhausted teacher has time to do is to fold the child's arms on the desk in front of him, place his head on them, and coax him to fall asleep again. But consider the conditions under which sleep is obtained. The child is in a close room – I have no hesitation in saying that not 20 per cent of the classrooms I saw in Manchester are properly ventilated – he is bent forward, his back is all crooked, and his body is all sideways. In this position he spends an hour or two hours of many a summer afternoon. If statistics could be obtained of the number of children in infant schools suffering from curvature of the spine, the matter might perhaps awaken the sleeping conscience of the education authorities. In winter sleep is not prevalent to quite the same extent, but the timetable usually provides a second dose of lessons on letters and numbers, and the only variety the day affords comes under the head of 'Occupations', 'Games' or 'Object-lessons'.

Let there be no mistake about these. 'My child loves looking at pictures; surely the children must enjoy object-lessons on pictures,' says the comfortable mamma; while papa recollects reading to himself at four years old, and has always been told that he gave no trouble at all when learning his letters. Quite so. But how were those letters taught, and in what position did he sit when holding the picture-book? Cuddled tight in his mother's arms, with encouraging terms of endearment in his ears and kisses showered on his curls, he babbled unreproved his own delightful version of the contents or meaning of each page. Moreover, boredom could be immediately relieved by a quick turn-over to the next picture, or a rush across the room; and, as a rule, he might change his occupation at will, and seek diversion elsewhere.

Compare this with the class system. One picture only is provided at a time, and is made to do duty for many days in the year. It is stuck on a blackboard. It cannot be handled, often it cannot be clearly seen. The talking is done by the teacher, not by the child, the subject and meaning are fixed by her explanation, and only one child at a time may respond to a question. The others must sit motionless, and with arms tightly crossed, waiting for the notice that, in many cases, never comes.

In a log book in Manchester the following entry was recently made by a man inspector: 'The babies should learn to sit still and attend.' That sounds dull, certainly, but what about the games? Games are opportunities for learning many virtues (see introduction to the Code, 1904). I would earnestly beg the reader's attention to this most admirably arranged book of platitudes, and I invite him to compare the sentiments expressed there with the methods that are actually in vogue in our schools. In a solemn ring, with anxious faces, and eyes fixed on the harassed face of the teacher, the children learn to personate one or other figure in the action song. 'It has to be perfect for the inspector at the end of the month.' Inspired by this motive and practised with labouring footsteps and faltering voices, the games often became as sad a performance as the lessons, and are treated quite as seriously by all who take part in them.

But there are still the 'occupations'. How many people know to what this refers? And how many would be willing to instruct in a 'manual occupation' a three-year-old baby? Paper-folding, stick-laying, bricks, chalk-drawing or Froebel's gifts have a real meaning and value when handled by a few children – say, half a dozen to a dozen – in presence of a trained specialist. 'Only she can manipulate her material with any beneficial effect to the children. But for such a purpose conditions far other than those prevailing in most infant schools are essential. Imagine one teacher with sixty babies to instruct. That is the number for which every certificated teacher in this country may be made legally responsible; though in fact these numbers are often exceeded, and in summer it is not unusual to find one woman with eighty, ninety or a hundred babies in her charge. So long as the average for the whole year is not above sixty there is no redress. In the last blue book the average number of children under the instruction of certificated teachers is given as 70·2 per head. I ask every mother, nurse or maiden aunt who reads these pages to place herself in imagination in this position, and I think that most people will allow that a teacher's life must necessarily be one of the most wearying and least satisfying.

The task given to them with these enormous classes is an impossible one.

Let me repeat it. A certificated teacher has sixty babies to instruct, many of whom are hungry, cold and dirty. In slum schools the parents are often drunkards, and the children's nights have been but short. They are heavy-eyed with unslept sleep. They are perched tier upon tier on hard benches one behind the other. Only one way of dealing with them appears physically possible, and the 'discipline' so dear to the heart of the man inspector becomes almost of necessity the end and object of a teacher's life. Every child must be made to resemble his neighbour as nearly as possible. To obtain this effect some sort of drill is required. It usually takes the following form: 'Fold arms' – 'Sit up' – 'Eyes on ceiling' (all the heads are raised) – 'Eyes on floor' (all the heads are bent) – 'Eyes to the right' – 'Eyes to the left' – 'Eyes on blackboard' – 'Eyes on me' (all the sixty baby heads are wagged in unison). 'Tommy Snooks is not attending to me. I sha'n't love you, Tommy Snooks. Now we must begin again, as Tommy Snooks is not a good boy.' Patiently the teacher repeats the same formula. Pathetically the whole class responds.

Then follows a second type of drill. We will suppose that every child has been provided with a small square of coloured paper, and that the timetable indicates 'Paper-folding' as the routine for twenty minutes twice a week throughout the year. 'I take my paper in my left hand.' All the children repeat the words. Then follows an interruption. Despite the fact that the teacher is going through the same movements as the class, it is easy at three and four years old to mistake one hand for another. She must therefore walk up and down the lines of her class removing the papers that are held in the right hand and placing them in the left. Meanwhile the children get tired. Little arms drop down – little pokes are given to little neighbours – the proceedings may even be diversified by a leg being placed on the desk, or a boot removed for nearer inspection. When the whole class has at last been reduced to uniformity of occupation, the teacher proceeds once more – 'I fold it over in the middle.' And so on. More interruptions ensue, while the ever patient woman goes from child to child, to see how near the middle the fold has been made. Step by step, accompanied by repetition after the teacher of an unvarying form of words, a result of some kind is obtained; and after weeks of practice the best specimens are carefully put aside 'to show the inspector'.

The subject of needlework requires separate mention. I have lately been employed in Manchester in making a special inquiry upon certain points connected with infant schools. For this purpose I visited ninety-three infant schools and obtained statistics which referred to 22,320 children. I am in a position to state that forty-five out of these ninety-three infant schools give lessons in needlework which last from forty-five minutes to an hour on end, and thirty-three schools have 'needle-threading' as an employment for children under five years of age. Consider what this means. Needles the size of bodkins are put into the hands of these babies, and ten, fifteen, and even twenty minutes on end are spent in threading them. Such an employment would be, one can imagine, trying at any age; but to oblige a little child of three or four years old to focus its eyes on a point, and guide its fingers sufficiently steadily to thread a bodkin is a most harmful and injudicious proceeding. A tendency to squint shows itself very markedly among the children of our poorer classes, and the greatest care should therefore be exercised in the choice of judicious occupations involving no strain to the eyesight. Lessons of forty-five minutes and an hour on end are far too long. With big classes the giving out and collecting of materials is wearisome to the teachers, and leaves but little time for the actual work. The subject is often begun at four years old, and these mites of children are forced to sit in a cramped position, using their undeveloped nerves and muscles in producing the required strip of hemming which custom has made obligatory. The teachers would be thankful to postpone instruction to a later age, but so long as specimens of work are asked for, examined and criticized by men inspectors the present system will continue.

The evil in Manchester is increased by the lack of proper desks; the children have constantly no support for their backs, the rooms are often cold and dark, and the inspector has no childish recollections of his own to arouse pity for the poor pricked little fingers or aching eyes. The constant glancing at the clock from far older children during needlework lessons is itself sufficient indication to a sympathetic observer of the strain from which they are suffering.

During both morning and afternoon one welcome break occurs; for 'an interval of not less than ten or fifteen minutes' is prescribed in the Code. The children troop into the playground, and those whose mothers are sufficiently careful to provide it produce newspaper parcels containing dry bread, cake, bread-and-jam or hard pudding, as the case may be. But in some schools the babies do not have the benefit of this interval. 'They take so long getting in and out of the room.' This makes it, in the teacher's opinion, desirable to remain indoors; while in cold weather the necessity of dressing the children is a real difficulty. Without assistance, one woman can hardly get sixty babies into hats and cloaks, and out of them again, within the specified time. We thus get the youngest children deprived of the change of air and scene which is so specially desirable in consideration of their tender years.

Are we not slaves to tradition – slaves to custom – slaves to our own regulations? Of what possible use is all this routine? In my opinion – and surely in this matter I may expect the support and sympathy of the women of this country – little children require nurses rather than teachers, and lady doctors rather than inspectors. By placing the infant schools entirely in the hands of men inspectors, the whole atmosphere has been made into a forcing-house for the schools for older scholars. Even where kindergarten methods are better understood, the teachers are hampered and hindered by a masculine love of uniformity and order. The discipline expected is military rather than maternal, and can only be maintained at the expense of much healthy, valuable, and, as far as the children are concerned, necessary freedom. The appointment announced in February will give universal satisfaction. Miss Lawrence has been made chief woman inspector to the Board of Education. It is earnestly to be hoped that this policy will be continued by the further appointment of a large staff of women inspectors, otherwise she will be hopelessly handicapped in the work she has undertaken. Up till now the number of women inspectors has never exceeded six, their position has been that of subordinate officers, and it has been impossible for them, both from their number and position, to render any revolutionary services to education.

23 Board of Education

from the Report of the Consultative Committee upon Questions affecting Higher Elementary Schools, 1906, pp. 6–13.

The strong bias within the education system created by the 1902 Act was sharply etched by the report which considered the needs of the higher elementary schools. Great stress was placed on 'character' and 'subservience', and the committee gave considerable weight to the characteristics which employers specified they would like to see in the products of such schools. Overall, the emphasis was that the education they received should make them 'efficient members of the class to which they will belong'.

The school and the need it is to fill

A 'Higher Elementary School', as contemplated by the Code, would provide education, between the ages of twelve and fifteen years, for the brighter children who have attended previously an ordinary public elementary school and who will, as a class, complete their day school education at the age of fifteen, and thereupon go out into the world to earn a living in the lower ranks of commerce and industry. For such children there must naturally be a kind of education that is likely to make them efficient members of the class to which they will belong. The first step towards a conclusion as to its character is to discover what are the qualities wherein, in the eyes of employers and of other persons qualified to express an opinion, children of this class seem to be deficient? Or, stated positively, what are the qualities they consider it most worth while to aim at developing? To arrive at any answer is, of course, to realize to some extent the object of a 'higher elementary school', and when this object has been broadly defined, the ground is clear for a consideration of the type of school most likely to effect it.

It would appear, therefore, that one of the first and most important questions to determine is, what are the particular qualities of character and mind that the school education of such children should be directed to develop?

In a general sense, moral qualities come first. Character is the primary aim of all education, and studies themselves lead up to it. Upon this ethical aspect the evidence of employers of labour has laid stress; they have been unanimous in the opinion that boys or girls entering their service should possess habits of discipline, ready obedience, self-help, and of pride in good work for its own sake whatever it may be. While this development of character is the general aim of all schools for all classes, and to that extent needs little more than a passing reference in a report dealing with a particular kind of education, its importance in connection with schools of the kind we have been considering has been brought prominently before us. The belief was expressed by one witness whose long experience entitles his opinion to weight, that these moral qualities are today far less commonly found among the working classes than they used to be thirty years ago, in spite of a larger number of schools and an increasing demand for the qualities themselves. He allowed that the change was due in part to social causes, but he thought that the schools had done less than they might have done to resist it. With such evidence before us, we desire to express our opinion, that if the education given to such children fails to encourage these moral qualities, the schools that supply it must be regarded as performing only a part of their function.

We pass all the more readily to consider the question of mental qualities, because we are convinced that the mental qualities which we desire to see encouraged must react favourably upon the habits of the children to the building up of character.

The evidence as to the mental qualities[1] which are most needed has been

1. 'Mental' qualities should be understood to include the exercise of the mind through and in conjunction with the hand.

contributed by two classes of witness: on the one hand the employers of labour – almost, without exception, men who interest themselves actually and keenly in the education of their employees – and the teachers and inspectors on the other. In one case evidence on this head was given by a witness who was not only an employer but a teacher also, whose knowledge of boys of this class has been further enlarged by many years' experience in the organization of a lad's club. The evidence was all of the same tenor, and the Committee are unable to resist the conclusion which has been pressed upon them from each direction that for boys and girls of this class habits of mind are far more important than any particular knowledge or degree of attainment. The employers generally are not satisfied with the present training of the elementary schools. 'It is a remarkable and suggestive fact,' said one witness, 'verified by my own observation when I acted as manager of our works in my early days, that the apprentices – lads of fourteen years of age, having only had inefficient elementary education beyond the three "R's" of that time – showed more self-activity and resource and greater use of the bodily senses than the boys do who come to us today.' This degeneration the witness attributed to a decay in pride of class and pride in work. The characteristics that employers most value and most deplore the lack of would appear to be *general* handiness (which is really to a large extent a mental quality), adaptability and alertness, habits of observation – and the power to express the thing observed – accuracy, resourcefulness, the ability to grapple with new and unfamiliar conditions, the habit of applying one's mind and one's knowledge to what one has to do. The employers, like the Navy, want 'handy men'. 'Whereas,' said one witness, 'the precise form of employment that will have to be entered upon cannot be foreseen from the beginning, and 90 per cent of the lads will have to accommodate themselves to the most suitable opening available, *general* handiness would be an advantage everywhere.' This was confirmed by a witness who said, 'It is very rarely that a particular class of work can be decided upon. A boy's career is fixed not by choice but by the accident of employment that offers itself.' Another employer referred with approval to teaching that he had seen abroad, where 'the system is to draw out more and more the thinking and reasoning faculties of the child, so that afterwards, whatever the mind is brought to bear upon, it is a mind equally prepared to receive or impart impressions'. The same witness particularly desired to see the mental faculties of the children rendered more capable of appreciating what they see and what they do when they come into the workshop. Another witness, also an employer, desired that a boy coming into his workshop 'should not be surprised to see all the things that are going on so much as wish to learn more about them'. 'Anything,' said another witness, 'that teaches exactness, absolute fidelity to a truthful standard, is of extreme value.' It was also remarked by an employer that the boys showed a lack of interest which told heavily against them: whereas 'an employer wants to see a lad taking pride in his work, to show a love for it for its own sake, with a capacity to feel its dignity and value'. A headmaster examined by the committee briefly suggested the emphasis which the employers put upon qualities as opposed to knowledge by quoting an employer who had said to him, 'Send me a boy who is accurate and intelligent; I do not care whether he knows how to keep books by this or that method; I do not want this at all.'

It is, of course, conceivable that what an employer is most anxious to secure in his workman or clerk would not be identical with what an unbiased person would most desire for the individual.[2] But the evidence of those interested in education and in the boys and girls themselves, apart from their market value as employees, supports the evidence of the employers. One of the Board's Inspectors of Elementary Schools maintained that the qualities to be encouraged are self-help, self-education; the children should learn to prepare work for themselves, that they should be expected to 'get up' lessons. Another inspector held that some of the qualities to be developed should be a 'really intelligent interest in and liking for the vocations in which they will be occupied for the rest of their lives'. They should be helped to form the habit of consulting books of reference, books for pleasure and profit; to speak and write with facility, and to recognize the practical value of accuracy and conciseness of expression. He would like to see self-help and initiative cultivated. The headmistress of a higher grade school laid stress upon the importance of arousing interest and, closely connected with this, of developing the power of observation. She illustrated her meaning by a reference to the teaching of botany, lately introduced into her school and now the most popular part of the school work. Her aim in introducing it was to make the girls self-reliant and observant. She claimed that her pupils have been very successful in after life. The stimulation of interest was also the key-note of the evidence given by a witness who deplored the fact that a boy leaving school at the age of fourteen is 'frequently not in the least fitted to do the work he is asked to do'. What knowledge he has he cannot apply; and what knowledge he lacks he shrinks from acquiring. 'When I take one of these lads into a night school and try to teach him I find that he shrinks from learning anything about his work. ... Arithmetic ... is absolutely repulsive to him.' But when a boy is told

2. Indeed, one employer frankly said that in his view, and for his ends, it was better that a boy should come to him as soon as he left the ordinary elementary school. This was an isolated opinion.

T—ECS—E

how his arithmetic applies to his work, and that by applying it he may make himself more useful in his trade,

gradually you may get him to see this, and then he will take it up cheerfully, but usually he has got it so driven into him to work without any interest that you cannot teach him in this way at all. . . . What is needed is to interest the boys . . . as soon as they are interested they will begin to work . . . they do not get interested in what they are doing . . . the fault is the lack of interest. . . . Ask them to look at the mantelpiece and draw it to scale . . . they would take immense interest in drawing the mantelpiece to a size smaller.

Apart, then, from the moral qualities – how essential they are is presupposed – it would seem clear to the Committee that the thing needed is not only knowledge but a right attitude of mind, a mind confident in its own power to observe and think and in the habit of observing and thinking – a mind in which interest makes for intelligence and intelligence for interest. This is a high aim that cannot be compassed in every case; yet it might, at any rate, be approached, if anywhere, in schools which will contain the brighter children. Its successful attainment will be due, of course, far more to the teacher and the character of the teaching than to the subjects taught; and this fundamental question of the teachers as the means of attaining it is discussed at a later stage in our report. It is sufficient for the present to have stated in general terms the qualities most to be desired, and to refer in passing to what we believe to be the most effective instrument in developing them. And we would suggest that such qualities are not merely the qualitities needed in a worker for the earning of livelihood; they are qualities as valuable to the individual as they are useful in the economic structure of society. They are essential as part of the individual's equipment for his work in the world, and are of intrinsic value for his own life and for his life in the home.

The character of the higher elementary school
Essential features

The Committee are in agreement as to the main features of a school intended to produce a result of this kind. Such a school should continue the general education that a child has already received in the ordinary elementary school: the course in the higher elementary school should develop in an unbroken progress the work already done. It should strengthen the foundations of primary education already laid, and upon those foundations attempt to build as good a 'general education' as the conditions of the case allow. Whatever else the higher elementary school may do for the children who attend it, it must attempt to do this first. The first necessity is to secure for each child as much 'humanity', as much accurate knowledge of general elementary fact, and as much mental power and manual aptitude as can be expected from a short course of instruction extending over three years at a comparatively early age, always recollecting that the course is the immediate preliminary to livelihood, and must accordingly receive a bent towards the special needs of the life which the child will at once enter. The course should consist of three threads or strands, roughly to be termed humanistic, scientific and manual, and, in the case of girls, domestic, and all higher elementary schools should give this threefold instruction. It is obvious, of course, in the circumstances, that the range of subjects must be strictly limited; a few subjects taught as well and suggestively as possible rather than a larger number treated superficially, and all as far as possible taught in relation to each other. The subjects that might be included under the three headings are dealt with in the part of this report entitled Curriculum.

At this stage it is important to make clear in general terms that the aim of a higher elementary school is to educate for life as well as for livelihood, for life in the home as well as for life in the outside world, for individual as well as for social life, and to indicate that its aim in this respect is identical with that of all schools which are not purely technical in scope. It is an additional reason for emphasizing this need of general education that children of the class who will attend higher elementary schools must depend for almost all of it upon their school education. In this respect they differ from those children of higher social standing whose general education is effected as much by the unconscious influences of home life as by conscious teaching in school. Not that we think the higher social status of parents means necessarily a keener interest in the education of their children or a home atmosphere necessarily more favourable to the development of the child in the direction towards which the best aims of school education tend. There is reason to suppose that as the conception of the purpose and value of education gradually penetrates more deeply into the structure of society as a whole so at the same time the conditions of home life in every class may come more and more into harmony with the ideals of school training. We cannot, however, ignore the fact that at present the effects of the educational system in this country upon the ordinary life and thought of those classes for whom higher elementary schools more especially provide are of a limited kind, and that in consequence the cooperation of parents cannot yet be counted upon to go very far.

Our view is well supported by the evidence of the various types of witnesses. . . . The evidence of the need and value of general education must be read in connection with that given more especially in regard to the desirability of introducing technical subjects of instruction, for, as a matter of fact, the evidence on these two correlative points has been elicited as a rule by almost the same questions. In the paragraphs immediately following, the evidence is presented as far as possible in a positive form.

To illustrate the necessity of securing that the foundations laid in the public elementary school are strong enough to build upon, it may be well to refer first to the evidence of a Manchester witness who draws his experience from service in a railway company, and from the lads' club with which he is connected. It must be remembered that he is speaking not of the brighter boys necessarily, and therefore it may be assumed that the deficiency which he has found to exist may in many individual cases be less glaring than it appears to be. He said, speaking of the usual run of boys in the employment of the company:

When I take him on to arithmetic and put some simple problems in fractions before him he knows nothing about it at all, and everything has to be explained to him from the beginning. I say, 'Write down a short letter'; often the boys are quite incapable of doing this: their writing is impossible. I say 'Read that report'; he cannot read it decently. It is not that he does not know the words, but he cannot put sentences quickly together.

To the question, 'Your experience is that the most important thing is a general education, and that you would not at that age venture on a more technical education,' the witness assented. 'What I feel most of all,' he said, 'is the necessity for general education.'

This necessity for general education was confirmed by a London engineering employer. He was asked, 'And you advocate very strongly a general system of training of a practical character, general knowledge, and general culture, which you think of great moment?' 'I think,' he said, 'especially with the class of boy we have in West Ham, that that is of very much more importance than anything else. We do certainly find that a boy who has had a better (general) education is likely to make better use of his opportunities and to make a better workman – a more intelligent workman.' And again, 'I think what we want is to make the training as broad and general and as thorough as possible.'

Another witness, who held that the scientific and manual instruction given in a higher elementary school was the more important feature, said, 'but at the same time I should continue the higher branches of what we call general education'.

One employer alone did not emphasize this point.

Among the witnesses other than employers the need of general education came out very clearly and was practically unanimous. The following extracts will be sufficient to show this:

The headmaster of a Municipal Secondary School, asked 'You think that a good general education is best?' replied 'Yes, certainly; as a headmaster I feel that very strongly. I believe that the same opinion is held generally by businessmen.'

Similarly: 'I would not allow any specialization except as subsidiary to a good general education. At least half the time should be devoted to a good general education.'

The headmaster of a secondary school in a country district was asked, 'You attach more importance to the general than the technical side of the schools, do you not? You think that the general side is the more valuable?' He said, 'Yes, I think there is a very great danger in specializing too much. . . . I would give them an extended course, a continued course, of what they have been doing.'

The Director of Education for a large town in the north of England, when questioned as to whether he thought the curriculum should be adapted to occupations, said, 'No, I think a good general education stands the best chance.' He added, 'What I should like to see is an improvement in the general education of the children.' And further, 'I think the technical school would rather have a boy with a good general education than with any special knowledge.'

The headmaster of a London higher elementary school said, 'We have nothing in view at present further than a good general education.'

An important official witness agreed that 'The more complete their general training the better it will be for them in the long run.'

One of His Majesty's Inspectors of Elementary Schools held that the higher elementary school should give the children a thorough elementary education. It should carry on the work of the elementary school, but it should do it more liberally and generally, on broader and freer lines. He agreed that in many higher elementary schools it is necessary to supplement the elementary work and begin it again. Again, to the question 'A great deal that is taught in the elementary school would be taught in the higher elementary school?' he said, 'Yes; only with a higher development and a more liberal conception of it.'

Whatever additions may be suggested by individuals, the evidence on the whole is unanimous that English subjects, elementary mathematics, elementary science, manual instruction and, in the case of girls, housecraft, should be included in the curriculum. Physical exercises and drill are taken for granted, and it has been suggested that, where possible, rifle shooting should be encouraged.

At the same time, this 'good general education' must, in our opinion, take the bent, on which its immediate usefulness depends, from the consideration that after leaving the higher elementary school the boy or girl will not proceed, except in a few individual cases, to a further course of organized school training; but will be obliged at once to take up some occupation. A considerable number, it is hoped, may after they leave school go voluntarily to evening classes;[3] but the great majority will have completed at the age of fifteen their regular schooling. We think it a principle of education that the nearer the pupil is to his entrance into life, the more steadily must the actual and practical needs of his occupation be kept in view, and the more decided therefore must be the bent of his education to that end. How far will the higher elementary school be affected by this principle, which bears on it very closely? This question is a difficult one, and we believe that the answer can only be suggested by considering it at length.

The Committee are agreed as to the nature of this practical bearing up to a certain point. Throughout the school the teaching of the different subjects should be illustrated by practical examples that are familiar to the children, so that they may be habituated to recognize the application of what is done in school to what is done outside and beyond the school. Further, examples might be drawn from the simpler aspects of the occupations that the children are likely to take up, so that they may see the possible bearing of their knowledge upon practical problems. In a district, for instance, where the bulk of the population are engaged in engineering industries a great many of the children will be to some extent acquainted with the sort of work that their fathers are doing. Even if the sons do not enter their fathers' occupations, they will nevertheless as children take some interest in the facts which at home they are constantly reminded of. Even supposing that at no stage in the course it should be desirable to introduce a technical subject as a matter of instruction, yet it is an advantage to encourage the practical way of looking at things, to encourage the attitude of mind which looks to practice for the illustration of theory and to theory for the explanation of practice; and this attitude may most easily and effectively be encouraged by the use as example and illustration of familiar practical or technical questions. 'I understand you to mean that really the important thing is not so much what the child learns at school, in view of its direct bearing upon his work afterwards, as the development of the kind of mind – the practical direction given to the education?' 'Entirely.' It seems to the Committee that in this way something may be done to stimulate interest and intelligence, for by this means the child will be enabled to answer the question 'What is the good of it?' What is learnt in school will become less meaning-

3. An inspector who gave evidence mentioned a town known to him where 60 to 70 per cent of the boys leaving public elementary schools go to evening schools.

less. The child will be provided with an instrument that he can himself apply to the understanding of everyday things, and whatever faculty of intelligence he may have will be developed by the added interest that he will be able to take. He will get an inkling of the connection between principles and practice, and each will give life to the other. If the habit of orderly observation can be fostered in his school time, it will continue to grow after his schooling is over. In a secondary school, where a boy stays until a later age, he has more time to realize for himself that what he is learning is not simply an end in itself, but also a means and an instrument. A conscious effort to engender this habit of mind is less necessary than it is in a case where school time is shorter and the pupils younger and their entry into the realities of life much closer at hand. Almost equally important – this practical reference, while it tends to answer the child's question, 'What is the good of it ?' will also help to answer the same question put by the parent. It should be obvious that a school which illustrates the principles that it teaches by reference whenever possible to familiar everyday things is a 'practical' school. And if a higher elementary school of the new type is at all successful in producing an intelligent interest in what is recognized as practical by the parents – if in any way it can show that it has made him even 'more useful about the house' – it may be supposed that they in their turn will begin to demand the kind of education for their children which is really needed. The demand on the part of the parents will then correspond to the need recognized by the organizing authority.

If [as a witness said] you tell a parent that the boy is working in manual work and really gaining a certain dexterity of hand, and that he is getting to know something about the science which underlies the industry he may have to follow, he says: 'Those are practical results, I can understand those things; I myself regret that I did not know something of scientific methods before I came to work; I should like my boy to know something about those things, certainly.' He feels that there is some tangible result in that for the time given to school life.

Such a character given to the teaching by the frequent employment of simple illustration, drawn, at any rate in part, from occupations that are familiar or will one day be so, may perhaps be called 'specialization of aim'. It is, of course, difficult to describe precisely the way in which the practical bent is to be given to the teaching of various subjects, and it is, after all, a matter which lies with the teacher, whose concern it should be to realize in each case the general principle enunciated. 'It is the way you teach rather than what you teach that matters.' A further discussion of this subject will come best in dealing with the curriculum and with the teachers.

A great deal of evidence has been pointed in the direction of giving a practical bent of this kind to the higher elementary school, and has confirmed our view that the children should be encouraged to apply their knowledge. The use of familiar and practical illustration has been advocated by a number of witnesses. An employer who complained of the lack of interest that he observed in boys employed in his works was asked: 'You think that interest could be developed by some practical kind of instruction?' 'Some stimulation, yes; that is to say, a clearer view really of the connection between what they are taught in school and what they are likely to do afterwards.' Manual instruction he thought desirable, 'provided that all along it is used as an illustration of theoretical studies'. He considered it less desirable if used as 'a preliminary to subsequent handicraft skill, which has to be acquired'. The illustrations, he thought, 'should be drawn from the factory or the industries with which the child is familiar'. Occupation should not be used as matter of instruction. 'I should use it for illustration.' 'The practical application of what he is learning should be apparent to the boy the whole time, even in the most elementary things.' The same opinion was expressed by a representative of the Scotch Education Department with regard to the aim of supplementary courses in Scotland. In answer to the question, 'I take it that we are right in thinking that the object of the supplementary course is to provide instruction with some direct relation to the future life of the boy or girl?' he said, 'It is to give a chance for the pupil to consider how his knowledge may be made to bear on his future life.' Illustration was instanced by one witness as a good means to encourage the realization of what is learnt. 'You get at them more easily' by illustration. It would lie with the teacher, he held, to choose suitable illustrations in accordance with local conditions. 'Anything you can do,' said another witness,

to impress upon a child the bearing of education upon the facts of life, or even upon the facts of labour and employment, I think most desirable. You cannot make the teaching too interesting, and mere abstract teaching is rarely interesting to children. I do not see how a child is to be taught the principles of the lever, for instance, unless you can explain them to him. A child would not be likely to evolve out of his own consciousness that a ladder being erected involved the principles of leverage, that a wheelbarrow being wheeled would involve the principles of leverage, and a teacher may make these things plain to a child by simple experiments. So far as that goes a teacher cannot be too profuse in his simple illustrations, but the illustrations should all be of an extremely simple nature and such as a child could absolutely understand.

Such methods, we hope, will stimulate interest and intelligence in every direction. It is peculiarly desirable, in view of their past training and their future life, that the children should become interested. 'When,' said one headmistress, 'I have been able to discover a point of interest, it has helped not only that particular subject, but other subjects as well.' It is important 'to find the point of interest, to help a girl to find her life's work afterwards in an educational way'. A witness assented readily to the question, 'The whole of your education is based upon awakening interest?' Later in life it is difficult to do this.

And while the desired result may be aimed at in part by this method, a corollary method consists in encouraging the children to work by themselves. 'The children would have,' said an Elementary School Inspector, 'to get up lessons and to do things for themselves much more than they have done in the elementary school.' They must teach themselves 'how to learn'. 'It is thought good,' said a witness, 'that the children [in supplementary courses] should study on their own account under the direction of a teacher.' Children from the elementary schools, where the conditions of teaching, and more especially the too large size of the classes, tend to produce a system of drill, of 'chalk and talk', are not accustomed, as a witness said, 'to think much about facts'. In the freer atmosphere of the higher elementary school at an age when the children are more capable of thinking, we believe that this method would be of the greatest educational value.

24 Board of Education

from the Report of the Consultative Committee upon Questions affecting Higher Elementary Schools, 1906, pp. 22–3.

The 1906 Report made clear the distinctions between secondary and elementary education. 'The two types of school' it suggested, 'prepare for different walks of life – the one for the lower ranks of industry and commerce, the other for the higher ranks and for the liberal professions.'

To round off and complete the general conception of a higher elementary school as it presents itself to the Committee, it will be useful to distinguish its character and function from those of a secondary school.

The higher elementary school is continuous with that of the public elementary school. The higher elementary school is 'end on', if the expression may be allowed, to the ordinary elementary school. As was well said by an elementary school inspector the lines of education in both schools are of the same gauge; they form 'a series'. The secondary school is not continuous in the same way with the elementary school; its course is, normally, preceded by a course of primary education in a preparatory school or department; but this primary education differs in character and method from the elementary instruction which the public elementary school affords. The difference between the higher elementary school and the secondary school extends downwards beyond the age of twelve, at which both schools admit pupils, and the difference is the same throughout the course. Though, for the purposes of grant, it may be convenient to consider that portion of the secondary-school course only which begins at the age of twelve, it must not be supposed that the secondary school course begins only at that age and not before. The difference is due, in the first place, to the age at which the pupil in the higher elementary school and the secondary school is assumed in each case to end his regular schooling. The maximum age limit in the higher elementary school is fifteen years; in the secondary school the course extends from twelve to sixteen, but this leaving age is not, as in the other case, a maximum, but a minimum. It is expected that the scholars in a secondary school will continue at school beyond the age of sixteen, and that they will stay four years at least. The four years make only the core of the period of school life. It follows that the plan of instruction may be laid out on different lines in the secondary school from those which the course in a higher elementary school of a maximum length of three years necessitates. Similarly, the boy who leaves a higher elementary school at fifteen is supposed to begin wage-earning at once; a boy who leaves a secondary school may often be supposed to pursue his education further. The higher elementary school completes the regular course of organized education; the secondary school not necessarily. The two types of school prepare for different walks of life – the one for the lower ranks of industry and commerce, the other for the higher ranks and for the liberal professions. Consequently, the higher elementary school can only afford to teach a limited number of subjects, and with a practical bias; the secondary school has time for more subjects and a more theoretical and academic method of teaching. Finally, but not least important, the home conditions of the pupils attending the two kinds of school are different, and while, in the case of the secondary school, the home life may be expected to supplement and strengthen the school instruction, or, at least, not to hamper it, in the case of the higher elementary school the home conditions at best, do little to favour the ends of school education, and at worst are antagonistic.

25 H. Ward

from the Divisional Inspector's Report upon Elementary Education in
Lancashire, Board of Education Annual Report, 1913–14, Appendix I,
1915, pp. 4–8.

*Educational reforms such as the raising of the school leaving age, and the
changing emphasis in teaching methods put a heavy premium on resources.
Local authorities were asked to transform their inherited school buildings
and provide many more services. In many cases, the pace of change rapidly
overtook the ability of such authorities to cope with the needs. Official
reports resound with the declamations of administrators and inspectors
for more resources. Here is just one example from many which could have
been selected.*

Lancashire County

The typical school in 1902 usually consisted originally of one very large
undivided room, with a few classrooms, one or two for each department,
and these either very small or else cumbrously large. Neither lighting nor
heating nor ventilation came up to modern standards, and very often,
especially in the towns, the schools were on two or three floors with awkward staircases and little accommodation for cloaks. The dominating idea
of schools built even within the last fifteen or twenty years was the use of the
school on Sundays, where the same large room served both for assembly and
worship, and for accommodating the numerous small classes into which
Sunday schools are commonly divided. The classrooms were for the
'select' classes, those of the young man and young woman. This type of
building served not at all badly when the ordinary staff of even a large
school was a head teacher, with perhaps one or two adult assistants, and a
set of pupil-teachers. The head teacher was in full control of almost the
whole school at once. The classrooms were large enough to accommodate
the pupil-teacher with his section for oral work; it is to be feared little pains
were taken to adapt the number of children to the size of the rooms and the
fact that twelve years ago in practically every school of this kind one could
find at least one if not all the classrooms furnished with 'forms', indicates
that under ordinary conditions of desking the rooms simply could not take
the numbers they were expected to contain. This kind of building was
almost universal among the Wesleyan and undenominational schools; it
prevailed very largely in the urban and semi-urban Church schools, and the
fairly numerous school chapels of the Roman Catholics were as awkward to
deal with. Though the older board schools commonly had classrooms of

some size, they also were often planned on the supposition that a large hall or schoolroom ought naturally to be occupied by several classes. Some of those in the towns are still so used.

The conditions of present-day teaching demand that if possible each class should have a separate room. But so prevalent is the type of structure just described and so unmanageable is it, that this ideal cannot at present be realized, and the presence of two classes in one room has perforce to be tolerated as a defect that is for the moment in many cases irremediable. Many of the worst schools have been closed. But very many more had to be adapted to the new requirements by partitions, by occasional enlargements of small classrooms and by surrender of space. Even these expedients have too often resulted in cramped conditions of teaching in the older schools; in particular there is usually little space for free movement for the younger children, and rarely is there room for suitable physical exercises indoors. This need for indoor space is particularly strong in Lancashire, where so many days are wet.

In Lancashire County on the 'appointed day' a very large proportion of the schools contained more or less serious defects of lighting and ventilation along with the prevailing drawback of inadequate classroom accommodation. In spite of the work accomplished before that date, in 1910 it was still necessary to schedule 205 schools for defects at least as serious as that of 'three classes in one room'. A 'building programme' was agreed upon with the Board of Education and the greater part of it has now been carried out. Only some thirty schools remain to be dealt with and in practically all these cases it is possible to report that the end is in sight. The amount expended by the authority since the appointed day in erecting and improving council schools (of which there are now 129) is over £400,000; fifty-four entirely new council schools have been opened since 1902; the majority of these replaced bad buildings, but the additional requirements of accommodation necessitated by a growing population have, on the whole, been promptly satisfied.

Manchester and Liverpool

The problems confronting Manchester and Liverpool were different from those of the counties. Thus each had a large number of buildings tolerably satisfactory, and it was customary to be constantly erecting schools to meet the needs of new population. But, in spite of the activities of the school boards for thirty years, during the course of which very many unsatisfactory buildings were replaced, there remained, and still remain, numbers of schools, voluntary and other, with the usual defects accentuated by urban conditions. Neither Liverpool nor Manchester has dealt with the intricate

problem of accommodation on a far-reaching or systematic plan or succeeded in framing a comprehensive and progressive scheme embracing the
improvement of old and the provision of new schools; and, though a good
deal has been accomplished in the way of meeting deficiences in accommodation and of replacing bad buildings, much remains to be done in both
directions.

Playgrounds

One question which is engaging the attention of managers and authorities
especially in the larger urban areas, is the provision of playgrounds. There
is little difficulty where schools are to be built in the suburbs, but where they
are required to replace bad buildings in the closely populated districts or
where old schools on restricted sites are to be reconstructed, it is hard to
secure the amount of space without which really free play is impossible and
physical exercises are cramped. For organized games, children can go further afield, to parks and open spaces. But for the unorganized play before
and after school and in the intervals, and for proper physical instruction,
upon which public opinion places an increasing value, adequate space in
the immediate neighbourhood of the school is essential. It is becoming
customary to place playgrounds on the roof and to make the fullest use of
any public recreation grounds which may be near at hand.

Temporary buildings

Two matters ought to have special attention in Liverpool and Manchester.
In both cities the old school boards began the practice of placing upon new
sites for schools temporary buildings of wood and iron. They were extremely
convenient; they could be rapidly put up and easily enlarged and they were
an index to the authority of the ultimate needs of the neighbourhood. But it
is difficult to keep these buildings properly warm in winter or properly cool
in summer; they are relatively costly and deteriorate rather quickly. It will
hardly be possible to dispense with their use entirely, but a systematic
attempt to replace them is needed. In Liverpool nine of these which were in
existence in 1903 are still in use. In Manchester there are nineteen, of
which eight have been up since 1905 or earlier; it is fair to say that five of the
Liverpool schools and four of the Manchester schools are on the way to be
replaced.

Noisy schools

The large increase in heavy motor traffic has brought into prominence,
especially in Manchester, the noisiness of many schools. Manchester is
paved with setts and it is alleged that no other form of pavement will suit

the kind of traffic that lumbers along its streets. Unfortunately quite a large number of schools are situated on or near main roads, and in some cases what was originally a bye-street has been converted into a busy thoroughfare by the erection of works. The schools affected are too numerous to be treated summarily and closed; but there is no doubt that, like insufficiency of playground accommodation, proximity to a noisy street should be a serious count against a school which is under criticism. The Manchester Highways Committee has consented to lay quieter pavements close to four schools as an experiment. This measure will no doubt mitigate though it cannot wholly remove the evil.

Progress in other towns

What has been said above in reference to the two counties and to Manchester and Liverpool is true to a varying extent of the other autonomous areas small and large. Steady progress has been made in Bolton, Burnley, Oldham, Blackpool, Rochdale. In Birkenhead the problem has been more systematically attacked than in most places, not only by providing accommodation for an increasing population, but also by dealing on a regular plan with premises that were defective. Salford has a fairly definite 'programme' for improving buildings, but the progress made up to the present, though sound, has not been considerable. Barrow is also behind in its provision of schools, but is on the point of erecting four new schools to take in the surplus from existing schools and to put out of use certain poor temporary buildings. [. . .]

In the case of authorities saddled in 1902 with a very large number of unsatisfactory buildings, comparison between those which have sincerely attacked the serious position before them and those which have not can hardly be avoided. In St Helen's for example (with a population of 84,410 and thirty-five schools in 1902) seven schools and two departments of schools have been closed, while eight schools and two departments have been built and opened. This borough has not only provided the school places necessary but to a large extent has put the existing buildings in an efficient state. Stockport had a bad name before 1902, though some of its reputation was undeserved. Since 1902 it has grown rapidly, especially in certain recently added areas (the population in 1911 being 108,682); but when the new authority came in, accommodation was deficient in quantity and certainly in quality. Some six schools have been closed and six large schools have been built, together with one temporary school and two new departments; two have been remodelled, another is planned and sites for two others are acquired. [. . .] Preston with a population of 112,989 in 1901 had, and continues to have, a number of poor buildings which are not yet replaced; though two new schools have been built on the outskirts, two schools and two departments have been built elsewhere, while others have been substantially improved. The population seems to be moving away from the centre of the town; thus schools which have many defects are fortunately not very full. The shifting of population complicates the question of providing new schools, and makes managers of the old schools unwilling to spend money on them. But in spite of the work accomplished the general standard of Preston remains low. So is that of Wigan, where, although many school premises are bad, only two schools and one department have been built since 1902.

26 Sir Samuel Hoare

Question Time, House of Commons, 22 March 1911.

Morant's reign at the Board of Education ended with the incident about the Holmes circular, a private report from his Chief Inspector which Morant inadvertently signed, authorizing publication. The report, which made strong criticisms about the quality of elementary-school teachers, caused a storm and was used by, among others, Sir Samuel Hoare, as a means of attacking the Liberal Government. Dozens of questions were asked in the House of Commons about the incident, to cause maximum embarrassment to the government. The one quoted below was tabled but never actually reached during debate, and therefore does not appear in Hansard. It was, however, answered personally and subsequently quoted in the Press.

To ask the President of the Board of Education, whether a circular, letter or written communication of any kind was issued by the Secretary, Assistant Secretary or Chief Inspector of the Board of Education on or about 6 January 1910, advising the Board's Inspectors to use their influence with local authorities to persuade them to restrict their important administrative appointments to candidates educated at Oxford and Cambridge.

The Honourable Member refers, presumably, to the Confidential Memorandum of Mr Holmes from which he read extracts in this House last night. That Memorandum was sent by Mr Holmes to his colleagues in April 1910, and this expression of his views first came to my notice in February 1911. They are his views and nothing more than that, and do not convey, either directly or indirectly, the advice suggested in the Question or any advice or instructions analogous thereto.

27 Edmond Holmes

from *What Is and What Might Be*, 1911, pp. 3-8.

On his retirement as Chief Inspector – shortly before the storm about his confidential Memorandum to Morant broke in Parliament – Holmes wrote a book which greatly influenced educational thinking, particularly in the elementary schools.

Salvation through mechanical obedience

The function of education is to foster growth. By some of my readers this statement will be regarded as a truism; by others as a challenge; by others, again, when they have realized its inner meaning, as a 'wicked heresy'. I will begin by assuming that it is a truism, and will then try to prove that it is true.

The function of education is to foster growth. The end which the teacher should set before himself is the development of the latent powers of his pupils, the unfolding of their latent life. If growth is to be fostered, two things must be liberally provided – nourishment and exercise. On the need for nourishment I need not insist. The need for exercise is perhaps less obvious, but is certainly not less urgent. We make our limbs, our organs, our senses, our faculties grow by exercising them. When they have reached their maximum of development we maintain them at that level by exercising them. When their capacity for growth is unlimited, as in the case of our mental and spiritual faculties, the need for exercise is still more urgent. To neglect to exercise a given limb, or organ, or sense, or faculty, would result in its becoming weak, flabby, and in the last resort useless. In childhood, when the stress of Nature's expansive forces is strongest, the neglect of exercise will, for obvious reasons, have most serious consequences. If a healthy child were kept in bed during the second and third years of his life, the damage done to his whole body would be incalculable.

These are glaring truisms. Let me perpetrate one more – one which is perhaps the most glaring of all. The process of growing must be done by the growing organism, by the child, let us say, and by no one else. The child himself must take in and assimilate the nourishment that is provided for him. The child himself must exercise his organs and faculties. The one thing which no one may ever delegate to another is the business of growing. To watch another person eating will not nourish one's own body. To watch another person using his limbs will not strengthen one's own. The forces that make for the child's growth come from within himself; and it is for him, and him alone, to feed them, use them, evolve them.

All this is

As true as truth's simplicity,
And simpler than the infancy of truth.

But it sometimes happens that what is most palpable is least perceptible; and perhaps it is because the truth of what I say is self-evident and indisputable, that in many elementary schools in this country the education given seems to be based on the assumption that my 'truisms' are absolutely false. In such schools the one end and aim of the teacher is to do everything for the child; to feed him with semi-digested food; to hold him by the hand, or rather by both shoulders, when he tries to walk or run; to keep him under close and constant supervision; to tell him in precise detail what he is to think, to feel, to say, to wish, to do; to show him in precise detail how he is to do whatever may have to be done; to lay thin veneers of information on the surface of his mind; never to allow him a minute for independent study; never to trust him with a handbook, a notebook or a sketchbook; in fine, to do all that lies in his power to prevent the child from doing anything whatever for himself. The result is that the various vital faculties which education might be supposed to train become irretrievably starved and stunted in the over-educated school child; till at last, when the time comes for him to leave the school in which he has been so sedulously cared for, he is too often thrown out upon the world, helpless, listless, resourceless, without a single interest, without a single purpose in life.

The contrast between elementary education as it too often is, and as it ought to be if the truth of my 'truisms' were widely accepted, is so startling that in my desire to account for it I have had recourse to a paradox. ' *Trop de vérité,*' says Pascal, '*nous étonne: les premiers principes ont trop d'évidence pour nous.*' I have suggested that the inability of so many teachers to live up to the spirit, or even to the letter, of my primary 'truism', may be due to its having too much evidence for them, to their being blinded by the naked light of its truth.

But there may be another explanation of the singular fact that a theory of education to which the teacher would assent without hesitation if it were submitted to his consciousness counts for nothing in the daily routine of his work. Failure to carry an accepted principle into practice is sometimes due to the fact that the principle has not really been accepted; that its inner meaning has not been apprehended; that assent has been given to a formula rather than a truth. The cause of the failure may indeed lie deeper than this. It may be that the nominal adherents of the principle are in secret revolt against the vital truth that is at the heart of it; that they repudiate it in practice because they have already repudiated it in the inner recesses of their thought. 'This people draweth nigh unto me with their mouth, and honoureth me with their lips; but their heart is far from me.' Tell the teacher that the function of education is to foster growth; that therefore it is his business to develop the latent faculties of his pupils; and that therefore (since growth presupposes exercise) he must allow his pupils to do as much as possible by and for themselves, place these propositions before him, and the chances are that he will say 'Amen' to them. But that lip assent will count for nothing. One's life is governed by instinct rather than logic. To give a lip assent to the logical inferences from an accepted principle is one thing. To give a *real* assent to the essential truth that underlies and animates the principle is another. The way in which the teacher too often conducts his school leads one to infer that the intuitive, instinctive side of him – the side that is nearest to practice – has somehow or other held intercourse with the inner meaning of that 'truism' which he repeats so glibly, and has rejected it as antagonistic to the traditional assumptions on which he bases his life. Or perhaps this work of subconscious criticism and rejection has been and is being done for him, either by the spirit of the age to which he belongs or by the genius of the land in which he lives.

Why is the teacher so ready to do everything (or nearly everything) for the children whom he professes to educate? One obvious answer to this question is that for a third of a century (1862–95) the 'Education Department' did everything (or nearly everything) for him. For a third of a century 'My Lords' required their inspectors to examine every child in every elementary school in England on a syllabus which was binding on all schools alike. In doing this, they put a bit into the mouth of the teacher and drove him, at their pleasure, in this direction and that. And what they did to him they compelled him to do to the child.

So far as the action of the 'Education Department' was concerned, this policy was abandoned – in large measure, if not wholly – in 1895; but its consequences are with us still. What conception of the meaning and purpose of education could have induced 'My Lords' to adopt such a policy, and, having adopted it, to adhere to it for more than thirty years? Had one asked 'My Lords' at any time during those thirty years what they regarded as the true function of education, and had one suggested to them (as they had probably never turned their minds to the question) that the function of education was to foster the growth of the child, they might possibly have given an indolent assent to the proposition. But their educational policy must have been dictated by some widely different conception. They must have believed that the mental progress of the child – the only aspect of progress which concerned educationalists in those days – would best be tested by a formal examination on a prescribed syllabus, and would best be secured by preparation for such a test; and they must have accepted, perhaps without the consent of their consciousness, whatever theory of education may be implicit in that belief.

In acting as they did, 'My Lords' fell into line with the universities, the public schools, the preparatory schools, the civil service commissioners, the professional societies, and (to make a general statement) with all the 'boards' and 'bodies' that controlled, directly or indirectly, the education of the youth of England. We must, therefore, widen the scope of our inquiry, and carry our search for cause a step farther back. How did the belief that a formal examination is a worthy end for teacher and child to aim at, and an adequate test of success in teaching and in learning, come to establish itself in this country? And not in this country only, but in the whole Western world? In every Western country that is progressive and 'up to date', and in every Western country in exact proportion as it is progressive and 'up to date', the examination system controls education, and in doing so arrests the self-development of the child, and therefore strangles his inward growth.

28 H. G. Wells

from *Joan and Peter: The Story of an Education*, 1918, pp. 212–13.

Holmes's dissatisfaction with current school practice was shared by many, including Morant, whose 1905 Handbook of Suggestions for the Consideration of Teachers and Others Engaged in the Work of Public Elementary Schools *was intended to act as a challenge for better teaching methods in the schools. Wells described the general apathy in the public schools with characteristic bluntness.*

Of course, Mr Mainwearing had no special training as a teacher. He had no ideas about education at all. He had no social philosophy. He had never asked why he was alive or what he was up to. Instinct, perhaps, warned him that the answer might be disagreeable. Much less did he inquire what his boys were likely to be up to. And it did not occur to him, it did not occur to anyone in those days, to consider that these deficiencies barred him in any way from the preparation of the genteel young for life. He taught as he had been taught; his teachers had done the same; he was the last link of a long chain of tradition that had perhaps in the beginning had some element of intention in it as to what was to be made of the pupil. Schools, like religions, tend perpetually to forget what they are for.

29 Board of Education

from the Annual Report of the Chief Medical Officer of the Board, 1908, Cd 4986, 1910, pp. 28–9.

A major development in welfare legislation was contained in the 1907 Education (Administrative Provisions) Act which not merely empowered local authorities, but legally bound them to carry out medical inspections on all school children, and specifically asked them to make provisions for their health. From this Act stems the first of a series of what has now become annual medical reports on the health of the nation's young. In 1908 when the first report appeared, the main issue was still malnutrition.

Scope of the work

Previously to the passing of the Education (Administrative Provisions) Act of 1907, a number of local education authorities had, as we have seen, undertaken some form of medical inspection. Such inspection, as might have been expected, had been of a somewhat limited and tentative character, following no well defined standard, and had been concerned only or chiefly with children selected from the school or class as being in some way obviously ailing or defective. The general routine, where such inspection was practised, has been for a medical man to visit the schools at intervals and examine more or less thoroughly those children submitted to him by the teachers or selected by himself. Such cases were, as a rule, but imperfectly followed up, and little or no account was taken of the necessities of school hygiene in any wide and comprehensive sense. Within these limitations, no doubt, good work was done and foundations were laid for the future, as has been pointed out in an earlier section of the present Report.

The fundamental principle of the new Act was, however, the medical inspection and supervision not only of children known or suspected to be weakly or diseased, but of all children in the public elementary schools, and this with a view to adapting and modifying the system of education to the needs and capacities of the children, securing the early detection of unsuspected defects, checking incipient maladies at their onset, and furnishing the facts which would guide education authorities in relation to physical and mental development of children during school life. This underlying principle has meant, in organization, that two broad requirements should be met. First, that all children should at some time or times in their school life come under medical inspection, whether they be physically healthy or unhealthy; and, secondly, that the medical inspection under which the children should pass should be as a rule not the maximum of clinical examination possible but the minimum necessary to detect such physical and mental defects as would unfit the children to receive the education provided by the State. I propose now to report on these two points.

The Act itself laid down that it was the duty of each local education authority to provide for the medical inspection of children (a) immediately before, or (b) at the time of, or (c) as soon as possible after, their admission to a public elementary school, and on such other occasions as the Board of Education direct. The examination of all children, of whatever age, on attention should be given to the whole question of physique and nutrition with a view to elucidation of the subject from a national health point of view. It would be well also in the next year's reports that medical officers should as far as possible group the children in the classes suggested in the Board's schedule, namely, good (meaning excellent), normal, below normal and bad, stating in as much detail as possible the data on which they classify. Lastly, while it is true that the question of nutrition must always remain, in large degree, a matter of individual opinion, and thus be incapable of summary or tabulation, it may be made a valuable test of progress both in individual children and in the children of an area, when they are examined by the same inspector.

Impossible though it is to make any numerical statement as to the percentage of children of any given area or living under any special conditions who might be classified as well nourished or as below normal or of poor nutrition, respectively, it is clear from the reports that there is a considerable number of children (rising in poorer districts to a serious proportion) who, in greater or less degree, exhibit evidences of malnutrition. Such children, though found in greater numbers in the larger industrial centres, are by no means confined to these. Many school medical officers comment on the causation of this condition of comparative malnutrition, all of them emphasizing the complexity of the factors producing it. This observation is undoubtedly true, and not only may the cause be complex in the case of a given individual child, but the different causes act in different degrees in the case of different groups of children, varying in large measure, according to the social status of the child. Thus, two children, each alike suffering from malnutrition, may have had the condition caused in the one case mainly by insufficient food and general neglect; in the other by unsuitable feeding and pampering. This, therefore, is yet another point on which it may be hoped that future work will throw light. In whatever manner this condition of malnutrition may be produced, the application of appropriate remedial measures is urgently required, since a satisfactory state of nutrition in the child is the first essential to sound physical health.

30 J. H. Palin

from 'The Feeding of School Children: Bradford's Experience',
Socialist Review, no. 1, March 1908, pp. 207–14.

*The battle to help undernourished, even starving children in the streets of the
larger cities became a political battle. The fight was really about interventionism,
and to what extent the State had a responsibility for the poor within its gates.
Many remained unconvinced, and the struggle was long and dour. In the north,
men like Robert Blatchford and women like the McMillan sisters pointed the
way. J. H. Palin recorded the battle as it took place.*

The genesis of the movement that led up to the question of child feeding
being brought within the range of practical politics, must be placed to the
credit of Mr Robert Blatchford and Miss Margaret McMillan. The first-
named by initiating the Cinderella Club movement did a greater work
than most people know of. Bradford among other places was profoundly
touched by Nunquam's eloquent appeal on behalf of Cinderella. All ranks
of society came forward and joined the Cinderella Club, which has done
most excellent work in systematically feeding and clothing the children of
the slums.

We, in Bradford, never do anything by halves, and it was soon discovered
that to give a child an occasional meal was not a good policy, while many
doubted whether they were not being actually guilty of cruelty in feeding
the child one day, and then allowing it to starve for weeks.

Consequently it was decided to sort out the worst cases by means of
inquiry and to feed these at the Club's own premises, and in the various
schools in the poorer districts for five days per week. This was successfully
carried out for several winters, hundreds of meals being given daily.

In the meantime the seed sown under very discouraging circumstances
by Miss McMillan, while a member of the Bradford School Board, had not
all fallen upon barren ground, and about five years ago the Labour Party
decided to place child feeding in the forefront of their Municipal Programme. The little group of our men on the city council lost no time in
forcing the question upon the notice of the City Fathers, and depicted such
a terrible state of things that they stirred one of the Fathers, a merchant
prince and philanthropist, to go to the Cinderella Club for information as to
the truth of the statements that had been made. Messrs W. Leach and Harry
Smith, the Secretary, were instructed to go over the material in the possession of the Club and prepare a report; this they did, and a very exhaustive
report was presented, which in addition to presenting facts and figures
showing the abject poverty of the people, also quoted statistics which proved

that there were upwards of 2000 children underfed and badly clothed, many of whom went breakfastless to school, and it further expressed the opinion that voluntary help could not cope with the matter. This report was fully discussed at a special meeting of the Club, and, although the majority of the members were opposed to the political faith held by the two young Socialists who presented it, they unanimously adopted it as an accurate statement of the position, and also passed a vote of thanks to the authors for its preparation.

When this report became public property it produced a profound sensation, and the ILP propagandists made full use of it, and urged Miss McMillan's oft-repeated argument that it was wasting money to try and educate a starving child. The city council had to do something to placate the feeling that had been aroused, and a conference of the leading citizens was called at the Mechanics' Institute one Sunday afternoon, and never in the history of the city has a more representative meeting been held. Cutcliffe Hyne, of Captain Kettle fame, rubbed shoulders with the street corner agitator; philanthropists, politicians and parsons had all come to hear the truth about this child feeding business from the lips of the teachers. What a story it was! No one present at that meeting unless made of stone could listen unmoved. The scene will never be effaced from my memory so long as I live. The teachers were drawn from every type of school, both provided and non-provided. They told us that it was not merely a winter question, or one that was very much affected by either good or bad trade; in summer they had children falling from their seats and fainting for want of food; they also incidentally told us very modestly of their own heroic efforts to deal with the worst cases out of their own slender means, and we came out of that meeting ashamed to look each other in the face.

Still, nothing was done, but with the advent of the municipal election campaign of 1904 the Education Committee appointed a sub-committee to go into the matter and report. Just before the election they reported and asked for authority to subsidize the Cinderella Club so that no child should go unfed, and the Liberals went to the electors with a halo round their heads. Despite this blanketing the Labour group was strengthened, but at the very first meeting of the Education Committee after 9 November, the Liberals rescinded the resolution to feed; but when this came before the City Council for endorsement the Labour men put up a good fight and the matter was referred back with instructions to feed. This was more than the upholders of the parental responsibility doctrine could stand; the war-drum was vigorously thumped by the Liberal wire-pullers, and, at a special meeting of the party, each Liberal member of the Council was pledged as a matter of loyalty to his party to support a resolution to rescind the previous decision, and on 13 December 1904, Mr Ald. H. B. Priestman, the leader of the Liberal party, moved the following resolution:

1. That it is the duty of the community to see that all children are sufficiently fed.

2. That the first responsibility of feeding the children rests with their parents and not with the ratepayers.

3. That voluntary effort is fully able and willing to feed children who are temporarily necessitous, by no fault of their parents.

4. That where the children of neglectful parents are not sufficiently fed, the duty of feeding them belongs to the Board of Guardians, who have power in proper cases (a) to recover the costs from their parents, (b) to prosecute neglectful parents, (c) in cooperation with the police, to remove the children from the custody of their parents and to place them in suitable homes.

5. That it is desirable that the question of providing meals at a small fixed charge covering the cost only for children attending the elementary schools should be considered.

6. That following these considerations the resolution regarding the feeding of necessitous children, passed at the City Council meeting on 29 November, be rescinded for the purpose of adopting a procedure in accordance with the above resolutions.

What a glorious fight it was, and how proud I feel at being privileged to take part in it. Led by Jowett and Hayhurst we raked capitalism fore and aft. We kept them at it from 3 p.m. to 2.35 next morning, but the Liberal forces had been well drilled, and, with a few honourable exceptions, they voted against us, and the children were handed over to the tender mercies of the Poor Law by forty-seven votes to twenty-nine recorded against the resolution I have quoted.

The first thing the Guardians did was to reduce the numbers by means of threatening notices and prosecutions in the County Court. This policy was efficacious in reducing the number that was being fed, owing to the parents withdrawing their children rather than take the humbug and insults that were meted out to them. In consequence of this, the greater number was not fed at all, and of the remainder a portion were fed out of a fund amounting to £3314 raised by the Mayor, and the rest were fed out of the rates by the Guardians. But in what a style they fed them! The children were kept outside the doors until all was ready, and when they were allowed to enter they came in without any semblance of order, to tables without cloths, without seats, to a ration consisting of a stale bun, a banana and half-a-pint of what they termed a beverage consisting of three parts water to one of milk. In the municipal elections of 1905, this absurd and totally inadequate system was so exposed by Jowett and others, that they distributed the children over the various little eating-houses that are to be found in the vicinity of every large mill, and although the conditions of serving were not much better, some of the children were better fed, as all the caterers did not care to make a profit out of them, and gave them full value for the 2d. paid by the Guardians. (This 2d. was translated by the Guardians into 3d. when recovering from parents.)

Thus things went on for the next twelve months, during which we sent Jowett to Westminster and I succeeded him on the Education Committee. Our little journal *Forward*, edited by Mr W. Leach, kept pounding away at the question and raising funds to defend the poor wretches who were being prosecuted and persecuted, with the result that all thoughtful people became sick and tired of the Poor Law and all its works so far as child feeding was concerned.

Then came that never-to-be-forgotten day when the fight was transferred to the floor of the House of Commons; how keenly we followed the speeches of Hardie, Crooks, and our true and tried colleague Jowett; how relieved we all felt when the Bill received the King's assent and became the law of the land. In due course the new Act came before the Education Committee, where I had been reinforced by Hartley, who had re-entered the Council the previous November. It was referred to the sub-committee, upon which I sat alone with only a few months' experience to guide me. Hartley came to the meeting; and although he could neither speak nor vote, I felt the value of his presence and support. The Director of Education reported that the Act was the most loosely drafted measure that had come under his cognizance, and expressed the opinion that if we spent money out of the halfpenny rate for plant and equipment we could not provide food, or vice versa. The Town Clerk was appealed to, and he supported the opinion of the Director of Education. I contended that the Act was intended to feed the children, and that it took for granted that we had already power to provide plant and equipment. The Liberal Chairman, Mr Councillor B. North, supported me, and the City Council was recommended to adopt the Act and seek the necessary power to levy the halfpenny rate. Mr Councillor E. J. Smith, a leading Liberal, and President of the Free Church Council, opposed it when it came before the Council, on the ground that private charity was not exhausted, and expressed the opinion that the Government had allowed the measure to become law not from conviction but from expediency. For once the Labour group kept silence; the battle had been won; no one else opposed, and the Act was adopted by an almost unanimous vote of the whole Council. Subsequently, the Education Department wanted satisfying as to the steps that had been taken to ascertain that private charity was exhausted before giving authority to impose the rate. The same gentleman appealed to the Lord Mayor to open a fund and make another appeal to the citizens to provide the money voluntarily, and when he met with a refusal succeeded in carrying a resolution instructing the Education Committee to make an appeal. This was done, and although the appeal was endorsed by the Lord Mayor and twenty pounds was spent in advertising, it only brought the sum of five pounds – from Mr Councillor E. J. Smith himself. Attempts were subsequently made to transfer the staff employed by the Guardians and to coopt outsiders nominated by various philanthropic societies, all of which we successfully resisted.

We then visited Manchester and Leeds, and saw what was being done in those places. In the feeding centre organized, equipped and worked practically single-handed by that grand old gentleman, Dr Hall, of Leeds, we became inspired by the ideas which led up to our present system of organization for the cooking and serving of the food. We were still faced with the problem of distributing it to the various dining-rooms. Having read an interesting account of how a London firm of caterers had successfully cooked in a central kitchen for a number of rich people who desired to dispense with a cook, and distributed the food to their customers in specially designed receptacles which kept it hot for some hours, I suggested that we should proceed on similar lines. Estimates were got out by the Superintendent of Cooking which supported the practicability of the idea. The Clerk of the Works was called in, and he designed receptacles which kept the food hot for hours after leaving the kitchen. We were then faced with the problem of suitable premises for a kitchen. Not daring to propose a new building, we had to make a survey of existing buildings under the control of the Committee. It was then discovered that the gymnasium at our Green Lane Schools was much too large for the number of children using it, and by partitioning off a portion we secured an excellent kitchen capable of supplying about 3000 meals per day. By merely cutting a hole in, and bringing a pipe through a partition wall, we were able to secure an abundance of steam from the boiler house attached to the school baths next door without any extra cost worth mentioning. The cost of fitting up the kitchen, including the purchase and fixing of three steam jacketed boilers, one with a capacity of 100 gallons, and two with a capacity of fifty gallons each, two very large gas ovens and one smaller one, two large porcelain baths for washing vegetables, one machine for cutting vegetables, two ingenious little machines for coring and paring apples, one machine for cleaning and paring potatoes, four thousand soup plates, four thousand dinner plates, forks and spoons, receptacles for conveying the food to the dining rooms, aprons and sleeves for the teachers and monitresses, have altogether cost about £600.

During the time the Committee were arranging these details Doctor Crowley was not idle. He first of all took a survey of the physical condition of the children in attendance at our schools, the result of which he gave in the form of a paper at the Northern Educational Conference held at Bradford in January 1907, in the course of which he stated that, based upon his personal examination of 2000 children, he estimated that there were at least 6000 children in our schools who were underfed. This curiously enough more than confirmed the Cinderella Club report of October 1904, and did much to spur the Committee into adopting the Act. He subsequently went into the question of the nutritious value of the food; such things as the amount of protein, fat, carbohydrate and salts contained in the food specified for each meal. A menu was drawn up in conjunction with Miss Cuff, the Superintendent of Cookery, which appeared to be an ideal one from every standpoint.

All that remained to be done was to ascertain what would be the effect upon the children and how they would take to such an unusual dietary and so on. At this juncture our first Lord Mayor, Alderman J. A. Godwin, stepped into the breach and offered to provide the cost of feeding forty children in accordance with the menu drawn up with two meals per day for a period of three months. The offer was gratefully accepted and the experiment was carried out in one of the poorer schools from 27 April to 24 July 1907. The experiment was not only useful as a practical guide to the character of meals provided, but also as an indication of the best methods to adopt in serving them.

The report presented to the Committee upon the result of the experiment is a most interesting and comprehensive one, and I would advise anyone desiring reliable information on the question, to obtain a copy from the Secretary of the Education Committee, Manor Row, Bradford, price 3d. plus postage. The experiment proved the estimate of the Superintendent of Cookery and the Secretary of the Cinderella Club of 1½d. per meal for dinner and 1d. for breakfast or tea to be correct. It was also found by carefully weighing each child every week that they gained in weight, on an average forty-nine ozs. per child. During the same period forty children taken from the same school, who were fed at home only gained twenty ounces.

31 Margaret McMillan

from 'London's Children: How to Feed Them and How Not to Feed Them', Independent Labour Party, 1909, pp. 6–12.

From their pioneering work among the poor of Bradford, the McMillan sisters went to the East End of London, where they opened their famous open-air school and ran their clinic. With these experiences behind her, Margaret McMillan was able to exert great influence on the future pattern of child care. In this, one of the very few pieces she committed to writing, she pamphleteered with a striking mixture of the intensely practical and the visionary. Her message was stark: 'We are,' she concluded, 'at grips with starvation.'

'Thanks be to God we eate plentifully, and be not gone crokyed and hungry as others are.' Old English Chancellor of the Exchequer.

It has often been noted that great reforms are brought about through the influence of passive, as well as humble beings, but it is especially true of schools that they owe much to the weakest scholars. The baby – the two- or three-year-old child – made the old discipline and methods of infant schools appear absurd at last in the eyes of all. The defective and abnormal child has stimulated the best kind of teachers to make studies that are resulting in improved methods. It is now the turn of the starveling to enter the arena, and it is pretty certain that his little person will be the centre of even a greater reform.

Three questions face the members of education authorities today in connection with the carrying out of the Act. They are, 'What are we to give the children to eat?' Also, 'Under what circumstances and surroundings are they to eat it?' And lastly, 'How and where is this food to be prepared, and how distributed?'

This little pamphlet is not written in order to give finished, perfect and authoritative answers to all these questions. The materials and the warrant for such dogmatic teaching cannot yet be claimed by anyone. In so far, indeed, as two of the three questions are concerned, only one or two education committees have any experience at all that is likely to be of great value, and these know quite well that every locality has to face a problem that is not exactly that of any other. A certain amount of experience is, however, already to hand, and so we may venture to offer a few suggestions as to the practical steps involved in carrying out a scheme of school meals in London.

What are the children to eat? 'Give them anything,' says the man in a hurry; 'if they're hungry they'll be glad of it.' But the famishing are not, as a rule, very hungry. Every organ is weakened as the result of starvation – more especially the organ that has to deal with food. The experience of the captains of Salvation Army shelters, as well as of teachers in slum schools, is that half-famishing adults and children sitting down for the first time for weeks to a good meal, eat little, and are on the sick list as the result of eating even a very small meal. Well-fed boys in public schools are ravenous – eager for 'hampers' from home, and ready to patronize tuck shops. The starving will often turn away from a good dinner.

In the first days the helpings should be small. It may be necessary to give on the first day or two only liquid – or light farinaceous food. After a short time, however, the symptoms of chronic starvation will pass off, and the child will seem to get hungrier every day.

To return, however, to our question. What kind and quantity of food does a child of school age require? Dr Clement Dukes has worked at the answer in the interest of the preparatory school boy. A child under fourteen (and over nine, we may say) requires, he declares, weekly

Starches	Bread	90 ounces
	Oatmeal	
Carbohydrates	Sugar	16
	Fat	2·5
	Butter	8
	Milk	20·0
	Soup	20
Proteins	Meat	64
	Fish	10
	Cheese	2

This dietary is interesting, not because we can attempt to supply it, but because it indicates the needs of growing children. The large quantity of meat – ¾ lb per day – indicates the great need of *protein* – which however, can be got from other foods, such as oatmeal, pea meal, lentils and cheese. The misfortune of the child of the poor is that, in many cases at least, he has always had to eat as if he were an adult. Although, needing only one-ninth part the protein and carbohydrate of a full-grown man, he requires one-half as much fat daily as the adult. Yet he may have had to eat from infancy just as his parents ate. No one was at hand to say that growing was a process that needed a good supply of fat. The food of many of our elementary school children has been dreadfully lacking in fat, and in protein. The results are before us.

We do not need the school doctor in order to learn that the wretched teeth, and soft twisted bones of thousands of poor school children are a symptom and result of a lean and starchy diet. But how rapidly a better diet may improve them, few can have realized, before Dr Ralph Crowley made his memorable experiments in child feeding in the spring and early summer of 1907. The record of this experiment is now familiar to many. Yet we may review the facts here. Dr Crowley gave two meals daily to the children with whom he made his experiment. Breakfast consisted of oatmeal porridge, not milled English meals, but genuine Scotch oats, and milk. Dinner, though not always including meat, had always the right amount of protein, in pulses (beans, lentils, peas) or cheese – also the right amount of fat (in butter, milk, etc.). The results were amazing. The children after a week of extraordinary gain in weight (one child actually gained over 3 lbs in a week!) attained a new level as it were in nutrition and began to grow healthily, gaining at the rate of 5 oz per week in weight. Formerly, when home fed they were, like their companions, gaining only 1 oz per week.

But there are well-nourished children who are very light and very small, and there are large and very heavy children whose output of energy is pitiable! But Bradford, and the Open-Air School of London – where children are fed regularly – can supply evidence of quite another kind. Dr Frederick Rose has had photographs taken of children entering the outdoor school, and other photographs some months later of the same children after they had enjoyed outdoor life and regular meals for some months. The mere gain in weight is weak evidence as compared with the change, or rather the transformation, visible in the faces of the children. In so far as some of the scholars are concerned it is a *new* soul that looks out from the young face, a soul whose very existence was formerly unsuspected. All signs of deterioration, the working, wrinkled forehead, the stolid eyes, the coarse lips even, have disappeared, and in their place is a calm, bright face, a face of dawning beauty and intelligence.

The point that needs to be emphasized is that imagination and intellect cost something. The brain and nervous system are expensive, draining the whole system as they do for nourishment. The Bradford Education Authority have really gone beyond mere teaching. They are trying to grow nervous systems. The food given in their dining halls is of the best quality.[1]

---

1. It is not therefore dear food. 'Luxurious' feeding is, of course, most unwholesome – more especially for children. The strongest men, and some at least of the more intellectual races appear to live simply. Oatmeal was the staple food of the Scottish people. The magnificent teeth of old Highlanders, and the massive skeletons found in old church yards, as well as the high thinking of the leaders of all ages prove that expensive foods are not necessary for fine structures.

It is prepared with great care and cleanliness. And last of all it is not *dull* and one might say '*stupid*' feeding. It is varied so that the same dinner is not set before a child twice in seventeen days. The average cost per head is from 1d. to 1¼d., though one dinner of the seventeen falls as low as three farthings without going below the standard in essentials. These figures apply, of course, to the mere cost of food, and do not include service and apparatus.

But it is not through the work of one authority, but through the efforts of many that all the problems of diet will be solved. An immense opportunity is now offered to raise the physique of the whole nation. To put children off in future with any kind of weak soup, to offer them any order of 'filling' pudding, to feed them with jam and starchy bread, will now mean the flinging aside of this opportunity.

The choice of the dining hall depends now on the school accommodation. In a few elementary schools in Bradford at least a dining-room is built. But in many schools, hall and classrooms are used, while halls are hired as in London for the use of some children. In Germany the gymnasium – which is to be found in every modern school – is used as a dining-room. The problem is largely one of service, however, as well as of space. Young monitors help in a wonderful way to get rid of the difficulty of service.

It is one of the misfortunes of the elementary school of today that a truly effective system of monitorships is almost impossible. The early age at which the children leave school baffles the teacher's efforts on every hand, yet in spite of this a beginning has to be made. The elder girls may be told in turn to lay the tables, serve the food, and attend to the little ones. It should be part of their duty to see that the infants come to table with clean hands and faces, and also with clean handkerchiefs. (Dr Kerr says that half of the education of a child of four consists in learning to use a handkerchief. Anyone with the smallest experience of little children in very poor neighbourhoods will bear him out in this saying. Speech troubles, throat and nose troubles are connected largely with the neglect of such training as a nurse or elder sister gives in this little matter in well-to-do-homes.) The dirty clothing of children in some areas is another great trouble. The table cloths can hardly be kept clean for a day, rubbed as they are by dirty sleeves. Some kind of cheap overall should be worn at table, until public opinion decides that these dirty clothes are not to be worn at all in schools. Elbow sleeves and aprons are worn today by the little monitors in Bradford schools – who are indeed in many instances models of neatness. Unfortunately, baths are not to be found in London elementary schools. It is therefore difficult to insist in every area on the keeping up of a high standard of cleanliness. With the help of school nurses and monitors it should be possible, however, to ensure that no child should sit down to table in a very neglected state.

The furniture should be fitted to the age and size of the children. The little ones should sit on small chairs at low tables, and should not be crowded together on forms. Otherwise the meal cannot have any educative value. It would be well, too, if the tables were fairly numerous, and in any case the groups should be well divided, and every group (of little ones) have its own monitor. Grace is sung in Bradford, and even the secularist can hardly fail to admit the great beauty and educational value of this custom.

The process of digestion, we are assured, begins in the mouth – and should begin *well* there. Many children bolt their food – more especially children who are stinted and hurried over their meals. Dr Hall, of Leeds, found that the slum children he fed did not chew at all, but swallowed their food whole. 'They put it in their mouths, and down it went like a letter going in a letter-box,' he said in amazement. Later, he had all the food cut up and minced fine so that it was eaten, like soup, with spoons. But this is not desirable. It is paying too little respect to the teeth. Every doctor insists that children should not be hurried in eating, that they should be encouraged to chew well, and that hard crusts should be given sometimes. Dr Henry Campbell thinks that the failure of learning to chew is one cause of adenoids, that it checks the circulation of the blood and lymph in such a way that the palate and mouth becomes misshapen. In any case it is a cause of other evils too numerous to mention.

Of course the school meal brings into prominence the sad fact that a great many children have bad teeth. It is a fact that some cannot chew. They having nothing to chew with. The nurses and monitors should see that the children clean the teeth after eating. At the school meal food that will help to make good teeth will be given, but, in the first years there will be sad revelations.

Manual training does not begin with woodwork or even with clay-modelling. It may be carried on all the time, and nowhere in a more educative way than at table. Many neglected children do not know how to use a knife or fork. They do not even know how to hold and use a spoon. But after a very little training they manage very well, and never lose the good, new habit. Here again, however, a great deal depends on space and *comfort*.

As a little child's *new* movements are *large* movements, he cannot make much progress at a crowded table. He wants space – even to learn to eat. After a little time he can manage even in crowds – but not at first.

Flowers and leaves to make the school table pretty will be a *very* good investment. But one need not spend the rate in order to make the school table look charming. The children can bring flowers at almost every season. After the first delicious shock the least fortunate accept the new and pleasant ways, and grow to resent ugly and unpleasant associations in eating – and that is education. Reading and writing are only convenient arts; but new habits and ways are something more, and something different.

For the well-to-do or wealthy child, meal times are usually hours of drill and discipline as well as of pleasure – unless of course he always eats in the nursery. Even then he has to sit up nicely, and to keep quiet, and to use his napkin. At the school table the children should sit up, but it is not advisable to insist on silence, since they are already subject *all* day to a discipline that may be necessary (in view of the large numbers) but is very repressive and certainly does not induce self-control. At dinner it should be relaxed – and what Mr Bray calls 'orderly disorder' should be encouraged. There should be no shouting – but plenty of smiles and laughter. An entirely new range of opportunity comes into view along with the school table. 'Does the sacredness of home depend on the family pudding' asks one reformer. The answer is that in a large measure it does. If the school meal is not carried out quite brutally, it must mean the making dear and sacred a larger group than is the family group. It seems that the members of groups, large and small, become known to each other in the breaking of bread.

This is one reason, too, why the teacher should sit at the head of the school table. Without her, or him, the whole venture will fail miserably on the educational side. The writer wishes to give her strong testimony that never in her experience has *any* effort to benefit school children been a success from which the teacher stood aloof. It is not to be expected that the school dining scheme will prove an exception to this rule. The question is not, 'Should the teacher be present?'[2] but 'How is her presence to be assured and her best services made available.' To begin with, nothing in the way of an attendant's duty should be required of teachers. They should *not* serve the food. They should not wait at table. They should not assist to bring in cans, plates, etc., or even help to marshal the children. They should simply enter as a mother or governess enters to preside, and to be the head, and, as far as possible to be the soul of the daily gathering. Again when dinner is over – they should have no duty but the duty of preparing by rest and recreation for afternoon work. Attendants, nurses, should be engaged

2. Let it be said again here that the child of the people is not essentially different as regards his needs from the child of the privileged class. What mother would say to her governess 'You need not preside at the school room meals. You have given lessons and this other duty is no concern of yours.'

for other duties, helped by monitors. Otherwise the educational side of all the work will be nil.

Needless to say, such perfectly natural, and home-like arrangements have not yet been made – even in Bradford. The initial difficulties have been faced there and are being conquered because of the help rendered by brave and self-forgetting men and women-teachers who have been willing to serve as well as teach the poorest children. (One of these is a highly qualified master in a secondary school, others are headmasters and mistresses with splendid records.) These receive now a small remuneration of 5s. a week for their work in the dining halls, but they could render a more valuable kind of service if they were entirely relieved of some of their present tasks.

Not the teacher alone, however, should break bread with the citizen of tomorrow. The school manager, the education committee member, the stranger within our gates might surely honour the children's table. Let one but think how little bright converse, how little change relieves the days of thousands of children who, week by week, year by year, hear at their movable eating hours nothing that stimulates or cheers – but only anxious questionings, sordid details of a hard life or in some cases it may be, bitter reproaches, breaking long spells of brutish silence. There *are* children who come down to lunch as people go to the theatre. Silent they are indeed, and well drilled. Yet how full of interest are the grave eyes they fix on the stranger who brings with him airs of a new life! Many a career has been fixed, and many a life directed by the words and presence of a visitor who is not talking to 'the children'. But to the little slum dwellers there are no such experiences. No relief comes, no new delight in the person of a guest. Yet he could listen and learn and enjoy as well as the other. It is life as well as bread that *all* our children want. In giving one of these we should at least attempt to give the other also!

32 Board of Education

from the Report of the Consultative Committee on Attendance at Continuation Schools, Cd 4757, 1909, p. 215.

Widespread poverty, and the continued use by industry of child labour, reduced education to a part-time affair for most children. A number of reports drew attention to the deleterious effects of such a system, and chronicled the results of such a compromise between the rights of the child and the needs of industry. Their findings were to be a major influence on the drafting of the 1918 Fisher Act.

The Committee find generally that there is urgent need for improvement in the educational conditions under which, in this country, boys and girls grow up from childhood, through adolescence, to adult responsibility. There are at any moment some 170,000 children between twelve and fourteen years of age in England and Wales who have left school and are not attending any form of weekday classes. Large numbers of other children, while still at the day school, are engaged in wage-earning occupations which injure their physical development and prevent them from deriving full benefit from such education as they receive. Out of the two million children in England and Wales who have passed their fourteenth birthday but are still under seventeen years of age, it appears that only one in four receives on weekdays any continued education. The result is a tragic waste of early promise. Through lack of technical training, hundreds of thousands of young people fail to acquire the self-adaptiveness and dexterity in handicraft which would enable them to rise to the higher levels of skilled employment. Through lack of suitable physical training, their bodily powers are insufficiently developed and their self-control impaired. Through lack of general training, their mental outlook remains narrow, their sympathies uncultivated, their capacity for cooperation in civic welfare stunted and untrained. In the meantime, modern industry in some of its developments is exploiting boy and girl labour during the years of adolescence. An increasing number of 'blind-alley' employments tempt boys and girls, at the close of their day-school course, by relatively high rates of wages which furnish opportunities of too early independence, but give no promise of permanent occupation and weaken the ties of parental control .

33 Board of Education

from the Report of the Consultative Committee on Attendance at Continuation Schools, Cd 4757, Appendix 8, 1909, pp. 255–8.

Replies of head teachers to a circular issued by the Halifax Education Committee in December 1908, asking for their views as to the effects of half-time labour

Forwarded by Mr W. H. Ostler, Secretary of the Education Committee

1 Mentally	2 Physically	3 Manners and behaviour
Akroyd Place School (boys) Half-timers – 99		
Retards progress, often destroys desire and endeavour, very few if any can keep pace with day scholars; and if there are any they are most exceptional cases.	Statistics of height, weight, and chest measurements of boys taken first when about 12 years old, and again six months later, show that in comparison with the day scholars the half-timers gain slightly in height but lose considerably in weight and chest measurement.	Deterioration.
Akroyd Place School (girls) Half-timers – 100		
Power of perception is dulled, and they cannot keep up with the work of the class.	They lose energy and doze over their work in the afternoon, and exhibit other signs of physical fatigue.	They soon become coarser in speech and rude in behaviour.
Battinson Road School (mixed) Half-timers – 32 girls, 28 boys		
In 85 per cent of cases mental development ceases, and no progress at all in school work is made; as compared with children of the same age the inferiority is soon marked.	Deterioration, and moral sense becomes stunted.	

Boothtown School (boys) Half-timers – 34

Boys who have been sharp and intelligent generally lose their mental alertness and become dull and drowsy.

The boys who work in the mill become pale, and have a tired, listless appearance. They are not as brisk in their physical exercises, and cannot compete with day boys of the same age in their games.

The deterioration in manners and behaviour is very marked amongst the half-timers who work in the factory. They become impertinent, and often resent correction. This I attribute to working and mixing with youths much older than themselves.

Boothtown School (girls) Half-timers – 30

Deplorable. Perhaps if the half-timers came to school always in the morning the evil effects might be minimized, but girls who have to begin work at 6 a.m. are too weary in the afternoon to profit much by the teaching in school.

Physical deterioration not so marked as the mental.

Bad.

Bradshaw School (mixed) Half-timers – 9 girls, 5 boys

During the first three months they fall away very much and never seem to properly regain their mental vigour whilst in school for their last year.

Children often become very pale and sickly, and for a number of weeks seem to be weary and show a dislike for any mental work.

In this much depends on the moral fibre of the children; some are not appreciably affected, but others are lower generally. I have not come in contact with a case of improvement.

Copley School (mixed) Half-timers – 9 girls, 8 boys

The mental life suffers from a kind of stagnation or inertia, resulting in indifference and apathy towards school work generally.

A weary, drowsy appearance is manifest, and the general physique becomes pale and indicative of loss of vitality.

The aims and ideals of the children are frequently completely changed, and lack of respect and courtesy is prominent.

1 Mentally	2 Physically	3 Manners and behaviour

Haugh Shaw School (boys) Half-timers – 34

Bad; boys previously ahead of their fellows soon fall hopelessly behind.	Cannot say; have not had a long enough experience. There is at least no improvement in physique.	Very bad effect. This shows itself almost immediately the boy has begun half-time, especially with those who go to the mill.

Haugh Shaw School (girls) Half-timers – 26

As a rule girls who are half-time are much less sharp, and have not the same interest in their work; have instances of bright, ambitious and exceptionally gifted girls as day scholars just the reverse as half-timers.	More listless, sleepy and less able to exert themselves, particularly in the afternoon.	Require more management, are much rougher, and have not at all a good influence on the class.

Lee Mount School (boys) Half-timers – 30

The mental abilities for the first three or four months certainly go down, and to such an extent that many have to be lowered a class during the remainder of their stay at school; they seldom equal the normal day boy.	Little difference is perceptible, but the tired weary look on their faces in the afternoon, and their consequent indifference is very obvious; some of them are fitter for bed than school.	Considerably deteriorated. Many lads nice as day boys are scarcely recognizable as half-timers. Their behaviour is contagious and contaminates the whole class.

Lee Mount School (girls) Half-timers – 21

The child keeps practically at a standstill for some time. After working from 6 a.m. to 12.30 she is fit for no mental work at school in the afternoon.	I do not notice much deterioration. Children are often languid at afternoon session at school. Needless to say, no pressure is made to bear upon the children.	In few cases do I notice much deterioration. I think the home and school surroundings have much to do in creating a moral atmosphere.

Mixenden School (mixed) Half-timers – 9 girls, 9 boys

The immediate effect is to put a stop for some time to further progress at school, and to cause a considerable amount of previously acquired knowledge to be forgotten. A more permanent effect is to dull the child's faculties.

In every case there is a diminution of vigour and energy. The child, boy or girl, loses colour, becomes less alert, and shows, expecially in the afternoon, evidence of fatigue.

There is a loss of gentleness, and of attention to the little politenesses of school life. The girls particularly deteriorate in this direction, tending to coarseness and rowdyism. The worst feature is the loss of responsiveness shown when a day scholar, and the consequent difficulty the teacher experiences in securing a right outlook upon things.

Moorside School (mixed) Half-timers – 24 girls, 17 boys

Half-timers make poor progress in class; they are easily out-stripped by day scholars who previously were their class fellows. Most of them lose ambition to excel and become dull and indifferent. Many of them cease to borrow books from the school library.

In all games of strength and skill the half-timer, and especially the mill employee, is no match for the day scholar – comparatively few are to be found on the school football teams (Moorside team is composed of eight day scholars and three shop boys). Rarely do half-timers make progress in swimming; all our best swimmers, with one exception, have been day boys.

Half-employment affects manners and behaviour considerably. The half-timer has less pride in appearance. He often neglects to clean his boots, or comes without a collar. He introduces bad language in the playground. He not infrequently smokes; he gets more spending money than other boys. He has a harmful effect on the tone of the school. Some girls bear up against it well, but it is safe to say that all fall in some degree in moral tone and stamina.

Northowram School (mixed) half-timers – 12 girls, 10 boys

An immediate and continued loss of menial grip. In long experience of evening school work, I have known very few half-timers who have not dropped out of the race after the first two years.

Loss of healthy colour, sleepy, little desire for vigorous exertion, most marked in physical exercises and games.

Most serious change, loss of tone, moral nature blunted; where possible would have them taught apart from the rest because of demoralizing effect thereon.

1 Mentally	2 Physically	3 Manners and behaviour
Queen's Road School (boys) Half-timers – 33		
A marked depreciation in alertness; the faculties become sluggish, especially in the afternoon. Fatigue and want of sleep are potent factors to contend with in our efforts to teach these boys.	The effect is not very appreciable, except in the deportment.	Generally the boys become sullen and disrespectful. There is an air of assumed superiority over the other boys, with a marked deterioration in morals and behaviour. The teacher's influence is almost nullified, and it is painfully apparent the boys have breathed a contaminated moral atmosphere.
Queen's Road School (girls) Half-timers – 30		
Detrimental in the majority of cases, as the girls are not as bright and active as they ought to be for the reception of knowledge; especially is this the case when the child attends school in the afternoon.	Judging from observation, with the exception of very few cases, girls are not affected physically.	Demoralizing as a rule. Their behaviour tends materially to lower the tone of a class.
Salterhebble school		
Half-time employment always has a deteriorating effect. It is difficult to secure continued mental effort from the children.	The children often show intense weariness in afternoon school, no doubt an evidence of overstrained physical powers. The less strong children become pallid after a short experience of factory life.	Here the deterioration is most marked. Rough behaviour and vulgar manners often result.

Salterlee School (mixed) Half-timers – 8 girls, 5 boys

Dulls their mental faculties invariably.	In almost every case great deterioration is noted after a few weeks' experience at the mill. This acts very prejudicially upon the school and lowers the tone.

Siddal School (mixed) Half-timers – 35 girls, 36 boys

A few weeks at the mills show a marked change in their mental powers. They undoubtedly deteriorate. Only a few recover perfectly.	Without any exception in manners, speech and behaviour the children are worse after becoming half-timers.

Sunnyside School (mixed) Half-timers – 32 girls, 22 boys

The bright child becomes mediocre, the average child dull, the dull child hopeless.	Deterioration in both respects very marked.
	Bodily development retarded. Evidence of insufficient sleep.

Wainstalls School (mixed) Half-timers – 10 girls, 11 boys

They begin to fall behind in their lessons at once. As a rule their interest slackens, and they show less intelligence. This may be due in part to ours being a small school. We cannot afford to make a half-time class, consequently they miss the continuity of the lessons.	So far as I am able to judge, I don't think the half-timer deteriorates much physically, though pale faces are more frequent among them. On the other hand, I cannot see any improvement.
	I regard this as the weakest point in the half-time system. The half-timer is much more difficult to deal with. He introduces morals which are unfit for a school. I am of opinion that the tone of this school would be considerably improved by the withdrawal of all half-timers.

1 Mentally	2 Physically	3 Manners and behaviour
Warley Road School (boys) Half-timers – 37		
The minds of the boys are so absorbed in new occupations and surroundings that the mind is not free to devote itself to school work. No progress is made at school for at least six months.	The boy's physical energies are so exhausted as to leave them unfit for school work.	By far the most serious is the effect produced on the morals. The half-timer becomes addicted to the use of coarse and indecent language as the result of mixing with adults who exercise no discretion in the presence of young boys.
Warley Road School (girls) Half-timers – 41		
Interest in school work dies when once the scholar goes half-time; consequently no further progress is made.	Girls are tired out at 2 p.m., having been working since 5.30 a.m. It must tell on the physique for the hours of sleep are considerably shortened.	The girls change for the worse in very short time. They assume a grown-up air and imitate their elders in the mill, their ideal being the overlooker. Sullenness, impertinence, slovenliness in dress and neglect of cleanliness of body are among the defects soon noticeable.
Warley Town School (mixed) Half-timers – 3 girls, 8 boys		
All are not affected alike. Some retain their interest in everything, others lose it as soon as they become wage earners.	Unfit for any severe effort, especially in the afternoon when morning has been spent in mills.	Do not improve.
Christ Church School (mixed) Half-timers – 12 girls, 10 boys		
Loss in alertness, less relish for mental work. Interest in school work suffers.	Effect is to make children languid and drowsy.	Bad; the effect is to coarsen. In the interest of the children I am strongly in favour of the abolition of half-time employment.

Parish Church School (mixed) Half-timers – 24 girls, 26 boys

This mainly depends upon the 'turn' in which the children attend school. Those half-timers who attend in the morning are equal to the day scholars in mental ability, but there is a falling off in those children who have spent the morning in the mill.

It is a striking fact, but children who have been irregular in consequence of general weakness, become so strong as soon as they reach the age of twelve, they are able to pass the doctor for half-time employment. Now that children do not commence working before reaching the age of twelve, one cannot see any difference between the day and half-time scholars. Some afternoons I find the half-timer very sleepy, but not so bad as those children who habitually go to bed at a late hour.

I am glad to say there is no falling off in this respect. Some years ago I heard of certain bad practices in connection with certain mills in which my scholars were employed, but I am glad to say that I had no further cause for complaint since the attention of the employers was drawn to the matter.

St Augustine's School (boys) Half-timers – 16

It causes them to become less alert, and to lose much of their former power of concentration. They therefore fall rapidly behind in their lessons.

Compared with day scholars, half-timers become weaker as a rule, and in the football team are often displaced by much younger boys. In some cases I have noticed an actual falling off in health and physique.

They rapidly deteriorate. The cases of bad language and moral offences I have had to deal with have been directly the result of half-time.

St Augustine's School (girls) Half-timers – 34

Affected by the kind of employment and the hour at which they commence their day's work.

Not affected so much now as when children began to work at a much earlier age.

Depends very much on the kind of employment and home influence.

St Mary's RC School (mixed) Half-timers – 25 girls, 31 boys

Have noticed want of mental vigour in most half-timers.

Have not noticed ill-effects except where overlookers are inclined to drive child workers.

Girls frequently become coarser in feelings and conduct.

1 Mentally	2 Physically	3 Manners and behaviour
Warley St John's School (mixed) Half-timers – 5 girls, 4 boys		
Varies. While some seem to get on quite as well as before they began to work, others fall back, and others again seem to change altogether, and are almost at a standstill.	Apparently very little effect.	Decided change for the worse.

34 H. Caldwell Cook

from *The Play Way: An Essay in Educational Method*, 1917, pp. 2-5.

Experiments in education were also under way. One of the most
influential was the work of H. Caldwell Cook, whose book, The Play Way,
became a source book for the philosophy of progressive education.

Why should there stretch such an abyss between the nursery and the class-room? Ah, yes, they tell us, but life is not going to be all a game. They must learn the *serious* side of things. By the life of the world! What could be more serious than child's play? I know of nothing so whole-hearted, so thorough, so natural, so free from stain, so earnest, as the spontaneous playing of a child. Take a child in the nursery and consider him beside these grave adults at their concerns. Compare a game of toy soldiers with the conduct of a campaign. The difference is in degree and not in kind. Consider whether the little maid in the day nursery is less engrossed in the care of her doll than the other maid in the night nursery is in the care of her baby. Do you play more fair at politics than we do at ninepins? And has any man as much care for the rules of the game in commerce, and as much respect for his oppon-ents, as he has in cricket? In the one it is a question of what he can make, in the other all is subject to fair play. I tell you that sincere endeavour and honesty of purpose can only be relied on under conditions that favour their continuance! Whether he be paid well or not, so long as a man's heart is in his work it is well with him and well for the work. Beyond that we cannot go. The force of extraneous need, or compulsion of any kind, however necessary it be, blunts honesty, dulls the zeal of whole-hearted endeavour; and if it come in much strength will spoil all. The child is the true amateur, he does a thing for the love of it. Among all workers he is the player, and alone is fit to stand beside the genuine artist, the self-sacrificing physician, and the inspired poet or seer. His hearty interest is a powerful engine which will carry a heavy load eventually to its appointed destination. What though you claim to know where that may be, and to know also of a shorter route? Is it not better to follow the engine that pulls the train, rather than drag it back, even though its route be roundabout? It may be that the way will prove more level and the countryside more beautiful. A child following his natural bent will play. His whole power is in play. Beware of trying to make rivers run up hills instead of flowing round them.

　To me it seems obvious where the trouble lies: the teacher works, whether consciously or unconsciously, on his own lines, and not in and for his children. The teacher may have a beautiful system, a course of work schemed, graded and ordered in admirable shape, and thoroughly approved by his or her chief, and by His Majesty's Inspector to boot. But what if the child's mind does not work orderly ? – which happens to be the case. What will His Majesty do then, poor thing ? What if a growing mind scorns systematic progress (which also is true), and leaps back and forth over the field of study, now shining with the brilliance of a light full focused, now showing as black as the back of a lighthouse lantern ? Let us have outline schemes by all means, but leave the details to the hour in which it shall be told us what we shall do. Let us remember that without interest there is no learning, and since the child's interest is all in play it is necessary, whatever the matter in hand, that the method be a play method. Otherwise there will be no guests at the table, and the feast will lie stale in our hands.

Much of what I have to say is obvious, but that is unavoidable, for the most well-accepted principles are generally ignored in practice. The conduct of most people is founded on the principles they most condemn.

I have said that when you consider a child you will find, as Stevenson says, that 'he intent, is all on his play-business bent': and, therefore, whatever you want a child to do heartily must be contrived and conducted as play. It may seem a strange thing to suggest that the boys and girls of the upper school should have as much play as the infants in the kindergarten, but this is what I do propose. Boys and girls nowadays have their play gradually thinned out until little is left to them as adults but a round of golf or a game of cards. When work and play are separated, the one becomes mere drudgery, the other mere pastime. Neither is then of any value in life. It is the core of my faith that the only work worth doing is really play; for by play I mean the doing anything with one's heart in it.

The Play Way is a means, but I cannot say what the end may be, except more play. In like manner the whole purpose of life for me, being no philosopher, is simply living. What I have now to say sounds very puerile, but I have no doubt the same could be found subtly said in many learned books. We must let ourselves live fully, by doing thoroughly those things we have a natural desire to do; the sole restrictions being that we so order the course of our life as not to impair those energies by which we live, nor hinder other men so long as they also seem to be living well. Right and wrong in the play of life are not different from the right and wrong of the playing-field. We must obey the clear rules; and what is more, have a sense of fair play, and, in chief, play with all our hearts in the game.

Is this foundation of the Play Way so simple as to need no statement ? Look in our nurseries, look in our schools, look in our fields, factories and workshops. Which of us has the chance to do thoroughly that which he has the desire to do ? But the right of every man to live a human life is daily becoming something more than a sentimental platitude. And when, long hence, every man shall find work to his hand that is noble to do, and leisure also to rest from his labours, there will be few found subtle enough to say where the work ends and the leisure begins. Work that is done with joy at heart, and leisure that is not wasted, merge into one as Play.

But my especial concern is with the schools. Can anyone say that life in school is so ordered as not to impair those energies by which the children live? If the children were moved by natural desire to do as we now make them do in school, then there would be no need of this same compulsion. Of the children's view of the work we give them is it not still true to say, 'Love goes toward love as schoolboys from their books'? And as for their view of the play we plan, who has not heard of that crowning indignity, compulsory games? 'Some boys, are by nature slack,' says the public-school man, 'and have to be brought up to scratch.' 'By nature they are the children of evil,' said the teacher of old time, 'conceived in wickedness and born in sin.' 'Many of us are born blind,' say I. 'Let us have the Play Way.'

35 Homer Lane
Paper read to the Little Commonwealth Committee after the Rawlinson Inquiry, 22 June 1918, pp. 253–67.

One of the most remarkable educational experiments of the time was conducted privately at a co-educational community in Dorset called The Little Commonwealth, under the inspired leadership of an American, Homer Lane. Lane dealt with delinquent adolescents, and sought to apply the principles of Freudian analysis to their problems. With the encouragement of the Home Office, he created a community in which the laws were made by the youngsters themselves, but in 1918, he was accused of misconduct (a charge of which an official inquiry fully cleared him) but which spelled the end of the experiment.

The distressing situation, in which you and all the others who have supported the Little Commonwealth during the past five years now find themselves, can only be tolerated by a conviction of the sincerity of those to whom you have entrusted your work, and a knowledge that the circumstances that have brought about the subject matter of this meeting are the result of errors, frankly admitted, rather than carelessness or lack of interest on behalf of the children under your care.

I beg of you, if it is possible under the circumstances, to place yourselves now in the position of the physician rather than that of the coroner; to conduct a diagnosis of the patient's ailments rather than a post-mortem examination of his remains.

I wish, at the very outset, to admit that the present position of this committee is due to a serious professional error on my part; an error which I will be grateful to you for examining in its proper relation to the content of your diagnosis.

The task which I will undertake is an exceedingly difficult one. The psychological principles upon which the Commonwealth has been built are comparatively new to the educational world. They involve the psychology not only of delinquent boys and girls but of insane persons and normal people as well. Any examination, then, of the psychological theories of the Commonwealth, if thorough enough to be convincing, must touch upon those feelings and instincts which are the base and foundation of morality and ethics and of social and spiritual consciousness as well; instincts and feelings which are common to every human being whether criminal, insane, normal or brilliantly successful in life. Could it be possible for you to explore this new area in psychological research as a detached intellect, with only reason and logic operative in reaching your conclusion, my task and yours would be infinitely easier. But your own deepest feelings and prejudices will probably intrude upon those conclusions both for and against, as the case may be, your arrival at a complete and detailed understanding of my error and of your responsibility for the future of your school.

I make this statement with conviction because of my own experience of violent opposition, years ago, to the acceptance of the identical theory that I now present to you: a theory that, because of the painful incidents that have led up to the necessity for this meeting, ceases, so far as I am concerned, to be a theory and becomes a science, the truth of which is within my own experience both as a badly educated individual and as a teacher.

Less than thirty years ago the pioneer in the science that is now being employed widely and successfully for the relief of insanity commenced a most profound and brilliant research into the content and processes of the instincts of mankind. He called that portion of the mind that lies beyond the threshold of consciousness the Unconscious Mind. This hitherto unexplored region is the laboratory of those instincts and feelings, physical, sensual, social and spiritual, out of which are developed the senses and perceptions which when conjoined with experience, produces consciousness of the Conscious Mind.

He conceived the theory that the Conscious Mind was, in all persons to a greater or less extent, victimized and thwarted in its efforts to regulate and control conduct by a mysterious and unknown function somewhere in the Unconscious that misdirected the life-forces into channels of effort and desire that might result in anything from unhappiness or failure in life-purposes to actual disaster according to the degree of the perversion of the affected instinct. Upon the adoption of this theory, and for the purpose of establishing a science and its technique, he conducted a new and most profound exploration into the instincts of man. His research brought him into contact with those fundamental and primitive feelings and desires that, with all life in every form, are common to every human being. He constructed a theory upon which he based his science and its technique.

This theory, being a theory only, one may adopt or modify as one perceives the truth in his own consciousness without affecting the technique of the science he has discovered.

Professor Freud's theory was that the fundamental instinct upon which other feelings and instincts in the Unconscious are based is the instinct and craving to create. When the deductions from this theory are applied to the most primitive in man for the purposes of research he states as his premise, in the fearless and direct manner of the true scientist, but in terms that immediately prejudiced even his own colleagues against his theory, that the fundamental instinct – the base of all instincts – is sexual. This premise and the associations of the term by which he designates it operates to this day as a deterrent of tremendous force to an investigation of the science he has created, particularly on the part of those who have the greatest need of such knowledge, viz: parents and teachers.

Professor Freud conducted his research in the interests of those persons who came under his care as a physician specializing in the treatment of mental diseases. The relief he and his students and followers have afforded to unfortunate humanity suffering from various forms of insanity is incalculable. Some of the almost instantaneous cures his science has affected seem almost miraculous. Indeed, it is the science and its techniques developed by Freud that is applied in the treatment of that most pitiable of all the misfortunes of the soldier known as shell-shock with such remarkable results. Still however the deep-rooted and harsh prejudice against the Freudian theory persists.

Now I have had the presumption to undertake to employ Freud's technique for the purposes of education, by a reverse process. He unravels the tangles in an unhappy and fruitless life, making the insane sane. I have tried to use his technique in education, in the building up of lives of joy and usefulness. He corrects insanity, I am trying to create sanity. He found that the great majority of his patients developed the symptoms of their several mental diseases during adolescence. It is obvious that in the treatment of my pupils I should find many evidences of mental abnormality, more or less developed, since I am dealing with persons well advanced in adolescence and who at the same time are delinquents. I must therefore use the Freudian technique in psychology in helping nearly every one of my pupils, in both directions, viz: to remove already formed obsessions and phobias from their paths, and then in a reverse process, re-educating and re-building.

So far as I am aware, no other teacher has attempted to employ the Freudian methods systematically in any school. I have not had the benefit of any other teacher's experience in a parallel effort. A recently published book by Oskar Pfister of Zurich, a pastor, is the first instance that has come to my notice of any other attempt to employ psychoanalysis for the improvement of normal people. Even Pfister has apparently not used the new psychology as an aid in academic education of the development of the social instincts that underlie these qualities that make for good citizenship.

If, then, I may assume that I am a pioneer in psychoanalytic education, may I not also assume the privilege of stating the premise upon which the technique of psychoanalysis rests for the purpose of practical application to education.

The Freudian premise starts with creation hunger or, in his own terms, sexual hunger, and proceeds in a straight line through various forms of desire and craving to high ethical and moral ideals as the ultimate goal of life.

I presume to re-state the premise in a form that more nearly realizes the truth as I have experienced it in practice as well as in theory, in the form of a cycle, viz: the fundamental instinct of all mankind, the basis of all instincts and feelings, the deepest point in the Unconscious, the starting-point of all motives is a titanic craving for spiritual perfection. Proceeding in the form of a cycle, this exalted craving passes, undiminished, through the various phases of evolution toward perfection in the order determined by nature's laws, from the primary compulsion to (1) create life, (2) maintain life, (3) protect life, (4) perfect life, proceeding until it reaches the completion of the cycle and arrives at (5) spiritual realization. The dynamic origin of the progression is derived from the instinctive spiritual impulses deep in the unconscious mind.

This cycle of the instincts may be crudely represented graphically as follows (see facing page).

The first point in the cycle, craving to create life or sexual hunger, is entirely submerged in the depths of the Unconscious in the individual until long after the other points, 2, 3 and 4 emerge into the conscious mind. The order of the emergence of the instincts into consciousness, then are as follows: first (2) craving to maintain life as seen in the conscious knowledge of the desire for nourishment; second, (3) craving for protection as seen in the conscious avoidance of danger; third (4) craving for perfection as seen

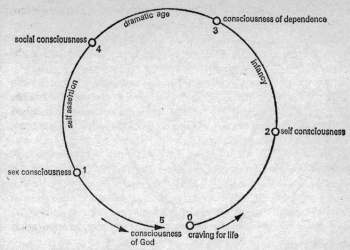

Figure 1 Cycle of instincts

in the desire for social relationships other than the instinctive one for the parent: fourth (1) craving to create life or sex consciousness; fifth, the completion of the cycle, unifying all the mental life in spiritual realization.

This cycle of consciousness may now be represented:

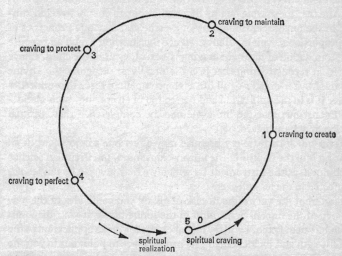

Figure 2 Complete mental cycle

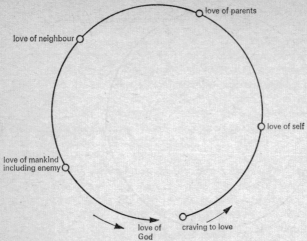

Figure 3 Love cycle

A third cycle, corresponding to the development of the mental life, representing the sublimation of craving, and called the love cycle may be constructed, see above.

However, in accordance with the law of nature that life must be created before it can be perfected, and because nature has made the whole of the life-cycle instinctive, the craving to create is, so far as the instincts are concerned, the first inexorable fact of life, and although instinctive and submerged in the unconscious mind has, nevertheless, dynamic properties of titanic proportions, even in infancy. Hence the startling Freudian premise that the foundation of desire or craving is sexual, even in the child. I have presumed in reconstructing that premise merely to recognize the Divine Will of the Master-creator of all life as the compelling force that underlies all desire. It is in the unification and perfection of all craving, both instinctive and conscious that the life-cycle may be completed – that spiritual realization may be achieved.

However much or little my premise may affect one's enjoyment of an exploration into the depths of the unconscious mind, the Freudian science and technique, as the instrument by which we may analyse its tendencies is not affected in the least degree.

I will attempt the very difficult task of giving you some idea of the new psychology of the unconscious mind in the limited time at your disposal; but it can be but a sketch. I will try to make clear to you its application to the Commonwealth and incidentally in its proper place to point out to you the serious professional mistake which I made as teacher, and which has caused the present painful position in which you as a committee are placed in your relations with the Home Office.

There are two kinds of mental life, both of which are active. One is conscious, the other unconscious. Therefore there are two kinds of thinking, one directed, the other undirected. The conscious mind is, in proportion to the unconscious mind, only about one-eighth as large in content. Therefore we do but one-eighth of our thinking with our conscious minds. The other seven-eighths of our thinking is undirected by our wills.

In other words, let the play as seen from the stalls in front of the stage represent the conscious mind, the whole of the mechanisms, rehearsals, properties, management, etc., etc., that precede the production of the play represent the unconscious mind. (That portion of our lives represented by the play, as seen from in front of the stage, is within the control of our wills: the much larger portion as represented by all that is behind the scenes. . . .) We create the motives and affects of our lives, wilfully, only on the stage of our conscious minds. Behind the scenes, in the instinctive, the plot and structure and management of our lives lie deep in the unconscious.

The content of our unconscious minds, being instinctive consists in craving or desire. This craving, being unaffected by our conscious moral or social concepts is unmoral – not immoral but unmoral. Freud designates this craving by the term 'libido'. This word in its derivation means lustful desire, and in its application to the titanic craving of the Unconscious as perceived in the Freudian premise is acceptable. But as I perceive the cravings of the Unconscious, although unmoral, they are by no means lustful as the term is commonly employed. However, inacceptable as the word may be as applied to the premise that I have constructed I feel compelled to use it as better representing the cravings of the Unconscious than any word I can invent.

The libido or instinctive life-craving is a positive dynamic force or love always seeking to attach itself to some object or purpose or person within the scope of the sense comprehension of its owner. Its most peculiar characteristic is its continual effort to gratify the conscious mind of its owner, irrespective of the moral and ethical code that exists within the consciousness. It supplies unmoral motives for conduct to the Conscious in whatever degree of disguise the Consciousness may demand for admission within its moral code. It need adopt no disguise for its desires when those desires are not in conflict with the ethical or moral code of the Conscious. Craving for food and bodily comforts are direct and undisguised; but desires for sensual gratifications that are in opposition to the ethical or moral standards inculcated in the Conscious by teaching or social conventions are disguised so as to pass these barriers with all the subtlety and skill of the

practised liar and dissimulator. It accounts for experiences in sensual gratifications that are in conflict with the codes of the Conscious in terms that
disarm criticism. Its impelling, insistent, never-ceasing voice is continually
urging the Conscious to remove all moral barriers to the gratification of its
cravings. It is plausible, compelling, never-tiring. It conceals a consciousness of guilt behind a camouflage of suspicion of guilt in others. It dis-
guises a sense of inferiority behind swagger and boasting and vain display.
It produces hypochondria as a cover for indolence and self-love. It conceals
unsatisfied ambition beneath a disguise of chronic bodily illness. It cloaks
the lack of definite purpose in life in a garment of restlessness and pursuit of
vain pleasures. In a thousand ways it impedes the conscious will in its striving for social and vocational success.

The libido has also a more positive and malignant faculty. When it
presents to the conscious mind some wish that is wholly inacceptable to the
moral consciousness and is sharply rebuked and repressed back into the
depths of its lair, it effects a complete forgetfulness in the conscious mind
of the inacceptable wish in its original form, but the energy emerges at
another point, in complete disguise as a mania or phobia or perhaps in
some of the innumerable kinds of hysterical obsessions. In its repertoire of
abilities is another very obliging quality. There are many authentic cases of
actual suspension of faculties as the result of a wish to avoid experience
that is painful to the Consciousness, such as deafness to avoid hearing a
scolding, nagging parent or teacher.

Incredible as it may seem to the layman, the evidence is indisputable
that every human being is to a greater or less extent victimized and thwarted
in the pursuit of his life-purposes by the libido in his unconscious mind.

But thanks to the brilliant and profound research of Professor Freud and
his colleagues, there is now a definite technique, widely practised by means
of which the content of the unconscious mind may be analysed, the libido
brought out into the open, and its tremendous forces directed toward the
service of the life-purposes of the individual and the welfare of society.

This technique as employed in the diagnosis and treatment of mental
abnormalities has been developed by means of a study of the innumerable
forms of undirected thinking to be seen in every person. Forgetfulness,
absent-mindedness, peculiarities of memory, speech impediments, hesitation for words, mispronunciation of words, faltering, misspelling,
eccentricities in dress, habits, peculiarities of gait, tastes in food, etc., etc.,
are all the manifestations of some particular and definite peculiarity of the
libido. Preferences in art, music, poetry have their origin in the feelings in
the Unconscious. Every act and gesture, however unconscious or spasmodic
it may be has a definite significance in the content of the unconscious

mind, and may be utilized in analysis as an indication of some peculiarity of the tendencies of the libido.

The most direct and intelligible expression of the desires of the libido, however, is to be found in dreams. That dreams have any meaning in the life of a person is not a new idea but one that many people will not accept at first hearing of such a fantastic assertion. Professor Freud, however, has developed a theory of dreams and a technique for interpreting their meaning that forms the basis of psychoanalysis. In the content of every dream there is an expression of some unfulfilled wish or desire of the unconscious mind. The wish must pass a censor in its emergence to the Consciousness and clothe itself in a form that will be acceptable to the moral or ethical faculty of the Consciousness. The disguise of the wish may be penetrated by means of the technique of dream analysis and the particular desire exposed. By this means the wish of the libido is discovered.

Freud does not recognize in his theory of dream analysis the presence of a spiritual wish in the Unconscious in symbolic form. But I am convinced that I have found in many dreams unmistakable evidence of spiritual conflicts as well as moral conflicts. These spiritual conflicts are usually clothed in symbols that in analysis associate definitely with the dogmas and forms of religious instruction. They are very closely allied with moral conflicts. This opens up a field for educational and psychological research much too vast for consideration here, but of greatest importance to teachers of religion. By analysis of dreams and associations proceeding from them, these sharply repressed and forgotten wishes of the libido which cause the complexes that produce insanity and hysteria, may be recalled to the conscious memory, the complex dissolved and a cure effected. Psychoanalysis is also employed with astonishing success in the treatment of hysterical forms of physical ailments and in the relief of persons addicted to immoral habits, by a constructive process called 'sublimation'.

The psychoanalyst, physician or teacher must exercise two distinct but related functions. First, he must diagnose his patients' difficulties. He, with the cooperation of his patient, explores the unconscious mind, analyses the tendencies of the libido, dissolves complexes or repressed wishes that are inacceptable to consciousness by re-awakening memory, discovers the particular manner in which each complex affects conduct and conscious effort, and educates the patient as to the thousand and one inclinations of his libido. This process is merely the diagnosis.

The second function or treatment consists in a process of redirecting the libido, now freed from unwholesome or futile pursuits, into channels of activity that will serve the life-purposes of the conscious mind. This function is called sublimation. As the word implies, the process is simply the elevation of the interests of the Unconscious to the higher emotions and efforts that will serve the purposes of realization of the ethical and moral ideals of the conscious mind.

The sublimation process is education, pure and simple. Every teacher, even those who have never heard of psychoanalysis, is attempting the sublimation of his pupil's libido. But the chief characteristic of the libido being, as it is, a tendency to attach its cravings to an instinctive and unmoral interest in the life-cycle, the non-analytic teacher, being unaware of the already existing attachments of the libido is, by his method, producing a titanic unconscious conflict in his pupil. This conflict between the moral conscious motive and the unconscious, instinctive cravings of the libido is the source of nine-tenths of the unhappiness and inefficiency in the world. If you at this moment recall incidents of forgetfulness in your own experience you will notice that you only forget those things in which there is an element of conscious distaste. If you suffer from procrastination you will find by self-analysis that you only put off doing those things that you consciously dislike doing. If a pupil dislikes history he is never good at that subject, and there is a definite organ for his dislike in the Unconscious. His failure is due to unconscious conflict. Every unconscious conflict in all persons – and no person is without them – has pathological effects. Whatever degree of inefficiency we, each of us, recognize in ourselves is due to unconscious conflict. The libido needs to be detached from some instinctive anti-social activity and re-directed toward the conscious life-purpose.

Does your boy hate arithmetic? He can be made to love it by analytic pedagogy. Is he rude and ungracious? It is conflict easily removable. Is he purposely annoying? He is suffering from an inferiority complex. His libido can be detached from its unwholesome goal. Does he bite his nails? Fidget in his chair? Has he an obsession for drumming with his fingers? Sucking the end of his pen? Teasing his brother or sister? Whistling? Throwing stones? Does he have a morbid interest in ghostly sights? Is he afraid of ghosts, burglars or goblins? All these things and thousands of others are inevitably the manifestations of unconscious conflicts raging within him and as such can be dealt with certainly and scientifically by analysis.

That period of life called by Ferrier 'the criminal age', by schoolmasters 'the storm period', by policemen a less polite but more expressive term – the period between the ages of eleven and eighteen is full of unconscious conflict. The libido is struggling against moral and social consciousness. The intensity of the struggle is determined by the degree of moral resistance that must be overcome by the libido in its craving for gratification.

If the moral consciousness is weak and artificial – not based upon experienced truths – conscious and but slightly resisted sexual perversion, purposeful lying, etc., etc., ensue.

If the social consciousness is founded upon an artificial base, such as the constant suppression of activity by the parent or teacher furnishes, obsessional thieving, hatred of parents or teachers, cruelty in its various forms, etc., etc., are the characteristics of conduct. The conflict is not intense – the libido speaks with a direct and but slightly disguised voice.

If on the other hand the moral consciousness is strong and the libido not already attached to other wholesome and love stimulating activities, the conflict between the instinctive craving and the conscious moral will is intense. The libido must disguise its effect in the conscious mind. The result is hypocrisy, fixation of libido upon the parent or obsessional love with hysterical symptoms, penuriousness, snobbery, priggishness, over-fastidiousness, sentimentality, competitiveness, etc., etc.

Masochism or self-torment and sadism or obsessional cruelty to others is a not unusual form in which the libido escapes detection and eludes the vigilance of a strong conscious sex-morality. Self-destruction and murderous tendencies are developments of masochism and sadism and are invariably the results of the unconscious conflicts that rage within us all through life, but most intensely during puberty and adolescence. These and other fruitful sources of life-long misery may be removed from the paths of our boys and girls by the introduction into our schemes of education of a scientific psychological basis for the moral and ethical structure we wish to erect.

The unhappy circumstances that brought about the necessity for this meeting today are the result of unconscious conflicts and sex perversities of citizens of the Commonwealth. One of my accusers is a pronounced sadist who has an obsessional fondness for Charlie Chaplin and his brutal comedy; the other is a masochist. These two mental diseases are more prevalent in the Commonwealth than in any other community which I have known. It is not difficult to account for this in the light of psychoanalytic knowledge as follows:

The conscious moral principles instilled deeply into the minds of the citizens of the Commonwealth by our form of self-government is so intense and so surely based upon logic and reason and experience that the libido which is definitely directed towards erotic or love objects, by the co-educational features of our school, must assume the deepest disguise in its power in order to evade the censor and affect the consciousness of the individual. Hence the prevalence of masochism or self-accusation in the Commonwealth.

These unfortunate incidents, in spite of the painful position in which we are all placed have the effect, in my own mind, of reaffirming my confidence in self-government, co-education and 'Commonwealth' principles in education.

Let me explain this paradox. It is at this point that I wish you to examine the error on my part that is responsible for the incidents that have given you so much anxiety during the past six months.

I must, if you are to understand the significance of my error, begin by explaining more fully one or two points in the technique of psychoanalysis.

No person can be successfully analysed against his will. 'Resistance' a technical term, invariably blocks the psychological processes. Not only must the patient accept analysis, but he must feel a positive desire for it. A negative or passive attitude does not yield successful results. The psychological attitude of the patient toward the analyst is called 'transference'. The process is as follows: In every person at all times there is a portion of unemployed or unattached libido. This is always directed toward some person or object or purpose in either a positive or a negative form. In the language of everyday life, we always unconsciously, perhaps, have some degree of love or hate for every person we meet, stranger or acquaintance. We 'transfer' to everyone who comes within the range of our senses. The psychoanalyst must first secure the 'transference' of his pupils libido or interest to himself. This transferred libido is invariably erotic or love-hungry irrespective of the sex of the analyst. This produces liking for, confidence in and trust of the analyst.

In other words the analyst accepts for the moment the affection and esteem of life-desire of his patient for purposes of diagnosis, and then, having dissolved complexes, re-awakened painful forgotten wishes in the memory, sends the libido or life desire on into vocational, professional, social, academic channels as the life interest of his patient may dictate.

'Resistance' disappears in proportion as 'transference' is effected. The libido of the patient is, at the will of the analyst, 'sublimated' into channels of happiness and content and success in life.

The identical psychological process takes place as between every boy and girl and the teacher, pastor, governess, or any person of either sex who is in a position of authority over him in either a positive or a negative sense.

The employment of a technical term to scientifically represent the normal relation between parent and child, teacher and pupil, physician and patient, pastor and parishioner, employer and employee – the use of the word 'transference' instead of the word we use in our everyday thoughts – love, confidence, respect, trust, loyalty, puts many unthoughtful people off. It associates, wrongfully, with hypnotism or some form of surrender of will to another. The psychological relationship between analyst and patient is the extreme opposite of hypnotism.

The patient transfers to his analyst, temporarily, as being for the moment the nearest person he can love, only that which belongs to the parent or the pupil's vocation, as the case may be according to his age and degree of independence.

The non-analytic teacher must depend upon chance or accident to dissolve the transference. His pupil is the victim of circumstances in so far as libido will attach itself to some interest or other, irrespective of morals or success in life. For the libido is unmoral until brought under the control of the consciousness.

The analytic teacher positively indicates the object or pursuit to the re-transferred libido. If the teacher refuses to accept the transference (love) of his pupil's libido, it may take a negative form and become hate. The transference is, however, inevitable.

I must make this point clear, even at the risk of boring you, for it is the critical point in analytic education, and the point at which my disastrous error occurred.

Those of you who have observed Montessori classes at work will have noticed that different teachers obtain different results in applying the same system. One teacher's class loves certain tasks and neglects others. Another teacher secures excellent results in the tasks that the pupils of the other teacher fail in, etc. An analysis of the teachers would explain the mystery in terms of transference. The teacher, herself, has interest in the things her pupils are successful in, and lacks interest in the activities which her pupils do poorly. The analysed teacher would then discover the cause of her pupil's failure, and by having knowledge in herself of her own unconscious dislike of those activities, would be able to dissolve that dislike and secure the transference of the child's libido to the hitherto disliked work.

I say the teacher would be able to dissolve her unconscious dislike for certain activities. Let me affirm this scientifically, as follows: Every teacher 'transfers' parental love to his or her pupil. The teacher's libido is (or should be) attached to the pupil, but not necessarily to the task the pupil is performing. Therefore, having secured conscious knowledge, through analysis, of her unconscious dislike of the distasteful work, it disappears at once because she sees the reflection of that dislike in her pupil.

I cite this as showing that re-transference of the pupil's libido is not accomplished, as in hypnotism, by word of mouth but by real, genuine libido-hunger of the teacher himself. If this is true, and I sincerely believe it to be so, every parent should have an analytic diagram of the unconscious of the teacher to whom he entrusts his child. The teacher who is coldly critical toward his pupil – does not love him, can never 'sublimate' that pupil's interests.

I would go a step farther still. The teacher who does not love the subjects he is teaching will find his lack of love reflected in his pupil's lack of accomplishment. Any 'analysed' teacher may 'sublimate' to love any subject that he thinks will benefit his 'first love', his pupil. Ergo: no one should teach who has not been himself analysed and through the process gained that true psychological insight which produces the 'Art of Teaching'.

Now I may confess my error and ask your forgiveness on a sound basis with all the elements exposed to view.

When, five years ago, I undertook the task of organizing the Commonwealth I was familiar to some extent with the theories and technique of psychoanalysis. I have always, up to a few weeks ago, felt a strong distaste for the responsibilities involved in making known to my pupils' conscious minds the fact of the transference of their libido to me as the 'nearest parent'. I knew that this transference was inevitable but I shrank from the responsibilities entailed by their consciousness of it. I devised a method of avoiding that responsibility that, until a few weeks ago, I sincerely believed in. The method was this: by allowing my pupils to create a community of their own, frame their own laws, administer their own courts, they being independent of their own parents' assistance through the wages scheme of the Commonwealth, I sought to secure transference from their own parents direct to their community without any intermediary in myself. (This seemed reasonable. The soldier transfers from his wife and children to his country.) I felt that by making myself a member of the community on equal terms with themselves, that whatever transference was made to me, personally, would be in their conscious minds an added love for their community. I felt that self-analysis by means of group criticism of each other as in the courts would become automatic. I hoped that the absence of adult and dogmatic moral authority would result in a minimizing of unconscious conflicts in the individual, and that the libido of each citizen would become firmly attached to the vocational, social and spiritual interests of the Commonwealth. I hoped and confidently expected that the Commonwealth would become the criterion of other schools as the result of its scientific use of all the powers of the mind. I confidently expected that the experiment would develop a scheme by which other schools might be similarly organized even though the heads were not psychologists. The technique of psychoanalysis is so difficult of mastery, the study of psychology occupies so much time and concentration, that I felt the great need of devising some method of bringing about mind-analysis automatically.

The events of the past six months have convinced me of the futility of trying to cut psychological corners in educational schemes. I now gladly abandon my beautiful scheme after five years' faithful adherence to it. Mr Rawlinson has completely dissolved my complex. I now see clearly that the adolescent must still have a parent-substitute to accept his libido temporarily for purposes of dissolving complexes and conflicts, before that libido can be transferred to the community in which he lives. The progress of the exalted craving that eventually brings about the completion of the life-cycle cannot be hurried. The adolescent is still a child.

This is the point at which my error occurred – the error that will account, reasonably, for a great many of the disappointments we have had in the citizens who have failed to achieve the standard of usefulness and character we had set for them.

I have been accused by my friends of 'genius' for dealing with children. It may now be seen, in the light of the psychological principles I have so imperfectly explained to you, that my relationship with my charges is logical, reasonable and scientific. Underlying the logic and reason and science is a libido that is firmly attached to the higher interests and happiness of all the citizens of the Commonwealth.

I and you and our boys and girls have suffered, in different degrees of suffering, because of my error but I hope that that error will not include, as one of its results, the abandonment of a sincere, although imperfect, attempt to employ the whole of the mind, instinctive as well as conscious, in the purposes for which the education of our children is undertaken.

36 Désirée Welby

from 'The Child and the Nation', *National Review*, November 1913, pp. 500–506.

Those who strove to improve the health and education of the young were not without their critics. These saw in the increasing provision for children a threat to 'the ideal of motherhood' and parental authority; an encroachment of the State on family life. 'The mother is no longer needed. The State has undertaken her work' complained Mrs Welby. Many agreed with her that intervention had gone too far, and that it was time to pause, before the character of the nation was sapped by a too-heavy reliance on State aid.

Most of us who watch with keen interest and sympathy the efforts of the various elements at work congratulate ourselves daily that the claim of the child has not been put forward in vain, that the nation is at last alive to its responsibilities and duties, that a freer, healthier, happier childhood awaits those that are to be.

Others there are perhaps among us who, while appreciating to the full the magnitude of the task in hand but looking beyond the immediate future, betray a not unnatural fear that in the very eagerness to sweep away present evils and obtain immediate results, there is danger of creating new and possibly greater difficulties, while running the serious risk of losing much that is valuable. Great objects are not attained without great sacrifices. Great movements for good have never been carried to a successful issue without the exaction of very heavy penalties. The price must always be paid, and while no one would grudge the time, labour and money that have been so lavishly expended of recent years, there are possessions in the keeping of every nation with (or from) which it cannot part except with grave danger and injury to itself.

In our eagerness to give the rising generation every opportunity, physically, mentally and morally, we have been led partly through ignorance, partly by necessity, to tamper with the sanctity of family relationship, to weaken parental responsibility, to substitute State aid for maternal instinct, thereby destroying one of the greatest incentives for good and loosening the whole fabric on which our social and community life is built up.

Year by year we see a lessening in the ideal of motherhood; year by year parental authority is being further ignored and abandoned; while year by year the State steps in, not to compel the parents to undertake their natural obligations, but to relieve them of their primary duties. The schools with their free feeding, medical inspection, visiting nurses, cleansing stations, boot clubs and housewifery centres have long ceased to be educational in the sense that we apply to book learning, but rather have turned themselves into institutions where children are trained, receive those personal attentions, and in many cases are supplied with the necessaries of life that should be the right and privilege of every parent to provide.

Then the early age at which so-called instruction begins has converted our infant departments into veritable nurseries, for in many cases the little pupils can scarcely walk or speak. Though they doubtless enjoy the toys and games generously provided, with the regulation periods of sleep, under the supervision of a kindly mistress, and the mothers are usually only too willing that the State should relieve them of the trouble of looking after their offspring, there is something fundamentally wrong in all this.

And again the training of the older girls in those domestic and household duties that used to be the pride and care of many a humble mother has now become a thing of the past. The mother is no longer needed. The State has undertaken her work. Though it will not be denied that in many cases the mothers had neither time nor inclination, and that there is material gain in a teaching and training that is certainly more thorough and systematic, on the other hand the mother and daughter, perhaps even the nation itself, are the poorer for the loss of that family intercourse, that individual and personal touch that is apart from any housewifery centre. Surely we have wandered far from the old belief that a child depends for its existence and upbringing not upon the State, but upon the instinct, care, intelligence and unselfish devotion of the parents. In relieving the father of his primary duty to provide for his family, in usurping the most sacred rights of the mother in constituting itself foster-parent, the State is in danger of inflicting a mortal blow to that home and family life which, as guardian of the nation's most cherished ideal, should have been its first duty to uphold and preserve.

But the cost is not limited to principle. In order to carry out the various social experiments to ensure such conditions that the rising and future generations may have a fair start necessarily involves vast expenditure. This entails heavy taxation, and in the levying of these taxes there has been very little wisdom or foresight. To meet the constant and increasing demands made in the name of social reform resort has been had to the most reckless finance, which has not only reacted adversely on industry, raised the cost of production, and created unemployment, but has destroyed all confidence and security, and by the very methods by which it was forced on an unwilling electorate has gone far to endanger that sense of responsibility and mutual trust which have hitherto characterized the relations between rich and poor.

Again, we cannot regard without grave misgiving the increasing tendency among the upper and middle classes to limit their families, which in countless cases is in direct consequence of the heavy financial burdens laid upon them. Every act of Parliament seems to react on them, new liabilities are heaped upon them, their difficulties increased, their profits further reduced. Having provided other people's children with the 'fair start', they now find it almost impossible to give anything like the same advantages to their own unless they altogether sink their social status. No wonder large families are becoming increasingly rare, and are a cause of condolence rather than congratulation. The good industrious working man is an equal sufferer with the class above him. He is too independent to accept the proffered State aid, he makes provision for his own children. Yet year by year he finds the cost of living going up, his rent is raised to meet the increase in the rates, his few luxuries are further taxed, not in order that the most deserving may benefit, but too often that the families of his wholly worthless companions may be supported. With one eye on the ballot-box, and driven by a wave of sentiment and humanitarianism, that is often as foolish as it is false, there has been no discrimination and very little foresight, with the result that we are in danger of producing from the wrong end. We are deliberately encouraging the least efficient, the least valuable, the least responsible, to increase and multiply, while compelling those who have an equal if not greater right to be considered to furnish the very means by which an indulgent State may see them through and undertake all future liabilities.

These are but a few of the great problems the far-reaching effects of which are as yet only dimly foreseen, but which compel the attention of all thoughtful people, raising as they do questions of vital issue for the future. In the great task we have undertaken for the regeneration of the race through the child, much has already been sacrificed, much is again demanded. Do the results so far justify the sacrifices that have been made? It would be well-nigh impossible at this stage to make adequate reply to this question, but as it is required of all trustees periodically to render account and present a balance sheet, so the nation as trustee for posterity must from time to time be ready to lay open its books, to show its record of loss and gain, to look at facts as they are, not as it would have them be. After some years of great effort, costly experiment, much display of public spirit and unselfish devotion, we have a right to ask ourselves – are we nearer the attainment of our great object, are we as a nation growing stronger, healthier, more responsible, more contented? It would be difficult to give an unqualified affirmative to either of these questions.

1. Are we healthier? Much may be legitimately expected of the great crusade against disease, whilst preventive and curative measures are already showing valuable results, which are again borne out in the steady decrease in the death-rate, especially among young children. On the other hand it may be maintained that through the advance of modern science and medical skill thousands of weakly and sickly lives are now kept going only to struggle out a weary existence and to give birth to others equally deficient. It may be after all that Nature, with her somewhat crude methods and rigid creed of survival of the fittest, is from the point of view of the nation and the individual the wisest and most humane.

The time and attention devoted to physical development, outdoor exercises and organized games, cannot be but beneficial, and yet it is significant that in order to obtain recruits both fighting services have had to lower their standards of requirements. How many young men and women of the present day are capable of doing continuous work that demands any great mental or physical effort without a breakdown more or less serious? With the exception of those industries where machinery has deliberately replaced labour, two are constantly employed where one was previously found to be sufficient. The cry is always for shorter hours and lighter work, and though this may be due more to the action of the trade unions and the prevailing idea that the worker has a right to greater freedom and the enjoyment of leisure hours than to actual incapacity to perform the allotted task, it is a fact that cannot be denied. The continual and increasing aggregation of the rural population into the great cities, and the consequent overcrowding and competition, the hustle and bustle of modern civilization with its nerve-racking noises, the practice in trades of 'speeding up', followed by long periods of depression and enforced idleness, cannot fail to tell adversely on the health of a people. Again it may be pleaded time and patience are necessary. You cannot retard the tide of civilization; you cannot make a people healthy by Act of Parliament, though you ensure every condition, inflict every penalty and cover the land with sanatoria. Prejudice is strong, ignorance colossal, and human nature, however adaptable, cannot be forced beyond a certain pace. New difficulties must arise, experiments are costly both in time and money, failures are certain, but if we would serve the real interests of the individual and the nation we should show the people not only what the State will do for them, but what they can do for themselves, and teach them to realize the personal element, the personal responsibility of every citizen, so far as lies within his power, to make and keep himself and his children sound in mind and body.

2. Is the sense of responsibility growing among us? It will not be denied that there is a great movement towards a wider recognition of duty and a deep desire for improvement, and there are many signs that give hope for the future. But among all classes we see far too much apathy, self-indulgence, shirking, dislike of any kind of preparation that involves the slightest sacrifice or personal inconvenience. There is a want of grit, perseverance, tenacity of purpose, the desire to see a thing through. But though there may be much that is unsatisfactory, we are not a degenerate people, and there is no need to join in the rather cheap pessimistic cry that we are going straight to the dogs. But as a nation we cannot stand still; we are not the only country in the world or even in Europe. There are others with an equal, if not greater, capacity for patriotism and self-sacrifice, and in the final test the fate of a nation is decided not only by the number of her 'Dreadnoughts' and Army Corps, but by the character of her people.

3. Contentment will scarcely claim a place among the virtues of this generation. But far from deprecating, many regard this as a hopeful sign, a necessary preliminary to all upward movement, and would have us believe that discontent is essential in order to stimulate and encourage a new order

of things. However this may be, the growing discontent among the young people of the present day does not tend to make either the home or the national life happier or easier. Among the masses the education given in the school is indirectly answerable for much that is unsatisfactory in the home. Educated beyond their station in a bewildering variety of subjects, the children too often grow up restless and dissatisfied, totally unfitted for the positions they have to occupy. On all sides, but especially among the young women, there is a want of balance, a strenuous straining after excitement and something new. Ideas are taken up and imbibed with feverish delight only to be immediately discarded for the next. Religion is losing its hold, while the beliefs which helped and inspired our forefathers have no meaning for the present generation. Contentment with their lot is the last thing sought or desired, a spirit which is fostered and kept alive by the literature of the day and the ceaseless activities of Socialist agitators and would-be reformers of every class and creed. We cannot look upon the tendencies of the youth of today without misgivings as to the future. The destruction of home life, the growing independence, the shirking of responsibility, the insistent demand of 'all for nothing' cannot fail to endanger the highest traditions of community life.

And yet in spite of all deep down in the heart of the people lies the convictions that the nation in its own way, in its own time, is moving towards something better, a nobler ideal of itself. In times of transition and experiment defects invariably appear uppermost, are always the more obvious, and in consequence assure an exaggerated importance. Time, faith, patience are needed; and again patience. Unfortunately in the carrying out of this great work of regeneration too much is left to the faddist and to the political opportunist, who, whatever their qualifications may be, lack two essentials – patience and foresight. The faddist is immersed in detail, the opportunist is always in a hurry; so while, on the one hand, we see the National schools yearly becoming more and more benevolent institutions, on the other, politicians are scouring the country purchasing the people's votes by promises for them and their children. The problem of the child and the regeneration of the race cannot be solved by a few Acts of Parliament, municipal regulations, or doles from education authorities. However materially they may and do assist, the true salvation of a people lies in the people themselves and in the realization of the powers they possess.

The State must do its part, but it has a right to demand, and should demand a corresponding effort on the part of the individual. The State has done much for the child; what shall the child do for the State? The State gives, the State should receive. Yet so little is this recognized among all classes today that it is openly acknowledged by political leaders that it would be fatal to the interests of their Party to advocate any form of compulsory service in defence of the country, which is, after all, but the first duty and highest privilege of citizenship.

Such is the growing spirit of the age, for which would-be reformers, doubtless with the best of intentions, are in no small way responsible. All those great qualities that make up the character of a people – self-sacrifice, self-reliance, self-restraint and self-respect – are not inculcated by an indulgent State undertaking all obligations while exacting no return, nor is it by advocating such methods that we can best render service to the individual and the nation. In the eagerness to repair past neglect, to sweep away crying evils and obtain immediate results irreparable mistakes are often made, much that is valuable is often sacrificed. We can but lay the foundations, others must build; we can but point the way for others to follow, and we should betray posterity and be false to our trust if, in the very earnestness of the desire to reach the wished-for end, we lose hold of any one of those great principles and ideals which, however incomplete and deficient they may appear to the present generation, have nevertheless raised us to the position of the greatest of all nations.

37 R. Blair

Prefatory Memorandum, in Cyril Burt, *The Distribution and Relations of Educational Abilities*, London County Council, 1917, pp. vii–xiii.

The appointment by the London County Council of Cyril Burt as its first educational psychologist paved the way for a rich vein of educational research, the findings of which had a considerable impact on educational policy. Tawney used Burt's findings in his 1922 report on secondary education, and both Hadow and Spens leant heavily on Burt's advice (see 65, 75 and 76). The introduction to Burt's first book after his appointment, The Distribution and Relations of Educational Abilities, *written by the Education Officer of the LCC at the time, provides an apt summary of the initial work, as well as reflecting the practical use that administrators would afterwards make of his research.*

Arising out of his immediate duties in connection with special (MD) schools and following on some previous inquiries, the results of which have already been published by the Council, Mr Burt has pursued his investigations into the distribution of educational ability among the whole of the children in the special (MD) schools and in the ordinary elementary schools within a representative borough.

It is obvious, from a mere turnover of the pages, that the memoranda have involved most extensive, arduous and painstaking work; a study of them has proved of the greatest interest and has convinced me of their wide and immediate usefulness to the practical teacher. The three memoranda indeed make a unique contribution to the scientific study of educational problems. To the best of my knowledge this volume is the first of its kind in Europe or elsewhere. Its basis is the London schools, and to that extent the value of many of its results is local, but its methods are universal and cannot but raise large issues in schools otherwise organized and among students of education in Europe and America.

Only a very few can, and only a very few need, carry out researches so extensive, and extract with such exhaustive care and fertile resource generalizations of such wide importance and usefulness from such a mass of complicated details. It is most gratifying to learn that Mr Burt found the teachers in the representative borough most willing to assist in his interesting though exhaustive task.

The memoranda offer some stiff reading. It may be expected that only the ablest teachers will master the details of methods and results; but there should be no teacher in the London service for whom the memoranda do not throw a flood of new light on old problems even on a first reading. The memoranda will no doubt stimulate a large number to repeat the inquiries, and they should certainly induce all to test the results, so far as this is possible within the limits of their own schools.

Mr Burt warns his readers continuously that his investigation has reached only a first approximation; an extensive application of his results and their consequent criticism should bring a continued inquiry to a closer approximation of the truth.

His first concern was the line which should mark off the special (MD) child from the normal or ordinary elementary school child. His investigations next led him into a study of the average attainments at each age of the normal children and the limits of deviation above or below that average. He then carries his readers through a long but deeply interesting study of backwardness and special aptitudes.

After many hours spent on Mr Burt's three memoranda I have been deeply impressed both by his methods and results. He has shown, by extensive inquiry, ingenuity and resourcefulness, how the principles and processes underlying the commonest school facts and operations can be revealed; and has initiated a group of investigations which, if continued extensively and intensively, should lift the practice of teaching from empiricism and lay it on a broad scientific foundation.

Every teacher who, even at a considerable distance, follows the spirit and conclusions of these investigations by so much helps to establish the claim that his profession is a learned one. Were the majority of teachers operating in the same spirit, a great impetus would be given to educational research which would result in lasting benefit to the schools.

The survey shows that in education there is a vast field for practical research. 'When the present crisis is over,' writes Mr Burt,

the nation will stand confronted with the task of social reconstruction. In preparation for this general overhauling one urgent item is the research for which I have appealed. To take the place of the ability that has been lost to the community, we have to discover the best methods of detecting fresh supplies of ability and the best means of training and utilizing it to the utmost of which it is capable. Scientific research in education is thus needed not only to enhance the practice and profession of teaching, but also to promote the welfare of the nation in the near future.

Several times Mr Burt has insisted that his suggestions and conclusions are tentative and provisional. Even so, many of them are of immediate practical value for those engaged in educational administration and particularly for the teachers in the schools, for example, in testing the value of their own classification. After much hesitation I have endeavoured to re-state some of his conclusions in a different order. I am fully conscious that in removing such conclusions from their context I have inevitably given them much baldness; and that in using as far as possible the less technical language to be found frequently in the body of the memoranda, I have lost much in precision. I hope, however, that in gathering the main conclusions together from the body of the text I have done something to assist those who will be unable to find time for an exhaustive study of memoranda which occasionally demand severe efforts on the part of their readers.

Educational abilities

Achievements in the subjects of the school curriculum appear to be determined by mental factors of two kinds:

1. *General educational ability*. A common factor entering into all school work. This common factor is not a simple but a complex capacity, partly dependent on a still more general intellectual factor, 'general intelligence' (all-round mental efficiency) and partly including other important factors such as long-distance memory, interest and industry. General educational ability determines performances in different school subjects in different degrees: such subjects as composition and perhaps problem work in arithmetic are intimately dependent on it, and, if suitably tested and marked, perhaps form the best measures of it.

2. *Specific educational abilities*. Special aptitudes confined to special subjects and groups of subjects. These apparently depend upon psychological factors, largely innate, but partly on moral factors determined by interest in the subject, the culture of the home, and the personality of the teacher.

Allowing for the influence of general educational ability, school subjects fall into four main groups, apparently dependent upon four specific abilities, complex, and nearly, though not entirely, independent:

(a) Arithmetical.
(b) Manual.
(c) Linguistic.
(d) Literary.

The specific abilities to some extent overlap. 'It is tempting to infer,' says Mr Burt, 'that the ordinary school curriculum views scholastic ability from almost every side.' It is equally tempting to suggest that the ring [see p. 59 of Burt's book – Ed.] predicts that there are gaps to be filled in between the linguistic and literary group and the manual group on the one hand, and the arithmetical group on the other.

Normal and backward children

1. On an average the normal child advances very nearly one standard in each successive year. The correlation between age and class, in the case of the normal child, is high but imperfect and may be roughly stated thus:

Age = Standard + 6.
Standard = Age − 6.

2. In educational ability normal children tend on an average to vary above and below the mean level for their age as follows:

At the age of five by just half a year;
At the age of ten by at least one year;
At the age of fifteen, in all probability, by nearly one and a half years;
and throughout by *about one-tenth of their age*.

Roughly speaking, these limits correspond with what in the memoranda is termed the Standard Deviation.

3. For practical purposes 'backward' may be taken to denote children who, though not 'defective', are yet unable in the middle of their school career to do the work even of the class below their age and are retarded by about 15 to 30 per cent of their age. In this sense the total number of backward children in the senior department of the borough investigated may be assessed at 10 per cent at the very lowest estimate. In the whole county the number of backward children between eight and fourteen is estimated as being at least from thirty to fifty thousand. Mr Burt has thus put an approximate measure (say 40,000) on a well-known problem. Efforts to deal with backward children, as distinct from defective, are still in their infancy, and are the result of the initiative of individual head teachers and inspectors rather than of any collective or central administrative act.

The tentative suggestions as to the causes and treatment of backwardness are fully set out later [see pp. 36–40 of Burt's book – Ed.] and should be read *in extenso*.

Mentally deficient children

Children in special (MD) schools are characterized more by backwardness in school work than by defective intelligence. Defective intelligence is usually accompanied by extremely defective attainments; but defective attainments are by no means an invariable index of an equal defect in intelligence [see pp. 16 and 17, particularly the paragraph at the top of p. 17]. Children in special (MD) schools often prove in the first instance to be school failures, and not always mental defectives in the narrower sense. The provisional diagnosis of educational backwardness and mental deficiency should be based primarily upon the child's performances with educational and mental tests.

1. The educational development of defectives is about twice as slow as that of normals, viz., about half a grade or standard per annum: in other words, the educational attainments of a 'defective' correspond, on an average to those of a 'normal' just over half his age. We have thus a simple rule for predicting the most probable degree of educational deficiency for any special school child of any given age. With defectives educational development is not only slower: it also seems to slacken and cease towards the end of the school career. Many, doubtless, arrive prematurely at the limit of their mental growth.

2. On an average, the deviation of the defectives from the normal level is about four and a half times the 'standard deviation' of the 'normals'. It is always in a negative direction, that is, towards a lower educational grade.

3. No child who has three-quarters or more of the educational attainments proper to his age should be even considered as a potential candidate for admission to an MD school. In the case of candidates who are retarded by less than 31 per cent of their age and therefore have over two-thirds of the normal attainments, evidence of deficiency in general intelligence or of emotional instability should also be required. Even for all who have more than half the normal attainments it is desirable to have such evidence; and this may often call for prolonged observation in a sorting class or clearing school.

The upper limits (in grades and standards) for candidates nominated for the statutory examination for admission to a special (MD) school are set out later [see table 16, p. 44 of Burt's book – Ed.].

With these limits the special school accommodation provided for defectives in London appears to be sufficient: were the backward children accommodated in special classes or in special schools of lower grade, the accommodation would be more than sufficient.

Candidates for central schools and junior county scholarships

Potential candidates for central schools should be advanced above the average by about 15 per cent of their age and potential junior county scholarship children by about 25 per cent.

General

1. Of children remaining in the ordinary elementary school after transfer of central school and scholarship children, some perhaps have not had an opportunity of developing their superior talent. This view corresponds with the more popular view that there is too much marking time in the top classes.

2. Between council and non-provided schools the differences in retardation are consistent and marked. In council schools there are 43·5 per cent below the level of their age. In non-provided schools there are 50·3 per cent, practically one-half. The discrepancy is greatest in the case of the girls. In their case the figures are 41·6 per cent (council schools) and 53·7 per cent for non-provided schools. Here is a subject of inquiry for inspectors and head teachers.

3. The investigation seems to confirm the hypothesis that mental abilities are distributed among the population according to the law of averages, i.e. they may, if a sufficiently wide field is taken, be arranged approximately according to the normal curve in the same way as distributions of height and weight.

If this position is established, important criteria will be available for guiding local authorities in such matters as the amount of special school accommodation to be provided and the number of scholarships to be awarded.

4. The differences between individuals tend to grow larger as the individuals themselves grow older. This view is again in accordance with the popular view and forms the sanction behind smaller classes at the top of the ordinary elementary school, and in central and secondary schools. The corollary to this conclusion – the increased differentiation manifested at higher ages – demands a corresponding increase of differentiation in the education thus provided: it also offers matters for much practical consideration. Mr Burt has put the same view differently in the statement: children classed together as infants may be unable to associate for joint work when nearly adult. The view harmonizes with the experience of teachers, but it is a good thing to have it put so tersely.

5. The main effect of teaching on educational ability is, as a rule, to increase the individual differences already present from birth.

6. If the child population and the community at large have profited by the establishment of special schools and classes for the educationally

incompetent, much more would they profit by refining the procedures for discovering and training those who are the most efficient for their age. Here, therefore, says Mr Burt lies a valuable field for future surveys and future research, and, let me add, for administrative action.

7. In a provisional survey of the results of an analysis of the psychological nature of scholastic abilities Mr Burt suggests the following conclusions:

1. The abilities and processes involved are far more complex than those who have written upon this subject commonly assume.
2. Similar results are reached by different children by very different mental processes; consequently a child who fails under one method of instruction will often succeed, if a brief study be made of his natural aptitudes and operations, and another mode of instruction adopted accordingly.
3. Similar subjects require very different abilities at different ages, and at different stages of progress.

8. The psychographs for special educational abilities reproduced between pp. 64 and 65 [of Burt's book – Ed.] are most interesting, and suggest great possibilities for the inquiring teacher.

In composition, reading and arithmetic schools or groups drawn from the poorest homes may be nine to twelve months or more behind those drawn from the best: they differ little, if at all, in manual subjects.

The sections on the overlapping of age-groups, on the distribution of age in school classes, and on the overlapping of classes [pp. 70–74 of Burt's book – Ed.] deserve to be read and re-read again and again by all teachers. Mr Burt points out that the most obvious reform would be (so far as administrative considerations permit) to reclassify for different subjects or groups of subjects. This reform, as is well known, is exacting much thought in secondary schools, but it has not become a practical issue in elementary schools, in which it should not be forgotten Mr Burt's investigations have lain and from which his conclusions have been drawn.

In Appendix 2 [of Burt's book – Ed.] will be found an ideal classification of children according to educational ability at each age.

38 An Officer Wounded on the Somme

'A National College of All Souls: The True War Memorial', *The Times*, 19 February 1917.

Throughout the war years, there were a spate of official reports, as well as private articles and pamphlets, about the need to reform education.

The very act of war inspired visions of a 'land fit for heroes'. One of the most moving, and the most pertinent, was published in The Times *under the title 'A National College of All Souls'. Its author remained anonymous.*

Consider the thousands of brave English people that have been consumed by sea and land within these few years who have not been rogues, cut-purses, horse-stealers, committers of burglary, nor other sorts of rogues, as some of our captains and men of war, to excuse themselves, do report. But, in truth, they were young gentlemen, yeomen and yeomen's sons, and artificers of the most brave sort, such as went voluntary to serve of a gaiety and loyalty of mind; all which kind of people are the flower and force of a kingdom.

Sir John Smith to Lord Burghley, on the Men in Flanders, January, 1589–90.

A little less than five hundred years ago, a great man desired to commemorate the end of one of the most miserable of wars in which the English nation was ever engaged. He endowed a college 'to pray for the souls of all those who fell in the grievous wars between France and England'. We stand for a moment where Chichèle stood, because we stand upon a world of graves. With a nobler cause we ought not to be content with a memorial less noble. We ought to perpetuate in peace the idealism of war, because that alone can deliver us from the selfish appetites that lie in wait for us in both. And if we desire to perpetuate it, how can we begin better than by founding upon it the educational system to whose influence generation after generation is submitted? It is no time for minimum standards, but for an effort corresponding to the sacrifice which it commemorates. A reconstruction of education in a generous and liberal spirit would be the noblest memorial to those who have fallen, because, though many of them were but little 'educated', it would be the most formal and public recognition of the world of the spirit for which they fell. It would show that the nation was prepared to submit its life to the kind of principles for which it thought itself justified in asking them to die.

A spiritual activity

The fundamental obstacle in the way of education in England is simple. It is that education is a spiritual activity which is not commercially profitable, and that the prevailing temper of Englishmen is to regard as most important that which is commercially profitable, and as of only inferior importance that which is not. The task of those who believe in education is correspondingly simple. It is to induce a larger number of their countrymen to believe, and if they believe it themselves, to believe more intensely, that spiritual activity is of primary importance and worth any sacrifice of material goods, and that, in fostering such activity, education, if not the most powerful, is at least the most readily available agency. Current speech and writing about educational progress is not more rapid, and that if only it will legislate more swiftly, and organize more effectively, the result will be that we shall all be 'better educated'. And, indeed, legislation and organization, which should be the mere groundwork and skeleton, are still only too much needed. But, unhappily, the matter is not so simple. To talk as though this or that 'reform' were the one thing needed is really to deceive ourselves because if it had not been for some internal obstacle, some blindness or apathy or recalcitrance within ourselves, the reform would have been made long ago, or the necessity for it would not have arisen.

The comparative indifference of English Governments to education – the idea, for example, that the shutting up of museums, not the shutting up of expensive restaurants, is the economy most worthy of England, or that any Minister will do for the Board of Education, because no one, thank Heaven! is likely to worry *him*, or that the most obvious way of meeting a shortage of labour is to allow the school life of children to be cut down, because after all, it does not really very much matter whether the children of agricultural labourers are educated or not – is merely a public and faithful interpretation of our attitude towards the things of the spirit, an attitude of sceptical, half-indulgent and half-contemptuous tolerance. It is the expression of the scale of values which rules in the minds of most individuals, and which, therefore, rules in the State. And we shall not make any serious progress until that scale is reversed, until the English people – and not merely 'the State' – is a little horrified at ignorance and vulgarity and stupidity. Courage is a great gift, and deserves to be reverenced, because it is so common, and reveals the true nature of man. But insight, respect for truth, and contempt for charlatanism, a lucid and piercing intelligence which appraises facts for what they are and sees through pompous pretences, are also great gifts. We do not reverence them at all in our ordinary life, and so we cannot command them, even when we would give anything to possess them. We cannot command them, because, as a nation, we value material possessions, and take pains to acquire them, more than we value and take pains to acquire spiritual qualities.

A change of heart

The first step towards educational reform, therefore, is not to start doing more energetically the kind of thing we used to do in the kind of mood we used to accept. The first step is to recognize that our mood itself, our attitude towards education, was wrong, and that we shall not be able to change the latter unless we abandon the former or at least recognize that it ought to be abandoned. The beginning for us, as for all barbarians, is to 'burn what we have adored, and to adore what we have burned'. True, education may be commended, and just now constantly is commended, on the ground that it is commercially profitable, that it leads to professional success, that it increases national wealth, that it is in a classic phrase 'our principal weapon in the coming commercial war'. Those who advocate it for such reasons are, doubtless, correct. But an interest in education which is elicited on these grounds is an insecure foundation for educational reform, because, if it is given for commercial motives, it will also be withdrawn for commercial motives, and because it is the nature of the mind to which such motives are of primary importance to take short views even of commercial profit, and to grudge the disinterested support of the pursuit of knowledge, the postponement of possessing to effort, of enjoyment to toil and thought, without which even material wealth cannot successfully be pursued.

Real wealth

Education is, no doubt, the best policy, in the same sense that honesty is the best policy. But no dishonest nation was ever persuaded to be honest by being assured that it would pay; for the reasons which make men dishonest are also the reasons which prevent them from understanding the advantages of honesty. They cannot recognize without themselves a law which they do not recognize within themselves. And the same is true of education. Who can doubt that education pays? Who can doubt that the mere increase in material wealth caused by the establishment of compulsory elementary education has covered many times the expenditure made upon it? But who can doubt that if the consideration of the profitableness of education had been the primary one, children would still have been working in factories at eight years of age, attendance at school would still have been voluntary, and the education rate would not, to quote Mr Forster, 'exceed 2d. in the pound'? The main need of our day, therefore, is not merely a keener appreciation of the pecuniary possibilities latent, or clamant, in particular kinds of scientific research, but a firmer determination to discard the spiritual crassness, the contempt for disinterested intellectual activity, by which, far more than by deficient commercial acuteness, such research, as well as more important things than scientific research, has hitherto been discouraged. And the task of educationists is not to flatter those who could pick over the treasures of earth and Heaven for a piece they can put in their purses – though they may toss them something glittering to play with now and then – but to persuade them that education is to be practised, like other spiritual activities, for itself, 'for the glory of God and the relief of man's state', and that, without education, rich men are really poor. Even then their countrymen may not ever believe in education so far as to make sacrifices for it, which is the only test of belief. But then, they do not believe in it now. They will at least come, in time, to respect it. And respect given for right motives is more estimable than patronage and popularity won by appealing to motives which are wrong.

Lessons of the war

It ought to be easier now than it was three years ago for English people to be persuaded that education is worth any sacrifice. It ought to be easier; because the war has been itself an education. Education is the most formal and public recognition of the claims of the spirit that the modern world has permitted, and the war has thrown certain spiritual tendencies into high relief. It has made moral alternatives intelligible by clothing them with personality. It has caused thousands of people, who are quite without hatred towards Germany, to ask themselves, 'What is it in the German attitude towards life which makes it intolerable to us ? Why is it that we feel that the cause of France and England is the cause of humanity ?' They ask this, and they answer, if they are French or English, that what is intolerable in Germany, what outweighs the many excellences of its learning and public spirit, is there is something in it which stamps what it touches with death, something which is the antithesis of individuality, of spontaneous personal aspirations and endeavour and sacrifice; a spirit which organizes men, but does not inspire them, which cultivates them, but does not love them, which makes a mighty State, but neither a democracy nor a Church; and that, while the characteristic sins of France and England are those of men, weakness and passion and thoughtlessness, the characteristic sins of Prussia, as she now is, are those of devils, intellectual arrogance, and a cold heart, and a contempt for what is lovable and pitiable and ridiculous in human nature.

The eternal struggle

Soldiers feel this, and because they feel it, and not merely because they care about persons like themselves in France or in England, they not only are willing, but conceive it their duty, to kill and be killed. But both they and we ought to feel more than this. We ought to recognize that the real struggle, in which this war is only an episode, is not merely between our own country and anything so unstable and transitory as modern Germany, but between permanent and irreconcilable claimants for the soul of man, and that what makes the German spirit dangerous is not that it is alien, but that it is horribly congenial, to almost the whole modern world. For the spirit of German Imperialism is too often the spirit of English and American industrialism, with all its cult of power as an end in itself, its coarse material standards, its subordination of personality to mechanism, its worship of an elaborate and soul-destroying organization; and the materialism, which in Prussia reveals itself in adoration of the power of the State, in England reveals itself in adoration of the power of money. The latter is not more noble, it is more ignoble, because less disinterested, than the former. If it is not so violent, it is more slyly corrupt, and, as far as the mass of mankind are concerned, almost as tyrannical. But whether it takes the form of military violence, or of commercial greed, the spirit of materialism is one, and the spirit which resists it is one. And if we feel that the absolute claim of personality, the preservation and development of spiritual freedom, are worth any sacrifice in time of war, we ought equally to feel that they are worth any sacrifice in time of peace. Now the sphere where the claims of personality are most clearly involved, and where what threatens them is most obviously the operation of materialistic motives, is the sphere of education.

Education offers, indeed, a kind of *experimentum crucis*, an issue on which our sincerity in the causes for which we claim to have taken up arms may be brought to the test. For, ultimately, the merits of a war are judged neither by the diplomatic correspondence which preceded it, nor by the efforts devoted to winning it, but by the kind of civilization which arises from it, and by the ability of the victor to establish not only over the enemy, but over himself, the authority of the principles for which he claimed to fight. If, as we claim, the cause of England is the cause of all the higher possibilities of the human spirit, then we ought to perpetuate that cause in our social institutions, the character of which must depend on the character of the education we give to all our sons and daughters.

39 Board of Education

from the Final Report of the Departmental Committee on Juvenile Education after the War, vol. 1, Cd 8512, 1917, pp. 3–5, 8, 31.

The report that shaped many of the recommendations in Fisher's 1918 Act looked into the conditions of children leaving school early, and attending only on a part-time basis. It made a strong plea for the school-leaving age to be raised to fourteen, and underlined the dead-end employment of many young people in industry and commerce.

The story, then, amounts to this. The aggregate enrolment in public full-time day schools (elementary, secondary and junior technical) reached its maximum of about 662,000 between twelve and thirteen, when it represented nearly 95 per cent of the total juvenile population of that age. During this year about 30,000 dropped out, mainly under the half-time system. About 185,000 dropped out at thirteen, about 85,000 between thirteen and fourteen, and about 266,000 at fourteen. Only about 84,000, or 13 per cent of the 650,000, are likely to have received any fragment of full-time education after the age of fourteen, and not more than 5 per cent can have received this in secondary schools. Between fourteen and eighteen these small numbers rapidly dwindle. Even the nominal elementary school age terminates at fifteen, and although secondary schools are supposed to keep their pupils at least until sixteen, they are really at the fullest between thirteen and fourteen. Even then they only get less than 6 per cent of the juvenile population, and between seventeen and eighteen this proportion has fallen to less than 1 per cent. Practically, therefore, public education after the elementary school leaving age is a part-time affair. And there is very little of it. In 1911–12 there were about 2,700,000 juveniles between fourteen and eighteen, and of these about 2,200,000 or 81·5 per cent, were enrolled neither in day schools nor in evening schools. The number who were being educated outside the purview of the Board of Education may be regarded at this stage as almost negligible. Here, then, are the two great causes of educational wastage; general disregard of the facilities offered by evening schools completes what early withdrawal from the day schools began. Statistics do not show the whole state of the case, and in interpreting them two additional points must be borne in mind. One is that, quite apart from the question of half-time exemption, many children, during the later years of their day-school life, are employed outside school hours in ways and to an extent which seriously interferes with their educational progress. The other is that even the meagre amount of evening-school enrolment does not represent anything like the same amount of continuous instruction from thirteen or fourteen up to eighteen. Many children enter evening schools during the session after they leave the day school, and then disappear. Many come after an interval of years, and have to spend their time in relearning what they had forgotten. Nor does an enrolment mean much. About 15 per cent of the students enrolled in evening schools for 1911–12 failed to complete the absurdly small minimum of fourteen hours of attendance during the session, and the average hours of attendance were no more than about fifty.

Summary table showing for the year 1911 the approximate numbers and percentages of children and young persons in England and Wales, at each year of age from twelve to eighteen, known to be under full-time or part-time instruction

Pupils classified according to the nature of instruction and the type of institution	Aged 12 and under 13		Aged 13 and under 14		Aged 14 and under 15		Aged 15 and under 16		Aged 16 and under 17		Aged 17 and under 18	
Type of institution	No.	%	No.	%	No.	%	No.	%	No.	%	No.	%
Under half-time instruction in public elementary schools	25,231	3·61	8,921	1·29								
Under full-time instruction in public and other elementary schools	597,612	85·43	421,869	61·08	48,378	7·05	7243	1·08	747	0·1	200	0·03
Under full-time instruction in state-aided and other secondary schools recognized by the Board of Education	32,709	4·68	36,455	5·28	30,722	4·47	20,628	3·08	11,522	1·71	4905	0·74
Under full-time instruction in schools working under the Regulations for Technical Schools and Schools of Art, etc.	419	0·06	1225	0·18	3016	0·44	1958	0·29	1318	0·20	811	0·12
Under part-time instruction in schools working under the Regulations for Technical schools and Schools of Art, etc.	6009	0·86	51,967	7·52	112,270	16·34	93,717	13·99	82,592	12·27	65,312	9·8
Pupil teachers and student teachers							4	0·00	1727	0·26	4603	0·69
Under instruction in universities							2	0·00	167	0·02	431	0·07
Total of above	661,980	94·64	520,437	75·35	194,269	28·30	123,552	18·44	98,073	14·56	176,345	11·45
Difference between the total above and the number of persons enumerated in the census of 1911	37,531	5·36	170,295	24·65	492,869	71·7	546,419	81·56	574,896	85·44	589,890	88·55
Total of persons enumerated in the census of 1911	699,511	100·00	690,732	100·00	687,255	100·00	669,971	100·00	672,969	100·00	666,235	100·00

Conditions of juvenile employment

No doubt, however, education and, still more, industrial training, are not confined within the four walls of a school; there is a discipline of the workshop and the office as well as of the classroom. Can it be assumed, then, that the conditions of juvenile employment were such as in themselves, and without the aid of formal schooling, to establish the character and develop the industrial efficiency of young citizens? The question is one which we cannot ask without a sense of irony, and its answer is written large in the records of former inquiries and in the sociological literature of the last decade. More than once already the country has gaped at it and passed it by. It is not for us to trace over again in detail the ground which has been covered by the Majority and Minority Reports of the Poor Law Commission, by Mr Cyril Jackson's Report on Boy Labour, which appeared as an Appendix to the Reports of the Commission, by the Report of the Consultative Committee on Continuation Schools, and by Mr R. H. Tawney's valuable Memorandum for that Committee. A brief analysis based on those documents must suffice.

Apprenticeship

The range of employment open to juveniles is a wide one, and any general statement of its conditions must be prefaced by the warning that these vary considerably in detail from industry to industry, from locality to locality, and even from business to business. At the top of the scale come the apprentices or learners; at the bottom many factory workers and others engaged in 'blind-alley' occupations. Apprentices are employed, not for their immediate commercial utility, but in order to maintain or increase at a future date the supply of skilled workmen in their industry. These, in theory, get a training which is of a practical kind, and has the advantage of being acquired in the atmosphere of business, not of a school. The fact that the age of apprenticeship is in some areas nearer sixteen than fifteen years of age unfortunately causes a considerable gap to intervene between the time when juveniles leave school and the time when they settle down to learn a trade. During this interval they have nothing but more or less casual occupations to fall back upon, and, when they finally enter their industries, are in most cases less well equipped than when they left school two years before. Moreover, apprenticeship does not by itself give a training which fits boys for modern industrial conditions. As a system of training, it was developed when industry was stable, methodical and regular, and it is not fully suited to an age when it is unstable, changing and irregular. A boy undertakes to serve seven years or five years in order to acquire a trade, but, after his skill has been laboriously obtained, it may

at any moment be rendered entirely unnecessary by changes in the organization of industry. What is required in addition to manual dexterity is
general industrial knowledge and intelligence which will enable him to
adapt himself to changing industrial conditions. But such general adaptability apprenticeship does not of itself give.

Blind-alley employment

Far worse, however, is the state of the large number of children in blind-
alley occupations. These are not engaged to learn a trade with a view to
practising it as adults, but are merely employed for their immediate commercial utility upon simple operations. The only reason for their employment is the fact that, as instruments of production, they are cheaper than
adults. As there is generally an unsatisfied demand for cheap labour, they
make good earnings in proportion to the cost of their maintenance, until
the point comes when they need adult wages. Their economic value in the
home renders them largely independent of parental control, just as the
law of school exemption renders them independent of social control. At the
mature age of fourteen they have become free competitors in the labour
market, and they use their freedom to the full. Many of them pass from job
to job at intervals of a few months; others find their way to the even more
complete economic independence of street trading. Their occupations
give them no kind of industrial training which will fit them for skilled adult
employment, and in many cases not even that general training of the
faculties which makes the intelligent and adaptable, even though unskilled,
labourer. Nor are these occupations necessarily an avenue even to unskilled
employment within the same industries. Most of those following them will
be dismissed whenever they begin to ask for an adult's wages. This is not
because they are inefficient workers or for any other personal or accidental
reason; it follows regularly and inevitably from the way in which the industries are organized. Either they have no adult workers or practically
none, or they can only absorb in adult employment a small proportion of
those employed as juveniles. The rest drop out, to become general labourers
at the best, or, at the worst, to join the ranks of the permanently or inter-
mittently unemployed.

Effects of the war

Upon this educational and industrial chaos has come the war, to aggravate
conditions that could hardly be made graver, and to emphasize a problem
that needed no emphasis. Many children have been withdrawn at an even
earlier age than usual from day schools, and the attendances at those evening schools which have not been closed show a lamentable shrinkage. We

are not prepared to say that much of the work which is now being done by juveniles in munition factories and elsewhere is in itself inferior to the work which most of them would have been doing in normal times, but there can be no doubt that many of the tendencies adversely affecting the development of character and efficiency have incidentally been accentuated. Unsuitable occupations in the distributive trades have largely been transferred from boys to girls. Parental control, so far as it formerly existed, has been relaxed, largely through the absence of fathers of families from their homes. Wages have been exceptionally high, and although this has led to an improved standard of living, it has also, in ill-regulated households, induced habits of foolish and mischievous extravagance. Even the ordinary discipline of the workshop has in varying degrees given way; while the withdrawal of influences making for the social improvement of boys and girls has in many districts been followed by noticeable deterioration in behaviour and morality. Gambling has increased. Excessive hours of strenuous labour have overtaxed the powers of young people; while many have taken advantage of the extraordinary demand for juvenile labour to change even more rapidly than usual from one blind-alley employment to another. Whether these conditions will be complicated by a shortage of employment for juveniles at the close of the war, it is not at present possible to foretell. But it is reasonable to suppose that there will in any event be a considerable dislocation of employment, in the sense that many juveniles will have to find occupations other than those in which they are at present engaged; and the process of adaptation to lower wages and normal prospects is not likely to be other than difficult and disturbing.

The search for remedies

What, then, are the remedies? In a sense there is only one remedy – *porro unum est necessarium*. But it is a pretty thorough-going one; nothing less than a complete change of temper and outlook on the part of the people of this country as to what they mean, through the forces of industry and society, to make of their boys and girls. Can the age of adolescence be brought out of the purview of economic exploitation and into that of the social conscience? Can the conception of the juvenile as primarily a little wage-earner be replaced by the conception of the juvenile as primarily the workman and the citizen in training? Can it be established that the educational purpose is to be the dominating one, without as well as within the school doors, during those formative years between twelve and eighteen? If not, clearly no remedies at all are possible in the absence of the will by which alone they could be rendered effective. [...]

The Committee's main proposals

We come now to our own suggestions. It is, we think, clear that there are two lines of advance which can be pushed forward concurrently. One is the strengthening of the existing system of compulsory full-time attendance at elementary schools; the other the bridging over of the period of adolescence by a new compulsory system of attendance at continuation classes. Early legislation is required:

(a) To establish a uniform elementary school leaving age of fourteen, which entails the abolition of all exemptions, total or partial, from compulsory attendance below that age.

(b) To require attendance for not less than eight hours a week, or 320 hours a year, at day continuation classes between the ages of fourteen and eighteen.

We do not, of course, contemplate that any child, who has already obtained statutory exemption, whether total or partial, when the new Act comes into operation, will be deprived of that exemption, or that any child, who has already reached the age of fourteen at that time, will be required to attend continuation classes. Thus the new obligation will only apply to each individual child who becomes fourteen at a date after it comes into operation, and as a result it will not be until the completion of four years that all juveniles between fourteen and eighteen will have come within its scope. This arrangement will not therefore recall to compulsory education any child who has previously passed the new leaving age, and it will at the same time enable authorities to plan the extension of their work by annual instalments. During the year after the Act begins to operate it will apply to all children between fourteen and fifteen during the second year to all between fourteen and sixteen, during the third year to all between fourteen and seventeen, and during the fourth and subsequent years to all between fourteen and eighteen.

We propose to deal separately with each of the suggested reforms, but before so doing we desire to emphasize the principle that they are really integral parts of one reform, and that juvenile education, to be effective, must be continuous and progressive, with whatever change of methods and of orientation, throughout both the full-time and the part-time stage. Much of the weakness of the present system is due to the interval of oblivion which often separates the elementary and the continuation schooling, and sometimes reduces the latter to the mere repetition of childish lore. At whatever age the child leaves the elementary school, there should be no gap between elementary and continuation teaching.

40 F. Potter, Ben Turner, W. McG. Eagar and the Rev. R. R. Hyde

from Evidence to the Departmental Committee on Juvenile Education after the War, 1917, pp. 38–9, 75.

F. Potter: the juvenile staff of the Great Western Railway

The juvenile staff of the Great Western Railway form about 10 per cent of the whole number of employees. There are some 6600 juveniles on the wages staff, i.e. those who are taken on without educational tests, including about 1300 apprentices) and about 1100 on the clerical staff.

The wages staff

The members of the wages staff are only required to show ability to read and write on joining. They include van boys, who are taken not before fourteen and who, if they remain with the Company, usually become car-men; engine cleaners, who are not taken before sixteen, and may ultimately become drivers; and messengers, lamp boys, etc., who at the age of eight-een or so become porters, goods porters, ticket collectors, etc., and ulti-mately rise to be signalmen, guards, station masters, etc.

Apprentices

Apprentices are employed for the most part at Swindon. They are en-couraged to attend evening classes for three evenings a week at Swindon Technical School up to the age of twenty-one. In the case of the appren-tices from outside who pay a premium, attendance at evening classes is made a condition of apprenticeship, but this has not been found practicable so far in the case of the sons of mechanics and others. Those who do best in the earlier years of the evening courses are selected to attend day classes for two afternoons a week. This day course extends over three years, and for each year's course there is a competitive examination, successful students passing on from one year to the next.

Clerks

Lad clerks have to undergo an entrance examination in arithmetic, dicta-tion and spelling. The first named subject is of an elementary character and is regarded as a test of accuracy only. Of late years there has been a deterioration in the results of this examination, 65 per cent of the candidates having failed on a recent occasion. Witness thought that lack of neatness and accuracy, and failure to give a good grounding in the rudiments of education, are the chief faults of present-day schools, having found a falling off in these respects since the time when most of the boys came from private schools.

Junior clerks are examined annually in the subjects of the entrance papers, together with shorthand and knowledge of railway matters, until they have passed the senior examination. This takes place at age eighteen to nineteen, and qualifies for appointment to the permanent staff, from which the heads of departments and other leading men are recruited. Clerks are encouraged to attend classes conducted by qualified members of the staff in subjects other than those with which they are engaged at the moment, and facilities are given for free attendance at lectures at the London School of Economics, to which the Company subscribe.

The school leaving age

Witness said that the majority of boys educated at public elementary schools leave between thirteen and fourteen. In many cases they take up casual employment (newspaper selling, etc.) before entering upon regular work. This period of irregular occupation is most prejudicial on educational and moral grounds. It may not be possible to require attendance beyond fourteen, but it would be advantageous for boys to remain at school till fifteen if they are unable to secure regular employment.

Instead of the present arrangements under which the byelaws as to school leaving vary in adjoining areas, attendance should be required universally up to fourteen. This would simplify the administration of the law and would establish fourteen as the commencing age of boy-labour. Railway companies do not, as a rule, employ boys under fourteen, and would be prepared to accept fourteen as the minimum age for employment.

The curriculum of the elementary school

Witness agreed that on the whole there has been improvement in the education given in elementary schools, especially in the larger towns. But often so many children leave between twelve and fourteen years of age that the top classes are too small to receive full attention, and the education in these classes is often the weakest part of the school. This is particularly true in rural districts. Witness suggested that special attention should be paid to the development of the powers of observation and the skilful use of the hands, by means of nature study and handicraft and the recording of the things seen and done; and to physical and moral training by suitable drill and exercises and by organized games and the encouragement of Scouting and similar movements.

Improved facilities for further education
The scholarship system

It is obvious that there will always be two groups of young people, viz., those who will form the rank and file, and those who are qualified to occupy positions of responsibility. This applies to both boys and girls, but in greater measure to boys. Speaking not only for the Great Western but for other railway companies, Witness said that every facility should be given to those showing good ability, good character and good intelligence to obtain the best possible education, in secondary schools or elsewhere for fitting them to employ their talents to the best advantage of themselves and the community. But the ordinary methods of examination in book knowledge are defective, and in many cases the differentiation is attempted at too early an age. The system of scholarships at secondary schools is good, but it does not catch all who would profit by more advanced education.

The rank and file should be fitted for carrying out their life duties with intelligence and for fulfilling their obligations as citizens.

Ben Turner: half-time employment

Witness said that half-time in the woollen trade is practically extinct. In the worsted trade it was gradually being abolished before the war, and in Huddersfield, Wakefield and the Colne Valley had disappeared, but since the war there has been a tendency to its increase in places where it still survived. The members of his Association disapprove the practice of half-time employment in the worsted trade.

The school-leaving age

Witness advocated the abolition of exemption on attendances at thirteen except in rare cases, where it should be granted for medical reasons or family sickness alone, and not for employment. This view is shared by most, but not all, of those whom he represents, a change of opinion having taken place owing to increased intellectual prosperity during the last two or three years. It had been shown by investigation that it is custom, as much as poverty, that takes children away at thirteen. Hard cases should be met by maintenance grants. Witness advocated a leaving age of fourteen; personally, he was in favour of fifteen, but thought that the time was not yet ripe for going to that age.

The Scottish system of fixed dates for leaving school would be good for the school. It might however produce a difficulty for the employer, who might not be able to absorb the children if they came to him in large batches; the fact that the present system is deeply ingrained in the habits of the people is another difficulty. Factory Certifying Surgeons should be replaced by the School Medical Officers, who have the advantage of possessing the records of school medical inspection.

Part-time continuation classes

Witness said that after a year or so the members of his Association would cheerfully accept compulsory Continuation Classes in the employer's time for (say) six hours a week up to the age of eighteen. Compulsory evening schools would be cruel institutions. If young people up to eighteen were taken from work for six hours weekly, some difficulties would arise in textile factories, but they would not be insuperable especially if the age were raised by steps, e.g. to sixteen for a beginning. Non-textile employers also would overcome the difficulty. Manufacturers are now seeing the need for promoting the education of children for the sake of developing trade.

If part-time day classes were universal only up to sixteen there should be day-trade schools for exceptionally brilliant children over sixteen. Trades unions would not object to a system of selection by merit for these schools.

The needs of the elementary school

The chief need of the existing system of primary education is the development of the upper classes by means of a system of higher standard or central schools, so as to avoid the marking time which frequently takes place between the ages of twelve and fourteen. There is also need for smaller classes, and for playing-fields, etc. The financial arrangements should be more fully nationalized; at present the burden on the rates is such that Local Authorities dare not reduce the size of classes to the extent necessary for proper teaching. Witness approved the extension of practical work, but did not believe in vocational training in the elementary school. Even for those able to remain full-time beyond fourteen he would not have strict vocational training from thirteen or thereabouts; vocational training in such instances should begin about sixteen.

W. McG. Eagar: effects of the War on employment

The neighbourhood of Bermondsey is a poor one, with very little skilled labour. Much work is done on wharves and in warehouses; many boys go to the City as messengers or for low-grade clerical work.

When war broke out there was a heavy fall in the demand for boy labour, followed soon by quick reabsorption of boys into industry and a rapid increase in wages. During the period of depression Witness's club made ready to open by day, but the boys soon got work, and nothing had to be done. Hours of labour increased considerably, many boys not finishing till seven, eight or nine. It is now practically unknown for a boy to receive less than 10s. weekly, and the maximum wage earned has risen considerably.

Many boys do heavier and more responsible work which was formerly done by men. As a rule they are not losing training which they would otherwise have had; their employment makes rather more demand on their intelligence, but is frequently beyond their strength. The demand for school children, though great, is not quite so marked now as it was last year. As a rule school children work for small employers, but at least one large firm in Bermondsey employs seventh standard children aged twelve to fourteen for three hours a night after ordinary office hours for a wage of 3s. 6d. or 4s. weekly. Witness thought that if half-time attendance at school were enforced on young persons up to eighteen the demand for the labour of school children would increase.

Effects on character and physique

Boys have risen in their own estimation, and are more independent both at home and at work. Premature responsibility has sometimes proved too much for them. The long hours of work have accentuated previous physical shortcomings. Boys now lie in bed to an unnatural extent, and take days off; Witness was sure that this is often due to exhaustion rather than idleness. Boys in school are said to be more unruly than before, possibly because of the presence of women on the staffs; the difficulties of women in preserving order may perhaps be due to the large size of classes. There has been a marked increase in the number of Labour Certificates granted in the local schools.

Much more money is being spent on clothes, jewellery, sweets and theatres. There is a good deal of gambling, though a certain amount of this has always gone on. There has been a marked increase in juvenile crime, which was especially pronounced in the early months of 1916, most of the culprits being school boys; there were very few girls of any age, or boys over fourteen. The increase is chiefly in crimes of lawlessness and adventure, such as stall robbing, which are often carried out in gangs. The police exercise great restraint; and magistrates are sympathetic, but hardly realize how low the standard of honesty is in the children's homes; juvenile crime should be tackled much more firmly from the angle of parental responsibility.

The evil influence of the cinema is somewhat exaggerated, though some films are depraving and the excitement is unwholesome. The craving for means of admission is responsible for a certain amount of juvenile crime. The haphazard enlistment, in the early days of the war, of mere children aged fourteen and upwards had a definitely mischievous effect. The absence of school masters, scout masters and club managers is partly responsible for the increase of crime. The absence of fathers appears to have no direct relation to the increase. More mothers than usual have been prosecuted for neglect.

Suggestions as to education and employment

1. If there is a great displacement of boys after the close of the war, training should be given to those who have been on munitions work, in order to bring them up to the level of improvers in skilled trades. If attendance at the classes is voluntary, maintenance grants will be absolutely essential, as otherwise the parents will be pressing the boys to earn.

2. If at the end of the war there is much unemployment among unskilled workers, there should be centres such as clubs to which they might go for instruction. Maintenance grants would be necessary. Attendance could hardly be made compulsory, but boys would probably go of their own accord when they got tired of walking about the streets. It would be most difficult to bring boys who had been in employment back to the elementary school, with the possible exception of those under fifteen.

3. No boy should work for more than say forty-four hours a week plus eight hours' overtime. Continuation schooling should be compulsory up to the age of seventeen, say two hours a day or ten per week, the teaching being vocational for boys in a trade and general for others. The schools might be held between 5 and 7 p.m.; Witness would not advocate classes from 3 to 5 p.m. if there was nothing to occupy the boys afterwards.

4. The Employment of Children Act 1903 (for children under fourteen) should be more strictly enforced. This would not be easy, as it is often impossible to discover whether a child is employed outside scheduled hours. A little more activity by inspectors however would improve matters considerably.

5. A Department of State should be created for the care and control of young persons. This Department might be linked on to the educational system, but should in any case be entrusted with all matters relating to their interests; it should be concerned with their protection as well as their training.

Rev. R. R. Hyde: the effect of present conditions on the character, discipline and training of boys

Witness had visited many controlled firms, including several of the largest employers of boy labour in the country, in connection with the question of the welfare of boys up to eighteen years of age. He had found a general feeling that boys are deteriorating in character on account of the present demand for their labour, and the high wages which in many places they are able to command.

This demand is not universal, however. It is true that in large towns where tradesmen have lost their men, and in centres where new munitions works have been erected, there is an increased demand for boy labour, and boys can earn high wages, but it is to be borne in mind that many opinions on boy labour problems which find expression today are based solely on knowledge of the quite abnormal conditions which are confined to one or two very large munitions centres. This cannot be emphasized too strongly. In a great many places the conditions are normal or nearly so, since the firms, in so far as boy labour is concerned, are continuing the work they were doing before the war. Where shell shops have been added to existing works, the additional labour is largely undertaken by women and girls. Boys have not taken the place of men to any great extent in large industrial concerns, though in shipyards and rolling mills, where the work is too heavy for women, boys of sixteen and upwards have been engaged in many cases to replace men.

The evil effect upon the boys' character is due to excessive wages and the consequent feeling of independence. Many boys are now working in gangs with men on jobs previously performed by adults. This is not good, especially as much adult labour of a low type is now engaged. Discipline is difficult to maintain. Foremen are harassed; and it is comparatively easy for a boy to throw up his work, since employers regard it as a waste of time to spend an afternoon in taking a boy before a tribunal. In several firms the percentage of boys leaving during the course of a year is between 60 and 70 per cent. A few firms, confined as a rule to definite difficult areas where social conditions are bad, are content to regard the boy as beyond redemption and make no attempt whatever to exercise any control or supervision. It is to be noted that the absence of the father, in spite of the belief that he exercised no control, has conduced to the present unsatisfactory attitude of the juvenile boy labourer.

41 H. A. L. Fisher

Introduction of the 1917 Education Bill, *Parliamentary Debates*, House of Commons, 5th series, vol. 97, 10 August 1917, cols. 795–811.

Fisher's Education Bill of 1917, which eventually reached the Statute Book in 1918, sought to remove the concept of 'part-timers' in schools, and greatly increase the provision of schooling for the majority of the population. In doing this, Fisher extended the powers of the local authorities. It was very much an 'enabling' Bill, which even its author did not envisage being fully implemented for many years. Very little of it, in fact, was ever translated into practice.

When a measure of far-reaching social importance is introduced by a Coalition Government in the height of a great European war and at a late stage of a busy and anxious Session, I feel that the House is entitled to assurances upon three points. It is entitled to be assured, firstly, that adequate provision will be given for the discussion of the measure; then that the Bill is urgently demanded and connected with the circumstances of the war; and lastly, that at a time when the preservation of national unity is a grave and dominant consideration, there is nothing in the Government proposals calculated to revive ancient party recriminations and controversies.

COMMANDER WEDGWOOD: There will be!

MR FISHER: It is because the Government feel that in this sphere of administrative action, so decisive and fundamental in its consequences, there should be no suspicion on the part of hon. Members that we are anxious to force the pace or to preclude a full and dispassionate criticism of our proposals, that I am standing at this Box this afternoon. We are aware that under the pressure of Parliamentary business it may not be possible for us to proceed very far with this measure during the current Session, but we are nevertheless desirous of taking this opportunity, while the Summer Recess is still in the future, of presenting our Bill for the consideration of the House and of the country. As to the second point, I admit that this Bill will not enable us to beat the Germans in 1918. Indeed, even if it were passed before Christmas many years must elapse before its provisions could yield their full fruit. But the measure is not obscurely connected with the circumstances of the war. It is prompted by deficiencies which have been revealed by the war; it is framed to repair the intellectual wastage which has been caused by the war; and should it pass into law before peace is struck it will put a prompt end to an evil which has grown to alarming proportions during the past three years – I allude to the industrial pressure upon the child life of this country – and it will greatly facilitate the solution of many problems of juvenile employment, which will certainly be affected by the transition of the country from a basis of war to a basis of peace.

I now pass to the third point. Is the measure controversial? I am a very raw Parliamentary hand, but I have noticed that there are members in this House who are not inexpert in discovering matters of controversy even in places where, to the eye of innocence, the fate of Empire is not conspicuously involved. I will not therefore prophesy, but I do sincerely hope that any controversies that may be excited with respect to the proposals which I am now about to lay before the House will not centre round the old question which in times past has excited so much warm debate in this House and in the country at large. I do not wish at this stage to raise what is known as the denominational question in any shape or form. I am not proposing to supersede or to revolutionize the educational settlement of 1902. That settlement was not perhaps exactly what my right hon. Friend would have made it if he had had a free hand, and many of us, from one point of view or another, would have wished it other than it is. I am aware that grievances under that settlement are still felt, that some of its principles are sharply contested in many quarters, and that attempts to adjust conflicting views have so far been unhappily frustrated, but I think I am representing the general feeling of this House and of the country when I say that at this particular moment it is especially to be desired that the members of the old religious controversy should not be fanned into flame, and that the question of education should be considered in the light of educational needs and of these alone.

At the same time, I would not desire the impression to go abroad that the Government ignore the spiritual aspects of education, or are indifferent to the strongly held views of those who, from one point of view or another, find fault with this or that feature of our existing system. I am not afraid of the denominational question. I hope and believe that, in the general improvement in the atmosphere which has been created by the war, parties may be brought closer together and that a settlement of the outstanding issues may be reached; but, quite apart from these issues, many of which may be solved without resort to legislation, there is a great and urgent need for development in our educational system, and I believe that this development will be more usefully and fruitfully considered if we can resolve to defer for future and separate discussion what is known as the denominational issue.

The Bill which I invite the House to consider assumes the administrative structure which was erected by the Act of 1902. It assumes that the business of carrying on the educational work of this country will continue to be entrusted to the authorities upon whom it was devolved by that Act. We do not even propose, except with special Parliamentary sanction, to merge the non-county boroughs and urban districts into the county. We feel that these smaller authorities have, in many cases, done their work well and that their continued existence is not incompatible with the formation of general and progressive schemes of education in the country as a whole. Nor do we propose to enlarge the powers of the boroughs and urban districts in the sense of making those authorities responsible for the provision of higher education. I am quite alive to the inconvenience and even embarrassment which has arisen, and still arises, in some places and at some times owing to the distinction between Part 2 and Part 3 of the Act of 1902, and I hope that some of the provisions of the Bill will operate to mitigate, if not entirely to remove, that inconvenience. But everybody knows that the reconstitution of public authorities and the consequent alteration in type of areas is a difficult and controversial business, and, unless it is essential for the proper development of education, I do not think that that work should be undertaken. In general, then, we adhere to the administrative ground work of 1902, because experience has shown that it has enabled a large educational advance to be accomplished and that it has been the means of enlisting a not inconsiderable army of persons who take an interest in education and who have by this time acquired a good deal of valuable experience in the management of schools.

The Bill which I am proposing to the House does not involve any radical alteration in machinery, though I should be greatly disappointed if it does not considerably modify the method of using that machinery and greatly increases its efficiency. Its object is to provide, under the better operation of the existing machinery – amended, it may be, in some directions, and extended in others – enlarged and enriched opportunities of education to the children of the poor. Let me add that, although the measure touches public education at many points, it does not profess to cover the whole field of educational reform. For instance, it does not affect the government of the universities, or of those institutions of secondary, technical and other higher education which are not maintained or aided by local education authorities. I am not proposing here to deal with the scholarship system, the training colleges or libraries; and the establishment of a satisfactory pension scheme for teachers in secondary, technical, and other schools, at present outside the State scheme of pensions, must be left to a separate measure.

There is another educational problem of great urgency which, after much anxious consideration, I have decided to exclude from the operation of the Bill. I have already made a passing allusion to it. In the three years of war some 600,000 children have been withdrawn prematurely from school and become immersed in industry. They are working on munitions, in the fields and in the mines. In a thousand different ways these children are contributing to our success in the war. Though they are earning wages, and in some cases high wages, let us make no mistake about it, these children are incurring a real sacrifice, the effects of which, in many cases, will be felt to the end of their lives. I ask the House to consider whether the nation has not incurred a special responsibility towards these children who have been brought in to help in the war, often in circumstances most adverse to the formation of stable character. There can be only one answer – that some special means must be found, either by administrative action or otherwise, whereby this responsibility may be adequately discharged.

Before I proceed to outline the leading features of the Bill, I would like very briefly to describe some aspects of the movements of opinion which, in the minds of the Government, have made a considerable measure of advance in education an absolute necessity. In the first place, attention has been increasingly directed to the close connection between educational and physical efficiency. One of the great dates in our social history is the establishment of the school medical service in 1907. We now know, what we should not otherwise have known, how greatly the value of our educational system is impaired by the low physical conditions of a vast number of the children, and how imperative is the necessity of raising the general standard of physical health among the children of the poor, if a great part of the money spent on our educational system is not to be wasted. That is one element in the movement of opinion. Another element is the growing consciousness that there is a lack of scientific correlation between the different parts of our educational machinery. We find an important and populous centre without a secondary school in any shape or form. We find an older and less important centre with four secondary schools. We discover that even where there is an adequate provision of secondary schools in an area there may be no provision of boarding scholarships such as may enable the abler children of the villages to take advantage of the schools in their neighbourhood, no provision of advanced teaching for the older pupils, and no provision of scholarships to the universities. Everyone realizes the elementary fact that some children, if they are only given opportunity, will profit most through modern languages and history, others by a scientific and technical education, and others again are destined by their natural turn of mind to profit most from an education based largely on the study of classical antiquity. But under our existing system we have no security that in any area of accessibility, to adopt a vague but convenient term, these various needs and aptitudes will be provided for. There is not even a reasonable probability that the child will get the higher education best adapted to his or her needs. The Act of 1902 no doubt contemplated area schemes for higher education, but the duty of considering the whole need of an area was left hanging in the air.

A third feature in the movement of opinion is the increased feeling of social solidarity which has been created by the war. When you get conscription, when you get a state of affairs under which the poor are asked to pour out their blood and to be mulcted in the high cost of living for large international policies, then every just mind begins to realize that the boundaries of citizenship are not determined by wealth, and that the same logic which leads us to desire an extension of the franchise points also to an extension of education. There is a growing sense, not only in England but through Europe, and I may say especially in France, that the industrial workers of the country are entitled to be considered primarily as citizens and as fit subjects for any form of education from which they are capable of profiting. I notice also that a new way of thinking about education has sprung up among many of the more reflecting members of our industrial army. They do not want education in order that they may become better technical workmen and earn higher wages. They do not want it in order that they may rise out of their own class, always a vulgar ambition, they want it because they know that in the treasures of the mind they can find an aid to good citizenship, a source of pure enjoyment and a refuge from the necessary hardships of a life spent in the midst of clanging machinery in our hideous cities of toil. I ask whether there is a single struggling young student in this country to whom a library of good books has not made an elemental democratic appeal.

Unlike the hard, the selfish and the proud,
They fly not sullen from the suppliant crowd
Nor tell to various people various things,
But show to subjects what they show to kings.

I will now descend to our specific proposal which may be conveniently, though not exhaustively, considered under six heads. Firstly, we desire to improve the administrative organization of education. Secondly, we are anxious to secure for every boy and girl in this country an elementary school life up to the age of fourteen which shall be unimpeded by the competing claims of industry. Thirdly, we desire to establish part-time day continuation schools which every young person in the country shall be compelled to attend unless he or she is undergoing some suitable form of alternative instruction. Fourthly, we make a series of proposals for the development of the higher forms of elementary education and for the improvement of the physical condition of the children and young persons under instruction. Fifthly, we desire to consolidate the elementary school grants and, sixthly, we wish to make an effective survey of the whole educational provision in the country and to bring private educational institutions into closer and more convenient relations to the national system. I will first, then, deal with our proposals as affecting the general framework of educational administration. We impose a duty upon the council of every county and county borough to provide for the progressive development and comprehensive organization of education in their respective areas and to submit schemes to the Board, and in order that this function may adequately be discharged we propose to remove the twopenny limit on the amount to be raised for higher forms of education which was imposed by the Act of 1902. The council of a county or county borough will, in other words, plan out an educational policy for its area. Before submitting its scheme to the Board the council will be required to consult the authorities having power in the county under Part 3 of the Act of 1902 with reference to the mode in which, and the extent to which, any such authority will cooperate with the council, and the Board will be informed as to the cooperation to be anticipated from any such authority. There will, we trust, be little difficulty in securing the degree of cooperation between the authorities within the county area which may be requisite for the representation of a combined and intelligent plan of educational organization from bottom to top. This, then, is the first point we desire to secure. We impose a duty on each complete authority to submit an area scheme, not for elementary education only, but for all forms of education. We impose a duty on the county authorities to consult the Part 3 authorities in their area. We impose duty on the Part 3 authority to cooperate with the Part 2 authority – that is to say, the authority for higher education – and, if required, to submit a scheme for the performance of its own duties and for cooperation with the Part 2 authorities. Finally, we liberate the county authority from the limitation of the twopenny rate.

But there are some educational problems which can be more conveniently considered in relation to areas larger than a county or county borough area and by bodies representing a wider constituency. The supply and preliminary education of teachers, for instance, could be best dealt with in relation to a large area. So probably could a scheme for scholarships to be held at the secondary schools or the universities. Or, again, the provision and utilization of secondary schools might be more scientifically planned out and with less fear of overlapping in a large area than in a small area. It is, of course, possible under the existing law for authorities to combine together for any one or all of such purposes, but it seems to me desirable that distinct statutory authority should be given for the formation of bodies which we may call provincial associations.

Now assuming that for some purposes it may be convenient to have larger areas than a county or county borough, one of two ways might be taken to effect this object. The country might be mapped out into eight or nine provincial areas, each provided with a council representing the local education authority of the area, together with representatives of the university and other interests; and wide powers, including the power to levy a rate, might be assigned to each of these councils. That, I understand, is the scheme advocated by Lord Haldane, who, of course, speaks on all educational questions with great authority. Or the Board might be empowered by Statute to provide for the establishment of provincial associations after consultation with the authorities concerned, the local educational authorities being empowered to delegate administrative and educational functions to these associations, and conversely the associations being empowered to exercise any functions so delegated. The Bill follows the second of these paths. We think that it would be premature to carve up England into provincial areas or to embark at once on such a very large scheme of devolution as the advocates of the former plan contemplate. We certainly cannot assume that the local education authorities would be willing to come into such a plan, so we think it wiser to look for our larger authority to a gradual process of coalescence fostered by the State, probably in the first instance with a view to some specific purpose or group of purposes, to which other purposes might in time be added.

We have, then, county and county borough authorities obliged to submit comprehensive schemes of education for their respective areas, and these may be gradually supplemented by provincial associations for those educational purposes which are most conveniently dealt with in relation to areas larger than those of county and county boroughs. But what do we mean by comprehensive schemes ? First, we want to make it plain that the education given in our public elementary schools is not to be considered an end in itself, but as a stage in the child's education destined to lead to a further stage. Secondly, we propose to require local educational authorities under Part 3 of the Education Act of 1902 to make adequate provision, either by special classes or by means of central schools, for what may be termed higher elementary education. We desire to meet the objection which is commonly, and not without justice, advanced against so much of the work done in our public elementary schools during the last two years – that the children are marking time, that their education is not bringing them on, that it does not fit them for their future calling. We desire to change all that, and our Bill provides not only for the introduction of practical instruction at appropriate stages, but for the preparation of children for further education in schools other than elementary, and for their transference at suitable ages to such schools.

I pass now to a series of proposals which are designed to improve and to strengthen our existing fabric of elementary education so as to secure for every child in the kingdom a sound physique and a solid groundwork of knowledge before the period when the part-time system begins. We propose to encourage the establishment of nursery schools for children under five years, and we empower the local education authorities to raise the age at which normal instruction in the elementary schools begins to six, as soon as there is an adequate supply of nursery schools for the younger children in the area. We propose to amend the law of school attendance so as to abolish all exemptions between the ages of five and fourteen, and we propose to place further restrictions upon the employment of children during the elementary school period. The first of these proposals rests upon the belief that children are introduced to the normal instruction of public elementary schools at too tender an age. At four or five years sleep and play are far more important than letters, and we feel that wherever the home is good the child should be encouraged to stay with his or her mother.

MR KING: What if the home is not good?

MR FISHER: We do not desire to compel the provision of nursery schools, but we propose to enable such schools, attendance at which must be voluntary, to be aided from the rates, and we believe that to the development of these schools, which will, I trust, often be open-air schools, we may reasonably look for a real improvement in the health of young childen. The second proposal involves as its consequence the abolition of what is known as the half-time system. This is a system which at the present moment mainly flourishes in certain parts of Lancashire and Yorkshire, where some 30,000 children between the ages of twelve and fourteen are permitted to divide their working day between the factory and the school. Originally the half-time system represented a concession to the claims of education. Boys and girls in Lancashire were released from the factory for a half-day's schooling at a time when, in other parts of the country, they were still deprived of all educational opportunities. Now the situation is reversed, and the child population in the half-time regions of the North suffers under peculiar and exceptional disabilities. The system, of course, has its defenders, as any system long continued, and become a habit must. The wages earned by the children are acceptable to the employers, but it is very difficult to see any grounds, apart from the convenience of cheap labour, upon which the continuance of this exceptional system can be defended. It is no argument to plead that the regions in which this system is practised are conspicuous for energy and intelligence. If such a statement be true, as I think it is, it only proves once more how native vigour may triumph over serious obstacles. I do not wish to be understood to be bringing any form of accusation against the employers of half-time labour, many of whom are most considerate to the claims of their workpeople.

But the system has been condemned by every educationist and every social reformer. It is bad for the physique of the children. It is injurious to the intellectual prospects of the half-timer. It has been shown that the work upon which the children are engaged is not such as to develop the higher forms of industrial activity, and it has been shown that when the half-time system is once admitted in the textile system it spreads to other forms of employment as well. We consider, then, that the time has come when in the general interests of the country and in the special interest of the children concerned, notice should be given that this system should, after a convenient interval, come to an end, and we consider that the termination of the war, when a large mass of new labour will be thrown on the market, will be a convenient period at which to terminate this undesirable custom.

The third measure for improving our elementary-school education is the further regulation of the employment of children during the period of daily elementary-school life. We desire a full period of school life, unimpaired by the competing claims of employment, for all children of the working population. At the present moment the value of our elementary-school education is gravely harmed by the work which is imposed upon children out of school hours. They are liable to be employed for three hours before the school opens and for some hours after the school closes, and the general opinion of my inspectors is that of all reforms affecting elementary education there is none more vital than the enforcement of strict limitation of the employment of children in their school-going days. This is not merely a question of scholastic efficiency. It affects the physical welfare of the race. We have now an overwhelming mass of evidence to the effect that the health of our children suffers from premature or excessive employment. You may trace the evil effects in diminished height and weight, in curvature of the spine, in cardiac affections, and in deficiency of the senses, especially the sense of vision, and in the bad dentition of our working classes. The reports of our school medical service are full of them.

Accordingly we propose that no child under twelve shall be employed for profit, and here we have already been anticipating by-laws passed in some of our large municipalities, and we further provide that no child under fourteen shall be employed on any day on which he is required to attend school before the close of school hours or after 8 p.m. on that day, or on other days before 6 a.m. or after 8 p.m. The House will observe that under this provision a child between twelve and fourteen may be employed between 6 a.m. and 8 p.m. on Saturdays and during school holidays, and, though we have come to the conclusion that there is something to be said for a little employment on days on which the school provides no regular work, we are fully sensible that this liberty may be abused in the future, as it has been in the past, and the Bill accordingly provides that the local education authority, if they are satisfied, on the report of the school medical officer or otherwise, that the child is being employed in such a way as to be prejudicial to health or education, may forbid or regulate that employment. We have also come to the conclusion that if the local education authority should decide that it would be wise to continue the elementary education either of the boys or the girls in the area, or of boys or girls following particular occupations in that area, up to the age of fifteen, they shall be empowered to do so.

SIR H. CRAIK: In the elementary schools?

MR FISHER: Yes. I now come to the most novel if not the most important provision in the Bill. We propose that, with certain exceptions defined in the Bill, every young person no longer under any obligation to attend a public elementary school shall attend such continuation school as the local education authority of the area in which he resides may require for a period of 320 hours in the year, or the equivalent of eight hours a week for forty weeks. The main exceptions are the following: attendance at such schools will not be required in the case of a young person who has received, to the satisfaction of the Board, suitable full-time instruction up to the age of sixteen, or has passed the matriculation examination of a university of the United Kingdom or an examination recognized as an equivalent to that, or is shown to be under suitable and efficient part-time instruction. In other words, we provide that every young person in the kingdom who has not received a full-time education up to the age of sixteen should receive a part-time education up to the age of eighteen, either in schools provided by the local education authority or in schools under their direction, such as the schools established by manufacturers in their works, or in schools providing satisfactory alternative instruction. We do not desire to discourage voluntary effort. On the contrary, we believe that very great benefit accrues from the recognition on the part of employers of their educational responsibilities towards their employees, and we believe that a great many more employers may be induced to start part-time schools connected with their own concerns, in view of the general obligations created under this Bill for some form of continued education throughout the period of adolescence.

There is another matter of great importance in reference to this proposal. The Bill provides that part-time instruction shall be given by day. It must be taken out of the employer's time, and provision is made to ensure that the young person who is required to attend continuation classes shall not be worked unduly long hours during the days on which the classes are held, and that he or she shall be given a reasonable interval for food, rest and washing between work and school. The classes then are to be held by day, and the pupils are to come to the schools in a fit condition to benefit by the instruction. It is further provided that the classes are not to be held on Sunday or any holiday or half-holiday which a young person is accustomed to enjoy. The proposal comes to this, that in general young persons who are not undergoing full-time instruction will be liberated from industrial toil for the equivalent of three half-days a week during forty weeks – two half-days to be spent in school, while one will be a half-holiday. I will now briefly explain how these continuation schools are to be set up and what are the governing ideas as to their educational purpose. The Bill devolves upon the local education authority, under Part 2 of the Education Act 1902, either separately or in conjunction with other local education authorities, the duty of submitting schemes for a system of continuation schools. The schemes must be submitted before an appointed day. Whatever the date may be, a liberal allowance of time must be granted to the local education authorities in which to think out a system appropriate to the special needs of the locality. No doubt the local education authority will consult, indeed, under the terms of the Bill they are compelled to consult, industrial and other interests, and it is contemplated that there may be a considerable variety of type in these schools.

The schools for the rural populations will no doubt be mainly held in the winter months, and one advantage of our local system of administration is that it enables these new schools to fit in with the varying industrial requirements of different regions. The character of the instruction will be partly physical. We feel that it is important to secure a physical minimum in the nation, and that this is just as important for girls as for boys. It will not be solely physical. We shall hope to continue the general education, the foundations of which have been laid in the public elementary school, and to give in addition vocational bias, the force of which will be graduated according to the age and occupation of the pupil. The details of the courses will, as I have already indicated, vary from locality to locality. The courses given in the rural districts will not be identical with those given in the towns, but the governing conception of the scheme will be identical over the whole country – the production of good citizens, able to make the most of themselves, and of the environment in which they are placed. And here I may be asked whether the spell of eight hours a week, or 320 hours a year is, in reality, sufficient to accomplish any substantial educational purpose, and why, the principle once admitted, a longer period has not been suggested. I need not say that on purely educational ground I should have preferred a larger amount of instruction, even if that amount had been confined to the age between fourteen and sixteen, but, after careful consideration, I came to the conclusion that the practical obstacles were too great, that it would be difficult, if not impossible, for us to provide, in a reasonable length of time, the requisite supply of teachers of ability, that the scheme, if it is to be made accessible to the working people, would have to be supplemented by a very large expenditure in maintenance allowances and buildings, and that it would involve too great a disturbance of the juvenile labour market.

At the same time, I should not like it to go abroad that I regard the period of eight hours a week either as ideal or as the necessary limit. I feel to the full the strength of the contention that young people, whatever may be their station in life, should primarily be regarded as subjects for education and not as parts of the industrial machine, and it may be that after the lapse of a few years it will become practicable, with the approval of Parliament, to extend the period of schooling in particular areas, or perhaps even for the whole juvenile population. The Bill makes provision for such a contingency. Meanwhile I trust that many of the students in our continuation schools will not be content with the statutory courses only. We also believe that many of them, once brought under this beneficial influence, will be more ready to join boys' and girls' clubs, boy scouts, girl guides, and other such wholesome associations, carrying with them intellectual and social advantages. We expressly empower, under this measure, local education authorities to provide school camps and social training with a view to the needs of this class of student. I confess I am a great believer in the value of school camps for boys between fourteen and sixteen, and I trust that this Bill may pass into law in sufficient time to justify the acquisition by the local education authorities for some of the material equipment for camp life which the War Office has so plentifully provided us.

MR D. MASON: Do you mean military camps?

MR FISHER: No, Sir; school camps. In asking the employers of this country to assent to these changes, the establishment of day continuation classes, the abolition of half-time in those regions where it still continues to exist, and the further regulation of employment during the period of elementary-school life, I am conscious that I am asking them to submit to readjustments in the organization of their industries which, in some cases, will be troublesome to effect, but I rest my appeal upon the broad ground of national advantage. We have reached a point in our history when we must take long views. We are a comparatively small country, we have incurred the hostility of a nation with a larger population and with a greater extent of concentrated territory and with a more powerful organization of its resources. We cannot flatter ourselves with the comfortable notion, I wish we could, that after this war the fierce rivalry of Germany will disappear and hostile feeling altogether die down. That in itself constitutes a reason for giving the youth of our country the best preparation which ingenuity can suggest. And there is another reason. We are extending the franchise, we are making a greater demand than ever before upon the civic spirit of the ordinary man and woman at a time when the problems of national life and of world policy upon which this House will be called upon to decide have become exceedingly complex and difficult, and how can we expect an intelligent response to the demands which the community propose to make upon the instructed judgement of its men and women unless we are prepared to make some further sacrifices in order to form and fashion the minds of the young?

I have the privilege of knowing many manufacturers in this country, and I have never found them reluctant to adopt a course in which their judgement discerned a balance of advantage to the nation. In many lands there is a permanent system of military conscription. The greater part of the young men of the nation is withdrawn from industrial work for the purely unproductive purpose of military exercises. We are proposing not a form of military conscription but a form of educational investment which will involve far less dislocation of industry, far less withdrawal of labour, and will be open to none of those powerful objections to which any system of military conscription is necessarily exposed. Even if we describe continued education as a tax upon industry it will be a comparatively small tax. In reality the word 'tax' is a misnomer. We cannot describe anything as a tax which has for its necessary effect an addition to the capital upon which the tax has been imposed. It is our contention that this will be precisely the effect of continuation classes, that what the nation spends with one hand it will get back with the other, and that our people will be stronger, more intelligent and better disciplined through some measure of educational control continued through the whole period of adolescence. And I would ask employers of this country who may be disposed to question the wisdom of this measure to reflect how greatly the success of industry depends on the character of their employees. A factory is like a ship, one bad hand rots the whole company. There is notoriously no gift more prized in a good firm than the capacity to pick out character. The employers of this country have a supreme interest in the formation of industrial character, and we believe that the measures which we propose will be calculated not only to arrest that process of degradation which is too often apparent after the close of the elementary-school period, but to give to the industrial character of our people just that additional measure of stability which it so pre-eminently lacks. The system will be good for boys, but even better for girls.

42 Lieutenant-Commander J. C. Wedgwood

from the debate in the 1917 Education Bill, *Parliamentary Debates*, House of Commons, 5th series, vol. 97, 10 August 1917, cols. 814–21.

The 'whiff of mid-Victorian social and political economy' as one MP described the speech, represented by the words of Lt.-Com.

Wedgwood in replying to Fisher's opening statement reflected the strong opposition to 'making the cattle think' in Wedgwood's crude terminology. Yet he made a good point; he exposed the duality in the government's thinking on education, which on the one hand presented reform as a measure to help the working classes, yet on the other saw it as a means of 'beating the Germans' both at war and in the longer-term economic struggle.

Though I have sat in this House for twelve years I have never before heard an education measure brought in, or education estimates argued, by a lover of education who is a specialist at his job. I think, however much I personally may differ from the proposals put before us by the right hon. Gentleman today, everyone of us is glad to find education handled by a man who, at least, is handling the job he likes. If personally I see in the Minister for Education less the able author of *The Republican Tradition in Europe*, and more the disciple of Lord Haldane and of that precious German, Dr Kirschensteiner, I, at any rate, am grateful for the fact that we have a man in charge of the educational work of the country who has an open mind, and who will be able to realize, I think perhaps better than he does at the present time, not the feeling amongst educational experts, but among the parents in this country – a man with a sufficiently open mind to modify the harsh provisions of the Bill he has outlined to us today. The fact of the matter is that both the present Minister of Education and all of us in this House during the last three years have got entirely out of touch with the constituencies. I do not suppose there is a quarter of the Members in this House who have made a speech on general political matters to their constituents during the last three years, and I am quite certain that the Minister of Education, or anybody present here today, has never made to his constituents one single speech which could justify his voting for increasing the age during which children are compelled to go to school. I have often spoken on this subject in my constituency, and indeed all over the north of Staffordshire, and I say with conviction that if this Bill could be voted on by the fathers and mothers – by the public generally – of North Staffordshire, it would inevitably be rejected. I believe that that holds in every other part of the United Kingdom today. When you propose to raise the school age universally to fourteen; when you propose further to give local authorities the power to raise the compulsory school age to fifteen; when you further say that two days a week for four hours a day education shall be compulsory up to the age of eighteen, and put that proposal before the people in the country who have got to obey that law, and not before Members of the House who have not got to obey that law, I think you will get a very different answer than the answer which will be given for the first reading or second reading of this Bill.

The fact is, it is not our children we are legislating for, but other people's children. We are not the people who will be affected directly by this Bill; it is other people who are not represented here at all. The working classes are represented, but there are no members of the Labour party here present. Of course we all represent their interests, but automatically we look upon education as the sort of education we have had, or our children have, without remembering we are legislating for other people who know much more about the details of this elementary education than we do. Let me put before the House clearly what is the point of view, as I understand it, of the working man, and, above all, the working mother. They have an extremely difficult time even now, when there is no want of employment, to make both ends meet. Every penny that goes into the houses of the working classes is reckoned on beforehand, and is of vital importance to keep body and soul together. The Minister of Education has pointed out the enormous improvement in the children's physique due to physical exercises. I quite agree with him, but the improvement that results from physical exercises will absolutely be wiped out if the parents and the children themselves are starved and cannot get sufficient sustenance. It is no good giving with one hand and taking away with the other. If you give the best physical training and the best intellectual training in the world, and these children have not had proper food, or enough of it, your educational system based upon such a fraud will manifestly fall to pieces. Every penny that goes into the working-class home at the present is of vital importance. If you curtail the wage-earning power of those children, you are doing a serious injury to the working-classes as a whole. Now you are proposing to raise the school age to fourteen and a little over, because I think it is proposed that if a child arrives at fourteen on the first day of the term, he has to remain till the end of the term. That alone is going to be a serious additional tax upon poor families who want every penny that their children bring in. Then you have the possibility of a body rather similar to ourselves in some county council, or more likely in some borough council, decreeing that the age shall be raised to fifteen – another serious tax upon the wage-earning powers of working-class families. Then you have the necessary loss of wages that must occur owing to two afternoons a week being taken up entirely by these continuation schools.

All these things have not only the direct effect upon the working-classes of reducing the income, and therefore reducing the body-building power – and it affects not only food but housing – but you have the indirect effect that you have already seen from the Compulsory Education Act of 1872.

that people will restrict their families more and more, the more you postpone the date at which children become a wage-earning factor in family
life. If you are going to postpone – not under this Bill indeed, but under the
provisions outlined by the Minister – wage-earning powers to eighteen, or,
possibly, if conscription comes along, to twenty-one, you are thereby
imposing a further restriction upon the birth-rate of this country. You are
making it a more undesirable burden to have a child, instead of giving the
people every inducement to incur the frightful dangers and risks of bringing
children into the world. I do not want the House to imagine for one moment
that I am not as keen as any member here to see the children of the working-
classes given a thoroughly efficient education and a much longer education,
but what I want to see is more opportunities and less compulsion. I ask the
House to consider for one moment, first of all, what would be the effect
now in certain working-class districts of removing the school attendance
officer and making education voluntary. I know districts in North Staffordshire where the whole district is inhabited by a fairly skilled class of working
men. I make bold to say that if you removed compulsion tomorrow, every
one of the children would go to school just as well as at the present time,
and you would be saved the burden in that area of the school attendance
officers, and all that inquisitorial interference that school attendance
officers involve. I believe more particularly in Scotland, where the parents
have a real competition to see that their children are well educated, there,
too, you would find the parents as a rule, and public opinion as a whole,
acting as compulsorily upon the education of the children as any amount of
Government rules and regulations. People have no conception of the pride
that the ordinary working-class family take in the education of their children. They take just as much pride in sending their children to the elementary school – or would if compulsion did not make all pride in that direction
ridiculous – as we do in sending our children to the best public school to
get as good education as we got in our time. Therefore, it seems to me, you
would be doing much better by education if you gave more freely opportunities for education. I believe you would find in those circumstances a
constantly dwindling band of parents who wished to exploit their children,
and a constantly increasing band of parents who wished to get the best
possible education for their children. Is it not better to induce people to
see that their children are better educated by giving them opportunities
than to try this absurd business of the police court ? In this Bill the child is
to be fined 5s. if he does not go to school. In that you will be introducing,
not to education, but to the police court a large number of young persons
about whom you are so solicitous. Even if we are all convinced that it is
necessary to introduce this new extension of compulsion into education,

surely it is our duty, sitting here in the seventh year of a moribund Parliament, to consult the people before we bring about this very drastic change in the domestic life of the vast mass of the people of this country.

Surely we are not now, after three years of divorce between the representatives here and their constituencies outside going to introduce a measure which will affect every man, woman and child in the land and affect them much more than the Corn Production Bill ? This is a question which ought not to be debated in the dying days of an old Parliament, and this measure should never pass into law under these circumstances. There is one particular reason why we ought to be extremely cautious about passing such a Bill as this into law at the present time. Everyone knows that there is industrial unrest below the surface. Everyone knows that, for the sake of victory, we should do nothing on earth that would in any way exacerbate that industrial unrest. I ask hon. Members, before voting for the second reading of this Bill and before imposing this measure upon the fathers and mothers of England to go into their own constituencies and have a meeting and try to find out what the people think about this question. I feel certain they would come back impressed with the vast unpopularity of such a drastic thing as this at the present time. I believe myself that it would do more to exasperate particularly the women, who are having a very bad time of it just now trying to obtain potatoes and sugar. Do not force this measure through in the teeth of the opinion of the people who are going to be affected, while the war is on, at a time when industrial peace is of enormous importance to our prospects in the war.

I can only regret that the Minister for Education, in his singularly lucid description of educational reform, did not devote slightly more attention to the question of compulsion instead of dismissing it in a single sentence as an impracticable suggestion to any scheme of education. Let me deal now with what I regard as the chief factors in these proposals apart from this compulsion of parents. It seems to me that this form of half-time education between the ages of fourteen and eighteen is a very serious danger to the liberties of England. It may be thought that that is putting it rather strongly, but I am convinced that the Minister for Education himself sees no such danger whatever in front of him at the present moment. The right hon. Gentleman was very insistent upon the fact that these extra four years of education were to be education which would create character and give to the future workers of this country not nimbleness and efficiency, but power to think, read, and derive advantage from all the great books of the past and the great thoughts of past thinkers. If I thought that would be the result of the scheme I might even swallow my objection to compulsion in order to secure it; but I know perfectly well, and I think the right hon. Gentleman knows at the back of his mind, that that is not the spirit that is moving the great employers of this country to accept half-time labour up to eighteen.

The development of character in their minds – I say it without hesitation – is not so much their object as the development of efficiency in that particular trade, conceal it how you like. If you take the children in the potteries and train them all to be useful potters, you are going to produce a more useful and efficient worker than you have at the present time, and they are going to be trained to create wealth quicker and better than they do now. If you put before the employers on the one hand a scheme which is going to develop in the children the power and capability of thinking for themselves and acting for themselves, and on the other hand a scheme which is going to turn out adjuncts to machines of invaluable efficiency, you are asking too much of human nature if you suppose the employers are going to go in for the first and not for the second. Surely hon. members have come across, over and over again, young men of the working classes who have climbed up the education ladder, and have gone to the universities, and at the end of their university career are faced with either going back to the mine or the shop or taking a government job or becoming a trade-union official. I know many of them, and I say unhesitatingly that these men, who have been to the university, have had character and the power of thought developed, and they are indeed men, and not cabbages. All this has developed in these men the theory of the anarchist, the hatred of the social injustice under which we live today.

If you make the cattle think they will become dangerous, and when the right hon. Gentleman tries to persuade the House that he is going to make the cattle think, I see at the back of his mind and at the back of the employer's mind not that the cattle may think, but that they may become more capable producers of wealth. I resent ministers and others coming here and pretending that they are going to teach the working classes to think for themselves when in the background there is this motive, connected, indeed, with a patriotic desire to beat the Germans at their own game; and I think we should look very carefully into any measure against which such a charge may be made. We are fighting the Germans at the present time; I hope we shall beat them, but I want to beat them much more than any other hon. Member because I want to stamp out this sort of scheme, and not be forced after peace by German competition into adopting all these vile schemes to keep the working classes up, that they may take part in the competition for wealth or territory. If we win this war, surely we shall revert to that form of thought and legislation which has made English people what they are. We have managed to win so far in this war because we have always been taught that we should act upon our own initiative and for ourselves, and not be compelled by inspectors, governments and experts how to order our whole lives. That is what has made us, and when I hear the Minister of Education coming here and in an eloquent peroration saying how the girlhood of today, or rather of tomorrow, will be looked after from the time she is four until she is eighteen, that her health will be studied, her body drilled, her mind drilled, that such a thing as that can be put before us as a desirable aim – and I would add that it does not begin only after birth, for the district visitor comes round before they are born and after they are born, and this constant State inspection of the individual begins before birth and does not end until they are eighteen, because at eighteen the youth goes somewhere else, and is looked after by a military tutor instead of by an individual tutor – or that this grandmotherly legislation can in the long run benefit England, I absolutely deny. It may make the nation temporarily more efficient, temporarily more German, temporarily better producers of wealth, a more docile and more disciplined population, but that in the long run England can benefit from such compulsion, from such legislation, as this I for one absolutely and totally deny.

43 Sir Henry Hibbert

from House of Commons, *Parliamentary Debates*, vol. 764, 5 June 1918, cols. 1637–8.

Sir Henry Hibbert, Member for Chorley, Lancs, moved the Lancashire Amendment which changed Fisher's Act from providing part-time continuation classes for all children up to eighteen down to sixteen. It is worth noting that Fisher, who spoke immediately after Hibbert (below), replied as follows: 'Everyone who knows the North of England is aware of the distinguished work which the hon. Member for Chorley has done in connection with the cause of popular education in Lancashire, and it is impossible that he should be associated with any proposal conceived in a spirit inimical to the interest of education.'

. . . both as an educationist and as a commercial man I recommend the selection of the fittest. I do not mean the selection of the fittest as it has been carried out up to now. I outlined a plan, and that was to examine the boys at twelve, which is the proper age to enter a secondary school, to examine them at sixteen and pick out your best, and examine them again at eighteen, and on the results of that examination send them either to a university or to a technical college. I would give liberal maintenance allowances, and I think you would see that process more considerably help the future prosperity both of the people and the trade of this country than you will under this Bill. Realizing that children develop sometimes at a later stage than others, I would further examine at the age of fourteen the children in the elementary day schools who have been unsuccessful at twelve, give them a fourth examination at sixteen and pick out the best, and again at eighteen, and as a result send them to a university or secondary school. I feel perfectly confident that that is the only true foundation upon which a scheme of education can be built up.

44 London County Council

from a Memorandum on the Education Act 1918, 1920, pp. 3–5.

One of the first local authorities to respond to Fisher's Act was the London County Council, and in its Memorandum, it very firmly rejected the scheme for part-education on the basis of the industrial lobby. London, like most other authorities, was mainly concerned with the need for industrial recuperation after the war, and its Memorandum left no doubt where its priorities lay.

The Education Committee of the Federation has been charged by the Council with the general consideration of the education of the country and its relation to the improvement of industrial efficiency. They have considered it necessary before dealing in detail with the training directly affecting industry to consider the general scheme of education and the alterations and improvements which may be necessary in it, particularly in the light of the proposals put forward by the President of the Board of Education.

At the very outset of their report the Committee wish to state quite categorically that they consider the extension, and still more the improvement, of the educational system of the country to be one of the greatest needs of the present time, and they will welcome any well-considered development of educational facilities for all children without distinction throughout the country. If any of their recommendations appear to fall short of this ideal, it is because they feel that at present it is impracticable to obtain all that may be desirable. They have accordingly decided to lay stress in their report on those reforms which they believe to be most urgent: firstly the improvement of elementary education; secondly, the provision of a full secondary education for the more able children, and, only after these measures have been taken, an improved general education for the remainder.

For the purpose of ascertaining the views of industry generally on the whole question of education the Committee circulated a memorandum with a questionnaire attached to all the members of the Federation and to the members of the affiliated associations. The recommendations of this report have been generally approved by very large majorities.

The Committee feel that it is essential for the well-being of the nation, and for industry in particular, that elementary education should be extended and very considerably improved. They accordingly support very heartily Mr Fisher's suggestion that compulsory education for all up to the age of fourteen should be established, and they put forward in the body of their report recommendations which they consider should be adopted in order to bring about an improvement in the elementary education which is at present provided.

The Committee are not, however, in agreement with Mr Fisher's proposal to impose compulsory part-time education at the present time on all children in this country up to the age of eighteen.

From the answers which have been received to the questionnaire it is evident that in every industry this proposal is viewed with great alarm, as the establishment of the new system would occur at the very time when it would be most essential for the industrial future of the country that the minimum of dislocation should take place.

At the same time the Committee feel that they are in general accord with Mr Fisher's views on secondary education, and they are entirely sympathetic to the principle that every child in the country of whatever class should have an opportunity of complete education if it is fitted to benefit by it.

They have, therefore, decided to recommend that, in place of Mr Fisher's proposals for compulsory part-time continuation education, a liberal system of whole-time education for elected children should be adopted as being more suited to the needs of the present time. They consider that more advantage would be obtained by giving a full-time course to those children most capable of benefiting by it than by a general system of part-time education under which the more able children would inevitably be kept back to the standard of those mentally inferior to them. They feel, moreover, very strongly that a period of eight hours a week taken out of working hours would impose a burden upon many industries which they would be quite unable to bear except as the result of a process of very gradual development. They would point out that in Germany this very difficulty was felt, and at the inauguration of the compulsory part-time system in that country provision was made for its adoption only for a very small number of hours a week, which could be gradually extended to suit the convenience of the various trades concerned and the prevailing local conditions. The regulations for establishing the scheme provided for a low compulsory minimum of two hours per week, with a maximum of eight hours per week, and between these limits power was given to make arrangements locally.

Attention is called to the fact that in many trades a very large proportion of the employees are under the age of eighteen, and if they were all withdrawn from industry for eight hours a week a very serious dislocation would occur, more especially in cases where the young worker is part of a group, whose operations would be interfered with during his hours of instruction.

The Committee have not considered fully the question of the education of girls. They feel, however, with respect to this, that from an industrial point of view it is more important that, where education is vocational, the vocation should be domestic life rather than handicrafts. They would also point out that in certain trades a considerable proportion of the employees are females, many of whom would leave the trade on marriage at, or soon after the age of eighteen.

The Committee in this connection would like to express their very warm support of a system of whole-time education for selected children similar to that established by the London County Council. The scheme which is outlined in this report adheres very closely to the principles which have been carried out by the Council with very excellent results. Under this system, the Committee are informed, every child who is mentally capable of benefiting by secondary education is enabled to obtain it, and until elementary education has been improved the Committee feel that it would be difficult to advance further at present than the Council have already gone.

In the foregoing remarks the Committee do not wish to rule out any future developments in the direction of establishing compulsory part-time education for those children who are not selected for the full-time secondary course. They suggest, however, that such extension should be adopted very tentatively and with the greatest caution. They would recommend very great elasticity in the regulations for establishing the scheme in order that it may be possible for the conditions to vary in different districts so as to suit the industries concerned and the local requirements.

The Committee, however, recognize the urgent need of improved physical training, for which an adequate supply of instructors can be expected after demobilization of the Army, and the necessity for this training to continue after fourteen if it is to attain its full value. They consider that a definite minimum of hours per week should be fixed, and that it should be left to each education authority to make arrangements that would best suit the conditions of different districts. It might be possible in many industries to arrange that part, at least, of these hours might be taken out of working time. The Committee strongly recommend that organized games should be included in any scheme.

General considerations

The Committee have throughout their report considered the question of educational reform more especially from the point of view of industry, and they would therefore draw attention to certain considerations which in their opinion should be borne in mind in any extension of educational facilities.

In consideration of the present dislocation of industry and the necessity of readjustment at as early a moment as possible after the conclusion of the war, the Committee feel that it is most essential that any extension of the time devoted exclusively to education should be very gradual in order to allow the necessary adjustment to be made in the labour markets.

At the same time they would very strongly advise that in selecting children for higher education care should be taken to avoid creating, as was done, for example, in India, a large class of persons, whose education is unsuitable for the employment which they eventually enter.

The Committee also feel that it would be very advisable to increase both the numbers, and in some respects the efficiency, of the teaching staff, before undertaking any considerable increase of facilities.

The Committee, therefore, while they do not wish to exclude the possibility of higher education being at some future date extended to all children, believe that more benefit will accrue to industry and to the country in general by concentrating upon an attempt to secure an improved compulsory elementary education for all children, together with a sound secondary education with full facilities for acquiring a knowledge of technical and commercial subjects, followed by a complementary university education for the necessarily limited number of children selected as best fitted to profit by it, than by any attempt to introduce prematurely a universal scheme of compulsory higher education, whether part- or whole-time.

Of the 2044 replies which have been received on this subject 1186 have approved the proposal of whole-time education for selected children, whereas only twenty-three are in favour of part-time education for all children. Two hundred and thirty-three firms suggest a combination of the two systems. The remainder, very largely consisting of the cotton industry, approved of a combination of whole-time and part-time education, provided that both are confined to selected children. It is considered by several industries that the adoption of the system of universal part-time education will be fatal to their future development and even to their continued existence.

The first part of the Memorandum is devoted, therefore, to suggesting the outline of a scheme which, in the opinion of the Committee, might secure the following three objects:

1. The provision of an improved elementary education for all children.

2. The provision of sufficient facilities to enable a selected number of really able children of whatever class to obtain a secondary education.

3. To enable the best of those who have obtained a secondary education to obtain a university or higher technical education.

General scheme of education

The Committee suggest that all children should receive a compulsory education up to the age of fourteen, and that this age should not be extended until sufficient teachers and facilities can be provided to enable this to be done efficiently, and until the labour market has adjusted itself to the new conditions. This is almost unanimously approved by nearly 2000 firms; in fact only six voted against it.

They consider that elementary education should consist firstly of a general elementary education more definitely concentrated than at present on the essential subjects. This stage should be completed by the normal children by the age of twelve. Special provision should be made for all backward children in order to prevent their impeding the progress of the normal children.

At the end of the school period in which they attain the age of twelve, the children should be divided into two classes.

1. *The more promising children*, who should pass either:
(a) Straight to a secondary school with the object of commencing a full course of whole-time secondary education laid out to cover a definite period of, say, four or five years.
(b) To a junior technical school with the object of undergoing a special full-time technical and vocational training calculated to fit them for the particular industry which their parents desire them to enter. This course should also cover a definite period of, say, three years.

The Committee consider that a much greater number of junior technical schools should be provided, especially in industrial districts, and that the nature of the training given in these schools should be largely determined by the character of the local industries.

2. *The less promising children*, who should continue in the elementary school until the end of the school period in which they attain the age of fourteen, receiving, however, during these last two years a more general training calculated rather to develop their character, general intelligence and powers

of observation than to increase their knowledge of educational subjects. Part of this training might be directly vocational and intended to fit the child for the particular industry which it will enter at fourteen. This would apply more especially to towns and districts which are almost exclusively engaged in one industry.

This subdivision is practically unanimously approved.

The Committee would suggest that this division of the second period of elementary education into two classes should be based either upon success or failure in attaining a fairly high standard by examination, or upon an analysis of the child's work and its results during the previous years, or by a combination of both these methods.

Every facility should, however, be afforded to those, who, while possessed of good ability, are late in developing, and who, for this or any other reason, do not proceed to second or junior technical schools at the age of twelve, to proceed to such schools later, and for this purpose considerable elasticity should be retained, and full opportunities should be given to children who leave school at fourteen to continue their education at voluntary continuation classes.

Secondary education or junior technical education; for selected children

The secondary and junior technical courses would necessarily be voluntary. Provision should, however, be made to recompense parents to some extent for the loss of the earning power of their children, in order to encourage as many of the selected children as possible to take these courses and to complete them.

The Committee attach the greatest importance to the completion of these courses by any child which commences them, and consider that every inducement should be offered to parents whose children have commenced a secondary junior technical course, to permit them to remain at school until it is completed. This should not, of course, impair the power of the education authorities to remove any child whose conduct or general progress is consistently unsatisfactory.

It is suggested that this inducement to parents might be offered by:

1. Providing for the entire education expenses of the child.

2. Allowing a graduated sum per week to any parent making declaration of the need of such assistance.

3. Rendering parents withdrawing their children without adequate reasons before the completion of the course liable to refund the money which had been granted to them.

45 London County Council

from a Memorandum on the Education Act 1918, 1920, pp. 27–8.

Though London rejected many of the major facets of the 1918 Act, it pursued improvements in secondary-school curricula and widened the scholarship system which Sidney Webb had introduced. The secondary-school curriculum described in the 1920 Memorandum makes interesting comparisons with Morant's view of secondary schooling (see 18).

When the Council became the Authority for higher education, a bias had been given to the curriculum of many of the London secondary schools, especially those with a small endowment, by the grants made under the technical intruction Acts of 1889 and 1891, which could be devoted only to science, art and modern languages. Thus, in a number of schools, particularly those connected with polytechnics and technical institutes, a disproportionate time was allocated to one or other of these subjects, and the qualifications of the teachers of them were often higher than those of other members of the staffs. Since the passing of the Education Acts of 1902 and 1903, which made it possible for aid to be given to any subject of the curriculum, these inequalities have been gradually redressed.

Another factor which unduly influenced the curriculum, especially in the lower stages, was the number of external examinations. These have been gradually reduced, so that today few London secondary schools present their pupils for an external examination before the age of sixteen. The whole conception of the secondary-school curriculum may be said to have been transformed. It is no longer regarded as a mere aggregate of subjects, determined, by a variety of circumstances, internal and external, but as an organism in which every part is vitally related to every other, and which evolves from within. The new schools created and maintained by the Council, while lacking the traditions and historical associations of the older aided foundations, have had the advantage of profiting from the first from this more liberal and balanced view of the curriculum. And the older schools, with the financial aid and the advice of the Board of Education and the Council, have shown themselves ready to adjust their schemes of work to the new conditions. All alike are seeking to give a training that is (1) humane on the literary, scientific and artistic sides; (2) physical, through organized games, drill and gymnastics, and remedial treatment; (3) practical, in the sense of being a preparation for the pupils' after careers; (4) social, through various recreative activities, out of school hours.

The core of the curriculum is increasingly to be found in the work of the four years between twelve and sixteen, the latter being the age (as already mentioned) at which the first external examination is now usually taken. Though there are naturally and rightly many variations in detail, the broad lines of the syllabus in the London secondary schools during this period are uniform. English is recognized as forming the basis of the scheme of work. It is no longer the Cinderella of the curriculum. Better methods of teaching grammar and composition, written and oral; increased attention to speech-training and phonetics; above all, a more liberal supply of good literature, and more enlightened ways of studying it, have given to English a new place and significance. The change has been partly due to the necessity of finding a means of literary culture for the large number of junior scholars who have entered secondary schools with little humane background. But it springs in the main from a new attitude to the mother-tongue as an instrument of liberal education. Among its results is the recognition of the great importance of the library in the school equipment.

With few exceptions secondary-school pupils learn at least one foreign language, usually French. The teaching of this subject has been largely influenced by the 'direct method', which lays predominant stress on the use of the spoken language. The method, even when not adopted fully, has done much to vitalize the work in French. It makes severe demands on the capacity and energy of the teachers, who have been helped to improve and keep up their qualifications by the provision of classes in phonetics, and of scholarships to enable them to attend holiday courses in France. The considered aim of the teaching is not merely to give a knowledge of French, but to familiarize the pupils with some of the general features of the Latin culture. In most schools a second language is taught, and is usually begun two years after the first. Where a modern language is taken, it has been usually German. What permanent effect the war will have on the place of German in the secondary-school curriculum, and on our national education generally, it is too soon to say. Italian and Spanish, both very important for literary and commercial purposes, can hardly as yet be said to be serious competitors with German for the place of the second language. This place is still mainly taken, not by a modern language, but by Latin. This might have been expected in the older 'aided' schools for boys, some of which were inheritors of the classical tradition. But it is noteworthy that not only in them and in the girls' 'high schools', but also in the new maintained schools, both for boys and girls, a considerable proportion of pupils are learning Latin. None the less the traditional methods of classical instruction have been modified. More effort is being made to familiarize boys and girls with a fairly wide range of Latin literature, and less attention is being given to Latin prose and to grammar. The direct method is used in some schools, but most teachers of Latin in London prefer the older system, with the modifications just mentioned. Except in the historic public schools, and in some of the girls' schools which follow similar lines of study, Greek has a small place in the curriculum. It is taken by pupils who are aiming at entrance classical scholarships, and until recently it has been a necessary subject for those who wish to proceed to the older universities.

The scope of history as a secondary school subject has been widened, though there have been difficulties in giving it an adequate place in the timetable. Social and industrial history have been dealt with, as well as political, though 'civics' as a separate subject has not made much way. The war will doubtless direct increased attention to modern European history. The historical textbooks in use in the schools have been greatly improved, and are often written by scholars of the highest standing. Much more use than formerly is made of pictures and documents for illustrative purposes. In some schools these have been collected and effectively arranged in special history rooms.

Geography, in spite of some good work, has scarcely yet secured its due place in the curriculum, partly owing to the lack of sufficient teachers with special qualifications in the subject.

It has already been pointed out that, owing to the operation of the Technical Instruction Acts, there has been less leeway to make up in the mathematical and scientific sides of the curriculum than in the humanistic. But here, too, there are developments to be noted. In all the new school buildings erected since the Council assumed control, and in the reconstruction of old buildings, careful provision has been made for laboratory instruction, with the result that the aided and maintained secondary schools enjoy adequate facilities for practical work in science. The tendency, if anything, has been to lay rather too much stress on laboratory instruction, and to neglect the wider aspect of science teaching. A reaction against this narrowing of the scope of the curriculum has now set in, and more attention is being paid to the broad generalizations of science, and to the relation of scientific knowledge to the problems of everyday life. During the last few years many schools have been endeavouring to create a real interest in science by forming a lending library of popularly written books on science for general reading. This is a valuable step forward.

In mathematics concrete methods of instruction have been introduced with good effect, and some of the methods used in the higher branches of mathematics have been introduced with good effect, and some of the methods used in the higher branches of mathematics have been introduced at an earlier stage in the curriculum. There is still room for improvement in the teaching of applied mathematics, and in the upper part of the school a good deal might be done by laying stress upon the relations of physics to mathematics.

During the period under review there has been a marked change in the attitude towards music and art as part of the secondary-school curriculum. They are no longer looked upon as 'extras', but as essential elements in a liberal education, though instrumental music, involving individual instruction, is necessarily taken outside of school hours. Manual training in woodwork and metalwork for boys, and domestic economy for girls, have been developed, and have been brought into closer relation with the more academic sides of the curriculum.

Far more attention has been given of late years to the physical well-being and development of the pupils. Large playgrounds have been provided. Organized games, drill and gymnastics occupy much time. Midday dinners have been arranged on the school premises at a minimum cost. A system of medical examination has been instituted. In fact, the most modern conception of a secondary-school curriculum is the application, to a wider extent than was possible in the ancient world, of *mens sana in corpore sano*. Social activities are also strongly in evidence.

In the maintained schools and in most of the aided schools the curriculum does not include in school hours the 'clerical' subjects of typewriting, shorthand and book-keeping, though the lack of facilities for learning them has led a good many pupils, especially girls, to leave school prematurely. What effect the day continuation schools may have on this somewhat difficult problem remains to be seen. In some boys' schools advanced commercial courses, including economics, industrial and social history, and modern languages, have been organized. Now that the University of London has instituted a degree in commerce, such courses will become increasingly important.

It is too soon yet to estimate the effect of the 'advanced courses' recently instituted by the Board of Education. They are as yet in a somewhat experimental stage. But there is every reason to expect that they will stimulate and systemize the work at the top of the school, and that they will do much to prolong the average of school life. The relation between these courses and the university examinations needs to be adjusted, if they are to have their full effect on the higher work of the schools.

It is perhaps the best testimony to the influence of the secondary schools on the intellectual and social life of London that at the present time they cannot accommodate the large numbers who are seeking admission to them. They have helped to create a demand which has outrun the supply. There has been a stirring of the waters, of which the end is not yet. London has at last listened to Matthew Arnold's insistent cry 'Organize your Secondary Education.'

46 London County Council

from a Memorandum on the Education Act of 1918, 1920, pp. 30–31.

The scholarship scheme

A comprehensive system of scholarships has been established. These scholarships may be divided into three classes: county scholarships, scholarships for students intending to become teachers, and technical and trade scholarships. In each case the scholarships, in addition to remission of fees, provide maintenance grants where the circumstances of the scholar make such assistance necessary.

The county scholarships provide a complete scheme, by which a boy or girl may proceed from the public elementary school at the age of eleven to the highest grades of education at a university, technical college, or other institution providing advanced training. Every boy and girl in an elementary school in London, who has reached a certain standard by the age of eleven, is required to sit for an examination in English and Arithmetic. On the result of this examination, combined with the reports from the schools, about 1600 to 1700 junior county scholarships are awarded each year, but the number is not limited. These scholarships, which are also open (under a condition as to income) to children not in attendance at elementary schools, are tenable at almost any secondary school in London, in the first instance for three years, and are renewable for a further period of two years, if the scholar is reported to be capable of profiting by further education, i.e., they are held as a rule till the scholars attain the age of sixteen. It has recently been decided that, in future, these scholarships shall be tenable for five years firm from the date of award. Boys and girls who do not succeed in obtaining junior county shcolarships at the age of eleven, have an opportunity of entering for supplementary junior county scholarships at the age of thirteen. The latter scholarships were introduced mainly for the benefit of children whose mental powers develop at a somewhat later age. At the age of sixteen, some of the scholars leave school for industrial or business pursuits; others are recommended for bursaries, and remain at secondary schools for a further year, or in some cases two years, with a view to entering the teaching profession; others obtain intermediate county scholarships which enable them to continue their education until the age of eighteen or nineteen. About 300 of these intermediate county scholarships are offered for competition each year. They may be competed for both by junior county scholars and by other pupils in secondary schools, whose parents' incomes do not exceed a certain limit. On attaining the age of eighteen, intermediate scholars or other eligible pupils in secondary schools may apply for senior county scholarships, which enable them to proceed to a university or a technical college for a three years', or in some cases a four or five years' course, of advanced study.

The scholarships for the preliminary education of teachers consist of probationer bursaries, bursaries and student teacherships. Probationer bursaries are usually tenable for three years; bursaries and student teacherships are, as a rule, tenable for one year each. Probationer bursaries are awarded at the age of thirteen or fourteen, but are confined to certain schools. Bursaries are open to pupils of all secondary schools. The age limits for bursaries and student teacherships are sixteen to eighteen. During the tenure of the bursaries, the scholars continue their education at the schools they have already attended. During the tenure of the student teacherships, they are engaged for the greater part of their time in receiving training in the art of teaching. At the end of the period of tenure, student teachers enter training colleges. In certain cases bursaries are given for a second year in lieu of student teacherships.

The technical and trade scholarships comprise the following: (a) scholarships in science and technology, to enable persons engaged in industry to devote themselves to full-time day instruction in technical colleges of university rank; (b) scholarships in art and artistic crafts, tenable at the day classes of schools of art or schools of arts and crafts; (c) evening exhibitions in art, science and technology; (d) trade scholarships for boys and girls, tenable at day trade schools; (e) scholarships in domestic economy, tenable at the day classes of polytechnics and technical institutes.

Important changes in the scholarship scheme have been approved by the Council since the passing of the Education Act 1918. These changes, which are fully set out in Part II, Chapter II§ III will not become operative as regards awards taken up in 1921.

47 Lord Percy of Newcastle
from *Some Memories*, 1958, p. 93.

The Fisher Act of 1918 subsequently came in for great criticism, much of it unfair. Eustace Percy, President of the Board of Education from 1924–9, who had to deal with the most financially stringent period the

Board ever experienced, later reflected on some of its shortcomings, as one who was faced with implementing its reforms.

Lloyd George ... started the new tradition of treating the field of education, which he had so recently undertaken to develop, as, for that very reason, the field also where economies in public expenditure could most easily be effected when the public purse strings had to be tightened. To that he was no doubt tempted by Fisher's miscalculations. Fisher had launched an ambitious programme of expansion, the cost of which he estimated at first at a mere £3,000,000; but in this estimate he had made no allowance for the inevitable improvement of teachers' salaries and pensions. The veteran secretary of the National Union of Teachers, Sir James Yoxall, had foreseen the consequent collapse and had not joined in the enthusiasm of his professional colleagues for Fisher's Education Bill, which he thought was an attempt to do too much in too many directions simultaneously. The increase in teachers' salaries flooded out most of Fisher's planned developments; and his last two years in office was a discouraging period of disappointed hopes. That was his legacy to his successor in 1922. A quarter of a century later Mr Aneurin Bevan was to make a miscalculation of almost precisely the same kind in creating a too sudden socialized National Health Service. It is, indeed, odd that statesmen never learn from the past and what they learn most slowly seems to be arithmetic.

48 R. H. Tawney

'Keep the Workers' Children in their Place', *Daily News*, 14 February 1918, reprinted in R. Hinden (ed.), *The Radical Tradition*, 1966, pp. 49–54.

The aftermath of the 1918 education debate gave R. H. Tawney the opening for one of the most devastating attacks on the reactionary wing of British industry ever penned. Tawney's essay is a model of sustained invective which clearly delineated the differences between the Labour and Liberal view of educational advance. But Tawney himself later departed from the Trades-Union policy of 'common schools' (see 51).

While the nation as a whole has seen in the Education Bill[1] the tentative

1. Leading to the 'Fisher' Education Act of 1918, which abolished all exemption from school attendance for children under fourteen, extended public provision for higher education, and proposed a system of compulsory 'continuation schools'.

beginnings of a new and more humane educational policy, there are those to whom the subordination of education to economic exigencies is still, apparently, an indisputable axiom. It would be unfair, no doubt, to attach too much weight to the Memorandum on Education recently issued by the Education Committee of the Federation of British Industries. Both in and out of the Federation there are a considerable number of employers to whom its naïve materialism will be highly uncongenial.

But the document is significant as the expression of a point of view which, though it is not representative, is not deterred by any false modesty from desiring to appear so, and which aims at intimidating the Government into abandoning the central element in its educational programme by the suggestion that the big battalions of industry have put their foot down. In thus attempting to mobilize the business interests against the children, the Federation of British Industries has unintentionally rendered a genuine service to the cause of educational reform. For it has revealed the motive and social policy which lie behind the opposition to the extension of higher education. They have only to be stated, in order to be rejected decisively by the public opinion of the community.

The days when education could be resisted by a direct frontal attack have passed, and the Education Committee of the Federation of British Industries is good enough to begin its Memorandum by assuring the public that it yearns for 'an improvement of the education system'. But it contrives, when it comes to the consideration of particular measures of educational reform, successfully to dissemble the affection which it feels for reform in the abstract. In particular, while it dwells on the need for better elementary education, and speaks feelingly of secondary education for 'the more able children', and demands a better system of training for teachers, it cannot accept the proposal which is the heart and kernel of the present Education Bill. Indeed, at the mere suggestion that all young persons should spend a small part of their time upon higher education, it cries and cuts itself with knives, quite like a person who is not fired by a passion for educational progress.

The Federation's first objection to the Education Bill is that unlimited supplies of juvenile labour are indispensable to industry, and that the proposals of that arch-Bolshevik, Mr Fisher, will shake to its foundations the fragile fabric of British industrial prosperity, 'A period of eight hours a week taken out of working hours would impose a burden upon many industries which they would be *quite unable to bear*, except as a process of very gradual development.'

Now it is true, of course, that any extension of education involves some industrial readjustment. It is also true that the lamentations of a certain section of employers over the prospective ruin of British industry have been part of the ritual which has accompanied the passage of every Education Act since 1870, and of every Factory Act since 1802; that experience has refuted these predictions as regularly as ignorance has made them; and that the 'burden' imposed by the present measure is insignificant compared with that borne by French and German employers before the war in the shape of military conscription. To suggest that British industry is suspended over an abyss by a slender thread of juvenile labour, which eight hours continued education will snap, that after a century of scientific discovery and economic progress it is still upon the bent backs of children of fourteen that our industrial organization, and national prosperity, and that rare birth of time, the Federation of British Industries itself, repose – is not all this, after all, a little pitiful ?

After fifty years of practical experience of the effort of raising the age of school attendance, the onus of proof rests upon those who allege that education will impede industry, not upon those who argue that education will stimulate all healthy national activities, and industry among them. Nevertheless, it may very readily be conceded that the establishment of a system of continued education from fourteen to eighteen will involve, like all other reforms, some practical difficulties. Very well, then; the Federation consists of practical men, to whom the nation may naturally appeal for assistance in overcoming them. What help do they offer ?

They offer, apparently, none. While well-known leaders of the cotton industry have been at pains to suggest how the circumstances of their particular trade might be adapted to meet the principle of the Education Bill, the attitude adopted in the Memorandum of the Federation of British Industries is one of frigid opposition to the whole policy of universal continued education. Education, it states, ought not to be extended beyond fourteen, 'until . . . the labour market has adjusted itself to the new conditions'. Of any consciousness, as is felt by an increasing number of employers, that there is an obligation upon those who organize industry to take pains to adapt it to the requirements of education, of any suspicion that fifty-five-and-a-half to sixty hours' labour a week may actually be excessive for children who have just left school, or that to stop education abruptly at fourteen is to stop it when it is just beginning to be most fruitful, or that there is a duty to the higher education to build a better world for all, there is, in this precious document, not a trace. The Bourbons of industry who drafted it have learned nothing and forgotten nothing. Europe is in ruins; and out of the sea of blood and tears the Federation of British Industries emerges jaunty and unabashed, clamouring that whatever else is shaken, the vested interest of employers in the labour of children of fourteen must not be disturbed by so much as eight hours a week.

But it is not merely for economic reasons that the Federation is opposed to higher education for all young persons. It is absolved from the necessity of proving that universal higher education is impossible because it does not really believe that universal higher education is desirable. Behind the objection based on the convenience of industry lies another objection based on the theory that all except a small minority of children are incapable of benefiting by education beyond the age of fourteen. It is not actually stated, indeed, that working-class children, like anthropoid apes, have fewer convolutions in the brains than the children of captains of industry. But the authors of the Memorandum are evidently sceptical as to either the possibility or the desirability of offering higher education to more than a small proportion of them.

In the manner of a European traveller describing a race which is too backward to count up to more than ten, it draws a sharp distinction between 'the more promising' child who is mentally capable of benefiting by higher education, and 'the less promising' child who is not. For the former there is to be full-time secondary education. For the latter there is to be elementary education up to fourteen, part of which, in the last two years of school life – a sinister suggestion – 'might be directly vocational and intended to fit the child for the particular industry which he will enter at fourteen'; and then full-time work in the factory. Nor is it contemplated that the children who are 'mentally capable of profiting by secondary education' will be more than a select minority. In a charming sentence, which reveals in a flash the view which it takes both of the function of the working classes in society and of the meaning of education, the Memorandum enters a solemn caveat against the dangers of excessive education. 'They would very strongly advise that in selecting children for higher education, care should be taken to avoid creating, as was done, for example, in India, a large class of persons *whose education is unsuitable for the employment which they eventually enter*.'

There it is, the whole Master Class theory of society in a sentence! One cannot refute it by argument, as one can refute the Federation's particular prophecies of the industrial disaster which would be caused by a more general diffusion of higher education. For this is not a question of fact, but of ultimate belief, and those who think that men are first of all men have no premise in common with those who think, like the authors of the Federation's Memorandum, that they are first of all servants, or animals, or tools.

One cannot, I say, disprove such a doctrine, any more than one can disprove a taste for militarism, or for drugs, or for bad novels. But one can expose its consequences. And its consequences are simple. They are some new form of slavery. Stripped of its decent draperies of convention, what it means is that education is to be used, not to enable human beings to become themselves through the development of their personalities, nor to strengthen the spirit of social solidarity, nor to prepare men for the better service of their fellows, nor to raise the general level of society; but to create a new commercial aristocracy, based on the selection for higher education of 'the more promising' children of working-class parents from among the vulgar mass, who are fit only to serve as the cannon fodder of capitalist industry.

This, then, is the subtle discovery which, as they pore over the lessons of the past three years, inspires in the Federation of British Industries bright hopes of a more profitable future. There are classes who are ends and classes who are means – upon that grand original distinction the community is invited to base its educational system. The aim of education is to reflect, to defend and to perpetuate the division of mankind into masters and servants. How delicate an insight into the relative value of human beings and of material riches! How generous a heritage into which to welcome the children of men who fell in the illusion that, in their humble way, they were the servants of freedom!

But why has the Federation reserved these revelations till now? If its gospel had been before the world in August, 1914, it might have reconciled us to the Prussian Government, which has long appreciated and practised it. Much money and several lives, both 'more promising' and 'less promising' – though perhaps the latter are hardly worth considering – might have been saved. As it is, it is just three-and-a-half years too late. The Federation must try again. And before it does so, let it read and digest the remark of Bacon: 'The Blessings of Judah and Issachar will never meet, that the same people shall be a lion's whelp and an ass between burdens.'

49 Labour Party

'Nursery Schools', a Memorandum prepared by the Advisory Committee on Education, 1919, pp. 21–2.

Just after the war and the passing of the Fisher Act, the Labour Party published proposals for the re-employment of young people. A special section of this Memorandum dealt with a demand for more nursery education.

Clause 19 of the Education Bill empowers local authorities to supply or aid the supply of nursery schools for children over two and under five years of age, and provides that the Board of Education may pay grants in aid of such schools.

Henceforward (once the Bill becomes law) it will be possible for local education authorities to establish and receive grants for nursery schools. If they are to do this extensively – and the need is great – the Board must use its influence to induce them to make the most of their new power. It has taken more than ten years to get local authorities to establish the comparatively small number of well-equipped school clinics which exist at the present time. We do not desire that the progress of nursery schools should be equally slow.

Further, local education authorities will not be able to establish nursery schools in the numbers required, nor will those established be of value unless a sufficient number of the right kind of teacher is forthcoming to staff them. This point is absolutely crucial. The staff of nursery schools most possess special qualifications and go through the special course of training needed to develop them. If they are of the right kind, nursery schools will be a success; if they are not, they will be a failure. But teachers with special qualifications needed do not exist in sufficient numbers at the present time, if indeed they exist at all, and cannot be created in a day. Unless clause 19 is to be a dead letter they must be trained, and trained as soon as possible. It is of urgent importance, therefore, that the Board of Education should state forthwith the nature of the qualifications which it will require from teachers in nursery schools, and of the training courses which it will recognize. When, and only when, that has been done, it will be possible for women who desire to take up this new and important work to prepare themselves for doing so.

The Labour Party desires, therefore, to urge on the Board of Education the importance, first, of making every effort to encourage local education authorities to establish nursery schools; and, second, to issue at the earliest possible moment a statement as to qualifications and training which may enable teachers for nursery schools to be trained in the necessary numbers. In bringing these demands to the attention of the Board, it would emphasize especially the following points:

1. However true it may be that the best place for children under five is the home, to keep them at home under present conditions is often neither practicable nor desirable. Many working-class mothers are at present overworked, and, of course, during the past three years the number of women who work in industry has largely increased. It is, therefore, of real importance that there should be public nurseries to which, if they desire,

mothers can take their younger children, and where they will know that they will spend the day amid healthy surroundings and under wholesome influences.

2. The development of nursery schools is the more important because local education authorities for several years past have pursued the policy of excluding from the elementary schools children between three and five years of age. In 1907, the children between three and five in the elementary schools of England and Wales numbered 459,034. In 1917, they numbered 209,272, or rather less than half. If this diminution had taken place by the choice of the parents it might have been welcomed. But it has not. It has been forced upon them by local education authorities. Provided that the *right kind* of school (i.e. not a school but a nursery) were available for young children, many mothers would be glad to make use of it.

3. Educational opinion is strongly in favour of the development of nursery schools. The Consultative Committee of the Board of Education reported in favour of an extension of them as long ago as 1908, and the Chief Medical Officer of the Board of Education in his last report (1916–17) emphasizes the importance of developing them. Since the report of the Consultative Committee was issued, several private experiments have revealed the enormous potentialities for good contained by nursery schools for young children. What young children require is fresh air, play, and rest, and this is what a nursery school offers them.

4. The development of nursery schools would tend greatly to raise the standard of physical health among the children of the country. The point is emphasized by the Chief Medical Officer of the Board of Education.

Facilities for treatment should be available for Nursery School children as readily as for others. The early treatment of physical defects usually yields far more satisfactory results than the treatment given after the defects have become established or habitual. *One reason for the provision of nursery schools is, indeed, to reduce the number of preventible defects now observed in entrants to the public elementary schools, and the underrated educational handicap and resulting incapacity.*

5. Though to ascertain the most suitable organization and arrangements of nursery schools must be a matter of time, it not premature to say that those which have already been established have proved that great benefits may be derived from them. Though nursery schools are still in the experimental stage, enough pioneer work has been done to prove their utility. What is now needed is for the Board of Education and local education authorities to build upon the tentative foundation already laid by private enterprise, to assist existing schools, and to promote the establishment of others.

6. In particular, it is essential that the Board of Education should encourage young women to undertake immediately, and in sufficient numbers, the training needed to qualify them for the difficult and responsible work of supplying the future staff of nursery schools. Certain suggestions for their training are included in the Appendix attached to this document. But the details are unimportant compared with the urgent necessity of enabling and encouraging recruits of the right quality to prepare for this branch of the profession.

For these reasons the Labour Party, believing that the Board of Education will agree with it in regarding nursery schools as an important and, indeed, indispensable part of the education system of the future, desires to urge the Board to encourage their establishment by every means in its power; and especially to facilitate the formation of a body of teachers with the requisite training and qualifications by defining now the qualifications which it will require in the teachers of nursery schools, the training and test of competence which it will recognize, and the grants which it will pay on account of prospective teachers in training institutions.

50 Board of Education

'The Question of Free Secondary Education', Report of the Departmental Committee on Scholarships and Free Places, 1920, pp. 12–17.

Even before Fisher's Act had a chance to be implemented, informed opinion began to move towards a more radical reorganization of secondary education. The Labour Party set up a committee under Tawney to formulate its own policy and a Board of Education report on the whole operation of scholarships and free places made its own views known in unequivocal terms.

That the State has a responsibility for the provision to its citizens of the means of education is a principle which it is needless for us to discuss. We do not question that it is a sound principle, but whether it be sound or unsound, it has, at any rate, been accepted and acted upon to an extent that places it now outside the sphere of controversy. Since 1891 the State has provided for free elementary education: since 1918 it has undertaken to provide free part-time post-elementary education; it already meets by central and local grants the greater part of the cost of secondary education in grant-aided schools; and now that State responsibility has gone so far it appears to us both natural and desirable that it should go further. The present condition of affairs in the matter of secondary education is transitional, and it has anomalous features, as transitional states are wont to have, that are unsatisfactory in themselves, and are harmful to the interests both of good education and good administration.

Apart from the provision of free places the education given in grant-aided secondary schools is already 'free' to a larger extent than is popularly realized. There are three ordinary sources of school income, public money in the shape of a grant from the Board or the local authority, income from endowments, and fees. Many schools are not endowed, and there are a few schools where no fees are charged. But in the schools where fees are charged fees meet only a part of the cost. The last published statistics dealing with school finance show that out of the total secondary school income of £2,663,661 the amount of £1,100,245 was contributed by fees. The burden on local and public funds amounted to £1,304,218.

When we remember further that in England 30 per cent of the pupils, and in Wales 42 per cent, pay no fees, the extent to which secondary education is already free is seen to be substantial. If our suggestion of an increase in the percentage of free places awarded on admission is accepted there is little doubt that just as the present 25 per cent rule has resulted in 30 per cent of free-place holders actually in the schools, because free pupils tend to stay longer at school than fee-paying pupils, so, after some years a higher percentage still will be reached, and to that extent secondary education will become free in a larger measure than it is today. Looking only to the terms of section 4 (4) of the Act, we cannot doubt that its effect must be to increase the number of free pupils in secondary schools whatever administrative steps may be taken to give effect to it.

It is not unnatural therefore that the evidence we have heard should constantly have raised in some form the question whether, either as an ultimate or as a prospective policy, it may be desirable to contemplate dispensing with the payment of all fees in secondary schools, and substituting for the present system what is usually known as free secondary education. We are not sure that this aspect of the free-place problem was intended to be included in our terms of reference, but we feel that it is so intimately connected with the questions we have had under consideration that we cannot ignore it in our Report.

The question arises all the more naturally in that the evolution of elementary schools offers a suggestive though not wholly analogous precedent. Elementary education has not always been free; it has become free since 1891. Further, the Act of 1918 makes provision for free part-time education continuing the education given by the elementary school.

It is true that the principle of compulsory attendance lies behind these types of free education, and supplies a definite basis for making them free. But to decline full financial responsibility for secondary education while accepting it for elementary and part-time post-elementary education is to emphasize an artificial and unsound distinction between the several stages of the educational process. Such a distinction seems to make the tacit assumption that school education is divisible into unrelated stages, that the first stage can be considered complete, and sufficient in itself, and that anything more than a part-time continuation is unessential and in the nature of a luxury. This is directly contrary to the weight of instructed opinion. The process of a good education is now generally regarded as one and indivisible throughout its successive stages. To a pupil capable of profiting by it secondary education is not unessential or a luxury, but a necessary and natural continuation of the elementary school course.

It is, we believe, on the clear recognition of this principle and on its consistent adoption in practice that the improvement of the educational system of the country in a large measure depends. Our present system neither recognizes it clearly, nor adopts it consistently. At present the State by accepting financial responsibility for some stages of the educational process while it refuses that for other stages no less beneficial in appropriate cases, tends rather to give to the principle a direct negative. We are of opinion, therefore, that sooner or later the State should be prepared to recognize the essential continuity of education by accepting the same financial responsibility in respect of secondary education that it has already accepted in respect of other and no more necessary stages and forms, and that in the meanwhile all steps for the immediate improvement of the financial basis of our secondary system, particularly in the matter of scholarships and free places, should be taken with that end in view.

Many, however, who would agree with these general considerations are doubtful whether the time is ripe for freeing the secondary schools. Some of our witnesses, for example, have urged that the effect of abolishing fees would be to drive a number of schools outside the national system, and have represented that the evil effects of this would be twofold. On the one hand the result might be to accentuate an undesirable segregation of social classes, and, on the other, many of these schools would be inefficient because they would be unable to command fees high enough to meet the cost of effective maintenance.

We recognize these possible dangers. With regard to the possibility that certain schools would be driven out of the national system, we think the extent of the danger may be exaggerated. The cost of maintaining a secondary school efficiently is now high and is likely to increase. It has to be remembered that in addition to the ordinary grants from public money the provisions of the Superannuation Act of 1918 are equivalent in effect to further, though indirect, grants from the State, and that it may become still more difficult for private schools to secure adequate staffing unless equivalent superannuation benefits are provided from their own resources. With regard to the possibility that the freeing of grant-aided secondary schools might result in a social cleavage we doubt whether enough weight has been attached to the importance of the distinction between some of these schools being free and all of them being free. There seems to be a feeling now that a school where fees are paid must be a better school than one that is free, and that the higher the fee the better the school, 'better' being understood partly in an educational partly in a social sense.

We doubt whether this feeling could long survive the freeing of all the schools now assisted from public funds. Similar apprehensions were felt when the admission of free-place pupils was first required in 1907 by article 20, but the almost unanimous opinion expressed to us by competent witnesses who had experience of the change was that, within a very short time, the free-place pupils were absorbed into the system of the schools, and that so far from the parents of fee-paying pupils now having any objection to their presence, it is commonly recognized that the schools benefit thereby.

We have also had before us the objection that if fees were no longer paid, and the schools became wholly dependent on public money and endowments, there might be a tendency, in the interests of a false economy, to a general levelling down of the schools. At present there are some secondary schools that represent a more advanced type of education than others and are proportionately more expensive to staff and maintain. Would there not be a danger that, if fees disappeared, such schools would be reduced to the more ordinary level?

We recognize this danger and do not minimize it. As one of our most experienced witnesses has said, uniformity is, perhaps, the greatest danger in education. No policy of freeing the schools would, in our view, be satisfactory if it did not imply a scale of grant compensating in full for the loss of fees and enabling schools of various types to continue to exist at least as successfully as before. A liberal scale of grants administered in a generous educational spirit would be essential. There is, of course, always the possibility that the increased control due in practice to any increase of financial responsibility may in the interest of administrative convenience lead to too uniform a system. Is it, however, certain that the payment of fees does in itself act as a check on this tendency? We doubt whether it does. On the other hand the acceptance by the State of fuller financial responsibility would enable it to require from the schools, with increased authority, satisfactory standards and conditions, particularly in the matter of accommodation and teaching staff.

It was further contended by some that to free the secondary schools might result in a lowering of the standard of admission, and so lead to a general levelling down of the educational standard. We do not think, however, that in the present great excess of the demand for secondary education over the supply of accommodation there is any reason to apprehend such a result. As long as the demand exceeds the supply, there must be some element of competition in the arrangements for admission, and competition may be relied upon to maintain the standard. It is generally recognized that under present conditions, with their strong element of competition, a large proportion of pupils who are unable to win a scholarship or free place are nevertheless capable of profiting to the full by secondary education. Further, if the supply of accommodation increases in proportion to the demand it may be argued with force that there will on the whole be no harm, but rather the reverse, in the consequent widening of the sweep of the net cast to catch pupils for the secondary schools. We contemplate also, and it is indeed one of our recommendations, that a standard of admission should be laid down, and the observance of this will protect the secondary system from any such ill consequence as that suggested.

There are, on the other hand, advantages in the ideal of free secondary education, to be set against the objections to which we have referred, that are obvious and important. The acceptance by the State of full financial responsibility would enable it, as we have said, to require from the schools, with increased authority, satisfactory standards and conditions. It would remove the reproach against the present method of financing secondary education, that it is based upon no fixed principle as to the distribution of the cost between the parent and the State. In doing so it would put an end to the fallacious notion in the minds of parents that by paying fees they are meeting the whole cost of their children's education, whereas in fact they are meeting only a part of it. The importance of this last consideration should not be underestimated. The fee-payer feels and sees the payment of fees; but payments made by the State on his behalf are made indirectly, and are not appreciated or seen. Fee-payers are tempted thereby to feel themselves entitled to more responsibility and influence in the sphere of secondary education than their contributions warrant. This is an unsatisfactory state of affairs, and the only complete remedy for it is for the State to complete the process, already far advanced, of freeing the secondary schools.

The simplification of the secondary school system, in relation to the free-place question, seems to us an important advantage. The view has been put to us that section 4 (4) of the Act, strictly interpreted, will be administratively impracticable if the practice of charging fees is maintained. Local authorities would be called upon first to determine who were the children 'capable of profiting' and then who among the parents of these children were unable to pay fees; and that this in practice would be an impossible task. Though we are not prepared to go as far as this, we cannot fail to see that an extension to the free-place system, such as we propose, reaches, at a great cost of energy, an end that could be reached in a simpler and easier way by abolishing fees. We do not contemplate that free schools would be open to any children who were not regarded as capable of profiting by the course provided, but we realize the difficulties and inconsistencies likely to be involved in discriminating between those who can and those who cannot pay fees.

The obvious practical difficulty in the way of freeing the secondary school is the cost. The liability that would be imposed upon public funds at present by the abolition of fees, although in itself substantial, is not a large one compared with the total cost of all forms of education. The amount received in fees for pupils in grant-earning secondary schools during 1912–13 was £1,100,245.[1] No later figures are available, and in recent years fees have been raised to some extent in many schools. The figure given is, however, at least a rough measure of the extra expense to be cast upon public funds, in respect of the loss of existing fees, but not, of course, in respect of any such extension of post-elementary education as we have suggested in chapter 4 of this Report.

It has, however, been put to us that in view of the urgent need for national economy and the inadequacy of the funds available for general educational purposes, this sum received in fees cannot at present be spared, and that public money is spent better at present in such ways, for instance, as aiding cleverer children and developing the much-needed alternative forms of post-elementary education, than it would be in relieving fee-paying parents. We admit that there is much force in the contention, and in the present state of the national budget are not prepared to recommend the freeing of the grant-aided secondary schools as an immediate policy. We do, however, feel that as a prospective policy, capable, we hope, of being made effective at a fairly early date, it is on the balance of advantage a desirable one.

1. Perhaps £2,000,000 now, in view of larger numbers and raised fees.

51 R. H. Tawney

from *Secondary Education for All: A Policy for Labour*, 1922, pp. 62–7.

*The Labour Party's policy on secondary education came out in
support of a continuous system of compulsory schooling, but in doing so,
it turned away from the earlier demands for common schools and tacitly
acknowledged that secondary schooling would take different forms. It
would take decades before the party moved back to its original policy of
'one school for all' or comprehensive education.*

Selection for higher education by means of scholarships has been for the
last twenty years the accepted policy of English education. The number of
children passing by means of them from primary to secondary schools,
though still small, has steadily increased, and if the schemes prepared by
local education authorities under the Act of 1918 are carried out, it will
increase more rapidly in the future. But the policy of selection may obviously
be given two opposite interpretations. If, as is hinted might be the case by
the Departmental Committee on Scholarships and Free Places, the effect
of it were that 75 per cent of the children in primary schools passed to secondary schools, then selection would be hardly distinguishable from
universal provision. When it results, as in certain areas today, in the pupils
in the secondary schools amounting to less than two per thousand of the
population, selection is hardly distinguishable from no provision at all.

One may, in fact, proceed either by inclusion or by exclusion, either by
endeavouring to ensure that all children other than the obviously sub-
normal shall pass at adolescence to some form of secondary school, or by
treating full-time secondary education as an exceptional privilege to be
reserved for children of exceptional capacity. The plan of development
suggested in the schemes of West Ham and of Gloucestershire would lead
in the first direction. The scheme of London County Council, or the views
expressed in the scheme of the Education Authority of Salford that a
'secondary school is intended for those who will prepare for some of the
more responsible positions in after life', or the opposition of the Federation
of British Industries to a wide diffusion of higher education on the ground
that it would 'unfit children for the employments they eventually enter',
or the proposal of the Select Committee on Education Expenditure to
restrict the access to secondary schools by raising their fees, would lead to
the second.[1]

1. Seventh Report from the Select Committee on National Expenditure (December,
1920), p. xiv. The committee appears to have been much shocked by the fact that 'the

On the view, primary and secondary education are stages in a single process through which all normal children ought to pass, because all, though in different degrees, will respond to them; the measure of the success of both is the heightened human capacity which they evoke. On the other view, the primary and secondary school represent, not stages of education, but systems of education. There must be facilities for passing from one to the other, for the brighter children of the working classes are needed to supply the educated *personnel* – the 'intellectual proletariat' – which modern industry, in its higher ranges, requires. But equality of educational provision up to sixteen is impossible of attainment and mischievous could it be attained. Industry needs cannon fodder as well as staff officers, and it is not desirable that the minds of the rank and file, even if capable of development (which the Federation of British Industries doubt), should be unduly developed. When the cream of intelligence has been skimmed off by scholarships, the mass of children must pass at fourteen to the factory with such part-time continued education (if any) as the exigencies of industry may permit.

The choice between these two views is the most momentous issue of educational policy before the nation. As far as the workers of the country are concerned, their decision has already been made. They demand neither central schools, nor part-time continuation schools, nor any other of the makeshifts by which it is sought to mitigate in detail the evil results of that organization on lines of class which is the tragedy of English education, while maintaining it in principle and in substance. They demand full-time secondary education for all normal children up to the age of sixteen. So to increase the provision for secondary education as to enable the majority of children to pass to a secondary school at eleven will obviously require an effort extending over a period of several years. But the measures taken now will depend upon the goal which is envisaged, and in insisting that the aim of development must be a universal system of secondary education up to sixteen, in insisting that it shall be, in the words of the Director of Education for Gloucestershire, 'a scheme which shall ultimately bring a complete secondary education within reach of everybody', the Labour Party is recommending nothing either extravagant or impracticable. It has on its side the expert opinion of many teachers, of educationalists, of a considerable number of those who are engaged in the practical work of educational

---

fees charged for secondary and higher education are very low, in fact far below the cost of the education which is afforded'. It apparently did not occur to it to inquire whether in any country, at any time, the policy of selling higher education at cost price (or, as the committee would presumably prefer, at a profit) has ever been adopted, and if not, why not?

administration. Its policy is framed not for the advantage of any single class, but to develop the human resources of the whole community.

The case for a development of education on these lines advanced by the educationalist is simple. From his point of view the intrusion into educational organization of the vulgarities of the class system is an irrelevance as mischievous in effect as it is odious in conception. 'Secondary education of the best kind,' states the Executive Committee of the Incorporated Association of Assistant Masters in Secondary Schools, 'should be open to all; and the time is long overdue for the removal of any restriction of opportunity for secondary education through accident of birth, social position or financial means. The removal of such restrictions we regard as an act of social justice.'[2] What the educationalist means by 'secondary' and 'primary' education has nothing to do with class stratification and the curious educational ritual which in England is annexed to it. It is adolescent education, and education which is preparatory to adolescent education. The capital message of educational theory, he would argue, is that the success of education is proportionate to the degree to which it is related to the facts of natural development. Hence it must be envisaged as a whole. The crucial point in development is adolescence. Hence the years from eleven should not be the fag-end of the primary-school course, but a period marked by new beginnings in education as in life. The foundations for specialization must be laid by a sound general education. Hence general education should last to sixteen, and children should not be encouraged to specialize, still less to enter industry, before it. The younger the children the more precarious and unreliable the classification of them according to the test of examination. Hence all classifications made (as in examinations for free places) should be purely provisional; no child should be excluded from a secondary education as a result of them; all children should pass as a matter of course at the appropriate age to the secondary school, just as all children have passed up to that age through the primary school. The educationalist, in short, looks forward with Professor Adams to developments under which, 'in twenty years' time, there would be one system of free education from the cradle to the grave, or for as long as we should desire it'.[3] He urges, in the words of Professor Nunn's report to the Education Reform Council, that 'though schemes of education necessarily take account of varying social conditions, their essential lines must follow the true lines of growth of human nature', that 'the present break at fourteen should not be regarded as an unalterable feature of the social system', and that 'the years from twelve to fourteen must be treated as

2. Resolution of 14 March 1921.

3. Lecture by Professor Adams, reported in *The Times Educational Supplement*, 12 November 1921.

part of a continuous course that in no case reaches its end earlier than the age of sixteen'.[4]

These general considerations are reinforced by the evidence resulting from the development of more exact measurements of intelligence than could be applied till recently. It is sometimes objected by persons without practical experience of educational questions that a wide extension of secondary education up to sixteen is not desirable, because all but a small minority of children – usually, it may be observed, a minority not in excess of the number being educated at the time when the objection is advanced – are not, as it is said, 'worth educating'. It is not necessary to point out that those who use this argument do not, apparently, regard it as applicable to themselves or to their own children, whose absolute 'worth' is assumed to be self-evident, or to emphasize the obvious fallacy of assuming that the value of education can be reduced to the terms of a profit and loss account, or to inquire into the precise nature of the calculus which decides that the child of, say, a mine owner is 'worth educating' up to twenty-one and that of a miner not 'worth educating' beyond fourteen, or to ask why, if it is worth while for the community to provide full-time education for a child up to fourteen, the age when it leaves the primary school, it suddenly ceases to be worthwhile for it to provide any further education whatever when that momentous date is passed. To those who ask, 'What use is secondary education to a working-class child?' the most obvious answer would appear to be to ask, 'What use' (since that is the formula favoured) 'has their education been to them?'

In reality, however, absurd as this view is on other grounds, the whole tendency of recent educational investigation has been still further to discredit it by emphasizing the immense mass, not only of average talent – and average talent is worth cultivating – but of exceptional talent, which is sterilized for lack of educational opportunities. It is true, of course, that not all children respond equally to the same methods and curriculum. Equality of educational provision is not identity of educational provision, and it is important that there should be the greatest possible diversity of type among secondary schools. But the theory that money spent on developing secondary education is likely to be wasted because the majority of children are not 'capable of profiting' by it finds no confirmation among educationalists or administrators. We have already referred to the statement of the Departmental Committee that 'practically all children, except the subnormal, are intellectually capable of profiting by full-time instruction up to sixteen or beyond'. Inspectors familiar with primary schools are stated to regard 25 per cent of the children as above normal, 50 per cent as normal, and 25

4. Education Reform, 1917. Report of Committee E.

per cent as below normal. Such estimates are obviously very rough. But they show at any rate that there is a widespread opinion among persons of experience that a great deal of educable capacity misses education. Since the entrants to public secondary schools from primary schools formed in 1918-19 only 9·4 per cent of the children between ten and eleven in the latter, it is evident that not only are we failing to cultivate the intelligence of *all* the children described as normal, but we are actually failing to provide higher education for almost two-thirds of those who are of exceptional intelligence!

52 H. A. L. Fisher

from *An Unfinished Autobiography*, 1940, pp. 114-17.

One of the most remarkable developments in higher education in England – and one that has been much envied abroad although copied almost nowhere – was the creation of the University Grants Committee, which acted as a buffer between central government and the sensibilities of academic freedom which were particularly sensitive in the twenties. One man who was much involved in setting up this unique institution was H. A. L. Fisher, when as President of the Board of Education he approached Chamberlain for government support for Oxford and Cambridge.

I believe that, when the history of our English education comes to be written no single step will be found to have contributed more effectively to the spread of the university idea through England than the decision of the Government in 1918 to allot eight millions to enable ex-Service men to enjoy the privileges of university education. Twenty-seven thousand students went to the universities with the aid of these state grants. As I examined every dossier I am in a position to affirm that this large body of students was drawn almost exclusively from families to whom the notion of a university career for one of their numbers would have seemed up to that time foreign, if not fantastic.

Though university education in England had been singularly retarded, it enjoyed one advantage denied to most foundations for the higher learning in other countries. No university in England, and this observation applies to Scotland also, had been founded by the State. Our ancient and modern universities were all the outcome of private enterprise. They were self-governing independent republics, free to direct their own studies and to enforce their own discipline. Oxford and Cambridge, until 1917, lived on their private endowments. The newer universities were from the point of view of finance not equally fortunate. Though private benefactions had played in every case a part in their foundation they could not afford altogether to dispense with assistance from public funds. They received help from the rates and taxes. The leading men of the city and the county were called in to share in the government of the civic university, and though the essentials of academic liberty were preserved the city fathers would occasionally take leave to comment on the proceedings of a body which they helped to form.

The boon of academic freedom was fully understood and widely valued. Even universities which accepted grants from the State would have sacrificed their parliamentary moneys without demur rather than submit to dictation from the government. Experience, however, showed that such dictation was never attempted. Yet, despite the encouragement to be derived from the fact, there were many, including the Vice-Chancellor of Oxford University at that time, who were vehemently opposed in the name of academic liberty to the acceptance of parliamentary money by the two national universities. I became, however, convinced early in 1917 that Oxford and Cambridge could not continue to discharge their functions or to cope with the developing requirements of applied science without help from the State. Their needs were crying. Without immediate financial aid it would have been impossible for them to carry on their current scientific work. Austen Chamberlain was fortunately Chancellor of the Exchequer. He was himself an alumnus of Cambridge and the son of the founder of Birmingham University. Few words were necessary to convince such a man of the needs of the two universities. After twenty minutes I left the Treasury Chambers with an assurance of a certain grant of £30,000 a year for each university pending the report of the Royal Commission, which we agreed between us must necessarily be set up.

Such an inquiry, indeed, was long overdue. The Report of the Commission would be a landmark in the educational history of the country. When I was fortunate enough to persuade Lord Oxford to accept the chairmanship I felt assured that its findings, whatever they might be, would be regarded as authoritative and would receive a full measure of parliamentary support.

The administration of the government grants to the universities and university colleges was entrusted, not to the Board of Education, whose jurisdiction did not extend over Scotland, but to a University Grants Committee composed of eminent academic people nominated in the first instance by the President of the Board of Education, but technically acting under the Treasury. The fear that government finance might involve government dictation has thereby been exorcised. The University Grants Committee has not indeed been without influence on academic policy. Having a synoptic view of all the universities and university colleges in Britain, it is in a position to make useful suggestions for the avoidance of overlapping and unnecessary duplication of effort and to communicate to one university experience gained from another. But the authority of the Committee has been by way of indirect influence only, and absolutely devoid of political bias.

53 Royal Commission on Oxford and Cambridge Universities

Cmd 1588, 1922, pp. 48–57.

It was the Royal Commission of 1850–52 which marked the initial victory of Parliamentary intervention into the affairs of the ancient universities; in 1922 this intervention produced the first modern inquiry into their affairs and saved the universities from ossification. It also marked the end of that era when universities were able to act with complete financial independence.

Owing to the change in the value of money, Oxford and Cambridge are no longer able to pay their way. The increase in the number of students to be taught, in the amount of instruction given to each student, in the variety of subjects in which teaching and research are conducted has been described in the previous sections. These developments have necessitated a great increase in staff and expenditure. Already before the war the financial situation was serious; many of the staff were underpaid and overworked, and not a few had no pension prospects; research, especially in the Humanities, was very poorly provided for; and difficulty was beginning to be felt in maintaining and staffing the libraries and museums. If these problems were present before the war, they have been rendered insoluble by the change in the value of money; but for the interim grant of £30,000 a year allowed by the State to each university for general purposes since 1920, it would have been impossible to continue their present work even provisionally. It is true that the gross incomes of some colleges have risen since the war, but the purchasing power of aggregate university and college wealth is much smaller, while the number of students of all sorts coming up to Oxford and Cambridge, and desiring to come, has enormously increased since 1914.

The first danger is the *effect of under-pay and the absence of a proper pension scheme on the quality of professors and fellows*. The present financial position, if unrelieved, must destroy the special value of Oxford and Cambridge to the nation, which lies in their ability to supply the highest type of intellect and training. The highest services cannot, save in exceptional cases, be obtained at the cheapest rates. If the level of pay and prospects at Oxford and Cambridge cannot share in the increases made since the war in most other professions and services, the type of teacher must decline.

Many professors and readers of both universities are inadequately paid; the average stipend is far below that due to the chief post in a branch of learning. There are several different scales of pay for professors, some entirely inadequate. There is no effective university pension scheme, though some colleges provide pensions for some professors. The absence of pensions is a very serious matter; till it is remedied, a retiring age cannot be fixed. Professors must often continue as now to serve till they are over seventy and eighty years of age, with the result that posts of the first importance, which ought to be filled by men in the maturity of their powers, are in some cases inevitably occupied by men in their decline, while the men fitted by their age and powers to be holding the post in succession fail to obtain promotion when it would be of most value to the university.

The system of pay and pension for fellows differs in different colleges at both universities; in some cases the pay is inadequate and the pensions are non-existent.

Under these conditions, it is beginning to be difficult to keep a sufficient supply of the best men, and it would become increasingly difficult if it were once believed by the younger men that the present conditions would be permanent, owing to a refusal on the part of the State to help the two senior universities.

For the last two generations the competition of other professions and lines of life has been constantly on the increase. The situation is, indeed, very different from what it was at the time of the previous Royal Commissions. Fellows are now allowed to marry, and in most cases wish to avail themselves of the privilege; and the usual type of 'don' is now a person who could command a high salary in many different walks of life. His choice no longer usually lies between the Church and the teaching profession. Well-paid professorships, all over the English-speaking world, are frequently offered to Oxford and Cambridge men. Excellent business openings are now available to successful students, particularly in science, sometimes with enormous salaries attached.

It is not, indeed, possible or desirable for the universities to compete pound for pound with offers of this last description but a living wage is necessary. People are ready to sacrifice higher salaries and even posts of greater power and influence in order to enjoy the amenities and the intellectual privileges and ideals of life at Oxford and Cambridge. But however anxious they may be to stay, few can do so except on terms enabling them to provide for a family and to educate their children. If this could be done before the war on an income of £500 or £600 a year in middle and later life, it cannot be done on those terms today. *Each University must be placed in a position to offer to all those who do its work a salary and pension prospects enabling a man to marry and bring up a family, with amenities and advantages of education like those of other professional families.* On that condition Oxford and Cambridge will be able in the coming era to keep enough of their best students to do their teaching and research – but not otherwise. That is the principle on which the proposals in this Report are based.

The second danger to Oxford and Cambridge is the *insufficient number of teachers* in proportion to the number of students and the variety of subjects; with the resulting evil of an *inadequate amount of time given to research*.

The highest type of university education cannot be provided wholesale. If the present number of students, or even the smaller number of students who were being taught in 1914, is in future to be taught without an increased staff, then either (a) the system of careful, personal instruction of the student by his tutor or supervisor must be abandoned, and much of the educational progress of the last two generations thereby permitted to lapse, or else (b) research must be starved. The existing resources of Oxford and Cambridge do not suffice to pay both for the tutorial system and for research.[1]

It is the second of these two evils that is at present chosen. It is research that suffers, except in the scientific schools where research and teaching are so closely interwoven that they flourish or decline together and share whatever funds are available. In the humane studies, the output of original work of Oxford and Cambridge, if not actually small, is deficient in relation to the intellectual ability of their members, and advanced teaching is not properly provided for.

The supersession of the private 'coach', though a very necessary reform, has had this attendant disadvantage, that college teachers of the highest

1. In this Report the word 'research' is used to include not only the actual study and collation of new mateiial, or the working out of scientific problems, but also the promotion of thought and learning in the widest sense, including (a) the self-education, study and thought, necessary before a student can decide on the particular branch of a subject for original work best suited to his powers; (b) a constantly renewed familiarity with the discoveries and views of others, both living and dead; (c) travel for purposes of study.

ability are now obliged to give much of their time to elementary instruction which ought to have been obtained before entrance. Research has consequently to suffer a neglect by which, in turn, the higher forms of teaching are impoverished, for the best teacher is one who imparts to his pupils his own sense of the living interest in their common subject; the subject should be regarded not as a fixed body of knowledge, but as a territory increased day by day with the accretion of new discoveries and new speculations. The proper interaction of teaching and research is of the very essence of the highest education.

Our proposals therefore aim at securing an *increase in the numbers of the staff*, some of whom will, like the *new professors and readers*, be devoted mainly to research and the assistance of researchers; while others will increase the number of the teachers, so that all teachers may have leisure for a certain amount of study, and many for a certain amount of original work.

In particular we desire to see opportunities created for the best of the students to have a period for research after taking the B.A. degree before they are absorbed for life in the engrossing demands of college teaching and administration.

The evils of the existing state of things in this respect have been very strongly condemned in the recently issued Report of the Prime Minister's Committee on Classical Education (p. 200).

Our proposals by way of remedy will be found below. It is enough here to point out that the necessary improvement cannot be effected on the present income of either university.

At the same early and critical period of a man's academical career, it is particularly desirable that he should travel and study abroad. Classics, history and modern languages cannot be properly studied in England alone. The materials as well as the inspiration are largely found overseas. But at present there is neither proper organization nor sufficient funds for this purpose, with the result that *pro tanto* the highest classical studies are discouraged, and history is provincialized. It is a disaster that, at a moment when we have become far more deeply involved than ever before in the affairs of countries overseas, our highest academical class is condemned through poverty to know little or nothing of life or learning outside this island.

In advocating further provision for research at Oxford and Cambridge, it must be understood that we do not favour the practice prevailing in Germany and other countries which have imitated her academic system, whereby great numbers of men and women sometimes of the second and third order of mind are encouraged to engage in research, often after an insufficient general education. But in this country many of the best minds are unable, or are not encouraged, to engage in the highest original work for which they are fitted, owing to the deficiencies in this respect of the two senior universities. This is a serious loss to the nation.

It may be relevant at this point to remark that the shortage of teachers and the consequent want of provision and leisure for research has a bearing on the dispute as to the *proper length of the terms* at Oxford and Cambridge. Complaint is sometimes made that the terms are too short. But many of the teachers plead that the only time they have for study and for original work is in vacation, although too many of them are obliged to devote even their vacations to the preparation of their lectures. It would certainly be disastrous to shorten considerably the period of vacation without largely increasing the number and leisure of the staff. Furthermore, in the interests of the students themselves, it is not desirable unduly to prolong the three regular terms, when debating and other societies, organized athletics and other events and interests, political and philanthropic and intellectual, valuable in themselves as part of education, infringe on the hours of solitary study.

But if and in so far as all the recommendations made in this Report for the further endowment and advancement of research are carried out, including a substantial increase in the number of teachers, we suggest to the universities that they should endeavour to effect an arrangement by which *twenty-four weeks a year of full term* should be reserved in which no examinations are held by the universities and colleges. But in making this proposal we do not desire to see any increase whatever in the number of lectures.

In connection with this question, it must be remembered that at Cambridge there is a *'Long Vacation'* lasting at least six weeks, during which an increasing number of the students voluntarily come into residence at very small cost to themselves, and use the libraries and laboratories for quiet study and for revision of what they have been taught during the year. This is particularly desirable for science students requiring laboratories; for many classical, linguistic and historical students travel or study abroad is better, where it can be afforded. The 'Long Vacation' at Cambridge does not involve heavy demands on the teaching staff, such teaching as is provided in science being chiefly done by junior teachers, while in the humanities there is practically no formal teaching except in law.

We suggest that opportunities for residence and study shall be equally available during the long vacation to students at Oxford.

The third danger arises to the universities from their present inability to provide new *laboratories and faculty rooms* when required, or even to keep the existing *libraries* and *museums* properly staffed and supplied with the new books and material requisite to study and research.

It is sometimes forgotten that, just as Science requires an expensive material outfit, so do classics, history, law and modern languages depend on the study of an ever fresh supply of books and learned periodicals in all languages. In these days, because new books cost so much, both teachers and students, who are on the average poorer than they used to be, depend more than ever on libraries. And for the same reason the libraries have not the funds to obtain as large a supply of books as they used to obtain year by year before the war. Even *the two great university libraries* are in a parlous condition for lack of funds and adequate staff; binding and cataloguing is falling into arrear, and the acquisition of foreign books neccessary for students is no longer adequate.

The Archaeological and Ethnological Museums, which are an essential part of the teaching apparatus of the universities, are in similar straits.

Not only are funds for the maintenance of these institutions lacking, but building and expansion, involving acquisition of new sites, are essential for libraries, museums, laboratories and faculty rooms, and the universities have not the funds to meet these necessities.

Another danger is inability to develop *new subjects of study* for lack of funds.

There must, of course, be a limit to such development, and Oxford and Cambridge cannot cover all branches of learning. But if the limitation became too narrow Oxford and Cambridge could not keep their place at the head of the intellectual world of the Empire, as was possible when classics and mathematics were considered to cover the main fields of study. It has been shown that the two universities have of recent years started a not wholly inadequate number of new schools, but these are not properly provided for today. Our proposals do not contemplate an immediate increase in the number of subjects taught, but are based on the principle of providing for those now existing. Judging by recent experience, the universities can be trusted to start new subjects as time and occasion demand, provided they are not now permitted to collapse beneath the financial weight of their present commitments.

Another danger is the danger to the accessibility of Oxford and Cambridge to poorer students. If help is not forthcoming from outside, the universities will be forced to *raise their fees* to an excessive degree that must exclude many students not only of the artisan but of the professional class. There is a danger that the universities may, against their will and policy be *forced back by their poverty on to the too exclusive patronage of the wealthy student, irrespective of his ability or industry*, in a way that must lower the intellectual standard now attained. The 'idle rich' student might revive.

It is, further, quite certain that without financial aid the extra-mural work must languish for want of funds.

The work of the women's colleges, particularly at Oxford, is also in danger for want of funds. The Oxford women's colleges have recently appealed to the general public for money to enable them to carry on, but the appeal has met with very inadequate success.

Character of the proposed grant

For the reasons given in the foregoing sections, we hold it to be certain that the two universities will decline in efficiency in the immediate future unless they are able to obtain more money, and that in fact they are only being saved from financial collapse by the Interim Grant of £30,000 a year each which has been allowed to them by Government since the war.

We recommend that each university receive, instead of the existing interim grant of £30,000, an annual grant of £100,000 a year, in addition to £10,000 a year for special purposes (women's education and extra-mural work), *and a lump sum for pension arrears,* in order to enable them to fulfil their functions to the nation in a satisfactory manner.

The *principal purposes for which we recommend a grant of public money* are as follows:

Proper salaries and pensions for university teachers, which should be a first charge on any public grant; secondly, the adequate maintenance of the university libraries and museums; the endowment of research and advanced teaching, including more professors, readers and university or faculty lecturers, and more research studentships for young graduates; the most pressing needs of maintenance in respect of laboratories and departmental libraries, as part of the apparatus of teaching and research; and the provision in both universities of a sites and buildings fund (it will be noted that for reasons of public economy we do not recommend a grant of capital moneys for buildings); we also budget for the needs of the non-collegiate bodies, for a grant towards women's education, and for aid for the extra-mural work of the universities and for adult students.

54 Committee on National Expenditure (Geddes)

from the First Interim Report, Cmd 1581, 1922, pp. 102–22.

In an attempt to deal with the growing economic crisis, a governmental committee was asked to look into national expenditure and cut it by £100 millions. The Geddes 'axe' proposed cuts in Naval estimates by £21 millions, the army by £20 millions, the air force by

*£5 millions and education by £18 millions. Altogether, it
recommended £87 millions in savings for the year 1922–3, and put paid
to most of the reforms outlined in the 1918 Education Act.*

Board of Education estimates

The estimates for the Board of Education are as follows:

1913–14 (actual expenditure) £14,369,000
1921–2   51,014,000
1922–3   50,600,000

It appears from estimates submitted to us that the total expenditure
from taxes and rates on education in Great Britain will in 1922–3 exceed a
total of £103,000,000. [...]

Not only has the cost of education increased enormously since 1913–14,
but the taxpayer, besides bearing his share of the increased cost, has had
to shoulder a proportion of the burden which would have been borne by
the ratepayer if the grant system had not been modified between 1917 and
1919.

Out of the total vote less than £1,000,000 is administrative expenditure
of the Board. By far the greater part of the vote of the Board of Education
is dependent in one form or another upon expenditure incurred by local
educational authorities (of which there are no less than 317 in England
and Wales) on a percentage grant basis, which, in our opinion, is a money-
spending device, but not an economical system. [...]

We draw particular attention to the following salient points:

Between 1913–14 and 1921–2:
The expenses chargeable to rates increased by 101 per cent.
The expenses chargeable to taxes increased by 239 per cent.
The total expenditure increased by 168 per cent.

For every £ of total expenditure:
In 1913–14 the taxpayer contributed 9s. 9d. and the ratepayer 10s. 3d.
In 1922–3 the taxpayer will contribute 11s. 6d. and the ratepayer 8s. 6d.

Apart from the change in the proportions of expenditure, the two
outstanding features in considering this estimate are:

1. The increase in teaching cost.
2. The increase in the number of pupils receiving secondary education. [...]

Elementary education

Expenditure
1913–14   £11,597,260

Estimates

1921–2   £36,998,713
1922–3   £36,723,961

Observations on the grant system

Elementary education represents over 70 per cent of the whole estimate. The very complicated grant formula ... has exhibited in a high degree the peculiar disadvantages attaching to the system of percentage grants to which we have drawn attention in the introduction to this part of the Report.

The net effect of the changes in the grant system is that the taxpayer, through the Exchequer, is today paying 55 per cent of the sums expended by local authorities on elementary education, as compared with 46 per cent in 1913–14. If the Exchequer share were reduced to the statutory obligation of 50 per cent the saving to the taxpayer in 1922–3 would be over £3,000,000.

Cost per child

The expenditure on elementary education in terms of cost per child is shown in the following table:

Cost per unit of average attendance

	1913–14		1919–20		1920–21		1921–2 (estimate)		1922–3 (forecast)	
	s.	d.	s.	d.	s.	d.	s.	d.	s.	d.
Salaries of teachers	60	10	120	11	155	1	166	3	168	0
Loan charges	11	4	11	11	11	11	12	0	12	0
Special services										
Schools for defective children	1	9	3	6	5	2	5	6	6	0
Medical inspection and treatment	1	2	3	7	5	4	6	0	7	0
Provision of meals	0	7	0	9	0	10	1	6	1	6
Administration	4	9	7	10	9	10	11	5	11	0
Other expenditure	16	1	29	1	40	10	41	8	42	0
Total	96	6	177	7	229	0	244	4	247	6
	£4 16 6		£8 17 7		£11 9 0		£12 4 4		£12 7 6	

Cost of teaching

The salary bill is directly affected by each of the following factors:

1. The number of children and the manner in which they are distributed among the school buildings of different sizes.

2. The size of classes.

3. The salary scales.

We suggest that economies should be effected under the above headings in the following directions:

Raising of the lower age limit. [. . .] As reduction in numbers is one effective means of reducing the cost of teaching, we recommend the raising of the lower age limit to six years. This should be made compulsory and not left to local option. [. . .]

The estimated saving to the taxpayer through the Exchequer in 1922–3 is £1,785,000.

Closing of small schools. [. . .] We are informed that a saving of £60,000 can be effected by closing schools below 100 pupils in London, and that an additional saving of £142,500 in salaries might be made in urban areas outside London. The larger proportion of such schools are in rural areas and further savings should be possible there, but no attempt has been made to estimate such savings.

Revision of the standard of staffing. On average over the whole country there were in June 1921 32·4 children to each teacher, which compares with 32·9 children to a teacher in 1913–14, and by itself involves an additional cost of £630,000.

We are informed that if the standard of staffing were revised in urban areas so that there were in future one teacher to each fifty pupils, the saving would be £8,282,000, of which £4,853,000 would accrue to the taxpayer. [. . .]

Teachers' salary scales. We are informed that the present scales were framed by the Burnham Committee, formed of representatives of the local authorities and of the teachers. The conclusions of the Committee are of direct importance to the taxpayer, who bears from 50 per cent to 60 per cent of the increased salaries granted, as well as the whole of any consequential increase in pension charges. [. . .]

The bill for teachers' salaries is now more than two and a half times the pre-war figure. The Burnham Report provides that if the official figure of the cost of living rises to a higher level than 170 per cent above pre-war costs, and remains there for six months, the scales shall be open to increase. It omits, however, any mention of reduction when cost of living falls. The index number at the date of the Burnham Report (September 1920) was 161, whilst it is now 103. Reductions on the ground of the falling cost of living have been accepted recently by most classes of the community and this process is continuing. [. . .]

Higher education

Expenditure
1913–14   £2,015,000

Estimates
1921–2   £8,970,000
1922–3   £9,765,000

Observations on the grant system

The administration of higher education is more complex even than that of elementary education. [. . .]

The system of grants for higher education resembles that for elementary education in general outline only.

Local education authorities have a statutory right to receive not less than 50 per cent of their expenditure on higher education if the substantive grants do not give them that amount. In practice nearly all these authorities are in receipt of the flat 60 per cent grant, and very few indeed are affected by substantive grants at all. On the other hand, non-LEA[1] institutions receive substantive grants on a *per capita* or other basis, and not a proportion of their expenditure.

Secondary education

Cost per pupil. We have been furnished with table opposite showing the cost per pupil in grant-aided secondary schools (LEA and non-LEA inclusive).

Some further light is thrown on the causes of the great growth in the cost of secondary education by the following particulars:

Grant-aided secondary schools

	1912–13	*1920–21*	*Percentage variation*
Number of pupils	175,752	339,308	+93
Number of teachers	10,506	17,894	+70
Average salary of teachers	£173	£332	+92

The number of pupils has thus nearly doubled. [. . .] A forecast for 1922–3 places the number of pupils at 385,000, an increase of 46,000 in two years.

1. LEA means local education authority. For simplicity all grants to non-LEA institutions have been treated as falling under higher education, though, in fact, a small proportion, less than £100,000, relate to elementary education.

Cost per pupil in grant-aided secondary schools

| | 1912–13 | | 1919–20 | | 1920–21 (estimated) | | 1922–3 (forecast) | |
	Cost per pupil		Cost per pupil		Cost per pupil		Cost per pupil	
Expenditure	s.	d.	s.	d.	s.	d.	s.	d.
Salaries of teachers	213	3	287	9	339	6	400	0
Loan charges	33	1	23	11	25	4	30	0
Provision for pensions	2	1	0	10	1	2	1	0
Maintenance of premises	46	0	65	3	84	6	84	0
Administration	10	10	13	7	17	8	17	0
Other payments*	26	3	40	0	51	10	52	0
Total expenditure	331	6	431	4	520	0	584	0
Deduct receipts								
Fees	123	10	147	8	154	0	180	0
Endowments	19	10	20	3	18	4	18	0
Miscellaneous	9	4	12	9	11	6	12	0
Total receipts	153	0	180	8	183	10	210	0
Net cost borne by LEA	178	6	250	8	336	2	374	0
	£8 18	6	£12 10	8	£16 16	2	£18 14	0

* Other payments include expenditure on books, stationery materials, library examinations, prizes, games, etc.

Up to 1920–21 the average salary per teacher in secondary schools had not increased so fast as in elementary schools, but the forecast given opposite shows a rapid increase under the operation of the Burnham Secondary-School scale. The average salary will shortly reach £389, an increase of of 125 per cent.

Free-place students and fee-paying students. The board's regulations provide that a minimum of 25 per cent of the places available shall be reserved for free-place pupils from the elementary schools, and we think that in present circumstances this should be limited to 25 per cent. [. . .]

We recommend the fees should be substantially raised and at the same time every effort should be made to reduce the cost of secondary education. Scholars, whether fee-paying or not, should not be allowed to continue to receive State-aided secondary education if they do not show ability and industry, and effective periodical tests should be applied to ensure this elimination.

Revision of grant list. The recent great increase in the cost of State subsidized education is alarming. The condition of affairs when taxes and local rates were drawn on only to pay for the elementary education of the children of the working classes has been abandoned. Schools which could hardly be considered as requiring State aid are now receiving assistance from the local rates and the taxpayer. [. . .]

Revised classification of schools. An extensive system has grown up under which local authorities, without assuming full control of non-LEA schools in their area, yet contribute to their cost. From the point of view of the Exchequer, schools of this kind throw an additional burden upon it as compared with LEA schools. [. . .]

We therefore suggest that where a school receives financial assistance from a local authority, the direct grant from the Board should cease and no further grant should be made to that school except through the supporting local authority as an intermediary.

This reform would save the Exchequer a charge of £500,000 per annum as compared with present conditions, and we think that with a closer financial interest in the matter the LEAs may effect further economies.

Technical schools

These schools are of the most varied description. The expenditure in 1921–2 passing through local authorities' accounts on technical education may be summarized as follows:

Senior technical schools	£1,500,000
Schools of art	550,000
Junior technical schools	250,000
Day continuation schools	540,000
Evening continuation schools	1,350,000
	£4,190,000

In addition to the above expenditure £142,000 is distributed by the Board in grants to non-LEA technical schools.

It appears to us clear that progressive developments should be postponed until the financial situation of the country is better, and we think that the cost should be capable of reduction. In many cases we feel convinced that instruction in certain subjects, not connected with any future occupation, is being given and we consider that unless activities of this kind can be made self-supporting they should be rigorously curtailed.

If a complete system of continuation schools is introduced, as contemplated in the Act of 1918, the additional charge can hardly be estimated at less than £10,000,000 per annum: and in addition, there is the ultimate pension liability of £2,500,000 referred to later.

Training of teachers

There are 18,542 full-time students in training to become teachers in elementary or secondary schools or teachers of domestic subjects. The average cost per resident and non-resident student to public funds is at present £79 per annum.

In 1922–3 it appears that, including part-time students, the expenditure from public funds would be at least £1,700,000, of which the taxpayer would pay £1,350,000.

If our suggestions as to the revision of the standard of staffing in elementary schools are adopted, a reduction of the expenditure on training should shortly be possible, though, in consequence of students who have commenced courses being still in residence, the full effect cannot be felt in 1922–3. The question of fees paid by students should also be reviewed. These today are about £30 per annum for residents, and £5 to £10 for non-residents, and should be brought into closer relation with the cost.

Aid to students

Many local authorities now grant maintenance allowance to students from elementary schools in order to enable them to continue their education at secondary schools, and scholarships to older pupils proceeding to the universities. The fees usually paid by the students may also be paid by the local authority. Such expenditure by the local authorities is, subject to certain restrictions, subsidized by the State to the extent of 50 per cent.

For 1922–3 the Board estimate that the expenditure of the local authorities for this purpose will be £950,000, which will require a Government grant of £475,000.

We understand that the Government grant towards these scholarships may eventually reach a maximum of £800,000 a year and we consider that the whole question of these grants should be reviewed.

In addition to subsidizing the activities of local authorities, the Board also grant direct certain scholarships, studentships and exhibitions, the cost of which in 1922–3 is estimated at £215,000. In our opinion these should for the present be limited to the present holders.

Recently the Board have introduced a State scheme of scholarships at the universities which is intended to supplement the efforts made in that direction by local authorities. This development, which is still in its infancy, appears to us another illustration of the readiness with which the State has accepted special obligations after it had provided fully for its liability by a percentage grant to local authorities, and we suggest that with the exception of the present holders of scholarships this scheme should cease. [...]

Miscellaneous expenditure

Sums to be provided under this head

To complete the examination of the vote, the following miscellaneous items must be considered.

	Estimate 1921–2	Estimate 1922–3
Scheme for assisting ex-officers and men at universities	£2,248,000	£1,090,000
Museums	269,000	210,000
Board's administration and inspection	963,000	900,000
Teachers' pensions	1,575,000	1,920,000
[. . .]	£5,055,000	£4,120,000

Museums

The museums under the Board are the Victoria and Albert, the Science Museum and Bethnal Green Museum. We suggest a rather greater reduction on 1921–2 figure, viz., to £195,000.

Administration and inspection

As regards the Board's administration and inspection, we are informed that a closer estimate has been made and that the Board agree that the figure of £900,000 can be reduced to £879,807. In view of our suggestion as to the simplification of the grant system, we think some further staff economies are possible, and therefore suggest a reduction to £850,000 at once and a larger reduction in the future.

Teachers' pensions

Expenditure, 1913–14	£176,000
Estimate, 1921–2	1,575,400
Estimate, 1922–3	1,920,000

Teachers' pensions are now provided entirely by the State, and no contribution is made either by the teacher himself or by his employers.

We have considered a suggestion that teachers' superannuation should be placed on a contributory basis. Under the pension system in force before 1918, which was confined to certificated elementary school teachers, contributions were made by teachers at a flat rate, which represented about $2\frac{1}{2}$ per cent of the average salary then current. The benefits under the present non-contributory scheme, which dates from 1918, apply to more teachers and are of much greater value than those under the old contributory scheme. We are advised by the Government Actuary that, expressed as a percentage of future salary, the value of the benefits under the present scheme to existing teachers, who are allowed to count their past service, ranges from 10 per cent of annual salary in the case of a man certificated teacher, aged thirty, to nearly 60 per cent of such salary in the case of a woman uncertificated teacher, aged fifty. The value of a teacher now entering the service is, on the average, approximately 8 per cent of annual salary.

The cost of the scheme, which will be £1,920,000 in 1922–3, will rapidly and continuously increase to a very high figure. The Government Actuary estimates that by 1929–30 it may reach £4,402,000 a year, by 1939–40 £7,667,000, and ultimately £9,584,000; and, further, if a complete system of continuation schools is put into operation, it will add a further £2,500,000 to the ultimate liability, making a total of £12,000,000 per annum. The present salaries of teachers in pensionable service aggregate about £50,000,000, whereas when the non-contributory scheme was introduced in 1918 they amounted to £20,000,000. Today, though the taxpayer pays the whole pension bill, the local authority has control of the pay, the age of retirement and promotion of the staff, but no financial interest in the pensions cost affected thereby – a most vicious principle.

The full cost to the taxpayer of the burden of teachers' pensions was clearly not appreciated when the arrangement was made, in fact the Government Actuary was not consulted.

We recommend that a full inquiry should be held with a view to placing the superannuation of teachers on a sound contributory basis under which the teachers and the authorities who employ them would each bear a due proportion of the burden.

Pending such inquiry we recommend that a 5 per cent levy should be paid by the teachers. On the reduced salary bill which would result from our previous recommendations this would yield £2,000,000 in 1922–3.

As shown above, the total of miscellaneous expenditure items can thus be reduced to £4,055,000, a saving of £65,000 apart from any contributions which may be levied in respect of teachers' pensions.

Financial effect of recommendations

Our suggestions on different portions of the vote would produce the following result:

Grant for elementary education	£26,573,000
Grant for higher education	6,050,000
Miscellaneous expenditure	4,055,000
	36,678,000
Deduct superannuation contributions	2,000,000
Net total	£34,678,000

This figure compares with the Board's estimate of £50,600,000. It may be added that there would be a consequential saving of £2,000,000 on the vote for the Scottish Education Department, making a total reduction on these votes of £18,000,000.

Grants to universities and colleges

1913–14, Actual Expenditure, £481,106 (including £37,483 for non-recurrent grants).

1921–2, Estimate, £2,000,000 (including £500,000 for a non-recurrent grant).

1922–3, Estimate, £1,200,000.

Before 1918–19, annual grants to universities and colleges were provided under many different votes. From 1919–20 onwards, the expenditure, apart from certain statutory grants to Irish universities (£84,000), has been collected under a single head. The Treasury now fix the sum to be provided each year, but as regards the details of its allocation among the universities, act on the advice of an independent committee of experts, known as the University Grants Committee.

For 1919–20, a sum of £1,000,000 was provided for recurrent grants, and this figure was increased to £1,500,000[2] in 1921–2. The Treasury have requested the University Grants Committee to frame their recommendations for 1922–3 so as to bring the expenditure within a total of £1,200,000, being 20 per cent less than the provision for the current year.

Correspondence between the Treasury and the University Grants Committee has been laid before us, in which the case is set out on the side of the Committee for a larger grant. We appreciate the importance of a due measure of State encouragement to universities, which greatly stimulates local support also, but the paramount consideration is national solvency, without which there can be no grants to universities at all. In all the circumstances we recommend that a sum of £1,200,000 – which is two and a half times the pre-war grant – should be provided in 1922–3, subject to any reduction which may automatically follow the transfer of responsibility for Irish universities and colleges.

2. In addition, a non-recurrent lump sum grant of £500,000 was made to enable universities to improve the superannuation provision for their teachers.

55 Lord Percy of Newcastle
from *Some Memories*, 1958, pp. 97–8.

Because of the continued pressure for economies, a particularly
tough Circular was issued in 1925, which forced local authorities to trim their
educational provision. It virtually put a surcharge on having children
under five in schools, and its harsh demands caused a storm of protest, as
its author describes below. (Incidentally, his memory slipped about the
year it was issued!)

In the early spring of 1926 [*sic*], after a series of meetings with a Cabinet
committee on economy, which brought me to the verge of resignation, I
issued the notorious Circular 1371 to local education authorities, proposing
a number of drastic checks on expansion. The storm of opposition which
this aroused shocked my colleagues and even surprised myself. It was my
first experience of a new sensitiveness in the enlarged post-war electorate.
It had become fatally easy to arouse immoderate expectations by the
use of even the most moderate language and equally immoderate resentment by even a temporary disappointment of those expectations.

Churchill was fond of recounting Haldane's skill in discrediting the
advocates of Army retrenchment in 1906 by staging a ceremony at which
King Edward bade a tearful farewell to a disbanded battalion of Scots
Guards; and I have sometimes wondered whether he suspected me of a
similar manoeuvre. For my circular was drowned in the flood of protests
and my colleagues left me free thereafter to pursue my policy as best I
could. But I would lay no claim to such political astuteness, even if I had
thought it honest. It was more influenced by a saying of Theodore Roose-
velt that all unpleasant political fences should be taken at a gallop. On the
whole I proved the advice to be sound on this occasion, though it was, I
think, on this occasion that Neville Chamberlain first took a strong dislike
to my style of horsemanship. Trevelyan warned me from the front Opposition bench that it could never be 'glad confident morning again'; but it is the
peculiarity of the educational hunting field that 'glad confident morning'
is altogether too exhilarating an atmosphere for a long run. In practice the
system of percentage Exchequer grants allowed local authorities to incur,
without effective Treasury control, liabilities which became at least as
much Treasury liabilities as municipal. It is extraordinarily difficult, in
such a riding school, for a minister to strike the right balance between the
use of the spur and bridle. My savage tug on the curb in 1926 was, no doubt,
bad horsemanship, and it nearly landed me in the ditch; but it made it,

perhaps, easier for me to strike something like the right balance over the next three years, and I think I can claim that, by the General Election of 1929, horse and rider had come to understand one another pretty well.

If I lost some political reputation by the incident, that was, on the whole, an advantage to my work. I had protested, I remember, to the Editor of *The Times* against the too frequent publication of my occasional addresses at school speech days and the like. They were the necessary local price I had to pay for getting personally to know schools and local authorities; but altogether too much was being made by the national press of what I thought of as 'Percy's daily platitudes'. After the flurry of 1926 I was glad to be able to get on with my work in the comparative obscurity to which political journalists tended to consign me for the next three years. To vary my metaphor, for the moment, from equitation to horticulture, schoolmasters will know what I mean when I say that education is a plant that thrives best in some shade, which may be why it is so seldom a favourite flower in any politician's garden.

56 Board of Education
Circular 1371, 25 November 1925, pp. 1–3.

The Board have been considering their probable estimates for the year 1926–7, and they wish to ask the cooperation of local authorities in meeting the situation which has arisen.

It will be the Board's duty to repeat for next year the attempt made this year to estimate closely the money necessary for educational services, and on this basis the Board have come to the conclusion that, if they were to provide for expenditure by local education authorities on new services without asking authorities to make any counterbalancing economies, their estimates, even after effecting certain economies in their own administration would reach the figure of £41,781,414, or £1,136,760 in excess of their estimate for ordinary services for the current year and £1,063,800 in excess of their actual expenditure on such services in the last completed year 1924–5.

The President of the Board has decided that in the present state of the national finances, he would not be justified in making so large a demand upon the taxpayer. He is, moreover, convinced that if the nation is to be able to finance new projects designed to provide additional facilities for higher education and to improve the instruction of the older children in elementary schools, it is essential that a clear understanding should be reached as to the amount of expenditure which public funds will be called upon to bear for the administration and maintenance of existing services.

The Board have attempted to review the factors governing the recent growth in local expenditure on education and the possibility of economies. It is observed that the expenditure of authorities in 1924–5 shows a total increase, as compared with 1923–4, of about £1,400,000, and that only a relatively small part of this appears to be attributable to the provision of new facilities. The increase of expenditure on administration, both elementary and higher, and on 'other' expenses of elementary education, is alone responsible for no less than £730,000 of this increase. It would appear that this expenditure on existing services offers a field for economies, and this field is extended by the reduction in the cost of salaries resulting from the Burnham Award. To these factors must be added the prospect of economies resulting from reorganization of schools, the gradual fall in loan charges, and the further administrative economies which may be expected to result from a simplification of the relations between the Board and local authorities.

Having regard to these facts and to the decision reached by H M Government that, in the existing state of the national finances, it is necessary to place a limit upon the demands to be made upon the Exchequer in the year 1926–7, the Board have decided that they can reasonably, and without detriment to the development of essential educational services, limit their grant to local education authorities as indicated below and ask local authorities, in this national emergency, to make corresponding economies. This limitation will still leave the Board's estimates at a substantially higher figure than in the present year.

While the grants which can be provided on this basis appear to the Board to be reasonable and to leave scope for the development of essential services, the Board cannot contemplate a return to the system of restrictions and controls associated with Circular 1190. They are themselves undertaking administrative economies involving the immediate reduction of the estimates for the Board's own administration to the 1923–4 level, and they believe that any attempt to impose detailed restrictions on expenditure would not only be incompatible with the spirit of the times, but would also entail a further complication of administration, instead of the simplification they desire to see. They therefore propose to adopt a policy of block grants and to ask Parliament to pass the necessary legislation for this purpose.

In accordance with these considerations a block grant will be fixed for each authority on the basis set out in the Appendix to this Circular. The grant so fixed will be guaranteed to each authority as a minimum for not less than three years from 1 April 1926, and will be paid in full, subject only to such conditions of grant as are indicated in the penultimate paragraph of this Circular. The benefit of any economies made by the authority will thus accrue to it in full. The grants will, of course, be adjusted in the year 1928–9 and subsequent years to carry out the provisions of section 9 of the Teachers' Superannuation Act 1925.

While the occasion for the introduction of this system is the present financial situation, the Board are convinced that a change in the grant system is essential, if local authorities are to be enabled to exercise their own judgement in the development of education, if that development is to be steady and continuous, and if administration is to be put on an efficient and economic basis. They had hoped to introduce a change of system gradually through the programme procedure, and they believe that this procedure may still be used to assist the change, but circumstances have compelled them to accelerate their decision, and the alteration in the grant system must of course affect the basis upon which authorities have been considering their programmes.

It is obvious that this change necessitates a corresponding change in the system of Regulations, etc., under which the Board's relation with authorities have hitherto been carried on and the Board have in fact been engaged for some months past in a reconsideration of the Code, Building and other Regulations. They would desire that in future their Regulations should be confined to those minimum requirements which may properly be prescribed as actual conditions of grant: that outside these actual conditions of grant the Board's action should generally take the form of advice given for the consideration of authorities: and that such advice should be directed rather to the maintenance and improvement of the general standard of education than to an investigation into the details of educational administration.

The Board recognize that changes of this far-reaching character must form the subject of consultation and discussion with authorities, and they will welcome the advice of authorities on the contents of this Circular, and in particular on any point where an alteration in the existing requirements of the Board would, in their opinion, assist administrative economies.

57 Advertisement, *New Statesman*

Advertisement *New Statesman*, 1 March 1924, reprinted in
W. van der Eyken and B. Gurner, *Adventures in Education*, 1969, p. 15.

Though the twenties was marked nationally by economic crises, it was also a period of fertile educational experimentation. One of the most

*influential was the Malting House School run in Cambridge between
1924 and 1929 by Susan Isaacs. The advertisement for the post – for
which she very nearly did not apply – appears below, followed by
an extract from her own writing, arising out of her experiences at the
school.*

Wanted. An Educated Young Woman, 18–27, to conduct the education of
a small group of children, aged $2\frac{1}{2}$–7, as a piece of scientific work and research.

A Liberal Salary – liberal as compared with either research work or
teaching – will be paid to a suitable applicant who will live out, have fixed
hours and opportunities for a pleasant independent existence. An assistant
will be provided when the work increases.

The advertisers wish to get in touch with someone possessing certain
personal qualifications for the work, and a scientific attitude of mind towards it. Previous educational experience is by no means required, but
training in any one of the natural sciences is a distinct advantage.

The applicant chosen would require to undergo a course of preliminary
training, six to eight months, in London. In part, at any rate, the expense of
this being paid by the advertisers. The advertisers would also welcome
correspondence from others with similar needs.

58 Susan Isaacs
from *Intellectual Growth in Young Children*, 1930, quoted from 8th edn,
1963, pp. 17–21.

On the basis of previous direct observations of the behaviour of young
children, as seen in their ordinary lives as well as in all types of school, it
was clear to me that children as intelligent as those in this group have a very
direct and active interest in everything that goes on in the general world
around them. They are eager to watch and 'find out' about all the concrete
events of the home and the street: the structure and arrangement of the
house, the drains and water supply, the electric light, the gas cooker and
fire, the telephone, everything connected with cooking and cleaning the
street drains, road-making and mending, the shops, motor cars and buses,
the policeman's way of directing the traffic, the railway station; the facts
of their own feeding and washing and digesting and excreting and growing,
and the whole cycle of life in animals and plants and the human family.

Active pleasure in looking at these things, and eager curiosity about them, is one of the most striking features of the minds of intelligent children of two years and more. It has quite as large a place in their spontaneous behaviour as their delight in stories and 'make-believe', in song and dance, and in all forms of 'self-expression'. And yet it has been very largely shut out of the tradition of schools for young children, even of progressive schools. Art and handicrafts, literature and music, have their due place; and our ways of bringing these to the experience of little children are now on the whole well based in child nature itself. But the child's pleasure in 'finding out', and his direct and active interest in the things and events of the physical and human worlds are largely neglected. They are not only hardly provided for; they tend to be actually inhibited by our emphasis on all the arts of 'self-expression', on the one hand, and on the importance of reading and writing, the mere tools of mediate experience, on the other.

The reasons for this are, of course, partly bound up with the history of the scholastic and verbal tradition in education as a whole. In many directions this tradition has now been amply corrected. Most of us are agreed in theory and practice about the great importance of the creative imagination, and of its expression in literature and handicraft, in music and drama and rhythmic movement. We are convinced of the value of the child's own practical activity in making things, as a means of harmonious growth. We know the technical value of activity in the three R's and ordinary school studies. And Dr Montessori has persuaded us to see how great a pleasure and how rich an education the young child can get from the 'exercises of practical life'.

But our awakening to these things seems for the time being to have exhausted our impulse to learn from the child. We seem to have stopped there, and to have refused to take seriously any other part of his behaviour as seen outside the walls of the schoolroom. As soon as we came to realize what a rich fantasy life the young child has, and how inevitably he looks out upon the world from the centre of his own personal feelings, we have behaved as if he did this all the time, and wanted nothing *but* fairies and fantasies. It is quite true, and a most significant truth, that the child's world is essentially a dramatic world. Undoubtedly, his direct interest in things going on around him in the home and the street has its roots deep in an intensely personal life. The records in this volume show how often and how readily the most active interest in things slips over into the dramatic play of father, mother and child; but they also help to show that their deeper sources do not prevent these interests from leading on to real experience, and from crystallizing out into forms of sustained inquiry, and delight in the actual process of discovery, which are at least anticipations of the genuine scientific spirit. The events of the real world are, indeed, often a joy to the child, as to us, just because they offer an escape from the pressure of fantasy.

The actual relation between the fantasy life and active intellectual interest in the real world of things and events is itself a profound psychological problem, and one which we had in mind throughout our work. I shall return to it in the later theoretical discussions. For the moment, I am emphasizing only the observable fact that intelligent children do show both a delight in the world of imagination and dramatic play, and in 'finding out' about the real world as seen in the things that go on around them in the home and the street. To see the one need not blind us to the other; to provide for the one should not lead us to thrust it upon children, nor to starve the other.

In discussing this problem in *The Function of the School for the Young Child*, I quoted an example of the gratuitous confusion of the child's understanding of real processes by adult conventions as to the child's needs which occurred with a highly intelligent and gifted boy of six years of age, who combined the qualities of the artist and the scientist in himself in the most delightful way. One day he experimentally opened the case of the piano, and spent hours examining its structure and watching the action of the hammer on the wire, and the relation of the striking of the key to the movement of the hammer. A day or two later he told me that his mother had said to him that 'when the hammer struck the wire, a little fairy that was in the wire came out and sang'.

Our failure to make any significant use of children's interest in discovery and in the concrete events of the physical and biological world has other roots also. Partly, of course, it is the outcome of quite mundane and practical considerations. It is, for instance, so much easier from the point of view of space, of staffing and equipment, to keep the children relatively inactive and to 'teach' them, than it is to arrange for them to 'find out'. It is so much simpler to teach them reading and writing, even by modern individual methods, to tell them stories, or even to teach them rhythmic movement, than it is to go with them to see a bridge being built or a road being mended, to trace the course of the telephone wires or water-pipes, or to wait patiently while they experiment with water or gas or fire or cooking things. Reasons of this kind, of course, account for the general lag of our practice behind our theory in every direction. We have acknowledged the importance of 'learning by doing' for many a long year; but really to let the child learn by doing would involve an immense advance in all the material setting of school life, as well as in the number of staff and variety of equipment. Perhaps the constant struggle which educationists have to maintain in order to make living realities of those principles which have already been surely grasped has prevented us from considering possibilities which can hardly be realized on any large scale for decades.

Another reason why we have overlooked this particular interest of young children, even in most of our theories of education, may perhaps be that the ways of the school tend to be dominated by the needs of the average children, rather than by the more intelligent. It may well be that this active interest in the real world is one of the distinguishing marks of the intelligent child, and that those of more average ability show it less. How far this is so would itself be worth inquiry; certainly this group of intelligent children, as well as others I have observed, showed a very lively curiosity about what things were made of, where they came from, and the way they worked. They did not, of course, show it all the time; like all children, they had plenty of dull stretches. But it was a recurring feature of their mental life, and there is no reason to think they are different from other children of the same intelligence, if placed under similar conditions.

It became, therefore, an integral part of our educational aim to provide for this as fully as for the more generally accepted needs of children. And this developed a view of the functions of the school for young children rather different from the one implicit in general practice. For me, the school has two main sorts of function: (a) to provide for the development of the child's own bodily and social skills and means of expression; and (b) to open the facts of the external world (the real external world, that is, not the school 'subjects') to him in such a way that he can seize and understand them. With the first purpose, everyone will agree; the second is a little more novel.

This is not, of course, the first time it has been suggested. The view has long been associated with the name and work of John Dewey. But it may be the first time, at least in this country, that it has been taken really seriously, and put into practice in the education of quite young children. We have long been familiar with the very young child's desire to touch and handle, to pull things to pieces, to 'look inside', to ask questions; but we have not taken much serious practical notice of all this, as regards the *direction* of our work, and our notion of what the school as a whole should be and do. We have been content to apply our new psychological knowledge of *how* the child learns, to the ways of getting him to learn the old things. We have not used it to enrich our understanding of *what* he needs to learn, nor of what experiences the school should bring to him. The school has on the whole remained a closed-in place, a screen between the child and his living interests.

And this is true in many respects of one of the most recent advances in education, the Montessori method. As I have already suggested, Dr Montessori has seen, in certain directions at least, that the young child is human, and ready to assimilate real human experience if it is graded for his needs and capacities. But, unfortunately, she has given her genius for devising technique to the narrow ends of the scholastic subjects. In the exercises for practical life her humanity broke through the conventions of the school; but even so, more for the purposes of practical necessity than for the purpose of knowledge. These practical exercises seem to be, with her, the field of morals rather than the field of intelligence. To us, the direct interests of the child in the concrete processes in the world around him seem far more significant in themselves, and as a medium of education, than knowledge of the traditional 'subjects' of the school-room. In other words, we see no reason to let the school and its conventions stand between the child and real situations in the world.[1]

59 Nathan Isaacs

'Critical Notice', *Journal of Child Psychology and Psychiatry*, vol. 7, 1966, pp. 155–8.

Despite the discussion on Montessori in the previous extract, the work and philosophies of Maria Montessori and Susan Isaacs were, and still are, often confused. The last article ever written by Nathan Isaacs – a book review which was actually published after his death in 1966 – clearly emphasized the differences between the two, and the meaning these differences held for teachers.

1. *The Montessori Method* (1964, pp. 377) (first published 1912).
2. *Spontaneous Activity in Education* (1965, pp. 355) (first published 1917).
3. *The Montessori Elementary Material* (1964, pp. 464) (first published 1917).
4. *Dr Montessori's Own Handbook* (1964, pp. 121) (first published 1914).

A revival in the United States of interest in the work of Dr Montessori has led to the republication of the above four volumes, described by her publishers as containing the 'four basic texts' for her insights and methods. These volumes (referred to below as (1), (2), (3) and (4) respectively) afford a very useful opportunity for a fresh look at her work; but the outcome as far as I am concerned is, I fear, mainly negative.

And this although I set out from a common platform with her. I believe that most of her searing critique of traditional pedagogy is justified, and I begin, just as she does, from the belief that education should be centred in

1. *The Forum of Education*, no. 5, p. 131.

the child and should offer a maximum of free scope for his own native powers of growth. It is because of Mme Montessori's vigorous and eloquent proclamation of these principles that she has been widely accepted as one of the main modern flag-bearers of progressive education. (So much so that the late Susan Isaacs actually began by calling her school in Cambridge a 'Montessori' one – though this did not last long, for the reasons referred to below.)

However, Montessori's books show that she also started from a number of other firm beliefs which carried her in a totally different direction from that of most English progressive educationists, and indeed, as it seems to us, a long way back towards the very yokes from which we have been so anxious to free children. Nevertheless, she states what she holds to be a conclusive case and as far as possible objective re-examination.

As one reads the books, one is struck immediately by a number of untenable pronouncements, inconsistencies and even wild statements; but putting all these on one side, I think that the positive case for her own distinctive views can be fairly summarized as follows:

After a professional medical training, she started on remedial work with defective children, and found in the ideas of Séguin and Itard an inspiration which she was able to carry much further, and which allowed her to bring her sub-normals to the educational level of average normal children in the Italian schools of the early 1900s. She therefore reasoned that if the method she had developed could achieve so much even for seriously defective children, what might they not be capable of doing for normal ones?

She found an opportunity of trying these methods out, and they worked. They differed radically from those practised in the ordinary schools, because they started from the child, and above all because their main criterion of effectiveness lay in carrying the child with them. He was given things to do, one after another, which he visibly enjoyed doing, but which at the same time trained him and carried him forward. In particular, these things to do consisted of materials and occupations which themselves halted him if he went wrong, but in turn readily permitted him to get himself right again.

Thus Montessori arrived at the conviction that everything which we wanted children to learn – reading, writing, arithmetic and all we normally mean by education – could be put into forms which truly responded to the child's own needs and strivings, and were thus inherently able to lead to joyous, yet disciplined, progress. In the light of her work with children from three years onwards she held that this was the right age to begin; but first of all with what she regarded as the all-important 'training of the senses': in every sort of discrimination, serial arrangement, classification and so on. After that, but before very long, the accepted school subjects of the three Rs, etc., could follow, but always by the same road of each individual child's own activities and mounting self-correction and self-education. Thus, as she saw it, her 'Montessorian' method simply consisted in giving to each child the kind of nutriment which his freedom needed in order to turn into self-propelling growth.

But what must here be noted is that however sharply the foregoing differs in *method* from conventional education, it fully accepts the latter's *assumptions and aims*. In fact it seeks to apply these from an even earlier age. Its most novel contribution lies in the preliminary early sense-training phase; but what is gained from this, as Montessori emphasizes over and over again, is not merely senses trained in all the above ways, but also the invaluable habits of discipline and obedience. These are indeed just what the conventional objectives of ordinary education need and normally rest upon. But whilst in the regular course they have to be vigorously *enforced*, Montessori claims that by her method and her early start she turns them into the natural pattern of the child's own life. It seems indeed as if these results of her method are those which she personally values most.

And so we come to the clear parting of the ways. All the above stands in diametrical contrast to both the aims and the methods of most progressive educationists in this country. It is not of course possible here to argue out this contrast, but only to note its existence and consequences. We begin, like Montessori, by focusing on the individual child and insisting that only he can really ensure his education. But we start from a quite different child psychology, a different child, a different way of education, and we end up with radically different results. For us 'sense training' is something superficial and relatively extraneous, which replaces the whole child by a small peripheral fraction of him, whilst 'discipline and obedience' are merely ways of making this radical deformation chronic. Children from the very beginning are individual selves and agents, doers and sufferers, in constant interaction with the world – human and physical – around them. They have on the one hand their intensely dramatic and fateful affective history, yet on the other also their cumulative intellectual story of actively exploring and manipulating their world, experimenting and effect-producing within it, learning about it and psychically building up its pattern. These are the ways in which all the time the process of living shapes them, but also by which they educate themselves. We, however, can vastly aid them in strengthening all the self-educative forces in themselves, thus enabling them to develop into independent individual personalities who can achieve constantly growing experience and understanding, skills and powers.

This kind of picture (which obviously owes much to both Freud and Piaget) necessarily points to an entirely different world from Montessori's, one quite incompatible with accepting hers, or practising her ways. But there remain of course her claims to those very remarkable results in her own world. If, by adopting her methods, they could be reproduced at will, those who continue to accept the assumptions and aims of conventional education would have a radical challenge to ponder. But even so there would still be the inevitable question how much Montessori's results owe to her personality (and personal influence over her close associates), and how much to her method as such. She certainly had the advantage of immense sympathy with the children she handled, and far higher standards of consideration than they were used to, but at the same time the firmness of someone who knew what she wanted and was determined to get it.

This, however, is all beside the point if one *aims* at something different. As Susan Isaacs wrote about Dr Montessori: 'Unfortunately she has given her genius for devising technique to the narrow ends of the scholastic subjects. . . . To us, the direct interests of the child in the concrete processes in the world around him seem far more significant in themselves, and as a medium of education, than knowledge of the traditional "subjects" of the schoolroom' (*Intellectual Growth of Young Children*, 1930, p. 21). Thus, though the Montessori material was always available at the Malting House School and occasionally turned to, it played only the minutest part in the total life, activities and achievements of the School.

An experienced teacher who had occasion not very long ago to visit several Montessori schools, spoke highly of the dedication of the teachers, but found the schools dull. I quote some outstanding points from her notes:

The stress all the time is on the individual child. . . . Every child is taught separately, and this means that there are long periods when the children sit or stand doing nothing while the teacher attends to one child. Although there is an emphasis on individual teaching, no allowances are made for individual differences and every child is expected to conform to the same pattern of behaviour and learning. There is no opportunity for the child to express himself individually in any kind of work.

Independence

Great stress again is laid on the development of independence in the child. He has to make his own choice of material, and in order to help him to do this the variety and amount of material offered is strictly limited so that he shall not be confused. No teacher is allowed to make any suggestions as to what he should choose. This meant in practice that amongst the youngest children a great many stood about and did nothing. . . . Although the children are allowed to choose their own material, they are not allowed to use it as they like. They are shown how to use it and must follow those directions. . . . Many children spent all their time wandering round after the teacher.

Creative work

This was practically non-existent. There was a certain amount of painting of patterns and cutting out of shapes in coloured paper. I was told that the children must never experiment with materials. Unless they could produce an end product which was acceptable to the adult, they were not allowed to use the material. They were shown how to produce an object and if they could not do that, they were considered not to be ready for that material and it was taken away. This I considered to be one of the worst aspects of the schools.

Concentrations

Except when the children were actually being taught by an adult, they only seemed to give half their attention to what they were doing. This was probably because the work presented no challenge to them. It was too easy.

Social behaviour

There was a good relationship between the teacher and the children, except that they were too dependent on her. Amongst the children themselves there seemed to be very little relationship. Even with the six year olds there was no cooperation, no help given to one another, and what exchange there was was largely aggressive!

These notes can naturally make no claim to be typical of every Montessori school; but they do seem to represent trends and risks inherent in the Montessori approach, and predictable from the basic theory. Dr Montessori and some of the disciples closest to her, could probably keep them in check; but they would assert themselves in typical forms as soon as these methods became more widely spread. And the master texts would not help too much to maintain either clear and balanced thought or consistent procedure. Consider the following quotations:

(1) The fundamental principle of scientific pedagogy must be indeed the liberty of the pupil; such liberty as shall permit a development of individual, spontaneous manifestations of the child's nature. If a new and scientific pedagogy is to arise from the study of the individual, such study must occupy itself with the observation of *free* children (p. 28).

We must check in the child whatever offends or annoys others, or whatever tends towards rough or ill-bred acts. But all the rest . . . must not only be permitted but must be *observed* by the teacher. . . . In our system, she must become a passive much more than an active influence, and her passivity shall be composed of anxious scientific curiosity, and of absolute respect for the phenomenon which she wishes to observe (p. 87). It is necessary rigorously to avoid the arrest of spontaneous movements and the imposition of arbitrary tasks. It is of course understood that here we do not speak of useless or dangerous acts, for these must be suppressed, destroyed (p. 88).

Pedagogy . . . is designed to . . . educate the senses. The method used by me is that of making a pedagogical experiment with a didactic object, and awaiting the spontaneous reaction of the child. This is a method in every way analogous to that of experimental psychology (p. 107).

(2) It must be remembered that the material of development affords graduated exercises passing from the most rudimentary sensory exercises to exercises in writing, calculating and reading. The children are free to choose the exercises they prefer; but of course, as the teacher initiates them in each exercise, they only choose the objects they know how to use. The teacher, observing them, sees when the child is sufficiently matured for more advanced exercises, and introduces them to him, or perhaps the child begins them for himself, after watching other children more advanced (p. 102).

The period when the child begins to be 'master of himself' and enters upon the characteristic phenomenon I have called the 'phenomenon of obedience'. He can *obey*, that is, he can control his actions, and therefore can direct them in accordance with the desires of another person (p. 104).

When invited by a single gesture to come and be measured, they obeyed in a wonderful manner, they evidently felt pleasure in obeying, and internal delight which came from the consciousness of being able to work, and of being ready to leave something that they liked doing, at a summons of something of a higher order (p. 115).

But what do we really mean by 'a development of individual, spontaneous manifestations of the child's nature'? As already noted, the child at say three is already the outcome of three years of continual interaction between the X that stands for his original constitutional self and the world around him, human and physical. This process cannot but continue, and the notion that 'scientific pedagogy' of all things demands a teacher passively absorbed in 'free' children is no better than a chimera. (If she is behind a one-way screen, she is not being a teacher, and even so, the child is constantly reacting to the situation he himself happens to be in.) However, Dr Montessori is very far from meaning what she says. Whatever tends towards rough or ill-bred acts must be checked, and even useless (to say nothing of dangerous) acts must be 'suppressed, destroyed'. And in any case the whole point of her pedagogy is that it is designed to *intervene actively* by educating the senses. The method used is moreover that of 'making a pedagogical experiment with a didactic object'. Oddly enough the *spontaneous* reaction of the child is then awaited, and this is said to be analogous to the method of experimental psychology. But the latter would obviously await the *induced* reaction of the child, and anyway without carefully designed controls would not venture to infer anything from the 'experiment'. But this is by the way. What is more important is that clearly the supposed pedagogical experiment is, as the next quotation shows, a whole graduated course of training by the teacher from the most rudimentary sensory exercises to writing, calculating and reading. And Dr Montessori is particularly proud of the extreme and indeed complete *obedience to another person* which her training produces.

It would be possible to multiply the inconsistencies and contradictions, and to bring in other quotations that make one murmur 'do I wake or dream?' (e.g. (1) 'The whole art of medicine is based upon an education of the senses' (p. 220). (3) 'It is the children between five and seven who are the word-lovers. . . . And they may be entirely carried away by their ecstatic, their tireless interest in the parts of speech' (p. 9). However, the outstanding fact is the flat incompatibility of her proclaimed gospel of freedom and spontaneity with her intensely directive doctrine of actual training. And, of course, also the quite untenable pretensions of a would-be 'scientific' pedagogy, which in fact has nothing in common with science, but is just another old-fashioned claim to have found the real elixir of pedagogic life, the one true pedagogy. However, all this is not to say that her detailed practical procedures do not still contain much that many working teachers could find useful and suggestive. Her lifelong passionate dedication to the cause of the child is moreover an unquestionable fact, and so, within the limits of her assumptions, is her continuous *rapport* with actual children and feeling for what they will respond to. We can continue to agree with her that 'by education must be understood the active *help* given to the normal expansion of the life of the child' ((1) p. 104) – even though we may think of very different modes of help to very different modes of expansion. Furthermore, there should be no two meanings about the following quotations from (4) 'If we could say: "We are respectful and courteous in our dealings with children, we treat them as we should like to be treated ourselves", we should certainly have mastered a great educational principle and undoubtedly be setting an example of good education' (p. 78), and again 'Kindness consists in interpreting the wishes of others, in conforming one's self to them, and sacrificing, if need be, one's own desire. This is the kindness which we must show towards children' (p. 79).

Only kindness is not enough, there must be true psychological understanding too, and by this criterion the main doctrine of the above four volumes does seem to me just to fail.

60 Board of Education

from the Report of the Departmental Committee on the Training of
Teachers for Public Elementary Schools, Cmd 2409, 1925, pp. 63–6.

*At a time when many rural areas were still using the pupil-teacher
system of recruitment to the profession, and elementary school teachers
had little more education than the children in their classes, a committee
under Lord Burnham pressed for a new deal in teacher education, and the
removal of the isolation that characterized the teacher's development. It
drew attention to the vast growth of the profession: 14,446 in 1870,
160,000 in 1924 and stressed the need to recruit an annual intake of some
8000 teachers to cope with the first of the 'bulges' – the peak of the
demographic wave entering the schools in the late twenties.*

It is not enough, as we have been reminded in evidence, that the teacher
should know just a little more than his pupils. The teacher in an elementary
school must know much more of his subjects than he will have to teach, but
he must also have a general sense of the relations which the subjects bear to
each other, of their place and extent in the world of knowledge, so that he
may convey or suggest to his pupils the main features of that world. After
all, boys and girls cannot get much knowledge of subjects before fourteen
or fifteen, but it is due to them that they should get some idea of the lines
and contours of the map as a whole. The main features should be known to
them, and we shall then have a more reasonable hope that some of them
may be stimulated to go exploring for themselves.

We surmise that considerations of this sort are partly responsible for the
striking unanimity of our evidence with regard to the desirability of providing adequate secondary education for those who will teach in elementary
schools. It has been put to us, and we think justly, that the preliminary
education of the intending teacher ought to be 'in the main current of
intellectual life'. On the moral side – the development of character and
personality – the arguments for the secondary school course are equally
good. The secondary schools as a whole provide not only the best available
general education, but opportunities in their corporate life for training
character and developing public spirit, which must serve the elementary
school teacher well. On the social side, that is in regard to the place taken
by teaching beside other professions in their service to the community, we
see no reason in principle why the future teacher should not receive his
whole education during adolescence in the way in which all other members
of the professional classes are educated.

We have found it interesting to note how the gradual raising of the school leaving age, and the rising standards of elementary education, have made the need of secondary education for intending teachers progressively more evident and have modified the organization of the system accordingly. From 1870 to 1893 the leaving age was ten, and from 1893 to 1899 it was eleven. This period of twenty-nine years saw the establishment of central classes for pupil-teachers, and then of the separate institutions known as pupil-teacher centres – special means of giving some secondary education to those who specially needed it. In 1899 the leaving age was raised to twelve. In 1922 it became fourteen as a result of the Act of 1918. This period of twenty-three years saw first the requirement that pupil-teachers should be relieved from employment for at least half their time to give them time for instruction, and that in towns they should not be recognized before sixteen; and next, the wide adoption of the plan of instructing them in secondary schools. In 1907 came the bursar system, providing for the continuous attendance of the intending teacher at the secondary school until seventeen, an arrangement in recent years adopted for pupil-teachers also. We have noted in the first chapter of this report that 85 per cent of the elementary school teachers now in the making pass through secondary schools.

All our witnesses have agreed that in principle a course of secondary education is desirable for future teachers in elementary schools. Some of them go further and urge that a course at a secondary school is an essential, without which no one should be considered qualified for recognition as a teacher. Some, on the other hand, state that such a condition is not practicable yet because it is not compatible with obtaining an adequate supply, and that, apart from grounds of expediency, there is advantage in maintaining some variety of approach to the profession.

Secondary education essential for all teachers, but attendance at a secondary school cannot yet be made obligatory

We have no hesitation in accepting the principle that a continuous course of general education continuing until the age of about eighteen or nineteen, is desirable for all teachers, and we think that is an ideal which ought to be realized within the next ten years. The bases of our opinion are, first, that those who are to teach boys and girls up to the age of fourteen, or even up to the age of eleven or twelve, cannot normally be expected to do it effectively unless they themselves have pursued a course of general education up to, say, eighteen, and that they cannot otherwise be fully ripe for subsequent training; and also that, if the teacher is to avoid narrowness of outlook, and be able to get a balanced view of elementary school work, and its purposes, in relation to the other practical activities of common life, he or she ought to spend perhaps the most formative period of education associated with contemporaries looking forward to many other careers. At the same time, we cannot ignore the opinion expressed to us by some witnesses who doubted whether it would be immediately practicable to make attendance at a secondary school a condition precedent to recognition as a teacher, in view of the large number of teachers needed annually and the limits of the existing secondary schools. A rough calculation will indicate the difficulty of numbers. Assuming that about 40,000 pupils in secondary schools now take a first examination annually, and that, of the 20,000 boys and 20,000 girls, 70 per cent of the candidates pass it (in 1923 the percentage was 69 odd), we get a reservoir of 14,000 boys and 14,000 girls from which to draw our annual supply of teachers. We suggested above that at least 6000 women and 2000 men represented roughly the annual need. Between the date of passing the examination and their recognition as teachers, whether certificated or not, some will fall by the way, and we must therefore assume, if we are to get in the end the required number of new teachers, that, say, 7500 women and 2500 men enter upon it each year. Is this expecting too much? To judge from the number of candidates seeking admission to women's training colleges at the moment it is not too much, so far as certificated teachers are concerned, but with regard to other grades the answer is not so clear. We have heard of no over-supply of uncertificated teachers. We have, however, to remember that the number of candidates taking a first examination is steadily rising, and that in a year or two it will probably reach 50,000 or more.

We may add that if the advantage of secondary education is to be considered an essential qualification for elementary-school teaching, the provision of secondary schools (not necessarily of one type, so long as they are schools planned to offer an organized course of education up to the age of about eighteen) must be made sufficient to furnish year by year the requisite number of new entrants to the profession without making unfairly large demands upon the total number of young people whose general education has been carried to this point, and upon whom the community has claims for maintaining the other professions as well. Further developments of the provision for secondary education in this country are continually being advocated, and are recognized by educational opinion as a whole to be necessary. From the standpoint of the needs of those who will staff the elementary schools of the country, we associated ourselves with the body of opinion which advocates an increase in this provision.

It may be well here to distinguish between the towns and the country districts. Witnesses from London and from Lancashire told us that they saw no reason why in those areas all future elementary school teachers should not pass through a secondary school. This is probably true of other urban, and largely urban, areas as well. Where it is not we should be disposed to consider it a sign that the secondary-school provision of the area is not sufficient for the area's needs generally. In any case, we feel little doubt that the development of secondary-school provision all over the country will before long cover the needs of supply in the urban areas. With the rural areas, however, the case as a whole is not the same, and it may remain different in certain districts for some time. For many reasons it is very desirable that the country districts should contribute men and women to the ranks of the profession; indeed no system of supply could be thought fair or reasonable which excluded them. But there are rural areas where it is impracticable to consider establishing a secondary school, and also where the difficulties of transport prevent children from attending existing schools. In such areas the obvious remedy appears to be the establishment of boarding hostels, and this arrangement is, as a rule, too expensive to be practicable yet, and does not always commend itself to parents, especially for their daughters.

Upon such considerations we come to the conclusion that the time is yet hardly ripe for limiting the profession to those who have passed through a secondary-school course. We are, however, of opinion that, as far as practicable, intending teachers should be educated in secondary schools, and we have therefore to discuss what precisely are the temporary alternatives which we think should be allowed.

61 Lord Percy of Newcastle

from *Some Memories*, 1958, p. 99.

The break at the age of eleven in our education system is normally attributed to the Hadow Report of 1926. But according to Lord Percy (see below), its origins were quite different.

I have never been sure of the origins of what came to be known as 'Hadow reorganization': the splitting of elementary schools into two stages, junior and senior, with a 'break' at about the age of eleven. I can only be sure that the policy did not originate with the Hadow report of 1926 on the *Education of the Adolescent*. My first memory of it is in a note on educational policy which I drew up for a group of Conservative Members of Parliament, for inclusion in the party's programme at the General Election of 1924. On the initiative of the Board's officials, it was propounded a few weeks later, as official policy in a circular (No. 1351) of January 1925. That I issued this circular without Cabinet, or even Treasury, sanction was characteristic, not so much of my own habits, as of the habits of educational administration in those days. The truth, I fancy, is that this policy had become a commonplace among educational administrators in England, as it had already long been in some continental countries, and that I took it up without quite realizing how far it would lead me. It was, in fact, to become the centre-piece of educational reform for the next thirty years. But it was far from being a commonplace among local authorities, especially those in rural areas, or among Anglicans or Roman Catholics who often viewed it as a threat to the entrenched position of Church schools; and it would never have 'caught on' with public opinion but for the powerful advertisement given to the idea in the Hadow report. Even with that advertisement, the popularization of the idea became my main and most uphill task in office.

62 Consultative Committee on the Education of the Adolescent (Hadow)

from the Report, 1926, pp. 89–90.

The Hadow Report on the Education of the Adolescent provided the first opportunity since 1920 to consider the whole area of post-primary schooling anew, and its recommendations, though not immediately implemented, have set the broad pattern of schooling that characterizes the system today. It recommended the raising of the school leaving age to fifteen – the depressed economy stifled this reform until 1944 – and, most radically perhaps, introduced the modern concept of the primary school, ending at eleven years of age.

Our fifth main conclusion is as follows: *At the age of 11 + pupils from primary schools should normally be transferred to a different school, or, failing that, to a different type of education from that given to pupils under the age of 11 +, though provision should be made in exceptional cases for the transfer of children at a later age, provided that their school course in the new institution lasts sufficiently long to allow of their deriving benefit from the transfer.*

We need not say more as to the desirability of beginning post-primary education at the age of eleven, nor need we emphasize the importance, which is obvious, of making provision for the transfer of children in exceptional cases at a later age. It is necessary, however, to explain why we think that the most desirable course, though it will often not be possible for some time to come, is that children should pass to a new school at the age of eleven. It is, briefly, that we desire to mark as clearly as possible the fact that at the age of eleven children are beginning a fresh phase in their education, which is different from the primary or preparatory phase, with methods, standards, objectives and traditions of its own. We want both them and their parents to feel that a hopeful and critical stage in their educational life is beginning in a school environment specially organized to assist it.

That result seems to us most likely to follow if they begin that new stage in a new school, and we were impressed by the evidence as to the advantage of transfer given by the representatives of certain areas (for example, Leicester) where arrangements for transferring all, or nearly all children, to intermediate or senior schools, are in force. The point was put very clearly by an inspector, who attributed the success of the Rutland Scheme to the following considerations, (a) that the buildings were new and completely separated from the schools already in existence, (b) that the staff was new, (c) that the curriculum was new and different from anything in the existing schools. He was strongly of the opinion that an *ad hoc* school would be better in nine cases out of ten for educating children after eleven years of age.

We recognize, of course, that there are arguments on the other side which deserve consideration: children become deeply attached to the elementary school which they have attended, and teachers are reluctant to lose them, though it is to be observed that the evidence submitted by the National Union of Teachers appeared to favour transference in many cases at 11+ to another school.[1] It seems to us on the whole, however, that the advantages, and that, wherever possible, arrangements should be made by local education authorities, as has already been done in some areas, to enable such transfer to take place.

1. A memorandum sent to the Committee by the National Union of Teachers, after suggesting that children should in some cases be transferred after the age of 11+ to junior technical schools, and in others should be grouped in senior departments, to be specially organized in existing elementary schools, continues as follows: 'In other cases, children would be transferred at the age of 11+ to another school building, and a form of organization where such transfer takes place would in many cases be preferable to the retention of the scholars in the school building where they passed the earlier years, as it is undesirable that pupils of the age of fifteen should be taught under the same roof as children under the age of eleven. Raising the school age to 15+ must lead either to the building of new schools or to the remodelling of existing schools, in order that full provision might be made by means of laboratories, work rooms, domestic service rooms and so forth, for the continued education of pupils to the age of 15+.'

63 Board of Education

from 'The New Prospect in Education', *Educational Pamphlets*, no. 60, 1928, pp. 5–12.

The reorganization called for by the 1926 Hadow Report was welcomed by the government, even though it created major problems of building and staffing. But it did not really get to grips with the major question that was now created; the shape and the future provision of a comprehensive secondary education policy for children who would be transferred at 11+.

There are three recommendations in the Report to which most attention has been directed:

1. That primary education should be regarded as ending at about the age of 11+, and that all children should then go forward to some form of post-primary education.

2. That this second stage should as far as possible be organized as a single whole within which there should be variety of types.

3. That legislation should be passed fixing as from 1932 the age of fifteen years as that to which attendance at school should be obligatory.

The first recommendation involves a drastic reorganization of the existing elementary-school system and to give effect to it is the most urgent, the most immediately practicable and at the same time the most revolutionary of the tasks set by the Report. The present pamphlet deals only with urgent problems which have to be faced at once and within the limits of the existing system, and it is therefore concerned primarily with this recommendation. But the second recommendation also is of immediate importance, for, quite apart from any possibility of future legislative changes which it would be out of place to discuss here, its acceptance involves a high degree of cooperation between all bodies concerned with the different types of schools for adolescent children, and particularly between local education authorities for higher and elementary education in boroughs and urban districts where the council is reponsible for elementary education only.

The Committee contemplated that schools dealing with the education of children over the age of eleven should include schools of the type now known as secondary, and, in appropriate cases, schools of the type of existing junior technical and selective central schools. Schools of all these types are definitely designed to meet the needs of selected children over eleven years of age, and the work of all of them is already clearly distinct from the general and unspecialized groundwork undertaken in the ordinary elementary schools. But to create facilities for the children now in these ordinary elementary schools to receive an education of the kind contemplated in the Report is a new task requiring a fundamental change in outlook.

It is true that the elementary schools have for many years not been content merely to provide an elementary education in the narrowest sense, as it might have been understood, for example, by the early pioneers of schools for the poor or even by those responsible for the early Education Acts. But efforts at extending the work have hitherto of necessity been directed in the main to the provision of more advanced instruction for a selected number of children. By the Education Act of 1918, Parliament required children to remain at school to the end of the term in which they reach the age of fourteen years, removing the various exemptions under which children had left before that age, and laid on all local education authorities the duty of providing practical and advanced instruction for the older children, including those who remain at school beyond the age of compulsion. This is the latest of many stages by which the age of compulsory school attendance has been raised during the last forty years, but the process has been so gradual that at no time has it been generally recognized as requiring any fundamental change in the machinery or outlook of the ordinary elementary schools. The Report makes it plain that some very valuable work is being done for the older children in these schools, but that, when all children now attend school for at least three years after reaching the age of eleven, it is in the highest degree wasteful not to recognize the claims of all these older children to receive an education suited to their special needs. The problem set by the Report is thus essentially different from that which has given rise to the extension of secondary-school provision and to the establishment of the junior technical and the selective central school. It is that of the adaptation of the existing elementary-school system so that all the older children, not a selected few, may receive an education suited to their age and special needs, practical in the broadest sense, and so organized as to allow for classification and differentiation between pupils of different types of capacity and of different aptitudes.

The secondary school, as we now know it, must continue as a school in which all will follow a curriculum including a foreign language, mathematics and a scientific subject, and in which the course will be planned for pupils remaining at school till at least the age of sixteen with definite provision for post-matriculation work by a substantial proportion of them. As more alternatives become available for pupils needing courses of different types, the more important will it be to maintain in their proper sphere the special standards of this traditional type of secondary education.

The junior technical school, varying in the details of its methods in different parts of the country, may be expected to retain its distinctive characteristic of providing an education with a strong bias in the direction of a definite industry or group of industries of local importance, and for this purpose it will always cultivate close relationships with the industries concerned.

The nature and extent of the provision made under these heads will clearly affect the methods adopted in any particular area for the establishment of senior schools for the great mass of the children. But the problem is in itself distinct, involving as it does a readjustment of the existing elementary school system, and being concerned in the main with the education of children within the period of compulsory school attendance. It is with a problem thus limited that the present pamphlet is concerned.

The need for more senior schools

Of all the local education authorities in England and Wales barely one-fifth have made any attempt to reorganize any part of their area so that all children are transferred at the age of 11 + to a senior school, and most of these authorities have not attempted to deal with more than a very small proportion of their schools. At the time when the Report of the Consultative Committee was issued there were on the rolls of public elementary schools in England and Wales 1,932,444 children over the age of eleven, of whom only 164,159 or 8·5 per cent were in senior departments (i.e. departments normally entered at the age of eleven or older) and most of these would be selective central departments taking only a few of the older children from the contributory area. Some progress has indeed been made during the past year, but almost the whole of the task of reorganizing the elementary schools still remains to be accomplished – the task of providing a senior school education for over 1,500,000 children or in the words of the Report (section 90):

emphasizing the fact that a new stage in education begins at 11+, by transferring as many children as possible at that age, not merely to a different type of teaching within the same school, but to another institution with a distinctive staff and organized definitely for post-primary education.

Clearly the desired result will not be achieved merely by altering the boundaries between departments within the school, for only in the very largest schools will there be enough children over the age of eleven to form a separate, properly classified senior school. We have now to conceive as the normal unit not the single school but the group. The first task is to contrive the creation of such groups out of schools designed, for the most part, on altogether different assumptions.

The case for a new organization

The difficult task of reorganization will never be accomplished – or will be of no real value – unless it is based on a conviction of the value of the changes proposed, and on a clear conception of their purpose. It may, therefore, be worth while, before dealing with details, to summarize briefly the reasons which appear to justify the demand that the problems and difficulties of a radical change in organization should be faced. The Report does not ignore the good work already done for the older children in many elementary schools, but its conclusion is that this good work is done under highly adverse conditions, and that teachers who attempt under the existing system to overcome the evil of 'marking time' are faced with a task of extreme difficulty. Many gallant attempts have been made, but all the experience gained from them emphasizes the advantage to be derived from an improved organization. Teachers, who have been able to obtain good results under the old system, will have far wider opportunities for good work under the new conditions contemplated in the Report.

The need for a further break in the school course, apart from that between the infants' department and the main school, has in recent years become more and more obvious. The older children need separate treatment just because they are older both in body and mind; they have a more independent outlook in life; they no longer require to be trained only in the general elements of education that all must master, but they also ask for an education suited to their own individual needs and capacities. If our objective is, as has been said, 'to prepare children for a life of active labour and social cooperation', it will be an enormous advantage if we can provide for their education during the last years of their attendance at school in an atmosphere and surroundings specially adapted to their needs, not hampered by the presence of younger children needing preparation and guidance of a different type.

The need for differentiation in the curriculum for older children

The needs of children of different capacities have to be met in different ways or we shall fail, as they grow older, to awake in them that active interest so essential to true education. It is not sufficient to provide 'advanced instruction' of a more or less literary type for a selected group of children, who would otherwise be 'marking time'; it is also our task to meet the needs of those children, whose outlook on life is more directly practical, or who wish to turn to some form of constructive work. If we cannot adjust our curricula so that they meet these varying needs, the compulsory attendance of the child at school becomes a mere constraint, which may well prejudice him for all time against educational influences. If classes are reasonably small, much can, of course, be done under any organization to adjust teaching methods to individual requirements, but only if the older children are collected in fairly large numbers in one school, will it, as a rule, be possible to provide alternative courses based on a clear recognition of the differences between children of different types. In a one-course school the child who should be following an alternative course becomes a retarded pupil, preventing the school from organizing even its one-course effectively.

The break at the age of 11 +

In the Board's Circular 1350, issued in 1925, it was stated that:

The age of eleven is increasingly recognized as the most suitable dividing line between what may be called junior and senior education. Its adoption for the purpose of school organization tends to a clearer definition of the aims and needs of the curriculum, and facilitates the training of the children on lines appropriate to their ages.

The same age is adopted in the recommendations of the Report, and there are important practical reasons for its acceptance. If the break be made later, the normal pupil, who leaves school at the age of fourteen, will not have a course in the senior school long enough to give him results of permanent value. Even on the basis of a break at 11 +, some of the children will receive all too short a course. If we fix an earlier age, most children will not yet have mastered the common essential elements, and it will be out of the question to carry out any process of selection; but eleven is roughly the age at which, under existing arrangements, it is most usual to select children for admission to secondary or central schools; it is the age at which those children who are most advanced in elementary subjects will find it most easy to embark on a new study of a foreign language or of mathematics, or of science on a more advanced syllabus.

Finally, in all but the most densely populated urban areas, senior schools must draw their pupils from a relatively wide area, if they are to be large enough to admit of suitable organization. It is reasonable to ask the child of eleven to travel somewhat further to school than his younger brother or sister and apart from the special difficulties of rural areas, it will usually be found possible to collect in one school enough children of this age to constitute a senior school of reasonable size. But with a lower age of transfer the schools would need to be nearer the children's homes and therefore more numerous; they would then contain fewer children in each age-group and classification would become more difficult.

There are thus strong reasons for making the break in organization at approximately eleven years, and we may regard it as possible at that age to make a reasonably satisfactory attempt to select children for different types of senior school. Classification at this age will not, of course, be regarded as permanent in all cases, and it will always be necessary to transfer individual children at a later age from one type of school to another.

Transfer to the senior school

In the first place, age is a better guide than scholastic attainments, for it is not true that the child who has failed to reach the school standard normal to his age can therefore best be taught with younger children. On the contrary, all the evidence shows that such a child will develop most rapidly if he is placed with other children of his own age in conditions which allow suitable special provision to be made for him. He needs the stimulus of a new environment, possibly even more than does the child of normal attainments, and his presence in a class of younger children is as harmful to them as to himself. Where schemes of reorganization have been carried out on the basis of a strict age division, it is often these retarded older children who have gained most conspicuously by the change. Instead of being a nuisance and a source of irritation in a class primarily concerned with younger children, they come into their own and receive the attention that they deserve, and as a result they often develop unexpected abilities. It is mere waste of valuable time to leave these children in the junior school till the age of twelve or thirteen; they, as well as the brighter children, should be transferred at the age of eleven, so that they may get the benefit of a course of reasonable length in the senior school.

Similar arguments can be quoted against the practice of promoting children of exceptionally good attainments before they reach the normal age of transfer. Such children are not necessarily suited either physically or mentally for association with older children, and the allegation that they will be wasting time if they are retained in the junior school is not, as a rule, borne out by experience. If children are transferred to the senior school on a strict age basis, the junior school is then freed from the burden of providing for retarded older children, the age-range of its classes is reduced to manageable proportions, and it is then far better able to provide for the continuous progress of its pupils up to the age of eleven. The school need not be confined to the work of any particular standard, but can make appropriate provision for the brighter pupils.

It is important that children should be transferred from the junior to the senior school at the age and at the period of the year at which pupils are admitted to secondary and central schools. Otherwise a child may be transferred twice within a period of twelve or thirteen months, and the senior school, instead of being able to concentrate on the provision of a coherent senior course for its pupils, will have a double objective; the organization of the course is upset, if some children leave the school after two or three terms, and the attention of the teachers is distracted by the preparation of those pupils for scholarship examinations. It is true that if children are transferred only once in the year there will be a difference of practically a full year in the ages of the youngest and oldest children promoted; but it will generally be found preferable to adopt this system, not only in order to avoid the double transfer of children going to secondary schools, but also to enable the senior school to organize its courses effectively. Pressure on accommodation has in some areas made it necessary to transfer children twice a year, but there are obvious difficulties in such an arrangement.

In order to obtain for all pupils a course of at least three years in the senior school, some authorities have fixed the age of transfer at ten and a half to eleven and a half; but it is of the first importance to secure that promotions to the different types of post-primary school should be made on the same basis and this will usually mean transfer at the age of $11+$, i.e. at some point between the eleventh and the twelfth birthday. It is recognized that on this basis not every child will spend a full three years in the senior school, but, if all transfers are made not later than the twelfth birthday, the loss should not be serious, and it should be the aim of the senior school to provide so good a course that children will remain to complete it.

64 Lord Percy of Newcastle

'The School Leaving Age', *Empire Review*, October 1929, pp. 265–70.

The problems of raising the school-leaving age were linked not only with the economy but with the need to completely reorganize secondary education. Lord Percy, as President of the Board of Education from 1924 to 1929, was unable to implement the Hadow recommendations during his tenure, and sketched out the situation shortly after leaving office.

There is an exasperating tendency in these days to make mysteries about education. Perfectly simple propositions upon which the common sense of mankind has long ago said the last word are wrapped up in phrases and made the subject of technical arguments. An instance is 'the raising of the school leaving age'. This is a phrase which stirs some men to unreasoning enthusiasm and others to unreasoning opposition. Yet surely the thing described by the phrase is simple enough.

Everyone knows that it is good for most children to stay at school continuously until fifteen, provided that the school gives them an education suited to their age and to the life they will have to lead on leaving school. Everyone knows that it is bad for children to stay at a school which cannot give them such an education, for at that age a boy or girl who is obliged to mark time deteriorates and is in danger of forgetting what he or she has already learnt. It is generally admitted that the elementary schools have found it difficult, if not impossible, to provide adequately for the older children who now attend them and would *a fortiori* not be able to provide adequately for children staying on for another year. It is, indeed, obvious that an educational system which attempts to deal with children from five to fourteen or fifteen years of age in one school is attempting an impossible task.

Consequently, no responsible person has ever suggested that children should be compelled to stay at the elementary school until fifteen. The accepted policy now is that senior schools should be organized for all children from eleven upwards. A comprehensive reorganization of the elementary-school system on these lines was launched by the late Conservative government and is now in progress. It must take time. The Hadow Committee suggested September 1932, as the earliest date by which it could be completed; the Association of Education Committees has suggested 1933. It certainly cannot be completed by April 1931, the date from which the present government have announced their intention to compel children to stay at school until fifteen. If, therefore, they carry out this intention, it will be impossible to regard the new measure of compulsion as an educational reform at the time when it first comes into operation.

Moreover, owing to abnormal circumstances arising out of the war, it will continue to be impossible to regard it in this light for some years after 1931. The high birth-rate of the first two years of peace will result in a 'bulge' in the senior school population between 1932 and 1937. The statistics have been published and it is needless to set them forth in detail. Suffice it to say that the number of senior school places required to provide permanently for all children between eleven and fifteen is approximately 2,200,000, or about 350,000 more than the number of senior children now in the schools. Of these all but about 100,000 will, in any case, be required in order to deal with children between eleven and fourteen in 1933, and the provision of 2,100,000 senior school places by 1933 was, therefore, the standard set before local authorities by the late government. But the number required to deal with children between eleven and fifteen will increase from nearly 2,300,000 in 1932 to over 2,500,000 in 1934, and will not fall again to 2,200,000 until 1938. It is certain, therefore, that, even if the organization of senior schools could be completed by 1931, they would be seriously overcrowded during the next few years.

We do not yet know the government's reply to these obvious objections, but, from the previous utterances of some members of their party, one may assume that their reply will be twofold. First, they will argue that local authorities will be moved to greater activity if they know in advance that they will have to provide accommodation for children between fourteen and fifteen by a certain date. Secondly, they will urge that, though the schools may be overcrowded during the 'bulge' period, it is precisely during that period that it will be most important to prevent the labour market being flooded by an abnormal surplus of juvenile labour – that, if we must in any case meet an abnormal situation during that period, it is, after all, better for a boy to stay in an overcrowded school than be launched on an overcrowded labour market. Let us examine these two arguments for a moment.

The first contains a fallacy so obvious that it would never have been seriously advanced if the Hadow Committee, in an unguarded moment, had not allowed it to slip into their Report. That Committee, reporting at the end of 1926, recommended the creation of senior schools for all children from eleven upwards and the retention of children in such schools for four years. They then recommended that Parliament, in order to stimulate local authorities, should pass anticipatory legislation in 1927 substituting fifteen for fourteen as the school leaving age as from 1932. But the Committee seem to have forgotten the fact that at present local authorities are under no statutory obligation to provide senior schools. Legislation merely substituting fifteen for fourteen as from a future date might stimulate local authorities to provide more classrooms in elementary schools, but it would not stimulate them to provide a new kind of school. Indeed, it might well have the exactly contrary effect. To add classrooms to existing schools is comparatively easy; to reorganize the whole school system requires elaborate planning and very hard thinking. If you wish to induce or compel someone to do two things, one easy and the other difficult, surely nothing could be more absurd than to warn him in advance that he must do the easy thing by a certain date and leave it to his discretion whether he does the difficult thing or not. Either legislation must be passed requiring local authorities to do both things, or legislation must be deferred altogether and local authorities must be induced to carry out the necessary work by ordinary administrative action. The late government adopted the second alternative and succeeded in getting the policy of reorganization generally accepted by local authorities. The present Government have apparently adopted neither alternative and contemplate that Parliament shall impose on the local authorities the statutory duty of providing accommodation for more children, but not the statutory duty of providing them with the kind of education that they need.

The second argument has much more force behind it, but it unfortunately betrays a misconception of the real problem of juvenile employment during the next decade. Even if there is no change in the law of school attendance the number of young persons between the ages of fourteen and seventeen inclusive in employment or seeking employment must, in any case, fall steeply from about 2,100,000 in 1930 to about 1,750,000 in 1933. If nothing is done, it will then rise again steeply to about 2,200,000 in 1937, after which it will fall once more to about 1,920,000 in 1940. It is this period 1934–7 that is the danger period. What is required, in the interests both of young persons and of industry, is a fairly steady flow of juvenile labour from the schools. If that flow increases or diminishes, it should do so gradually. But the raising of the school leaving age in 1931 will accentuate the fluctuations we have described. Instead of a fall of 350,000 between 1930 and 1933 we shall have a fall of about 780,000 between 1930 and 1934. This fall will still be followed by a temporary rise of 450,000, and this rise will take place in three years instead of four. The rise will, in its turn, still be followed by a fall of about 250,000, but in 1940 the figures will still be more than 200,000 above the low level to which industry will have had to adapt itself in 1934. If we desired to raise the school leaving age, not primarily on educational grounds, but in order to regulate the flow of young persons into the labour market, the obvious policy would be that recommended by the Balfour Committee in its recent final report, i.e. to raise the age gradually by one term a year over three years, and the proper time for beginning this process would be 1935, when it would flatten out the upward curve in the middle of the decade. If this were done, the number of young persons in employment or seeking employment after the steep fall between 1930 and 1933 would be approximately as follows:

1933	1,750,000
1934	1,810,000
1935	1,720,000
1936	1,770,000
1937	1,790,000
1938	1,690,000
1939	1,620,000
1940	1,540,000

There are fluctuations here but they are, at any rate, much less violent than those which we should otherwise have to face and the general trend is steadily downwards. Moreover, the gradual raising of the school-leaving age at this time would also fit best with the fluctuations of the school population, since in no year except 1937 would the local authorities have to provide for more than 2,200,000 senior scholars and in 1937 the excess would not be much greater than 50,000.

All these figures are, of course, only approximate estimates, but they are a fair indication of the problem.

The government's policy must, therefore, be pronounced a short-sighted one. It will withdraw a certain number of young persons from the labour market just at the time when there will be the greatest shortage of juvenile labour and the greatest demand for it; it will not provide many of those so withdrawn with an education suited to their age; it will do nothing to meet the serious juvenile employment problem which will arise in the middle of the next decade, but will rather accentuate it; and it runs the risk of diverting the attention of local authorities from their main task of systematically reorganizing education to the easier task of hurriedly providing a certain number of extra classrooms.

There remains the question whether, apart from these questions of time and method, it is justifiable or desirable to compel children to remain longer at school. The answer is that, if suitable opportunities of education are once provided for older children, there will almost certainly arise a demand from parents themselves for a compulsory raising of the school-leaving age. Broadly speaking, it may be said that industry as a whole, with certain important exceptions, would prefer to recruit boys at fifteen rather than fourteen. That, at least, is the steadily increasing tendency. The main exceptions are the textile industries, farming and the retail trade (but not the department stores); but such exceptions can be dealt with by the expedient already recognized in the Education Act, whereby exemptions from school attendance can be given, in certain circumstances, to boys entering particular industries. Where such a tendency exists, experience shows that the parents who wish, in increasing numbers, to keep their children longer at school begin to demand that the State shall protect them from the competition, as it were, of parents whose children, leaving school at the earliest possible moment, are supposed (often erroneously) to snap up the best jobs. It may be doubted whether the State would be justified in imposing a further measure of compulsion upon unwilling parents, whatever may be thought of the educational advantages of a longer school life; but compulsion designed to impose on some unwilling parents and employers generally is in line with accepted principles of State policy and there is little doubt that a compulsory raising of the school-leaving age on these lines will be demanded and must be brought into force at the proper moment in this country, as it has already been in many other countries. But this presupposes a system of education which attracts on its own merits before it applies compulsion, and it is this essential condition that the government appear to have forgotten.

In these circumstances, what is the proper attitude to adopt towards the government's proposals? Not an attitude of opposition in principle to a longer school life; and not an attitude of unreasoning panic about its cost or its effect on industry. As to cost, apart from the question of maintenance allowances, it need not cost much more to teach all children between eleven and fifteen after 1937 than it will cost to teach all children between eleven and fourteen in 1933, and it will actually cost less to teach children for four years somehow than to teach them for three years well. The attitude of educational reformers should rather be to insist that, if the government introduces legislation to keep children compulsorily longer at school, that legislation shall cover all the steps necessary to provide them with a good education. It must, in particular, definitely recognize the principle of senior schools and must give the Board of Education and the local authorities power to take voluntary bodies into active partnership in providing such schools. Space will not permit us to develop this thesis, but what is required is nothing less than a comprehensive revision of the Education Act and of the financial relations between the State and voluntary bodies responsible for Church schools. In no other way can the reform of education be carried out. Legislation on these lines was promised by the late government for the present Parliament and much work was done on its preparation. These are thorny problems which a minority government might well fear to tackle, but legislation aimed at a bold solution of them might convert the government's hasty and ill-conceived pronouncement into the prelude to a real educational reform. The attitude of other political parties should, therefore, surely be, on the one hand, to insist that the problem must be approached as an educational one, not as a rough and ready expedient for 'keeping the boys back' from competition with their elders in the labour market, but, on the other hand, to offer the government whole-hearted support in carrying through a comprehensive revision of the Education Act in which the question of the proper length of school life shall occupy its proper place as an important consideration but as subordinate to the supreme question of providing a good education.

65 Consultative Committee on the Primary School (Hadow)

from the Report, 1931, Appendix III, p. 258.

Official reports like those of the three Hadow Committees on adolescence, the primary school and nursery schooling leant increasingly on the evidence of psychologists and, in particular, on the work of Cyril Burt at the London County Council. The following is an extract of his evidence to the Hadow Committee on the Primary School, making the case for what ultimately came to be known as 'streaming'.

From the point of view of educational organization, one of the most important facts revealed by intelligence tests is the wide range of individual differences, and its steady expansion from year to year. At the age of five, children are spread out between the mental ages of about three and seven – a total range of four or five years. By the age of ten the range has doubled; and probably goes on enlarging until the end of puberty.

Older children, therefore, differ far more widely in intellectual capacity than younger children. During the infant period they can be grouped together without much regard to their different degrees of mental endowment. At the age of eight or nine, however, to put together in a single room all those who are of the same age would be to organize a class that was extremely heterogeneous. By the age of ten, the children of a single age-group must be spread over at least three different standards. And by the age of twelve the range has become so wide, that a still more radical classification is imperative. Before this age is reached children need to be grouped according to their capacity, not merely in separate classes or standards, but in separate types of schools.

Special intellectual abilities

For most of the more important special abilities, standardized psychological tests have now been devised; and accurate measurements have been obtained by applying these tests to children at successive ages of school life. No longer have we to content ourselves with vague impression or personal observation for judging the characteristics of any one period of development. The mental difference between one age and another can be precisely measured. The results so obtained may here be briefly reviewed.

The outstanding result is this. Between the ages of seven and eleven all intellectual activities appear closely correlated one with another. Towards puberty, indeed, these intercorrelations tend to diminish. But, during the period with which we are concerned, one central underlying factor tends to determine the general level of the child's ability. This discovery seems of itself to disprove the older view that special intellectual capacities emerge suddenly at different ages, or develop more rapidly at one period than at others. The mere fact that one such fundamental function underlies all concrete intellectual activities, and determines their efficiency, is presumptive evidence against the view that mental development could consist in the successive appearance of a number of isolated faculties one after the other.

66 A. S. Neill

'Freedom', from *That Dreadful School*, 1937, reprinted in Gillian Avery (ed.), *School Remembered: An Anthology*, 1967, pp. 153–61.

Pitted against the national philosophy of selecting children on ability tests, and segregating them into categories, were the 'progressive' schools, including Bertrand Russell's school at Beacon Hill and, most notably, A. S. Neill's Summerhill. Here is Neill, on the subject of Freedom, offering a radical alternative to the type of educational thinking contained in the official documents.

Lessons in Summerhill are optional. Children can go to them or stay away from them – for years if they want to. There is a timetable for the staff, and the children have classes according to their age usually, but sometimes according to their interests. Personally I do not know what type of teaching is carried on, for I never visit lessons, and have no interest in how children learn. We have no new methods of teaching because we do not consider that teaching very much matters. Whether a school has an apparatus for teaching long division or not is of no significance, for long division is of no importance whatever.

Children who come as infants attend lessons all the way, but pupils from other schools vow that they will never attend any beastly lessons again. They play and cycle and get in people's way, but they fight shy of any lessons. This sometimes goes on for months, and the recovery time is proportionate to the hatred their last school gave them. Our record case was a girl from a convent. She loafed for three years. The average period of recovery from lesson-aversion is three months.

Strangers to the idea of freedom in the school will be wondering what sort of a madhouse it is where teachers smoke while they teach and children play all day if they want to. Many an adult says: 'If I had been sent to a school like that I'd never have done a thing.' Others say: 'Such children will feel themselves heavily handicapped when they have to compete against children who have been made to learn.' I think of Jack who left us at the age of seventeen to go into an engineering factory. One day the managing director sent for him.

'You are the lad from Summerhill,' he said. 'I'm curious to know how such an education appears to you now that you are mixing with lads from the old schools. If you have to choose again, would you go to Eton or Summerhill?'

'Oh, Summerhill, of course,' replied Jack.

'But why? What does it offer that the public schools don't offer?'

Jack scratched his head.

'I dunno,' he said slowly; 'I think it gives you a feeling of complete self-confidence.'

'Yes,' said the manager dryly, 'I noticed it when you came into the room.'

'Lord,' laughed Jack, 'I'm sorry if I gave you that impression.'

'I liked it,' replied the director. 'Most men when I call them into the office fidget about and look uncomfortable. You came in as my equal . . . by the way what department would you like to change into?'

This story shows that learning does not matter, that only character matters. Jack failed in his Matric. because he hated all book learning, but his lack of knowledge about Lamb's *Essays* or the trigonometrical solution of triangles is not going to handicap him in life.

All the same there is a lot of learning in Summerhill. I don't suppose a group of twelve year olds could compete with a state-school class of equal age in – say – neat handwriting or spelling or vulgar fractions. But in an examination requiring originality our lot would beat the other hollow. We have no class examinations in the school but sometimes I set an exam for fun. In my last paper appeared the following questions:

Where are the following: Madrid, Thursday Island, yesterday, God, love, my pocket screwdriver [but alas, there was no helpful answer to this one], democracy, hate, etc.

Give meanings for the following: the number shows how many are expected for each: Hand (3) . . . only two got the the third right—the standard measure for a horse. Bore (3) . . . club bore, oil well bore, river bore. Shell (3) . . . seaside, 'That was Shell that was', undertaker's word for coffin. Brass (4) . . . metal, cheek, money, department of an orchestra . . . 'The stuff that Neill is stingy with in his workshop' was allowed double marks as metal and cheek.

Translate Hamlet's to be or not to be speech into Summerhillese.

These questions are obviously not intended to be serious, and the children enjoy them thoroughly. Newcomers, on the whole, do not rise to the answering standard of pupils who have become acclimatized to the school, not that they have less brain power, rather because they have become so accustomed to work in a serious groove that any light touch puzzles them.

This is the play side of our teaching. In all classes much work is done, and if for some reason or another a teacher cannot take his or her class on the appointed day there is usually trouble. David, aged nine, had to be isolated the other day for whooping cough. He cried bitterly. 'I'll miss Roger's lesson in Geography', he protested furiously. David has been in the school practically from birth, and he has definite and final ideas about the necessity of having his lessons given to him. A few years ago someone at a meeting proposed that a culprit should be punished by being banished from lessons for a week. The others protested on the ground that the punishment was too severe.

My staff and I have a hearty hatred of all examinations, and to us the Matric. is anathema. But we cannot refuse to teach children their Matric. subjects. Obviously as long as the thing is in existence it is our master. Hence Summerhill staff is always qualified to teach to the Matric. standard. Not that many children want to take Matric.; only those going to the university do so. I do not think they find it specially hard to tackle this exam. They generally begin to work for it seriously at the age of fourteen, and they do the work in about three years. I don't claim that they always pass at first go. The more important fact is that they try again.

Boys who are going in for engineering do not bother to take Matric. They go straight to training centres of the Faraday House type. They have a tendency to see the world before they settle down to business or university work. Of our old boys, three are in Kenya, two of them coffee-farming; one boy is in Australia, and one in British Guiana. The story of Derrick Boyd may become typical of the adventurous spirit that a free education encourages. He came at the age of eight and left after passing his Matric. at eighteen. He wanted to be a doctor, but his father could not at the time afford to send him to the university. Derrick thought that he would fill in the waiting time by seeing the world. He went to London Docks and spent two days trying to get any job – even as a stoker. He was told that too-many real sailors were unemployed, and he went home sadly. Soon a fellow schoolmate (of Summerhill) told him of an English lady in Spain who wanted a chauffeur. Derrick seized the chance, went out to Spain, built the lady a house or enlarged her existing house, drove her all over Europe, and then went to the university. The lady decided to help him with his university fees and living. After two years the lady asked him to take a year off to motor her to Kenya and there build her a house. He is there now, and the latest news is that he is to finish his medical studies in Capetown.

Larry, who came to us about the age of twelve, passed Matric. at sixteen and went out to Tahiti to grow fruit. Finding this an unpaying spec. he took to driving a taxi. Later he passed on to New Zealand, where I understand he did all sorts of jobs, including driving another taxi. He passed on to Brisbane University and three weeks ago I had a visit from the Principal of that university, who gave an admiring account of Larry's doings.

'When we had a vacation and the students went home,' he said, 'Larry went out to work as a labourer on a sawmill.'

But I promised to be as honest as I could and I must confess that there are Old Boys who have not shown enterprise. For obvious reasons I cannot describe them, but our successes are always those whose homes are good. Derrick and Jack and Larry had parents who were completely in sympathy with the school, so that the boys never had that most tiresome of conflicts, the thought: Which is right, home or school? And looking at the children we have today I am convinced that the successes will be those whose parents are in agreement with us . . . when the child comes young enough.

Breakfast is from 8.15 to 9, and the staff and pupils fetch their breakfast from the kitchen hatch which is opposite to the dining-room. Beds are supposed to be made by 9.30 when lessons begin. At the beginning of each term a timetable is posted up. Children are divided into classes according to their age and interest; the classes being called by Greek letters. Thus Corkhill in the laboratory may have on Monday the Betas, on Tuesday the Gammas and so on. Max has a similar timetable for English, Cyril for Mathematics, Roger for Geography, my wife for history. The juniors usually stay with their own teacher most of the morning, but they also go to chemistry or the art-room. There is, of course, no compulsion to attend lessons, but if Jimmy comes to English on Monday, and does not make an appearance again until the Friday of the following week, the others quite rightly object that he is keeping the work back, and they may throw him out.

Lessons go on until one, but the infants and juniors lunch at 12.30. The school has to be fed in three relays, and the staff and seniors sit down to lunch at 1.45. Afternoons are completely free for everyone. What they all do in the afternoon I do not know. I garden, and seldom see youngsters about. I see the juniors playing gangsters, but some of the seniors busy themselves with motors and radios and drawing and painting. In good weather they play games. Some tinker about in the workshop, mending their cycles or making boats or revolvers.

Tea is at four, and at five various activities begin. The juniors like to be read to; the middle group likes work in the art room – painting, linoleum cuts, leather-work, basket-making, and there is usually a busy group in the pottery; in fact the pottery seems to be a favourite haunt morning and evening. The Matriculation group works from five onwards. The wood and metal workshop is full every night.

There is no work, that is, no organized work, after six or six-thirty. On Monday nights the pupils go to the local cinema on their parents' bill, and when the programme changes on the Thursday those who have the money may go again. Pocket money is given out on Thursday for this reason.

On Tuesday night the staff and seniors have my psychological talk. The juniors have various reading groups then. Wednesday night is lounge night, that is dance night. Dance records are selected from a great pile . . . and as the lounge is next door to our sitting-room I dread Wednesday nights, for the tunes that the children like are to me simply a dreadful noise. Hot Rhythm is about the only thing in life that makes me feel murderous. They are all good dancers, and some visitors say that they feel inferior when they dance with them.

Thursday night has nothing special on, for the seniors go to the cinema in Leiston or Aldeburgh, and Friday is left for any special events such as play rehearsing. Saturday night is our most important one for it is General meeting night. Dancing usually follows, and Sunday is our Theatre evening. . . . Our system of self-government has gone through various phases and changes. When we had six pupils it was a kind of family affair. If Derrick punched Inges he would call a meeting and we would all sit round and give our opinions. We had no jury system; the verdict and sentence were given by show of hands. As the school grew bigger this family method gradually changed, and the first change was the election of a chairman. Following that came trial by jury, a jury elected on the spot by the chairman. The culprit had the right of challenging any member of the jury, but this seldom happened; only occasionally would one hear the protest: 'I won't have Bill on the jury, for he's a pal of Pat's' (Pat being the plaintiff who got punched).

During the last year or two we have had another form of government. At the beginning of each term a government of five is elected by a vote. This sort of cabinet deals with all cases of charges and acts as a jury, giving punishment. The cases are read out at the general Saturday night meeting, and the verdicts are announced. Here is a typical example of such a procedure:

Jim has taken the pedals from Jack's cycle because his own cycle is a dud and he wants to go away with some others for a weekend hike. The government after due consideration of the evidence announces that Jim has to replace the pedals and be forbidden to go on the hike. The chairman says: 'Any objections?'

Jim gets up and shouts that there jolly well are (only his adjective isn't exactly 'jolly').

'This isn't fair he cries. 'I didn't know that Jack ever used his old crock of a grid; it has been kicking about among the bushes for days. I don't mind shoving his pedals back but I think the punishment unfair. I don't want to have the hike cut out.'

Follows a breezy discussion. In this it transpires that Jim should have a weekly allowance from home, but it hasn't come for six weeks and he hasn't a bean. The meeting votes that the sentence be quashed and it is duly quashed. But what to do about Jim ? Finally it is decided to open a subscription fund to put Jim's bike in order . . . and he sets off on his bike happily.

Usually the government's verdict is accepted both by the culprit and the community. On appeal I cannot remember a government sentence being increased. The ordinary procedure on an appeal is for the chairman (nearly always a pupil) to elect a jury to decide the appeal, and in the case of Jim and the bike the jury had disagreed and had left the decision to the general vote.

Certain classes of offences come under the automatic fine rule. If you ride another's cycle without permission there is an automatic fine of six-pence. Swearing down town (but you can swear as much as you like in the school grounds), bad behaviour in the cinema, climbing on roofs, throwing food in the dining-room, these and others are automatic fine rules. Punish-ments are nearly always fines . . . half a pocket-money or miss a cinema. When, recently, Paxton Chadwick (Chad) was tried for riding Ginger's bike without permission, he and two other members of the staff, who had also ridden it, were ordered to push each other on Ginger's bike ten times round the front lawn. Four small boys who climbed the ladder of the builders erecting the new workshop were ordered to climb up and down the ladder for ten minutes on end. A jury never seeks advice from an adult, well, I can remember only one occasion when it was done. Three girls had raided the kitchen larder. The government fined them their pocket-money. They raided the larder again that night, and the jury fined them a cinema. They raided it once more, and the government was gravelled what to do. The foreman consulted me.

'Give them tuppence reward each,' I suggested.

'What ? Why, man, you'll have the whole school raiding the larder if we do that.'

'You won't,' I said. 'Try it.'

They tried it. Two of the girls refused to take the money, and all three were heard to declare that they would never raid the larder again . . . they didn't for about two months all the same.

. . . In our government meetings all academic discussions are eschewed: children are eminently practical, and theory bores them. They are concrete and not abstract. I once brought forward a motion that swearing be abolished by law, and I gave my reasons . . . I had been showing a prospective parent round with her little boy. Suddenly from upstairs came a very strong adjective: the mother hastily gathered her son to her and went off in a hurry.

'Why,' I asked in general meeting, 'should my income suffer because some fathead swears in front of a prospective parent ? It isn't a moral question at all; it is purely financial. You swear and I lose a pupil.'

My question was answered by a lad of fourteen.

'Neill is talking rot,' he said. 'Obviously if this woman was shocked she didn't believe in Summerhill, and even if she had sent her boy, the first time he came home saying Bloody or Hell she would have taken him away.'

67 Committee on National Expenditure
from the Report, 1931, pp. 46–51.

The Depression forced the Labour government to set up a Committee under Sir George May to consider cuts in public spending, and its recommendations, involving slashing economies in education which were to have repercussions for many years, were adopted by the new National Government. Exchequer grants towards new buildings were stopped, teachers' salaries were once again pruned, and many progressive schemes had to be abandoned.

The estimated cost of teachers' pay in 1931 in England and Wales is £42,900,000 for elementary teachers (towards which the State pays in general 60 per cent or £25,740,000), and £11,250,000 for secondary and technical teachers (towards which the State pays 50 per cent or £5,625,000). The total State contribution in England and Wales is thus £31,365,000. In Scotland, the State pays into the Education (Scotland) Fund 11/80ths of this contribution, or £4,313,000. The total State grant payable in Great Britain as regards teachers' remuneration is thus £35,678,000.

As in the case of police, the salaries of teachers before the war varied widely in the different areas. After the war, their salaries were considered by the Burnham Committee with a view to securing 'an orderly and progressive solution of the salary problem in public elementary schools by agreement, on a national basis, and its correlation with a solution of the salary problem in secondary schools'.

The Burnham Committee issued a series of reports, first establishing a provisional minimum scale, then recommending standard scales for elementary teachers and dealing with the distribution of these scales over the various education authorities, and later recommending scales for secondary and technical schools.

The provisional minimum scale, recommended when the cost of living was about 125 per cent above pre-war, on a rough average approximately doubled the pre-war pay of assistant teachers and more than doubled that of head teachers. When the later recommendations were made, the cost of living had risen appreciably further, being about 164 per cent above pre-war, and the standard scales meant extra remuneration to elementary teachers of 159 per cent above the pre-war average (i.e. they were roughly two and a half times pre-war). Provision was made that if the cost of living rose above 170 per cent above pre-war, a bonus should be granted but no provision was made for a reduction if the cost of living fell.

The scales thus fixed were to hold good for the four years, 1 April 1921, to 31 March 1925. Their full effect was not, however, felt at once as the increase necessary to bring each teacher to his right position in the new scales was given in three equal annual instalments, i.e. the full scheme could not have been in operation until the year beginning 1 April 1923.

In the autumn of 1921, the Geddes Committee considered education expenditure. By this time, the cost of living had fallen appreciably and the Committee commented on the fact that while reductions on the ground of the falling cost of living had been applied to most classes of the community and the process was continuing, the striking fact about teachers' salaries was that their increases had suffered no check with the large fall in the cost of living and were still automatically increasing.

The Geddes Committee clearly contemplated substantial cuts in elementary, secondary and technical teachers' salaries.

No action was, however, taken at the time on the Committee's implied recommendation that the teachers must in the national interest face the prospect of substantial modifications in their rates of pay. The view was apparently held that alteration at that moment would involve a breach of faith.

In 1922, however, with a further fall in the cost of living, it became obvious that the full Burnham rates were no longer justified, and the teachers decided on 29 December 1922, to accept a reduction of salaries of 5 per cent from 1 April 1923. This reduction was continued by consent for the year 1924–5.

At this point, reference must be made to teachers' pensions. Before the war, the scale of pensions was inadequate, and towards these inadequate pensions the teachers contributed £3 12s. od. a year (men) and £2 8s. od. a year (women). In 1918, the contributions were abolished and the scheme of pensions was improved, being approximated to the Civil Service scheme. The pensions were paid entirely by the State. The Geddes Committee criticized a scheme under which the local authority had control of the pay, age of retirement and promotion of the staff, but no financial interest in the pensions cost. They recommended that a 5 per cent levy should be paid by teachers towards their pensions, and this recommendation received legislative sanction from the 1 June 1922. In considering the pension deduction then imposed in its relevance to salary comparisons, it should be borne in mind that the scheme of 1918, even with the contributions imposed in 1922, is more favourable to the teachers than their pre-war contributory scheme.

The Burnham scales were due for review in 1925. In 1923, negotiations were commenced and the local authorities demanded reductions of 15 per cent, then 12 per cent, then 10 per cent as an all-round reduction before considering details. These negotiations, however, broke down, and the determination of the review to be made was referred to Lord Burnham as arbitrator. The awards then made effected a reduction on a salary bill of some £50,000,000 of a net sum of less than £500,000 or under 1 per cent.

The difference between the figures in the last table and the figures for 31 March 1930, thus shows the effect of the 5 per cent reduction in 1923-5 and the further alterations made on review from 1st April 1925, viz. a total reduction on the average salary of all teachers compared with the full Burnham scales of 6·1 per cent.

The scales fixed in 1925 were subject to review after 31 March 1931, on one year's notice. Notice has now been given to terminate them as from 31 March 1932, and we understand that consideration is now being given to revised scales.

Before examining the scales in more detail, we turn to the method of review. Teachers are engaged and paid by the local authorities and the settlement of their salary scales is regarded as a matter for negotiation between representatives of the teachers and local authorities. The interest of the State arises through the payment of percentage grants. In theory the State is not committed to payment of grant on the full scales and it need not only recognize for grant purposes such scales as it thinks reasonable. Various reasons have been urged in defence of this position. But whatever its theoretical justification may be, it appears to us from a practical point of view to be indefensible. The State is clearly in a very difficult position if

| | Certificated | | All certi- | All uncer- | All supp- | Total | Total | All |
	Men	Women	ficated	tificated	lemented	men	women	teachers
Average salary at								
31 March 1914	£147	£103	£118	£58	£40	£139	£82	£97
31 March 1922 (Burnham scales in first year)	337	261	284	146	96	326	215	241
31 March 1923 (Burnham scales in second year)	346	270	294	151	97	336	224	251
31 March 1924 (Burnham scales in full operation but by this time subject to 5 per cent reduction)	337	266	289	147	96	328	221	248
31 March 1930	334	254	279	143	98	324	217	245

The full effect of the Burnham scales, had they come into operation without deduction, can be ascertained by adding 1/19th to the averages on 31 March, 1924

| | Certificated | | All certi- | All uncer- | All supp- | Total | Total | All |
	Men	Women	ficated	tificated	lemented	men	women	teachers
Average salaries on 31 March 1924, increased by 1/19th	355	280	304	155	101	345	233	261

Note: The salaries of certificated teachers in 1914 were subject to pension contributions of £3 12s. od. per annum (men) and £2 8s. od. per annum (women).

There were no pension contributions in 1920 or 1921. As from 1 June 1922, the salaries of pensionable teachers (this includes all the classes in this table except the supplementary teachers) were subject to a pension contribution of 5 per cent. The figures in these tables show the salaries before deduction of any pension contributions.

it attempts to pay grants on scales lower than those to which representatives of the local authorities and the teachers have agreed, or which have been determined by an arbitrator. In practice, the position must work out that local authorities and teachers determine the salaries and the State has to pay 60 per cent, or in some cases more (in the case of elementary teachers), of the bill.

The least reform which appears to us to be essential is that the State be a party to the negotiations and should place before the negotiators the important national financial considerations which arise on the settlement of a matter involving so heavy a charge on the taxpayer. But in present circumstances, more than this appears to us to be necessary. In the present financial situation, it appears to us essential that the government must itself announce to the negotiating body that grants will only be paid on the assumption that there is an overall cut in the total cost of a prescribed percentage. [. . .]

It is clear from the circumstances under which the Burnham Committee originally considered its recommendations, and in particular from their proposal that a bonus should be paid if the cost of living rose above a figure of 170 per cent above pre-war that their scales were framed in the light of a cost of living very near the post-war peak. The fall in the cost of living from 170 per cent above pre-war down to the present level of 45 per cent above pre-war is a fall of just over 46 per cent. [. . .]

The remuneration of secondary teachers has followed lines closely comparable with those of elementary teachers. A table on similar lines to that given earlier for elementary teachers earlier in our report is on page 332.

It is clear from this table that the pay of graduates has followed very closely that of elementary teachers. The pay of non-graduates appears from the average figures to have been reduced more than that of the other classes, but we understand that this is due to changes in classification having been made between 1924 and 1930, and not to the scales having been modified to a degree different from the others.

In the case of technical teachers, there is a wider variety of qualification included in the group than in the case of elementary teachers and secondary teachers. The bulk of the technical teachers are paid on the secondary teacher scales, but a number of special posts exist.

The indications we have given of the effect of change in the cost of living on teachers' salaries all point to a reduction in the neighbourhood of 30 per cent. Having regard to the practical difficulty of enforcing so large a reduction even though it may be justified, and to the gradual adjustment to a higher standard of living which must necessarily have followed the increasing purchasing power of their salaries, we cannot recommend so high a

	Graduates			Non-graduates		
	Men	Women	Men and Women	Men	Women	Men and Women
Average salary						
31 January 1914	£225	£151	£194	£165	£123	£139
31 March 1922 (first year of Burnham scales)	451	343	400	357	272	301
31 March 1923 (second year of Burnham scales)	461	359	413	376	289	319
31 March 1924 (Burnham scales in full operation but by this time subject to 5 per cent reduction)	442	348	399	365	282	310
31 March 1930	436	348	397	330	256	278
31 March 1924 increased by 1/19th	465	366	420	384	297	326

reduction. *We feel, however, after balancing the relative claims of the teacher and the taxpayer and ratepayer that 20 per cent is the minimum reduction which should be made. We would point out that on the average as regards elementary teachers, this cut will still leave them with more than double their pre-war remuneration.*

We recommend that provision should be made within the existing arrangement for the salaries as reduced to be reviewed from time to time in the light of any change of conditions there may be in the future.

68 Committee on National Expenditure

from the Report, 1931, pp. 191–200.

The total net expenditure of local education authorities in England and Wales on elementary and higher education within the purview of the Board of Education has increased since 1913–14 from £30,010,000 to £83,690,000 (estimated) for the current year. In 1921–2 the total reached a maximum of £73,146,000: it then declined to £67,602,000 in 1923–4. In the last eight years, therefore, there has been an increase of £16,000,000 and apart from the raising of the school-leaving age (which was estimated to involve an additional expenditure of £6,250,000 in the first full year rising to £8,000,000 in the year 1935–6) it is estimated that the total net expenditure of local education authorities will have increased by a further £3,500,000 by 1932. [. . .]

Many causes have conduced to this rapid expansion not the least of which has been the great transference of charge from the administering authorities to the Exchequer and the placing of a powerful lever in the hands of the Board of Education in the form of percentage grants. In using this lever to urge on local authorities the Board have admittedly had behind them a weighty force of public opinion. Educational progress has been a popular plank in election platforms since the war and we fear that a tendency has developed to regard expenditure on education as good in itself without much consideration of the results that are being obtained for it and of the limits to which it can be carried without danger to other, no less vital, national interests.

Since the standard of education, elementary and secondary, that is being given to the child of poor parents is already in very many cases superior to that which the middle-class parent is providing for his own child, we feel that it is time to pause in this policy of expansion, to consolidate the ground gained, to endeavour to reduce the cost of holding it, and to reorganize the existing machine before making a fresh general advance.

First among the changes that we consider necessary in the interests of efficient administration we would place the reduction in the number of authorities by the concentration of all educational functions, as far as local authorities are concerned, in the hands of the county and county borough councils. There are 317 local education authorities for elementary education and 146 local education authorities for higher education. The authorities for elementary education consist of London, sixty-two counties (excluding London), eighty-three county boroughs, 131 boroughs and forty urban districts, making a total of 317. The authorities for higher education consist of London, sixty-two counties (excluding London) and eighty-three county boroughs, making a total of 146.

The local bodies which are local education authorities for elementary but not for higher education are now 131 boroughs which, according to the Census of 1901 had populations of more than 10,000 and forty urban districts which had populations of more than 20,000. (These are commonly known as 'Part III Areas' because their duties are primarily those imposed on them by that part of the Education Act 1902.) Consequently the sixty-two counties which are authorities for elementary education do not comprise the same areas as the sixty-two counties which are authorities for higher education, because they only administer so much of the areas as remain after the 131 boroughs and the forty urban districts have been taken out of them. As authorities for higher education, however, the sixty-two counties comprise the whole area within the county boundaries excepting only that of the county boroughs. We do not question the high efficiency in their limited sphere of many of the minor authorities now exercising powers over some part of the educational field, but the service is now developing under the recommendations of the Hadow Committee in a manner which is rapidly breaking down the old distinction between elementary and higher education. The dividing line of the future will be less between elementary and higher education than between education under and over eleven years of age. As long as the Part III areas remain there will be overlapping jurisdiction, competition and confusion in the education of the older children. [. . .]

It would be an essential part of this reform that the county councils and county borough councils should take over from the Board of Education the entire responsibility for supervising and helping, where necessary, private educational effort in their areas.

These changes would remove the chief obstacles to bringing this service within the block grant system set up under the Local Government Act. Under that system the element of local responsibility would be increased and the Board of Education would be able to substitute a general advisory supervision of the service for its present meticulous control.

We realize however that such reforms will take a considerable time to effect and we accordingly submit recommendations for such temporary adjustments as seem to us desirable in the meanwhile.

Elementary education

The existing main grant for elementary education is given by the formula:

1. 36s. a child in average attendance.

2. 60 per cent of teachers' salaries.
50 per cent of special services, maintenance allowances, and as regards the period 1 September 1929 to 31 August 1932, loan charges and other expenditure on reorganization and development.
20 per cent of remaining expenditure.

3. From the sum of (1) and (2) is subtracted the produce of a rate of 7d. in the £ for the area.

4. If the result is less than 50 per cent of the net expenditure the grant is made up to this proportion.

This formula originated with the proposals of the Kempe Committee of 1914, but the percentage element in the formula recommended by that Committee was limited to 40 per cent. The increase to 60 per cent in the case of the teachers' salaries was given in order to induce local authorities to increase the general standard of teachers' remuneration. That object has not only been fully achieved but in our view there is now urgent need for a reduction. We recommend in chapter 3 of this report that this reduction should be not less than 20 per cent. *Inasmuch as the increase of teachers' salaries was made the occasion for raising the percentage grant towards such expenditure we now recommend that the benefit of this reduction should be secured to the Exchequer by reducing the grant to 50 per cent.*

At the same time the special increase of grant in respect of loan charges and expenditure on reorganization and development incurred during the three years 1929–32 should be withdrawn forthwith subject to the honouring of existing commitments.

Were the existing minimum limit of the grant of 50 per cent (under (4) above) to continue in force, these recommendations would be inoperative in the wealthier areas of the country, because any reduction of grant thereunder in these areas would be made up under the guarantee. This would be quite unjustifiable. [. . .]

In making these recommendations, which involve loss of grant to the richer authorities and the loss of a possible saving to all, we have taken into account the fact that the reduction of the produce of the rate of 7d. in the £ in consequence of the derating of industrial and agricultural property under the Local Government Act did in fact result in an increase of about £1,000,000 in the education grant, which we understand was entirely additional to the relief intended to be given to local authorities as set forth in the financial memorandum attached to the Local Government Bill.

Another exception to the plain working of the elementary education-grant formula is afforded by a limited group of necessitous areas. Prior to 1930, areas which after receipt of the formula grant would have had a rate burden for this service exceeding 3s. 6d. in the £ were given an extra grant of 50 per cent of the excess; the amount so distributed in 1929 being £250,000. Thus any additional expenditure attracting the ordinary formula grant of 50 per cent or 60 per cent fell as to 75 per cent or 80 per cent on the Exchequer. It is not surprising to find that under this strong incentive to expenditure the cost of education in many of these areas has risen to a very high figure. Owing to the alterations made by the Local Government

Act this basis of distribution is no longer workable and pending the formulation of a new scheme the distribution has been stereotyped on the 1929–30 basis with an addition of 20 per cent. We have already pointed out that many of these areas are financially too weak to form suitable independent units of administration and the majority would be merged in larger areas under the reforms recommended above. *Pending this – in our opinion the only proper remedy – we recommend that any revised basis of distribution should avoid the strong incentive to expenditure contained in the old scheme.* We recognize that in so doing it will in all probability be necessary to widen the field of distribution of the grant and on this account we have allowed for some increase of the existing amount of £300,000.

Higher education

Higher education comprises a wide field of activities. In so far as these are carried on by local authorities the State contributes one half of the cost that would otherwise fall on the rates. To other bodies the State makes various grants on a capitation basis. Complete information as to the cost of higher education in this country is not available. The net expenditure of local education authorities in recent years is shown in the table opposite.

Prior to the war the Exchequer contribution towards this expenditure was in the main on a capitation basis but under the Education Act 1918, it was placed on a 50 per cent basis. Up to 31 March 1930, £807,000 of the grant was paid through the local taxation account, the balance being provided on the Board of Education vote, but since that date the whole amount has been so provided.

The Geddes Committee commented on the 'extreme rapidity' with which this expenditure was expanding at the time of the inquiry, the preliminary estimates for 1922–3 being as high as £16,200,000. The national movement in favour of economy brought the actual expenditure for that year down to £11,655,000, and it was not till 1927 that the expenditure of 1921 was exceeded. Since then the growth has averaged £1,000,000 a year. Part of this growth has been the result of the transfer of schools from the category of those aided directly by the Board of Education to that of schools aided by the local authority (with the assistance of a State grant). This transfer followed the recommendation of the Geddes Committee that no school should receive grant through both channels.[. . .]

Under the operation of the percentage grant to local education authorities the Exchequer will obtain one half of the saving in teachers' salaries as far as their own institutions are concerned. Steps should be taken to secure a similar saving to the Exchequer as regards institutions aided by local education authorities. Grants to bodies other than local education author-

Higher Education

Net expenditure of local education authorities over a series of years in hundreds of pounds

Year beginning 1 April		1913–14	1921–2	1922–3	1923–4	1924–5	1925–6	1926	1927	1928	1929	1930 LEAs October Ests.	1931 Assumed Board of Education Est.
Colleges etc. for the training of teachers			457	378	324	330	325	317	309	288	282	332	320
Secondary schools	Details		5295	4912	4496	4743	4980	5029	5568	6176	6471	6894	7200
Technical, etc., schools	not		3670	3153	2938	3143	3368	3334	3610	3733	3967	4196	4300
Loan charges	avail-		640	717	720	718	751	832	956	1110	1250	1483	1660
Administration and inspection	able.		672	648	605	664	714	726	735	703	712	751	750
Aid to students			1383	1571	1589	1621	1695	1769	1870	1982	2099	2257	2320
Other expenditure			334	276	194	195	202	231	191	261	252	442	450
Employers' pension contributions											*276	*271	*293	400
Total		4403	12,451	11,555	10,866	11,414	12,035	12,238	13,239	14,529	15,304	16,648	17,400

*These contributions are in respect of teachers in maintained institutions only, and exclude any aid given by local education authorities to non-local education authority institutions to meet the cost of such contributions.

ities are mainly on a capitation basis. We recommend that the rates of grant be revised to give the Exchequer the benefit of one half of the saving to the anticipated on teachers' salaries in these cases also. The total Exchequer saving to be made in the field of higher education from the reduction of teachers' salaries we estimate at about £950,000.

In addition we consider that steps should be taken to slow down the rapid growth of expenditure from public funds on secondary education resulting both from the provision of additional schools and also from the steady increase in the proportion of free places in such schools. Since 1920 the number of free places in secondary schools has practically doubled, while the number of fee payers has shown little change. [. . .]

Plans for new schools already approved and in course of erection are estimated to bring the above total up to about 440,000, of which roughly one half will be free places.

Taking into account the very large provision for secondary education made in institutions not aided from public funds and the certainty of a marked decline in the number of children of secondary school age in the near future owing to the heavy fall in the birth-rate since 1920, we consider that this provision should in present financial circumstances be regarded as adequate.

We are further of the opinion that a large proportion of the total expenditure can and should be met from fees charged to parents who can afford to pay them. The present system under which certain local authorities have been allowed to free their schools entirely – and, through the percentage grant, to throw one half the cost of this local benefit on to the country generally, which has not adopted this policy – seems to us inequitable. This situation will be fully met by the general reform of educational administration and grants recommended above, but in the meantime we think that the existing policy in regard to fees should be reviewed. While local authorities should be free to charge, or not to charge, fees as they choose, we suggest that the State grant to any area with an average fee income per scholar below the national average for the preceding year, should be based on the assumption that that average fee income is in fact received. *We recommend further that the grant of a free place should be conditional on the parent being able to show that he cannot afford even a modified fee.* In other cases the scale of fees should be increased more nearly to the standard of what the parent would be willing to pay to a private school. In these ways we consider that it should be possible to increase the total income from fees by not less than 25 per cent, or roughly £1,000,000, of which one half should be secured to the Exchequer by the operation of the 50 per cent grant or by an alteration in capitation rates.

Finally, reference must be made to the fact that on existing policy the

Exchequer charge in respect of education is estimated to be about £2,250,000 more in 1932 than in 1931. £350,000 of this will be required for the rapidly growing charge for teachers' pensions and a considerable further sum may be needed to meet other unavoidable commitments, but we trust that if local authorities recognize the urgent need for economy at the present time, the increase will be limited to £1,000,000. [. . .]

None of the reductions we recommend involves the withdrawal of any educational facility now being afforded.

Grants to universities

The State grants to universities are made on the recommendation of a Treasury Committee from a Special Vote. In 1922 the total sum available for distribution (which had been increased from £1,250,000 to £1,500,000 in 1920) was reduced on the recommendation of the Geddes Committee to the previous figure of £1,250,000, but the increase of £250,000 was again made on a review in 1925. On the next quinquennial review in 1930 the total sum was further increased to £1,750,000 for the next five years. We understand that in so far as the increased grants have been applied by universities to recurrent needs they have gone largely to increase salaries. *Having regard to our recommendations in other fields of education we consider that this extra £250,000 should be discontinued.*

69 Board of Education

Circular 1421, 15 September 1932, pp. 1–2.

One immediate outcome of the May Committee's proposals was a change in the 'free place' system of secondary schooling. Parents of children offered a place were now expected to pay, according to their earnings. For the first time, the 'means test' was introduced into secondary schooling.

Secondary schools

Enclosed herewith are revised draft Regulations for secondary schools. In revising the Regulations the Board have felt bound to take account of two criticisms which have recently been made with increasing force, viz., that (a) the system of admitting pupils free to secondary schools without any regard to the capacity of the parents to pay is needlessly wasteful of public funds, and runs counter to the principle, now generally accepted, that where educational awards are made by public or quasi-public bodies the amount of any assistance given should vary according to the circumstances of the successful candidates, (b) the fees charged often bear but a small proportion to the cost of the education provided, and are frequently not adequate having regard to what parents can afford to pay.

In formulating a scheme designed to meet these criticisms the Board have been principally concerned to maintain the facilities which local education authorities and governors at present offer to poor parents to obtain for their children the benefits of secondary education, and for this purpose will continue to have regard to varying local conditions.

At present a proportion, and sometimes the whole, of the places in a school are filled by competitive examination, the successful candidates at which are admitted free. Under the new Regulations fees will be charged in all schools and, while places (in future to be called special places) will continue to be filled by open competition, the parents of pupils successful in the competition will be expected to pay the school fee, except when their circumstances justify its remission either wholly or in part. The provisions of the new Regulations contemplate that the number of special places to be offered in any area will ordinarily be similar to the number of free places at present offered.

The Board recognize that it would not be reasonable to expect that the conditions for the special remission of fees should be uniform for the whole country. They contemplate for complete exemption from fees an income limit of £3 to £4 a week in the case of a family with one child, plus an addition of 10s. for each additional child, or any alternative scheme having equivalent effect. In considering proposals put forward for approval, they will have regard to the particular circumstances of the area in question and the rate of fee to be charged.

In order to meet the criticism mentioned in (b) above, Authorities and Governors should review the fees now charged in their schools. The Board do not desire to lay down any uniform standard, but they consider that it would be not unreasonable to look for some increase where the fee is at present below fifteen guineas a year; and while regard must necessarily be had to the fees at present charged, they will ordinarily hesitate in future to approve a fee of less than nine guineas.

Where so desired, arrangements may properly include provision for some reduction of fees for pupils over sixteen who have passed an approved first examination.

Where a school contains a preparatory department the Board consider that the fee charged to pupils in that department should be either the school fee or fifteen guineas, whichever is the higher.

The Board are aware of the problems presented by any proposal for obtaining increased fee income from existing pupils, particularly in the absence of a solution of any legal difficulties which may be involved, but in view of the financial exigencies of the time they think that the propriety of asking parents of pupils already in the schools on the 1 April 1933, to pay the increased fees, where they can afford to do so, may reasonably be considered. In the case of pupils admitted in January 1933, at the existing fee, parents should be warned that the fees are liable to be increased from 1 April following. In the case of pupils admitted after 1 April 1933, authorities and governors will wish to consider how far provision should be made for the review of initial awards where there is a change in the parents' circumstances.

It is not proposed that the arrangements referred to above should normally apply to schools in receipt of direct grant, since the fees in such schools are in general relatively high, and variations of fee or of the proportion of free and fee-paying pupils do not affect the grant payable by the Board to such schools. Accordingly, article fifteen of the draft Regulations reproduces in substance the provisions of the existing Regulations.

If the new arrangements are to be brought into operation on the 1 April 1933, it is important that the proposals of authorities and of governors of schools not in receipt of direct grant, should be submitted for the examination and approval of the Board not later than 1 January 1933, and the Board accordingly hope that authorities and governors in consultation will give the matter their early consideration.

70 George Orwell

'The Private School', from *A Clergyman's Daughter*, 1935, pp. 181–9, reprinted in Gillian Avery (ed.), *School Remembered: An Anthology*, 1967, pp. 104–14.

Between the developments within the State system of schools and the handful of 'experimental' schools there existed another, darker and largely unknown area of private schools; unregistered and uninspected, in which an earlier view of childhood was held captive. George Orwell, who had had some experience of teaching and cheap private schools, drew attention to this world, particularly in his early novel, A Clergyman's Daughter, *in which he portrayed the cloistered air of private education in the guise of Mrs Creevy's Ringwood House Academy for Girls Aged 5–18.*

Presently the sound of feet on the gravel outside, and of squeaky voices in the schoolroom, announced that the girls were beginning to arrive. They came in by a side door that was left open for them. Mrs Creevy got up from the table and banged the breakfast things together on the tray. She was one of those women who can never move anything without banging about; she was as full of thumps and raps as a poltergeist. Dorothy carried the tray into the kitchen, and when she returned Mrs Creevy produced a penny notebook from a drawer in the dresser and laid it open on the table.

'Just take a look at this,' she said. 'Here's a list of the girls' names that I've got ready for you. I shall want you to know the whole lot of them by this evening.' She wetted her thumb and turned over three pages: 'Now, do you see these three lists here?'

'Yes,' said Dorothy.

'Well, you'll just have to learn those three lists by heart, and make sure you know what girls are on which. Because I don't want you to go thinking that all the girls are to be treated alike. They aren't – not by a long way, they aren't. Different girls, different treatment – that's my system. Now, do you see this lot on the first page?'

'Yes,' said Dorothy again.

'Well, the parents of that lot are what I call the *good* payers. You know what I mean by that? They're the ones that pay cash on the nail and no jibbing at an extra half-guinea or so now and again. You're not to smack any of that lot, not on *any* account. This lot over here are the *medium* payers. Their parents do pay up sooner or later, but you don't get the money out of them without you worry them for it night and day. You can smack that lot if they get saucy, but don't go and leave a mark that their parents can see. If you'll take *my* advice, the best thing with children is to twist their ears. Have you ever tried that?'

'No,' said Dorothy.

'Well, I find it answers better than anything. It doesn't leave a mark, and the children can't bear it. Now these three over here are the *bad* payers. Their fathers are two terms behind already and I'm thinking of a solicitor's letter. I don't care *what* you do to that lot – well, short of a police court case, naturally. Now, shall I take you in and start you with the girls? You'd better bring that book along with you, and just keep your eye on it all the time so as there'll be no mistakes.'

They went into the schoolroom. It was a largish room, with grey-papered walls that were made yet greyer by the dullness of the light, for the heavy laurel bushes outside choked the windows, and no direct ray of the sun ever penetrated into the room. There was a teacher's desk by the empty fireplace, and there were a dozen small double desks, a light blackboard, and, on the mantelpiece, a black clock that looked like a miniature mausoleum; but there were no maps, no pictures, nor even, as far as Dorothy could see, any books. The sole objects in the room that could be called ornamental were two sheets of black paper pinned to the walls, with writing on them in chalk in beautiful copperplate. On one was 'Speech is Silver. Silence is Golden', and on the other, 'Punctuality is the Politeness of Princes'.

The girls, twenty-one of them, were already sitting at their desks. They had grown very silent when they heard footsteps approaching, and as Mrs Creevy came in they seemed to shrink down in their places like partridge chicks when a hawk is soaring. For the most part they were dull-looking, lethargic children with bad complexions, and adenoids seemed to be remarkably common among them. The eldest of them might have been fifteen years old, the youngest was hardly more than a baby. The school had no uniform, and one or two of the children were verging on raggedness.

'Stand up, girls,' said Mrs Creevy as she reached the teacher's desk. 'We'll start off with the morning prayer.'

The girls stood up, clasped their hands in front of them, and shut their eyes. They repeated the prayer in unison, in weak piping voices, Mrs Creevy leading them, her sharp eyes darting over them all the while to see that they were attending.

'Almighty and everlasting Father,' they piped, 'we beseech Thee that our studies this day may be graced by Thy divine guidance. Make us to conduct ourselves quietly and obediently; look down upon our school and make it to prosper, so that it may grow in numbers and be a good example to the neighbourhood and not a disgrace like some schools of which Thou knowest, O Lord. Make us, we beseech Thee, O Lord, industrious, punctual and ladylike, and worthy in all possible respects to walk in Thy ways: for Jesus Christ's sake, our Lord, Amen.'

This prayer was of Mrs Creevy's own composition. When they had finished it, the girls repeated the Lord's Prayer, and then sat down.

'Now girls,' said Mrs Creevy, 'this is your new teacher, Miss Millborough. As you know, Miss Strong had to leave us all of a sudden after she was taken so bad in the middle of the arithmetic lesson; and I can tell you I've had a hard week of it looking for a new teacher. I had seventy-three applications before I took on Miss Millborough, and I had to refuse them all because their qualifications weren't high enough. Just you remember and tell your parents that, all of you – seventy-three applications! Well, Miss Millborough is going to take you in Latin, French, history, geography, mathematics, English literature and composition, spelling, grammar, handwriting and freehand drawing; and Mr Booth will take you in chemistry as usual on Thursday afternoons. Now, what's the first lesson on your time table this morning?'

'History, Ma'am,' piped one or two voices.

'Very well. I expect Miss Millborough'll start off by asking you a few questions about the history you've been learning. So just you do your best, all of you, and let her see that all the trouble we've taken over you hasn't been wasted. You'll find they can be quite a sharp lot of girls when they try, Miss Millborough.'

'I'm sure they are,' said Dorothy.

'Well, I'll be leaving you, then. And just you behave yourselves, girls! Don't you get trying it on with Miss Millborough like you did with Miss Brewer, because I warn you she won't stand it. If I hear any noise coming from this room, there'll be trouble for somebody.'

She gave a glance round which included Dorothy and indeed suggested that Dorothy would probably be the 'somebody' referred to, and departed.

Dorothy faced the class. She was not afraid of them – she was too used to dealing with children ever to be afraid of them – but she did feel a momentary qualm. The sense of being an imposter (what teacher has not felt it at times?) was heavy upon her. It suddenly occurred to her, what she had only been dimly aware of before, that she had taken this teaching job under flagrantly false pretences, without having any kind of qualification for it. The subject she was now supposed to be teaching was history, and, like most 'educated' people, she knew virtually no history. How awful, she thought, if it turned out that these girls knew more history than she did! She said tentatively:

'What period exactly were you doing with Miss Strong?'

Nobody answered. Dorothy saw the older girls exchanging glances, as though asking one another whether it was safe to say anything, and finally deciding not to commit themselves.

'Well, whereabouts had you got to?' she said, wondering whether perhaps the word 'period' was too much for them.

Again no answer.

'Well, now, surely you remember *something* about it? Tell me the names of some of the people you were learning about in your last history lesson.'

More glances were exchanged, and a very plain little girl in the front row, in a brown jumper and skirt, with her hair screwed into two tight pigtails, remarked cloudily, 'It was about the Ancient Britons.' At this two other girls took courage and answered simultaneously. One of them said 'Columbus', and the other 'Napoleon'.

Somehow, after that, Dorothy seemed to see her way more clearly. It was obvious that instead of being uncomfortably knowledgeable as she had feared, the class knew as nearly as possible no history at all. With this discovery her stage fright vanished. She grasped that before she could do anything else with them it was necessary to find out what, if anything, these children knew. So, instead of following the timetable, she spent the rest of the morning in questioning the entire class on each subject in turn; when she had finished with history (and it took about five minutes to get to the bottom of their historical knowledge) she tried them with geography, with English grammar, with French, with arithmetic – with everything, in fact, that they were supposed to have learned. By twelve o'clock she had plumbed, though not actually explored, the frightful abysses of their ignorance.

For they knew nothing, absolutely nothing – nothing, nothing, nothing, like the Dadaists. It was appalling that even children could be so ignorant. There were only two girls in the class who knew whether the earth went round the sun or the sun round the earth, and not a single one of them could tell Dorothy who was the last king before George V, or who wrote *Hamlet*, or what was meant by a vulgar fraction, or which ocean you crossed to get to America, the Atlantic or the Pacific. And the big girls of fifteen were not much better than the tiny infants of eight, except that the former could at least read consecutively and write neat copperplate. That was the one thing that nearly all of the older girls could do – they could write neatly. Mrs Creevy had seen to that. And of course, here and there in the midst of their ignorance, there were small, disconnected islets of knowledge, for example, some odd stanzas from 'pieces of poetry' that they had learned by heart, and a few Ollendorffian French sentences such as 'Passez-moi le beurre, s'il vous plait' and 'Le fils du jardinier a perdu son chapeau,' which they appeared to have learned as a parrot learns 'Pretty Poll'. As for their arithmetic it was a little better than the other subjects. Most of them knew how to add and subtract, about half of them had some notion of how to multiply, and there were even three or four who had struggled as far in long division. But that was the utmost limit of their knowledge; and beyond, in every direction, lay utter, impenetrable night.

Moreover, not only did they know nothing, but they were so unused to being questioned that it was often difficult to get answers out of them at all. It was obvious that whatever they knew they had learned in an entirely mechanical manner, and they could only gape in a sort of dull bewilderment when asked to think for themselves. However, they did not seem unwilling, and evidently they had made up their minds to be 'good' – children are always 'good' with a new teacher; and Dorothy persisted, and by degrees the children grew, or seemed to grow, a shade less lumpish. She began to pick up, from the answers they gave her, a fairly accurate notion of what Miss Strong's regime had been like.

It appeared that, though theoretically they had learned all the usual school subjects, the only ones that had been at all seriously taught were handwriting and arithmetic. Mrs Creevy was particularly keen on handwriting. And besides this they had spent great quantities of time – an hour or two out of every day, it seemed – in drudging through a dreadful routine called 'copies'. 'Copies' meant copying things out of textbooks or off the blackboard. Miss Strong would write up, for example, some sententious little 'essay' (there was an essay entitled 'Spring' which recurred in all the older girls' books, and which began, 'Now, when girlish April is tripping through the land, when the birds are chanting gaily on the boughs and the dainty flowerets bursting from their buds,' etc., etc.), and the girls would make fair copies of it in their copybooks; and the parents to whom the copybooks were shown from time to time, were no doubt suitably impressed. Dorothy began to grasp that everything the girls had been taught was in reality aimed at the parents. Hence the 'copies', the insistence on hand-writing, and the parroting of ready-made French phrases; they were cheap and easy ways of creating an impression. Meanwhile, the little girls at the bottom of the class seemed barely able to read and write, and one of them – her name was Mavis Williams, and she was a rather sinister-looking child of eleven, with eyes too far apart – could not even count. This child seemed to have done nothing at all during the past term and a half except to write pothooks – page after page of pothooks, looping on and on like the man-grove roots in some tropical swamp.

Dorothy tried not to hurt the children's feelings by exclaiming at their ignorance, but in her heart she was amazed and horrified. She had not known that schools of this description still existed in the civilized world. The whole atmosphere of the place was so curiously antiquated – so reminis-cent of those dreary little private schools that you read about in Victorian novels. As for the few textbooks that the class possessed, you could hardly look at them without feeling as though you had stepped back into the mid-nineteenth century. There were only three textbooks of which each child had a copy. One was a shilling arithmetic, pre-war but fairly serviceable, another was a horrid little book called *The Hundred Page History of Britain* – a nasty little duo-decimo book with a gritty brown cover, and, for frontis-piece, a portrait of Boadicea with a Union Jack draped over the front of her chariot. Dorothy opened this book at random, came to page 91, and read:

After the French Revolution was over, the self-styled Emperor Napoleon Buona-parte attempted to set up his sway, but though he won a few victories against continental troops, he soon found that in the 'thin red line' he had more than met his match. Conclusions were tried upon the field of Waterloo, where 50,000 Britons put to flight 70,000 Frenchmen – for the Prussians, our allies, arrived too late for the battle. With a ringing British cheer our men charged down the slope and the enemy broke and fled. We now come on to the great Reform Bill

George Orwell **347**

of 1832, the first of those beneficent reforms which have made British liberty what it is and marked us off from the less fortunate nations, etc., etc.

The date of the book was 1888. Dorothy, who had never seen a history book of this description before, examined it with a feeling of approaching horror. There was also an extraordinary little 'reader', dated 1863. It consisted mostly of bits out of Fenimore Cooper, Dr Watts and Lord Tennyson, and at the end there were the queerest little 'Nature Notes' with woodcut illustrations. There would be a woodcut of an elephant, and underneath in small print: 'The Elephant is a sagacious beast. He rejoices in the shade of the Palm Trees, and though stronger than six horses he will allow a little child to lead him. His food is Bananas.' And so on to the Whale, the Zebra, the Porcupine and the Spotted Camelopard. There were also, in the teacher's desk, a copy of *Beautiful Joe*, a forlorn book called *Peeps at Distant Lands*, and a French phrase book dated 1891. It was called *All you will need on your Parisian Trip*, and the first phrase given was 'Lace my stays, but not too tightly.' In the whole room there was not such a thing as an atlas or a set of geometrical instruments.

At eleven there was a break of ten minutes, and some of the children played dull little games at noughts and crosses or quarrelled over pencil cases, and a few who had got over their first shyness clustered round Dorothy's desk and talked to her. They told her some more about Miss Strong and her methods of teaching, and how she used to twist their ears when they made blots on their copybooks. It appeared that Miss Strong had been a very strict teacher except when she was 'taken bad', which happened about twice a week. And when she was taken bad she used to drink some medicine out of a little brown bottle, and after drinking it she would grow quite jolly for a while and talk to them about her brother in Canada. But on her last day – the time when she was taken so bad during the arithmetic lesson – the medicine seemed to make her worse than ever, because she had no sooner drunk it than she began singing and fell across a desk, and Mrs Creevy had to carry her out of the room.

After break there was another period of three-quarters of an hour, and then school ended for the morning. Dorothy felt stiff and tired after three hours in the chilly but stuffy room, and she would have liked to go out of doors for a breath of fresh air, but Mrs Creevy had told her beforehand that she must come and help get dinner ready. The girls who lived near the school mostly went home for dinner, but there were seven who had dinner in the 'morning-room' at tenpence a time. It was an uncomfortable meal, and passed in almost complete silence, for the girls were frightened to talk under Mrs Creevy's eye. The dinner was stewed scrag end of mutton, and Mrs Creevy showed extraordinary dexterity in serving the pieces of lean to the 'good payers' and the pieces of fat to the 'medium payers'. As for the three 'bad payers', they ate a shamefaced lunch out of paper bags in the schoolroom.

School began again at two o'clock. Already, after only one morning's teaching, Dorothy went back to her work with secret shrinking and dread. She was beginning to realize what her life would be like, day after day and week after week, in that sunless room, trying to drive the rudiments of knowledge into unwilling brats. But when she had assembled the girls and called their names over, one of them, a little peaky child with mouse-coloured hair, called Laura Firth, came up to her desk and presented her with a pathetic bunch of browny-yellow chrysanthemums, 'From all of us.' The girls had taken a liking to Dorothy, and had subscribed fourpence among themselves, to buy her a bunch of flowers.

Something stirred in Dorothy's heart as she took the ugly flowers. She looked with more seeing eyes than before at the anaemic faces and shabby clothes of the children, and was all of a sudden horribly ashamed to think that in the morning she had looked at them with indifference, almost with distaste. Now, a profound pity took possession of her. The poor children, the poor children, the poor children! How they had been stunted and maltreated! And with it all they had retained the childish gentleness that could make them squander their few pennies on flowers for their teacher.

71 **Board of Education**
from the Report of the Departmental Committee on Private Schools, 1932, pp. 63–8.

The concern expressed by Orwell and others about the conditions of private schooling was considered by a committee under Alderman (as he was then) J. Chuter Ede in 1932. There were about 10,000 private schools in the country at the time, teaching some 400,000 children, but the list of 'Secondary Schools and Preparatory Schools Recognized by the Board as Efficient' contained only some 611 schools, most of them public schools. Obviously, the Board's List was only touching the surface of the problem, and the committee recommended registration of all schools, demanding certain minimum standards. Many of its recommendations were finally included in the 1944 Act.

Most of our witnesses suggested that private schools should be registered. This term, however, is used in many different senses and the exact purpose of registration must therefore be carefully considered. If we had recommended that the local education authorities or the Board of Education should be empowered to determine whether a school complied with the minimum requirements, it would have been convenient to make registration the main instrument of control. A school would be registered only if it reached the necessary standard and it would be struck off the register if it afterwards fell below this standard. The only question for a Court of Law would be whether the proper procedure had been followed and whether the school was, in fact, registered or not. The interpretation of the minimum requirements would be outside the province of the courts. Registration would thus be an act performed by the appropriate authority which would grant or refuse the proprietor's application after inspecting the school.

If, however, as we believe, the question whether the minimum requirements are fulfilled must be determinable in the courts, registration of this type is not essential to the scheme of supervision and there is much to be said for avoiding it altogether. It would cause several minor difficulties, into which we need not enter as there are more important considerations. In the first place it is almost certain that, under this type of registration, registered schools would come to be regarded as having been positively approved by the registering authority and this is undesirable because many schools would have to be tolerated which are not sufficiently satisfactory to receive any form of public recognition. Secondly, registration would depend on information supplied by the proprietor and upon the conditions found at inspection. It would be difficult to avoid requiring the proprietor to apply for an amendment of the registration if, for example, he increased the numbers in the school after extending the premises. It might become necessary in practice to fix for each school the maximum number of pupils and the age range and sex of the pupils. Strictly to prevent all unauthorized changes a plan of the premises would have to be registered. Thus changes of a kind frequent in private schools might cause a great deal of administrative work harassing both to the proprietors and the inspecting authorities. It may be possible to suggest means of avoiding this danger but there would always remain much risk of this type of registration proving a frequent source of restriction and irritation. Against bad schools it would, admittedly, be a useful weapon, though not a strong one if the courts are to have the last word. We conclude therefore that, in order to minimize administrative work and to avoid the possibility of mistaken and unnecessary interference with the running of schools which are fully meeting the minimum requirements, the type of registration adopted should not be such as to constitute in itself a form of administrative control. In general the right to inspect a school at any reasonable time without notice and the power to obtain the closure of a bad school by taking action in the courts should be relied upon as the means of preventing abuses.

In our view therefore the only purpose of registration should be to secure the notification of the existence of a school, and the submission of some essential particulars. These might be of much the same character as are now required under section 155 (1) (b) of the Education Act 1921. In the case of an existing school the responsible person should be required to register the school by completing a registration form and sending it to the local education authority. Any person proposing to establish a new school should be required to register it in a similar way on or before the date of opening. In order to prevent the register becoming too much out of date during the intervals between inspections a periodical, perhaps annual, renewal of the information on the registration form, would be desirable. Changes of address and closures for any considerable length of time (otherwise than for holidays) should be notified immediately in order to avoid fruitless visits by inspectors. Registration would thus be an act performed by the proprietor and not by the authority and therefore would not convey any kind of recognition or appoval.

Failure to register should be an offence. The local education authority should have the general duty of ensuring that schools duly register and of prosecuting proprietors if they omit or refuse to register their schools.

Choice of inspecting body

Our witnesses differed strongly on the question who should inspect private schools. The County Councils Association, the Association of Education Committees and the Association of Municipal Corporations took the view that under the Education Acts the local education authority were charged with the general supervision of education in their area and should therefore have at least the primary responsibility for inspecting private schools. The Association of Directors and Secretaries for Education put forward the same view but their witnesses said that the Association was not unanimous. All four Associations recognized that some local education authorities had no suitable staff for this purpose and that many would not have enough private school work for a full-time inspector. Some authorities, they thought, might cooperate to employ one inspector, while others might invite the Board of Education to take over this work. On the other hand the association representing inspectors employed by local education authorities (the National Association of Inspectors of Schools and Educational Organizers) considered that the schools should have a right of choice between inspection by the Board and inspection by the authority in areas where local inspectors were employed and should be inspected by the Board in other areas. They thought that many authorities would find it difficult to obtain suitably qualified inspectors.

Representatives of private-school associations, of teachers' associations (except the Association of Head Masters), and of the Froebel Society, the New Education Fellowship and the Parents' Association, were on the whole opposed to inspection by the local education authorities. The private-school representatives were insistent that the schools should at least have a right to choose inspection by the Board of Education; some of them considered this the best solution; others, while willing to accept it, would prefer that all inspection should be undertaken by the Board.

The local authority representatives argued that those authorities which had a suitable staff, not necessarily of inspectors but of persons with good educational qualifications and some experience of teaching, would be able to supervise the least satisfactory schools very closely, whereas the Board's supervision would necessarily be distant and infrequent. They pointed out that many private schools had already been placed open to the inspection of the local education authorities and that the few authorities which had been active in this matter had established friendly relations with the private schools in their areas. They felt that it would be derogatory to the authorities to suggest that they were not competent to administer such minimum requirements as we have proposed.

The private-school representatives feared that local inspection might be biased by personal interests or considerations of local politics; they alleged for example that some local authorities were opposed in principle to private enterprise in education. They were reluctant to mention any specific instances and the representatives of the local education authorities assured us that these fears were unfounded. Nevertheless this point was so strongly pressed that we do not think it can be disregarded. Such occurrences would not be impossible though no doubt they would be rare. This appeared to be the chief cause of the opposition of private school witnesses to local inspection. They also pointed out, however, that the obligations on private schools would be more uniformly interpreted if inspection were wholly, or mainly, in the hands of the Board and that inspectors belonging to the national inspectorate had wider experience and would be better able to understand and help the private schools.

In discussing details of a scheme of supervision with our witnesses much of our time has been given to this question. We have come to the conclusion that the only solution likely to meet with sufficiently general acceptance is to give private schools a right of choice between inspection by the Board of Education and inspection by the local education authority, though for certain reasons we qualify this right in one respect later in our recommendations.

Some witnesses representing private schools suggested that there should also be a choice of inspection by a university and possibly also by some *ad hoc* body. It is evident, however, that a duty of inspection which is ultimately concerned with the enforcement of statutory obligations cannot properly be delegated to any body not responsible to Parliament. Some of us also consider that universities might be inclined to view education in schools from the angle of university requirements and to be guided too much by the curriculum of the school certificate and other examinations for which they are responsible. Universities may, no doubt, be relied upon to employ inspectors with experience of teaching and some knowledge of private schools, but they have no regular staff of inspectors and there is much to be said for the view that inspection is a separate art which can be acquired by practice. The majority of us therefore consider that there should be no further right of choice.

The question has been raised whether the local education authorities concerned with private schools should be the authorities of counties and county boroughs only or should be all the authorities which have powers in respect of elementary education. In the former case the counties would be concerned with private schools throughout the whole of the area in which they have powers for higher education. Most of the arguments are drawn from a wider controversy remote from our terms of reference, but there is a general feeling that a much larger proportion of the counties and county boroughs than of the authorities for elementary education only are adequately equipped for inspecting private schools. For this and other reasons a majority of us consider that in principle such new powers as we propose should be reserved to the counties and county boroughs; a minority of us, supported by local authority witnesses, are of the opinion that since our proposals primarily concern children who are under the school-leaving age, these powers must necessarily be allocated to all local education authorities for elementary education so long as the present statutory division of functions between the two types of authority remains.

Procedure for the closure of a school

If a school, when inspected, is found to fall short of the minimum requirements, it is clearly desirable that time should be allowed for improvement. In practice no doubt some time would be spent on informal persuasion, but we recommend that the procedure for closing a school should include a formal warning followed by an interval of six months before action is taken to compel it to close.

The final action usually suggested by our witnesses is to prosecute the proprietor for failing to comply with the statutory requirements. If the action were successful he would be convicted and incur a penalty. He would thus become a person convicted of an offence against the law. In many cases, however, the proprietor's failure to comply with the statutory requirements might be due primarily to incompetence rather than to any wrong intention, and conviction of an offence against the law would be undesirable if it could be avoided. We consider that it would be preferable to give the authority concerned power to apply to a court of summary jurisdiction for an order for the closure of the school. Under this procedure the proprietor would learn whether the decision of the court was favourable to him or adverse without the risk of incurring a conviction. He would only be convicted of an offence if he failed to obey the order.

We have recommended that the schools should have a right to choose between inspection by the Board of Education and inspection by the local education authority. If a school inspected by the local education authority fails to fulfil the minimum requirements, the duty of applying for a closure order should rest with the local education authority. Local education authorities already possess powers for undertaking legal proceedings in connection with school attendance; they may appear by means of their clerk or an authorized member of the authority, and their officers have much experience in these matters. The Board of Education at present possess no corresponding powers or experience and the question who should undertake legal proceedings in respect of a school under the Board's inspection is not without difficulty. One solution, but not, we consider, a satisfactory one, would be for the local education authority to be required to undertake the proceedings, relying upon information supplied by the Board and upon the Board's inspectors as witnesses. We think, however, that authorities would naturally be reluctant to take action against any school about which they possessed no first hand information through their own officers.

After much consideration we have come to the conclusion that it should rest with the Board to carry out the duty of applying for a closure order in the case of a school under their inspection which fails to fulfil the minimum requirements, and that the Board should be provided with the necessary powers in the simplest possible form. Objection might indeed be taken to a government department frequently appearing in legal proceedings against private individuals throughout the country, but we do not consider that there would be any likelihood of such a result of our proposals. The utmost use of methods of advice and persuasion in preference to legal compulsion is a long established tradition of the Board's administration, and in general this is equally true of the administration of local education authorities. Provided that there existed reasonably effective powers for closing unsatisfactory schools by legal compulsion in the last resort, we are convinced that the number of cases which would actually reach the courts under our proposals would be very small.

72 Cyril Burt and Susan Isaacs

'The Emotional Development of Children up to the Age of Seven Plus', from the Board of Education Report of the Consultative Committee on Infant and Nursery Schools, Appendix III, 1933, pp. 244–51.

Modern practices in child rearing influenced the Hadow Committee's inquiry into nursery schooling and offers a remarkable contrast to the situation that faced the McMillan sisters (see 31) or Mrs Bathurst (see 22). Part of the Memorandum prepared by Cyril Burt and Susan Isaacs actually became the basis for a chapter in the Hadow Report.

Of all the general features that mark the behaviour of the child during the first two or three years of life the most obvious and the most significant is the great strength of feelings and impulses as compared with the weakness of understanding and the power of control. Only gradually does the ordered world of physical objects and social realities come before the child's comprehension. For long he remains a creature of imperious wishes and intense emotions.

Experimental research has recently thrown much light on the nature and growth of the young child's instincts and emotions. Watson's work on fear and rage in infants, for example, seems at first sight to establish a suggestive fact, namely, that these feelings can be automatically called out by relatively simple and definite stimuli; fear, by the sudden loosening or lowering of the child's physical support or by a sudden loud noise; rage, by the forcible inhibition of the infant's movements. Subsequent work, however, has somewhat modified this view, and made it appear too simple. Valentine's studies have shown that the infant's responses are never quite so mechanical as Watson's descriptions have implied. After the very earliest days, it is always the total situation to which the child responds, rather than the single simple stimulus. The presence or absence of the mother, for instance, may entirely determine whether or not the child will respond to a particular stimulus with symptoms of fear or dismay. A more recent investigator has studied sleeping habits of children aged two to four; and has similarly demonstrated that during the day time the length of sleep and the readiness with which children fall asleep is largely affected by their personal response to the particular adult in charge. There is little doubt that the same also holds good, though perhaps not quite so strongly, of the younger child.

Nevertheless, Watson's observations of the special kinds of stimuli most liable to produce fear in the young infant, and his demonstration that one of the most certain ways of provoking rage is to inhibit the child's movements, whether by rough handling or by tight garments, still remain unquestioned, and are highly significant for education.

One instructive study has lately been made by Washburn of the smiling and laughing of infants during the first year. It has been shown that there are definite phases in the development of both responses. From the eighth to twentieth week, the infant will respond with a smile to another's smiling; but from the twentieth to fortieth week, negative responses predominate, probably because the child is then becoming more aware of strangers as such. After the fortieth week the smile can again readily be called out. Laughing appears later than smiling. It is more stereotyped in its pattern, and seems more closely connected with the primitive emotions and the expression of feeling generally; smiling, on the other hand, has the character of a communicative, adaptive response, and thus marks the beginning of a social reaction.

At birth and throughout the first two or three years the child's emotional life centres chiefly in the nutritive impulses of his body. His first affection for his mother, and his first feelings of loss or thwarting, are experienced in connection with the way she nurses and feeds him. It is through the same fundamental relations that he gleans his first knowledge of her as a person. He learns to know his mother through his mother's breast. Later, when she begins to train his excretory functions in accordance with social standards, his emotions of love or fear and anger become closely coupled with these experiences as well.[1]

To treat the training either of the feeding responses or of the excretory habits as a problem of purely physiological and local mechanism is a serious educational mistake. By his behaviour in regard to these functions the child manages to express either his trust and love or his anger and defiance; and such feelings are readily stimulated by the way in which he is

1. The close association between the emotional life and the alimentary processes has been demonstrated by such work as Cannon's on *Bodily Changes and Pain, Hunger, Fear and Rage*, as well as by direct observation of those situations which call out emotional responses in the infant and young child.

handled during these recurring situations, quite as much as by his general relation towards the adults who have charge of him.

From the point of view of mental hygiene, therefore, it is of great importance that a sound technique in managing the infant while serving his physiological needs and training his excretory habits, should be acquired by those who attend to his needs. Regularity in the times for feeding and in the opportunities for voiding are essential; equally important are a gentle mode of holding him and a calm and confident manner. Quiet, positive encouragement, showing the child what to do and how to do it, is far more effective than scolding or punishment, or emphasis on what he should not do. Successes should be emphasized; failures should be minimized; and above all, any feeling of shame or hostility should be avoided.

It is equally essential for mental health in later childhood that the process of weaning should be properly accomplished. There is reason to believe that a normal period of breast-feeding is as important for mental as for bodily health, that too early a weaning is to be avoided, and that the change over from breast to bottle or spoon should be graduated according to the special emotional requirements of each individual child.

The normal time for weaning falls in the third quarter of the first year. Just before this period there is a significant change in the instinctive responses of the child. Together with the first appearance of the teeth, there appears a marked inclination towards biting. This change may bring with it a general alteration in the child's whole emotional attitude; in particular there often is a marked increase in the destructive impulses. With the ordinary well-cared for infant such impulses find a harmless satisfaction in biting food, bone rings, and the like, and, later on, in destructive and constructive play with bricks or sand. Thus exercised, they cause but little trouble. If, however, during the early months the child suffers from undue thwarting in regard to the routine of feeding, then the biting impulses may be greatly heightened and become a vehicle of rage and defiance. Later difficulties over excessive destructiveness in the nursery-school period may often be traced to unsatisfactory conditions during the weaning period. These are but a few of the observable facts which illustrate the great psychological importance of a proper handling of emotional situations such as arise out of the nutritive processes during the first year of life.

The second year sees a considerable increase in the variety and vividness of emotion. Difficulties may now arise even in children who, throughout their first year, have been comparatively placid. A recent investigation into anger in children has shown that the frequent outbursts of anger, no matter what their cause, rises to a definite peak during the second twelve months. During this period, a number – perhaps the majority – of children go through a phase of obstinate self-assertion, stubbornly resisting almost every demand which adults make upon them. It would seem as if now, for the first time, the child discovers himself as an independent person, and so needs to affirm himself defiantly and wilfully against his environment. Only in this way can he begin to learn in which directions he is allowed to be independent and self-determining, and in which directions it is more satisfying in the long run to acquiesce. A brief spell of perversity is normal; but the tendency may persist unduly in those who are severely punished or who feel thwarted by the absence of any opportunity for self-determination and self-help.

During this second year the common phobias of childhood, including night terrors, may make their first appearance. In a few they may give ground for anxiety; but as a rule, with calm and sensible treatment, they die gradually away.

Difficulties in regard to feeding now take the form of idiosyncrasies of taste, of reluctance to chew or swallow solid food, or of a general moodiness with regard to food. If there is no ill-timed attempt to ride rough-shod over the child's preferences, no excessive fuss on the part of the adults when he is disinclined to eat, the trouble may vanish spontaneously by the end of the second year.

Another characteristic of this period is thumb sucking; but again it soon loses its attraction when the child's skill and interest in the external world find scope for development.

All through these first two years what is most distinctive in the child's emotional attitude is his intense attachment to his parents. Other children interest him, but are often treated as merely rivals. Indeed, rivalry with playmates over the sharing of toys or over the attention of grown-ups may be very acute. But in the main it is mostly to adults that the child looks for his emotional satisfactions.

Observers who have approached the study of the young child from many different angles are all agreed upon one outstanding point: namely, that the emotional intensity of the young child's life reaches its zenith about the end of the third year. At this age, every emotion the child undergoes is felt with a vividness and a strength that is never again experienced either in later childhood or in adult life; from this stage onwards experience and the integration of impulses tend more and more to control and moderate the child's emotional excitement. This early vividness and intensity are seen with every type of feeling. The child's rage at being thwarted, his fears, his phobias, his night terrors, his love and devotion towards mother or nurse, his sense of loss if they leave him, his jealousy and feelings of jealousy towards other children, all are violently felt and vigorously displayed. In its quick changes and warm and shifting colours, his emotional life is kaleidoscopic. From laughter to tears, from affection to hostility and back again, is but a momentary step. What the child cannot do as yet is to organize his conflicting impulses into restrained, stable, consistent behaviour.

In the home, all these feelings with their varied content are shown with a demonstrativeness that is undiluted. In the nursery school they never appear so fully or so vividly: there the presence of a greater number of persons leads to a wider diffusion of feeling; and further, the child's emotions are naturally less keen and acute towards other adults than towards his own mother or nurse. Nevertheless, even in the nursery school the tiny child of three is very ready to show rivalry with other children, and evinces a perpetual desire to cling to grown-ups for shelter or attention. By the middle of his fourth year, however, his close attachment to adults and his jealous suspicion of other youngsters grows less and less marked: a more positive and active interest in play-fellows appears and becomes progressively established.

The control of emotional impulses is due mainly to the formation of what the psychologist terms sentiments. Groups of emotions become associated and organized about central ideas. Those ideas are, to begin with, ideas of persons – almost invariably those whom the child meets daily in his home circle; later they may be ideas of concrete but inanimate things, such as the child's own property or playthings; later still, and for the most part after the period with which we are here concerned, they may relate to more abstract conceptions and form the centre of an enthusiasm for certain games, for particular school subjects, for particular modes of conduct, for ideals of virtue and the like.

In popular conversation, we speak of these sentiments as the 'love for' this or that object; and we say how important an influence is exercised on conduct by this child's love for his mother or another, by that child's love for her pretty clothes. Affection for a doll, respect for a teacher, family pride, attachment to the old home, loyalty to a school, a passion for reading, a liking for ball games, self-love or self-respect – these are all sentiments; and the germs of them may be successively sown during the years that elapse from birth to six or seven, or later. Some sentiments, as we shall see in a moment, may be sentiments not of love but of hate; most early sentiments are mixtures of both. Unfortunately, common language has no convenient general term: the technical use of the word 'sentiment' strikes the non-psychological as a little forced. Perhaps the best simple word would be 'interests'. It is, then, the development of rich and permanent interests that is the chief agent in stabilizing the child's emotions and rendering his conduct more coherent.

Of these interests or sentiments the earliest, as a rule, is the child's sentiment for his mother (or for the nurse who takes his mother's place). Its formation starts in the first few weeks of babyhood. At the outset his interest in his mother is primarily an interest in the source of food and of comfort; but soon he begins to 'love' her in the more ordinary sense of the word. This means not merely that he will experience a passing emotion of affection whenever she is present to his eyes; it implies that he gradually builds up a permanent disposition to feel a whole cycle of various emotions according to the changing circumstances. When his mother is happy, he feels happy too; if she suffers, he feels sorrow; if he fancies she is in danger, he begins to feel fear; if someone ill-treats her, he grows angry; if she neglects him for her husband or for a younger child, he grows jealous. Thus a complete system of feelings – joy, sorrow, fear, anger, affection and the like – becomes attached to the thought of his mother. Such an organized sentiment tends to regulate his passing impulses and feelings in a more consistent fashion.

Sometimes, however, the emotions aroused by one and the same person may come into conflict. While his mother nursed and protected him, the emotions she aroused were mainly pleasurable. So soon as he has learnt to walk and to show some degree of independence, his mother may find it necessary to thwart or restrain his actions, and this may arouse a feeling of anger or of fear: the germ of hate thus appears. The word 'hate' may seem a strong one to use in this connection; but it is scarcely too strong if we consider, not the overt manifestations, but the half-unconscious tendencies to which such feelings give rise. Usually these more unpleasant emotions get repressed, and so remain more or less unconscious. And in this way the sentiment comes to resemble what the psychoanalyst has taught us to call a 'complex'. Hence, in the organization of the child's feelings there may be dangers as well as benefits. It is often within his own home that he first learns to hate as well as to love. But whatever form they take, his early emotional attitudes towards the members of his family will largely determine his later emotional attitudes to other persons whom he meets in afterlife. It is, therefore, supremely important that the way in which the child's own parents treat him should be sane, scientific and consistent. The process can be traced step by step. The habitual response of the child to his parents will affect his reactions towards the adults whom he meets in the nursery school, and their treatment in turn will influence him afresh for the rest of his days. His feelings towards his own brothers and sisters will affect his feelings towards his playmates when he meets them outside his own home; and once more his new experiences in school will correct or confirm the habits started already.

Of all these sentiments the most important, the master-passion, is the child's own sentiment for himself. From the attitude and utterances of other people, from the way they react to his everyday behaviour, he gradually builds up a notion of himself as a distinct and interesting personality of a particular sort. This notion may develop into a kind of ideal which he may endeavour to live up to or live down to. The emotions attached to it may be selfish emotions or purer and more enlightened emotions. Accordingly, the way the child is praised or punished, allowed to gain confidence and a sense of self-reliant independence, or crushed into timidity and diffidence, or, it may be, allowed to regard himself as the domineering centre around which the whole household revolves – these early forms of treatment and the very names or nicknames he is given may produce a lasting and ineradicable effect upon his moral character. Accordingly, where the parents' attitude is unwise, or where the relations between the two parents are themselves strained, unhappy, or excessively emotional, there the more orderly environment of the nursery school, with calm dispassionate treatment, may save the child from the permanent ill-effects of an unwholesome environment at home.[2]

There is both room and need for first-hand investigations into these processes. A few have already been attempted. Professor Katherine Bridges has made a detailed study of the way in which a young child's emotional attitude towards other children alters,[3] and is influenced by successive changes in his development and surroundings. At three or earlier the first response of the child to other children is commonly one of suspicion and dislike. This gradually gives way to a kind of experimental hostility, in which the child shows his interest by behaviour more or less aggressive. Where there are opportunities for cooperative play, this aggressive stage is succeeded in its turn by an active pleasure in doing things together with the other youngsters. At first the opportunities will not be fully seized and the play will not be genuinely cooperative play. The children play happily in the presence of each other; yet, before the age of four and a half, they still tend, on the whole, to play individually. Each follows his own pursuits; and, if he tries to get others to join in, it is usually in an attempt to make them follow his particular notions. Spontaneous groups formed among children at this period are nearly always small; generally they consist of two or three, hardly ever of more than four. Whenever half a dozen or so are present, they quickly break up into small and separate groups. Limited and occasional as it is, however, such playing together provides the ground out of which the social impulses gradually begin to spring up. The children gain an

2. See Flugel, *Psycho-Analytic Study of the Family*.
3. *The Social and Emotional Development of the Pre-School Child*.

actual experience of 'togetherness'; and the foundation is thus laid for true social reciprocity in later group life.

In these spontaneous groupings one significant feature is the way in which rivalry flashes out between the smaller groups, whether in make-believe or in earnest, much as it formerly flashed out between individuals, though now in milder form. The child's initial hostility to all other children but himself is dealt with first in this fashion; it is as it were pushed further outwards, away from his immediate friends in his own special group, and on to other groups in his neighbourhood. In these early years, however such groupings are always unstable and temporary: at any moment, through the outbreak of quarrels or petty disputes, they are liable to break down. The leadership of an adult who understands how to direct children's activities will sustain a genuine group-feeling far more durably and far more stably than the children left to themselves.

The hostility that so constantly obtains among the tinier children springs from various sources. A squabble may arise over the possession or the use of some toy or apparatus, over the leadership of the group, the choice of the game or the fashion in which it is to be played, and most significant of all, out of a sharp competition for the friendship and attention of other children. Sometimes it will spring from no cause in the outer environment, but rather from the momentary peevishness or unhappiness of one child who for some internal reason is moody or ill-humoured. Much of this early antagonism and aggression tends to fade away as the children in a particular group gain the experience of playing together, building up a common history, and learning to trust each other. As each child achieves an increasing skill, he becomes better able to cooperate with his fellows.

Towards the close of this period, therefore, the amount of sustained friendly play and genuine cooperation amongst children, though still restricted, is much greater than was possible during the preceding years. As a result, by the end of his fifth year, the child has become more stable in his private emotional life; this in turn reacts on his dealings with others. His social relations with the rest of his group thus grow more and more settled and reliable. Further, these active friendships with other children serve to detach him from his exclusive dependence on adults, and so usher in the initial stages of that gradual change which culminates in the typical attitude of the older child of nine or ten. Characteristically enough, during the years that intervene children are much more concerned with, and much more affected by, the opinion and feelings of other children like themselves, than they are by the approval or disapproval of adults.

Between the child under five and the child of six or seven no difference is perhaps so striking as the difference in general emotional attitude. In its essence, the change is a continuation of what has been going forward ever since the period of most intense emotional conflict – the age of three or thereabouts. But the cumulative effect of the intervening processes produces a distinct re-orientation of the child's mind, gradual but complete. The new standpoint is now slowly consolidated and fixed; and, as he passes from one stage to the other, the child's whole outlook expands and his insight grows deeper as well as broader.

The most conspicuous feature is his increasing detachment from his parent. More and more the child turns away from his father, mother, and, indeed, from adults generally, and looks rather for his chief emotional satisfactions to the outside world – most of all to other children. By slow degrees he ceases to regard other youngsters simply as rivals for the love and attention of grown-ups, and comes to treat them as allies. Feeling as he does his own insufficiency against the prestige and the authority of the adult, this sense of comradeship comes as a great support to him: it enables him to look on adults with a more open and discerning eye, and so behave towards them in a more temperate fashion and with greater self-control.

The new alliance with other children thus gradually builds up a new reserve. During the infant-school period the child grows far less demonstrative. His parents or his teachers may even complain that they are losing his confidence. Actually the change implies a definite progress in emotional stability. The quickly shifting moods of love and hostility, of jealousy and friendship, so characteristic of the youngster up to the age of five, give way to attitudes more lasting in quality and quieter in tone. Three influences contribute to lessen the intensity of his feelings. First, his circle of acquaintances among both children and adults grows wider and wider. And with this goes an increase in the variety of contacts that he makes not only with persons but also with things and with ideas – an expansion which now becomes possible through the enlargement of his own skill and interests. Secondly, both in the spontaneous associations of free play and in the regularized competitions or organized games, his feelings of hostility and rivalry are now turned outwards – away from his own immediate playmates to other children or towards other groups. He thus becomes capable of active friendship, and can participate on equal terms in the pursuits of others. Thirdly, emerging out of the two previous influences, there is an increasing organization in the child's social relations. His behaviour, both towards young and old, no longer rests on the impulse of the moment; it is based on a scheme of attitudes, which fit more and more closely to the special requirements of time, place and person. Something like a moral code is beginning to grow up.

Recent studies of the moral development of young children have revealed an important change. In the earlier years children's moral judgements and their notions of just punishment are far more severe and absolute than later on. Before the age of five or six the whole pattern of their emotional and social life is founded on the relation of parent and child, of authority and obedience (or disobedience). Towards six or seven years, however, a morality of equals begins gradually to develop; and, little by little, the virtues of loyalty, friendship and tolerance gain meaning for the child. His moral values as a whole grow more tempered and balanced, and show a closer connection with his real experience. They will, of course, still be entirely concrete and immediate; as yet all abstract moral judgements are beyond the range of his comprehension.

73 G. C. M. M'Gonicle and J. Kirby

from 'The Physical Condition of Elementary School Children', *Poverty and Public Health*, 1936, pp. 41–50.

Despite the changes in child rearing reflected in the 1933 Hadow Report, the incidence of chronic physical ailments among young children remained high. The annual medical reports issued by medical officers of health allowed a personal report to state (below) that some 17 per cent of children throughout the country coming into schools at the age of five needed immediate medical treatment.

Never in the history of the world have such opportunities for medical and sociological research been offered as those presented by the school medical service, and, were teamwork among the members of local staffs more highly developed and directed by far-seeing, broad-minded men, problems which have baffled science for generations might be solved in the course of a decade. Individual effort is handicapped because it is individual, and mistakes are made by the individual worker which, in teamwork, would be avoided. Checks and counter-checks on accuracy are needed and, in the case of the isolated investigator, the personal element may assume too great an influence.

In spite of these handicaps much valuable individual work is being done. The massed results of the whole of the school medical inspection work carried out each year throughout England and Wales are published annually by the Board of Education. The annual reports entitled 'The Health of the School Child' provide a mass of information which enables a general picture of the physical condition of the elementary-school population to be visualized. The information in these reports is of inestimable value.

One of the most striking facts adduced from a study of these reports and of the reports of individual local education authorities is that the five-year-old child, on admission to school, suffers from defects, similar in number and kind, to those found in the eight- and twelve-year-old groups of children.

The physical defects discovered in school children have originated, very largely, during the five years preceding entry into school. This is a finding of fundamental importance, for it follows that efforts directed to prevent their occurrence must be initiated during the pre-school years.

Routine medical inspection of elementary school children is carried out three times during the child's school life. Each child is medically examined at five years of age as an 'Entrant'; at eight years as an 'Intermediate'; and at twelve years as a 'Leaver'.

In 1933 the average attendance at all elementary schools in England and Wales amounted to 6,049,284 children. The actual numbers on the registers of these schools was 5,639,000. The average attendance was, therefore, approximately 90 per cent of the total number on the register. The number on the registers of elementary schools represents 93 per cent of all children of ages ranging from five to fourteen years.

The human material available for examination and assessment by the school medical officer represents a very large proportion of the childhood of the land.

During 1933 the number of elementary school children medically examined as 'routines' totalled 1,855,499. Of the 1,855,499 children examined that year 303,199 were found to be suffering from defects of a nature requiring immediate medical treatment – a percentage of 17·33.

Table 1 **Percentages of elementary school children found at routine medical inspection in 1933 to require medical treatment**

Entrants (5 years old)	16·26
Intermediates (8 years old)	18·58
Leavers (12 years old)	17·21

The percentages in the three age groups are shown in Table 1.

These findings are less than would have been discovered thirty years ago but their magnitude is disquieting. Bad as these results are, they do not present a complete picture of the physical condition of our childhood. It must not be assumed that the remainder are free from defect.

These findings do not include the results of dental inspection nor do they contain the large group of children in which defects of a less severe degree are detected. The less severe defects are recorded by the school medical officer upon the child's schedule card but are marked 'for observation'.

During 1933 the number of elementary school children dentally inspected by qualified dentists totalled 3,303,983. The number found to require dental treatment was 2,263,135 – a percentage of 68·5.

We have seen that 17·3 per cent of the 1,855,499 children medically examined as routines in 1933 required immediate medical treatment; a further 261,763 of this total were discovered to be suffering from defects of a less serious nature and were scheduled 'for observation'. This represents 14·0 per cent of the total number medically examined.

If to this figure of 14·0 per cent is added the 17·3 per cent of children who have defects requiring immediate medical treatment it appears that **31·3** per cent of all routine examiners possess physical defects. This figure takes no account of dental defects or of defective vision in the entrant group (five year olds). The defects discovered and recorded are fairly obvious defects, and meticulous search by experts for aberrations from normality always yield a much higher figure. This will be referred to later.

A large additional number of elementary school children are examined each year. This group consists of children who for the most part suffer, or are thought to suffer, from defects that are obvious to non-medical observation. This extra group of children is known as 'special' and consists of those whom the teachers, attendance officers, or school nurses consider to require medical examination because of some obvious or suspected defect, or who present some abnormality, such as defective hearing, that precludes them from taking full advantage of the education provided.

Table 2

	No. of med. exams	No. of defects	
		requiring treatment	For observation
Special	1,239,427	486,777	88,706
Routine	1,855,499	303,199	261,763
Totals	3,094,926	789,976	350,469

Total defects = 1,140,445
            = 36·8 per cent of all children examined

The number of 'special examinations' during 1933 was 1,239,427. In this large group 486,777 children were found to have defects requiring treatment – a percentage of 39·0 per cent and 88,706 (7·0 per cent) to have defects of a less severe nature and marked 'for observation'.

These figures show that a total of 3,094,926 children came, during 1933, directly under the observation of the school medical officer. This represents 61 per cent of the average attendance in elementary schools.

The results of these examinations are shown in Table 2.

There remain about 590,000 absentees. Truancy is no longer a serious cause of absenteeism, but, especially among older girls, a considerable number remain at home to help in the housework, particularly if the mother is sick or ailing. How large this number may be is not known. The commonest cause of absence from school is illness, which may be of a temporary nature, such as a cold, influenza, infectious disease. Also a considerable number of children are temporarily excluded on account of being contacts of infectious disease. The ailments which cause absenteeism are rarely seen in the course of his work by the school medical officer. Children suffering from severe colds, influenza and infectious disease are nearly always absent from school and so do not come under his observation.

The defects discovered by special examinations are not entirely comparable with those found on routine inspections. Many of the defects found among the 'specials' are of a temporary character and cannot reasonably be characterized as physical defects. For instance, inflammation of the eyes and impetigo may be of a purely temporary nature and may, if properly treated (or even if untreated), leave no permanent defect.

The conclusion may fairly be drawn that 36·8 per cent of all children examined during 1933 presented some deviation from normal *at the time of examination*, but it is not reasonable to state that this percentage of school children suffer from permanent physical defects. It is a very difficult matter (and, in practice, impossible) to separate permanent from temporary conditions.

74 Education Act (1936)

pp. 1–4.

A particular exercise in governmental compromise was the attempt in 1936 to raise the school-leaving age to fifteen from 1 September 1939, while acquiesing to the argument that many children would be better off at work. The Act therefore introduced the notion of 'beneficial employment' and thereby created so many loopholes in the law it was supposed to be promulgating that it would largely have negated its good intentions. It stands as a monument to the different pressures – educational, social, industrial – that shaped the system during the century, but the war intervened before the power of the Act could be tested.

1. 1. Subject to the provisions of this Act, the age of fifteen shall be the age up to which byelaws under Part IV of the Education Act 1921 (hereinafter called 'the principal Act'), shall require parents to cause their children (unless there is some reasonable excuse) to attend school.

2. The amendments set out in the First Schedule of this Act (being amendments consequential on the provisions of the last preceding sub-section) shall be made in the enactments specified in that schedule.

3. Any byelaw in force on the appointed day requiring the parents of children to cause them to attend school up to any age less than fifteen years shall have effect as if for that age there were substituted the age of fifteen, and any provision of a byelaw in force on the appointed day whereby any children between the ages of fourteen and fifteen may be exempted from attendance at school shall cease to have effect.

4. This section shall not apply in the case of children born on or before the first day of September, nineteen hundred and twenty-five, and the principal Act and any byelaws made thereunder shall have effect with respect to those children as if this Act had not been passed.

2. 1. Byelaws relating to school attendance shall not apply to any child who has attained the age of fourteen and in respect of whom an employment certificate within the meaning of this section has been granted by the local education authority in the area in which the child resides (hereinafter called the issuing authority), and is for the time being in force.

2. An employment certificate shall be granted to the intended employer of the child, if the issuing authority are satisfied that the parent of the child desires the employment for the child and are also satisfied, after consultation with the local committee for juvenile employment, if any, and after consideration of the health and physical condition of the child, that the employment will be beneficial to the child.

3. Every employment certificate shall state the date from which it is to have effect, and that date, unless in any particular case owing to exceptional circumstances the issuing authority otherwise determine, shall not be a date falling in a school term.

4. The issuing authority in determining whether any employment will be beneficial shall have regard as well to the prospective as to the immediate benefit to the child, and in particular to

(a) The nature and probable duration of the employment, the wages to be paid, and the hours of work.

(b) The opportunities to be afforded to the child for further education.

(c) The time available to the child for recreation.

(d) The value, in relation to the future career of the child, of any training or other advantages afforded by the employment.

and the determination of the authority shall be conclusive.

5. The issuing authority shall, as a condition precedent to the grant of a certificate, require such undertakings from the employer as they think necessary

(a) In connection with all or any of the matters mentioned in paragraphs (a), (b) and (c) of the last preceding subsection.

(b) For enabling the authority to satisfy themselves that the employment has not, by reason of any change in the conditions of the employment or for any other reasons, ceased to be beneficial to the child.

and shall specify in the certificate the terms of any undertaking so given.

6. Before granting a certificate relating to employment in the area of another local education authority, the issuing authority shall, unless arrangements made between the two authorities otherwise provide, give notice to that other authority of their intention to grant the certificate, and if the other authority, within seven days of the receipt of the notice, notify the issuing authority that they would not themselves hold the employment to be beneficial for children residing in that area, or that the date from which the certificate is to have effect should be determined so as not to fall in a school term of that area, the certificate shall not be granted in relation to the employment in that area, or the said date shall be determined as aforesaid, as the case may be:

Provided that no parent or employer shall incur any liability by acting on the faith of an employment certificate granted by a local education authority by reason only that the certificate was granted in contravention of the provisions of this subsection, or in breach of any arrangements made with any other local education authority.

7. Where the parent of a child attending a secondary or other school has made a contract with a local education authority or other body whereby he undertakes that the child shall continue to attend school until at least the age of fifteen years, no employment certificate shall be granted with respect to that child without the consent of that authority or body.

75 Consultative Committee on Secondary Education (Spens)

from the Report, 1938, pp. 122-4.

The importance of new psychological thinking in education was indicated in the Spens Report, which emphasized, largely on the evidence of Cyril Burt, the change from faculty psychology to a developmental approach (see 72). But psychologists also felt able to say, as in the extract below, that it was possible 'at a very early age to predict with some degree of accuracy the ultimate level of a child's intellectual powers' which justified not only the eleven plus, but the segregation of children into different types of secondary school.

Until about thirty years ago it was commonly assumed by psychologists and educationists that the salient feature in mental development was the successive emergence of specific intellectual faculties – sensation, movement, speech, memory, imagination, reasoning – each appearing at fairly definite periods in the child's life. It was held that all these faculties could, and should, be trained as they emerged. Thus the main function of the infant school was conceived to be the training of the senses and of the power of speech and movement; the task of the primary school for children under the age of eleven was to train their memory and to rely on this for the acquisition of the fundamental subjects. Inasmuch as reason and imagination were not supposed to mature until adolescence, the special function of the secondary (grammar) school was to train the rational and imaginative faculties through literature, languages and mathematics. It was supposed that at this stage the mind could best be developed by a basic education of a humanistic type providing a general foundation of culture, applicable to every child without regard to individual differences or to subsequent specialization of careers. The theory that the mind is composed of distinct intellectual faculties each in a separate organ of the brain and maturing at fairly specific periods has now been generally abandoned. Moreover, careful research has thrown a good deal of doubt on the view that the mind as a whole and its several faculties can be trained merely by exercising them. Education rather consists in developing specific habits, memories, ideas, forms of manual and mental skill, intellectual interests, moral ideals, and a knowledge, not merely of facts and conclusions, but also of methods. Furthermore, the application of mental tests to children at successive years of school life has shown that intellectual growth in general and in its more specific aspects is not spasmodic, but remarkably uniform up to the time that development ceases. Memory and the power to reason steadily improve from a very early age, and mental development in every direction is continuous. Even when individual children appear to display new talents or special gifts at a fairly definite date, it is probable that such changes are the outcome of emotional rather than intellectual causes, being due to the acquisition of new interests rather than to the emergence of fresh aptitudes. For administrative and other reasons, it may be advisable to transfer children from one school to another at the age of eleven and generally to delimit instruction into separate phases; nevertheless, education, like mental development, should form one continuous process, and the education of the adolescent child should be the culmination of all that has gone before.

Intellectual characteristics: general intelligence

From the point of view of modern psychologists the most noticeable feature of the period after the age of eleven on the intellectual side is the gradual retardation and ultimate arrest in the development of ' general intelligence ', or in other words, in the maturing of those measurable capacities which have hitherto evolved at a fairly uniform speed and in close association with one another. Certain qualitative changes in the child's personality, particularly the apparent emergence of specific aptitudes and interests, become noticeable after the age of eleven, though these may probably be attributable more to temperamental and environmental causes than to any spontaneous ripening of fresh capacities.

Intellectual development during childhood appears to progress as if it were governed by a single central factor, usually known as 'general intelligence', which may be broadly described as innate all-round intellectual ability. It appears to enter into everything which the child attempts to think, or say, or do, and seems on the whole to be the most important factor in determining his work in the classroom. Our psychological witnesses assured us that it can be measured approximately by means of intelligence tests. General intelligence, if assessed in this manner, is seen to increase fairly steadily up to the age of about twelve, but thereafter the speed of increase begins perceptibly to decline, from the age of about sixteen further growth in general intelligence, as shown by performance tests, appears to be very small, and this early completion of intellectual maturity is probably due to the same causes as the completion of physical development. Psychologists are confident that there are wide individual differences in the development of general intelligence. For instance, there is evidence to show that the abler child continues to develop, though at a comparatively slow pace after puberty, till later than the average child. The less able child, and still more the mentally deficient child comes earlier to a final stage in the development of general intelligence. *We were informed that, with few exceptions, it is possible at a very early age to predict with some degree of accuracy the ultimate level of a child's intellectual powers, but this is true only of general intelligence and does not hold good in respect of specific aptitudes or interests. The average child is said to attain the effective limit of development in general intelligence between the age of sixteen and eighteen.* Our psychological witnesses explained that this statement, which is sometimes misunderstood, does not imply that older boys and girls stop learning or that their acquired attainments, as distinct from their innate capacity, do not continue to increase. The child's general intelligence, which has been increasing up to the age of about sixteen to eighteen, has, in the view of modern psychologists, then practically attained its maximum.

76 Consultative Committee on Secondary Education (Spens)

'Administrative Problems' from the Report, 1938, pp. 291-2.

The Spens Committee was the first to give some thought to the idea of comprehensive schools, but their conclusions were not encouraging, and they were the first to raise the arguments which, in one form or another, were held against the idea throughout the fifties and sixties. Despite describing the schools as 'interesting' and 'attractive' it plainly did not take the Spens Committee long to dismiss the concept.

We have discussed at some length in the Introduction to this Report the interesting and attractive proposal for a multilateral type of secondary school. We recognized the many benefits that would accrue when children after the age of eleven were being educated together in the same set of buildings: how in such a school the transfer of pupils at various ages to courses of teaching most suitable for their abilities and interests would be facilitated, and how great an advantage there might be in the close association of children differing in background and objective. *With some reluctance we have come to the conclusion that we could not advocate the adoption of multilateralism as a general policy.* Among the reasons which led us to this decision were the necessarily large size of multilateral schools in general; the relatively small number of children who would be available for the sixth form; and the possibility that in this country we might find, as has occurred elsewhere,[1] that the prestige of the academic 'side' would

1. Dr I. L. Kandel, Professor of Education, Columbia University, stated in his evi-

prejudice the free development of the modern school form of secondary education. To these we might add one further reason, important to the administrator, that the general adoption of the multilateral idea would be too subversive a change to be made in a long established system, especially in view of the extent to which this system has been expanded in recent years by the building of new grammar schools and technical schools, and also in view of the success with which the ancient framework of the system has, on the whole, borne the strains and stresses to which it has been subjected by the growth of the new type of modern school.

We do not wish to deprecate experiments in multilateral schools, especially in areas where the last-mentioned difficulties do not arise, as in areas of new population. We hope, too, that the various difficulties may be surmounted in sparsely populated rural areas where a grammar school and a modern school may be formed into a multilateral school. The advantages of a multilateral school might, in these cases, be held to outweigh its disadvantages, or the disadvantages might be ameliorated through the personality of a headmaster conscious of the pit-falls which, experience has shown, have most to be avoided.

77 Committee of the Secondary Schools Examinations Council on Curriculum and Examinations in Secondary Schools (Norwood)
from the Report, 1943, pp. 2–4

The concept of children falling into three educational types, which grew out of the psychological evidence of the thirties and the deliberations of previous committees, hardened in the Norwood Report into certainty.

dence: 'The problem is not simplified even in such a country as the United States, where the single or comprehensive high school, organized end-on with the elementary school, has attempted to meet the needs of all the adolescent population and to provide curricula and courses suited to the capacities of each individual pupil.

... It is beginning at last to be admitted that the single school may cater to the average but it does justice neither to the bright nor to the dull pupils, that the attempt to provide general cultural and vocational courses side by side in the same institution tends to militate against the success of both. ... Although opportunities for academic, semi-academic and vocational training are provided, the academic courses seem to be preferred by the majority of parents and pupils, despite the fact that manual occupations enjoy a higher status than in less democratic countries.'

This swing towards the more academic 'side' had been personally observed, too, in American schools and elsewhere by several members of our Committee.

'Our point is,' said the report, 'that rough groupings, whatever may be their ground, have in fact established themselves in general educational experience.' The tripartite system of secondary education was here confirmed and justified.

Variety of capacity

One of the major problems of educational theory and organization has always been, and always will be, to reconcile diversity of human endowment with practical schemes of administration and instruction. Even if it were shown that the differences between individuals are so marked as to call for as many curricula as there are individuals, it would be impossible to carry such a principle into practice; and school organization and class instruction must assume that individuals have enough in common as regards capacities and interests to justify certain rough groupings. Such at any rate has been the point of view which has gradually taken shape from the experience accumulated during the development of secondary education in this country and in France and Germany and indeed in most European countries. The evolution of education has in fact thrown up certain groups, each of which can and must be treated in a way appropriate to itself. Whether such groupings are distinct on strictly psychological grounds, whether they represent types of mind, whether the differences are differences in kind or in degree, there are questions which it is not necessary to pursue. Our point is that rough groupings, whatever may be their ground, have in fact established themselves in general educational experience, and the recognition of such groupings in educational practice has been justified both during the period of education and in the after-careers of the pupils.

For example, English education has in practice recognized the pupil who is interested in learning for its own sake, who can grasp an argument or follow a piece of connected reasoning, who is interested in causes, whether on the level of human volition or in the material world, who cares to know how things came to be as well as how they are, who is sensitive to language as expression of thought, to a proof as a precise demonstration, to a series of experiments justifying a principle: he is interested in the relatedness of related things, in development, in structure, in a coherent body of knowledge. He can take a long view and hold his mind in suspense: this may be revealed in his work or in his attitude to his career. He will have some capacity to enjoy, from an aesthetic point of view, the aptness of a phrase or the neatness of a proof. He may be good with his hands or he may not; he may or may not be a good 'mixer' or a leader or a prominent figure in activities, athletic or other.

Such pupils, educated by the curriculum commonly associated with the grammar school, have entered the learned professions or have taken up higher administrative or business posts. Whether the curriculum was designed to produce men of this kind we need not inquire; but the assumption is now made, and with confidence that for such callings a certain make-up of aptitudes and capacities is necessary, and such make-up may for educational purposes constitute a particular type of mind.

Again, the history of technical education has demonstrated the importance of recognizing the needs of the pupil whose interests and abilities lie markedly in the field of applied science or applied art. The boy in this group has a strong interest in this direction and often the necessary qualities of mind to carry his interest through to make it his life-work at whatever level of achievement. He often has an uncanny insight into the intricacies of mechanism whereas the subtleties of language construction are too delicate for him. To justify itself to his mind, knowledge must be capable of immediate application, and the knowledge and its application which most appeal to him are concerned with the control of material things. He may have unusual or moderate intelligence: where intelligence is not great, a feeling of purpose and relevance may enable him to make the most of it. He may or may not be good at games or other activities.

The various kinds of technical school were not instituted to satisfy the intellectual needs of an arbitrarily assumed group of children, but to prepare boys and girls for taking up certain crafts – engineering, agriculture and the like. Nevertheless it is usual to think of the engineer or other craftsman as possessing a particular set of interests or aptitudes by virtue of which he becomes a successful engineer or whatever he may become.

Again, there has of late years been recognition, expressed in the framing of curricula and otherwise, of still another grouping of pupils, and another grouping of occupations. The pupil in this group deals more easily with concrete things than with ideas. He may have much ability, but it will be in the realm of facts. He is interested in things as they are; he finds little attraction in the past or in the slow disentanglement of causes or movements. His mind must turn its knowledge or its curiosity to immediate test; and his test is essentially practical. He may see clearly along one line of study or interest and outstrip his generally abler fellows in that line; but he often fails to relate his knowledge or skill to other branches of activity. Because he is interested only in the moment he may be incapable of a long series of connected steps; relevance to present concerns is the only way of awakening interest, abstractions mean little to him. Thus it follows that he must have immediate returns for his effort, and for the same reason his career is often in his mind. His horizon is near and within a limited area his movement is generally slow, though it may be surprisingly rapid in seizing a particular point or in taking up a special line. Again, he may or may not be good with his hands or sensitive to music or art.

Within this group fall pupils whose mental make-up does not show at an early stage pronounced leanings in a way comparable with the other groups which we indicated. It is by no means improbable that, as the kind of education suitable for them becomes more clearly marked out and the leaving age is raised, the course of education may become more and more supple and flexible with the result that particular interests and aptitudes may be enabled to declare themselves and be given opportunities for growth. That a development of this kind yet lies to great extent in the future does not preclude us from recognizing the existence of a group whose needs require to be met in as definite a manner as those of other groups.

Types of curriculum

In a wise economy of secondary education pupils of a particular type of mind would receive the training best suited for them and that training would lead them to an occupation where their capacities would be suitably used; that a future occupation is already present to their minds while they are still at school has been suggested, though admittedly the degree to which it is present varies. Thus, to the three main types sketched above there would correspond three main types of curriculum, which we may again attempt to indicate.

First, there would be a curriculum of which the most characteristic feature is that it treats the various fields of knowledge as suitable for coherent and systematic study for their own sake apart from immediate considerations of occupation, though at a later stage grasp of the matter and experience of the methods belonging to those fields may determine the area of choice of employment and may contribute to success in the employment chosen.

The second type of curriculum would be closely, though not wholly, directed to the special data and skills associated with a particular kind of occupation; its outlook and its methods would always be bounded by a near horizon clearly envisaged. It would thus be closely related to industry, trades and commerce in all their diversity.

In the third type of curriculum a balanced training of mind and body and a correlated approach to humanities, natural science and the arts would provide an equipment varied enough to enable pupils to take up the work of life: its purpose would not be to prepare for a particular job or profession and its treatment would make a direct appeal to interests, which it would awaken by practical touch with affairs.

Of the first it may be said that it may or may not look forward to university work; if it does, that is because the universities are traditionally concerned with the pursuit of knowledge as such. Of the second we would say that it may or may not look forward to the universities, but that it should increasingly be directed to advanced studies in so far as the universities extend their orbit in response to the demands of the technical branches of industry.

78 Committee of the Secondary Schools Examinations Council on Curriculum and Examinations in Secondary Schools (Norwood)
from the Report 1943, pp. 14–16.

At the beginning of the century secondary education meant grammar-school education: forty years later secondary education officially so recognized and named means the education provided in secondary schools which inherit the grammar-school tradition. In these years, however, secondary education has gradually altered its meaning so as to denote a stage in the educational process rather than a type of educational programme. This alteration has been brought about, partly, by change in educational theory and ideals, partly by the increased demand for a stage of education which would go beyond the 'elementary' or primary stage. Into the causes of that demand we need not inquire.

The secondary schools, being the sole repositories of recognized secondary education, have had to provide for the needs of the pupils who entered them. They have in our opinion faithfully maintained their inheritance, but at the same time they have had to enlarge their horizon immeasurably to cater for very diverse abilities and interests; none the less they have been confined by limitations arising partly from their own nature and partly imposed from without. Because they have been asked to do too much and to serve too many ends, there has inevitably been compromise. Yet the very need to do justice to their various kinds of pupils has forced into the foreground the importance of the principle of child-centred education. Hence the search for new curricula; hence the pressure to relax examination regulations, for under existing conditions the schools cannot suggest that some of their pupils should not seek the certificate sought by the rest. Meantime a curriculum on the whole suited to some is condemned because it is unsuited to others. That the schools have done their utmost to do justice to all their pupils is undeniable, but there comes a time when adjustment achieves nothing more and when compromise defeats all ends.

The time has come, we believe, when the real meaning of secondary education, the significance of child-centred education, the value of the grammar-school tradition, the difficulties of the present secondary schools should all be recognized and admitted. This means that within a framework of secondary education the needs of the three broad groups of pupils which we discussed earlier should be met within three broad types of secondary education, each type containing the possibility of variation and each school offering alternative courses which would yet keep the school true to type. Accordingly we would advocate that there should be three types of education, which we think of as the secondary grammar, the secondary technical, the secondary modern, that each type should have such parity as amenities and conditions can bestow; parity of esteem in our view cannot be conferred by administrative decree nor by equality of cost per pupil; it can only be won by the school itself.

From one type of education to another there should be ease of transfer, particularly, though not exclusively, in the early stages, for the transition from primary to secondary education is not a break but a process in which special interests and aptitudes have further opportunity of declaring themselves and of meeting with appropriate treatment.

Only on some such reorganization of secondary education can the needs of the nation and the individual be appropriately met. The existing secondary schools would continue to perform their proper task without distraction; the secondary technical schools would receive an access of pupils well able to profit by the courses which they provide; the modern schools still in process of formulating their aims and methods would gain the scope necessary to them to fulfil the promise which they already show, and we do not regard it as impossible that eventually pupils of over 16+ may be found in them. What we are concerned with here and now is that the three main types of secondary education would be free to work out their own spheres of usefulness; all would gain and not least the individual child.

... We propose to set out our view of secondary education as it might be reorganized, and it will be convenient if we sketch first in general terms the main outline of our proposals, and discuss the proposals later at greater length.

Preliminary sketch

At the age of 11+, or earlier in some cases,[1] a child would pass into one of the three types of secondary education which we have postulated, secondary

1. 11+ is a term of art; it means that the able child would go on at 10+, the average child at 11+, and some children would more appropriately go on at 12+.

grammar school, secondary technical school, secondary modern school. This first classification of pupils would necessarily be tentative in a number of cases, for the diagnosis of special interests and skills demanding a curriculum suited to them takes time. The next two years would be spent in what for convenience we call the 'lower school' of one of the three types of school, and during these years a generally common curriculum would be pursued, though within limits there would be some variation. During these years the special interests of the child would be studied and, if desirable, transfer would be recommended. After two years a review of all pupils in the lower school of all types of school would be made; promotion into the higher forms of the school in which a pupil found himself at 11 + would not be automatic, unless that were the right school for him. From the age of 13 + to 16 + a pupil would pursue a course of study suited to his abilities in the type of school which could offer it. This course would lead either to employment and to part-time continued education up to the age of 18 + or to whole-time continued education culminating in the university or in institutions offering opportunities for further study. We regard it as important that the doors to further study should be kept open along as many paths as possible, regard being had to the maintenance of the standard of such further study. The full secondary grammar-school course we consider to extend to 18 +, but we think it essential that pupils from secondary technical schools should have greater opportunity of going on to places of advanced study than at present, and we are conscious that pupils who have left at 16 + or so and in later years show ability to profit from full-time advanced study should be able to gain admittance to it; their case is borne in mind in later proposals relating to examinations. On educational grounds we are in favour of a break of six months, in which boys and girls between the ages of eighteen and nineteen years would render public service interpreted in a broad sense, and the recommendations which we make allow for such a period. Before this break comes pupils going on to universities and other places of advanced study would have taken the examinations necessary to secure admission and financial aid, and would take up residence after the period of service. Finally, we would envisage greater facilities for adult education much more widely conceived and distributed than at present, believing that without part-time education and adult education the work of the schools must necessarily be incomplete.

79 George Orwell

from 'The Lion and the Unicorn', 1941, reprinted in *Collected Essays, Journalism and Letters*, vol. 2, pp. 76–80

One of the most influential developments in England, and one that can hardly be documented, was the rise of the middle classes.
Much of the shaping of educational policy over the century can be explained in terms of this social mobility, and of the aspirations and fears that accompanied it. Orwell chronicled them with a deft precision.

One of the most important developments in England during the past twenty years has been the upward and downward extension of the middle class. It has happened on such a scale as to make the old classification of society into capitalists, proletarians and petit-bourgeois (small property-owners) almost obsolete.

England is a country in which property and financial power are concentrated in very few hands. Few people in modern England *own* anything at all, except clothes, furniture and possibly a house. The peasantry have long since disappeared, the independent shopkeeper is being destroyed, the small businessman is diminishing in numbers. But at the same time modern industry is so complicated that it cannot get along without great numbers of managers, salesmen, engineers, chemists and technicians of all kinds, drawing fairly large salaries. And these in turn call into being a professional class of doctors, lawyers, teachers, artists, etc., etc. The tendency of advanced capitalism has therefore been to enlarge the middle class and not to wipe it out as it once seemed likely to do.

But much more important than this is the spread of middle-class ideas and habits among the working class. The British working class are now better off in almost all ways than they were thirty years ago. This is partly due to the efforts of the trade unions, but partly to the mere advance of physical science. It is not always realized that within rather narrow limits the standard of life of a country can rise without a corresponding rise in real wages. Up to a point, civilization can lift itself up by its boot-tags. However unjustly society is organized, certain technical advances are bound to benefit the whole community, because certain kinds of goods are necessarily held in common. A millionaire cannot, for example, light the streets for himself while darkening them for other people. Nearly all citizens of civilized countries now enjoy the use of good roads, germ-free water, police protection, free libraries and probably free education of a kind. Public education in England has been meanly starved of money, but it has nevertheless improved, largely owing to the devoted efforts of the teachers, and the habit of reading has become enormously more widespread. To an increasing extent the rich and the poor read the same books, and they also see the same films and listen to the same radio programmes. And the differences in their way of life have been diminished by the mass-production of cheap clothes and improvements in housing. So far as outward appearance goes, the clothes of rich and poor, especially in the case of women, differ far less than they did thirty or even fifteen years ago. As to housing, England still has slums which are a blot on civilization, but much building has been done during the past ten years, largely by the local authorities. The modern council house, with its bathroom and electric light, is smaller than the stockbroker's villa, but it is recognizably the same kind of house, which the farm labourer's cottage is not. A person who has grown up in a council housing estate is likely to be – indeed, visibly *is* – more middle class in outlook than a person who has grown up in a slum.

The effect of all this is a general softening of manners. It is enhanced by the fact that modern industrial methods tend always to demand less muscular effort and therefore to leave people with more energy when their day's work is done. Many workers in the light industries are less truly manual labourers than is a doctor or a grocer. In tastes, habits, manners and outlook the working class and the middle class are drawing together. The unjust distinctions remain, but the real differences diminish. The old-style 'proletarian' – collarless, unshaven and with muscles warped by heavy labour – still exists, but he is constantly decreasing in numbers; he only predominates in the heavy industry areas of the north of England.

After 1918 there began to appear something that had never existed in England before: people of indeterminate social class. In 1910 every human being in these islands could be 'placed' in an instant by his clothes, manners and accent. That is no longer the case. Above all, it is not the case in the new townships that have developed as a result of cheap motor cars and the southward shift of industry. The place to look for the germs of the future England is in light-industry areas and along the arterial roads. In Slough, Dagenham, Barnet, Letchworth, Hayes – everywhere, indeed, on the outskirts of great towns – the old pattern is gradually changing into something new. In those vast new wildernesses of glass and brick the sharp distinctions of the older kind of town, with its slums and mansions, or of the country, with its manor-houses and squalid cottages, no longer exist. There are wide gradations of income, but it is the same kind of life that is being lived at different levels, in labour-saving flats or council houses, along the concrete roads and in the naked democracy of the swimming-pools. It is a rather restless, cultureless life, centring round tinned food, *Picture Post*, the radio and the internal combustion engine. It is a civilization in which children grow up with an intimate knowledge of magnetoes and in complete ignorance of the Bible. To that civilization belong the people who are most at home in and most definitely *of* the modern world, the technicians and the higher-paid skilled workers, the airmen and their mechanics, the radio experts, film producers, popular journalists and industrial chemists. They are the indeterminate stratum at which the older class distinctions are beginning to break down.

This war, unless we are defeated, will wipe out most of the existing class privileges. There are every day fewer people who wish them to continue. Nor need we fear that as the pattern changes life in England will lose its peculiar flavour. The new red cities of Greater London are crude enough, but these things are only the rash that accompanies a change. In whatever shape England emerges from the war, it will be deeply tinged with the characteristics that I have spoken of earlier. The intellectuals who hope to see it Russianized or Germanized will be disappointed. The gentleness, the hypocrisy, the thoughtlessness, the reverence for law and the hatred of uniforms will remain, along with the suet puddings and the misty skies. It needs some very great disaster, such as prolonged subjugation by a foreign enemy, to destroy a national culture. The Stock Exchange will be pulled down, the horse plough will give way to the tractor, the country houses will be turned into children's holiday camps, the Eton and Harrow match will be forgotten, but England will still be England, an everlasting animal stretching into the future and the past, and, like all living things, having the power to change out of recognition and yet remain the same.

80 Sir William Beveridge

from the Report on Social Insurance and Allied Services, Cmd 6404, 1942, pp. 7–8.

Orwell's comments indicate how much of what was strictly educational policy was shaped by events and aspirations that lay completely outside the field of education. In many ways, the most important document on education was the 1942 Beveridge Report, and especially its concern to free the family from want. Social security and educational advance could achieve together what neither could do singly; hence the Beveridge proposals were as important to the 1944 Education Act as that legislation was to subsequent educational development.

The way to freedom from want

The work of the Inter-Departmental Committee began with a review of existing schemes of social insurance and allied services. The plan for Social Security, with which that work ends, starts from a diagnosis of want – of the circumstances in which, in the years just preceding the present war, families and individuals in Britain might lack the means of healthy subsistence. During those years impartial scientific authorities made social surveys of the conditions of life in a number of principal towns in Britain, including London, Liverpool, Sheffield, Plymouth, Southampton, York and Bristol. They determined the proportions of the people in each town whose means were below the standard assumed to be necessary for subsistence, and they analysed the extent and causes of that deficiency. From each of these social surveys the same broad result emerges. Of all the want shown by the surveys, from three-quarters to five-sixths, according to the precise standard chosen for want, was due to interruption or loss of earning power. Practically the whole of the remaining one-quarter to one-sixth was due to failure to relate income during earning to the size of the family. These surveys were made before the introduction of supplementary pensions had reduced the amount of poverty amongst old persons. But this does not affect the main conclusion to be drawn from these surveys: abolition of want requires a double redistribution of income, through social insurance and by family needs.

Abolition of want requires, first, improvement of State insurance, that is to say provision against interruption and loss of earning power. All the principal causes of interruption or loss of earnings are now the subject of schemes of social insurance. If, in spite of these schemes, so many persons unemployed or sick or old or widowed are found to be without adequate income for subsistence according to the standards adopted in the social surveys, this means that the benefits amount to less than subsistence by those standards or do not last as long as the need, and that the assistance which supplements insurance is either insufficient in amount or available only on terms which make men unwilling to have recourse to it. None of the insurance benefits provided before the war were in fact designed with reference to the standards of the social surveys. Though unemployment benefit was not altogether out of relation to those standards, sickness and disablement benefit, old-age pensions and widows' pensions were far below them, while workmen's compensation was below subsistence level for anyone who had family responsibilities or whose earnings in work were less than twice the amount needed for subsistence. To prevent interruption or destruction of earning power from leading to want, it is necessary to improve the present schemes of social insurance in three directions: by extension of scope to cover persons now excluded, by extension of purposes to cover risks now excluded, and by raising the rates of benefit.

Abolition of want requires, second, adjustment of incomes, in periods of earning as well as in interruption of earning, to family needs, that is to say in one form or another it requires allowances for children. Without such allowances as part of benefit or added to it, to make provision for large families, no social insurance against interruption of earnings can be adequate. But, if children's allowances are given only when earnings are interrupted and are not given during earning also, two evils are unavoidable. First, a substantial measure of acute want will remain among the lower paid workers as the accompaniment of large families. Second, in all such cases, income will be greater during unemployment or other interruptions of work than during work.

By a double redistribution of income through social insurance and children's allowances, want, as defined in the social surveys, could have been abolished in Britain before the present war. As is shown earlier, the income available to the British people was ample for such a purpose. The plan for Social Security set out in Part V of this Report takes abolition of want after this war as its aim. It includes as its main method compulsory social insurance, with national assistance and voluntary insurance as subsidiary methods. It assumes allowances for dependent children, as part of its background. The plan assumes also establishment of comprehensive health and rehabilitation services and maintenance of employment, that is to say avoidance of mass unemployment, as necessary conditions of success in social insurance. These three measures – of children's allowances, health and rehabilitation services, and maintenance of employment – are described as assumptions A, B and C of the plan; they fall partly within and partly without the plan itself, extending into other fields of social policy. They are discussed, therefore, not in the detailed exposition of the plan in Part V of the Report, but in Part VI, which is concerned with social security in relation to wider issues.

The plan is based on a diagnosis of want. It starts from facts, from the condition of the people as revealed by social surveys between the two wars. It takes account of two other facts about the British community, arising out of past movements of the birth-rate and the death-rate, which should dominate planning for its future. The first of the two facts is the age constitution of the population, making it certain that persons past the age that is now regarded as the end of working life will be a much larger proportion of the whole community than at any time in the past. The second fact is the low reproduction rate of the British community today; unless this rate is raised very materially in the near future, a rapid and continuous decline of the population cannot be prevented. The first fact makes it necessary to seek ways of postponing the age of retirement from work rather than of hastening it. The second fact makes it imperative to give first place in social expenditure to the care of childhood and to the safeguarding of maternity.

81 Board of Education

'Proposed Reforms', from the White Paper on Educational Reconstruction, Cmd 6458, 1943, pp. 7–11.

The White Paper on Educational Reconstruction after the war set out the government's own views on what should be done in the way of reforms, and many of the ideas contained in it found themselves in the 1944 Act. It remains an impressive document, and includes many reforms which never saw reality, and hints at the first doubts about a rigid division between three types of secondary school. It also firmly advocated the raising of the school-leaving age.

General provisions

It is intended that the raising of the school-leaving age to fifteen, postponed in 1939, should be brought into effect as soon as possible after the war, but without the arrangements for exemptions made in the 1936 Act, and that provision should be made for a further extension to sixteen at a later date.

It is proposed that the statutory system of public education shall cease to be severally administered for the purposes of elementary education and higher education respectively. It will be organized in three progressive stages to be known as primary education, secondary education and further education, and a duty will be placed on each local education authority to contribute towards the mental, moral and physical development of the community by securing the provision of efficient education throughout those stages for all persons in the area capable of profiting thereby. For the fulfilment of the duties thus laid upon them local education authorities will be required to make a comprehensive survey of the existing provision and the present and prospective needs of their areas and to prepare and submit to the Board development plans which will give a complete picture of the proposed layout of primary and secondary schools. In respect of all such schools, whether provided schools or non-provided schools (hereinafter called county and auxiliary schools respectively), the plan will indicate the future organization, the nature of the education to be given in the various types of secondary schools, and the alterations to the premises needed to bring the schools up to the standards to be prescribed in Regulations of the Board. It will also contain information about the general arrangements to be made for the transport of pupils to and from school. Provision will be made for the Board, when they have approved the development plan, to make an education order for the area which will specify the steps which the authority is required to take by way, amongst other things, of maintaining existing schools, improving existing schools and providing new schools, and will contain a timetable to which the authority will be required to conform in taking these steps.

The parent's duty will no longer be confined to causing his child to be efficiently instructed in the three Rs; his duty will be to cause his child to receive efficient full-time education suitable to the child's age and aptitudes.

Children under compulsory school age

Primary education covers the period up to the age of eleven or twelve. For the younger children, though it is not proposed to lower the age at which attendance becomes compulsory – and no other country has a lower age than five – is is proposed to substitute for the present power of local education authorities a duty to provide, or aid the supply of, such nursery schools as in the opinion of the Board may be necessary. It is now considered that the self-contained nursery school, which forms a transition from home to school, is the most suitable type of provision for children under five. Such schools are needed in all districts, as even when children come from good homes they can derive much benefit, both educational and physical, from attendance at a nursery school. Moreover, they are of great value to mothers who go out to work, and also to those who need relief from the burden of household duties combined with the care of a young family. It is, however in the poorer parts of the large cities that nursery schools are especially necessary. The authors of 'Our Towns', in describing the conditions which were brought to light by the evacuation of 1939, said that nothing had impressed them so often or so deeply as the need to multiply these schools in the poor quarters of the towns, from which they should spread and be provided for the children of all parents who desire to use them. There is no doubt of the importance of training children in good habits at the most impressionable age and of the indirect value of the nursery school in influencing the parents of the children. There is equally no doubt of the incalculable value of the schools in securing medical and nursing care, and the remedial treatment of defects which may be difficult to eradicate if they are left untreated until the child enters school in the ordinary way at the age of five. Though it is not proposed that local education authorities should cease to have the power of providing for children from three to five by means of nursery classes in infants' schools, it is hoped that new provision for children under five will be mainly in nursery schools which, in addition to providing a more suitable environment for young children, are nearer to the home than large infants' schools and give less opportunity for the spread of infectious diseases. While the nursery school will normally provide for children between the age of two and five, children who are not yet ready for transfer to the infants' school can be retained till a later age.

Infants and juniors

It is generally accepted that, wherever numbers make it possible, there should be separate schools for infants and juniors respectively, because of the different methods of approach appropriate to the training of the younger and older children in the primary stage. This principle will be observed in considering the local education authorities' development plans, which will also make provision for the new schools and for the improvements necessary in the premises of existing schools in order that they may offer the space, facilities and amenities suitable for the full mental, social and physical development of young children. The reform of the system of secondary education and the adoption of other arrangements for the classification of the children at eleven and subsequently will go a long way towards enabling the junior schools to devote themselves to their proper task. It is further an essential element in the proposals to secure a progressive reduction in the size of classes in infants' and junior schools, as the supply of teachers and buildings permits.

Secondary education

At about the age of eleven comes the change from the junior to the senior stage. At present all children of the appropriate age and standard enter for the Special Place examination and, from what has been said previously, it is clear that there is urgent need for reform. Accordingly, in the future, children at the age of about eleven should be classified, not on the results of a competitive test, but on an assessment of their individual aptitudes largely by such means as school records, supplemented, if necessary, by intelligence tests, due regard being had to their parents' wishes and the careers they have in mind. Even so, the choice of one type of secondary education rather than another for a particular pupil will not be finally determined at the age of 11, but will be subject to review as the child's special gifts and capacities develop. At the age of thirteen, or even later, there will be facilities for transfer to a different type of education, if the original choice proves to have been unsuitable. The keynote of the new system will be that the child is the centre of education and that, so far as is humanly possible, all children should receive the type of education for which they are best adapted.

If this choice is to be a real one, it is manifest that conditions in the different types of secondary schools must be broadly equivalent. Under present conditions the secondary school enjoys a prestige in the eyes of parents and the general public which completely overshadows all other types of school for children over eleven. Inheriting as it does a distinguished tradition from the old English grammar school it offers the advantages of superior premises and staffing and a longer school life for its pupils. Since 1902, when local education authorities were first empowered to provide or aid secondary education, there has been a rapid expansion. In 1904 there were 86,000 pupils; today there are 514,000, of whom considerably more than half are in schools provided by local education authorities. The success of the schools in dealing with this extension has been remarkable. The traditional curriculum has been widened and adapted to meet the ever-increasing variety of demands and, helped by the introduction in 1917 of the School Examinations system, an education has been evolved which in the main meets the needs of the more promising pupils. But in spite of this success, the schools are facing an impossible task. An academic training is ill-suited for many of the pupils who find themselves moving along a narrow educational path bounded by the School Certificate and leading into a limited field of opportunity. Further, too many of the nation's abler children are attracted into a type of education which prepares primarily for the university and for the administrative and clerical professions; too few find their way into schools from which the design and craftsmanship sides of industry are recruited. If education is to serve the interests both of the child and of the nation, some means must be found of correcting this bias and of directing ability into the field where it will find its best realization.

Compared with the grammar schools the senior schools have a recent history. Growing originally out of the upper forms of elementary schools, they received an impetus from the new emphasis on advanced instruction given in section 20 of the Education Act 1921 and from the recommendations of the Hadow Report. Today they are one of the main elements of post-primary education. Lacking the traditions and privileged position of the older grammar school they have less temptation to be 'at ease in Zion'. Their future is their own to make, and it is a future full of promise. They offer a general education for life, closely related to the interests and environment of the pupils and of a wide range embracing the literary as well as the practical, e.g. agricultural, sides. In many areas admirable examples exist of fully developed senior schools, but they are still too few in number. The further advance of schools of this type depends on a longer school life for the pupils, a more complete reorganization, better buildings and amenities, and a more generous scale of staffing.

Junior technical schools came into being in 1905 and their success has been remarkable. Planned to give a general education associated with preparation for entry to one or other of the main branches of industry or commerce they have grown up in close relation to local needs and opportunities of employment. But their progress in numbers has been comparatively slow and their chances of attracting the most able children *vis-à-vis* the grammar schools have been adversely affected by the fact that they normally recruit at the age of thirteen. With altered conditions, and with a more rapid development in the future, they hold out great opportunities for pupils with a practical bent.

Such, then, will be the three main types of secondary schools to be known as grammar, modern and technical schools. It would be wrong to suppose that they will necessarily remain separate and apart. Different types may be combined in one building or on one site as considerations of convenience and efficiency may suggest. In any case the free interchange of pupils from one type of education to another must be facilitated.

A particular problem arises in respect of the class of school known as the direct-grant secondary school. These schools, of which there are at the present time 232, exercised an option in 1926 in favour of capitation grant direct from the Board in preference to receiving their financial aid through the local education authorities. The list includes a wide variety of schools ranging from those schools which are an integral part of the local provision to those which, to a considerable degree, have non-local connections. It is not possible here and now to reach a conclusion about the future of these schools as a class. Some of them will no doubt be attracted by the financial provisions applicable to auxiliary schools; in any case a number of them fall within the scope of the inquiry of the Fleming Committee, the report of which may be expected to have an important bearing on the problem. Meantime the postponement of a decision on the future of this group of schools will in no way prejudice the general reconstruction of secondary education described in the preceding paragraphs.

In one direction a new departure may be looked for. Hitherto, apart from the provision made at certain country grammar schools for pupils from remote homes, boarding education has been restricted, either to those children whose parents are able to send them to the public schools or to children who have to be removed from their homes because they are destitute, defective or delinquent. There is no reason why the benefits of a boarding education should be thus limited, and it is widely held that such facilities should be extended within the ambit of the state system. This need not mean the building of a large number of new boarding schools since there is likely to be a surplus of accommodation that can be used for this purpose after the war. The whole question of boarding education is at present under consideration by the Fleming Committee.

It is in terms of the wider conception of secondary education outlined above that legislation will be cast. The leaving age will be raised. A duty will be placed on local education authorities to provide such variety of instruction as may be desirable in view of the different ages and aptitudes of the pupils and the different periods for which they may be expected to remain at school. Power will be given to authorities to provide, maintain and assist boarding schools and hostels, where these are found to be necessary or desirable. Reorganization will be completed, and conditions in the modern schools will be assimilated to those in the existing secondary schools, in such matters as standards of accommodation and the size of classes. All types of secondary school will be conducted under a single code of regulations, as recommended in the Spens Report, instead of under separate regulations as at present. Lastly, the prohibition of fees will be extended to all secondary schools for the maintenance of which the local education authorities are responsible. The justification for continuing fees in any type of maintained secondary school will disappear when they are all brought together in one general system. Provision will, however, be made for boarding fees to be charged in appropriate cases.

But laws cannot build better human beings and it is not the machinery of education so much as its content that will count in the future. Already in one direction a start has been made. The curriculum of secondary schools, and especially that of the grammar schools, will be the subject of a report by the Norwood Committee. Public opinion will, undoubtedly, look for a new approach to the choice and treatment of school subjects after the war. In particular, consideration must be given to a closer relation of education in the countryside to the needs of agricultural and rural life and, more generally, to creating a better understanding between the people of the town and of the country. A new direction in the teaching of history and geography and modern languages will be needed to arouse and quicken in the pupils a livelier interest in the meaning and responsibilities of citizenship of this country, the Empire and of the world abroad. Education in the future must be a process of gradually widening horizons, from the family to the local community, from the community to the nation, and from the nation to the world.

82 Board of Education

from the White Paper on Educational Reconstruction, Cmd 6458, 1943, pp. 18–20.

Compulsory part-time education

It is a common criticism of our present full-time education which for most children ceases at about the age of fourteen, that its effects are thin and liable to wear off quickly once the child has left school for work. The reason for this is not difficult to see; to borrow the language of photography, the process of education for the vast majority of children offers at present an example of 'under-exposure, under-development and insufficient fixing'.

As things now stand, the great mass of pupils leaving the elementary schools do not pursue any formal education and much of the work of the schools inevitably runs to waste. When every allowance has been made for those – possibly one in six of young persons aged fifteen to eighteen – who of their own initiative attend evening institutes or technical schools, and for those who may be associated with one of the various voluntary organizations which provide a training for adolescents through their social and recreative interests in their leisure hours, it remains true to say that, in the normal course, hundreds of thousands of boys and girls are left without the supervision and help that they need during the most critical years in the formation of characters and the training of mind and body.

Something will be done to remedy the defect of 'under-exposure' by the extension of school life to fifteen; but this extension, and even the further extension to sixteen, will not give full value unless steps are taken to consolidate the results. The continued supervision of the health of young people after their full-time schooling has ceased, and the encouragement and the provision of opportunity to develop their capacities and their interests, are alike essential if the best is to be made of the nation's youth. There is common agreement that, had the provisions for day continuation schools of the Act of 1918 been operated, many of the problems of the adolescent would largely have been solved.

From the point of view of the country's manufacturing industry, agriculture and commerce, the training afforded by a system of part-time education in conjunction with employment is long overdue. The initial and natural advantages that gave this country, almost for the asking, its place of preeminence in world manufacture and world markets have long been fading. More and more in the future will it be necessary to rely on the capacity, adaptability and the quality, of our industrial and commercial personnel. Had fuller attention been given earlier to the all-important question of the training of young workers, some of the difficulties experienced by the services and by industry during the present war would have been markedly less acute.

The principles of the Act of 1918 relating to day continuation schools, will be adapted to meet the requirements of the post-war world. The term 'day continuation school' will be abandoned and the institutions required for this purpose referred to generally as young people's colleges. It is important to make clear that what is in view is no 'going back to school', a mere extension on a part-time basis of previous full-time schooling, but the entry on a new phase of life and development.

All young persons from fifteen to eighteen will be required to attend an appropriate centre part-time, unless they are in full-time attendance at school, or otherwise under suitable part-time instruction. A number of firms already have schools in connection with their factories for the training, both general and vocational, of their young employees, which have proved of the greatest value to the young people themselves and to the whole life of the undertakings. These schools are in some cases conducted and financed entirely by the firms concerned, and in others with financial assistance from public funds. In some instances schools are provided in works but are conducted and maintained by the local education authority. Provision will be made for the requirement to attend an appropriate centre to be discharged at such works schools, subject to their satisfying the Board and the local education authority as to the content and quality of the training provided and being open to inspection.

The hours of attendance at young people's colleges would be taken from the hours of employment as regulated by existing law, or by any subsequent industrial legislation. At first at any rate attendance would be limited to a day a week or its equivalent. This is clearly a minimum, and it is held by some that the first introduction to employment might well be on a half-time basis. The new service can, however, only be established by stages and developed gradually, and provision within the limits now contemplated will present a sufficiently considerable task. The full age range will be built up gradually, children of fifteen attending in the first year of operation; in the second year those of fifteen and sixteen, the full range fifteen to eighteen being attained in the third year following the appointed day for bringing the relevant sections into force.

In rural areas weekly attendance might often be impracticable, and in such areas provision may be made for comparatively short but continuous residential courses in the 'dead' season. Centres so provided would be available at other times for use as camp schools, and as holiday camps and centres for children and young persons from the towns. This will lay the foundation of an appreciation of country life and pursuits.

Special arrangements will be made for young persons serving at sea, a matter to which the shipping industry has already been giving consideration.

The question will naturally be asked – 'Given this time for further education what use will be made of it ?' The young persons concerned will be engaged in a wide variety of occupations – some training for one of the skilled crafts or in employment for which definite training is necessary: some in employment in which no high degree of skill or training is required, and others in non-progressive occupations, commonly called 'blind alley', which do not lead on to adult employment. It must be remembered too that girls largely look to leaving factory, shop or office to get married and set up homes of their own.

For all alike some basic elements should be included in their training. Provision must be made for their physical well-being through physical training and remedial exercises and instruction in health and hygiene. The school medical service will be extended to cover them and, working in conjunction with the proposed State Medical Service, should have a marked effect on the health and physique of the nation. Other essential elements will be training in clarity of expression and in the understanding of the written and the spoken word, together with some education in the broad meaning of citizenship – to give some understanding of the working of government and the responsibilities of citizens and some interest in the affairs of the world around them.

When basic requirements have been met, the remaining hours may well be devoted to a variety of subjects according to individual needs and capacities. For young persons of both sexes in all appropriate cases the time may be used for technical or vocational education related to their employment. For others there would be a variety of courses including handicrafts, and the domestic arts, designed to stimulate their interests, keep their minds alert and create within themselves resources of satisfaction and self-development. In the case of those whose early employment is of the 'blind-alley' type, attention would be given to the further training that will assist them to transfer to more permanent work.

It will be all important that the lessons of past experience should not be forgotten. To obviate one of the causes of the previous failure to operate the Act of 1918, the appointed day for the start of compulsory part-time education should be the same for the whole country. In the second place the new system must not start under the handicap of poor and inconvenient premises, which are dispiriting to the staff, command little respect from the students, and carry no prestige with the public. The problem of accommodation may be met in different ways in different instances. In some cases provision for the young people's college may be combined with much needed extension of technical college accommodation. In many cases separate buildings will be required, or provision may be made on the lines of the village colleges of Cambridgeshire. In general, the young people's colleges should look to the future rather than to the past, i.e. they should be associated with provision for adults and adult activities rather than with the schools which the young persons have left.

83 Board of Education

'The Recruitment and Training of Teachers', from the White Paper on Educational Reconstruction, Cmd 6458, 1943, pp. 26–7.

Legislation can do little more than prepare the way for reform. It will rest with the Board and the local education authorities and, not least, with the teachers working in the schools, to translate its aims into practice. That there will be needed the services of a large body of teachers with very varied qualifications is obvious. But it is not merely a larger number of teachers that will be required but a larger number of teachers of the right calibre. It would be deplorable if the necessary corps of teachers could be obtained only at the expense of lowering existing standards. It depends almost entirely upon the quality of those who staff the schools whether the reforms proposed will be merely administrative reforms or whether they will, in practice, work out as real educational reforms.

These questions of the supply and the training of teachers for the future are now being investigated by the McNair Committee. It is not possible to predict what the recommendations of this Committee will be. Some things, however, are so patently wrong with the present system of recruiting and training teachers that an expert inquiry was long overdue.

The teaching profession is at present recruited almost exclusively from those boys and girls who enter grammar schools and remain there until they are seventeen or eighteen years of age. But only about one in seven of the nation's children reach the grammar schools and of these only about a quarter stay until they are seventeen. There is at present no systematic provision to enable boys and girls in senior schools to continue their education and subsequently prepare for the teaching profession if at, say, fifteen years of age they express a desire to do so; and yet the war has revealed that the ability and the character required of teachers is not to be found exclusively in the boys and girls in the grammar schools. Steps must also be taken to ensure that potential teachers in the grammar schools shall not be lost to the profession, as they frequently now are, because owing to straitened financial circumstances parents feel the necessity of withdrawing their children early from school.

Further, the educational history of too many teachers is alike: school to training college or university and back to school, without any break. Few teachers, except those in technical colleges, have had experience of life other than as students and teachers. Plans must be laid to secure that the teaching profession represents, so far as is practicable, a cross section of the interests and experiences of society at large. Travel, experience of affairs, participation in some form of social service – all these enhance the contribution which a man or woman can make to the schools. Industry, commerce and other callings should contribute their quota to the teaching profession; and it should not be so true as it is today that once a teacher means always a teacher. It is not reasonable to suppose that, if the country treats its teachers well, there will be any dearth of men and women of ability and character to meet the demands of a reconstructed educational system.

A larger number of teachers means more training facilities. What the future relationship of the universities to the training of teachers and what the future of the training colleges should be cannot be predicted in advance of the results of the McNair inquiry. But two things can be said without fear of contradiction. In the first place it is clear that, if teachers are to meet the needs of children and young persons under the reformed educational system, they must be educated men and women of responsibility whose training has introduced them to a full life which they will be encouraged to maintain, and indeed develop, during their professional careers. In the second place, it is a matter of history that the training college system has links with a past which by no means offered prospective teachers such a life; and it is well known that some colleges are reluctant to break with these narrow traditions.

Many improvisations will have to be made immediately after the war in order to secure the teachers required for re-establishing the schools on a firm basis and so laying the foundations for permanent reforms. There are many men and women now serving in the Forces or elsewhere whose experience and devotion would greatly enrich the education of children. Short intensive courses of training will be provided for them, and also for those whose training before they were called up was so slight as not to justify their taking up work in the schools immediately on demobilization. Generous financial provision will be made under the 'Further Education and Training Scheme' to enable them to prepare for the profession. The problem of adjusting the supply of teachers to rises and falls in the school population is one with which the Board are familiar. Though the magnitude of the problem on this occasion differentiates it in degree from similar ones with which they have had to deal in the past, the fact that the various reforms necessitating increases of staff will be introduced by stages will make it one of manageable proportions.

The task is to present the challenge of the educational service to as wide an audience as possible, to ensure that those in the Services and elsewhere whose minds are turning to teaching get opportunities for study and discussion which will keep their interest alive, and to have available, when their release from military or other duties arrives, a wealth and variety of training facilities to meet all needs. These matters are already being taken in hand, but final plans cannot be made until the course of events is clearer. With a reformed system the power and influence of those who educate the young will be much increased, and the teachers of the future must therefore be of the calibre to discharge their great responsibilities to the lasting benefit of children and of society.

84 Lord Percy of Newcastle

from *Some Memories*, 1958, pp. 96–7.

The passing of the 1944 Education Act was, as with the Acts of 1870, 1902 and 1918, the triumph of a single man. Forster, Morant, Fisher and Butler had to fight to get their legislation on to the statute book, and in the case of the 1944 Act, it was a near thing. Churchill himself was unenthusiastic, as Lord Percy later revealed in his memoirs.

To tell the truth, Churchill's feelings about education have often reminded me, then and since, of Porson's famous comment on Gibbon's attitude to Christianity; he seemed to 'hate it so cordially that he might seem to revenge some personal injury'. In fact, of course, this was just the contempt felt by the really self-cultured genius for forms of boyhood schooling from which he himself felt he had derived no benefit. That contempt was, no doubt, accentuated by a generous disdain for the squalid sectarian controversies which had defaced educational policy during the first ten years of his political life, and he hardly realized how almost completely those squalors had evaporated since the war. Moreover, in all his varied experience, he had never administered a department which had to deal with local governments; and he was impatient of this kind of administration. His imagination would have been caught by the use of the taxpayer's money to build and staff some great national institution; but he could see no political or national advantage in the making of grants in aid of municipal institutions, from which the municipalities would reap most of the credit – whether it were the extension of the great Manchester College of Technology or the improvement of what he once described to me, in one of his baroque moments, as 'village schools with a few half-naked children rolling in the dust'. Churchill's country owes much to his baroque moods, but it is unfortunately not a style of architecture that suits educational building.

But, if I thus criticize two of my Conservative colleagues, their prejudices were shared by the older members of all parties. I think, for instance, that both Mcdonald and Snowden shared with Churchill the impatience of the self-educated man with formal school education. All three were ready to encourage less formal schemes of adult education; but none of them had much sympathy with the reforming zeal of the younger men of their parties. It was much the same with the Liberal party. Asquith, to the day of his death, could see no point in the Act of 1902, and was unconscious of the renaissance of secondary education which it introduced. In this field, more than in most others, the war years had been a real dividing line between new and old schools of thought.

85 Education Act (1944)
'The Three Stages of the System', pp. 4–6.

The 1944 Act not only introduced the Hadow idea of primary schools, but created the Ministry of Education, and tried to provide a coherent system by emphasizing the need for nursery schooling and for special schools, as well as further education. But it remained vague about secondary education.

7. The statutory system of public education shall be organized in three progressive stages to be known as primary education, secondary education and further education; and it shall be the duty of the local education authority for every area, so far as their powers extend, to contribute towards the spiritual, moral, mental and physical development of the community by securing that efficient education throughout those stages shall be available to meet the needs of the population of their area.

Primary and secondary education
Provision and maintenance of primary and secondary schools
8. 1. It shall be the duty of every local education authority to secure that there shall be available for their area sufficient schools

(a) For providing primary education, that is to say, full-time education suitable to the requirements of junior pupils.

(b) For providing secondary education, that is to say, full-time education suitable to the requirements of senior pupils, other than such full-time education as may be provided for senior pupils in pursuance of a scheme made under the provisions of this Act relating to further education:

And the schools available for an area shall not be deemed to be sufficient unless they are sufficient in number, character and equipment to afford for all pupils opportunities for education offering such variety of instruction and training as may be desirable in view of their different ages, abilities and aptitudes, and of the different periods for which they may be expected to remain at school, including practical instruction and training appropriate to their respective needs.

2. In fulfilling their duties under this section, a local education authority shall, in particular, have regard

(a) To the need for securing that primary and secondary education are provided in separate schools.

(b) To the need for securing that provision is made for pupils who have not attained the age of five years by the provision of nursery schools or, where the authority considers the provision of such schools to be inexpedient, by the provision of nursery classes in other schools.

(c) To the need for securing that provision is made for pupils who suffer from any disability of mind or body by providing, either in special schools or otherwise, special educational treatment, that is to say, education by special methods appropriate for persons suffering from that disability.

(d) To the expediency of securing the provision of boarding accommodation, either in boarding schools or otherwise, for pupils for whom education as boarders is considered by their parents and by the authority to be desirable:

Provided that paragraph (a) of this subsection shall not have effect with respect to special schools.

9. 1. For the purpose of fulfilling their duties under this Act, a local education authority shall have power to establish primary and secondary schools, to maintain such schools whether established by them or otherwise, and, so far as may be authorized by arrangements approved by the Minister, to assist any such school which is not maintained by them.

2. Primary and secondary schools maintained by a local education authority, not being nursery schools or special schools, shall, if established by a local education authority or by a former authority, be known as county schools

and, if established otherwise than by such an authority, be known as voluntary schools:

Provided that any school which by virtue of any enactment repealed by this Act was to be deemed to be, or was to be treated as, a school provided by a former authority shall, notwithstanding that it was not in fact established by such an authority as aforesaid, be a county school.

3. Subject to the provisions hereinafter contained as to the discontinuance of voluntary schools, every school which immediately before the commencement of this Part of this Act was, within the meaning of the enactments repealed by this Act, a public elementary school provided otherwise than by a former authority shall, if it was then maintained by a former authority, be maintained as a voluntary school by the local education authority for the area in which the school is situated.

4. Primary schools which are used mainly for the purpose of providing education for children who have attained the age of two years but have not attained the age of five years shall be known as nursery schools.

5. Schools which are especially organized for the purpose of providing special educational treatment for pupils requiring such treatment and are approved by the Minister for that purpose shall be known as special schools.

6. The powers conferred by subsection (1) of this section on local education authorities shall be construed as including power to establish, maintain and assist schools outside as well as inside their areas.

86 Education Act (1944)
'Compulsory Attendance', p. 29.

Not only did the Act raise the leaving age to fifteen, but it contained within it the desire, and machinery, for adding yet another year to compulsory schooling. Yet it would be a quarter of a century before that wish was finally realized.

35. In this Act the expression 'compulsory school age' means any age between five years and fifteen years, and accordingly a person shall be deemed to be of compulsory school age if he has attained the age of five years and has not attained the age of fifteen years and a person shall be deemed to be over compulsory school age as soon as he has attained the age of fifteen years:

Provided that, as soon as the Minister is satisfied that it has become practicable to raise to sixteen the upper limit of the compulsory school age, he shall lay before Parliament the draft of an Order in Council directing that the foregoing provisions of this section shall have effect as if for references therein to the age of fifteen years there were substituted references to the age of sixteen years; and unless either House of Parliament, within the period of forty days beginning with the day on which any such draft as aforesaid is laid before it, resolves that the draft be not presented to His Majesty, His Majesty may by Order in Council direct accordingly.

87 Education Act (1944)
'Further Education', pp. 33–8.

Some of the most ambitious and radical proposals within the new Act dealt with the concept of continuation schooling first raised in the 1918 Act. Inspired by the work of Henry Morris in the Cambridgeshire county colleges, it foresaw a day when all young people would be attending some form of education until the age of at least eighteen. Like its 1918 predecessor, the ideas were never implemented.

41. Subject as hereinafter provided, it shall be the duty of every local education authority to secure the provision for their area of adequate facilities for further education, that is to say
(a) Full-time and part-time education for persons over compulsory school age.
(b) Leisure-time occupation, in such organized cultural training and recreative activities as are suited to their requirements, for any persons over compulsory school age who are able and willing to profit by the facilities provided for that purpose:

Provided that the provisions of this section shall not empower or require local education authorities to secure the provision of facilities for further education otherwise than in accordance with schemes of further education or at county colleges.

42. 1. Every local education authority shall, at such times and in such form as the Minister may direct, prepare and submit to the Minister schemes of further education for their area, giving particulars of the provision which the authority propose to make for fulfilling such of their duties with respect to further education, other than duties with respect to county colleges, as may be specified in the direction.

2. Where a scheme of further education has been submitted to the Minister by a local education authority, the Minister may, after making in the scheme such modifications if any as after consultation with the authority he thinks expedient, approve the scheme, and thereupon it shall be the duty of the local education authority to take such measures as the Minister may from time to time, after consultation with the authority, direct for the purpose of giving effect to the scheme.

3. A scheme of further education approved by the Minister in accordance with the provisions of this section may be modified, supplemented or replaced by a further scheme prepared, submitted and approved in accordance with those provisions, and the Minister may give directions revoking any scheme of further education, or any provision contained in such a scheme, as from such dates as may be specified in the directions, but without prejudice to the preparation submission and approval of further schemes.

4. A local education authority shall, when preparing any scheme of further education, have regard to any facilities for further education provided for their area by universities, educational associations and other bodies, and shall consult any such bodies as aforesaid and the local education authorities for adjacent areas; and the scheme, as approved by the Minister, may include such provisions as to the cooperation of any such bodies or authorities as may have been agreed between them and the authority by whom the scheme was submitted.

43. 1. On and after such date as His Majesty may by Order in Council determine, not later than three years after the date of the commencement of this Part of this Act, it shall be the duty of every local education authority to establish and maintain county colleges, that is to say, centres approved by the Minister for providing for young persons who are not in full-time attendance at any school or other educational institution such further education including physical, practical and vocational training, as will enable them to develop their various aptitudes and capacities and will prepare them for the responsibilities of citizenship.

2. As soon after the date of the commencement of this Part of this Act as the Minister considers it practicable so to do, he shall direct every local education authority to estimate the immediate and prospective needs of their area with respect to county colleges having regard to the provisions of this Act, and to prepare and submit to him within such time and in such form as may be specified in the direction a plan showing the provision which the authority propose to make for such colleges for their area, and the plan

shall contain such particulars as to the colleges proposed to be established as may be specified in the direction.

3. The Minister shall, after considering the plan submitted by a local education authority and after consultation with them, make an order for the area of the authority specifying the county colleges which it is the duty of the authority to maintain, and the order shall require the authority to make such provision for boarding accommodation at county colleges as the Minister considers to be expedient: the order so made for any area shall continue to regulate the duties of the local education authority in respect of the matters therein mentioned and shall be amended by the Minister, after consultation with the authority, whenever in his opinion the amendment thereof is expedient by reason of any change or proposed change of circumstances.

4. The Minister may make regulations as to the maintenance, government and conduct of county colleges and as to the further education to be given therein.

44. 1. This section shall come into operation on such date as soon as practicable after the date determined by Order in Council under the last foregoing section as the Minister may by order direct.

2. It shall be the duty of the local education authority to serve upon every young person residing in their area who is not exempt from compulsory attendance for further education a notice (hereinafter referred to as a 'college attendance notice') directing him to attend at a county college, and it shall be the duty of every young person upon whom such a notice is served to attend at the county college named in the notice in accordance with the requirements specified therein.

3. Subject to the provisions of the next following subsection, the requirements specified in a college attendance notice shall be such as to secure the attendance of the person upon whom it is served at a county college

(a) For one whole day, or two half-days, in each of forty-four weeks in every year while he remains a young person; or

(b) Where the authority are satisfied that continuous attendance would be more suitable in the case of that young person, for one continuous period of eight weeks, or two continuous periods of four weeks each, in every such year.

And in this section the expression 'year' means, in relation to any young person, in the case of the first year the period of twelve months beginning with the first day on which he is required by a college attendance notice served on him to attend a county college, and in the case of every subsequent year the period of twelve months beginning immediately after the expiration of the last preceding year:

Provided that in respect of the year in which the young person attains the age of eighteen the requirements specified in the notice shall be reduced to such extent as the local education authority think expedient for securing that the attendances required of him until he attains that age shall be as nearly as may be proportionate to those which would have been required of him during a full period of twelve months.

4. If, by reason of the nature of the employment of any young person or of other circumstances affecting him, the local education authority are satisfied that attendance in accordance with the provisions of the last foregoing subsection would not be suitable in his case, a college attendance notice may, with the consent of the young person, require his attendance in accordance with such other arrangements as may be specified in the notice, so, however, that the requirements specified in the notice in accordance with such arrangements as aforesaid shall be such as to secure the attendance of the young person for periods amounting in the aggregate to three hundred and thirty hours in each year, or, in the case of the year in which he attains the age of eighteen, to the proportionately reduced number of hours.

5. Except where continuous attendance is required, no college attendance notice shall require a young person to attend a county college on a Sunday or on any day or part of a day exclusively set apart for religious observance by the religious body to which he belongs, or during any holiday or half-holiday to which by any enactment regulating his employment or by agreement he is entitled, or, so far as practicable, during any holiday or half-holiday which is allowed in accordance with any custom of his employment, or between the hours of six in the evening and half past eight in the morning:

Provided that the Minister may, on the application of any local education authority, direct that in relation to young persons in their area or in any part thereof employed at night or otherwise employed at abnormal times this subsection shall have effect as if for the reference to the hours of six in the evening and half past eight in the morning there were substituted a reference to such other times as may be specified in the direction.

6. The place, days, times, and periods, of attendance required of a young person, and the period for which the notice is to be in force, shall be specified in any college attendance notice served on him; and the requirements of any such notice in force in the case of a young person may be amended as occasion may require either by the authority by whom it was served on

him or by any other local education authority in whose area he may for the time being reside, so, however, that the provisions of every such notice shall be such as to secure that the requirements imposed on the young person during each year while he remains a young person shall comply with the provisions of the last three foregoing subsections.

7. In determining what requirements shall be imposed upon a young person by a college attendance notice or by any amendments to such a notice, the local education authority shall have regard, so far as practicable, to any preference which he, and in the case of a young person under the age of sixteen years his parent, may express, to the circumstances of his employment or prospective employment, and to any representations that may be made to the authority by his employer or any person proposing to employ him.

8. The following persons shall be exempt from compulsory attendance for further education, that is to say

(a) Any person who is in full time attendance at any school or other educational institution (not being a county college).

(b) Any person who is shown to the satisfaction of the local education authority to be receiving suitable and efficient instruction either full-time or for such times as in the opinion of the authority are equivalent to not less than three hundred and thirty hours instruction in a period of twelve months.

(c) Any person who having been exempt under either of the last two foregoing paragraphs did not cease to be so exempt until after he had attained the age of seventeen years and eight months.

(d) Any person who is undergoing a course of training for the mercantile marine or the sea fishing industry approved by the Minister or who, having completed such a course, is engaged in the mercantile marine or in the said industry.

(e) Any person to whom, by reason of section one hundred and fifteen or section one hundred and sixteen of this Act, the duties of local education authorities do not relate.

(f) Any person who attained the age of fifteen years before the date on which this section comes into operation, not being a person who immediately before that date was required to attend a continuation school under the provisions of the Education Act 1921.

88 National Association of Labour Teachers

'The Comprehensive School: Its History and Character', 1948,
pp. 7–16.

*The major issue of the late forties and early fifties turned on the nature of
secondary education, a debate that has run throughout the century and
remains unresolved even today. A review of the discussion was prepared
by the National Association of Labour Teachers and summarized the
position of those who strongly advocated the move to a reorganization of
secondary education along comprehensive lines.*

In January 1936, the Presidential Address of Dr Terry Thomas to the
Incorporate Association of Headmasters included:

In most instances the secondary school held a complete cross-section of society
... the multiple-bias secondary school was the only one which could produce a
coherent community where trades, professions and classes had learned to
understand and respect the point of view of the others.

The Annual Council Meeting of the Incorporated Association of Assistant
Masters, in the same month, carried a resolution urging the Government to
proceed along certain lines, including: 'Reorganization of all education
from the age of 11 + as secondary education on the basis of the multilateral school.' These, and many other, examples of agreement with the idea
of real, as opposed to Hadow, 'secondary education for all' caused disquiet
among the defenders of the *status quo* – the system based on class and
privilege. The Consultative Committee of the Board, now under the
chairmanship of Sir Will Spens, was asked to prepare and issue another
Report. The Spens Report, published in 1938, developed Hadowism by
adding the suggested provision of what has been called 'secondary-
technical' education, to be given in a third type of 'secondary' school
styled the technical high school. The tripartite system first proposed in
1868 was now complete!

The NALT at once replied to the Spens Report in a pamphlet entitled
'Social Justice in Public Education', in which were exposed the inconsistencies of the Report. The Report paid lip service to the 'idea of multilateralism', which should, it said, pervade the whole system, and it actually
recommended multilateral schools in sparsely populated areas, but it
advanced a number of unconvincing arguments against the adoption of
multilateral schools as a general policy.

It would appear that the 'powers behind the throne' at the Board were
dissatisfied with the Spens Report and sought stronger support for the

system of three types of school – the 'tripartite' system. Some of the Board's officials themselves wrote a 'Green Book' in 1941 which strongly defended the class system of education, and a Special Committee was appointed, under the chairmanship of Sir Cyril Norwood, to supplant the Spens Report by one which was more favourable to traditional orthodoxy. If this was not the deliberate intention, it was certainly the result.

The Norwood Report, published in 1943, began by making the claim that children at the age of eleven can be divided into 'three rough groupings':

The pupil who is interested in learning for its own sake, who can grasp an argument or follow a piece of connected reasoning, who is interested in causes ... the pupil whose interests and abilities lie markedly in the field of applied science and applied art – he often has an uncanny insight into the intricacies of mechanism whereas the subtleties of language construction are too delicate for him ... the pupil who deals more easily with concrete things than with ideas – his mind must turn its knowledge to immediate test, and his test is essentially practical.

These three types of children fitted most conveniently, of course, both quantitatively and qualitatively, into the proposed grammar, technical high and modern schools. As Professor Barnard remarks: 'The history of English education is full of examples of theoretical arguments advanced to justify an already existing state of affairs.'

Professor Cyril Burt, in the *British Journal of Educational Psychology*, disposed effectively of the pretentious nonsense of the Norwood Report: 'This view entirely reverses the facts as they are known to us ... the proposed allocation of all children to different types of school at the early age of eleven cannot provide a sound psychological solution.' But the Norwood Report provided the desired pseudo-authoritative justification of the 'Green Book' and the Board proceeded to publish a White Paper on the same lines, planning separate grammar, technical high and modern schools.

The Norwood Report also influenced teachers' organizations, some of which modified their earlier attitude of agreement with the policy of the multilateral school by suggesting that 'experiments' might be conducted in their provision, on not too large a scale, and with due caution. The defenders of class and privilege had good reason to be grateful to the Norwood Committee and its chairman – a former head master of Harrow.

The attitude of the Labour Movement

There is ample evidence of the consistent advocacy of the comprehensive school by the Labour Movement, and for the recollection of those now charged with local administration we select the following:

Trades Union Congress

In a 'Statement on the Spens Report' the TUC said:

The separation of the three types of school is, in the view of the TUC, also bound to perpetuate the classification of children into industrial as well as social strata. So long as the three types of school remain separate, it is inevitable that the grammar-school pupils will continue to look upon the black-coated job as their natural right; that the technical high school will tend to be regarded as the training ground of foremen and of highly skilled workers in the engineering and building trades; while pupils leaving the modern schools will have to be content with what jobs are left. And these questions will be decided when the children are yet only eleven years old. So long as this stratification of children at the age of eleven remains, it is in practice useless to talk of parity in education or of equality of opportunity in after life.

True, the Report proposes that the content of the curriculum in each of the three types of school should have sufficient in common during the first two years to facilitate such transfers between schools as may be found to be desirable when children reach the age of thirteen. It is known, however, that when experiment in transfers between post-primary schools have been tried they have not been successful.

These considerations caused the TUC to propose in their evidence to the Committee that there should be one roof as well as one Code. By this is meant that instead of the three separate types of school proposed in the Report, there should be one all-in type of school for secondary education and that within these schools there should be sufficient diversity of curriculum to provide for all children over the age of eleven. We believe that a policy of multilateral schools is the only way of bringing about educational parity and that approach to social and industrial equality which we may properly expect our education system to contribute to the society in which we live.

On educational grounds alone there are good reasons why multilateral schools should be preferred to separate specialized schools. It is good that children with differing interests and tastes should mix freely together and should come to understand and respect each other, each widening the outlook of the other. It is good that the brightest children should mix with those not so bright. In these relationships both sides will gain from the mixing. In a system of separate schools these good results cannot be brought about.

In 1943 the TUC repeated these arguments and hoped that 'the Board will undertake really substantial experiments in the way of multilateral schools'.

The Workers' Educational Association

The Multilateral School, which was recommended to the Committee by the Associations of Secondary School Teachers, and by the TUC, would obviously go far towards ensuring equality of status for the various sides of education in the years eleven to sixteen ... the encouragement of the setting up of a number of multilateral schools throughout the country would be a convincing proof, on the part of the Board, of a genuine desire to secure a Single Code not merely on paper but in actual practice.

The Labour Party

The following resolutions were passed by the Labour Party Annual Conference in the years mentioned:

All schools for children over eleven to be brought under a common code of regulations for secondary schools, with common standards of accommodation, staffing, etc., and for the Board to encourage, as a general policy, the development of a new type of multilateral school which would provide a variety of courses suited to children of all normal types (1942).

Mr Harold Clay moving the resolution on behalf of the Executive, said: 'We advocate the application of the common school principle. We believe that it is sound that every child in the State should go to the same kind of school.'

Schools for all children over eleven to be brought under a common code of regulations for secondary schools. A new type of multilateral school should be developed (1943).

This had formed part of a seventeen-point educational programme pressed upon Mr Ralph Butler, President of the Board of Education, by a sub-committee of the Executive, which waited upon him on 25 February 1943.

Newly built secondary schools to be of the multilateral type wherever possible (1945).

Miss Alice Bacon accepting the resolution on behalf of the Executive, said: 'We say also that as far as secondary education is concerned we favour multilateral schools.'

This Conference urges the Minister of Education to take great care that he does not perpetuate under the new Education Act the undemocratic tradition of English secondary education, which results in all normal children born into well-to-do homes being educated together in the same type of school, while the abler children in working-class families are separated at the age of eleven from their less gifted brothers and sisters. This Conference draws attention to the fact that on four occasions during the last five years it has passed resolutions emphasizing the need for the rapid development of a new type of multilateral or common secondary school, taking a complete cross-section of children of secondary-school age without selection, and providing a comprehensive curriculum suited to children of varied capacities and tastes. It calls upon the Minister to review the educational system in order to give real equality of opportunity to all the nation's children (1947).

The 1944 Act – and after

The Butler Act of 1944 repeated the device of the Hadow Committee of 'calling' all education from the age of eleven to that of sixteen 'secondary', but provided that the leaving age would be raised to fifteen. The Act itself makes no reference either to the tripartite system or to comprehensive schools, and it is to administrative circulars and ministerial publications that we have to look for a declaration of policy.

In 1945 the Ministry published *The Nation's Schools: Their Plan and Purposes*, and it became clear that the permanent officials still clung tenaciously to the tripartite system. This pamphlet provoked a storm of protest. Labour members of the House of Commons urged its withdrawal, but in December 1945, the Ministry followed it with a circular which was almost as injurious. Circular 73 specified the accommodation which should be provided in the three types of school and actually discouraged experiments with multilateral schools by requiring local authorities to design them 'so as to be capable of effective separation and adaptation into smaller units if occasion arises'.

The NALT therefore submitted to the Annual Conference of the Labour Party in 1946 the following resolution, which the Conference carried by a large majority:

This Conference, in view of the fact that many educational development schemes are being based on the pamphlet 'The Nation's Schools', urges the Ministry of Education to repudiate this pamphlet, since the policy laid down in it conflicts with the educational policy of the Labour Movement.

Faced with growing and wide-spread opposition, the official element adopted a device which may have been calculated to spread confusion in the ranks of their opponents. The device, simple but effective, was to change the labels of the babies in their cradles. What the Labour movement had always advocated as 'multilateral' schools were now officially called 'comprehensive' schools; but the term 'multilateral' was retained to describe a school with three entirely separate streams – a tripartite system housed in one building or in separate buildings on one site. More than one local authority has walked into this trap and is happily planning the ministerial tripartite multilateral school in the fond belief that they are implementing Labour's policy!

Other authorities, however, are planning a complete system of 'comprehensive schools'. The LCC in its Development Plan recalls that 'such a system of omnibus schools, variously described as multilateral, comprehensive or cosmopolitan, is universal in large urban areas in the United States'. The LCC discusses the old tripartite system and its defects, and meets the objections raised in the Spens and Norwood Reports to the comprehensive school.

In Scotland the term 'omnibus school' is preferred. The Scottish Advisory Council, in 1947, published a report in which the following paragraphs are particularly worthy of note:

We have taken account of the tripartite organization proposed for England ... such a scheme has the obvious attraction of administrative tidiness ... we consider that there are decisive reasons against its adoption. ... The whole scheme rests on an assumption which teacher and psychologist alike must challenge – that children of twelve sort themselves out neatly into three categories to which these three types of school correspond. It is difficult enough to assess general ability at that age: how much harder to determine specific bents or aptitudes with the degree of accuracy that would justify this three-fold classification. Status does not come with the attaching of a name or by a wave of the administrative wand, and the discussion to date has left the position of the modern school neither defined nor secure. Indeed, it seems clear to many that the modern school will in practice mean little more than what is left once the grammar and technical types have been housed elsewhere, and that the scheme will not end in tripartite equality but in a dualism of academic and technical, plus a permanently depressed element. But even if the tripartite scheme were wholly feasible, is it educationally desirable? If education is much more than instruction, is in fact life and preparation for life, can it be wisdom thus to segregate the types from an early age? On the contrary, we hold that school becomes colourful, rich and rewarding just in proportion as the boy who reads Homer, the boy who makes wireless sets and the boy without any marked aptitude for either are within its living unity a constant stimulus and supplement one to another. ...

If this system of selection (i.e. for three different types of school) gives the educationist an unquiet conscience, it has likewise given many a good Scots parent a sore heart. It is easy to accept the general truth that only a certain proportion of children are capable of profiting by a certain type and range of education; but it is very hard for any of us to admit the particular truth, the galling truth, that our own boy or girl is one of those who are not. Can we then expect that the best type of working-class parent, earnest, provident and properly ambitious will readily acquiesce in what they regard as a slamming of the door of opportunity at the very outset? ... Moreover, the resentment of the parent at the refusal of choice of school is sharpened by the knowledge that the selection procedure is not consistently applied throughout the whole social range. He notes that the economically more favoured sections of the community secure by the payment of fees precisely what is denied to himself, the right to ignore the educational verdict at twelve and send his child to the school of his choice, to follow a curriculum that promises to lead to the more desired kinds of career.

The foregoing is an admirably frank appraisal of the social, as well as the educational, issues involved. The tripartite system does mean that the grammar schools are to be the training ground for the professions, for the university, for the administrative and managerial strata in society (after the 'public' schools have taken their pick), and that their portals may only be entered as the result of intense competition at the age of ten or eleven. The Ministry has suggested that the parents of these children should be invited to express their willingness to keep them at school until they are eighteen. The technical high schools will cater for roughly as many who are destined, in the words of the T U C 'to be foremen or highly skilled workers in the engineering and building trades'. The modern schools will continue to do what they can, with a shorter course and a less specialized staff of teachers, for the anonymous great majority. The governing class, secure in the knowledge that its sons can still be trained in the 'public' schools to carry on the family tradition, can thus be assured of a sufficient supply of competent administrators and technicians, carefully selected at the age of eleven and can hope the 'the masses'will be persuaded that their children are in fact receiving an equivalent educational opportunity in the modern schools.

After all, as the Vice-Chancellor of Oxford said on New Year's Day, 1948: 'They must have the courage to say that the best education could not be given to every child. Equal educational opportunity was a popular catchword that could not be realized.' Our readers are reminded of the quotation with which we began, dating from 1807!

Organization and curriculum

The comprehensive school, taking all children who are not sub-normal, from the age of eleven, has to cater for a wide range of ability, and later on, for very different aptitudes. If the primary schools are to be freed from the incubus of the Special Place examination, no serious attempt must be made to assess either general ability or special aptitudes at the age of ten or eleven. Apart from some knowledge which may be passed on in reference to, say, 10 per cent, as particularly bright and 10 or 15 per cent as rather backward, the new pupils will be largely an unknown quantity. They must therefore at first be grouped in classes without any particular 'grading'. This is as well for children not only respond quite unexpectedly to a new environment, but change in very many ways including general ability as assessed by 'intelligence tests' – as they grow older Any initial grading will soon be out of gear.

Each class, therefore, must begin as a 'random selection' of children whose potentialities are as yet unrevealed. It is the business of the school to convert this random selection into a coherent community within the larger community of the school as a whole. It may be found desirable, after a few months, to regroup from the classes for certain activities, but the cohesion of the class community should be preserved for most purposes. The L C C defines the purpose of the comprehensive school as that of giving 'a liberal education, ministering to three main types of interest – cultural interests for the enrichment of personal leisure, vocational interests in preparation for the successful gaining of a livelihood, and community interests leading to responsible participation in the duties of citizenship'. It is 'community interests' which can best be fostered between the ages of eleven and thirteen. Training in social living will be frustrated if over-emphasis on the response to instruction is allowed to destroy the entity of the class.

Whatever the size of the school – whether it has an annual intake of three, five or ten classes – the nature of the course taken up to the age of thirteen will be the same, comprising the 'core curriculum', without any specialization.

In discussing the subsequent organization of the school it would be altogether out of place here to be precise or dogmatic. No one wishes to see schools deprived of their initiative or freedom to experiment. The size of the school, the area in which it is situated, the physical amenities it offers, the nature of its staffing – these are some of the factors which will differ from school to school. Certain general principles, however, are inherent in the idea of the comprehensive school, and these may be simply stated.

By the age of thirteen, that is to say after two years in the school, a good deal will have been learned about each child. These two years provide the opportunity for careful study and assessment. It is necessary, therefore, that the size of each class shall not exceed thirty, and it is desirable that a member of the staff with some knowledge of the techniques involved in child study and the ways in which it can be placed on record should be given some responsibility for this 'junior section' of the school. At the end of the second year it will be possible to make some rough assessments of ability and aptitude, and to decide on the basis of this knowledge how many, and which, 'special studies' the child may with advantage be advised to undertake.

There should be no question of segregating pupils into separate 'streams' or 'sides', for there are many activities included in the common-core curriculum which all can pursue together as a class. But a number of 'periods' in the week can now be assigned during which activities outside the common core can be pursued, the pupils regrouping for this purpose. The most able children may be allowed and encouraged to engage in four or five special studies. The least able children will probably attempt only one, spending the remainder of these special study periods in a consolidation of the common core. Between these two extremes there will be variants. Such a scheme calls for time tabling which may be very complicated, but this is already the case in many existing large secondary schools and offers no insuperable difficulty.

The number of special studies and the time devoted to them will depend inevitably upon the size of the school and the adequacy of its staffing. It is here that the really large school, such as is planned by the L C C, will have an advantage, but the principles can be put into practice quite successfully in a school of 600 pupils.

The Scottish Report suggests in detail an allocation of time for nine different groupings in a school of 600 pupils, providing for: no special bias, two-language or one-language; technical bias, one-language or no language; domestic science bias, one-language or no language; commercial bias, one-language or no language; less able pupils. In a larger school there would be no need to multiply the number of groupings, but it would be possible to have parallel groups between which grading could be arranged.

English, social studies (an integration of history, geography and civics), music, art, science, physical education and religious instruction all appear in the Scottish scheme in each of the nine groupings. These activities represent the common-core curriculum, for which the identity of the class can be retained. Those who protest that the interests of the most able pupils will suffer if they have to work at the pace of less able children in the class should recall the experiments conducted in France and Germany – and on a small scale in England – which were the subject in 1935 of a report by the International Bureau of Education, and in particular of a psychological study written by M. Piaget as an appendix to that report. It is true, no doubt, that teachers may be called upon to modify their technique of class instruction, but they will themselves gain from the necessity of thinking anew about the ultimate purpose of their work.

If it be found that schools of 600 pupils fail to provide sixth forms of economic size, it is to be remembered that each local authority will have a number of such schools and that for the purpose of sixth form work these may be regarded as a single unit, pupils interchanging according to the special bias of sixth-form staffing and equipment in a given school.

It is high time, moreover, that we forgot the unverified assumption that only a small percentage of our children have sufficient native ability to move on to advanced work of quite a high standard. It is an assumption which is easily made by all who wish to restrict opportunity to a small minority. Dr Alexander stipulates that an 'intelligence quotient' of 120 should be the minimum requirements for admission to a grammar school, this representing only 11 per cent of the age group, and that even some of these may be justifiably excluded if they fail to reach a 'persistence rating'. It is just this kind of mathematical recreation, so disdainful of social and human values, which the comprehensive school will drive into deserved oblivion. Many of our greatest men – statesmen, scientists, artists, soldiers – would have failed to satisfy such pseudo-scientific tests, the purpose of which is to create an intellectual aristocracy, an élite, by excluding from opportunity as many as possible.

The British nation cannot afford to neglect the latent talent of any of its children, whatever be the depth of their parents' purse or the social status of their parents, by adopting a system which pretends to discover what is undiscoverable at the age of eleven or twelve, or thirteen or even more. It is the virtue of the comprehensive school that it provides a continuous opportunity for every child, throughout the whole of his school course, to enjoy the kind of education for which he is at any stage in his development best suited.

89 Marion Richardson

from *Art and the Child*, 1948, pp. 40–45.

The pioneering work of countless teachers in developing the style and methodology of primary-school teaching, coupled with new architectural innovations, made the English primary school a post-war success story. One of the features of their work was in art, crafts and music, and in this sphere, they owed a great deal to Marion Richardson, best known for her handwriting exercises, but whose creative approach to children ranged over the whole field of arts and crafts.

I have now recorded as simply as I can the story of my early years of teaching in Dudley. The freedom and happiness of the atmosphere there had made it possible for the children to develop an art which was essentially their own, but which was none the less the result of their partnership with me. I was indeed charged with exercising too strong a personal influence and with imposing something of my own which produced a family likeness in the children's work. But for my part I found each child's work so individually characteristic that when I looked at the painting, I saw the child herself. And yet, while this was so, I, too, saw the family likeness. There was in the work as a whole a manner so unmistakable as to mark it as a little local school of painting. I welcomed it. To me it was both natural and kindling.

How can I explain it? We were members of a community with its own strong customs and conventions (it isn't Christmas unless the windows have been cleaned); and the drawings were in the Dudley dialect, traditional, intimate, indigenous to the soil, and mysteriously revealing. These things counted for much, and within the studio itself influences of the same sort were at work: even the way I cut the paper, the colour combinations and limitations I suggested, and the method of glazing colours over a thin transparent wash. These, and a hundred seeming trifles so slight that I can feel rather than describe them, united to produce a native style, a painting idiom through which the children became articulate; for it provided that framework or form which is one of the necessities of art. And they were encouraged to criticize and discuss their own and one another's work. They were always expected to make a written valuation, even if only a word or two, on every drawing they did. A vernacular developed. 'Right or wrong.' 'This is just what I saw.' 'It was there, but it disappeared.' 'The colours are false and made up.' 'Too big or too small,' and so on. Each week the best work was shown on the studio walls. In these ways something passed from one child to another, and I am quite sure that the less capable were helped by feeling, however unconsciously, that everyone can paint. I only know that all had the confidence to try.

We were, then, interdependent, and although I was as self-effacing as I could be, I knew that the children relied upon me rather as an orchestra relies upon its conductor.

They would say that I opened a door for them. This meant that they preferred to be given a subject rather than find one of their own. Once in possession of the all-necessary mind-picture to which my description gave birth, they were directed, steadied and settled. Every moment of the lesson was purposefully spent, while if called upon to work without such guidance they would try first one thing and then another, and in the end achieve little or nothing at all.

Visitors to Dudley who liked our work would sometimes suggest that the Dudley children were specially unsophisticated, and that I should find another type of child less teachable. This gave me an uneasy feeling. Would my ideas transplant? I knew that I must put this to the test.

For some years, teaching had completely satisfied and filled my mind. I related every artistic experience to it, and in my search for material and inspiration everything was grist to my mill. At length, however, the time did come when I felt the need for reflection and study. At this point I had infinitely good fortune of being invited by Margery Fry to spend a term with her and her brother Roger in London. This meant freedom from responsibility, and the opportunity for quiet thought as to what my next field of work should be. I shall never forget the first sight of the house that was now for a time to be my home. On the right as one entered there was a long room lighted at both ends by large windows. The walls were mottled in rich reddish tones, and were hung, to my surprise and delight, with some of the pictures that I had seen years before at the Post-Impressionist Exhibition. The sun streamed into the room that autumn afternoon, and I knew I had time to satisfy my first enchanted curiosity before my host and hostess arrived. In this room artists and critics gathered to discuss the burning controversies of the day. They brought with them contemporary pictures, and during the next few months it was as an enraptured onlooker that I sometimes had the opportunity of being present.

It was at about this time that the London Day Training College opened a graduate course for art students, and I had the happiness of being asked to become one of the tutors. This was a part-time appointment and left me free, not only to undertake other work in or near London, but, best of all, to return to Dudley for two days at the end of each week.

Every Monday I went to Benenden, a public school for girls high up in a lovely part of the Weald of Kent, and on Wednesday mornings I went to Hayes Court, a delightful private school where also the children were fortunate enough to have wide opportunities. On Tuesdays I supervised the students' school practice, and on Wednesday afternoons we were visited in the College by groups of boys and girls from neighbouring elementary schools. On Saturdays, through the introduction of an American friend, a class was collected for me in a lovely country house in Northamptonshire. This was now my weekly programme of work. I do not recall having myself taken any steps to arrange it, but it offered the very opportunity I needed; for, during the week, I met children from almost every kind of home. How slight and skin-deep were the external differences that might seem to divide them, how lasting the links that united them as children! In looking at their drawings one could always say, 'Only a child could have done this,' but never more.

I think the children themselves enjoyed my varied programme almost as much as I did, for I took with me the work of one group to another. We had so much to recount. Those who were taught at home listened with breathless interest to everything I could tell them about the children who went to school, while on Thursdays, when I returned to Dudley, work was not allowed to begin until I had given a sort of News Letter of what was going on in London and in that dreamland where children had ponies to ride and servants and nurses to wait on them, and where footmen came to carry and change the paint-water.

Wednesday afternoon with the students and children was also usually given up to painting, but we had a colour game which is described here in detail because it has not been mentioned elsewhere.

We met in a large light studio at the top of the building, where conditions were almost perfect for experiment and research. Here there was space for a valuable piece of colour-training apparatus, for which I had collected many hundreds of duplicate skeins of wool. At each end of the room hung a huge holland sheet divided into ten sections. In these sections the skeins were arranged in groups. White and nearly white, yellow, orange, red and pink, blue, green, violet and purple, buff and brown, grey and black, mottled and marled. On one sheet the skeins were permanently fixed and numbered; on the other the duplicates were detachable, looped over curtain hooks and, of course, unnumbered. One version of the game was played by dividing the children into small teams in charge of a student. On the word 'Go', each child was shown a skein; its number having been recorded, she was told to run to the end of the room, find its pair, unhook it, and return with it. Only the subtlest differences divided certain of the skeins, yet some of the children showed an almost uncanny power of memorizing colour. I recall one occasion when, in the fifteen minutes we generally gave to this game, one little boy who could not read made nineteen right choices out of nineteen. When I asked him how he did it, he did not seem to know; but, after a few moments of puzzled reflection, he answered, 'I look at it, and then say to myself, "Is it light ? Is it dark ? Is it neither ?" ' An explanation which hardly seemed to account for his success.

We occasionally challenged members of the College staff to a colour contest, which the children enjoyed because they were invariably easy winners. We never had the opportunity of discovering whether our learned competitors would have had more success if given more training.

One afternoon, I was suddenly aware that a child was looking into my eyes with rapt attention. 'They have little speckles in them and are just like one of the sock wools at the end of Set 6,' she told me. I often wish now that I had recorded more of the children's remarks and conversation concerning colour. One other story does come back to me. I thought a child was being really wasteful with the paints, and asked him why he kept mixing colours and washing away what he had made. 'I want a colour I can't find,' he told me, and, pointing to a sort of wine shade, he said, 'It is that, only blue.'

It was good to watch the rapid growth of the children's power of recognizing and remembering differences, and the way in which this game awakened a new interest in colour and paints. This was reflected in the growing refinement with which the children used all their materials.

90 Ministry of Education

from *Primary Education*, 1959, pp. 216-22.

Work of the kind described by Marion Richardson in the previous extract was given official approval and encouragement in a Ministry handbook in 1959. Most of the sections dealing with arts and crafts were drafted by Robin Tanner, an inspector with the Ministry who had himself pioneered such work in the primary schools of Oxfordshire.

It was not until the years following the First World War, however, that there was any particular awakening to the potentialities and resources of children. Since the end of the nineteenth century Franz Cizek had been working in Vienna with a rare intuitive understanding of children's approach to drawing and painting; and to many who saw the exhibitions of his pupils' pictures in this country in the early twenties this work was a revelation. English boys and girls, educated under different conditions, would probably not work in this way, but surely the discovery that children have an art of their own – in some respects akin to the art of primitive peoples – would also be shared here. Educational thought at the time was beginning to lead teachers to consider children as growing and maturing individuals, each with his peculiar gifts and personality. The moment was certainly ripe for those teachers, scattered throughout England in towns and villages, who believed in art and craft as the birthright of every boy and girl, to go ahead, and this they did. Many encountered opposition and prejudice, and there was for a while great difficulty in finding suitable materials with which to work. Yet that great educational advance of which they were a part is now generally recognized as one of the major revolutions of this century in the teaching of young children.

To the vision, courage and skill of Marion Richardson teachers owe a profound debt. Her struggle to liberate children's urge and power to paint pictures and make patterns culminated in the memorable London exhibition of 1938, when once and for all it was established that some boys and girls are essentially artists.

Only very slowly, however, out of the old ideas of 'industry' and 'imitative arts', and the entirely separate ideas of 'drawing' and 'handwork', there emerged the conception of art and craft considered as one broad aspect of living. The direct vision and creative attitude of the child surely did not need to stop at painting and pattern-making but might be given an outlet also in the great traditional crafts. The section of the *Handbook of Suggestions* (1937) on art and craft opens with this statement:

Design – the common ground of the arts and crafts. The chief purpose in combining the hitherto separate chapters on 'drawing' and 'handwork' and substituting for them a single chapter with the title 'art and craft' is to stress the importance of design, which forms the common ground shared by handicraft with drawing and every other form of graphic art. ... Whatever he creates or interprets, the artist seeks to achieve something that will cause both in himself and in others a feeling of satisfaction – similar perhaps to what we experience in our response to the works of nature – through the use of design appropriate to the medium he has chosen. So, too, the crafts, which are primarily concerned with the making of serviceable things in various materials, have each its own technique. The good craftsman, whilst suiting his material to the particular end he had in view, seeks, like the artist, to arouse similar feelings of satisfaction by the use of appropriate design. Thus, design – the character of which is determined, in each art, by the experiences it expresses and the medium employed, and in each craft by its practical purpose and the material used – provides a link between the arts and the crafts.

Yet it must be admitted that today, while the majority of young children have opportunities to paint freely, craftwork falls far behind. Trivial occupations, sometimes using spurious materials and often only those that have been 'manufactured', without much relation either to a genuine craft or to the interests and attitude of children, tend to usurp the place of true craft teaching; and the whim of the moment or the use of some fashionable new material too often dictates what is done. It is then that craft degenerates into a merely manual process in which mind and spirit have no part, whereas it should be thought of as the whole creative process by which a carefully made design or plan is achieved. But where, on the other hand, children's visual sensibility and feeling for material are encouraged from the start, and they paint a picture, model in clay, create a costume, arrange some flowers, paint or print a pattern, or explore the possibilities of all manner of raw materials, including native ones such as rush, straw, willow, wood, wool and clay, with equal zest and sense of purpose, they happily never see any division nor indeed much distinction between these activities. They grow in their respect for materials, for their inherent qualities and the ways of using them; and because they love making things they bring all their imagination and power to whatever absorbs them at the moment.

The foolish separation between art and craft in our present-day life which has led to the making of so much that is ugly to look at and unpleasant to use should be a warning. We know that if an artist is not a craftsman the less artist he, and we also know that a craftsman worthy of the name is always an artist. Indeed, printing is as much a craft as weaving is an art. The education of children should surely aim at fulfilling their creative powers as both artists and craftsmen; and at the same time it should foster their growth as discerning people, able to choose and select, to discriminate between the true and the counterfeit, to reject the shoddy and false and hold fast to that which is good – in short, to form first-hand judgements, to grow in critical awareness and in the capacity to enjoy the arts and crafts of mankind.

Children as artists and craftsmen

Do you remember, when you were first a child,
Nothing in the world seemed strange to you?
You perceived, for the first time, shapes already familiar,
And seeing, you knew that you had always known
The lichen on the rock, fern-leaves, the flowers of thyme,
As if the elements newly met in your body,
Caught up in the momentary vortex of your living
Still kept the knowledge of a former state,
In you retained recollection of cloud and ocean,
The branching tree, the dancing flame.[1]

Thus a poet makes articulate what in some measure we all feel; and since the writer is an English woman, brought up in the northern parts of these islands, it is naturally with things indigenous to them that she most closely identifies herself, though the thought she utters is universal. The Austrian poet, Rilke, searches into the recesses of early childhood and finds this same affinity – almost kinship – with the things about him in his home:

The sugar bowl, the glass of milk
Would never waver the way people would waver.
The apple lay. Sometimes it did me good
To hold tight to it, a hard ripe apple –
The big table, the coffee cups that never moved.
They were good, they quieted the year.
And my toys did me good too, sometimes.
They were by me like the other things, as sure as they
Only not so peaceful. They stood, as though half way
Between me and my hat, in watchfulness forever.
There was a wooden horse, there was a rooster,
There was the doll without a leg.
I did so much for them
I made the sky small when they looked at it.
Since, almost from the start, I understood
How alone a wooden horse is. You can make one,
A wooden horse, one any size:
It gets painted, then you pull it,

1. From 'Message from Home' by Kathleen Raine, from *Collected Poems*.

And it's the real street it pounds down then.
When you call it a horse, why isn't it a lie?
Because you feel that *you're* a horse, a little,
And grow all maney, shiny, grow four legs. . . .
And wasn't I wood, a little, too,
For its sake, and grew hard and quiet
And looked out at it from an emptier, woodier face?[2]

For every child there would seem to be something of this oneness with the elemental, universal materials of the natural world of stone and wood, of leaves and flowers, together with this intense identification with those man-made things that are his daily comfort and his companion from the start. And since what any one child feels and sees about him will not be quite like that of any other we are each of us unique in this respect. The home and the world outside it make their mark on each one.

Through the ages it has been the life and labour of the land and its own native character that have permeated most deeply, and given our art and craft – whether professional or in the popular idiom of the people – its essential quality. The weather, the soil, the vegetation and wild life, the variety of the scene, all these have given to men's work a peculiarly indigenous character. Even today, when the local idiom often seems submerged under industrial development, English children remain essentially English. While they share with boys and girls the world over certain needs and characteristics, they nevertheless retain, in their approach and in their way of using materials, something that is deeply embedded in their native culture. True, the influences upon this culture from beyond these islands have been many and continuous, but each in its turn has been so completely assimilated as to become an inherent part of tradition. There may be few vestiges of folk art alive in England today, yet wherever they are still found they are unmistakeable. Perhaps it is the craftsmanlike respect for the materials chosen, the restraint of subtlety of the colour, or the loving attention to detail that shows itself; be that as it may, such work could not have been produced elsewhere: it has emerged from a certain way of life lived in a certain place with long traditions and where certain materials are ready to hand. And this has significance for the teacher, who may not always understand why, for example, a small meticulous drawing made with a fine point may sometimes satisfy a child's need more completely than the now familiar large painting in bold powder colour. It is clearly possible for adults greatly to influence the work of children and for mere passing fashion to dictate what they shall do; yet, when they can feel free to be themselves,

2. From *Requiem on the Death of a Boy* by Rainer Maria Rilke (translated by Randall-Jawell).

children often surprise us by what they choose to do and how they set about it. Moreover, since a child brought up in, say, a Northern industrial city or a new housing estate sees and experiences a life very different from that of a coastal village in the South West or a quiet suburb of a cathedral town in the Midlands, the paintings he makes and the things he constructs may be expected to show in some degree the peculiar impact of his environment. But the point must not be pressed too far. It is those common attributes and needs among children that will concern teachers most. For instance, in the two-dimensional world of their paintings, problems of recession may not interest many; and proportion, in the adult sense, is not their concern. What the camera reveals is not what they attempt to reveal. Drawing, painting and making things are for them a means by which they not only explore their world and learn, but through which they also express and sometimes communicate their emotions and ideas.

This is not to suggest that boys and girls are receivers of some heavenly gift that their less fortunate teachers must be careful not to sully! On the contrary, if children are to grow to the full they need to be helped specifically and consistently to use this native language that we call art. The teacher needs to see that it is a fundamental basis for learning and maturing. Like all forms of language, its use involves effort: there must be respect for the materials employed if they are to be properly handled as instruments of ideas. Above all, children have to be helped to observe and see; and their school environment and their experience within it should together lead them to see with a growing acuteness and discernment, with finer appreciation and subtler feeling. Children cannot be expected to grow in visual awareness unless they are taught. Their nature is such that if they are merely surrounded by attractive materials and then 'allowed to develop on their own' they fail to develop but rather repeat a performance *ad nauseam* and with diminishing effort and sincerity of feeling. Art and craft are not mere recreation; they involve hard work and constant effort to master materials and techniques as they are appropriate to children's growing needs and powers. It must be recognized that laziness and slovenliness can mar what they paint or make no less than what they do in any other field; and a sense of progression is as necessary here as in every other aspect of education.

The teacher can neither impose an adult standard nor leave children to flounder. Nor can he hope to find that they will conform to any theory of art. It must be recognized that a way of teaching that makes for freer expression on the child's part also allows for freer expression on the part of the teacher, who must therefore sedulously avoid using the child as a vehicle. The influence of the teacher is undeniably necessary. Just how far it should extend must be decided by the individual, who must face the possibility of a child expressing what is more the teacher's than his own if it penetrates too deeply. What is certain is that it is temptingly easy for a teacher to put too much of himself into the work of his children, and often this happens without his having even realized it.

The essence of the artist is his uniqueness: no two children are alike. Within any group there will be some who, by virtue of their innate sensibility, will see far further and work with much greater expressiveness than others; while some, and especially those with a meagre background, will respond only haltingly to what is offered them. But, undoubtedly, the experience of an education in learning to see must be provided for all children – not as an isolated 'subject' or as a set of skills to be practised, but as a very means of learning and living.

The pleasures of looking, seeing and making begin very early in the life of a child. Whatever his background, the materials composing it make some impact upon him, and from the start he uses for his enjoyment those means that might be called without extravagance the equipment of the artist.

91 Central Advisory Council for Education (Crowther)

'Why the School-Leaving Age should be Raised: The Benefit to the Individual', from the Report, 1959, pp. 108–16.

A strong and lucid argument for the raising of the school-leaving age to sixteen was made by the Crowther Committee in 1959, when it considered the educational provision of the fifteen to eighteen year olds in secondary education. Although it went on to support its case with arguments about the national interest, it admitted that 'our main case is not economic at all. It rests on the conviction that all boys and girls of fifteen have much to learn, and that school and not work is the place for this.'

There are two main arguments for raising the school-leaving age. One starts from the social and personal needs of fifteen year olds, and regards education as one of the basic rights of the citizen; the other is concerned with education as a vital part of the nation's capital investment. As far as the former argument is concerned, nothing has happened in the last twenty years, or could happen, which would weaken our agreement with the view of John Dewey that what the best and wisest parent wants for his own child the community must want for all its children. A boy or girl of fifteen is not sufficiently mature to be exposed to the pressures of the world of industry or commerce. He needs an environment designed specifically to develop his powers, and not one in which he finds a place only, or mainly, in so far as an employer can make use of him. Our reasons for believing that the promise of secondary education for all, made in the Act, cannot be redeemed without education for all to the age of sixteen are set out at length in this chapter. The second argument, that educational advance is a form of capital investment that serves the national interest, is the concern of chapter 12.

What ought to fix the end of compulsory school life? Presumably nobody now wants to reduce the age to twelve, as it was not so long ago; and few would want to keep everybody at school until eighteen. Compulsion should, therefore, presumably stop at some point between twelve and eighteen. But where? There can, of course, be no universally right age since boys and girls vary widely in their rate of physical, emotional and intellectual growth. The most and the best that Parliament can do is to fix the age which will be right for most people. Should it be fifteen or sixteen? That, in broad terms, is the decision that faces the country; though, as we shall see in chapter 13, there are a number of different ways in which the definition can be framed. We are, of course, discussing only the minimum leaving age. Clearly the abler boys and girls should continue their full-time education for a number of years beyond that point. But what about the rest? Is there reason to believe that by leaving school at fifteen they are leaving with an essential job unfinished? We have already given that as our opinion. In this chapter we attempt to set out why we think so.

The years of adolescence

A change in vocabulary can be significant. The primary-school teacher thinks and speaks naturally and appropriately of children; the secondary-school teacher does so at his peril well before the school-leaving age is reached. By around thirteen, pupils have reached the stage of growth when any word that harks back to childhood is misleading and resented. They think and speak of themselves as 'teenagers' and the word, though not yet standard English, is descriptive enough of the troubled and exciting time of adolescence which lies half within and half beyond the school life of most English boys and girls. Not long ago it lay almost entirely beyond. As late as 1917 a Departmental Committee reported that 'in many localities . . .

the effective leaving age approximates rather to thirteen than to fourteen';
while in the old senior elementary school of the inter-war years only one of
the three years lay in the teens. Not only has school life been extended
upwards, but the onset of puberty is earlier than it used to be. Medical
evidence given to us made it clear that menstruation in girls has over a long
period of years gradually been beginning earlier in most western countries,
and there is no doubt that boys also mature earlier. Of course, the physical
changes are spread over a wide belt of years with great individual variations,
but for most children they are nearly complete by the time of leaving school.

But this is not true of the emotional and social consequences of puberty.
The problems they raise are made more difficult by the earlier emotional
development of girls. Few girls leave school before they are conscious of the
attraction of the opposite sex. But, on the whole, the boys in whom they are
interested are not those of their own age, although 44 per cent of all pupils in
secondary schools are in mixed forms. For boys, a personal interest in girls
is usually still in the future when they leave school, though only just over the
horizon. Another year at school would pretty certainly bring it within the
term of school life. But boys and girls alike are already, while still at school,
subject to the frequent mood swings, and mingled brashness and tender-
ness, assertiveness and deep uncertainty – all that April weather of the soul
which marks the time of adolescence. Coming to terms with one's new self
is a difficult and lengthy process, complicated by the fact that sexual maturity
precedes by several years emotional and social maturity.

This is surely the period in which the welfare of the individual ought to
come before any marginal contribution he or she could make to the national
income. Going to work may be the right thing for the adolescent; but, if so,
it should be justified on this ground and not by any reference to industry's
need of juvenile labour or to the family's need of additional income. A
sympathetic employer and a wise foreman may provide just the unsenti-
mental guiding hand a teenager needs, but there can be no guarantee that
he will find them, since industry does not exist for the sake of the teenager.
His main need at this age is not of course to be protected, still less to have
everything his own way, but he does still need an environment that is
designed for him. School is such a world, but is it the right world for the
ordinary boy or girl who is rising sixteen? Can it provide for him, and not
only for his abler brothers and sisters, a sufficiently progressive and demanding programme to feed his mind, hold his interest, develop his sense of
responsibility and provide him with growing independence, including the
opportunity to make and profit by mistakes? We think it can, and in some
instances does. We are very far, however, from asserting that this is yet
generally the case.

The adolescent's needs

One of the marks of the secondary-school period is the greater physical skill and control which come to boys and girls in their teens. This is one reason for the specialist teaching,[1] and specialist rooms, in secondary schools – the gymnasium, the stage, the craft shops, the housecraft rooms, the laboratory and the art room. Many boys begin to be able to work to fine limits in the woodwork and metalwork shop; in the art room they are not satisfied unless they can attain a conscious mastery of technique. Some will soon exhaust their interest or competence in one or more directions, but few in all. Most specialist teachers of these subjects will agree that a gratifyingly large proportion of their pupils are not only still learning at the end of the course, but really beginning to go rapidly ahead. They leave school at a time when the law of increasing returns is operating. They are not only gaining skill, but insight. Many teachers of these specialist subjects would cheerfully give up the first year, or possibly even two years, of the secondary course if they could be allowed one more at the end. The course is over too soon. Not only does it finish when there is still more to be learned – that would be true whenever it occurred – but too often it really is an end. Seed has been sown but the crop will not ripen.

Side by side with this growing physical competence, this approach to adult standards of performance, goes an intensified interest in the 'real' world. For boys especially this is apt to be the world of machines. For thousands of years the tools were simple enough – the skill lay in the hands which used them. Now it lies as much in the mind – the mind of the mechanic who looks after the machines as well as the mind of the designer. It is fostered by the delight that so many boys experience in tinkering with a motor-cycle or in constructing a radio set. This mechanical ability is far more widespread than would have seemed credible a generation ago. Every man needs, for himself and for society, as much of this scientific, or more properly, technological knowledge as he can master. Essentially it is a secondary, not a primary-school subject, and it is not one in which many boys and girls will have begun to reach the limit of their competence by the age of fifteen. It is probably true, also, that many boys find technological subjects their easiest and most natural approach to science both as a body of knowledge and as a method of acquiring it. By cutting off compulsory

1. Specialist teaching (i.e. teaching by a master or a mistress who teaches virtually only the one subject he has been specially trained to teach) should not be confused with specialization in sixth forms (i.e. the system by which a pupil spends the greater part of his time on a few closely related subjects).

education at fifteen we lose the opportunity fully to exploit this mechanical interest in the service of scientific understanding.

Inevitably there is a strong vocational flavour to what boys and girls value most in secondary education. Before the end of the present secondary course they have reached the stage when they desire to see the relevance of what they are doing in school to what they will be doing when they leave school. They are anxious to see a purpose in education, and this anxiety seems to us wholly natural. It should be neither ignored nor played down, but used to enlist their cooperation. There is, of course, a great deal more to life than earning a living, and it is natural that the strength of the vocational test of relevance will vary a good deal between individuals, and that it should be more frequent in boys than in girls, for a good many of whom wage-earning is likely to seem a more temporary preoccupation. Teachers have always been conscious that education has a value in the world to which their pupils are looking forward, but they have not perhaps always been sufficiently concerned to make what they teach manifestly relevant to it. This need has become more apparent now that the senior pupils are older. But our belief that what is taught should be, and appear to be, relevant to the world outside school does not imply that every skill which an employer would like a worker to possess should be taught in school. There are many tricks of the trade which are best learned in the trade, and many skills which are insufficiently educational to be worth a place in the curriculum, at any rate before the minimum leaving age.

The passionate interest that many girls feel in living things can be as strong an educational incentive as the love of machines. It is not for nothing that biology is the main science taught to girls, as physics and chemistry are to boys. The same forces, whether innate or social does not matter, probably determine the fact that girls show a more conscious and avowed interest in personal relations than boys do. To the primary-school child, characters in fiction and history alike are either black or white, heroes or villains for his admiration or his hate. He plays at being them. To the secondary-school girl, imaginary characters are like real characters, like herself. The interaction between her real character and their imagined characters is subtle and two-sided. This analytical and introspective interest in literature in the widest sense – in everything that tells a human story – is not found in most girls at the beginning of the secondary course; it is there before the end; but, once again it needs to be, and could be, developed much further than is possible by the age of fifteen. Too many girls' reading interests are needlessly left fixed for life within the covers of a hopelessly unreal romantic love novel. Often enough reading in any serious sense soon disappears.

Over half the modern school boys and girls interviewed for us by the Social Survey had at one time belonged to a public library; only 16 per cent still belonged two years after leaving school.

It is true that there is a broad distinction between boys' and girls' interests which is rightly reflected in curriculum planning, but the point should not be over-stressed. It is sometimes almost implied that no girl is interested in physics or mathematics, and no boy in biology or English literature. This is, of course, nonsense; and, even if true, it would be something to be corrected, not accepted. It should not be accentuated, as we think it sometimes is in co-educational schools, by the tendency for mathematics, physics and chemistry to be taught by men, and therefore to be regarded as boys' subjects, and for English, history and kindred subjects to be taught by women and to be looked on as more suitable for girls. Of course this is bound up with the shortage of women science and mathematics graduates and with the relatively greater difficulty of finding women teachers for co-educational than for girls' schools. It may, therefore, often be unavoidable at present.

Another subject or group of subjects, which is characteristic of the secondary stage, is foreign languages. It may be only tradition and the lack of qualified staff which prevents their being started in the primary school; but they are now wholly, and would always be mainly, a matter for the secondary school. We are not concerned to argue that all boys and girls should study a foreign language; but we note that a good many modern schools, especially girls' schools, are teaching one with success. It is important that the numbers should grow. Teaching a foreign language is one of the surest ways of awakening a sensitivity to the use of words. It is not only through the discipline of vocabularies and translation that learning a foreign language improves a pupil's knowledge of English, but also in a more general way through arousing an awareness of words and their meaning, and of the structure of sentences. Once reading has been mastered, far too many pupils, especially boys, take English for granted and regard it as a something which comes by nature, which it is fussy to try consciously to improve; communication in a foreign language can never be taken for granted. There are also, of course, strong social reasons for teaching a foreign language, especially now that foreign travel is within the reach of so many. But these are not, in our view, the main reasons for the place of languages in the curriculum. They have a strictly educational task to perform – and it can be much more fully performed by sixteen than by fifteen.

Standards of life

We turn to another aspect of education. If primary and secondary schools have been doing their job properly, boys and girls will have grown up in a society which has without fuss or preaching taught them to respect and practise a way of living which is certainly higher than much of that with which they are familiar through the world of entertainment; and, unfortunately, in many instances also better than a good deal of what they meet in the streets and even at home. There is no cause for complacency – indeed we are clear that much more thought needs to be given to what can be done in the secondary years – but at least this rather negative praise of what the schools accomplish can, we think, be substantiated. If children have learned to treat one another with consideration and respect, they have a good foundation on which as teenagers they can build when the strong winds of sexual attraction begin to ruffle the relatively placid waters of pre-adolescent companionship. A boy or girl, chameleon-like, is quick to take on the moral characteristics of the environment in which he finds himself. He finds one way of living appropriate at school, another in the streets. If the schools are to do their duty of moral education efficiently – and one strong stand in the tradition of English education even sees this as their main duty – they must come into the open with full and frank treatment of ethical problems, so that boys and girls may perceive that the way of living they have been taught to respect at school is not only appropriate there, but relevant everywhere. This is a task which cannot be hurried; it also is not one of the things that can be finished at fifteen.

It is not only about right and wrong that boys and girls need explicit and frank discussion in which all points of view can be expressed. Adolescence is a period of uncertainty, unwelcome uncertainty, about life as a whole and about man's place in the universe, about what is real, what is true, what is the purpose of it all, and what matters. The adolescent is just as conscious of the different metaphysical assumptions that are made in different circles as he is of different ethical assumptions. He knows, though he could not explain it, that philosophy, religion and behaviour are related to one another. The adolescent needs help to see where he stands, but it must be given with discretion and restraint. He does not want to be 'told', but he wants a guide, and a guide who will be honest in not over-stating a case. There is no period of life when people more need what the Education Act means when it refers perhaps rather unhappily, to 'religious instruction', and no period when it is more difficult to give. What is true of ethics and philosophy is true also of politics. The fact that politics are controversial – that honest men disagree – makes preparation for citizenship a difficult matter for schools. But it ought to be tackled, and not least for the ordinary boys and girls who now leave school at fifteen and often do not find it easy to see any argument except in personal terms.

The assertion of independence

One of the main problems raised at the beginning of this chapter was whether a school can provide for the gradual increase of independence which is necessary to adolescent boys and girls, or rather whether it can carry the process far enough to give them some real experience of standing on their own feet at a time when the friendly support of the school is still there to see that the conditions are favourable and that no serious harm occurs. Certainly there is a demand for the independence which money can buy. Boys, and to a less extent girls, are prepared to work for it. Over half the boys in the Social Survey had held paid jobs while still at school – and this was true alike of modern, technical and grammar school pupils. Do the schools accept this fact and draw the necessary conclusions from it in the way in which they treat senior boys and girls at school ? Some schools are much more successful than others in this respect, but the interviews carried out by the Social Survey showed that one-fifth of the boys and one-quarter of the girls who left school as soon as they could gave as their main reason for leaving the fact that they disliked school or some aspect of it. Do they feel that school is holding them down, instead of bringing them up ? They are not likely to tolerate a situation in which they are treated nearly as adults at home and nearly as children at school.

The Social Survey showed that 46 per cent of the boys and 60 per cent of the girls who left modern or all-age schools had no further full-time or part-time education. But it would be quite wrong to suppose that education could do nothing more for these boys and girls. To realize how much undeveloped talent there is in quite ordinary people one has only to look at the experience of the armed forces. The job of the present-day infantryman, for instance, calls for an adaptability and resource which would have surprised the army of a hundred or even fifty years ago. The challenge produces the response. Indeed it was always so. Those occupations, such as the fisherman's, which have called for more than the average capability, have found it. The experience of the test expedition in the Duke of Edinburgh's Award has shown that some boys whose official intelligence rating is very low have been able successfully to meet the considerable demands it makes on what would normally, and rightly, be regarded as intelligence. Why has this talent been left undeveloped ? It is partly caused by the fact that until recently boys and girls left school while they were mere children, and so yesterday's late-developers rarely got a chance; partly because the scope of education was often defined in too narrow and abstract terms to elicit the qualities of practical wisdom, and partly because of the very large classes which were normal until recently, and are not yet by any means things of the past. But where schools have developed fifth-year courses, they have found that their pupils, so far from marking time, have advanced with an unexpected rapidity.

Secondary education is, then, in our view essentially the education of the adolescent. And adolescence coincides much better physically than it does psychologically with the present length of the compulsory secondary course. Until they are sixteen, boys and girls need an environment designed for their needs. Each extension of the school-leaving age obviously brings the schools increasingly difficult emotional and social problems, especially perhaps with the education of girls. But the difficulty of the problems is no reason for refusing to face them, though it is a reason for considering very carefully what qualities are needed in the teachers who will have to deal with them. We may hide, but we do not solve, teenage problems simply by letting boys and girls leave school. Indeed, we condemn many of them to do without the help they need. It is true that the protective side of education is likely to be quite ineffective if the educational side is unsatisfying, but we are convinced that there are sufficient important, fresh educational interests which can be aroused in boys and girls during their teens which are today often left only half-exploited, or barely touched upon, when they leave school.

We conclude that the promise of secondary education for all cannot be redeemed unless it is continued for all to sixteen. This does not, of course, mean that simply keeping all boys and girls at school until they are sixteen will automatically provide them with a secondary education worthy of the name. We recognize that some schools are already discovering how to provide it for completely unacademic pupils, but we know how few they are, though their number is growing. There is much to be done if the schools are to be ready for a higher school-leaving age by the date we recommend.

92 Ministry of Education
from Circular 8/60, 31 May 1960, pp. 1–2.

*The fifties and sixties were marked, in education, by a crucial
shortage of teachers. 'Teacher supply' was the major problem facing
successive Ministers of Education, and in 1960, the Ministry had to
place an official ban on the provision of any more nursery schooling in an
effort to reduce the demands for teaching staff to so-called 'non-essential'
work. The ban, with various elaborations, was to stay in effect for twelve
years.*

There is no change in the circumstances which have made it impossible to
undertake any expansion in the provision of nursery education. The
Minister wishes, however, to consolidate the current guidance on this
subject and to bring it up to date, especially in view of the recent development of part-time education. Circulars 175, 202, 280 and 313, Administrative Memoranda Nos. 103, 120 and 129, and paragraph 17 of Circular 350,
are cancelled.

The attention of authorities is drawn to the definition of 'nursery class'
in Regulation 3 (1) of the Schools Regulations, 1959, as 'a class mainly for
children who have attained the age of three years but have not attained the
age of five years'. The provisions of this circular apply to all such classes,
whether or not they were regarded as nursery classes before the coming
into operation of these regulations.

Policy

Authorities are required by section 8 (2) (b) of the Education Act 1944
to have regard 'to the need for securing that provision is made for pupils
who have not attained the age of five years by the provision of nursery
schools or, where the authority considers the provision of such schools
to be inexpedient, by the provision of nursery classes in other schools'. It
has not, however, at any time since the Act came into operation been possible to undertake any expansion in the provision of nursery education.

The White Paper on Secondary Education for All, issued in December
1958, announced a five-year programme devoted principally to the improvement of secondary education and also emphasized the urgent need to
reduce the size of classes in both primary and secondary schools. No
resources can at present be spared for the expansion of nursery education
and in particular no teachers can be spared who might otherwise work with
children of compulsory school age.

At the same time the Minister values the excellent work being done in nursery schools and classes, and is anxious to ensure its continuance, both for its own sake and as a base for expansion in the future when the time comes for a full application of the principles set out in the 1944 Act. He believes therefore that authorities will best carry out their statutory responsibilities at the present time by maintaining the provision of nursery education at its present level wherever conditions are satisfactory, by securing advances in the already high quality of the service and in the effective use of current resources.

Thus the Minister cannot encourage authorities to propose any new nursery schools, except by way of replacement where existing buildings have to be taken out of use, or any enlargement of nursery schools which would require increased staff according to the standards set out in Part IV of this circular; but equally he would deprecate any proposal to discontinue an existing school working in satisfactory conditions and meeting a clear need.

In the case of nursery classes the Minister is especially concerned to ensure that teachers are not diverted from the teaching of older children. There may be infant schools with declining numbers of pupils which find themselves with spare accommodation which would be suitable for nursery classes and it may appear that such classes could be satisfactorily staffed. The Minister is convinced, however, that over the whole area of an authority any net increase in the number of pupils under compulsory school age must, if adequate staff is provided, reduce the supply of teachers available for older children.

93 Jean Floud, A. H. Halsey and F. M. Martin

from *Social Class and Educational Opportunity*, 1957, pp. 139-49.

A direct attack on the concept of the 'pool of ability' and on the socially divisive effects of selective secondary education was made by the budding social science of educational sociology in the late fifties. Research from a number of quarters drew attention to the waste of human talent and the deprivation of opportunity afforded by the educational system, and pointed up the continuing class bias within that system. The work of Floud, Halsey and Martin was a pioneering effort in the field, and preceded the enormously influential reader, Education, Economy and Society *(1961) which appeared a few years later, and brought together a mass of evidence on these themes.*

Our inquiries took as their starting point the account of the history of the social distribution of educational opportunity which emerged from the investigation into occupational selection and mobility undertaken at the London School of Economics in 1949. The object was to look more closely than was possible on a national scale into the part played by the educational system in the process of social selection, and at the impact of the Education Act of 1944 on the particular role of the grammar schools. This is an account of the first stage of the work which is being undertaken in a traditionally prosperous district in the south of England – the south-west Educcational division of Hertfordshire – and in an industrial county borough in the north – Middlesbrough, Yorkshire – which has had a chequered economic history and in which educational reform has had to face greater material difficulties.

In the years of our inquiry in both areas, virtually the full quota of boys with the necessary minimum IQ from each occupational group in the population were awarded places in grammar schools. If by 'ability' we mean 'measured intelligence' and by 'opportunity' access to grammar schools, then opportunity may be said to stand in close relationship with ability in both these areas today. Though they are not in any strict sense representative areas they are by no means untypical of their kind, and we may reasonably conclude that in very many, if not in most, parts of the country the chances of children at a given level of ability entering grammar schools are no longer dependent on their social origins.

The story of educational change leading up to this achievement in south-west Hertfordshire and Middlesbrough illustrates the way in which the social and educational pressures of the national situation worked themselves out under very different local conditions.

In the nineteenth century educational provision was frankly viewed in terms of occupation and class. Secondary education led to middle-class occupations; elementary instruction was for workmen and servants. If a conspicuously able child of the working class received the education appropriate to middle-class children, he owed it to success in the competition for scarce scholarships provided by private charity. In south-west Hertfordshire and Middlesbrough, as elsewhere, scholarships were provided 'to enable boys and girls of exceptional ability to proceed from the elementary schools to the Endowed schools', and in the early days of the educational ladder the middle-class prerogative was anxiously watched. In 1904, the headmaster of the Watford Grammar School saw 'no element of difficulty or danger' in having 10 per cent of his scholars drawn from the elementary schools; in his opinion it constituted sufficient provision 'for enabling poor boys of exceptional ability to rise from the elementary to the secondary schools'.

In the generation which followed the 1902 Act there was an unprecedented expansion of secondary education in which the grammar schools in south-west Hertfordshire and Middlesbrough played their part. In 1892 there were well-informed complaints of public apathy towards 'intermediate' education, but thirty years later, the situation had been transformed. Every year after the First World War a greater number of parents sent their children to the secondary schools as fee-payers. Competition for the safety and prestige of a black-coated job was growing keener and a secondary education became an indispensable investment to secure a good occupational prospect. The provision of free secondary education was related to the demand for fee-paying places when in 1907 official policy stipulated that a number of free places should be provided annually in schools on the Grant List proportionate to the total number of pupils admitted in the previous year.

Even before the First World War more than one-quarter of the growing total number of places in the grammar schools in both areas were open to competition. As the proportion grew, after the war, the middle-class and lower middle-class character of the schools was undermined, slowly in south-west Hertfordshire and quite rapidly in Middlesbrough, by the inflow of pupils of working-class origin. To some observers equality of opportunity already appeared to be a reality in the 1920s. Lord Birkenhead went so far as to claim that 'the number of scholarships from the elementary schools [is] not limited, awards being made to all children who show capacity to profit'.

The assumption that the educational ladder was for the exclusive use of the gifted poor became more and more unreal with each increase in the provision of places open to competition, and the expansion of the grammar schools had profound effects upon the social composition of the primary, then called 'elementary', schools. These schools, and through them the competition for free places in grammar schools, were always open to those of the middle and lower middle classes who cared to use them. The small minority of parents who could afford to realize higher aspirations for their children sent them to independent schools, and others used the private schools and the preparatory departments of the grammar schools. But an increasing number sent their children, especially their sons, through the rough and tumble of the elementary schools.

The result was that as the scholarship ladder widened it carried an increasing number of middle-class boys, and the competitive strength of working-class boys declined. After 1933, when economies were introduced to meet the economic depression, a place won in competition meant, more often than not, partial rather than total remission of fees, and the selection examination was opened to children attending private schools as well as public elementary schools. Boys of middle-class origin, and particularly those from lower middle-class families of clerks, small business people, tradesmen, etc., took up an increasing share of fee-paying places; they also improved their competitive strength with every increase in the number of places open to award. The long-term decline in the competitive strength of working-class boys was as marked in south-west Hertfordshire, where the proportion of places open to award remained virtually constant up to the Second World War, as in Middlesbrough, where, by 1937, 80 per cent were open to award. The abolition of fees in 1945 accentuated the decline in both areas.

The effect of these developments on the social composition of the schools themselves naturally depended upon the proportion of places open to competition. In south-west Hertfordshire the grammar school was the undisputed preserve of middle class, and especially of lower middle-class boys who, by 1939, represented two-thirds of the annual intake. When all places were opened to competition in 1945, these boys suffered severe competition and today constitute only one-third of the entry. In Middlesbrough working class boys formed 40 per cent or more of the annual intake throughout the decade after 1935, and abolition of fees has not brought about any drastic change in the social composition of the schools such as has taken place in south-west Hertfordshire.

It is obvious that the number of working-class boys entering the grammar schools each year has been increasing fast, and that there are more in the schools today than ever before. Nevertheless, the probability that a working-class boy will get to a grammar school is not strikingly different from what it was before 1945, and there are still marked differences in the chances which boys of different social origins have of obtaining a place. Of those working-class boys who reached the age of eleven in the years 1931–41 rather less than 10 per cent entered selective secondary schools. In 1953 the proportion of working-class boys admitted to grammar schools was 12 per cent in Middlesbrough and 14 per cent in south-west Hertfordshire. Thus, approximately one working-class boy in eight was admitted in Middlesbrough, as compared, for instance, with nearly one in three of the sons of clerks; and approximately one working-class boy in seven in south-west Hertfordshire, as compared with nearly one in two of the sons of clerks.

Our findings as to the social distribution of measured intelligence are closely consistent with those of earlier inquiries, and provide an adequate explanation of these differences. Virtually the full quota of boys with the requisite minimum I Q from every class was admitted to grammar schools and the distribution of opportunity stands today in closer relationship to that of ability (as measured by intelligence tests) than ever before. Yet the problem of inequality of educational opportunity is not thereby disposed of.

We have considered some of the material and cultural differences in the environment of the children who succeed, as distinct from those who do not succeed, in the selection examination for secondary education, and we have shown how the success of children varies with the distribution of these features of the environment even at the same social level. Since measured intelligence is so closely related to the results of the selection procedure our findings are relevant to the problem of the influence of environment on intelligence test scores. But this was not our direct concern, and the features of the environment we have selected for study cannot, of course, be regarded as social determinants of intelligence. Nevertheless, though they touch on less fundamental problems, certain conclusions do emerge concerning the part played by differences of environment in the social distribution of educational opportunity.

In the past, the problem of social waste in education could be seen in comparatively simple terms, for gross material factors overshadowed all others. Poverty caused ill-health and poor attendance; facilities for study could not be provided in slum homes, nor proper instruction given in overcrowded schools; grammar-school places were refused by parents who could not afford to forgo adolescent earnings. But the influence on the distribution of educational opportunity of the material environment in which children live at home and are taught at school before the age of selection is tending to diminish in importance in face of the general prosperity and the measures of social reform which are characteristic of post-war Britain. Social factors influencing educational selection reveal themselves in more subtle forms today.

The present situation at its most favourable is illustrated by the position in south-west Hertfordshire where a generally high minimum degree of material comfort is enjoyed at all social levels. In that area, in 1952, material conditions in their homes did not, at a given social level, distinguish the successful from the unsuccessful candidate in the selection examination. At a given social level, the children who secured grammar-school places were not those whose parents earned the highest income, nor those who enjoyed superior standards of housing. On the other hand, differences in the size of the family, and the education, attitudes and ambitions of parents were reflected in the examination performance of children in all classes. In Middlesbrough the situation was less favourable. In 1953 in that area, purely conditions at home still differentiated the successful from the unsuccessful children even at the same social level. If poor parents were favourably disposed towards their children's education this attitude was less likely than in south-west Hertfordshire to be reflected in the performance of their children in the selection examination. Moreover, the traditional association between poor homes and poor schools persists in Middlesbrough, and places an additional handicap on the child of poor but educationally well-disposed parents. There is still scope for attack on gross economic disabilities. In south-west Hertfordshire, however, virtually everyone enjoys an adequate basic income and good housing which, together with the security of the social services, provide something like the basic ingredients of a middle class or at least lower middle-class existence. The influence of the home on children's educational prospects is more subtle, and the problem of developing and utilizing their ability to the full is educational rather than social.

Once the grosser material handicaps are eliminated, the size of the family emerges as the most important single index of the favourable or unfavourable influence of home environment on educational prospects. Very little is known as to what determines the size of families at different social levels, but there is no doubt about the existence of a relationship between family size and educational opportunity. This relationship obviously has its economic aspect, even in the Welfare State. It is a well-established fact, however, that children from small families, at all social levels, tend on the average to do better in intelligence tests and therefore also in the selection examination for secondary education. Dr Nisbet has suggested that the child of a large family learns verbal skills less effectively from his peers than does the child of a small family from adults, and that he carries the handicap at least until the age of eleven. But the evidence from Middlesbrough suggests that the educational disadvantages of a large family are far less marked for the children of Catholic parents, and if generally true this would cast doubt on the notion that there is some distinctive quality of educational value in the environment of a small family. It may be suggested that family limitation amongst Catholic parents does not correspond so closely to intelligence as it tends to do amongst non-Catholic parents, so that the average level of ability of children from large Catholic families is likely to be higher than of those from large non-Catholic families. In fact, the mean IQ of the children of Catholic unskilled workers, who constituted the largest single social group amongst the Catholic children, was found in 1953 to be slightly higher than that of others at this social level. This finding cannot be interpreted without more information, particularly as to the geographical origins of Catholic parents, and their length of residence in Middlesbrough. Recent immigrants to the area might be temporarily employed in occupations below their capacities, so that their offspring might show greater ability than the average for the unskilled group. However that may be, this problem, and others in the same field of the relations between social class, family environment and educational opportunity, can only be effectively examined through intensive inquiry into children's home environment on case-study lines.

The social waste at the point of selection indicted by Kenneth Lindsay in the 1920s has today been pushed forward *into* the grammar schools where it now occurs at the threshold of the sixth form. In both areas, as nationally, there are marked differences, according to their social origins, in the length of school life and opportunity for further education enjoyed by children at the same general level of ability. It is possible that material differences in home background come into their own again here, even in south-west Hertfordshire, underlying and reinforcing differences of attitude to the value of an extended secondary course and further education on the part of parents and children alike.

However, it seems doubtful, on the evidence available to us, whether parents can be held wholly responsible, at least so far as their early intentions are concerned, for the wastage of children from secondary schools before or when they reach the age of sixteen. It is evident that their strength of purpose as well as their capacity to make sacrifices on behalf of their children's education varies from class to class. But there has undoubtedly been a post-war revolution in parents' attitudes towards their children's education, especially at the bottom of the social scale. The frustration of parents whose children are sent to other secondary schools despite their wish that they should attend grammar schools is not confined to the middle classes. The frustrated minorities of skilled and unskilled working-class parents in Middlesbrough and south-west Hertfordshire were proportionately not so very much smaller than in the lower middle class, and in absolute numbers they were, of course, much larger. Moreover working-class parents who said that they wished their children to attend a grammar school also said, in the great majority of cases, that they were willing to keep them at school at least until the age of sixteen; and a surprisingly large proportion contemplated a leaving age of eighteen or over (one-quarter in Middlesbrough and nearly one-third in south-west Hertfordshire). Admittedly, the proportion of middle-class and lower middle-class parents contemplating a six- or seven-year secondary course for their children was larger and it is often argued that it would be expedient to take this into account in making the selection, at least at the borderline of differences in ability. But it would be difficult on ethical and political grounds to justify such an evasion of a problem which should be regarded as an educational challenge to the schools. Each generation of more or less able children allowed to leave school before or immediately after completing the minimum course (or denied admittance because of their suspected intention of doing so) ensures a recurrence of the wastage in the next generation, even allowing for the possibility that in a number of cases parents may regret their own lack of educational qualifications and encourage their children to take opportunities which they themselves missed.

It is tempting to regard the problem as merely one of 'assimilation' into selective secondary schools with a distinctive tradition and rather specific educational aspirations. The secondary grammar schools, despite considerable regional variety in their social composition, are by tradition schools serving the middle classes. Their traditions and ethos tend to be foreign to the boy or girl of working-class origins and the problem of assimilation is a real one. A small and highly selected minority of working-class free-place pupils may be expected to be assimilated – to become in effect socially mobile, accepting school values, making the most of the course by remaining at school at least until the age of sixteen or, in some cases, until a later age and going on to full-time further education. But when, as is now the case, the grammar school is open to a much wider population, assimilation is more difficult and this approach to the problem becomes less and less fruitful.

The precise nature of the hindrances placed by their home background in the way of educating working-class children in grammar schools urgently needs investigating both for its own sake as an immediate problem of educational organization, and for the light it would throw on the problems and possibilities of the comprehensive school. But in the long run, the problem must be viewed as part of the broader question of the interaction of homes and schools generally – of the influence of the home at each social level on the educability of children in schools of particular types and with particular traditions and aims. The problem of equality of educational opportunity is now more complicated than when it took the simple form of the need to secure free access to grammar schools on equal intellectual terms. With the expansion of educational opportunity and the reduction of gross economic handicaps to children's school performance, the need arises to understand the optimum conditions for the integration of school and home environment at all social levels in such a way as to minimize the educational disadvantages of both and to turn their educational advantages to full account.

94 C. A. R. Crosland

'The Influence of Education', from *The Future of Socialism*, 1956,
pp. 188–90, 196–207.

*The work of the social scientists was interpreted in political terms by
Anthony Crosland into a policy supporting the reorganization of secondary
education along comprehensive lines and, more questionably, but politically
irresistible, the absorption of the private (i.e. public) schools. It was
this policy which he carried with him to the Ministry of Education in
January 1965 when he became Secretary of State for Education and
Science in the Labour government.*

The school system in Britain remains the most divisive, unjust and wasteful
of all the aspects of social inequality. First, it denies even the limited aim of
equal opportunity. Before the war, it did so to an extent which now seems
almost fantastic, so that a high proportion of children had no access to
secondary education of any kind. Of boys born between 1910 and 1929
only 14 per cent of those from State elementary schools achieved a secondary
education, compared with 89 per cent of those from private primary schools.
Taking the occupational status categories described in chapter 8, a boy
from categories 1–3 had five times the chance of a grammar school education
as a boy from categories 6–7 (and thirteen times the chance of reaching a
university) – and this without reference to boys educated at independent
schools. Part of the cause of this deplorable situation was directly economic–
even when a working-class child did win a free grammar school place, his
parents often could not afford to take it up. But mainly it was due to governmental apathy and meanness.

The 1944 Education Act set out to make secondary education universal;
and formally it has done so. Yet opportunities for advancement are still not
equal.

First, the intention was, since it was recognized that the grammar schools
would retain their superior quality and hence their differential advantage as
an avenue to the better occupations, to throw open this advantage, by
abolishing fees and standardizing entry procedures, to all social classes on
equal terms. This aim has not yet been fully realized. The class distribution
of the grammar-school population is still markedly askew. An investigation
in 1951 showed that the middle class was still heavily over-represented:[1]
the upper working class, with one-third of grammar-school places, now

1. That is, over-represented from the point of view of equality and justice – not necessarily, as things now are, from the point of view of efficiency.

reasonably well represented: but the lower working class, with only 15 per cent of places, still heavily under-represented.[2] And not only do proportionately more middle-class children enter the grammar schools, but once there they do much better. Children from professional and managerial families account for 15 per cent of the total population, 25 per cent of the grammar-school population, and 44 per cent of the sixth-form population. 'From the children of [such] parents at one extreme to the children of unskilled workers at the other there is a steady and marked decline in performance at the grammar school, in the length of school life, and in academic promise at the time of leaving.'[3]

These contrasts are much larger than can be explained on genetic grounds. No doubt the proportion of high-IQ children is greater amongst the middle class than amongst the working class; but given the far higher absolute numbers of the latter, one would still expect them to show significantly better results than they do. The explanation must be looked for partly in social influences – the less educated parents, the more crowded (and noisy) homes, the smaller opportunities for extra-curricular learning, of working-class children: and partly in financial factors – a child continuing at school is still a heavy financial strain on working-class parents, and one which could at least be mitigated, and early leaving thus discouraged, by more generous maintenance payments and an extension of family allowances. But, for the present, equal opportunity is subject to definite limitations.[4]

But the question of grammar-school places is relevant only to the above-average child. Matters are much worse when we turn to the average child. The least we can ask for is that all ordinary children, irrespective of social background, should enjoy a good primary and secondary education in decent buildings, with classes of reasonable size, and up to a reasonable age. This the children of better-off parents enjoy in the independent schools. But many working-class children, owing to the appallingly low quality of parts of the State educational system, are still enjoying nothing of the sort.

The handicap arises mainly from overcrowding and bad buildings. The deficiencies on these two counts are by now notorious. The select Committee on Estimates wrote in 1953 that 'at every point they were confronted with overcrowding, lack of schools, a shortage of teachers, and often rapidly deteriorating and even dangerous school buildings. . . . The condi-

2. A. H. Halsey and L. Gardner, 'Social mobility and achievement in four grammar schools', *Brit. J. Sociology*, March 1953.

3. *Early Leaving* (HMSO, 1954).

4. This is quite apart from the notorious inequalities of opportunity deriving from the unequal *geographical* distribution of grammar-school places.

tion into which many of the older schools in the country have fallen is the worst feature. Some of them are no better than slums. No doubt matters are gradually – though very gradually – improving; and the situation will be greatly eased when the population 'bulge' has finally left the schools in the early 1960s.

But one cannot speak of even an approach to equal opportunity until the average size of class in State schools has been substantially reduced: the 'all-age' schools, which still deny a proper secondary education to over 700,000 children, have been reorganized: the black-listed slum schools have been closed down: the many structurally sound but grimly forbidding Victorian Gothic schools in industrial towns have been improved: the school-leaving age raised: and County Colleges opened as envisaged in the 1944 Act. This is, of course, simply a matter of money and resources, on which something is said later in the chapter. [. . .]

The implementation (though it is not clear that it was the intention) of the 1944 Act was in terms of a tripartite secondary school system – grammar, secondary modern and technical – the three streams being divided out by a selection at 11+. Although there was supposed to be 'parity of esteem' between the three types of school, it was recognized that the grammar schools would long retain their superiority; and the 11+ examination, combined with the abolition of grammar-school fees, was intended to provide an equal opportunity for all children to enjoy this superior advantage.

It was precisely because the advantage was so superior that the 11+ examination assumed such overwhelming importance, both objectively and subjectively, in the years following the war. Not only did the grammar school often start with a long-standing prestige, while the secondary modern started with none; not only did it offer an immensely superior education at a time when the secondary modern school was being improvised, usually from scratch, and in wholly unsuitable buildings: but it also represented the main, if not the only, avenue to well-paid, non-manual, high-status occupations. This reflects the fact that as the small man and the self-employed give way to the large-scale managerial structure, and as technical proficiency becomes increasingly essential, educational qualifications (which in this context mean a grammar-school background) become more and more the indispensable condition of rising in the social scale.

We have here a microcosm of what a national elite system of education, based on competitive entry, might look like. One thing cannot be doubted, that it would be exceedingly unpopular. The 11+ examination came to be bitterly disliked and resented. It was thought that a child's whole future was decided on a single day's test.[5] No doubt much of the dislike was based on ignorance or exaggeration. The results were in fact never decided on a single day's test. Immense care was commonly taken over borderline cases. There was always provision (though often imperfect) for re-testing and transferring 'late developers'. And the better secondary modern schools began increasingly to provide advanced courses and thus a route to the higher occupations.

But there was quite sufficient truth in these intuitive fears to give them a genuine validity. Nor were they assuaged by the seeming justice of the process of selection – indeed this may actually have exacerbated the resentments. At any rate the depth of these fears and subsequent resentments and the intense mental and nervous strain imposed on parents and children alike by the knowledge of what was at stake, strongly underline the argument that equal opportunity, if combined with marked educational and social disparities, will not create a society which is contented and deemed to be just.

There are also, of course, strong practical objections to segregation at 11. It is conceded that mistakes in selection are inevitable, and indeed occur on a wide scale.[6] The question is whether any practicable provision for later transfer can adequately correct them, given the upheaval involved in changing schools, the social disgrace for children who are graded downwards, and the pressure on overworked headmasters and education officers. Nor is it clear that there is any logic in this particular tripartite division – that there are in fact three clearly-marked types of child, which can be neatly sorted and labelled in this way: or even if there were, that the numbers in each could be accurately predetermined, as they must be if separate schools are to be built for them. The whole business has a distinctly arbitrary air.

If we add to these drawbacks, inherent in the segregation of grammar-school children, the parallel drawbacks which would attach to a still further selection for free places in the public schools; and if in addition to the practical drawbacks we consider the divisive and stratifying effect, wholly unknown in most other advanced countries, of educational segregation at wide varying levels of social prestige and advantage, then we must surely incline, as socialists, towards a 'comprehensive' system of educa-

5. The middle and upper classes, if they have girls of university age, are now gaining an inkling of what the 11+ examination is like from the extremely competitive conditions of entry into women's colleges at Oxford and Cambridge.

6. How fallible the selection process is can be judged by the fact that 24 per cent of the grammar-school population leave at fifteen and only 17 per cent avail themselves of the hard-won opportunity of staying until eighteen (*Early Leaving*).

tion, under which all children would ideally share the same broad experience at least up to the official school-leaving age. Indeed if the argument of previous chapters is accepted, this would seem, if we had a free choice in the matter, a condition of creating an equal and 'classless' society.

Comprehensive schools in principle

In fact we do not have a completely free choice, since we inherit an elaborate non-comprehensive school structure, which cannot be forcibly dismantled. For this and other reasons the Labour Party could never impose a comprehensive system rapidly on the entire country. Nevertheless we have some choice in the matter; and we must therefore consider the arguments commonly brought against comprehensive secondary education.

The most forceful opposition spokesman has been Dr (now Sir) Eric James.[7] He bases his case on a passionate belief in the importance of 'leadership' – an importance greater than ever now that the range of social problems has become so wide and complex. The nurture of potential leaders, he argues, must be the first concern of the educational system; this requires their segregation into separate schools; and any egalitarian sentiment must give way to this overriding aim.

No reasonable person would deny that leadership is important. But general statements do not advance matters very far. For instance, how wide a gap in status is required between the leadership elite and the rest of the community? How do we weigh the need for leadership against other social 'goods', such as democracy, or equality, or group participation? And, more fundamentally, can we so precisely delineate the qualities needed for leadership that we could, even if we so wished, build our entire educational structure round them?

Dr James lists these qualities as high intelligence, an intensive academic education, integrity, courage, judgement, stability, tact and perseverance.[8] But some of the most effective leaders in history have been illiterate, academically moronic, dishonest, unstable, neurotic, if not actually insane or epileptic. Even if we exclude 'bad' leaders and confine ourselves to 'good' ones, we still find a great many of the latter, indeed probably a majority who have had no intensive academic education (and still more who have had no tact). In fact the above is just a list of 'optimum' leadership qualities so vague and general that almost anything can be read into it.

All we can say about leadership is that as an absolute concept it has little or no meaning. The quality of leadership is specific to particular situations; 'what makes for good leadership in one situation may actually militate

7. *Education and Leadership* (1951).
8. The qualities, evidently, of a successful headmaster.

against it in another';[9] and group psychology has not advanced to the point where we can be sure of how to elicit the leadership qualities required by different situations.

However, we have to make common-sense judgements; and surely all the evidence is against the view that the type of leadership required today is likely to be the type encouraged by an elite system of education. No doubt Plato and Arnold were all very well in their day; but it would be distinctly odd if educational systems adapted in the one case to an idealized oligarchy of philosopher-kings, and in the other to the needs of a far-flung British Empire, were equally well adapted to a democratic, egalitarian, mid-twentieth-century society.

Most people would, I suppose, agree that leadership today called for three attributes, apart from a list of desirable moral qualities: it must be characterized by good judgement in public affairs, it must be technically efficient, and it must be democratic. The first attribute, more than ever necessary by reason of the growing scope and complexity of public action so rightly stressed by Dr James, does not obviously demand an intensive academic education. It requires a measure (no more) of brains and intelligence, a 'feel' for situations, a sense of the possible, great psychological intuition, and a knowledge of public affairs. It does not require exceptional academic attainments, as anyone who has been both in academic life and politics well knows, nor, so far as one can see, a special, separate education; indeed, if anything, one would suppose the opposite both *a priori* and judging by the lack of this practical wisdom amongst so many contemporary intellectuals.

On the question of technically efficient leadership, there is often a misunderstanding. It is sometimes said that the selective education of the most talented children is essential to Britain's survival in a competitive and technical world. But what this survival calls for is simply a great deal more expenditure on research, applied science, technical colleges and so on; and this does not require segregated secondary schools of the type suggested, as the example of the US clearly shows. And there is a more general confusion here. Where Britain lags behind the US is not in the calibre of the top academic or 'grammar-school' section of the population, but in the *average* technical ability lower down the scale. From this point of view we positively need less concentration on an educational elite, and more on the average standard of attainment. It is here that Britain is always weakest; and America gains competitively far more from having eight times the proportionate number of students in (often second-class) universities,

9. J. A. C. Brown, *The Social Psychology of Industry* (1954, p. 221). The whole of Dr Brown's chapter on 'Leaders and Leadership' is highly relevant to this issue.

than Britain gains from having public schools and grammar schools.

Lastly, the democratic quality of leadership. Dr James argues that segregation along Platonic lines represents a 'profoundly democratic conception', since it provides equal opportunity without regard to birth or wealth.[10] Certainly this is more democratic than segregation without equal opportunity, such as we have at present. But this is scarcely the relevant comparison, and one cannot reasonably maintain that any system of segregating a particular group of children, however chosen, into superior schools offering superior prospects, is more democratic than a system in which all children share broadly the same education. And whichever is the more democratic conception, the latter is surely more likely to foster democratic attitudes.

We cannot, I think, yet be at all sure what system of education is most likely to generate the type of leadership which we require; indeed it is not altogether clear, in our rapidly changing society, what type of leadership we do require. But prima facie judgements, and a consideration of the experience of other countries, certainly do not point unequivocally to a Platonic elite.

One may be allowed to ignore other arguments, allegedly of principle but in fact rather emotional, such as that to object to an 'aristocracy of learning' is to display 'social prejudice', or a bias in favour of mediocrity, or 'a purely political' attitude, or an indifference to the needs of individual children and hence to the requirements of the community.[11] We may assume that neither set of protagonists is more prejudiced, political or callous than the other; but that they simply differ on how various values are to be weighed, how the community can best be organized, and how the needs of children *as a whole* can best be met. Nothing is to be gained by the use of prejudicial language.

10. But so far as Plato himself is concerned, most people would prefer Mr Crossman's judgement. 'Plato's philosophy is the most savage and the most profound attack upon Liberal ideas which history can show. It denies every axiom of 'progressive' thought and challenges all its fondest ideals. Equality, freedom, self-government – all are condemned as illusions which can only be held by idealists whose sympathies are stronger than their sense' (R. H. S. Crossman, *Plato Today*, 1937, p. 132).

11. It seems hard that socialists should have to bear the entire brunt of this disapproval, since many highly respectable non-socialists have also objected to an aristocracy of learning. Even so impeccably constituted a body as the Fleming Committee regarded 'any segregation of the particularly gifted children of the country as altogether unfortunate. . . . If school is to be a true community, it must contain children of varying intellectual qualities. . . . Any attempt to make use of the schemes which we propose in order to segregate the abler children and to send them to boarding schools would be socially and educationally wrong.' They therefore rejected 'without hesitation' any idea of a competitive examination for the free public-school places (p. 71).

Comprehensive schools in practice

But many people still object to the idea of comprehensive schools, not necessarily on grounds of principle, but simply because they fear the results may be bad in practice. The most common fears are, generally, that standards will be lowered, and the clever child held back to the pace of the average child: and specifically that if the school is to cater adequately for advanced and sixth-form study, it must be vast in size – Dr James mentions a figure of 5000 – and so sacrifice any intimate, personal quality, and all chance that the headmaster will know all his pupils personally.

These are matters to be determined factually; and in this country, with (at the time of writing) only some fourteen comprehensive schools as yet in being, there is naturally no conclusive evidence. But a careful study of the experiments to date affords at least preliminary evidence; and this does not bear out the fears expressed. There is no sign of any levelling-down of standards, and some evidence even of the reverse. The main reason is that the comprehensive schools have not, as many feared (and some hoped) that they would, mixed children of different abilities in the same class, but have adopted a system of testing and differentiation designed to produce homogeneous classes of more or less similar standards of attainment.

This has shocked some comprehensive enthusiasts, who had hoped for a system of 'social promotion' on the American model, with virtually no grading by ability.[12] But both common sense and American experience suggest that this would lead to a really serious levelling-down of standards and a quite excessive handicap to the clever child. Division into streams according to ability, remains essential.

This does not mean, as some critics suggest, that the whole experiment is then a waste of time, since this selection by ability will reproduce all the evils alleged against the 11 + examination. This is to get the matter out of perspective. The object of having comprehensive schools is not to abolish all competition and all envy, which might be rather a hopeless task, but to avoid the extreme social division caused by physical segregation into schools of widely divergent status, and the extreme social resentment caused by failure to win a grammar (or, in future, public) school place, when this is thought to be the only avenue to a 'middle class' occupation. That division and that resentment bear no relation whatever to the effects of grading *within* a single school, with the possibility of re-grading at any time simply by moving across a corridor. One has only to think of the present public schools, where it could hardly be maintained that the divisions and resent-

12. Some of them, their heads perhaps a little turned by too much sociology, even insist on classes being known not by numbers, but by the teachers' names, lest any mark at all of superior or inferior status be conferred. This is simply egalitarianism run mad.

ments created by failure to get into the sixth form, or to become a prefect, are in any way comparable with those caused by failure to win a grammar school place.

So far as the sixth-form argument is concerned, the evidence is necessarily inconclusive. It is not true that all comprehensive schools will in fact be vast; most of those now projected are for well below 1500 pupils, and some for only 500–600. Even supposing the average size to be 1000, it is not clear to the layman, given a reasonable devolution, that this must be disastrous. Many public schools are of a comparable size; and most of their products whom I know had little personal contact with their headmaster for which they now seem none the worse. At any rate, the existing comprehensive schools appear to provide for advanced work at least as adequately as do most grammar schools; and this is a criticism which so far, at least, must be regarded as non-proven.

Much of the argument against comprehensive schools proceeds by analogy. The critics point to the low standards characteristic of many American high schools. These low standards are not in dispute. But there are many possible explanations besides the comprehensive character of these schools: for example, the anti-highbrow and anti-academic (anti-egghead') tradition of American life, the acute shortage of teachers (especially male teachers), the low quality of many of the teachers (amounting sometimes almost to illiteracy),[13] the insistence on automatic 'social promotion' by age-groups and the lack of grading by ability, an excessive attachment to Deweyism and 'life-adjustment' education at the expense of more basic academic disciplines, the overwhelming preference for vocational courses, and so on.[14] All or any of these influences, none of which are or need be reproduced in English comprehensive schools, may be responsible for the lower standards.

This is confirmed by the experience of Sweden, which has recently embarked on the experiment of replacing a tripartite by a comprehensive system of education. (Indeed the comprehensive schools are actually to embrace primary as well as secondary age-groups.) This experiment appears to be proceeding most successfully. The size of school varies from 200 in rural areas to 1200 in Stockholm; and no one suggests that a much larger size is necessary to ensure an adequate grammar school stream. Educa-

13. 'Can Our Teachers Read and Write?' *Harpers' Magazine*, November 1954. Of course it is not intended to suggest that these low standards are universal; but the average teaching standard is certainly lower than in England.

14. The range of subjects taught is often distinctly bizarre – from driver education and consumer buying at one end, to the study of 'boy and girl friendships', 'one's own personality', and 'plans for marriage' (for senior pupils only) at the other. I have taken these examples from an actual high-school prospectus.

tional standards have been maintained. There is no disagreeable status gap or resentment between the different streams. And all the major political parties are supporting the experiment. Taking Sweden and America together, it seems clear that the results of comprehensive education are not uniquely determined by the fact of 'comprehensiveness', but depend mainly on the cultural traditions of the country concerned.

And surely the analogy of the pre-war public schools is relevant. Many of them then bore a close resemblance to a comprehensive school. They were often extremely large – certainly too large for the head to know each individual boy. They taught all faculties – they had, that is to say, the equivalent of grammar, secondary modern and technical streams. They took all intellectual levels, and not simply the top 15 per cent or 25 per cent; indeed with a few notable exceptions, such as Winchester, almost any child, unless an imbecile, could find a place. No doubt the average level of intelligence was higher, owing to the more favourable parental background; but the dispersion was probably not significantly less. Yet the educational results were excellent, even in lesser-known schools where no exceptional heredity factor was at work. It seems that many of the anti-comprehensive arguments are not consistent with a belief in the virtues of the mixed fee-paying public school.

A Labour educational policy

Were we starting *tabula rasa*, I should therefore strongly favour a non-segregated, comprehensive system of schools, with other schools, not indeed abolished, but existing merely as an oblique appendage to the national system, as they do in most other countries, and not as a separate, nationwide top stratum, as in England. The social arguments for this solution seem to me irresistible, the educational arguments against it inconclusive.

We are not, however, starting *tabula rasa*, but with segregated schools already established and strongly entrenched; and even if they were not, we could still not drive straight on to the objective, for the ground ahead is studded with obstacles – the shortage of suitable buildings, the state of public opinion, and the fact of local educational self-determination.

Thus even within the state sector there can be no question of suddenly closing down the grammar schools and converting the secondary moderns into comprehensive schools. These latter require a quite exceptional calibre of headmaster, of which the supply is severely limited: a high-quality staff for sixth-form teaching – again a factor in limited supply: and buildings which would have to be converted, are quite unsuitable. Until and unless the proper supply conditions exist, it would be quite wrong to close down grammar schools of acknowledged academic quality. The result would simply be a decline in educational standards, and discredit on the whole experiment.

Not that this would be possible, in any event, so long as we have local autonomy in educational matters. Only a minority of education authorities at present favour a large-scale conversion to a comprehensive pattern; and no one proposes that the remainder should be coerced. It would, moreover, be absurd from a socialist point of view to close down the grammar school, while leaving the public schools still holding their present commanding position. This would simply intensify the class cleavage by removing the middle tier which now spans the gulf between top and bottom. It is curious that socialists, so often blind to the question of the public schools, should fail to see that 'parity of esteem' within the State sector, combined with a continuation of independent schools outside, will actually increase the *disparity* of esteem in the system as a whole.[15]

What, then, can be done? First, a Labour government should explicitly state a preference for the comprehensive principle, and should actively encourage local authorities – and such advice carries great weight – to be more audacious in experimenting with comprehensive schools in the light of the marked success, described in Dr Pedley's survey, of the experiments to date.[16]

Secondly, where new comprehensive schools cannot or will not be built, the object must be to weaken to the greatest possible extent the significance of the $11+$ examination, and the rigidity of the prestige and physical barriers inherent in the present tripartite stratification. This is partly a matter of money and resources. As new secondary modern and technical schools are built and staffing ratios improve, thus narrowing the gap in standards and general ambience, so the desperate, universal obsession with a grammar school place will weaken. It is partly a matter of facilitating later transfer, so that the 'last chance' atmosphere now attaching to the $11+$ examination is dissipated. And it is partly a matter of severing the present direct and unique link between grammar school and superior occupation – by creating 'grammar-school streams' in secondary modern schools, encouraging the taking of subjects in General Certificate, instituting 'special courses' of a more advanced nature, facilitating late transfer into the sixth-form at grammar schools, and so on. But perhaps the most important step, directly in fostering 'parity of esteem', and indirectly in encouraging these

15. At least until the esteem of the State sector is relatively much higher than it is today.

16. But with the important proviso, in large cities which are divided into rather clearly marked one-class neighbourhoods, that the catchment-areas are so drawn as to straddle neighbourhoods of different social standing.

other reforms, would be the raising of the school leaving age to sixteen.

All this is to some extent a second-best. Late transfers from one school to another are not in general satisfactory; and considering the leeway to be made up, the secondary modern school will not easily achieve parity of esteem. But these changes will at least increasingly break up the present rigid, tripartite pattern – the more so as local authorities experiment with bilateral and other new types of secondary school. Diversification is at least one route towards equality.

But we still face the problem of the independent schools. One important change for the better, as I suggested earlier, may be the gradual closure, as we achieve more equality of wealth, of private preparatory schools, and the disappearance of one early and influential source of class insemination. In the independent secondary schools, the existence of 75 per cent free places will of course weaken their present stratifying influence.

The problem is then twofold. First, these schools must not be allowed to become the breeding-ground of a new, superior intellectual elite. This requires that we carefully attend to the admonition of the Fleming Committee, that the free places in these schools should not go only to the cleverest children, but should be spread amongst a wide cross-section, with a preference, naturally enough, for those who want, or seem apt for, a boarding-school education. And in the long run it requires, in my view, that some of these schools should be converted to other educational uses – as high schools for advanced tuition, short-term boarding establishments, junior universities, adult education centres, and the like.

But a huge gap in social prestige will remain for many years to come. Closing this gap is simply a matter of standards in the State sector, and hence ultimately of priorities in national expenditure. It is true that an air of unreality, even of absurdity, now attaches to this statement. This is because it has so often been made in the last few years, especially in perorations, where it was always sure of a round of applause; but nothing has ever been done to implement it. Only if performance really matches promise – only if, that is, the Labour Party gives education a much higher priority than in the past, and comes to see it as a far greater significance to socialism than the nationalization of meat-procuring or even chemicals – only then will the reality take shape in the form of bricks and mortar, more and better teachers, a longer school life in ample, imaginative surroundings.

Gradually, the schools which children go to will become, as in the United States, not an automatic function of brains or class location, but a matter of personal preference and local accident. The system will increasingly, if the Labour Party does its job, be built around the comprehensive school.

But even in the large non-comprehensive sector, all schools will more and more be socially mixed; all will provide routes to the universities and to every type of occupation, from the highest to the lowest; and it will cease to occur to employers to ask what school job-applicants have been to. Then, very slowly, Britain may cease to be the most class-ridden country in the world.

95 J. W. B. Douglas

from *The Home and the School*, 1964, pp. 120–22.

The arguments of 'equality of opportunity' were reinforced in the sixties by a powerful and influential piece of research in which a national sample of 5000 babies born in 1946 were followed up throughout their youth. The study, under the charge of Dr J. W. B. Douglas, provided convincing evidence that however well-intentioned, the administration of a selective secondary education system led to considerable 'wastage' of ability, especially among working-class children.

Do late transfers to grammar schools or the award of technical school places reduced the social inequalities of 11 + selection?

It has been estimated that, 'even the use of best methods of allocation that, on the basis of our present knowledge can be devised is likely to involve errors in the allocation of approximately 10 per cent of the candidates'. Yet transfers from secondary modern to grammar schools are rare and are, in any case, largely a matter of filling the vacant desks left by pupils who have moved from grammar to other types of school. In so far as they effect the social class differences in educational opportunity, they increase rather than diminish them. The highest proportion of transfers is in the upper middle class, the lowest in the lower manual working class; indeed, of the pupils who do transfer, half come from the middle classes, and this is a far larger proportion than would be expected by chance.

The earlier description of the hazards of secondary selection took no account of the award of places in technical schools. The reason for this omission is that a considerable number of children do not reach these schools until they are thirteen years old; the results of the selection examinations give, therefore, only an imperfect account of the part played by these schools in secondary education. In 1961 we obtained further details of schooling, and so are also able to look at the technical school awards. A total of 5·2 per cent of fourteen year olds were in technical schools and the question is how far shortages of grammar school places are offset by increased opportunity at the technical school level.

It could be argued that social-class differences in educational opportunity are less than they appear in this study, for although manual working-class children get fewer grammar-school places than their measured ability would entitle them to, they largely make up for this disadvantage by the greater number of places they obtain in technical schools. Even if the technical schools are regarded as the equivalent of grammar schools, the manual working-class children are still less well provided for than the upper middle-class children of similar measured ability. Those in the lower manual working classes, for example, get only 85 per cent as many places in grammar and technical schools as do an equivalent group of upper middle-class children. The lower manual working-class boys do better; they get 98 per cent of the places that would be expected for a group of upper middle-class boys of equivalent measured ability, whereas the lower manual working-class girls get only 73 per cent.

If these figures are regarded as showing equality of educational opportunity for the boys, it can be only in a very special and highly restricted and restrictive sense. In the upper middle class there are fourteen pupils in grammar schools for every one in a technical school, whereas in the lower manual working class, there are only two pupils in grammar schools for every one in a technical school. This is a distribution of selective secondary school places that can hardly be justified in terms of social equity or, for that matter, of national interest. Why should a level of ability which leads in one social class to the grammar schools and the universities, lead in another to the technical schools with restricted opportunities for further education and a pattern of early leaving?

96 Committee on Higher Education (Robbins)

'The Pool of Ability', from the Report, 1963, ch. 6, pp. 49–54.

The growth in post-war secondary education led, inevitably, to pressure to expand higher education and the number of university places. The Robbins Report which was to set the seal on this demand, created ten new universities overnight, and endorsed a university boom to parallel the developments chronicled by Webb and Lord Haldane at the turn of the century. But Robbins had to tackle two key questions: were there really

Committee on Higher Education (Robbins)

enough talented young people coming forward to benefit from an expanded
university sector, and if there were, could they put a number to it ?

It is sometimes argued that growth in the number of those able to benefit
from higher education is something that is likely to be limited in the for-
seeable future by biological factors. But we believe that it is highly misleading to suppose that one can determine an upper limit to the number of
people who could benefit from higher education, given favourable circumstances. It is, of course, unquestionable that human beings vary considerably in native capacity for all sorts of tasks. No one who has taught young
people will be disposed to urge that it is only the difference in educational
opportunity that makes the difference between a Newton or a Leonardo
and Poor Tom the Fool. But while it would be wrong to deny fundamental
differences of nature, it is equally wrong to deny that performance in
examinations or tests – or indeed any measurable ability – is affected by
nurture in the widest sense of that word. Moreover, the belief that there
exists some easy method of ascertaining an intelligence factor unaffected
by education or background is outmoded. Years ago, performance in
'general intelligence tests' was thought to be relatively independent of
earlier experience. It is now known that in fact it is dependent upon previous experience to a degree sufficiently large to be of great relevance. And once
one passes beyond tests of this kind and examines for specific knowledge
or aptitudes, the influence of education and environment becomes more
and more important.

Considerations of this sort are important at all stages of education, but
especially at higher stages. For by then the effects of earlier education and
environment in moulding and modifying fundamental biological equipment have produced a cumulative effect. It is no doubt true that there are
born a number of potential 'firsts' whose qualities are such that they win
through whatever their environmental disadvantages, and another,
considerably larger, number who, if trained by the most famous teachers in
history, would still fail their examinations. But in between there is a vast
mass whose performance, both at the entry to higher education and beyond
depends greatly on how they have lived and been taught beforehand.

Of this we have received ample evidence both from our witnesses and
also from a survey we conducted of a sample of men and women aged twenty-
one in August 1962. One of the purposes of this survey was to throw light
on the factors affecting the achievement of school children and their entry
to higher education. The Crowther Report had already indicated the close
association between a father's level of occupation and the educational
achievement of his children at school. As Table 1 shows, our survey con-

Table 1 **Percentage of children born in 1940–41 reaching full-time higher education: by father's occupation, Great Britain**

	Father's occupation	Full-time higher education		No full-time higher education	All children	Numbers (= 100 per cent)
		Degree level	Other			
Boys and Girls	Non-manual (boys and girls)					
	Higher professional	33	12	55	100	15,000
	Managerial and other professional	11	8	81	100	87,000
	Clerical	6	4	90	100	38,000
	Manual (boys and girls)					
	Skilled	2	2	96	100	248,000
	Semi- and unskilled	1	1	98	100	137,000
	Non-manual (boys)	15	4	81	100	70,000
	Manual (boys)	3	2	95	100	189,000
	Non-manual (girls)	9	10	81	100	70,000
	Manual (girls)	1	2	97	100	196,000

Source: Survey of twenty-one years olds.

Notes: 1. The table shows the proportion of children born in 1940-41 who had reached higher education by 1961-2.

2. The figure for total numbers in each group are population estimates based on the survey. The table excludes those whose fathers' occupations were not known and whose fathers were unoccupied or dead.

firmed that the association with parental occupation is, if anything, still closer where higher education is concerned. For example, the proportion of young people who enter full-time higher education is 45 per cent for those whose fathers are in the 'higher professional' group, compared with only 4 per cent for those whose fathers are in skilled manual occupations. The underlying reasons for this are complex, but differences of income, and of the parents' educational level and attitudes are certainly among them. The link is even more marked for girls than for boys.

Clearly the economic circumstances of the home are very influential: even in families of the same occupational level, the proportion of children reaching full-time higher education is four times as high for children from families with one or two children as from those where five or more children have claims on the family's resources. Thus a continuing growth in family incomes is likely to increase still further the demand for higher education. There is also a very important influence from the educational background of the parents (although this is, of course, related to their social class or occupation). As Table 2 shows, the proportion reaching full-time higher education is eight times as high among children whose fathers continued their own education to the age of eighteen or over as among those whose fathers left school under sixteen.[1] These facts suggest that, just as since the war more children have stayed on at school for a full secondary education, so in

Table 2 **Percentage of children born in 1940–41 reaching full-time higher education: by father's age on completing full-time education Great Britain**

Father's age on completing full-time education	Full-time higher education		No full-time higher education	All children	Numbers (= 100 per cent)
	Degree level	Other			
18 or over	32	11	57	100	22,000
16 or 17	14	7	79	100	41,000
Under 16	2	3	95	100	491,000

Source: Survey of twenty-one year olds.

Notes: 1. The table shows the proportions of children born in 1940-41 who had reached higher education by 1961-2.

2. The figure for total numbers in each group are population estimates based on the survey. The table excludes those whose fathers' ages for completing full-time education were not known.

turn more of their children will come to demand higher education during the 1970s. The desire for education will tend to spread as more and more parents have themselves received a fuller education.

This in itself is, of course, no guarantee that the quality of students will be maintained if there is an increased entry. There is, however, impressive evidence that large numbers of able young people do not at present enter higher education. Table 3 gives some of the results of a recent Ministry of

1. When a similar analysis is done in relation to the mother's educational level the differences are nearly as great as those shown in Table 1.

Education survey of school leavers which, at our request, was extended to provide information on parental occupation and on performance at the age of eleven. Column 1 shows that, of grammar-school leavers with a given measured ability at the age of eleven, the proportion obtaining the qualifications for entry to higher education varies widely according to their social

Table 3 **Percentage of leavers from maintained grammar schools having two or more passes at Advanced level: by grading in 11 + and father's occupation, England and Wales, 1960–61**

Grading in 11+	Father's occupation	Percentage of leavers of all ages who have 2 or more A-levels (1)	Percentage of leavers of all ages who leave aged 18 and over (2)	Percentage of leavers aged 18 and over who have 2 or more A-levels (3)
Upper third	Professional and managerial	57	55	79
	Clerical	44	39	74
	Skilled manual	38	40	77
	Semi- and unskilled	21	23	81
Middle third	Professional and managerial	33	42	63
	Clerical	18	29	56
	Skilled manual	18	27	59
	Semi- and unskilled	10	15	58
Lower third	Professional and managerial	14	32	43
	Clerical	16	22	58
	Skilled manual	10	18	51
	Semi- and unskilled	4	7	53
Transfer from secondary modern school		15	29	49
All groups at 11+	Professional and managerial	37	46	67
	Clerical	26	32	64
	Skilled manual	22	29	65
	Semi- and unskilled	11	17	56
All children		24	31	65

Source: *Statistics of Education*, 1961, supplement to Part 2, Table 13.

background. Children of manual workers are on average much less successful than children of the same ability in other social groups. This is largely because they leave school earlier. A comparison of columns 1 and 2 of the table shows that the proportion of children of manual workers who stay on to the age when the General Certificate of Education at Advanced level is normally attempted is smaller than the proportion of middle-class children who actually achieve two passes at Advanced level. But as may be seen from column 3 of the table those children who do stay on are on average as successful as children of the same ability in other social groups.

While the reserves of untapped ability may be greatest in the poorer sections of the community, this is not the whole of the story. It is sometimes imagined that the great increase in recent years in the numbers achieving good school-leaving qualifications has occurred almost entirely among the children of manual workers. This is not so. The increase has been as great among the children of professional parents, where the pool of ability might have been thought more nearly exhausted. In these groups the performance of children of a given measured ability has in fact continually improved. The desire for education, leading to better performance at school, appears to be affecting children of all classes and all abilities alike, and it is reasonable to suppose that this trend will continue.

The quality of primary and secondary education and its organization also affects the proportion of children who emerge as capable of entering higher education. Reductions in the size of classes, and the lengthening of the period of higher education for school teachers, should both tend to increase the number of those who achieve good qualifications at school. It is probable that courses leading to the General Certificate of Education will continue to become more widely accessible. The evidence suggests that the degree to which children experience an academic environment has a major influence on whether they make the best of their talents. Table 4, for example, shows how in 1960 the proportion of children going into the sixth form varied between areas of differing grammar-school provision. Where the provision was liberal, some 12 per cent of children stayed on, compared with only 7 per cent in areas of relatively low provision.

During the later 1950s, when this group of children reached the statutory school-leaving age, there were comparatively few schools, other than grammar schools, that offered academic courses leading to the General Certificate of Education. Since then the number has been continually increasing and the habit of staying on may also be expected to grow.

Finally it should be observed that fears that expansion would lead to a lowering of the average ability of students in higher education have proved unfounded. Recent increases in numbers have not been accompanied by an increase in wastage and the measured ability of students appears to be as high as it ever was.[2]

Table 4 **Percentage of children aged seventeen at school in different types of local education authority area: by grammar-school provision and social-class composition, England and Wales, January 1960**

	'Social class' of the area			All areas
Grammar-school provision in the area	High	Middle	Low	
High	14·5	10·6	10·7	12·3
Middle	10·8	9·5	7·9	9·5
Low	*	7·9	6·4	7·2

Notes: 1. The categories used are:
(a) for grammar-school provision, the percentage of thirteen year olds in grammar schools in 1955:
High   23·1 per cent and over
Middle   18·1 per cent–23·0 per cent
Low   Under 18·1 per cent
(b) for social class, the percentage of occupied and retired males aged fifteen and over in the Registrar General's Classes I and II in 1951:
High   22·1 per cent and over
Middle   14·6 per cent–22·0 per cent
Low   Under 14·6 per cent
2. Each figure in the table is a simple (unweighted) average of the percentages found in all the authorities in the category in question.
3. In the category marked * there are only two authorities.

In short we think there is no risk that within the next twenty years the growth in the proportion of young people with qualifications and aptitude suitable for entry to higher education will be restrained by a shortage of potential ability. The numbers who are capable of benefiting from higher education are a function not only of heredity but also of a host of other influences varying with standards of educational provision, family incomes and attitudes and the education received by previous generations. If there is to be talk of a pool of ability, it must be of a pool which surpasses the widow's cruse in the Old Testament, in that when more is taken for higher education in one generation more will tend to be available in the next.

2. Moreover, the performance of manual working-class students at university is as good as that of middle-class students.

97 Committee on Higher Education (Robbins)

'The Total Number of Places for Home Students', from the Report. 1963, ch. 6, pp. 65–6.

Table 1 shows the minimum number of home students in all forms of full-time higher education for whom it is necessary to plan.

Table 1 **Number in thousands of home students for whom places will be needed in full-time higher education, Great Britain, 1962–3 to 1985–6**

1962–3	195
1965–6	262
1970–71	312
1975–6	396
1980–81	507
1985–6	(632)

Note: The figure for 1962–3 shows the actual number of students (provisional data).

These figures involve what to many will seem a startling increase in numbers, and we must therefore repeat that they make no allowance for any relaxation in the standards required to gain places: if there are 507,000 places in 1980 this will make provision only for students not one whit less eligible in terms of school-leaving attainments than those being admitted today. The estimates reflect chiefly the growth in the age groups (requiring some 50,000 more places), and in the proportion of the age group qualifying for entry (this will call for 190,000 more places). They also allow about 45,000 more places for the extra proportions we expect to apply, and about 25,000 more places for modest increases in the average period of study.

That these numbers are only the bedrock on which policy should be based is confirmed by referring again to the implications of our assumptions about the degree of competition. The present standards, both in universities and in training colleges, are, by common consent, considerably higher than the standards of the thirties and are almost certainly higher than those of the early fifties. In the thirties many students entered with qualifications below the present minima: in the early fifties the minimum qualifications were generally the same as at present, but a higher proportion of those who possessed them were admitted. Yet it would be difficult to contend that the number receiving higher education in those decades contained an undue proportion of students incapable of substantial benefit from the process.

Above all, our projections may not have allowed sufficiently for any increased tendency of children, and especially of girls, to stay on at school so as to seek entry to higher education. At the present time in England and Wales, only six girls obtain two or more passes at Advanced level in the General Certificate of Education for every ten boys who do so; in Scotland the equivalent ratio is eight girls to ten boys. Moreover, over the last few years the proportion of boys staying on has if anything risen more sharply than that of girls. It seems possible that the tendency for girls to stay on may gain momentum, and this might become a major feature of the future educational scene. We should greatly welcome a tendency for more girls to stay on at school, if only from the national point of view of making better use of what must be the greatest source of unused talent at a time when there is an immediate shortage of teachers and of many other types of qualified person. If staying-on increases faster in the future than in the past, to that extent our estimates of places will prove too low.

We started this chapter by stressing that our estimates were inevitably attended by uncertainties and the possibility of error. We have tried to base them on as secure a statistical foundation as possible and have explained our assumptions at various stages. We are confident that the projections give the right order of magnitude, and that they are if anything on the conservative side. The result shown in Table 1 will mean that by 1980 this country should be providing entry to full-time higher education for about 17 per cent of the age group. This is only half the proportion of young people who at present enter full-time higher education in the United States. We have no figures that would entitle us to make comparisons with what they and other leading countries will be providing by 1980. But, if the plans of other countries for the years up to 1970, discussed in the last chapter, give any guide, our targets will only be in line with what is likely to happen elsewhere.

98 Central Advisory Council for Education (Newsom)

from *Half Our Future*, 1963, pp. 7–8.

Despite the recommendation of the Crowther Committee of 1959 to raise the school-leaving age to sixteen, the economic crisis of 1961 brought no government response. In 1963, the Newsom Report, which had the brief of looking at the education of the less-academic adolescent, repeated the plea for raising the leaving age. A year later, Sir Edward (now Lord) Boyle, then Secretary of State for Education, announced: 'It is the government's intention that the school-leaving age should be raised to sixteen in 1970–71'; a year later than Newsom advised. The reform was delayed again, but eventually became fact in 1972–3.

Our terms of reference imply, and the whole argument of our report assumes, a school-leaving age of sixteen for everyone. We have again considered the position with great care, and we have unhesitatingly come to the same conclusion as the Council reached in 1959: 'This is a duty which society owes all its young citizens.' The evidence presented to us makes it clear that in the last few years there has been a marked strengthening of conviction in this matter, both among those professionally concerned with education and among the interested general public. The percentage of pupils who voluntarily remain at school beyond the minimum age of fifteen has doubled in the secondary modern schools since 1958,[1] and this in itself testifies to an increasing confidence in the schools and to a belief on the part of many parents in the value of a longer education for their children. Already in some modern schools, pupils are voluntarily remaining not only for a fifth but for a sixth year, and we have little doubt when the formal school-leaving age is raised to sixteen, there will be more pupils voluntarily choosing to stay to seventeen and even eighteen.

But the decision to raise the school-leaving age should not therefore continue to be deferred and progress left to follow its voluntary course. There are still too many boys and girls who, otherwise, will leave at the earliest permissible moment, whatever their potential abilities, because outside pressures are too much for them. Again and again teachers confirm that the pupils with whom we are especially concerned stand to gain a great deal in terms of personal development as well as in the consolidating of attainments from a longer period of full-time education – but it is just these boys and girls who most readily succumb to the attractions of the pay-packet and the bright lights it commands.

1. In 1962, rather more than one-sixth of the age group in secondary modern schools for the country as a whole, and a very much higher percentage for some individual schools and areas. The demand for a longer education is also reflected in the proportion of pupils staying on in the comprehensive schools, and account must be taken of the pupils in full-time courses in further education, particularly in areas where it has been a matter of local policy not to provide fifth-year courses in the modern schools. It must be noted, however, that only 45 per cent of all fifteen year olds in 1961–2 were in any kind of full-time education, at school or in colleges of further education, and quite certainly the great majority of these were not the pupils with whom this report is essentially concerned.

Besides, in the national economic interest we cannot afford to go on waiting. Others are already ahead of us. It is true that we start school a year earlier than most other countries, but there is no reason to assume that the majority of our children are ahead of other people's at the age of fifteen when they leave school. In the United States nearly two-thirds of the population are at high schools until the age of eighteen, and there is currently much concern over 'the drop-outs', many of whom have stayed at school till sixteen. France, with problems of shortages of teachers and of accommodation comparable with our own, has already raised the school-leaving age from fourteen to sixteen for all the pupils who started school in or after 1959.

The French procedure of naming the date on which the higher leaving age will become operative well in advance strongly commends itself to us. In this country, we cannot now afford to wait another ten years until boys and girls who have not yet entered the primary schools become fifteen. But, if the decision were taken quickly, a leaving age of sixteen could be made operative for all pupils who enter the secondary schools in or after 1965: that is, the first year of full-time compulsory education up to the age of sixteen would be 1969–70. The Crowther Report urged the claims of the years 1966–9, when the secondary schools will experience a relative easing in the pressure of numbers, as the most apt for introducing the higher leaving age. The chance of using that spell is virtually gone, but in 1970 at least the actual numbers of boys and girls who will reach the age of fifteen, and who would be the first to be affected by the new provision are relatively low – 655,000 compared with 663,000 in 1969 and with 738,000 in 1975. There would be advantage in making the change when the first age group to be affected is relatively small. There are, in any case, undoubted advantages in taking the decision and announcing the date five years in advance: in this way, the pupils and their parents know from the beginning of the secondary course where they stand, and both teachers and administrators can make their plans with a definite goal ahead.

99 Ministry of Education

from the Report of the Working Party on Schools' Curricula and Examinations, 1964, pp. 9–12.

One of the few major innovations concerning actual educational practice consisted of founding the Schools Council, and it is notable that this new machinery, which brought the schools and the examining bodies together,

*was largely the achievement of a civil servant, Derek Morrell. Morrell, who
was later described in* New Society *as 'one of the great reformers in the
government' was also largely responsible for drafting the Children and
Young Persons Act of 1969, the year of his death, when he was
Assistant Under-Secretary of State in charge of the Children's
Department within the Home Office.*

We were appointed by a representative held in London on 19 July 1963. This was
convened by the Minister of Education to consider a proposal to establish a
Schools Council for the Curriculum and Examinations.

Our terms of reference were defined in the following resolution, which
was adopted unanimously by those present at the meeting:

This representative meeting held in London on 19 July 1963

1. Notes there is wide support for the proposal to establish cooperative machinery
in the fields of the school curriculum and examinations.
2. Appoints a working party comprising, under the chairmanship of Sir John
Lockwood, one representative of each of the bodies present at the meeting,
together with assessors and a secretariat appointed by the Minister of Education,
to consider how effect could best be given to the matters discussed and to make
recommendations.
3. Agrees to reconvene to consider and reach conclusions on the working party's
recommendations.

It was also agreed that the Association of Chief Education Officers should
be represented on the working party, and that all member interests should
be authorized to nominate both full and alternate members.

We have held four meetings, and we now submit our report. Our main
conclusion is that there is a need for new cooperative machinery in the
fields of the schools' curricula and examinations, and we make recommendations for establishing such a body. We suggest that it should be called the
Schools Council for the Curriculum and Examinations, and that it should
include representatives of all the interests principally concerned. We also
propose that it should be set up in time to take over the functions of the
present Secondary School Examinations Council from the beginning of
the 1964–5 academic year.

Aims and principles

We considered first the principles which should govern the relationship
between the schools and other bodies whose decisions and actions may
affect their work.

We noted that it has long been accepted in England and Wales that the
schools should have the fullest possible measure of responsibility for their

own work, including responsibility for their own curricula and teaching methods, which should be evolved by their own staff to meet the needs of their own pupils. We reaffirm the importance of this principle, and believe that positive action is needed to uphold it.

The responsibility of the individual schools for their own work is not, however, an exclusive responsibility. It has inevitably to be exercised within a wider framework which takes account of the general interest of the community, both local and national, in the educational process. Within this general framework, individual schools have to take a wide range of particular decisions on educational content and methods.

The work of the schools also has to be related to the requirements of the many and varied establishments of higher and further education to which many of the pupils will go on leaving school, and to the training arrangements and entry requirements of a wide range of professional bodies and of employers generally. There is thus a complicated, and constantly changing, relationship between the work of the schools and many particular outside interests.

The responsibility placed upon the schools is a heavy one. If it is to be successfully carried, the teachers must have adequate time and opportunity for regular reappraisal of the content and methods of their work in the light of new knowledge, and of the changing needs of the pupils and of society. A sustained and planned programme of work is required, going well beyond what can be achieved by occasional conferences and courses, or by the thinking and writing of busy teachers in their spare time.

We concluded therefore that there was no need to define a new principle in relation to the schools' curricula and examinations. Our task was rather to examine how far the existing principle is being realized in practice, and whether new arrangements are needed to uphold and interpret it.

The outlines of the problem

We are unanimous in recognizing the existence of a problem. There are differences of view on questions of detail, but general agreement on the main outlines. Influences are at work which could in time seriously diminish the responsibility of the schools for their own work; the pressures are already severe in the secondary schools, particularly at the level of the sixth form.

These influences are not sinister. No one is consciously seeking to erode the schools' responsibilities. Indeed, great strides have been made since the turn of the century in freeing the schools from detailed supervision of their work by local and central government: at both levels, the role of the Inspectorate has become advisory rather than supervisory.

The problem is basically one of inadequate coordination where different areas of responsibility touch or overlap, and of an inadequate effort in research and development. There is, for example, insufficient coordination between the development of curriculum content and teaching techniques and policy on examinations, and between the entry requirements of higher and further education and the work of the schools. The resolution of these and other problems is hampered not only by the lack of standing co-operative machinery for studying them, but also by a combination of inadequate information about the existing state of affairs, insufficient research to define new possibilities and insufficient development work to demonstrate practical applications of possible new solutions.

The result is that the schools, and particularly the secondary schools, find that the opportunity for independent initiative and experiment is being reduced by a complex of decisions and pressures which they cannot sufficiently control or influence. They consider, in our view rightly, that the underlying trend is towards an excessive standardization of their work, and away from that variety of syllabus content and teaching methods which is desirable if our educational system is to be in any real sense alive. They also consider, and again we agree with them, that if the scope for innovation by the schools were increased, they would not be able to take full advantage of the new possibilities without a larger effort in research and development, in which the teachers must be enabled to play a full part.

In short, our conclusions on the nature of the problem are as follows:

1. The present arrangements for determining the curriculum in schools and the related examinations are not working well: in particular, teachers have insufficient scope for making or recommending modifications in the curriculum and examinations.

2. Different arrangements are needed to achieve the balanced cooperation of the teachers, the local education authorities, the Ministry of Education, the establishments of higher and further education, and others, in a continuing process of modifying the curriculum and examinations.

3. More resources and more effort should be devoted to cooperative study, research and development in this field.

The nature of the new machinery

We considered next the nature of the new machinery which we believe to be needed. We noted that the Minister of Education had, in February 1962, established a new unit within his Department, known as the Curriculum Study Group. This brings together members of Her Majesty's Inspectorate, local education authority inspectors or organizers, specialists from institutes of education, teachers and administrators for the close and continuous full-time cooperative study of curriculum and examination problems. We welcome this initiative. We also welcome the Minister's subsequent proposal that the range of problems which are the concern of the Curriculum Study Group should be remitted to a body more fully representative of the education service as a whole, and that this body should be supported in its work by interdisciplinary study teams on the model of the Curriculum Study Group. This approach has worked well in the limited context of the new Certificate of Secondary Education examinations, where the relationship between the representative Secondary School Examinations Council and the examinations team of the Curriculum Study Group has enabled the Council to make very thorough preparations for launching the new examinations, based on preliminary studies and research, and on the organization and assessment of trial examinations.

We consider, however, that four main requirements must be met by any plan to extend these new cooperative arrangements to cover the whole field of the schools' curricula and examinations. These are as follows:

1. Control of the new cooperative machinery should be vested in a body fully representative of all those principally concerned. A suitable title for this body would be the Schools Council for the Curriculum and Examinations.

2. The character of the new body should be that of a free association of equal partners who would combine to promote, through cooperative study of common problems, the pursuit of common objectives. The Schools Council would not, in other words, be advisory to the Minister of Education alone: it would be advisory to all its member interests. These interests would retain unimpaired their right to take decisions within their own areas of responsibility but they would seek, through the agency of the Schools Council, to coordinate their decisions in harmony one with another. Authorities and bodies in membership of the Council would, of course, be free to delegate such of the executive functions to the Council as they might consider desirable, just as the Minister now delegates to the Secondary School Examinations Council some of his functions as central coordinating authority for secondary school examinations. We would expect this particular arrangement to continue if and when a Schools Council for the Curriculum and Examinations were set up.

3. The Schools Council should have control of its own work. It should be free to select its own subjects of study, to publish its findings and recommendations, and should have full operational control of its own staff. Where a member interest requested the Council's advice on matters of particular

concern to the member interest concerned, publication of the Council's advice would, however, be a matter for agreement between the Council and the member interest making the request.

4. The new body should be regarded as complementary, and not alternative, to existing agencies for research and development. There is a need for cooperation among those concerned in defining problems for research, and in making a more effective use of research findings. But there is equally a need for more work undertaken on their own initiative by schools, groups of schools, local education authorities, institutes of education, bodies such as the National Foundation for Educational Research, professional associations and others.

On the assumption that all concerned will be prepared to accept these four requirements, we recommend that a Schools Council for the Curriculum and Examinations be set up.

100 C. A. R. Crosland

from the Woolwich Polytechnic Speech, 27 April 1965.

Two years after the Robbins Report on Higher Education had quantified the need for the expansion of the system, and had put forward plans for doing so, the Labour Secretary of State for Education, Anthony Crosland, officially launched the 'binary system', promoting a duality in higher education between the independent universities and the locally controlled F. E. sector. Of his Woolwich speech Crosland afterwards commented: 'I began by making an appalling blunder. . . . It came out in a manner calculated to infuriate almost everybody you can think of, and in public relations terms it did considerable harm to the policy. The more I thought about it subsequently, the more I became utterly convinced that the policy was right . . . but the Woolwich speech put people's backs up quite unnecessarily, and I had to fight the policy through against a great deal of very strong opposition, including some in the Labour Party.'

In their great report, the Robbins Committee pointed out that it would be a misnomer to speak of a *system* of higher education in this country; and they posed the fundamental question as to whether it was desirable that there *should* be such a system. Their conclusion deserves to be quoted:

Higher education, is so obviously and rightly of great public concern, and so large a proportion of its finance is provided in one way or another from the public purse, that it is difficult to defend the continued absence of coordinating principles and of a general conception of objectives. However well the country may have been served by the largely uncoordinated activities and initiatives of the past, we are clear that from now on these are not good enough. In what follows therefore we proceed throughout on the assumption that the needs of the present and still more of the future demand that there should be a system.

The Government accepts this conclusion. We believe that there must be a system in the sense defined, with 'coordinating principles and a general conception of objectives'. And in Britain the system must be based on the twin traditions which have created our present higher education institutions. These are broadly of two kinds. On the one hand we have what has come to be called the autonomous sector, represented by the universities, in whose ranks of course, I now include the colleges of advanced technology. On the other hand we have the public sector, represented by the leading technical colleges and the colleges of education.

The Government accepts this dual system as being fundamentally the right one, with each sector making its own distinctive contribution to the whole. We infinitely prefer it to the alternative concept of a unitary system hierarchically arranged on the 'ladder' principle, with the universities at the top and the other institutions down below. Such a system would be characterized by a continuous rat-race to reach the first or university division, a constant pressure on those below to ape the universities above, and a certain failure to achieve the diversity in higher education which contemporary society needs.

To be precise, we prefer the dual system for four basic reasons.

First, there is an ever-increasing need and demand for vocational, professional and industrially based courses in higher education – at full-time degree level, at full-time just below degree level, at part-time advanced level, and so on. This demand cannot be fully met by the universities. It *must* be fully met if we are to progress in the modern technological world. It therefore requires a separate sector, with a separate tradition and outlook within the higher education system.

Secondly, a system based on the ladder concept must depress and degrade both morale and standards in the non-university sector. If the universities have a 'class' monopoly as degree-giving bodies, and if every college which achieves high standards moves automatically into the university club, then the residual public sector becomes a permanent poor relation perpetually deprived of its brightest ornaments, and with a permanently and openly inferior status. This must be bad for morale, bad for standards, and productive only of an unhealthy rat-race mentality.

Thirdly, it is desirable in itself that a substantial part of the higher education system should be under social control, directly responsive to social needs. It is further desirable that local government, responsible for the schools and having started and built up so many institutions of higher education, should maintain a reasonable stake in higher education.

Fourthly, we live in a highly competitive world in which the accent is more and more on professional and technical expertise. We shall not survive in this world if we alone down-grade the non-university professional and technical sector. No other country does so – consider the Grandes Ecoles in France, the Technische Hochschule in Germany, Leningrad Poly in the Soviet Union. Why should we not aim at this kind of development? At a vocationally oriented non-university sector which is degree-giving and with an appropriate amount of post-graduate work with opportunities for learning comparable with those of the universities, and giving a first-class professional training. Let us now move away from our snobbish caste-ridden hierarchical obsession with university status.

For all these reasons we believe in the dual pattern. The university sector will continue to make its own unique and marvellous contribution. We want the public sector to make its own equally distinctive but separate contribution. And between them we want – and I believe we shall get – mutual understanding and healthy rivalry where their work overlaps.

The Government have already made a number of policy decisions which reflect this philosophy. We have decided that, with one possible exception, there should be no new universities or accessions to university status for about ten years. In the field of teacher training, we have decided that the number of places should be greatly expanded, and that the colleges of education should remain under the administrative and financial control of their present sponsors. And for the technical colleges, we see a distinctive and growing place in higher education, of which I shall say more later. These decisions have laid the foundation for our policy on higher education and will determine the shape of the dual system which we wish to see developed.

I hope that what I have said so far will go some way to still the doubts and anxieties which have recently been expressed in the technical-college world. I know what these doubts have been. Did not the Robbins Committee condemn us to a subordinate role, some are asking? Could we not perhaps improve our status, ask others, by imitating the universities, or transferring some of our work to them, or even, possibly, by seeking absorption by them? Is our method of government consistent with the dignity of higher education institutions? And what exactly is our role?

In case some doubts still linger, I shall now try, within the philosophy of the dual system which I have just described, to elaborate our answers to them.

I shall talk mainly about the colleges which are engaged in higher education. The general public knows far too little of this system; too many people, recalling perhaps their own youth, think of it in terms of night school. The facts are these. In the technical, commercial and art colleges of England and Wales, there were in 1963 130,000 students taking courses at the higher education level – 50 per cent more than in 1958 and more than in the universities. About 33,000 were taking full-time or sandwich courses and nearly 12,000 were taking courses leading to degrees or diplomas in technology. The figures for 1964 will almost certainly show a substantial increase.

These courses are of varying length; they are both full time and part time; and they cover many and diverse subjects. But they all come within the 'further-education tradition' which has been so well described in the recent ATTI report on 'The Future of Higher Education within the Further Education System'.

The underlying assumption, is that the student's primary motivation is the profession he intends to follow. He is committed to a profession from the outset and his course of study is closely integrated with his professional work. He is given direct experience of professional practice at an early stage in his course . . . . He and the staff who teach him maintain close contact with the profession and, as a rule, many of his teachers have themselves spent time practising the professional occupation for which they are preparing him. . . . The technical-college tradition is to maintain close contact with the world of employment and to provide higher education in which education and professional experience are obtained concurrently in a single integrated course.

Within this valuable tradition, the colleges have a threefold role to play as institutions of higher education. First, they will provide full-time and sandwich courses for students of university quality who are attracted by the more vocational tradition of the colleges, and who are more interested in applying knowledge to the solution of problems than in pursuing learning for its own sake. Up till now such students – and the staff who teach them – have been discouraged because in most colleges, though not of course in Woolwich such studies could not lead to a degree unless there happened to be a relevant external degree. The students often faced the unhappy dilemma: of either abandoning a course in one of the applied arts or sciences in favour of a more academic course because only the latter would qualify them for a degree; or of sticking to their chosen course, but foregoing a degree with all it implies in our society as a mark of achievement and prestige.

This difficulty – and with it a major obstacle to the achievement of higher status by the leading colleges – has now been removed by the creation under Royal Charter of the Council for National Academic Awards. The Council will realize in practice the principle laid down by Robbins that equal academic awards should be given for equal performance. It has already been announced that in deciding whether a course qualifies for a CNAA degree, the test will be whether it is comparable in standard and quality with a university course. [. . .]

I am especially glad that the Council shows itself determined to support the continued development of the sandwich course – first in the technologies and then in business studies and other fields. The sandwich-course concept is now well established in the former field; but in subjects outside science and technology it is scarcely known save in a very few colleges and firms. [. . .] With the encouragement of the Council, the colleges can now develop a range of suitable courses for the growing number of students with a background in arts and social studies for whom they will need to provide.

These are fields in which there are big opportunities for innovation and experiment. As compared with technology and science, they are relatively new fields for most of the colleges. But this should not necessarily be a disadvantage. At least there will be no incubus of precedent to hamper thinking. And the colleges start out with important assets – in particular; their close relations with industry and the professions, and their long experience of courses which stress practical relevance rather than pure scholarship.

What might this mean in terms of arts and social studies? Here some highly promising developments seem to be on the way. Much thought is being given to what I might call professionally oriented courses intended to prepare students not only for careers in business and commerce, but also for other professions such as social work and librarianship. We shall need a wide range of such courses. And we shall also need courses for students who are not ready to commit themselves to a particular profession, but who want a preparation for the various careers which are open to arts and social studies graduates – public administration, journalism, broadcasting, as well of course as teaching and business.

The Robbins Committee gave modern languages as an example. They pointed out that the traditional honours course does not meet the practical needs and interests of many would-be language students; and they foresaw a growing scope for courses with a special emphasis on fluency in the use of languages combined with background study of the countries concerned. There must be similar rethinking in other subjects, and I see ample scope for imaginatively devised courses which break with traditional patterns without sacrificing quality. I know that the Woolwich Polytechnic has already developed a course in overseas marketing. So when it comes to the need for innovation, I am preaching to the converted; and you will agree with me that we have only scratched the surface of such possibilities, and that we shall certainly find an infinite variety of possible courses.

But in pursuing this aim, the leading colleges must surely build on their own proud tradition of service to industry, business and the professions, and not set out simply to duplicate the provision in the universities. As the ATTI Report points out, if they seek merely to extend the number of external degree courses they offer, they will come to be regarded as places for students who fail to get into university. Of course they should not try to be different just for the sake of being different. But they should exploit their own traditions and standards of excellence, and develop the fields in which they can make their own distinctive contribution to meeting society's needs.

So much for the first function, in which the colleges complement the work of the universities. Their second function, of vital importance today, falls outside the normal scope of university work. They have the primary responsibility for providing full-time and sandwich courses which, while falling within the higher education field, are of a somewhat less rigorous standard than degree level courses. It is here that the colleges meet the needs of the thousands of young people who will occupy the all-important intermediate posts in industry, business and the professions – the high-level technicians and middle managers who must support the scientists, technologists and top managers in a modern community. These students, both for their own sake and for obvious social and economic reasons, must have a full share of the resources of the colleges, and not be neglected through preoccupation with the first category of student. A college would betray its trust if, in the mistaken pursuit of supposed status, it were to regard these students as of lesser importance.

Thirdly, there are the tens of thousands of part-time students who need advanced courses either to supplement other qualifications, or because for one reason or another they missed the full-time route. There are immense fields of talent and aspiration here; common justice and social need combine to demand that they should be harvested.

101 Department of Education and Science

from Circular 10/65, 12 July 1965, pp. 1–6.

With a Labour government returned to power in 1964, the way was at last clear to reorganize secondary education along non-selective lines; a philosophy which the trades unions had first advocated some eighty years previously. Many authorities had already established comprehensive schools, but now the new Secretary of State, Mr Anthony Crosland, provided a circular which formally 'requested' local authorities to submit schemes of reorganization. There was political pressure and argument for the word to be changed to 'require' but Crosland decided to offer the local authorities the less demanding verb, in the knowledge that many of them were already prepared to 'go comprehensive'.

The organization of secondary education
Introduction

It is the Government's declared objective to end selection at 11 + and to eliminate separatism in secondary education. The Government's policy has been endorsed by the House of Commons in a motion passed on 21 January 1965:

That this House, conscious of the need to raise educational standards at all levels, and regretting that the realization of this objective is impeded by the separation of children into different types of secondary schools, notes with approval the efforts of local authorities to reorganize secondary education on comprehensive lines which will preserve all that is valuable in grammar-school education for those children who now receive it and make it available to more children; recognizes that the method and timing of such reorganization should vary to meet local needs; and believes that the time is now ripe for a declaration of national policy.

The Secretary of State accordingly requests local education authorities, if they have not already done so, to prepare and submit to him plans for reorganizing secondary education in their areas on comprehensive lines. The purpose of this Circular is to provide some central guidance in the methods by which this can be achieved.

Main forms of comprehensive organization

There are a number of ways in which comprehensive education may be organized. While the essential needs of the children do not vary greatly from one area to another, the views of individual authorities, the distribution of population and the nature of existing schools will inevitably dictate different solutions in different areas. It is important that new schemes build on the foundation of present achievements and preserve what is best in existing schools.

Six main forms of comprehensive organization have so far emerged from experience and discussion:

1. The orthodox comprehensive school with an age range of eleven to eighteen.

2. A two-tier system whereby *all* pupils transfer at eleven to a junior[1] comprehensive school and *all* go on at thirteen and fourteen to a senior comprehensive school.

3. A two-tier system under which *all* pupils on leaving primary school transfer to a junior comprehensive school, but at the age of thirteen or fourteen *some* pupils move on to a senior school while *the remainder* stay on in the same school. There are two main variations: in one, the comprehensive school which all pupils enter after leaving primary school provides no course terminating in a public examination, and normally keeps pupils only until fifteen; in the other, this school provides GCE and CSE courses, keeps pupils at least until sixteen, and encourages transfer at the appropriate stage to the sixth form of the senior school.

4. A two-tier system in which *all* pupils on leaving primary school transfer to a junior comprehensive school. At the age of thirteen or fourteen *all* pupils have a choice between a senior school catering for those who expect to stay at school well beyond the compulsory age, and a senior school catering for those who do not.

5. Comprehensive schools with an age range of eleven to sixteen combined with sixth form colleges for pupils over sixteen.

6. A system of middle schools which straddle the primary–secondary age ranges. Under this system pupils transfer from a primary school at the age of eight or nine to a comprehensive school with an age range of eight to twelve or nine to thirteen. From this middle school they move on to a comprehensive school with an age range of twelve or thirteen to eighteen.

The most appropriate system will depend on local circumstances and an authority may well decide to adopt more than one form of organization in the area for which it is responsible. Organizations of types (1), (2), (5) and (6) produce schools which are fully comprehensive in character. On the other hand an organization of type (3) or (4) is not fully comprehensive in that it involves the separation of children of differing aims and aptitudes

1. The terms 'junior' and 'senior' refer throughout this Circular to the lower and upper secondary schools in two-tier systems of secondary education.

into different schools at the age of thirteen or fourteen. Given the limitations imposed by existing buildings such schemes are acceptable as interim solutions, since they secure many of the advantages of comprehensive education and in some areas offer the most satisfactory method of bringing about reorganization at an early date. But they should be regarded only as an interim stage in development towards a fully comprehensive secondary organization.

Against this general background, the Secretary of State wishes to make certain comments on each of the systems described above:

Orthodox comprehensive schools, eleven to eighteen. There is now a considerable volume of experience of all-through comprehensive schools; and it is clear that they can provide an effective and educationally sound secondary organization. If it were possible to design a new pattern of secondary education without regard to existing buildings, the all-through comprehensive school would in many respects provide the simplest and best solution. There are therefore strong arguments for its adoption wherever circumstances permit.

In practice, however, circumstances will usually not permit, since the great majority of post-war schools and of those now being built are designed as separate secondary schools and are too small to be used as all-through comprehensive schools. There is, of course, some scope for building new schools of this type; and it should be borne in mind that such schools need not be as large as was once thought necessary to produce a sixth form of economic size. It is now clear that a six- or seven-form entry school can cater properly for the whole ability range and produce a viable sixth form. In rural areas or in small towns where only one secondary school is needed its size will inevitably be determined by the number of children for whom it must cater; and this may well not support a six-form entry school. But wherever a six-form entry is possible, within the limits of reasonable travelling for secondary pupils, it should be achieved.

It will sometimes be possible to establish a single comprehensive school in buildings designed for use as separate schools. But any scheme of this type will need careful scrutiny. If buildings are at a considerable distance from each other, or separated by busy roads, the disadvantages are obvious. Even where they are close together the amount and type of accommodation available may cause groupings of pupils which are arbitrary and educationally inefficient. It is essential that any such school should make a satisfactory timetable, deploy its staff efficiently, economically and without undue strain, and become a well-knit community.

There are examples of schools which function well in separate buildings, and there will often be advantages to offset the disadvantages mentioned above. For example, the sharing of different premises by a single school may ensure that all the children enjoy at least part of their secondary education in a new building. Moreover additional building already approved or likely to be included in an early programme may help to overcome the drawbacks of the initial arrangements.

Two-tier systems whereby all pupils transfer at eleven to a junior comprehensive school and at thirteen or fourteen to a senior comprehensive school. Two-tier systems consisting of junior and senior comprehensive schools, each with its own head teacher, and with automatic transfer of all pupils at thirteen or fourteen, have two clear advantages over other two-tier systems. They avoid discrimination between pupils at the point of transfer; and they eliminate the element of guesswork about the proportion of pupils who will transfer to the senior school. They may, it is true, produce problems of organization, particularly where a senior school is fed by more than one junior school. If pupils are not to suffer unnecessarily from the change of school, the schools involved will have to cooperate fully and positively in the choice of curriculum, syllabus and teaching method. In the interest of continuity all the schools will have to surrender some of their freedom. But this system is attractive in that it will often fit readily into existing buildings; and it can develop into an all-through system of orthodox comprehensive schools in the course of time as new buildings become available.

A two-tier system under which all pupils transfer at eleven to a junior comprehensive school and at thirteen or fourteen some pupils move on to a senior school while others remain in the junior school. The two main forms which this system may take have been described above. That in which the junior comprehensive school keeps pupils only until fifteen can clearly be no more than an interim arrangement; there must eventually be automatic transfer of all pupils from the junior to the senior school.

If local circumstances rule this out for some years then at the very least there should be a reorganization of the junior schools to make satisfactory provision until sixteen for those pupils who do not transfer at thirteen or fourteen. Such provision will certainly have to include courses leading to the CSE examination; whether it should also include GCE Ordinary level courses is a more open question. Where staffing permits, there is much to be said for including GCE courses in the junior schools. This gives an added stimulus to the work and to the teaching; it gives intellectually able pupils who do not transfer an opportunity nevertheless of gaining the qualifications which they would have won if they had transferred; it makes it easier for them, through gaining GCE Ordinary levels, to transfer in due course to the sixth form in a senior school or to a college of further education and it reduces the danger of creating social differences between junior and senior schools, with the junior schools regarded as 'poor relations'.

Whatever dividing line is drawn between the junior and the senior school, the Secretary of State will expect certain conditions to be observed:

(a) It is essential, if selection is not to be reintroduced, that transfer to the senior school should be at parents' choice.

(b) Guidance to parents on transfer should be given on an organized basis and should not take the form of advice by one teacher only.

(c) Guidance should ensure that children who would benefit from a longer or more intellectual course are not deprived of it by reason simply of their parents' lack of knowledge of what is involved. The parents must have the final decision; but parents from less educated homes in particular should have a full explanation of the opportunities open to their children.

(d) The junior school must be staffed and its curriculum devised so as to cater effectively for the whole ability range in the first two or three years. This is of great importance whatever transfer age is chosen; but with a transfer age of fourteen it becomes critical. The more able children must not be held back or denied the range of subjects and quality of teaching which they would have enjoyed in a grammar school. Equally their needs must not be met at the expense of other children.

If these conditions are met schemes of this type have the merit of fitting comparatively easily into existing buildings and of taking full account of parental choice at the point of transfer. They are therefore acceptable as transitional schemes. But eventually as has been made clear, the Secretary of State expects that all two-tier systems involving optional transfer at thirteen or fourteen will give way to systems under which transfer is automatic.

Two-tier systems whereby all pupils transfer at eleven to a junior comprehensive school with a choice of senior school at thirteen or fourteen. These differ from the schemes described above in that the junior comprehensive school has the same age range for all its pupils. No children remain in it beyond the age of thirteen or fourteen. All pupils then have a choice of senior school: one senior school will aim at Advanced level and other sixth-form work, while the other will not take its pupils beyond Ordinary level, although the dividing line between the schools can be drawn at different points and they may overlap. The comments made above apply equally to schemes of this kind.

Comprehensive schools with an average age range of eleven to sixteen combined with a sixth-form college for pupils of sixteen and over. Two conceptions of the sixth-form college have been put forward. One envisages the establishment of colleges catering for the educational needs of all young people staying on at school beyond the age of sixteen; the other would make entry to a college dependent on the satisfaction of certain conditions (e.g. five passes at Ordinary level or a declared intention of preparing for Advanced level). A variation of the sixth-form college pattern is that which attaches the sixth-form unit to one school; under such an arrangement pupils from schools without sixth forms can transfer to a single sixth form at another school.

A sixth-form college may involve disadvantages for the lower schools; there are few obvious arguments in favour of comprehensive schools with an age range of eleven to sixteen. Children in this age group may lose from a lack of contact with senior pupils of sixteen to eighteen. There is a danger that the concentration of scarce specialist teachers in the sixth-form college will drain too much talent away from the schools. Some teachers may find unattractive the prospect of teaching the whole ability range in a school offering no opportunities for advanced work and many teachers express a preference for work in schools catering for the whole secondary age range.

But the possibility of loss to the lower schools has to be weighed against possible gains to pupils in the sixth-form colleges. The risk of draining away teaching talent from the lower schools may be outweighed by the concentration of specialist staff in the colleges, thus ensuring their more economic use: a point of particular importance while the present teacher shortage continues. The loss to the younger pupils from lack of contact with sixth formers may be outweighed, not only by the greater opportunities for leadership which the younger pupils themselves will have in the lower school, but also by the gain to the sixth formers from their attaining something of the status and freedom from traditional school discipline enjoyed by students.

It is essential that no scheme involving the establishment of a sixth-form college should lead to any restriction of existing educational opportunities for young people of sixteen to eighteen. Where authorities are considering the establishment of sixth-form colleges they should review all the educational needs of the sixteen to eighteen group in their area and the provision they have hitherto made for them, both in sixth forms and in colleges of further education. Where, in the light of this review, it is proposed to establish sixth-form colleges, the relationship between these colleges and colleges of further education, and their respective functions, will require careful consideration to avoid unnecessary duplication of resources and to ensure that the best use is made of the educational potential of each.

In this country there is so far little experience on which to base final judgements on the merits of sixth-form colleges. Nevertheless the Secretary of State believes that the issues have been sufficiently debated to justify a limited number of experiments. Where authorities contemplate the submission of proposals, he hopes that they will consult with his Department at an early stage.

An organization which involves middle schools straddling the primary-secondary age ranges. Section 1 of the Education Act 1964 makes it legally possible for new schools to be established which cater for an age range covering both primary and secondary schools as defined in section 8 of the Education Act 1944. The establishment of middle schools with age ranges of eight to twelve or nine to thirteen has an immediate attraction in the context of secondary reorganization on comprehensive lines. In the first place such schools seem to lead naturally to the elimination of selection. In the second they shorten the secondary school span by one or two years and thus make it possible to have smaller all-through comprehensive schools.

Notwithstanding the prima facie attractiveness of middle-school systems the Secretary of State does not intend to give his statutory approval to more than a very small number of such proposals in the near future. This is for reasons relating to the age of transfer from primary to secondary education.

102 Central Advisory Council for Education (Plowden)

'Educational Priority Areas', from *Children and Their Primary Schools*, 1967, vol. 1, ch. 5, pp. 50–65.

One of the major innovations in educational thinking was the idea, central to the Plowden Report of 1967, that policy should positively intervene in the social inequalities inherent in society. It designated criteria whereby certain areas might qualify for 'positive discrimination' and coined the term Educational Priority Area. It demanded urgent and dramatic relief to be given to these areas, in terms of better school facilities, more teachers and greater resources. The government responded with an immediate £16 million programme, and an Urban Aid scheme to help local authorities combat the problems of inner city decay was set in motion. A large research project to consider ways in which these communities might best be helped was also launched.

In a neighbourhood where the jobs people do and the status they hold owe little to their education it is natural for children as they grow older to regard school as a brief prelude to work rather than an avenue to future opportunities. Some of these neighbourhoods have for generations been starved of new schools, new houses and new investment of every kind. Everyone knows this; but for year after year priority has been given to the new towns and new suburbs, because if new schools do not keep pace with the new houses some children will be unable to go to school at all. The continually rising proportion of children staying on at school beyond the minimum age has led some authorities to build secondary schools and postpone the rebuilding of older primary schools. Not surprisingly, many teachers are unwilling to work in a neighbourhood where the schools are old, where housing of the sort they want is unobtainable, and where education does not attain the standards they expect for their own children. From some neighbourhoods, urban and rural, there has been a continuing outflow of the more successful young people. The loss of their enterprise and skill makes things worse for those left behind. Thus the vicious circle may turn from generation to generation and the schools play a central part in the process, both causing and suffering cumulative deprivation.

We have ourselves seen schools caught in such vicious circles and read accounts of many more. They are quite untypical of schools in the rest of the country. We noted the grim approaches; incessant traffic noise in narrow streets; parked vehicles hemming in the pavement; rubbish dumps on waste land nearby; the absence of green playing spaces on or near the school sites; tiny play grounds; gaunt looking buildings; often poor decorative conditions inside; narrow passages; dark rooms; unheated and cramped cloakrooms; unroofed outside lavatories; tiny staff rooms; inadequate storage space with consequent restriction on teaching materials and therefore methods; inadequate space for movement and PE; meals in classrooms; art on desks; music only to the discomfort of others in an echoing building; non-soundproof partitions between classes; lack of smaller rooms for group work; lack of spare room for tuition of small groups; insufficient display space; attractive books kept unseen in cupboards for lack of space to lay them out; no privacy for parents waiting to see the head; sometimes the head and his secretary sharing the same room; and, sometimes all around, the ingrained grime of generations.

We heard from local education authorities of growing difficulty in replacing heads with successors of similar calibre. It is becoming particularly hard to find good heads of infant or deputy heads of junior schools. We are not surprised to hear of the rapid turnover of staff, of vacancies sometimes unfilled or filled with a succession of temporary and supply teachers of one kind or another. Probationary teachers are trained by heads to meet the needs of their schools but then pass on to others where strains are not so great. Many teachers able to do a decent job in an ordinary school are defeated by these conditions. Some become dispirited by long journeys to decaying buildings to see each morning children among whom some seem to have learned only how not to learn. Heads rely on the faithful, devoted and hard working regulars. There may be one or two in any school, or they may be as many as half the staff, who have so much to do in keeping the school running that they are sometimes too tired even to enjoy their own holidays.

We saw admission registers whose pages of new names with so many rapid crossings out told their own story of a migratory population. In one school 111 out of 150 pupils were recent newcomers. We heard heads explain, as they looked down the lines, that many of those who had gone were good pupils, while a high proportion of those who had been long in the school came from crowded, down-at-heel homes.

The educational needs of deprived areas

What these deprived areas need most are perfectly normal, good primary schools alive with experience from which children of all kinds can benefit. What we say elsewhere about primary-school work generally applies equally to these difficult areas. The best schools already there show that it is absurd to say, as one used to hear, 'it may be all very well in a nice suburb, but it won't work here'. But, of course, there are special and additional demands on teachers who work in deprived areas with deprived children. They meet special challenges. Teachers must be constantly aware that ideas, values and relationships within the school may conflict with those of the home, and that the world assumed by teachers and school books may be unreal to the children. There will have to be constant communication between parents and the schools if the aims of the schools are to be fully understood. The child from a really impoverished background may well have had a normal, satisfactory emotional life. What he often lacks is the opportunity to develop intellectual interests. This shows in his poor command of language. It is not, however with vocabulary that teaching can begin. The primary school must first supply experiences and establish relationships which enable children to discriminate, to reason and to express themselves. Placing such children in the right stance for further learning is a very skilled operation. But those who have done remedial work will be aware of the astonishing rapidity of the progress which can be achieved, particularly in extending vocabulary, once children's curiosity is released. The thrust to learn seems to be latent in every child, at least within a very wide range of normality. But however good the opportunities, some children may not be able to take advantage of them. Failure may have taken away from them their urge to learn.

A teacher cannot and should not give the deep, personal love that each child needs from his parents. There are ways he can help:

1. He can relieve children of responsibility without dominating them in a way which prevents them from developing independence. Deprived children may have been forced into premature responsibility. They are often given the care of younger children and are free to roam, to go to bed or to stay up, to eat when and where they can. This produces what is often a spurious maturity. Confidence can be encouraged by tasks which are fully within their capacity. A measure of irresponsibility has to be allowed for: it will pretty certainly come later, and in a less acceptable form, if not permitted at the proper time.

2. A teacher can do much by listening and trying to understand the context of the questions the children ask. It will be much easier if he knows the child's family and the neighbourhood surrounding his home.

3. Children in deprived neighbourhoods are often backward. There is a risk that an inexperienced teacher will think there is not time for anything but the three Rs if the child is not to be handicapped throughout his life. This is quite wrong. These children need time for play and imaginative and expressive work and may suffer later if they do not get it at school.

4. Teachers need to use books which make sense to the children they teach. They will often have to search hard for material which is suitable for downtown children.

5. Record keeping is especially necessary for teachers in schools in deprived neighbourhoods. There is so much coming and going by families that a child's progress may depend very much on the amount and quality of information that can be sent with him from school to school.

Hope for the future

In our cities there are whole districts which have been scarcely touched by the advances made in more fortunate places. Yet such conditions have been overcome and striking progress has been achieved where sufficiently determined and comprehensive attack has been made on the problem. In the most deprived areas, one of HM Inspectors reported, 'Some heads approach magnificence, but they cannot do everything. . . . The demands on them as welfare agents are never ending.' Many children with parents in the least skilled jobs do outstandingly well in school. The educational aspirations of parents and the support and encouragement given to children in some of the poorest neighbourhoods are impressive. Over half of the unskilled workers in our National Survey want their children to be given homework to do after school hours; over half want their children to stay at school beyond the minimum leaving age. One third of them hoped their children would go to a grammar school or one with similar opportunities. The educational aspirations of unskilled workers for their children have risen year by year. It has been stressed to us that the range of ability in all social classes is so wide that there is a great reservoir of unrealized potential in families dependent on the least skilled and lowest paid work. A larger part of the housing programme than ever before is to be devoted to rebuilding and renewing obsolete and decaying neighbourhoods. The opportunity must be seized to rebuild the schools as well as the houses, and to see that both schools and houses serve families from every social class. It will be possible to make some progress in reducing the size of classes in primary schools in these areas as well as elsewhere. Colleges of education which have taken a special interest in deprived areas report that their students respond in an encouraging fashion to the challenge of working in these neighbourhoods. Most important of all, there is a growing awareness in the nation at large, greatly stimulated, we believe, by our predecessors' reports, of the complex social handicaps afflicting such areas and the need for a more radical assault on their problems. These are the strengths on which we can build. How can they be brought to bear ?

We propose a nationwide scheme for helping those schools and neighbourhoods in which children are most severely handicapped. This policy will have an influence over the whole educational system, and it colours all the subsequent recommendations in our report. It must not be put into practice simply by robbing more fortunate areas of all the opportunities for progress to which they have been looking forward; it can only succeed if a larger share of the nation's resources is devoted to education. So far reaching a set of proposals must be firmly rooted in educational grounds, yet the arguments for them inevitably extend beyond this field into many other branches of the nation's affairs. Before explaining these proposals we give a brief outline of the reasoning which led us to make them.

Educational assumptions and policies

Our study of these problems compelled us to consider the process of economic and social development and the contribution made to it by the schools. Industrial development in many respects is the motor of social progress. We recognize that there are limits to the resources that can be mobilized for education and the primary schools. But it does not necessarily follow, as many have assumed, that the fruits of economic growth, together with the present pattern of public services, will in time give every child increasing opportunities of contributing to the nation's progress. It does not follow that education, because its development depends in the long run on the growth of the economy, must therefore follow in its wake, rather than contribute to the promotion of growth. Nor does it follow that a 'fair' or 'efficient' distribution of educational resources is one that provides a reasonably equal supply of teachers, classrooms, and other essentials to each school child in each area. Nor does it follow that the government's responsibility for promoting progress within the limits permitted by these resources must be confined to encouraging development in the most capable areas, spreading word of their progress to others, and pressing on the rear-guard of the laggard or less fortunate whenever opportunity permits. Though many of these assumptions are already being questioned or abandoned, our own proposals are unlikely to convince those who still accept them, and we must, therefore, challenge each in turn.

During the Second World War there was a considerable improvement in the living conditions which bear most directly upon children in deprived groups and areas. In spite of this there has not been any appreciable narrowing of the gap between the least well off and the rest of the population. This is most obvious among children, particularly those in large families. 'It is ... clear that, on average, the larger families in all classes, and also those containing adolescents and children, constitute the most vulnerable groups nutritionally.' Signs of rickets have recently been reported again from the slums of Glasgow; mortality among children during the first year of life has fallen sharply since 1950, but the difference between social classes remains great. Much the same goes for stillbirth rates which, in different social classes 'despite a dramatic wartime fall, were as far apart in 1950 as in 1939'. Meanwhile 'class differentials in perinatal mortality are as resistant to change as those of infant mortality. The results of the (Perinatal Mortality) Survey suggest, indeed, that the gap may be increasing rather than narrowing.' The Milner Holland Committee's study of housing conditions in London covered a period in which this country probably achieved a faster rate of economic growth that it has ever experienced before, and an area in which conditions are generally better and improving faster than elsewhere. But it showed that progress has been most rapid in those parts of the town where conditions were already best. In less fortunate neighbourhoods there has been less improvement and in some respects an appreciable deterioration. Families with low incomes and several young children were among those who suffered most.

If the fruits of growth are left to accumulate within the framework of present policies and provisions, there is no assurance that the living conditions which handicap educationally deprived children will automatically improve – still less that the gap between these conditions and those of more fortunate children will be narrowed.

The contribution made by education to economic development poses complicated questions, upon which systematic research has only recently begun, and we cannot present firm conclusions about it. Comparisons with other countries – all of them more recently industrialized than Britain but all now at a similar stage of economic development – suggest that we have not done enough to provide the educational background necessary to support an economy which needs fewer and fewer unskilled workers and increasing numbers of skilled and adaptable people. One example can be drawn from a pioneer piece of research in comparative educational achievements. This compares mathematical skills at several stages of secondary education. It shows that in the early stages England was distinguished, from other countries not by the average standard attained (which was closely similar to the average for the other countries compared) but by the scatter of its results. English children achieved more than their share of the best results, and more of the worst results. Our educational system, originally moulded by the impress of Victorian economic and social requirements, may not yet have been fully adapted to present needs. In the deprived areas with which this chapter is concerned too many children leave school as soon as they are allowed to with no desire to carry their education further and without the knowledge to fit them for a job more intellectually demanding than their father's or their grandfather's. Yet they face a future in which they must expect during their working life to have to change their job, to learn new skills, to adapt themselves to new economic conditions and to form new human relationships. They will suffer, and so will the economy; both needlessly. It should not be assumed that even the ablest children can surmount every handicap. They may suffer as much as any from adverse conditions.

If the schools are to play their part in resolving and forestalling these problems much of the action required must be taken at the secondary and higher stages of the system. But this action cannot be fully effective if it does not touch the primary schools. Recent research has shown how early in the lives of children the selective processes begin to operate. There are primary schools from which scarcely any children ever take a secondary-school course which leads them to O-level in G CE. Children of good potential ability enter them, but the doors to educational opportunity have already closed against them when their schooling has scarcely begun. Reforming zeal and expenditure directed to later stages of education will be wasted unless early handicaps can be reduced.

The schools unaided cannot provide all the opportunities their pupils deserve, or create the labour force this country needs. Industry, and the authorities responsible for housing, planning, employment and other services must also play their part. But, from the earliest stages of education, the schools enlarge or restrict the contribution their pupils can make to the life of the nation. Money spent on education is an investment which helps to determine the scope for future economic and social development.

Our argument thus far can be briefly summarized. As things are at the moment there is no reason why the educational handicaps of the most deprived children should disappear. Although standards will rise, inequalities will persist and the potential of many children will never be realized. The range of achievement amongst English children is wide, and the standards attained by the most and the least successful begin to diverge very early. Steps should be taken to improve the educational chances and the attainments of the least well placed, and to bring them up to the levels that prevail generally. This will call for a new distribution of educational resources.

The distribution of resources

The principle that certain local authorities (but not districts within local authorities) should receive special help from the rest of the community is already recognized. At the national level the government takes needs into account when distributing grants to local authorities for educational and other purposes. The basic grant consists of so much per head of population plus so much for each child under fifteen years of age. The supplementary grants allow for:

The number of children under five.
The number of people over sixty-five.
School children in excess of a prescribed proportion.
Density.
Sparsity.
Declining population.
Metropolitan areas.

There is also a formula that increases the grant paid to authorities with lower rateable values and reduces it for wealthier ones. The same principle of district priorities applies to educational building programmes. The needs of districts with a growing population come first; the next buildings to be sanctioned must be for the purpose of making good the deficiencies of existing schools. This principle can also be seen at work in the distribution of teachers. Local education authorities with an exceptionally high proportion of immigrant children may apply for an addition to their quota of teachers.

Redistribution of resources within local authority areas has been less marked. 'Equality' has an appealing ring, 'discrimination' has not. It is simpler and easier, for example, to defend staff–pupil ratios that are roughly the same in each school than to explain why they should be better in some and to decide which are to be the favoured. Even so, more and more local authorities do discriminate. They look with a more generous eye on schools whose 'social need' is greatest, as reckoned by the free dinner list, by the proportion of children who do not speak English at home, or (which may be an even better guide) by the opinion of experienced teachers and administrators. These schools may be allowed an extra teacher or more non-teaching help, or a slightly bigger ration of 'consumable stocks'.

These are no more than a tentative beginning. The formulae for allocating grants are designed to equalize the financial resources of poorer and wealthier authorities. But equality is not enough. The formulae do not distinguish between the districts within authorities' areas in which children and schools are most severely handicapped. These districts need more spending on them, and government and local authorities between them must provide the funds. Permission is required before the money can be spent on what is most needed – additional teachers and better buildings. The authority's quota must be raised before extra teachers can be engaged. and additions to the building programme must be sanctioned by the Department of Education. Even if this happens the battle is not over. Some authorities whose need for teachers is great find it impossible to recruit for deprived schools the teachers to whom they are entitled. The vicious circle continues.

A study of the educational expenditure of eighty-three county boroughs has been made for us by Mr B. P. Davies. He compared the way money was spent with the evidence about the needs of each borough. He found no link between the amount spent on primary schools and their pupils and the social character of the area they served. In general, deprived areas were neither more nor less likely than others to get a bigger share of the total expenditure. A large proportion of expenditure was devoted to the salaries of teachers, whose distribution is subject to quota rules, and to the provision of those essential services which give little scope for variation. Other services, on which an education authority has great scope for independent decision, often tended to have more spent on them in those boroughs where the needs appeared to be less urgent. There are signs of this in the expenditure on nursery schools, and (less clearly) on child guidance. The same applied to school meals where parental preferences exert an influence. More striking, perhaps, was the persistence of these patterns. The boroughs in which expenditure was generally low were much the same in 1960–61 as they were in 1950–51.

Educational priority areas

The many teachers who do so well in face of adversity cannot manage without cost to themselves. They carry the burdens of parents, probation officers and welfare officers on top of their classroom duties. It is time the nation came to their aid. The principle, already accepted, that special need calls for special help, should be given a new cutting edge. We ask for 'positive discrimination' in favour of such schools and the children in them, going well beyond an attempt to equalize resources. Schools in deprived areas should be given priority in many respects. The first step must be to raise the schools with low standards to the national average; the second, quite deliberately to make them better. The justification is that the homes and neighbourhoods from which many of their children come provide little support and stimulus for learning. The schools must supply a compensating environment. The attempts so far made within the educational system to do this have not been sufficiently generous or sustained, because the handicaps imposed by the environment have not been explicitly and sufficiently allowed for. They should be.

The proposition that good schools should make up for a poor environment is far from new. It derives from the notion that there should be equality of opportunity for all, but recognizes that children in some districts will only get the same opportunity as those who live elsewhere if they have unequally generous treatment. It was accepted before the First World War that some children could not be effectively taught until they had been properly fed. Hence free meals were provided. Today their need is for enriched intellectual nourishment. Planned and positive discrimination in favour of deprived areas could bring about an advance in the education of children in the 1970s as great as the advance in their nutrition to which school meals and milk contributed so much.

Every authority where deprivation is found should be asked to adopt 'positive discrimination' within its own area, and to report from time to time on the progress made. Some authorities contain schools or even one school of this kind where deprivation is so serious that they need special help. Most of these schools and areas are already well known to teachers, administrators, local inspectors and HM Inspectors. Local knowledge will not be sufficient to justify decisions which are bound on occasion to be controversial. Objective criteria for the selection of 'educational priority schools and areas' will be needed to identify those schools which need special help and to determine how much assistance should be given by the government. Our National Survey showed the prime importance of parental attitudes, and it might be thought that a measure of these attitudes could be devised. But the data for the selection of priority schools and areas must be readily available, without additional surveys, and in any event the validity of answers given by parents with the education of their children at stake might fairly be questioned. The criteria required must identify those places where educational handicaps are reinforced by social handicaps. Some of the main criteria which could be used in an assessment of deprivation are given below. They are not placed in order of importance, nor is any formula suggested by which they should be combined. They may require further study. The criteria are:

Occupation. The National Census can report on occupations within quite small areas, and, for particular schools, the data can be supplemented without too much difficulty. The analyses would show the proportions of unskilled and semi-skilled manual workers.

Size of families. The larger the family, the more likely are the children to be in poverty. Wages are no larger for a married man with young children than they are for a single man with none. Family size is still associated with social class, and men with four or more children tend to be amongst the lowest wage earners. Family size also correlates with the results of intelligence tests – the larger the family, the lower the scores of the children. The children are liable to suffer from a double handicap, both genetic and environmental – the latter because, it is suggested, they have less encouragement and stimulus from parents who have more children amongst whom to divide their attention. Those earning the lowest wages often make up their incomes by working longer hours. Often, too, their wives have less time and energy to devote to their children. Family size likewise correlates with nutrition, with physical growth and with overcrowding, and is therefore an apt indicator (when allowance is made for the age structure of the local population, and particularly the number of mothers of child bearing age) of the poor home conditions for which schools should compensate. The National Census, supplemented by the schools censuses made by the education authorities, would provide the information required.

Supplements in cash or kind from the State are of various kinds. Where the parents are needy, children are allowed school meals free. The proportions so benefiting vary greatly from school to school, and afford a reasonably good guide to relative need. The procedures laid down are designed to give free meals according to scales similar to those used by the Ministry of Social Security. Another criterion of the same type is the number of families depending on National Assistance, or its future equivalent, in a particular locality. The weakness of these criteria taken by themselves is that some people do not know their rights or are unwilling to seek them.

Overcrowding and sharing of houses should certainly be included amongst the criteria. It will identify families in cramped accommodation in central and run-down areas of our cities. It is a less sure guide than some others because it may miss the educational needs of some housing estates and other areas which can also be severe.

Poor attendance and truancy are a pointer to home conditions, and to what Burt long ago singled out as a determinant of school progress, the 'efficiency of the mother'. Truancy is also related to delinquency. The National Survey showed that 4 per cent of the children in the sample were absent, on their teachers' assessment, for unsatisfactory reasons.

Proportions of retarded, disturbed or handicapped pupils in ordinary schools. These vary from authority to authority according to the special school available and the policies governing their use. But, everywhere, the proportions tend to be highest in deprived districts. It is accepted that special schools need additional staff, and the same advantages should be extended to normal schools with many pupils of a similar kind.

Incomplete families where one or other of the parents is dead, or not living at home for whatever reason, are often unable to provide a satisfactory upbringing for their children without special help.

Children unable to speak English need much extra attention if they are to find their feet in England. This is already recognized in arranging teachers' quotas, but should also be used as a general criterion.

All authorities would be asked to consider which of their schools should qualify, to rank them according to criteria such as those we have listed, and to submit supporting data. Advice would also be available from HM Inspectors of Schools. In this way the Department of Education and Science would have full information both about the social and the educational needs of the schools and areas. Many of the criteria would be closely correlated. With experience, the data required could be simplified so as to ease administration; but meanwhile, a wide variety of criteria should be employed. The schools near the bottom of the resulting rankings would be entitled to priority. We envisage a formal procedure enabling the Secretary of State for Education and Science to designate particular schools or groups of schools as priority schools or areas. Those so designated would qualify for the favourable treatment described later in this chapter. Local education authorities would submit regular reports on these schools to the Secretary of State for the purpose of determining what progress was being made, how long their designation should continue, which aspects of the programme were proving most effective, and what further steps should be taken.

Special groups

However good the information secured, and however extensive the experience gained in using it, the administration of this policy would always call for wise judgement and careful interpretation. An infallible formula cannot be devised. Severe deprivation can be found among particular groups which are unlikely to be singled out by such criteria. Canal-boat families are an example. Another are the gypsies whose plight is described in Appendix 12. They are probably the most severely deprived children in the country. Most of them do not even go to school, and the potential abilities of those who do are stunted. They tend to be excluded by their way of life and their lack of education from entering normal occupations and confined to others that compel continual travelling. Thus, unless action is taken to arrest the cycle, their children will in turn suffer educational deprivations which will become increasingly severe in their effects as general standards of education rise. The age distribution of this group bears a telling resemblance to that of England in 1841 and so does their education or lack of it. The numbers of gypsy children are small – those of compulsory school age probably amounting in total to less than four thousand. But they are increasing, and in the next twenty years their numbers are likely to double. In their own interests and in the nation's they merit help of the kind we recommend. Yet the criteria listed above would not select them. They move too frequently to be accurately recorded in census data, they are too seldom in school to appear in figures (of free school meals, for instance) derived from the school population, and the districts in which they are found, particularly the rural areas surrounding the South Eastern and West Midland conurbations, are unlikely to contain many educational priority areas.

Another group of children which would not be identified by the suggested criteria are from Army and Air Force families in areas with large service populations. There is evidence of serious backwardness among them and of high turnover of pupils and teachers.

The case of the gypsies illustrates another aspect of the policies required in educational priority areas. Improved education alone cannot solve the problems of these children. Simultaneous action is needed by the authorities responsible for employment, industrial training, housing and planning. There will be similar, though less extreme, needs for coordinated action on behalf of other groups deserving priority. The experience of those engaged in the 'war on poverty' in the United States gives warning

of the disappointments which sometimes follow from attempts to improve
the education of the poorest which are not coupled to an effective attack on
unemployment. Where there are plans for new centres of economic
growth in the less prosperous regions, extra resources for education should
be temporarily concentrated in areas where the whole pace of development
is likely to be increased. In such places, joint operations of this kind could
before long go far to eliminate educational deprivation.

More teachers

Once educational priority areas have been selected, the next step must be
to give them the help they need. Each authority would be asked not only
to say which schools had been selected, and why, but also what it proposed
by way of remedy. The most important thing is to bring more experienced
and successful teachers into these areas and to support them by a generous
number of teachers' aides. Until there are more teachers all round, the
possibility for increasing their numbers in these schools will, of course, be
limited. But a beginning could be made, and the right framework created
for the future. To start with, quotas should be raised for authorities with
educational priority areas. But the schools in greatest need often cannot
recruit their full complement at present, and to increase it, if that were all,
would do nothing but cause irritation. Additional incentives are needed. We
therefore recommend that there should be extra allowances for teachers and
head teachers serving in schools in difficult areas. In many ways their work
is already more arduous than their colleagues'. They will in future be
expected to assume yet further responsibilities, not only in making contact
with parents but also in arranging activities for their children outside the
normal limits of the school day, and in collaborating with other local social
services. Teachers in such schools deserve extra recognition and reward,
and to give it to them would be one way of achieving something even more
important, greater fairness between one child and another. The government
has already reached the same conclusion in its search for means of recruiting
doctors to the less popular areas; financial incentives are being offered to
those who are willing to work in them. Salary incentives, of course, present
difficulties for the professions concerned, but we believe that the teachers,
who understand better than most the urgency of the need, will be prepared
to accept the remedies their medical colleagues are already adopting.

The Dame Jean Roberts Committee on Measures to Secure a More
Equitable Distribution of Teachers in Scotland studied these problems
independently and we were unaware that they had reached similar conclusions until our own Report was nearly completed. They call in their
report for the designation of individual schools in which the scarcity of

teachers is particularly severe, and for the payment of an additional £100 a year to all teachers serving in these schools. Our scheme differs from the Scottish plan in one important respect. The criteria we recommend are all social, not educational, so that priority schools and areas will not lose their privileged status, whether they have enough teachers or not, until the social conditions improve. As we understand the Scottish proposals, designation as a school of temporary shortage is to be subject to annual review and the additions to salaries will be paid only during the time when the school is so designated.

There is an important distinction between 'mobile' teachers, often young and sometimes still unmarried, and the 'immobile', who are more often married. Many authorities have succeeded in attracting back to work women teachers who had resigned after marriage, and the more who return the better. But the schools to which they go are often those near their own homes, and therefore in middle-class neighbourhoods not in the queue for priority. Each woman who returns could release an additional mobile teacher for priority areas, but that will not be achieved unless more carefully drawn distinctions can be made between the mobile and immobile, and the quotas to be applied to each. The principle underlying these arrangements should be that authorities must employ every immobile teacher in their areas before drawing on mobile teachers who may be available for the priority areas. The administrative difficulties of such an arrangement are considerable, but while teachers remain so scarce every effort should be made to overcome them.

There are two obvious problems about this scheme which should be mentioned. The first is the risk that, while the black areas may become white, the neighbouring grey areas may be turned black by an exodus of teachers attracted by salary incentives. But the fact that the priority areas will seldom, if ever, cover a whole authority will be a safeguard. They will usually consist of much smaller districts, some containing one or two schools only, within the territory of an authority and the authority can exercise considerable control over the recruitment and deployment of its teachers and ensure that a balance is maintained between the claims of all its schools, good and bad. The second concerns our proposals for different rules of employment of mobile and immobile teachers. The Department of Education and Science does not know where the immobile live, especially if they left teaching some years ago. This information might be collected by local education authorities. This should form the basis of information for the Department, who should modify its quota arrangements to take into account the varying resources of immobile teachers in each area.

Priority areas are not the kind of place where teachers normally live. Yet those whose homes are near their pupils' can often do a better job than those who travel great distances. They belong to the same community; they can understand their background better. What is more, the creation of vast one-class districts from which all professional people are excluded is bad in itself. Sustained efforts ought to be made to diversify the social composition of the priority areas. Many professional workers feel the need to start buying a house early in their careers because mortgage terms may be more favourable, and because once they own a house it is easier for them to secure another one if they move elsewhere. Their needs should be recognized by the housing and planning authorities. There should be a mixture of houses for renting, for owner-occupation and for co-ownership, and cost-rent schemes run by housing associations. As our inquiries showed, many authorities can, and some do, provide housing for teachers and others whose claims derive not from the urgency of their housing needs but from the contribution they make to the community which provides the houses. The housing needs of families in badly overcrowded places are likely to be more urgent than those of teachers; but their children will not get the education they deserve if teachers are systematically excluded from the locality. The Dame Jean Roberts Committee urges, and we agree, that local education authorities 'should be allowed greater freedom than at present to purchase, and if necessary to adapt, houses to let to teachers willing to serve at shortage points. Expenditure incurred on the purchase and adaptation of such houses should not be regarded as a charge on an authority's capital investment allocation for school building.' We agree with this. It does not follow that any help with housing would entitle teachers to subsidies designed for tenants with lower incomes. The Dame Jean Roberts Committee recommended also that there should be travel allowances for teachers working in difficult areas at a distance from their homes. We recommend that local authorities consider this.

Colleges of education

Teachers in training also have a part to play. In our visit to the United States we were much struck by the value of linking teacher-training establishments with schools in deprived areas. In some cities young teachers are attracted to such places and helped to settle down there by the appointment of special consultants who regularly visit new teachers in schools where the conditions are difficult, support them in their work, and are available on call to give advice. On a smaller scale, the benefits of such links can already be seen in England. We urge that colleges should be asked to establish wherever possible a continuing link with schools in priority areas. Students should be sent to them for a part of their teaching practice. We also hope that in many of these areas a generously equipped teachers' centre can be set up for the in-service training of teachers already working there, partly staffed by the affiliated college of education and partly by local inspectors, HM Inspectors and experienced local teachers and heads. The improved staffing ratio we recommend should make an in-service training programme possible. Longer courses to equip teachers for work in the priority areas could be run from such centres and in colleges of education, and be recognized for purposes of Burnham allowances. Over the years this work would help to build up a body of knowledge about the best ways of teaching children in socially deprived neighbourhoods. Cooperation for research purposes with university departments and with colleges of education would also enable the successes, and failures, of the whole venture to be properly assessed.

Buildings

The shortage of buildings is going to be as acute as the shortage of teachers. New building is committed for several years ahead to keep pace with the birth-rate and the rise in the school-leaving age. There will not be much to spare for the priority areas in the immediate future. Our criteria should be given great weight when determining which of the schools with old and out-of-date buildings is to be replaced first. It would also help if the element in the total building programme reserved for minor works were increased specially for the benefit of these areas. Schools in the greatest plight could be given preference, for the improvement of lavatories and wash places, and for modifications to classrooms. They also should be frequently redecorated. There is urgent need for decent staff rooms to replace those ones thought good enough sixty years ago, if indeed there were any at all. In making estimates of the cost involved we have assumed that an average of £5000 should be spent on each of these schools. Some will need more; others will need very little. What goes into the building is likewise important. The need for extra 'consumable stocks' has already been mentioned. Additional books and audio-visual equipment of various kinds, including television sets and tape-recorders, would be particularly valuable in these schools.

Nursery education

We argue in chapter 9 that part-time attendance at a nursery school is desirable for most children. It is even more so for children in socially deprived neighbourhoods. They need above all the verbal stimulus, the opportunities for constructive play, a more richly differentiated environment and the access to medical care that good nursery schools can provide. It will be many years before they are generally available. The building of new nursery schools and extensions to existing schools should start in priority areas and spread outwards. As a minimum we suggest that all children aged four to five who live in the areas should have the opportunity of part-time attendance and that perhaps 50 per cent should have full-time places (although their need for a gradual introduction is the same as that of all other children).

Other priorities

The development of social work carried out in conjunction with the schools is discussed in chapter 7. This too should be concentrated first in the priority areas.

It might be thought that our proposal for community schools, made in the previous chapter, would be hardest to implement in these districts. But in many of them the demand for centres for activities outside the home of various kinds is keen, as the existence of university settlements and similar bodies shows. It will take special skill to seize these opportunities and use them for educational purposes. But the gains that could be made in mutual understanding between teachers and parents through the work of a well run community school in a priority area make the scheme well worth trying.

First steps

Local education authorities which have a number of priority schools will not be able to embark on a policy of positive discrimination until they know what help they can get from the central government. The nation's supply of the principal resources required – teachers and school buildings – is known and committed, several years in advance, often to other parts of the educational system. We must, therefore, think in terms of an immediate programme, on which a start can be made without waiting for additional resources or major changes in existing plans, and after that a longer-term programme to follow.

The principles on which we have based the immediate programme are as follows:

1. A start should be made as quickly as possible by giving priority to the schools which by our criteria contain the 10 per cent of most deprived children. Starting at 2 per cent in the first year this percentage should be reached within five years. The additional budget for these areas should not engross the entire increase in educational resources available for the whole country, year by year. There must be a margin permitting some improvement in the schools serving the rest of the population.

2. The programme should begin as quickly as possible at varying dates for different elements in the system (teachers' aides, for example, may be available sooner than an overall increase in the school building programme).

During a period to start in 1968 and to reach its peak in 1972 the following steps should be taken in educational priority areas (or in individual priority schools):

1. The staffing ratio should be improved so that no class need exceed thirty.

2. Additions to salary of £120 (as are given to teachers of handicapped children or those with other special responsibilities) should be available at the rate of one for every teacher in the priority areas. But it would be open to local education authorities to award these increases according to any plan approved by the Department of Education and Science as being likely to improve education in the designated schools. The additional resources should be used flexibly; for example, an allowance might be allocated to a remedial teacher specializing in helping these schools, or allowances might be withheld and become payable only after a brief qualifying period. They would not, of course, be paid to staff working mainly in other schools. These arrangements will require an amendment of the Burnham Report.

3. Teachers' aides should be provided to help teachers, on the lines described in chapter 24, but at the more generous ratio of one aide for every two classes in infant and junior schools.

4. Those educational priority schools with poor buildings should be allocated, within the first five years, a minor building project. The average cost between all priority schools might be £5000 though some will need little or no new building.

5. The full provision for nursery education should be introduced for children aged four and five as proposed in chapter 9 of this Report. A higher proportion than in the rest of the country will attend full-time (up to 50 per cent).

6. Research should be set on foot to determine which of these measures has the most positive effect as a basis for planning the longer-term programme.

7. We estimate that by 1972–3 the educational priority areas will add £11 million to the total current costs of the maintained primary schools. It is clear therefore that the total of Exchequer grants to local authorities will have to be increased to take account of this. It is not for us to plan the mechanism for the distribution of these grants. A new specific grant for authorities containing priority areas may be required, on the lines of the proposed grant to authorities with large numbers of Commonwealth

immigrants; or the formula for the distribution of the new rate support grant might be modified.

A continuing policy

The longer-term programme will call for additional resources, over and above those at present allocated to education. Our proposals are not intended to be a once-for-all expedient. The lead in the ratio of teachers to pupils which the priority areas should have attained by 1972 must be maintained. It is suggested they should be restricted to an arbitrary figure of 10 per cent of the population initially, in order to provide a serious test of the effectiveness of different elements of priority within the resources that can be found without depriving the rest of the country scope for improvement. It will be much longer before reliable conclusions can be reached about the outcome, but already by 1972 it should be easier to decide how far and in what way to extend the programme. The need may well be shown to go beyond 10 per cent of children. The Council's last report estimated that just under a fifth of modern school pupils were in 'problem areas', very similar to what we describe as educational priority areas.

The arguments for this policy are general, and apply to whole districts that have been educationally handicapped for years. They are not confined to primary schools and apply to secondary schools as well. But a start should, in our view, be made in primary schools. They have long had less than their share of new building and their classes have always been larger. Since they draw their pupils from smaller catchment areas they feel the full impact of social conditions in their immediate neighbourhood, whereas rather more secondary schools can draw from a mixture of neighbourhoods, with the more fortunate offsetting the less.

Conclusion

Positive discrimination accords with experience and thinking in many other countries, and in other spheres of social policy. It calls both for some redistribution of the resources devoted to education and, just as much, for an increase in their total volume. It must not be interpreted simply as a gloss upon the recommendations which follow in later chapters. This would not only be a misunderstanding of the scheme; it would destroy all hope of its success. For it would be unreasonable and self-defeating – economically, professionally and politically – to try to do justice by the most deprived children by using only resources that can be diverted from more fortunate areas. We have argued that the gap between the educational opportunities of the most and least fortunate children should be closed, for economic and social reasons alike. It cannot be done, unless extra effort, extra skill and extra resources are devoted to the task.

103 Central Advisory Council for Education (Plowden)

from *Children and Their Primary Schools*, 1967, vol. 1, ch. 10, pp. 135–6.

The Plowden Committee drew attention to a strange administrative anomaly that existed in the entry to primary schooling, whereby summer-born children might receive up to three terms less early schooling than children born in the autumn. Combined with the practice of 'streaming' in some junior schools, this had the effect of 'trapping' children in the lower streams, with the result that a predominance of summer-born children transferred to secondary schools with poor academic attainment.

The choice of five as the age at which children must begin school was made almost by chance in 1870, but the Consultative Committee reported in 1933 that it was working well in practice, and thought there was no good reason for modifying the law. But, with the exception of Israel and a few states whose educational systems derive from ours, the United Kingdom is alone in the world in fixing so early an age. In most countries it is six; in some seven. This sharp contrast makes it right for us to consider carefully the grounds for admitting children to school, when they are so much younger.

Children are born every day of the year. In England they are admitted to infant schools at intervals of four months (most countries have one yearly intake), and promoted to junior schools or classes only at intervals of twelve months. They must go to school at the beginning of the term after their fifth birthday; they are promoted to the junior school (or junior classes) in the September following their seventh birthday.

Table 1 shows that:

1. There is a considerable difference in age and in the length of time children have been at school when they are promoted to the junior school. Either annual admissions, or termly promotions, would remove one or other of these differences; it is the combination of the two which imposes a double difference.

Disadvantages of termly entry

There is evidence both from our witnesses and research that children born in the summer, who are younger and have a shorter time at school than others before they are promoted, tend to be placed in the 'C' stream of those junior schools which are organized in this way. The National Foundation for Educational Research (NFER) study of streaming found that 'the A streams had the highest average age and the lowest ability streams the youngest'. The difference persists. One county borough has found that a high proportion of the pupils born between September and December gained grammar-school places compared with those born between May and August. The latter often have to transfer to junior school before they have finished learning to read. Their new teachers, not always realizing their relatively late start, may believe them to be slow learners, expect less of them and often in consequence get less from them. The 'age allowances' made in selection procedures cannot offset their psychological handicap.

Table 1 **Compulsory education in infant schools under present arrangements**

Month of birth	Age of child in Autumn term	Age of child in Spring term	Age of child in Summer term	Age of child in Autumn term	Age of child in Spring term	Age of child in Summer term	Age of child in Autumn term	Age of child in Spring term	Age of child in Summer term	Length of schooling on promotion
Sept.–Dec.	5	5	5 to 6	6	6	6 to 7	7	7		8 terms
Jan.–April		5	5	5 to 6	6	6	6 to 7	7		7 terms
May–Aug.			5	5	5 to 6	6	6	6 to 7		6 terms

In many schools there is either a spare classroom in the first term of the year, or the rooms are over filled in the summer. Few authorities staff the infant schools on summer numbers and fewer still will do so as staffing problems increase. For this reason it is common to find that children are promoted each term. This practice has been encouraged by authorities who have often provided two-form entry schools with one especially well equipped room for the admission class. Its teacher's task is unrewarding. She helps children to adjust to school and gets to know their parents; but, before she can use this knowledge, the children are transferred to another teacher. She feels the lack of a group of 'old hands' among the children to show newcomers how things are done.

The shuffle up of children from admission classes often affects the whole school. Children and teachers may have to get used to a new class each term. The effect on young children may be serious. The teacher is to them something like a parent. Nobody would like to change parents once a term; children in infant schools should not have to change teachers at this rate. A minority of schools avoid this problem by the form of organization known as vertical grouping. But this would not be acceptable in all schools.

It seems, therefore, that termly entry results in unsatisfactory organization in the infant school and has serious disadvantages for the summer-born children. This view was endorsed by many of our witnesses and by the sample of teachers whom we invited to comment on the age of entry. We recommend, therefore, that all children should begin compulsory schooling in the same period of the year and that this should be in the autumn term. Even though the children born in the summer would be younger than the rest, they would have the same number of terms as other children in the infant school.

104 J. W. B. Douglas, J. M. Ross and H. R. Simpson

'School Leaving and GCE Results', from *All Our Future*, 1968, pp. 23–5.

The class bias within the education system was further illuminated by the continuing longitudinal survey which had earlier drawn attention to the 'wastage' associated with the 11+ exam. (see 19). It found that among children matched for academic ability, middle-class children were twice as likely to stay on at school than were working-class children, a finding which confirmed the decision to raise the school leaving age.

The boys and girls in the National Survey reached fifteen early in March 1961 and those who left school at the minimum age did so at Easter, one term before the end of the academic year. Approximately half the pupils left school at the earliest opportunity and a further 10 per cent at the end of the summer term. After this there was a year during which relatively few left, followed by a further substantial fall-out at the end of the five-year secondary school course at sixteen years four months; 24 per cent of the boys and 23 per cent of the girls were still in full-time education at sixteen and a half years either at school or college. The fall-out during the fifth year included some entering trade apprenticeships that by tradition begin at sixteen and end at twenty-one. Apart from these, the number of mid-fifth-year leavers is small, for most of those still at school or college at the beginning of the year were intending to sit some O-level examinations. For convenience we shall use the terms 'completed the session 1961–2' and 'began the session 1962–3'. The first includes all those who would normally have had the opportunity to sit the O-level examinations after a five-year secondary school course (or four years in Scotland). The second refers to those who were still at school one term later, in other words, those who stayed on after the normal age of sitting the O-level examinations. The majority of these would be entering the sixth form.

The heavy losses through early leaving occur largely in the manual working classes – only 36 per cent of the lower manual working-class pupils remained at school after the statutory leaving age. Owing to this differential fall-out there is a rapid change in the social background of those still at school after the age of fifteen. This is shown by the increase in the proportion of upper middle-class pupils from 5 per cent of all those at school up to the age of fifteen, to 12 per cent of all those completing the session 1961–2 and to 15 per cent of those starting the session 1962–3.

One reason why the middle-class boys and girls stay on longer at school is that they are academically more able, and even when comparisons are made between pupils of similar measured ability and attainment, the social class differences are still marked. This even holds for the pupils of high ability,[1] and is in contrast with our findings at the point of secondary selection. At the age of transfer pupils of high ability had an equal chance of reaching grammar schools from whatever social class they came. But there is a heavy loss even at the highest levels of ability through relatively early leaving from the poorer families. Thus 50 per cent of the lower manual working-class pupils of high ability have left school by the end of the session 1961–2, compared with only 10 per cent and 22 per cent respectively of the able upper and lower middle-class pupils. From this it is clear that many manual working-class pupils, who have the ability to benefit from a sixth year at school or college, are failing to do so.

Social-class differences are even greater among those at the borderline level of ability for grammar-school entry.[2] 38 per cent of this group started the session 1962–3 and of these 53 per cent are middle class. Indeed over four-fifths of the upper middle-class pupils at this level of ability were still at school at the beginning of the academic year 1962–3, compared with one-fifth of the lower manual working class. Even at the lower-ability ranges the majority of upper middle-class pupils remain at school after the minimum leaving age; 69 per cent of those whose scores show them to be of average ability or just below stayed at school at least until the end of the session 1961–2 and 42 per cent were still at school one term later –

1. The term 'pupils of high ability' will always refer to those with aggregate test scores of sixty or more at fifteen years (i.e. the top 16 per cent).

2. The borderline level includes those pupils with aggregate test scores of fifty-five to fifty-nine in the fifteen-year tests.

the corresponding percentages for the lower manual working class are 12 per cent and 4 per cent.

The above figures probably understate the loss of academic talent through early leaving for they are based on assessments of ability and attainment made at fifteen, just before the pupils reached the statutory leaving age. The test results at eight or eleven might have given a more realistic picture of the potential ability of these pupils; the figures already given are however striking enough as they stand.

The social-class pattern of leaving may be summarized by saying that the upper middle-class pupils were two and a half times as likely to stay on after the minimum leaving age as the lower manual working-class pupils, four times as likely to complete the session 1961–2 and nearly six times as likely to start session 1962–3. Part of these differences is explained by the higher measured ability of the upper middle-class boys and girls, but even when groups of similar ability are compared, the upper middle-class pupils were approximately twice as likely to stay on at each age.

105 Schools Council

from *Raising the School Leaving Age*, Working Paper no. 2, 1965, pp. 8–12.

Faced with the imminent raising of the school-leaving age to sixteen, and the inherent fact that this would mean a full five-year course of secondary education for a new population of children, schools were faced with the question: 'What kind of education?' The new Schools Council gave the problem top priority, and launched a series of major inquiries (see 106) to discover the characteristics of this new group.

Thought must start with the pupils themselves. And this involves imagination as well as knowledge and experience. Indeed it is a basic argument of this Working Paper that success in the development of new curricula, courses and methods may depend very largely on the realization that many existing assumptions derive from experience of pupils far less mature than those who, from 1970–71 onwards, will complete five instead of four years of secondary education. It is suggested that this greater maturity provides a major opportunity to develop an approach to secondary education which will differ from the present approach more, and certainly more importantly, in the range and quality of the work that is attempted, than in its quantity. More of the same will not bring success. It is not the 'extra year' that makes the difference; the opportunities of a five-year course are totally different from those of a four-year course. They require new assumptions, attitudes and understandings, and a new approach to the development of a five-year course which will be truly secondary in character.

The possibility of true secondary education begins when the pupil realizes that he is no longer a child, and becomes aware of himself – of his needs, satisfactions and expectations – and of his relationships with other people and with his environment outside the narrow circle of family, neighbourhood, peer group or school. It is part of the nature of this awareness that it involves him in taking decisions which are adult, or near adult, in character; for example: to become positively involved in his own education, because he sees its relevance to his own interests, needs and expectations from life, or deliberately not to become involved, because he does not see personal relevance in the life and work of the school.

The difference between the acceptance of childhood and the self-conscious awareness of the adult gives a clue to the real distinction between the primary and secondary modes of learning. The natural curiosity of the younger child, and his relatively undiscriminating desire to discover, to explore and to compete, provides the good teacher, working with healthy children from normal home backgrounds, with a lively basis of interest and motivation upon which to build. The young adult, on the other hand, is using his growing awareness of himself, of other people and of his environment, as a basis for decisions, many of them of life-long importance, about the kind of person he intends to be, the nature of his relationships with other people, his interests, motives, adaptation to his environment and his expectations from life. Secondary education, in the true sense of the word, then becomes possible, though its guidance will always be a difficult and delicate operation.

The question 'When does this transition occur?' is fundamental to an understanding of the ideas put forward in this Working Paper. It occurs, of course, at different ages for different people, and at different ages in the same person in different activities. There is no sharp break between childhood and an adult awareness; there is a period of transition of varying length. Indeed, for a few the transition to a fully adult state over a large field of activities is never realized. For most of the pupils who will be affected by the raising of the school-leaving age, it seems likely that the transition gathers momentum later rather than earlier, in the course of their third and fourth years of secondary education. By the fifth year, their personal and mental maturity will make heavy demands on the teacher's understanding and knowledge – markedly heavier than for fourth-year leavers at the present leaving age.

From many points of view, the most important aspect of the transition is that the young adult begins to claim, as of right, freedom of choice. And perhaps the most important aspect of true secondary education is the opportunity it offers to help the students lay the groundwork of a mature understanding of the processes, limitations and consequences of making different choices. The groundwork is no easier to lay than the superstructure is to build. Each requires some degree of insight, some exercise of thought and some effort at formulation.

In many other respects, secondary education may be seen as a continuation of the primary stage. The treatment will be different, but many of the main strands are essentially the same: for example, the development of powers of body and mind, self-expression, the acquisition of knowledge and the learning of skills. To the child, these can be ends in themselves. But to the mature adult, they are tools to be used for human purposes, both personal and social, which may be judged good or bad, better or worse. Whether for child or adult, they grow simply by use.

If the distinctive task of secondary education is to help the pupils make the judgements, or choices, which will determine the use they make of whatever capacities their parents, their school and their environment have enabled them to develop, this involves adding to the pupils' equipment both a telescope and a microscope. They need a telescope with which to look back in time in order to see something of the choices which men have made in the past, the reasons why these choices were made, the consequences which followed, and the ways in which men have evaluated both choices and consequences. They also need to point the telescope forward in time in order to acquire some vision, albeit personal, of where they themselves, and humanity in general, are heading. And they need a microscope, with which to gain insights into their own experience, and into the choices which they themselves and their contemporaries face in the here and now. Mature judgement arises when both telescope and microscope are used to the full, when what is seen is compared, ordered and discussed with others by a use of reason, skill, knowledge, imagination and sensitivity of feeling, and when it is realized that the resulting judgements or choices are a matter of personal responsibility, frequently involving commitment in the face of uncertainty.

The possibility of helping the pupils who are the concern of this paper to enter the world of ideas, to use powers of reason, and to acquire even the beginnings of mature judgement, may seem to contradict the experience of many teachers. Indeed it may carry an almost revolutionary ring to some, and this accounts for the tentative character of many of the ideas put forward in this Working Paper. It is often said that these pupils are not interested in ideas; they cannot handle abstractions; they cannot verbalize; they make choices by comparing immediate satisfactions; they are only interested in people and concrete situations. It is just these assumptions which the raising of the school-leaving age gives all in the sphere of secondary education the opportunity to challenge. For the more able pupils, now staying on voluntarily in increasing numbers, the fifth year has revealed powers which many did not suspect. When, for some 60 per cent of the pupils, schooling stops often before the fourth year is out, and before a sufficient maturity is reached, possibilities for development may be undiscovered. This is the basic assumption which the Newsom Report asks us to make when it calls for a change of heart in our attitudes towards the slower learners.

In thinking about what is desirable, and practicable, in developing new curricula and courses for the young school leaver, the standpoint of this Working Paper is thus that some existing assumptions, though soundly based on current experience, may be invalid in the situation which will follow the raising of the school-leaving age. There is evidence from further and adult education, and from the experience of those few schools which have successfully held appreciable numbers of the less able pupils for a fifth year of secondary education, that doors can be thrown open where current experience of a four-year course might suggest that they must remain closed. There is also evidence from primary education that practically all pupils can acquire insights into abstract ideas, and a capacity to work with them (particularly by oral means), if doors are opened through the use of teaching methods which build on the pupils' present experience and supply new forms of experience which help them to discover for themselves the powers of their own minds. And there is evidence that adults of quite low educational achievement often have to try to sort out complex ideas, and that many of them do so with astonishing success once they feel the need for – and therefore set about the business of acquiring – attainments (for example, a wider vocabulary: relevant concepts: powers of reasoning) more highly developed than customary opinion in educational circles has allowed them. The challenge, and the opportunity, of the five-year course is to open more of these doors, at least to some degree, for the majority of ordinary pupils.

Implications for the curriculum

There are however conditions to be met if this is to be possible. The pupil, or young student, will not be best placed to play his full part if the purposes of the teachers are hidden from him, or if they appear to be derived from a scholastic tradition which is valid for other people, but not for him. If the work he is asked to do is simply to memorize facts about the English legal system at work, he will form no idea about the Rule of Law; nor, lacking the concept which embodies, relates and explains the detailed information he is given, will he be likely to remember the facts. And if he is taught skills – and this applies particularly to the use of his mother tongue – without adequate explanation of, or opportunities to discover for himself, the human purposes which they can serve, he will acquire them less readily; and, later on, if vocational motivation or leisure interests give him a personal reason for wanting to acquire a high level of skill, he may (and often does) complain that he was badly taught.

If it is unsafe to carry forward into the new situation some assumptions derived from experience of the pupils of lesser maturity now completing only four years of secondary education, others can be carried forward with a greater degree of confidence. The first and without doubt the most important is that a central and abiding interest of most young adults is people. They are deeply interested in themselves; they are deeply interested in their relationships with other people.

Here, then, is a vital core of interest ready to hand. And educators need have no hesitation in using it as the central theme and motive for new curricula, pervading and relating all the separate courses, and having its influence upon organization and methods throughout the school. For there is wide agreement that a man's understanding of himself, and of Man, is of the first importance in the education of ordinary pupils. To quote from the Newsom Report:

The field in which it is most important that ordinary boys and girls should learn to exercise a common sense judgement quickened by imaginative insight is that of personal relations. Their greatest service to the community, and there is none greater, will be as men and women who can be relied on to make a success of their own lives and by the quality of their living to bring up their children to do the same. This is not something that can be taken for granted or left to traditional methods of indoctrination. In a contracting world, where all men are neighbours but by no means necessarily friends, everybody needs an education of the imagination and the will to enlarge the area of his concern and acceptance of responsibility (paragraph 315).

It is therefore basic to the ideas put forward in this Working Paper that some understanding, however limited, of human nature and conduct, and of the means which men use in developing concepts of value, and in using the physical world for valued human purposes, takes on greater and greater precedence the older the pupils become. The older they are, the nearer they come to taking charge of their own lives – and they know it, and want help of the right kind in facing up to the challenges which they will meet.

More is however at issue than simply relating the work of the schools to the pupils' own view of their needs, to their own central interests, and to their own evaluation of what is relevant. These are the points of departure, and at least half the task is that of finding starting points, methods of work and materials for assisting the process of learning which, so to speak, come right home to the pupils. But the other half of the task is to carry the pupils forward, so that what is taught has relevance not only to the pupils' present condition, but also to at least the next stage in their future development and understanding.

The teacher must necessarily see more deeply than the pupil can, partly because he is older, better educated and longer experienced, but also because he is trustee for a social view of what is good and useful, the full implications of which lie far beyond the pupils' present experience. This experience may well give the pupils insights into the likely personal relevance of skills and certain other elements in the curriculum. But they will be left prisoners of their own experience if the teacher cannot find a way of so enlarging their vision and understanding that they come to see value for themselves in gaining some understanding of Man's total experience, and with it some capacity to contribute to its further enlargement.

What is at issue is, therefore, the bringing of the best traditional view of what constitutes a liberal education within the grasp of ordinary people. When every man is King how does he become enough of a philosopher to wield power wisely ? When every man is aware, as all are today at least in some degree, of the complexity of the world in which we live, how can every man be helped to gain some kind of access to a complex cultural inheritance ? How can all be brought to have some kind of hold on their personal lives, and on their place in, and contribution to, the various communities – family, neighbourhood, club, occupational, national and international – in which they play a part ? And what are the limits to what the schools can hope to achieve ?

For there are, of course, limits to what the schools can usefully attempt. If it is true that doors to the world of ideas can be opened for these pupils, once their greater maturity while still at school makes this possible, it is equally true that these doors open later than for others and that, even with a leaving age of sixteen, there will be less time for the schools to help those who learn more slowly. Indeed, it may well turn out that the biggest challenge will occur in the fourth rather than the fifth year of secondary education. A degree of impatience to be off and away must be expected to develop in the fifth, as it now does in the fourth year of the course.

Nor is it suggested that the task which the teachers face is to find the right answers all at once. The task is rather to make the best of all the opportunities presented by the raising of the school-leaving age to raise the level of the platform upon which the next generation of teachers, parents and others can build. The young pupil who is helped by his school to provide a home environment for his children better than his own makes it that much easier for a future teacher to consolidate and improve on the advance, however marginal. The ability to discriminate between pop music which is mawkish, sentimental or boorish, and that which evokes, however crudely, genuine human feeling, represents a gain in sensitivity that is worth having. The ability to see, however dimly, that the pay packet is not the only possible criterion for industrial action; the ability to solve a few more personal problems; to take rather more personal responsibility; to cooperate a little more readily with others in meeting human needs; all these are gains, which will make it easier for future parents, teachers and others to secure even larger gains in the education of successive generations of children.

In building new curricula and courses, it is therefore important to find the right balance between too little and too much. It will be better to convey some understanding of a few large ideas of central importance than to run far ahead of the pupils' grasp and perseverance by attempting more than they can cope with, whether in quantity, complexity or level of difficulty. And it is the quality of the pupils' understanding that matters, not the volume of remembered fact. Indeed, the one follows the other. Facts will be remembered only if they have been organized and understood.

Nor is there any place for the 'integrity of the subject', if by this is meant some corpus of factual knowledge confined within strict subject boundaries. The true integrity of the subject, highly relevant to the present challenge, resides in its distinctive ways of inquiry, of asking questions about and seeking to explain some aspect of the human condition or of human experience. Subject areas possessing this kind of integrity can strongly reinforce one another in conveying the understandings that are sought. A topic, if important enough to justify the expenditure of time, can usefully appear in several different subject syllabuses, each of which contributes to the pupil's total understanding, its distinctive methods of inquiry, and relationships with other topics. Such reinforcement is of the greatest importance with the slower learners.

The view of the curriculum put forward in this paper is therefore holistic. It is suggested that it should possess organic unity, and that the organizing principle most likely to provide a sound basis for development is the study of Man, and of human society, needs and purposes.

106 Schools Council

from *Inquiry 1*, 1968, pp. 45, 218–19, 221.

As part of its inquiry into the problems of raising the school-leaving age, the Schools Council commissioned the Government Social Survey to carry out a study into the differences in attitudes and expectations of education between middle-class and working-class families. The findings revealed the 'culture clash' existing between many pupils and their teachers in the nation's classrooms.

Both fifteen-year-old leavers and their parents very widely saw the provision of knowledge and skills which would enable young people to obtain the best jobs and careers of which they were capable as one of the main functions that a school should undertake. Teachers, however, very generally rejected the achievement of vocational success as a major objective of education. It is evident therefore that conflict and misunderstanding may arise between the short-term viewpoint of parents and pupils who are concerned with starting work in the immediate future and the long-term objectives of teachers who see their responsibility as preparing pupils for the whole of their future lives.

The majority of teachers considered that very important aims of school life should be to develop the characters and personalities of pupils, to teach them ethical values and to help them to become mature, confident and successful in their personal relationships. These objectives received a good deal of support also from fifteen-year-old leavers, particularly girls, and even more from their parents, the exception being personality and character development which parents and youngsters less often saw as a school responsibility.

Other practical aspects of everyday living such as management of money, being able to speak well and easily and to put things in writing easily were very generally wanted by fifteen-year-old leavers and their parents. Among girls there was a great demand to learn things which would be useful in running a home. Fifteen-year-old leavers more generally than later leavers wished their education to include things which would be of practical value in everyday life, they more often wanted to be helped in their personal development and in making the most of themselves.

On the whole they attached only moderate importance to the role of the school in developing their interests and increasing their awareness of what was happening in the world. They saw little value in school visits other than for careers purposes, or in extra-curricula activities such as school clubs, holidays or residential courses. Parents, however, appeared more generally to look to the schools to provide spare time interests and acceptable outlets for the energies of the young and in this they were generally supported by the school staff. [. . .]

The diagram (on page 513) shows the average scores for the two subgroups, fifteen-year-old leavers and those staying on at school, on each of the six-attitude dimensions, the five school-objective dimensions and the six for values, interests and home backgrounds. Again on each dimension the average for the whole sample of youngsters is zero. It can be seen that fifteen-year-old leavers differed most of all from those staying on at school in the quality of their home backgrounds which were much less favourable for leavers; in being very much less inclined to have any intellectual or academic interests; and in being much more generally of an active than a sedentary bent and more interested in practical-constructional activities than were stayers. They also showed differences from those staying on at school on a number of other dimensions, although to a lesser degree. They tended to come from larger families and more overcrowded homes. On the whole they occupied their leisure time less satisfactorily than did the stayers and more easily became bored or gave their parents cause for anxiety. They were more inclined than stayers to resent school discipline, they were less identified with and interested in school life, they considered their subject curricula less useful and interesting and their behaviour in school was more likely to be considered unsatisfactory by their teachers. Even more than those staying on they wanted their education to be concerned with preparing them for their working life but they were less anxious than stayers that it should be concentrated on improving their career prospects. They more generally wished the school to help them to develop as people and to make the most of themselves and they wanted to learn things which would be useful in everyday life.

107 Department of Education and Science

'In-Service Training', from the White Paper *Education:
A Framework for Expansion*, Cmnd 5174, 1972, p. 18.

*A relative decline in the numbers passing through the education system
provided the opportunity – the first since the State system came into being –
of concentrating more attention on the quality of teaching rather than
its quantity. 'In-service training', the essential demand of a committee
under Lord James which looked into teacher training, was accepted by the*

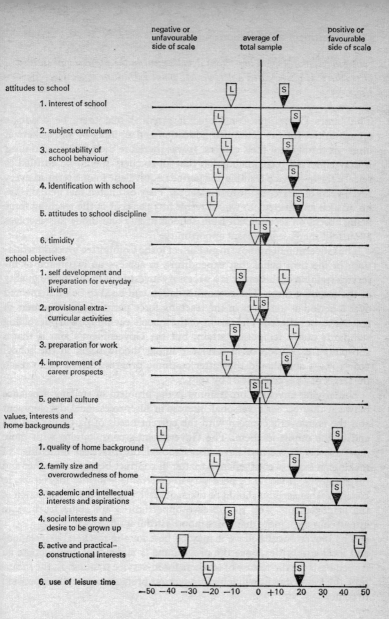

L = Youngsters leaving school at fifteen   S = Youngsters staying on at school

Figure 1 Comparison of average scores of fifteen-year-old leavers and stayers on dimensions of attitudes to school, school objectives, values, interests and home backgrounds

T—ECS—R

government, marking an important development in the professional status of teachers. It also created a new growth point within the education system itself.

The James Committee considered it essential that there be adequate opportunities for the continued education and training of all teachers at intervals throughout their careers. It was therefore their leading and most widely endorsed recommendation that all teachers should be entitled to release for in-service training for periods equivalent to one term in every seven years of service in the first instance. They estimated that actual take-up of such an entitlement would result in 3 per cent of the teaching force being absent on secondment from schools at any one time; this involves a fourfold increase in present opportunity.

The Government propose to give effect to the Committee's recommendation, in the firm belief that expenditure to achieve an expansion of in-service training of this order is a necessary investment in the future quality of the teaching force. The recommendation will need to be implemented over a period as increases in the teaching force permit larger numbers of teachers to be released. The raising of the school-leaving age will put staffing standards under temporary strain, but the Government's aim is that a substantial expansion of in-service training should begin in the school year 1974–5 and should thereafter continue progressively so as to reach the target of 3 per cent release by 1981.

Underlying any such programme is the problem of striking a balance between the teacher's personal interest in his professional development and the employer's concern with the current needs of particular schools and of the pupils in them. The Government's consultations with those most closely concerned have also exposed the practical difficulties of making an express entitlement a matter of contract between a teacher and his employer. It would be necessary to determine priorities for release, to consider what account should be taken of service before the introduction of the arrangements, and to preserve opportunities for some teachers to attend courses of more than three months in duration.

The Government believe it may be best for the teachers' associations and local authorities, once the programme is under way, to negotiate an agreed basis for the release of teachers for in-service training. In the meantime the Government will look for vigorous preparation for the expansion to come.

108 Department of Education and Science

Circular 2/73, 'Nursery Education', 31 January 1973, pp. 1–8.

Probably the most dramatic content of the 1972 White Paper, Education: A
Framework for Expansion, *was the provision it made for the expansion
of pre-school provision. The details of the government's thinking were
contained in the subsequent Circular, given below, asking for local
authority plans to implement this expansion within a number of months.
The government pledged to provide £30 millions in the period 1974–6
to begin a programme of provision, and aimed at meeting the Plowden
targets of 75 per cent of four year olds and 35 per cent of three year olds
enjoying part-time schooling (and another 15 per cent on full time) by 1982.*

The Secretary of State for Education and Science and the Secretary of
State for Wales announced on 6 December in Cmnd 5174 that they intend
to expand nursery education at a rate which would enable provision to be
made by 1981–2 (i.e. January 1982) up to the limit of the scale estimated as
necessary by the Central Advisory Councils in 1967 in the Plowden and
Gittins Reports. The purpose of this Circular is to give guidance to local
education authorities in England and Wales on the scale and nature of this
expansion, on the provision of staff and buildings and on related matters.

Numbers

To provide full-time education for 15 per cent of three and four year olds,
and part-time education for 35 per cent of three year olds and 75 per cent
of four year olds will require up to 250,000 additional full-time equivalent
places in 1982. This figure, which allows for the growth in the number of
places for under-fives, including rising-fives, on present trends from
300,000 now to 450,000 in ten years time, should be regarded as a maximum.
It represents the basis on which the Government is planning to make
resources available up to 1982. It may need to be revised in the light of new
forecasts of the child population or of indications that the demand for
nursery education is lower than that estimated by the Central Advisory
Councils. It should also be noted that the figure does not allow for the
provision of additional places for children of rising-five in primary schools
over and above those provided for four year olds on the scale indicated
above.

Nature of provision

The objective is to make nursery education available for children whose
parents want it from the beginning of the term after their third birthday,

until the term after their fifth birthday. Demand for places for three year olds is likely to be much smaller than for four year olds but provision should be made for both. Resources will not be available for additional provision for two year olds in nursery schools or classes.

The Secretaries of State endorse the view expressed in the Plowden Report that for the majority of children aged three and four part-time attendance at school on five mornings or five afternoons a week may often be educationally preferable to full-time attendance. The number of part-time pupils in nursery schools and classes has grown from 4000 in 1960 to about 70,000 in 1972 and the Secretaries of State expect most of the additional provision to be based on part-time attendance. But for a minority of children aged three and four, estimated in the Plowden Report at 15 per cent as an average over the whole country, full-time provision is desirable for both educational and social reasons. In areas of social deprivation a higher proportion of full-time provision may be appropriate.

For practical reasons it may also be necessary to make full-time provision for some children whose homes are scattered over a wide rural area. Circumstances and problems vary widely from place to place, and authorities should study alternative solutions to determine those best suited to their area. In some cases, for example, full-time attendance on two or three days may be preferable to part-time attendance every day.

Local education authorities in Wales will need, in making their provision, to have due regard to the linguistic character of their areas.

There are educational advantages in enabling most children attending school below the age of five to do so at the school which they will attend after five. This avoids a change of school and enables educational development to be planned as a whole from three to four to the beginning of the junior- or middle-school course. Nursery provision within primary schools is also more economical to provide and maintain than separate nursery schools. For these reasons, although nursery schools already in existence or at an advanced stage of planning should continue, it is recommended that most additional places should be provided in units attached to primary schools so far as their sites allow.

In planning new primary schools under major building programmes, whether to meet rising numbers or to replace old buildings, local authorities should ensure that account is taken of the need to provide education for children under five. The Architects and Building Branch of the Department of Education and Science, in consultation with the Welsh Education Office, is taking part in a development project for an infants school which incorporates a nursery unit. Information on the design of this project will be published in a Design Note as soon as possible.

Disadvantaged children

Nursery education is particularly valuable as a means of reducing the educational and social disadvantages suffered by children from homes which are culturally and economically deprived. It is for this reason that the Secretaries of State have concentrated the resources available for nursery education in areas of social deprivation eligible for the Urban Programme. Recent research findings confirm that such children are greatly helped in two ways. The first is through increasing the interest of the parents, particularly mothers, in such a way that they understand more of their children's development, are able to assist them at home and cooperate with the teachers at school. The second is through educational programmes which enrich the children's experience and thereby directly offset their environmental handicaps. In making plans for providing nursery education throughout their areas authorities are accordingly asked, in consultation with social service departments and voluntary bodies to give priority to meeting the needs of these children, while ensuring that in any one class a balance between them and other children is maintained.

It is important that children from economically and culturally deprived homes should not be put at a further disadvantage because their parents are uninformed about nursery education or diffident about taking the steps necessary to secure a place in a nursery unit. It may be desirable to take positive steps to publicize the expansion of provision in areas of social disadvantage so as to encourage parents whose children are most in need of nursery education to apply for the places available.

It may also be desirable that headteachers should be given guidance on the selection of children for places in nursery units until supply matches demand. Authorities will be in the best position to judge in consultation with headteachers, what criteria of individual need should be applied in their area and to decide how much control they wish to exercise over the detailed arrangements in individual schools.

Handicapped children

The importance of early education for children who are handicapped has long been recognized. Nursery education enables immediate measure to be taken to offset the educational disadvantages imposed by any form of handicapping condition; and it provides an ideal opportunity for the prolonged and systematic observation of a child so that a precise assessment can be made of his future educational needs. It is also a valuable source of support and advice for parents to help them to develop a constructive attitude towards their child's disability. For some handicapped children aged two and over a special school is appropriate. But provided that a suitable balance is maintained and that staffing and other arrangements are appropriate, less severely handicapped children can often be educated along with other children in nursery schools and classes.

Staffing

The present ratio of staff (teachers and nursery assistants) to children in nursery classes, excluding headteachers of the primary schools to which they are attached, is about 1: 13. There are wide local variations in the employment of teachers and nursery assistants, but over the country as a whole about one-third of the staff are teachers and two-thirds are nursery assistants.

A ratio of 1:13 is generally acceptable except when some of the children require special help. But the Secretaries of State hope that the proportion of qualified teachers will rise steadily so that by 1982 they account for at least one half of the total staff, and that they are supported by trained nursery assistants. Together with this change, and the improvements referred to below, the expansion of provision for under-fives will require the employment by 1982 of upwards of 25,000 teachers compared with the 10,000 now teaching pupils in these age-groups. It will be necessary to plan for a suitable share of teacher training places to be devoted to training for the younger age-groups and to attract students to fill them as opportunities for teaching children under five are seen to be expanding. It should then be possible for many of the additional teachers required to be recruited direct from appropriate courses in colleges or departments of education. For others, men as well as women, with experience mainly of teaching older children, who wish to turn to nursery education, suitable in-service training will need to be developed. Finally, the organization of nursery classes on a part-time basis should make it possible to attract back into teaching some married women who do not want to work full-time.

Even with the rise in the ratio of children to nursery assistants (the corollary of the lower pupil–teacher ratio), a substantial expansion in the number of nursery assistants will be required. Courses leading to a certificate of the NNEB will continue to provide the main source of training nursery assistants. The arrangements for these courses are at present under review by the NNEB and by the Departments concerned. Meanwhile the Board can be expected to give sympathetic consideration to any special arrangements for the practical training which may be necessary for particular courses. In considering the possible expansion of courses, authorities will no doubt wish to consult appropriate members of HM Inspectorate.

The role of parents

Nursery education should supplement, not replace, what a child learns at home. The experience of the playgroup movement shows that parents often wish to be closely involved in the education and growth of other young children as well as their own; and both recent research and long experience of nursery teachers demonstrate that under professional guidance parents can play a valuable part in a school or unit and by so doing can come better to fulfil their own role as parents. Authorities are asked to do everything possible to extend opportunities for collaboration, particularly through the provision of amenities which make it easier to welcome parents into schools and which enable parents to participate in their work. Teachers themselves, especially any who enter nursery work for the first time, may need opportunities for study, observation and training. A short list of references to research and experiment in these fields is given in Appendix A to this Circular. It is also recommended that authorities should provide opportunities in colleges of further education and elsewhere for parents to learn more about young children.

The role of playgroups

The Secretaries of State recognize the value of the contribution of the playgroup movement to the education of the under-fives in both England and Wales and they hope that the development of playgroups will continue. Some playgroups may immediately become maintained nursery classes, linked to local primary schools. Until nursery education is more widely available, other playgroups may be assisted by authorities, through cash grants, the loan of equipment, and the advice of the authority's nursery and infant specialists. These playgroups should also be associated with local primary schools and thereby enjoy the support of qualified teachers who would be able, by virtue of their training, to help identify any children with learning or other difficulties which call for fuller investigation. There may be others again for which there will be a continuing need, alongside the maintained provision. In consultation with social service departments, authorities should consider carefully the role of playgroups when preparing plans for the expansion of nursery provision in their area.

Admission of children under five to the reception classes of primary schools

In a number of areas the decline in the numbers of children over five and the improvement in the supply of teachers have already made it possible for local authorities to admit to primary schools not only rising-fives (over 150,000 in January 1972) but also other four year olds in addition to those in nursery classes. Provided that the accommodation is suitable for young children and that adequate staff and equipment are available, this is a welcome development and, with a further fall in primary-school numbers and more teachers, it will be feasible on a growing scale as a step towards the provision of nursery education for most four year olds.

At the same time authorities should ensure that the hours of attendance, staffing, programmes, accommodation and equipment for these children under five are equivalent to those appropriate to nursery classes. They are also asked to ensure that children are not normally transferred as soon as they are four from nursery schools to the reception classes: for those who start in a nursery school at three, the continuity of up to two years' education can be very valuable. Moreover, a nursery school in which all the pupils are of one age group lacks opportunities for younger and older to learn from each other.

Research

Restrictions on the scale of provision have inevitably limited research into the content of nursery education and the development of new teaching programmes. Nevertheless some significant contributions, especially in the field of language development, have recently been made by the Educational Priority Areas Action Research Project and by the Compensatory Education Project and the Pre-School Education Project, the last two sponsored by the Schools Council. A wealth of material relevant to early childhood is available from other sources, notably from the longitudinal study undertaken by the National Children's Bureau for the Government, the findings of which for the years from birth to seven have recently been published. Materials and approaches recently developed in other countries, particularly the USA deserve study, and area training organizations and teachers' centres have a valuable part to play in disseminating knowledge of them. The Secretaries of State will consult appropriate bodies before deciding what further research and development should be undertaken into the content of nursery education. They also propose to set up a research programme to monitor the development of the new provision.

Buildings

To provide up to 250,000 additional places by new building or adaptation by 1982 will require substantial building programmes, beginning in 1974–5 and running at the rate of £15m. a year (starts) for the first two years. (Some authorities may be able to use part of their existing minor works allocations for 1972–4 in order to make an earlier start.) The programmes will take the form of earmarked additions to minor works allocations and to block allocations. Authorities are asked to consider what additional provision will be required to meet by 1982 the likely demand described in paragraph 1 and to inform the Department of Education and Science or the Welsh Education Office in due course. Meanwhile they are asked to inform them by 18 May 1973 what volume of work they wish to start both in 1974–5 and in 1975–6. Details of individual projects are not required, but in their plans and estimates of cost authorities should have regard to the advice given in Design Note No. 1 and to the present cost limit of £305 for a place in a nursery class. The allocations for both years, which will be made during the summer, will cover both county and voluntary schools: at a later stage the approval for grant purposes of individual projects at voluntary-aided schools will follow the normal procedure. Authorities are asked to consult the voluntary school authorities at an early stage both about their role during the decade as a whole and about their part in the programmes for their first two years.

In assessing their requirements for new building, authorities will need to take into account the prospective size of pre-school age-groups and the number of children under five for whom they expect to be providing places by 1974, after allowing for those approved under the Urban Programme, and for changes in primary school rolls which will enable them to use existing accommodation for children of nursery-school age, subject to the safeguards mentioned above. As indicated in Appendix B, this information should accompany proposals for new building in 1974–5 and 1975–6.

The total size of allocations to individual authorities in 1974–6 will depend partly on the demand for new places assessed on the basis outlined above. It is intended that all authorities should ultimately be enabled to meet demand up to the limits described above, although the pattern of attendance within areas may vary according to demand and social need. However the Secretaries of State intend to weight the initial allocations in favour of authorities with areas of greatest social need in order that deprived children, including some who are handicapped, may be the first to benefit from expansion of nursery education. Allocations will therefore depend also on the general social characteristics in each area. The definition of an area of social need will be similar to that used in the Urban Programme, broadened in order to reflect the social deprivation that exists in some new housing areas and rural areas as well as in inner city areas and declining industrial communities.

HM Inspectorate

HM Inspectorate will be glad to assist authorities by discussing how best to apply in their own areas the policy set out in this Circular.

Department of Education and Science

Finance

Estimates of relevant expenditure for rate support grant for 1973–4 have already been determined. These assume a continuation of the recent rate of growth in the number of under-fives in schools. The expansion foreshadowed in this Circular is not likely to entail significant additional expenditure until 1974–5 on loan charges and running costs, which will be reflected in estimates of relevant expenditure for that and subsequent years.

Virtually all the resources available for education under the Urban Programme have been used to increase provision for the under-fives in deprived areas. Now that it is possible to authorize a general expansion of nursery education the Secretaries of State believe it is right to concentrate Urban Programme expenditure elsewhere in the education service, and further guidance on this will be given to authorities shortly. Phase VII of the Urban Programme announced in Home Office Circular No. 91/1972 and covering expenditure on capital projects starting in 1973–4 will be the last to include projects for nursery schools or classes. Beyond this the expansion of nursery education to meet the targets set by the Secretaries of State will not be eligible for specific grant either on capital or recurrent expenditure.

Local government reorganization

Existing local education authorities will retain full responsibility for the education service in their areas, including the planning of the programme described in this Circular, in the period between the 1973 elections for the new councils and 1 April 1974. The new authorities will be responsible for the execution of the programme, and the Secretaries of State hope that the existing authorities will consult them during this transitional period. However, it is recognized that at a later stage the new authorities may wish to modify some of the assumptions on which the original plans are based. Full guidance on practical issues arising from local government reorganization was given in Circular No. 1/73.

Circular No. 8/60*

Circular No. 8/60 and its addenda are withdrawn.

* See p. 431 in this volume.

Further Reading

One could draw up a vast list of recent books that have described, in one way or another, the development of the English education system. Most of them offer a fairly rapid guide from the 1870 Act, which some take – falsely in my view – to be the start of the State system, through the main educational legislation. They are thick on the ground, and I would not presume to differentiate among them. In the following short list, I have merely mentioned some books that I have particularly enjoyed, and to which I have returned on numerous occasions. They form an entirely personal list, and I am therefore able to write about them with affection. But their mention here – and the exclusion of other, equally good, works – should not be considered as more than an idiosyncratic first reading list for those who want to look behind the official documents at the wider historical implications involved in the shaping of our education system.

T. W. Bamford, *The Rise of the Public Schools*, Nelson, 1967.
A detailed, but magnificently readable and genuinely interesting, study of a hackneyed theme. Bamford presents a lot of original research material on his subject, and does so with humour and clarity.

Rodney Barker, *Education and Politics 1900–1951*, Oxford University Press, 1972.
A recent study of the Labour Party, which contains much fresh detail and a lively and provocative interpretation which is a refreshing change from so much of the stilted writing that appears on this subject. It also has the merit of being brief without being cursory.

S. J. Curtis, *History of Education in Great Britain*, University Tutorial Press, 1961 edn.
A detailed and rather tedious tome, which nevertheless covers every essential facet so often glossed over by more readable writers. One cannot escape from its essential scholarly probity. A reference book rather than a good read.

Elie Halévy, *Imperialism and the Rise of Labour (1895–1905*, vol. 5, *History of the English People in the Nineteenth Century*, Ernest Benn, 1961 edn.
Nobody who wants to understand the complexities underlying the 1902

Education Act can ignore Halévy's brilliant chapter on 'The Problem of National Education' in his classic history, or the following chapter on the birth of the Labour Party. Much of the data he presents, and the insights he offers, have not been improved upon after nearly half a century of research and discussion. And if not read for the scholarship or the historicism, then simply admire the lucidity of the prose and the skill with which he organizes the mass of his material.

Maurice Kogan, *The Politics of Education*, Penguin Education, 1971.
There is remarkably little written on the actual decision-making process in education, and this study arising out of full-length discussions with two outstanding education ministers in post-war Cabinets, is a pioneering work that tries to draw aside a little of the veil. If it does not bite as deeply as one might have hoped, it is nevertheless a fascinating insight into a little-known world. And well-written to boot.

J. Stuart Maclure, *Educational Documents, England and Wales, 1816–1963*, Chapman & Hall, 1965.
An indispensable guide to the major educational reports, from a Parliamentary Committee on 'The Education of the Lower Orders' to the Plowden Report (in the revised edition). It has the great merit of providing the essential passages without the dross which makes most of them unreadable.

J. Stuart Maclure, *One Hundred Years of London Education, 1870–1970*, Allen Lane, 1970.
A lively history of the great LCC and its doings, gently working through a great mass of material to present a coherent and important story. There is a great deal of interesting detail for the specialist, and some superb photographs.

P. W. Musgrave (ed.), *Sociology, History and Education: A Reader*, Methuen, 1970.
Although this contains a number of essays outside the scope of this volume, it also has some very readable and provocative pieces, including the editor's own discussion of technical education in the critical period at the turn of the century. An important volume, in that it firmly links, as its title implies, a critique of education in relation to the social and economic situation of the time.

Malcolm Seaborne, *Education: A Visual History*, Studio Vista, 1966.
Although this is basically a picture book (with some really splendid photographs) it also contains a very good, synoptic introduction which, while it deals with education throughout the ages, inevitably gives a good deal of space to the period covered in this volume.

Brian Simon, *Education and the Labour Movement, 1870–1920,*
Lawrence & Wishart, 1965.
This volume, by our best educational historian, is both compulsive
reading to those interested in the subject, and the most comprehensive
treatment of this particular angle available anywhere. Rich in original
source material, it is essential reading for anyone who wants to
understand the period. The companion volume, covering the period
1780–1870, is well worth reading as background information, and a
third volume, covering the twenties and thirties, is to be published
shortly.

British Journal of Educational Studies.
Since its foundation in 1952, this journal has been published twice a year,
in May and November, by Faber. It now appears three times a year, and
consistently carries the most detailed and interesting studies in depth on
historical matters. It is notable that many of the pieces in Musgrave's
Reader (see above) first appeared in the *Journal.* The articles, however,
are aimed at the specialist rather than the novice.

Acknowledgements

For permission to reproduce copyright material acknowledgement is made to the following:

The Controller of Her Majesty's Stationery Office for all Crown copyright material quoted; the Estate of H. G. Wells for extracts from *Joan and Peter: The Story of Education* by H. G. Wells; to *Nineteenth Century and After* for 'Our Undisciplined Brains' by C. C. Perry; the *Monthly Review* for 'The Outlook for British Trade' by Sir H. E. Roscoe; *Nineteenth Century and After* for 'The Disadvantages of Education' by O. Eltzbacher; the Fabian Society for 'The Education Muddle and the Way Out' from *Fabian Tract;* the Trustees of the Rt Hon. Lord Passfield for 'The Making of a University' by Sidney Webb from the *Cornhill Magazine*; Hodder & Stoughton Ltd and W. and F. Haldane for an extract from *An Autobiography* by Richard Burdon, Lord Haldane; *Nineteenth Century and After* for 'The Need for National Nurseries' by Katherine Bathurst; Constable Publishers for an extract from *What is and What Might Be* by Edmond Holmes; the *Socialist Review* for 'The Feeding of School Children: Bradford's experience' by J. H. Palin; Independant Labour Party for an extract from 'London's Children: How to feed them and How not to feed them' by Margaret McMillan; the author and William Heinemann Ltd for an extract from *The Play Way: An Essay in Educational Method* by H. Caldwell Cook; to the *National Review* for 'The Child and the Nation' by Désirée Welby; the Inner London Education Authority for 'Prefatory Memorandum' by R. Blair from *The Distribution and Relations of Educational Abilities* by Cyril Burt; Eyre & Spottiswoode Ltd for extracts from *Some Memoirs* by Lord Percy of Newcastle; George Allen & Unwin Ltd and Pantheon Books Inc. for an extract from *The Radical Tradition* by R. H. Tawney; George Allen & Unwin Ltd for an extract from *Secondary Education for All: A Policy for Labour* by R. H. Tawney; Routledge & Kegan Paul Ltd and Schocken Books Inc. for an extract from *Intellectual Growth in Young Children* by Susan Isaacs; the *Journal of Child Psychology and Psychiatry* for 'Critical Notice' by Nathan Isaacs; the *Empire Review* for 'The School Leaving Age' by Lord Percy of Newcastle; A. P. Watt & Son for an extract from *That Dreadful School* by A. S. Neill; A. M. Heath & Co. Ltd and Mrs Sonia Brownell Orwell for an extract from *A Clergyman's Daughter* by George Orwell; Victor Gollancz Ltd for an extract from *Poverty and Public Health* by G. C. M. M'Gonicle and J. Kirby; A. M. Heath & Co. Ltd and Mrs Sonia Brownell Orwell for 'The Lion and the Unicorn' by George Orwell from *Collected Essays, Journalism and Letters*, vol. 2; the Socialist Educational Association for 'The Comprehensive School: Its History and Character' by National Association of Labour Teachers; the University of London Press for an extract from *Art and the Child* by Marion Richardson; Cedric Chivers Ltd for an extract from *Social Class and Educational Opportunity* by J. Floud, A. H. Halsey and F. M. Martin; Jonathan Cape Ltd for an extract from *The Future of Socialism* by C. A. R. Crosland; MacGibbon & Kee Ltd for an extract from *The Home and the School* by J. W. B. Douglas; Peter Davies Ltd for an extract from *All Our Future* by J. W. B. Douglas, J. M. Ross and H. R. Simpson.

Index

Adolescence, 211, 422–30, 462–3,
    504–10
Adult education, 378, 393
Age
  of employment, 46, 163, 207, 214,
    228
  and intelligence, 198–201, 370–71
  of school
    compulsory, 226, 227, 316, 385,
      398–9
    leaving
      economic considerations, 314–19
      14 years, 45–6, 207, 212, 227,
        243
      15 years, 214–15, 229, 308, 366–8,
        389, 398
      16 years, 398, 422–44, 462–3,
        502–4
      18 years, optional to, 229, 233, 240,
        422
  of transfer to secondary school, 138,
    243, 306–7, 313–14, 387–8,
    see also Comprehensive schemes
A-levels
  and social class, 457–9
American education, 445–9, 463
Anarchy, 237
Apprenticeship, 102, 128, 209–10,
    213
Aptitudes, 309, 311, 370, 373–5,
    385
Art, value of in education, 413–22
Arts in further education, 112,
    472
Assessment to replace
    examination at age 11, 386
ATTI report, 471, 473

Backwardness, 198–9, 243, 492
Birmingham University, 25, 105, 108
    113–14, 118
Blind-alley employment, 163, 206,
    209–10, 392
Block grant, 289–90, 334–9
Board of Education
  function of, 65, 69–72, 93–4, 284, 334
  publications
    circulars, 288–9, 305, 339–40
    education expenditure, 276–86,
      327–32, 332–9
    regulations, 98–105
    reports, 94–8, 137–8, 148–9, 162–72
      206–12, 302–5, 306–7, 320–21,
      348
    white papers, 384–93
Boarding, 32–3, 388–9, 401
Boards, school, 56–62, 65, 69, 75–8,
    87–8
  London, 72–3
Booth, Charles, 33
Boyle, Lord, 462
Bradford, school meals, 150–55
Bristol, 57, 114, 118, 119
'Bulges', 315, 317, 442
Burnham Committee, 279, 302, 327–31
Bursaries, 249, 250, 303
Burt, Cyril, 369
Business studies, see Commerce
Butler (1944 Education Act) 395–403
    407, 408

Cambridge university, 105–8, 114,
    269, 270–76
Cambridgeshire village colleges, 393,
    399

Certificate of Secondary Education, 467

Character
effect of early employment on, 164–72, 210–11, 217–19, 221
training in higher education, 127, 504–7, 511

Charlottenberg, 26, 111, 116

Children working, 23, 36, 222–4,
part-time from school, 162–73, 207–11, 213–14, 216–19

Churchill, Sir Winston, 395–6

Citizenship, education for, 224, 230, 392, 509

Class, see Social class

Cockerton judgement, 72–3

Co-educational community, 175, 186–9

Commerce, education for, 102, 112, 242, 248, 472

Community schools, 497

Comprehensive (Multilateral) education
curriculum, 410–13
encouraged in 1938, 371–2
Labour party policy for (1956), 449–52
need for, 404–10, 443–4
principles for, 444–9
schemes for, 474–80

Compulsory education, 86, 212, 234–5
further, 403
part-time, 240, 390–93,
see also Age, School

Conscription, 223

Continuation schools, 162, 212, 216, 218, 224, 229–31, 240, 391

Cost of education
1901, 26–7, 56–8, 79
1922, 276–86
1925, 287–90
1931, 327–39
free secondary (1920), 258–63

improvement in educationally deprived areas, 498–9
new (1903) universities, 113
see also Grants

Council
local authority, 57–60, 65–9, 76, 82–3, 222, 334
for National Academic Awards (CNAA), 472
Schools, 463–8, 504–10, 511–12

County schools, 397

Craft, 248, 413

Crosland, Anthony, 474

Crowther report, 454

Curriculum
comprehensive school, 410–13
'extra year', 504–10
primary school, 96, 214
secondary school, 245–9, 375–6, 389, 464–8

Defects (physical) in children, 122, 124, 158, 159–60

Degree courses in technology, 471–3

Delinquency, 175–89, 491

Denominational schools, 56, 59, 67–8, 84, 88

Deprived areas, 480–99, 517

Diet, 157–9

Direct-grant schools, 98–9, 103, 341, 388

Disabilities, schools for, 397, 517–18

Discrimination, positive, 489–99

Douglas, J. W. B., 502–3

Drill in infants schools, 124

Drink, 53–4

Dual system in higher education, 468–73

Durham university, 114, 118

Economies necessary in education costs, 276–86, 287–8, 288–90, 327–39

Education
ability, see Intelligence

Acts
  1870, 75, 98
  1889, 76, 88
  1902, 73–94, 113, 119, 126, 221–3,
    226, 230
  1918, 219–51
  1936, 366–8
  1944, 384–9, 395, 431
  administration of, 55, 62–71, 221,
    223, 224
  see also Board of education, Local
    authority, Ministry of Education
  costs see Costs
  function of, 130–33, 144–7, 186,
    202–6, 221, 224, 389, 392, 505–12
  half-time, 164–72, 206–8, 215, 227–8
  National Minimum, 71–2
  stages of, 384, 396
  see also Elementary, Secondary,
    Tertiary, Further education
  unnecessary, 28–31, 233
Educational priority areas, 480–99
Elementary (later primary) education
  see Primary school
Elementary higher education see
    Higher elementary education
Eleven +, selection for transfer to
    secondary schools, 306–10, 312–13,
    405, 409–10, 442–4, 502–4
Employers providing education, 229
Employment, juvenile
  'beneficial' as exemption from
    school, 366–8
  effects of, 164–72, 210–11, 217–19,
    221
  half-time system, 164–72, 207–15,
    227–8
  need for, 36, 128, 209–11, 317–19
  proposals to limit, 228
  see also Continuation schools
Endowments, 76, 119
English, teaching of, 102, 104, 246
Evening classes, 73, 100, 134, 207,
    390
Examinations

for secondary education, 238–9
  'special places', 340, 386, 410
  see also Scholarships, Selection
  in secondary schools, 229, 457–9,
    464–8, 502–4
Exeter university, 114
'Extra year' curriculum, 504–10

Family allowance, 338–84
Feeding habits, beneficial, 160–62
Fees for secondary education, 259–63,
    280, 338, 340–41, 435, 440
  abolished, 389
Fisher, H. A. L.
  1918 Education Act, 162, 206,
    criticism of, 233–8, 238–9, 239–45,
    251
  University grants, 266–70
Fleming Committee, 389, 451
Forces families, 492
Forster
  1870 Education Act, 63–4, 75, 204
    395
France, 205, 463
Free places in secondary schools,
    259–63, 280, 338, 339–41, 389,
    451 see also Scholarships, Selection
Freudian theory, 176–83
Froebel, 120, 123
Further education, 215, 396, 399–403,
    468–73
  see also Adult education,
    Polytechnics, Universities

Geddes commission, 328–9, 336
General Certificate of Education
  see A-levels, O-levels
Genius of uneducated leaders, 28–31
Germany, 20, 26, 205–6, 240
Girls
  education, 45–6, 104, 131, 230, 241,
    392, 461
  working, 219
Gloucester secondary education
  scheme, 265–6

Government
  administration of education, *see*
    Board of Education, Ministry of
    Education
  self, in progressive school, 325–7
Grading, 410
Grammar school, 369, 372, 387,
  452–3
  see also Direct grant school
Grant-aided schools, 258, 261, 280
Grants
  from local authority
    maintenance during higher
      education, 215, 218, 244, 283
    see also Scholarships, Free places in
      secondary schools
  from state
    to ex-Service men, 268, 284, 394–5
    to local authority
      block grant, 289–90, 334–9
      capitation scale, 120
      'elementary' education, 94, 278–9
      'higher' education, 258, 280,
        281–2
      nursery school, 255–6
      supplementary maintenance, 283
      for teachers' salaries, 279, 327–32
    to universities, 268–70, 276, 286,
      339
    for university education, 522
Great Western Railway, 213–14, 215
Gypsies, 492

Hadow Reports, 195, 305, 363
Haldane, Lord, 225
Half-time education, 164–72, 206–8
  215, 227–8
Halifax
  half-time labour in, 164–72
Handicapped children, 517–18
Higher education *see* Further
    education, Higher elementary
    education, Secondary education
Higher elementary education, 127–37,
  137–8, 226

Holmes, Edmond, 143
Home conditions and educational
    dependence on *see* Social class

Imperial College of Science and
    Technology, 116–17
Income
  and scholarships, 249, 250, 338–41
Independence, 217, 298, 311, 360,
  429
Individual approach to teaching,
  297–301
Industrial schools, 47
Industry
  education requirements, 240–41,
    252–4, 264–5, 318, 390–93
  juvenile labour requirements, 23,
    162–3, 207–11, 213–14, 216–19,
    220, 222, 228, 240–41
Infants
  emotional and social development,
    354–63
  mortality, 37–8
  schools, 96–7, 120–26, 305, 369, 386
  see also Nursery education
Inspection, 128–30, 137, 139–43, 218,
  350–54, 465–6
Intelligence
  as basis for secondary school selection,
    267, 320–21
  general, 197–201, 370–71
  need for military, 20–23
  and social class, 432–9
Interest
  as basis for learning, 134, 136–7,
    173–5, 291–5

James committee, 444–7, 514
Junior school, 305, 386
Junior secondary school *see* Technical
    school
Juvenile
  crime, 217
  employment, 23, 36, 164–72, 206–19,
    222–24

Lancashire, 139–43, 227, 238–9
Languages, 104, 112, 246–7,
    472–3
Latin, 104, 246
Leavers, school, 502–4, 511–12
Leeds
  school meals in, 154
  university, 114, 115, 118
Leicester transfer scheme, 307
Leisure occupation, 399
Libido, 181–9
Liverpool
  elementary schools, 140–42
  university, 105, 108, 109, 113–18
Local education authority
  child employment control, 228
  education costs, 288–90, 327–33
    see also Grants
  elementary (primary) schools, 56–69,
    83–9, 90–94, 148–9
  further education, 399–403
  nursery schools, 226, 255, 515
  secondary schools, 76–8, 81, 221–5,
    316, 396–8
  teachers' pay, 327, 329
  voluntary schools, 79–80
    see also Councils
London
  county council,
    elementary education, 85, 93, 158,
      159, 195–6
    secondary education, 239–45, 245–9,
      249–50, 409, 411
  school board, 68–9, 72–3, 78
  school of Economics, 112, 214, 433
  university, 27, 57, 105, 108–14
    see also Imperial College of Science
      and Technology

McMillan, Margaret, 150–52
McNair committee, 393
Malnutrition, 32–3, 148–9, 151,
    156–62
Malting House school, 291
Managers, school, 88, 91–2

Manchester
  pollution in, 33–6
  schools in, 57, 65, 119–26, 140, 154
  university, 105, 108, 114, 118
    see also Victoria University
Manual instruction in higher
    education, 131, 132, 135–7, 248
Maths in secondary schools, 247–8
Means test, 339–41
Medical inspection, 148–9, 223, 228,
    248, 363–6, 392
Mentally deficient children, 199–200
Middle class, 379–81
Military
  efficiency and intelligence, 19–23,
    30–31
  recruits, 38–43
Ministry of Education
  creation in 1944, 396, 463
Monitors, 159
Montessori teaching method, 187, 292,
    294–5, 295–301
Morant, Sir R. L., 94, 143
Morrell, Derek, 464
Morris, Henry, 399
Mothers
  importance to children, 122, 190,
    218, 354–5, 359, 517
  working, 45, 50–51, 53, 219, 250,
    385
Multilateral education see
    Comprehensive education
Museums, 203, 284
Music, 112, 248

National
  characteristics, 20–23
  economy and education
    1922, 274–86
    1925, 287–90
    1931, 327–39
  survey of social class and secondary
    education, 452–3, 483, 502–4
Needlework in infants school, 96,
    124–5

Newcastle upon Tyne, 57, 118
Newsom report, 507, 508
Nottingham, 57, 113, 114
Nursery education
  in elementary schools, 119–26,
    226–7, 385
  restriction of, 431–2
  in separate schools, 255–8, 385–6,
    496–7, 515–22
  social growth in, 358–63

O-levels
  and social class, 502–4
Overcrowding in homes, 33–4, 50,
    441, 491
Oxford university, 105–8, 114, 269,
    270–76

Parents, 80–81, 96, 131, 135, 244, 517,
    519
  see also Mothers
Part-time
  elementary education, 164–72, 206–8,
    215, 227–8
  further education, 473
  secondary education see
    Continuation schools, Evening
    classes
Physical
  ailments of elementary children, 122,
    124, 158, 159–60, 363–6
  effect of child labour, 164–72, 217,
    223, 227
  enquiry into deterioration (1904),
    33–55
  training, importance of, 241–2, 245,
    248, 257
Playgroups, 519
Plowden report, 516
Policy of drift, 59–61
Pollution, atmospheric, 35–6
Polytechnics, 468–73
Poverty, 32–4, 44–54, 480–84
Practical education, 131, 132, 135–7,
    245, 291–301

Primary school
  administration, 56, 58, 74–8, 81,
    90–94, 99, 396–8
  children under five in, 119–26, 519–20
  compulsory, 212
  cost of, 277–9, 288, 334–6
  curriculum, 214
  departments see Infants
  1918 improvements, 239, 242–3
  need to continue, 200, 206, 226,
    309
  see also Continuation schools,
    Evening classes, Secondary
    education
  purpose of, 74–6, 81, 95–8
  teacher training for, 302–3
Private schools, 32–3, 341–8, 348–54
Progressive schools, 321–7
Psychoanalysis, 183–9
Psychology
  in child rearing, 356–63,
  in education, 176–89, 195, 369–71
Public schools, 22, 24, 410, 449
Pupil teachers, 303

Rawlinson inquiry, 175, 189
Reading university, 105, 114, 118
Religious education, 74, 80, 92–3,
    97–8
Research needed
  educational priority areas, 480, 498
  nursery education, 520
  scientific, 25, 109, 273
Robbins report, 472
Rural areas, 214, 230, 305, 388, 391
Rutland secondary school scheme, 307

Sandwich course, 471–3
Scholarships, 215, 225, 245, 249–50,
    258–64, 283
School
  age, see Age, Compulsory education
  buildings, 84–5, 139–45
  camps, 231
  certificate, 387

meals, 50, 150–56, 159–62, 248
  see also Nursery education, Primary
    school, Secondary education
Schools Council, 463–8, 504–10,
  511–12
Science
  in education, 98, 108–10, 131, 132
    247
  need for, 21, 25–7
Scotland, 219, 235, 269, 409, 412
Secondary education
  administration and cost, 57–8, 59,
    70, 76–8, 225, 280–82
    fees, 259–63, 280, 338, 340–41, 389,
      435, 440
    free places, 259–63, 280, 338,
      339–41, 389, 451
    grants, 98–9, 103–4, 336–9
    age of transfer, 138, 243, 306–7,
      313–14, 387
    see also Comprehensive education
  curriculum 104, 245–9
  distinct from primary education,
    396–7
  grades of, 102, 137–8, 308–10, 371–2,
    387–8
    see also Grammar education, Higher
      elementary education, Technical
      education, Comprehensive,
      Tripartite education
  illegal, 73
  need for, 25–7, 225, 239, 259–63,
    265–8, 302–5, 396
  part-time, 229–32
  regulations, 98–104, 464–6
  selection for, 238–44, 263–8, 308, 310,
    474
  and social class, 432–9, 440–44,
    452–3, 455–9, 460–61, 502–3
Secondary modern schools, 378, 387–8
Selection
  for secondary school, 238–44, 263–8,
    308, 310
    end of, 474
  for university, 242–3

Sheffield university, 118
Social class
  and education, 138, 232, 245, 248,
    358–63
  and secondary education
    attitude to, 511–12
    selection for, 131, 254–5, 260,
      433–42, 454–7, 480
    national survey, 452–3, 502–4
    merging of, 379–81, 381–4
    see also Middle class, Working class
Social studies in polytechnics, 472
Social work through schools, 497
Southampton university, 105, 114
Special (M D) schools, 195, 397,
  398
Spens report, 195, 389, 406, 422
Staffordshire, 233–4
State
  care for children see Nursery schools
    criticism of, 189–95, 233–8
  education costs, see Costs
  intervention in poor homes, 45
  social services, 381–4
  university support, 268–77
Streaming, 320–21
Summerhill school, 321–7
Sweden, education in, 448–9
Syllabus see Curriculum

Tanner, Robin, 417–22
Tawney reports, 195, 258–61,
  264–8
Teachers
  appointment/dismissal, 91, 93
  nursery, 256, 518
  pensions, 284–5, 329, 518
  pupil ratio, 123–4, 279, 499, 518
  qualification, 79
  quality questioned, 143, 145–6
  salary, 284–5, 287–8, 327–32, 339
    incentive in deprived areas, 493–6,
      498–9
  at school meals, 161–2
  supply, 75, 78, 431, 493–5

Teachers—*continued*
  training
    elementary, 78–9, 81, 225, 302–5
      scholarships for, 249–50
    extended, 393–5, 470
    nursery, 518
    in service, 512–14
Teaching
  effect on intelligence, 200–201
  'extra' year, 505–11
  methods, 143–7, 173–5, 297–301
Technical education,
  colleges for *see* Polytechnics
  industrial acts controlling, 57, 70,
    76
  institutes for, 100
  schools (junior secondary), 81, 282–3,
    308, 310, 374–8
  selection for *see* Selection
Termly entry, disadvantages, 500–502
Tertiary education, 113
Trade
  scholarships, 250
  unions, 216, 251, 405, 406
Training colleges, 394–5, 470, 495–6
Transfer in secondary schools, 377,
  378, 443, 451, 452
Tripartite system, 372–6, 377–8, 405,
  410, 442
Truancy, 491

University
  compared with polytechnics, 469–73

education for, 102, 242–3, 378
grants committee, 268–70, 286
new (1903), 105–14, 115–18
new (1963), 453
old, 23–7
  see also Cambridge, London,
    Oxford, Victoria
Urban aid scheme, 480, 517, 522

Victoria university, 25, 105, 114, 115,
  118
Vocational training, 134–7, 216, 218,
  230, 469, 470
Voluntary schools, 56–61, 67–8,
  75–80, 83, 87, 94, 398

Wales, 82, 118
War, 20–23, 201–6, 210–11, 220,
  223
Webb, Sidney, 55–72, 117, 245
'Whiskey' money, 58, 65, 66
Women
  needed in education administration,
  66–7, 126
  see also Mothers
Working class
  criticism of state help to, 189–95,
    233–8
  in secondary schools, 354–5 265,
    435–6, 440–43, 452–3, 502–3
  social improvement in, 379–84

Yorkshire, 105, 227

Adventures in Education
Willem van der Eyken and Barry Turner

An attempt to rewrite the history of education, to explore in depth various experiments started by educational pioneers, and to examine how and why they succeeded and failed. This book, with its rich vein of source material, indicates that the legislators follow rather than lead the real pioneers.
Allen Lane; Pelican edition available 1974

The Pre-School Years
Willem van der Eyken

This is about the education of children during the most crucial period in their intellectual and emotional development, their first five years, and the virtually irreversible nature of the changes which are nurtured in the pre-school child. Most importantly, it is about the extraordinary educational neglect of these children in a society which acknowledges their importance.

'*The Pre-School Years* deserves serious and urgent attention, and the author is to be congratulated on a wise, lively and valuable piece'
The Times Educational Supplement

A Penguin Education Special

County Hall
The role of the Chief Education Officer
Maurice Kogan with Willem van der Eyken
in conversation with Dan Cook, Claire Pratt and George Taylor

In this book, three educational administrators, who have spent their
working lives running our schools, talk openly and in absorbing
detail about the role of the Chief Education Officer.

A Penguin Education Special

The Politics of Education
Edward Boyle and Anthony Crosland
in conversation with Maurice Kogan

Edward Boyle and Anthony Crosland are two of the most able and
influential men to enter politics since the war. In these conversations
with a former official who worked for both of them, they analyse in
depth the role of the political head of the education service.
'One of the best studies . . . of the process and problems of decision
making in politics' *The Times*

A Penguin Education Special

Other related books from Penguin Education

Centuries of Childhood
Phillippe Ariès

The questions around which this book revolves are no less than the origins of modern ideas about the family and about childhood. Before the seventeenth century a child was regarded as a small and inadequate adult; the concept of 'the childish' as something distinct from adults is a creation of the modern world. The change involved far-reaching implications for the family, for education, and for children themselves. 'It will come as no surprise to the reader,' writes Philippe Ariès, 'if these questions take us to the very heart of the great problems of civilization, for we are standing on those frontiers of biology and sociology from which mankind derives its hidden strength.'

Centuries of Childhood is by now a classic. It must surely rank as one of those books which, among changing fashions, emphases and perspectives, retain their power to illuminate our perception of childhood – its possible nature and its relation to other social forms. It is also a subtle and skilful piece of demographic history. In the course of his analysis, Ariès includes much fascinating material on such diverse topics as dress, the history of games and pastimes, attitudes towards sex and early ideas about education.

Half Way There
Report on the British Comprehensive-School Reform
Second Edition
Caroline Benn and Brian Simon

Half Way There first came out as the Conservative Government
came in, during June 1970. In the wake of political decisions taken in the
educational sphere since that date, are we now any *more* than 'half way
there'? The changeover to a non-selective system of secondary
schooling continues, the 11-plus examination is universally condemned
– yet astonishingly, by the middle of the decade it is likely that no
more than 20 per cent of children aged fourteen will be in schools
that are genuinely comprehensive

As the arguments continue, as comprehensive schemes are adopted or
rejected, there is an ever greater need for a book such as this, now
widely recognized as the most detailed and authoritative analysis of the
new British secondary schools. For this second edition Caroline Benn
and Brian Simon have added to their extensive original research two
follow up surveys which chart the very positive trend away from
streaming, and examine the character and growth of comprehensive
sixth forms. There is also a new chapter on national policy developments
since 1970, and the text has been revised and brought up to date
throughout. *Half Way There* remains an absolutely essential book for all
those who will teach in, send their children to, or share responsibility for
the comprehensive schools of the future.

'The most important and detailed book yet published on comprehensive
education in Britain' *The Times*

The Special Child
Second Edition

Barbara Furneaux

The Special Child shows how a wide range of handicapped children
– autistic children, children with language difficulties, slow-learners, those
suffering from cerebral palsy or deafness or emotional insecurity have
been haphazardly placed in the limbo of hospital wards where all too
often treatment is perfunctory, stimulation lacking and training a
matter of dreary repetition.

With cogency and compassion the author demonstrates that in fact
each child's problem is unique and that with specifically personalized
care a tremendous amount of suffering and human loss can be
prevented. Drawing on her own experience as well as on research findings,
she puts forward an unanswerable case for increased allocation of
resources to prove that 'dull' children need not remain dull and that to a
significant extent even the most handicapped child is educable.

For the second edition Barbara Furneaux has revised and expanded
her book to take into account the transfer of responsibility for the
education of mentally handicapped children from Health to Education,
and the publication of the Government White Paper which argues for
radical changes in the quantity and nature of provision. She also
analyses the early findings of one of the most important attempts at
genuine community care for the mentally handicapped – the Wessex
Experiment.

'Her lucid and yet compassionate approach sets a valuable standard
for those engaged in similar work' *Child Education*

Children in Distress
Second Edition
Alec Clegg and Barbara Megson

Two out of every hundred children have to be given direct help by the State – whether it by psychiatric, social or medical. But are these the only children 'in distress'? What about those children who do not qualify for State help?

Alec Clegg and Barbara Megson estimate that perhaps 12 per cent of our children desperately need help, but do not qualify to receive it. *Children in Distress* paints an agonizing picture of child distress, based on the authors' long experience in educational administration. They argue that it is the schools – in daily contact with the children – that are the agencies best suited to help this large and saddening section of our child population

For the second edition the authors have updated their text throughout. In particular the chapters on teaching methods and school welfare and counselling have been rewritten, and new material has been brought in on the latest developments in the field of pre-school education.

'This book, containing a wealth of information and ideas based on the experience of very many schools, can help teachers who want to help their problem pupils, but just do not know how to start. It can help them, probably more than any other single volume'
The Times Educational Supplement

Education for a Change
Community Action and the School
Colin and Mog Ball

This is a simple book. It is also an uncompromising one. It is the first Education Special written not merely for adults, but also directly for the consumers of education themselves. It is a book about youth taking matters into its own hands, on its own terms.

Colin and Mog Ball show how community service, once doomed as a worthy alternative for 'early leavers' on Thursday afternoons, can be transformed into a potent agent for radical change. They describe experiments which have taken activities out of the hands of the professionals and placed them with the young – for example, tutoring in schools. They show how community action can spread across the whole curriculum, through and beyond the school, bringing young people and adults together in genuine participation. The only skill required is willingness: the motto is 'helping one another' instead of the pervasive 'survival of the fittest'.

On behalf of the bored, the frustrated and the isolated, *Education for a Change* demands for the young the opportunity of becoming 'the investigators of the inadequacies of the system in which they are enmeshed, the callers for an education that will have some meaning in the life they are to lead'.

The School That I'd Like
Edited by Edward Blishen

In all the millions of words that are written annually about
education, one viewpoint is invariably absent – that of the child,
the client of the school. It is difficult to think of another sphere of
social activity in which the opinions of the customer are so persistently
overlooked.

In December 1967 the *Observer* organized a competition for
secondary school children to remedy this, and invited essays on
'The school that I'd like'. We publish a selection of the entries here.
They constitute a passionate and sustained attack upon our present
educational order. Their intelligence and originality are rivalled
only by their unanimity. The writers demand to be allowed to think,
to encounter head on the raw material of learning, to be at risk, to
escape from boredom into the joy of discovery, to be partners in
their education. No one will read this selection without feeling some
shame at what we have done to these children. Who will answer
them? Who will explain to them why they should not have what they
demand?

'I am tired of hearing that the hope of my country lies in my
generation. If you give me the same indoctrination . . . how can
you expect me to be any different from you?' *15 year old girl*

'Fascinating . . . the sense of bursing adventure comes through
on every page' *The Times Educational Supplement*

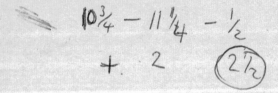

$$10\tfrac{3}{4} - 11\tfrac{1}{4} - \tfrac{1}{2}$$
$$+\ 2 \qquad \boxed{2\tfrac{1}{2}}$$